797,885 Books

are available to read at

Forgotten Books

www.ForgottenBooks.com

Forgotten Books' App
Available for mobile, tablet & eReader

ISBN 978-1-332-59211-1
PIBN 10102665

This book is a reproduction of an important historical work. Forgotten Books uses state-of-the-art technology to digitally reconstruct the work, preserving the original format whilst repairing imperfections present in the aged copy. In rare cases, an imperfection in the original, such as a blemish or missing page, may be replicated in our edition. We do, however, repair the vast majority of imperfections successfully; any imperfections that remain are intentionally left to preserve the state of such historical works.

Forgotten Books is a registered trademark of FB &c Ltd.
Copyright © 2015 FB &c Ltd.
FB &c Ltd, Dalton House, 60 Windsor Avenue, London, SW19 2RR.
Company number 08720141. Registered in England and Wales.

For support please visit www.forgottenbooks.com

1 MONTH OF FREE READING

at

www.ForgottenBooks.com

By purchasing this book you are eligible for one month membership to ForgottenBooks.com, giving you unlimited access to our entire collection of over 700,000 titles via our web site and mobile apps.

To claim your free month visit:
www.forgottenbooks.com/free102665

* Offer is valid for 45 days from date of purchase. Terms and conditions apply.

English
Français
Deutsche
Italiano
Español
Português

www.forgottenbooks.com

Mythology Photography **Fiction** Fishing Christianity **Art** Cooking Essays Buddhism Freemasonry Medicine **Biology** Music **Ancient Egypt** Evolution Carpentry Physics Dance Geology **Mathematics** Fitness Shakespeare **Folklore** Yoga Marketing **Confidence** Immortality Biographies Poetry **Psychology** Witchcraft Electronics Chemistry History **Law** Accounting **Philosophy** Anthropology Alchemy Drama Quantum Mechanics Atheism Sexual Health **Ancient History Entrepreneurship** Languages Sport Paleontology Needlework Islam **Metaphysics** Investment Archaeology Parenting Statistics Criminology **Motivational**

OF

EDUCATION IN INDIA

IN

1886,

WITH SPECIAL REFERENCE TO

THE REPORT OF THE EDUCATION COMMISSION.

BY

SIR ALFRED CROFT, K.C.I.E., M.A.,
DIRECTOR OF PUBLIC INSTRUCTION, BENGAL.

1888

CONTENTS.

CHAPTER I.—PRELIMINARY.

PARA.		PAGE
1.	Object of the Report	1
2.	Scope of the Report	ib.
3.	Period covered by the Report	2
4.	Divisions of the Report	3
5.	Order of Subjects	4

CHAPTER II.—EDUCATION IN INDIA FROM THE CLOSE OF THE YEAR 1881-82 TO THE CLOSE OF THE YEAR 1884-85.

I.—SCHOOLS AND SCHOLARS.

6.	General Statistics of Attendance, 1881-82 to 1884-85	5
7.	Definition of Public and Private Schools	5 & 6
8.	Private Schools from 1881-82 to 1884-85	6 & 7
9.	Public Schools and Colleges from 1881-82 to 1884-85	7 & 8
10.	New Classification of Schools in 1883-84	8
11.	Summary of Progress, 1881-82 to 1884-85	8 & 9
12.	Provincial Returns of Schools and Colleges, 1881-82 to 1884-85	9
13.	Provincial Returns of Primary Schools	10
14.	Provincial Returns of Schools other than Primary	10 & 11

II.—EXPENDITURE.

15.	General Statistics of Expenditure, 1881-82 to 1884-85	11
16.	General Statistics: Tuitional and Non-tuitional Expenditure	12
17.	General Statistics: Provincial Expenditure	12—14
18.	Expenditure from Provincial Revenues: Tuitional	14 & 15
19.	Expenditure from Provincial Revenues: Non-tuitional	15 & 16
20.	Expenditure from "Other Sources"	16
21.	Character of Local or District Funds	17
22.	Expenditure from Local Funds	17—19
23.	Expenditure from Municipal Funds	19 & 20
24.	Distribution of the Increase from Public Funds	20
25.	Expenditure from Fees	ib.
26.	University Fees	20 & 21
27.	Provincial Increase in Pupils and Tuition-Fees compared	21—24
28.	Expenditure from Subscriptions, Endowments, and other Sources	24 & 25
29.	Proportionate Expenditure from Various Sources	25 & 26

III.—COLLEGIATE EDUCATION.

30.	The Indian Universities	26 & 27
31.	The Madras University	27
32.	The Bombay University	28
33.	The Calcutta University	28 & 29
34.	The Punjab University	29 & 30
35.	Arts Colleges, English, 1881-82 to 1884-85	31 & 32
36.	Attendance of Students in Arts Colleges, 1881-82 to 1884-85	32
37.	Grade of Arts Colleges, 1881-82 to 1884-85	32 & 33
38.	Expenditure on Arts Colleges, English, 1881-82 to 1884-85	33—35
39.	Results of University Examinations, 1881-82 and 1884-85	35—37
40.	Increasing Success of Non-departmental Colleges	37 & 38

52. Secondary Schools for Girls, 1881-82 to 1884-85	51 & 52
53. Expenditure on Secondary Schools for Boys, 1881-82 to 1884-85	52—54
54. Secondary Education, Madras, 1881.82 to 1884-85	54 & 55
55. Secondary Education, Bombay, 1881.82 to 1884-85	56 & 57
56. Secondary Education, Bengal, 1881.82 to 1884-85	57
57. Secondary Education, North-Western Provinces and Oudh, 1881-82 to 1884-85	57 & 58
58. Secondary Education, Punjab, 1881.82 to 1884-85	58
59. Secondary Education, 1881-82 to 1884-85 : Other Provinces	58 & 59

V.—PRIMARY EDUCATION.

60. Primary Schools for Boys, 1881-82 to 1884-85	59—61
61. Schools under Public Management	61 & 62
62. Aided Schools: Bengal	62 & 63
63. Aided Schools: Bombay	63 & 64
64. Aided Schools: Punjab	64 & 65
65. Aided Schools in other Provinces	65—66
66. Unaided Schools	66
67. Primary Schools for Girls, 1881-82 to 1884-85	67 & 68
68. Primary Schools: Results of Public Examinations	68 & 69
69. Expenditure on Primary Schools, 1881-82 to 1884-85	69 to 72

VI.—SPECIAL INSTRUCTION.

70. Training Schools, 1881-82 to 1884-85	73
71. Training Schools for Masters	73 & 74
72. Training Schools for Mistresses	74
73. Training Schools in Madras	74—76
74. Training Schools in Bombay	76
75. Training Schools in Bengal	77 & 78
76. Training Schools in the North-Western Provinces and Oudh	78 & 79
77. Training Schools in the Punjab	79 & 80
78. Training Schools in Burma	80 & 81
79. Training Schools in other Provinces	81 & 82
80. Technical and other Special Schools	82
81. Schools of Art	82 & 83
82. Medical Schools	83 & 84
83. Engineering or Surveying Schools	84 & 85
84. Industrial Schools	85—88
85. Other Special Schools	88 & 89

CHAPTER III.—EDUCATION IN INDIA IN 1886.
SECTION I.—GENERAL SUMMARY.

86. Method of the Chapter	90
87. General Statistics of Attendance, 1884-85 to 1885-86	90 & 91
88. Proportion of Scholars to population, 1885.86	91 & 92
89. Schools classified according to standard of instruction	92—94
90. Scholars classified according to stage of instruction	94 & 95
91. General Estimate of Progress in 1885-86	95 & 96
92. Schools classified according to Management	96—98
93. Race and Creed of Scholars	98—100
94. Meaning of the School-going Age	100 & 101

CONTENTS.

Para.		Page
103.	Code of Rules for Inspectors	114—116
104.	District and Municipal Boards	116 & 117
105.	Recommendations of the Commission as to District and Municipal Boards	117 & 118
106.	Action taken on the foregoing Recommendations	118 & 119
107.	District and Municipal Boards in Madras	119 & 120
108.	Expenditure by District and Municipal Boards in Madras	120 & 121
109.	District and Municipal Boards in Bombay	121—123
110.	Expenditure by District and Municipal Boards in Bombay	123 & 124
111.	District and Municipal Boards in Bengal	124—126
112.	Expenditure by District and Municipal Boards in Bengal	126
113.	District and Municipal Boards in the North-Western Provinces and Oudh	126 & 127
114.	Expenditure by District and Municipal Boards in the North-Western Provinces	127
115.	District and Municipal Boards in the Punjab	127 & 128
116.	Expenditure by District and Municipal Boards in the Punjab	128 & 129
117.	District and Municipal Boards in the Central Provinces	129 & 130
118.	Expenditure by District and Municipal Boards in the Central Provinces	130
119.	District and Municipal Boards in Burma	130 & 131
120.	Expenditure by Municipal Committees in Burma	131
121.	District and Municipal Boards in Assam	131 & 132
122.	Expenditure by District and Municipal Boards in Assam	132
123.	Local Boards in Berar and Coorg	132 & 133
124.	Educational Expenditure of District Boards	133
125.	Educational Expenditure of Municipal Boards	134
126.	Enactment of an Educational Code	134 & 135
127.	Other Controlling Agencies	135

Section III.—COLLEGIATE EDUCATION.

128.	Character of Collegiate Education	136
129.	Changes in University Regulations	136—138
130.	Arts Colleges, English, 1885-86	138 & 139
131.	Classification of Arts Colleges according to Management	139 & 140
132.	Expenditure on Arts Colleges, English, 1885-86	140
133.	Expenditure from Public Sources	140 & 141
134.	Expenditure from Fees	141—143
135.	Proportion of Fee-receipts to total Expenditure	143 & 144
136.	Expenditure from other Sources	144
137.	Results of University Examinations in Arts, 1885-86	144 & 145
138.	B. A. Examination: Courses in Literature and in Science	145—147
139.	Popularity of the two Courses	147 & 148
140.	Comparative Success of Government and other Colleges	148
141.	M. A. Examination	149 & 150
142.	B. A. Examination	150
143.	Provision of Scientific Instruction	150 & 151
144.	The Relation of Government to Collegiate Education	151
145.	Recommendations of the Commission as to Collegiate Education	151—153
146.	Extension of Collegiate Education	153 & 154
147.	Grants to Aided Colleges	154 & 155
148.	Employment of Indian Graduates	155
149.	Withdrawal of Government from the direct Management of Colleges	155 & 156
150.	Other Recommendations regarding Colleges	157
151.	Oriental Colleges	157 & 158
152.	The Punjab Oriental College	158—160
153.	The Calcutta Sanskrit College	160

Section IV (a).—SECONDARY EDUCATION.

154.	Character and scope of Secondary Education	161
155.	Different classes of Secondary Schools	161 & 162
156.	Secondary Schools for Boys, 1885-86	162 & 163
157.	Secondary Schools, English: Attendance	163
158.	Secondary Schools, English: Control	163 & 164
159.	Secondary Schools, Vernacular	164 & 165
160.	Different Departments in Secondary Schools	166
161.	The teaching of English in Secondary Schools	166 & 167

168. Action taken on this Recommendation	.	178—183
169. Qualification of Teachers	.	183—185
170. Fees in Secondary Schools	.	185 & 186
171. Scholarships in Secondary Schools	.	186—188
172. The further extension of Secondary Education	.	188—192
173. Withdrawal of Government in favour of private Managers	.	192—194

SECTION IV (b).—PRIMARY EDUCATION.

174. Character and scope of Primary Education	.	195 & 196
175. Primary Schools for Boys, 1885-86	.	197 & 198
176. Systems of Primary Education: Departmental Schools	.	198 & 199
177. Board Schools	.	199—201
178. Aided Schools	.	201—203
179. Unaided Schools	.	203 & 204
180. Primary Education in Burma	.	204—207
181. Provincial Standards of Examination for Primary Schools	.	207 & 208
182. Comparative progress as tested by Public Examinations	.	208—211
183. Expenditure on Primary Schools for Boys, 1885-86	.	211—213
184. Comparative cost of Primary Schools	.	213—215
185. Comparative cost of Primary Schools and Primary Departments		215 & 216
186. Recommendations of the Commission as to Primary Education	.	216 & 217
187. Superior claims of Primary Education upon public effort and public Funds		217—219
188. Action taken by the Local Governments	.	219—223
189. Agencies and means for extending Primary Education	.	223—226
190. Special measures for aboriginal and backward races	.	226—231
191. Methods of aiding Primary Schools	.	231 & 232
192. Revision of Standards in Primary Schools	.	232—234
193. Physical, Moral, and Religious Instructions	.	234
194. Fees and Exemptions	.	235 & 236
195. Night Schools	.	236 & 237
196. District and Municipal Boards	.	237 & 238
197. Other recommendations as to Primary Education	.	238

SECTION V.—SPECIAL INSTRUCTION.

(a) TRAINING SCHOOLS.

198. Character and Scope of special Instruction	.	239
199. Training Schools for Masters, 1885-86	.	239 & 240
200. Training Schools for Mistresses, 1885-86	.	240
201. Expenditure on Training Schools	.	241 & 242
202. Training Schools in Madras	.	242 & 243
203. Training Schools in Bombay	.	243 & 244
204. Training Schools in Bengal	.	244—246
205. Training Schools in the North-Western Provinces	.	246
206. Training Schools in the Punjab	.	246 & 247
207. Training Schools in Other Provinces	.	247
208. Recommendations of the Commission as to Training Schools	.	248
209. Special Requirements for Teachers in Secondary Schools	.	248—250

(b) OTHER SCHOOLS OF SPECIAL INSTRUCTION.

PARA.	PAGE
216. Cost of Professional Colleges, 1885-86	255 & 256
217. Results of University Examinations	256
218. Technical and other Special Schools	256 & 257
219. Schools of Art	257 & 258
220. Medical Schools	258
221. Engineering and Surveying Schools	258 & 259
222. Industrial Schools	259 & 260
223. Other Schools	260
224. General Schemes of Technical Instruction	261
225. The Madras Scheme	261—263
226. The Bombay Scheme	264—266
227. The Bengal Scheme	266—274
228. General remarks on Technical Instruction	274—277

Section VI.—FEMALE EDUCATION.

229. Difficulties in the way of Female Education	278 & 279
230. Primary Schools for Girls, 1885-86	280
231. Secondary Schools for Girls, 1885-86	281 & 282
232. Higher Education of Women: the Countess of Dufferin's Fund	282
233. Race and creed of Girls at Schools	282 & 283
234. Expenditure on Girls' Schools in 1885-86	283 & 284
235. Female Education in different Provinces	284—288
236. Recommendations of the Commission as to Female Education	288 & 289
237. Action taken on these Recommendations	289
238. Grant-in-aid Rules	289 & 290
239. Mixed Schools	290 & 291
240. District and Municipal Boards	291 & 292
241. Teachers in Girls' Schools	292 & 293
242. Zenana Agencies, &c.	293

Section VII.—EDUCATION OF SPECIAL CLASSES.

(a) EUROPEANS AND EURASIANS.

243. Need of special measures: Lord Canning's Minute	294
244. Lord Lytton's Minute	294 & 295
245. Archdeacon Baly's Report	295 & 296
246. Resolution of the Government of India thereon	296—298
247. Draft Code for European Schools in the Bengal Presidency	298—301
248. Provisional Introduction of the Draft Code	301 & 302
249. Confirmation of the Code	302 & 303
250. Extension to other Provinces	304
251. Results of its Introduction	304 & 305
252. Attendance in European Schools	305 & 506
253. Expenditure in European Schools	306 & 307
254. Improvement in Standard of Instruction	307 & 308
255. Alleged defects of the Code	308 & 309
256. The Bruce Legacy	309—311

(b) MUHAMMADANS.

257. Muhammadan Education: its Early Difficulties	311 & 312
258. Report of the Education Commission	312—314
259. General effect of the Commission's proposals	314
260. Progress of Education among Muhammadans	314 & 315
261. Classification of Muhammadan Pupils	315
262. Progess of Muhammadans in different Provinces	316
263. Success at University Examinations	316
264. Recommendations of the Commission as to Muhammadans	216—318
265. Action taken in Madras	318 & 319
266. Action taken in Bombay	319 & 320

Section VIII.—PRIVATE INSTITUTIONS.

270. Meaning of the Term	323
271. Recommendations of the Commission as to Indigenous Schools	323 & 324
272. Extent of Indigenous Instruction, 1885-86	324
273. Provincial Returns of Private Schools	324 & 325
274. Private Schools in Madras	325 & 326
275. Private Schools in Bombay	326
276. Private Schools in Bengal	326 & 327
277. Private Schools in the North-Western Provinces	327
278. Private Schools in the Punjab	327—329
279. Girls in Private Schools	329

Section IX.—DISCIPLINE AND MORAL TRAINING IN SCHOOLS AND COLLEGES.

280. Recommendations of the Commission	330
281. Boarding Houses: Inter-school Rules	330 & 331
282. A Moral Text-Book for Colleges	331 & 332
283. Action taken on these Recommendations	332 & 333
284. Discipline in Schools in Bengal	333 & 334
285. Recent Inquiries by the Government of India	334 & 335

Section X.—EDUCATIONAL CONFERENCES.

286. Co-operation between the Department and Private Managers	336
287. Revision of the Grant-in-aid Rules	336 & 337
288. Permanent Consultative Boards	337 & 338
289. Educational Conferences: Madras	338—340
290. Bombay	340 & 341
291. Bengal	341 & 342
292. North-Western Provinces and Oudh	342 & 343
293. Punjab	343 & 344
294. Other Provinces	344
295. General Results	ib

STATISTICAL TABLES.

(See separate Index at their commencement) . . . . . . 351—363

No. 199.

Extract from the Proceedings of the Government of India in the Home Department (Education),—under date Simla, the 18th June 1888.

READ—

Despatch from Her Majesty's Secretary of State for India, No. 43, dated the 23rd April 1885, directing the preparation of a general annual Education Report.

Despatch to Her Majesty's Secretary of State for India, No. 64, dated the 15th March 1887.

Letter to the Hon'ble Sir Alfred Croft, No. 124, dated 18th May 1887.

Read also—

Letter from the Hon'ble Sir Alfred Croft, No. 2, dated 1st April 1888, submitting the General Report in question.

RESOLUTION.

IN the Resolution No. $\frac{10}{309}$, dated 23rd October 1884, recorded in the Home Department, the Governor General in Council reviewed the Report of the Education Commission, and laid down for the future guidance of Local Governments and Administrations the broad lines of the Educational policy which the Government of India desired to pursue. That Resolution met with the general concurrence of Her Majesty's Secretary of State, who, in expressing his approval, communicated the following instructions to the Government of India. "In order to stimulate the efforts of the various authorities in the promotion of education on the lines now laid down, it would, I think, be well if Your Excellency in Council would direct the preparation of a general annual report, embracing the important features of the several provincial reports (including Madras and Bombay), and transmit copies of the same to the Secretary of State, with a Resolution by the Government of India reviewing such general report."

2. For reasons into which it is unnecessary to enter here, it was found desirable to postpone the preparation of the first General Report required by the Secretary of State until last year, when the work was entrusted to Sir Alfred Croft, K.C.I.E., Director of Public Instruction in Bengal. It was at first anticipated that the Report would be completed in three months; but after entering on the undertaking, Sir Alfred Croft found it necessary to collect from Local Governments information of various kinds which was not supplied in the departmental reports, but without which the special report called for would lose much of its value. Considerable time elapsed before all the information was collected; and it was not until last April that the report was submitted to Government. In his letter of the 1st April 1888, cited in the preamble, Sir Alfred Croft explains the cause of the delay; and the Governor General in Council, while regretting the delay, very readily believes that it was not due to any want of industry or attention on the part of the writer of the report. The report as now submitted is an able and full exposition of the educational condition of British India; and the Governor General in Council desires to thank Sir Alfred Croft for the careful manner in which he has carried out his instructions.

3. These instructions were devised to secure a report which should be a compendium of the information supplied by the different Local Governments, as regards the condition of education in each province, the methods and organization by which it is imparted, and the extent to which effect is being given to the recommendations of the Education Commission. Sir Alfred Croft has carried these instructions into effect by writing an introductory chapter, giving

an outline of the history of education from 1881 (the year for which statistics were supplied to the Education Commission) to 1885; and by then presenting a comprehensive view of the state of education in each province from the statistical, financial, and administrative points of view.

The Governor General in Council does not think it necessary to make any examination of the merely introductory portion of the Report; and the following remarks are, therefore, directed to presenting a general view of the present state of education in India, with such references to the earlier statistics as may be necessary to illustrate the progress made. As the statistics for 1886-87 are now in the possession of the Government of India, they will be quoted with a view to supplement the information furnished in the Report, and to bring that information up to date.

4. Education in British India is conveyed through the medium of two classes of Institutions: Public Institutions and Private Institutions. A Public Institution is defined to be "a School or College in which the course of study conforms to the standard prescribed by the Department of Public Instruction, or by the University, and which either is inspected by the Department or regularly presents pupils at the Public Examinations held by the Department or the University." A School or College not coming within the above definition is called a Private Institution.

As may be inferred from the preceding definition, the information available regarding Private Institutions is neither exhaustive nor reliable. Such information as exists is set forth in chapter VIII of the Report; and shows that the instruction imparted in Private Schools is, as a rule, less systematic and efficient than that imparted in similar schools controlled by the Department. It is not intended in this Resolution to dwell at any length on the character or progress of the education conveyed in these private schools; but, in order to present a general view of the condition of education in India, it is desirable for the moment to ignore the difference between the two classes of Institutions, and to combine the statistics of attendance at both.

5. Proceeding on this plan, it will be seen that in 1881-82, the earliest date touched by the Report, there were in British India 94,989 Institutions of all grades attended by 2,451,989 pupils. Between 1882 and 1885 there were considerable fluctuations, both in the number of Institutions and of students attending them; the most marked fluctuation being exhibited in the Province of Bengal, where over 14,000 rudimentary schools, attended by more than 120,000 pupils, were excluded from the public class without apparently being enumerated in the private class of schools. But, notwithstanding this, the total of Institutions stood in 1885-86 at 122,367, and the attendance at 3,325,080. The following year the institutions numbered 127,116, and the pupils 3,343,544. The broad fact which emerges from a comparison of these statistics is that in the five years ending with 1886-87 the number of educational Institutions of all sorts in British India increased by one-third, while the number of pupils increased by a still larger proportion.

6. The progress of education within the last five years, which the preceding figures evidence, has been marked; but, viewed with reference to the population as yet untouched by our educational agencies, the progress made still leaves a great deal to be desired. In Western countries it is commonly assumed that children of a school-going age form 15 per cent. of the population. In paragraph 94 of the Report, Sir Alfred Croft seem inclined to hold that for India that proportion is somewhat less than the reality. Assuming, however, that the conventional 15 per cent. is correct for India, it appears from a consideration of the census statistics that only one child out of every ten of a school-going age is actually under instruction. This low percentage is due to the extreme backwardness of female education. The case in regard to males is not nearly so bad; for while of females of a school-going age, not one in fifty (less than two per cent.) is at school, there are 19 males out of every hundred, or nearly one-fifth of the male population of a school-going age, under instruction of some form or other. In the opinion of the Government of India, the proportion of the male population under

instruction cannot, having regard to the circumstances of the country, be considered otherwise than satisfactory.

7. Passing from the consideration of the educational satistics in their widest aspects, to the question of the general character of the instruction imparted, it is at once apparent that to the enormous mass of children the instruction conveyed is of the most elementary kind. Broadly speaking, the system of education administered in British India operates through three grades of institutions : Primary Schools, Secondary Schools, and Colleges. The Primary School aims at teaching the elements of reading and writing, and such simple rules of arithmetic and land measurement as will enable the peasant in a purely agricultural country to look after his own interests. This is not a very ambitious programme ; but, at the present time, it meets the wants of 94·5 per cent of the entire school-going population. The Secondary Schools, in which an advanced instruction in the vernacular and a substantial knowledge of English are conveyed, claim an attendance of 5·1 per cent. of that population, while the remainder (about ⅓ per cent.) supplies students to all the colleges which impart the highest English education, or teach the various professions of Law, Medicine, and Engineering.

8. The preceding remarks, made with a view to indicating the relative extent of rudimentary and advanced education in India, will be more significant and intelligible if supplemented by a citation of the statistics of actual attendance at the various classes of schools. Beginning with the lowest or Primary class, it appears from the Report that in 1881-82 there were 86,269 Public Primary schools attended by 2,156,242 children (2,070,963 boys and 85,279 girls). There were also Private schools of this class, the precise number of which is not apparent; but it probably did not exceed 4,000 attended by some 50,000 children. The grant total of Primary schools, public and private, five years ago, may therefore be taken at 90,000 in round numbers, attended by 2,200,000 children. In 1885-86, the number of schools had increased to 111,117, and the attendance to 2,811,934. The returns for 1886-87 show that there were in that year 114,303 schools, and 2,806,472 pupils, the decrease in attendance being chiefly due to a temporary cause, the operation of which has now diminished, namely, the disturbed condition of Lower Burma. These totals show that on the whole there is an increasing appreciation of that form of education which is most useful and essential for the great mass of the people.

9. Incidental reference has been made to the number of girls attending Primary schools in 1881-82; and, before passing on to the statistics of secondary and collegiate education, it may be well to indicate here the progress which, during the last five years, has been made in this the elementary stage of female education. So far as can be gathered from the Report, there were in 1881-82, excluding private elementary institutions for which separate statistics are not available, 2,678 elementary schools for girls which were attended by 85,279 pupils. In 1885-86, the number of schools for girls had increased to 5,210 (including 873 private schools), and the attendance to 134,749 (12,251 pupils in private schools). In 1886-87, the number of girls' schools had reached 6,281 (including 1,767 private schools), and the attendance 149,922 (including 17,205 pupils at private institutions). It is interesting to note that for every Mahomedan girl at school there are from three to four Hindu girls, which is in accordance with the proportion which the two great creeds bear to each other both in the general and in the school population. These figures are, indeed, insignificant when compared with the total female population of a school-going age; but they seem to the Governor General in Council to be satisfactory as indicating the fact that steady, if slow, progress is being made. It must be remembered that it is difficult to overrate the obstacles to be overcome in promoting female education in India.

10. Secondary education is the connecting link between Primary or Elementary, and Collegiate or University education. It is imparted in two classes of school, the middle and the high school; the instruction conveyed in the latter being of a more advanced character than that imparted in the former. While the middle school has always a vernacular basis thereby touching the Primary system, the high school concerns itself mainly with education through the medium of English alone, and reaches the Collegiate course.

In 1881-82, there were 3,932 secondary schools for boys attended by 215,731 pupils (149,265 attending the English and 66,466 the vernacular side). In 1885-86, the schools numbered 4,083 and the pupils 394,508 (264,918 receiving a purely English education); while in 1886-87, there were 4,160 schools and 404,189 students, of whom 271,654 were in the exclusively English division. It thus appears that during the last five years the number of male pupils receiving a purely English education introductory to a University course has increased by about 80 per cent.; while the number of boys receiving a superior mixed English and vernacular education has doubled. It should also be added that there were, in 1886-87, 7,678 advanced private schools, attended by 77,379 students learning Persian, Arabic, Sanskrit, or some other Oriental classic. It may, the Governor General in Council considers, be confidently stated that the progress of secondary education in India during the last five years has been very satisfactory, and that it is now established on a sound and prosperous footing.

Among females, the progress of the higher or secondary education is of course much less marked than among males. The secondary schools for girls, which in 1881-82 numbered only 190, attended by 6,366 pupils, had in 1885-86 increased to 349, attended by 23,904 pupils, and in 1886-87 to 357 schools, attended by 24,904 pupils. These figures are only satisfactory because of the promise, slight though it be, which they afford of better things.

11. The third and highest division of the Indian educational system is the Collegiate Section comprising Arts, Law, Medicine, Engineering and teaching. By Collegiate education is to be understood the education of those students who, having successfully passed through the secondary course, are studying in a College, affiliated to the University, one or other of the courses prescribed by the University for its higher examinations. In 1881-82, the number of Colleges in India was 85; and the attendance consisted of 7,582 students. In 1885-86, the number of Colleges had increased to 110, and the attendance to 10,538. In the following year, the latest for which statistics are available, there were 114 colleges, attended by 11,501 students. In 1881-82 there were 67 Arts Colleges (English and Oriental) attended by 6,037 students; in 1885-86, 86 Colleges attended by 8,127 students; and in 1886-87, 89 Colleges attended by 8,764 students. Law Colleges numbered in 1881-82, 12 with 730 students; in 1885-86, 16 with 1,371 students; and in 1886-87, the same number of Colleges with 1,602 students. In 1881-82 there were 3 Medical Colleges with 476 students; in 1885-86, also 3 Colleges with 584 students; and in 1886-87 the number of Colleges had risen to 4, and the number of students to 654. Engineering Colleges which in 1881-82 numbered 3 with 330 students rose in 1885-86 to 4 with 447 students; and in 1886-87 while the number of Colleges remained the same as in the previous year, the number of students increased to 474. There was also a College for professional teaching in the Madras Presidency in 1885-86 and 1886-87; the number of students was 9 in the former year and 7 in the latter. The history is thus, from a statistical point of view, one of progressive development.

12. The advance made in the number of schools for special instruction other than training schools has been satisfactory. Medical schools, the course of study in which is not so advanced or thorough as in Medical Colleges, were eleven in number in 1881-82 and were attended by 830 pupils. The number rose in 1885-86 to 16, with 1,227 pupils, and in 1886-87 to 18, with 1,388 pupils. Law Schools had not been established in 1881-82; but four years later there were four such schools attended by 45 pupils. In 1886-87 the schools fell to two, but the students rose to 90. There were only 9 Engineering and Surveying schools in 1881-82, with 310 pupils; but in 1885-86 there were 15, with 558 pupils, and 14 in 1886-87 attended by 616 pupils. Reference will be made in a later portion of this review to the subject of technical education.

13. The foregoing remarks have reference to education generally; but there are two classes in India for whose education it has been at different times suggested that special measures are required. These classes are the children of Europeans and Eurasians, and Muhammadan children. The subject of the education of the children of the domiciled European and Eurasian communities

was excluded from the deliberations of the Education Commission, because it had already received the serious consideration of the Government of India. The conclusion arrived at was that contributions from private sources towards the maintenance of European Schools should be supplemented by grants-in-aid from Government, regulated by the educational progress made by each school, and without reference to denominational distinctions. A School Code embodying these principles was prepared under the circumstances detailed in paragraphs 247-250 of the report of Sir A. Croft. This Code has been extended to the North-Western Provinces and Oudh, the Punjab and the Central Provinces, while portions of it have been introduced into the Code in force in Madras.

14. The records of attendance of European and Eurasian children show that the working of this grant-in-aid system has been productive of satisfactory results. In 1881-82 the number of pupils at school, excluding those at private institutions, was 18,750; in 1885-86 it had risen to 22,634, and in 1886-87 to 23,031. As the Bengal Code at present stands, the grants are dependent on the results of the annual examination of individuals. The Governor General in Council does not regard this plan with unalloyed satisfaction, inasmuch as in his opinion experience tends to show that the system under which grants-in-aid are made to depend on examination of each individual student in the school results in pupils being "crammed" for examinations instead of being properly grounded in their studies. Such a system, especially when applied to pupils whose studies have not yet taken any particular direction—in other words, have not been specialized—must, in the opinion of His Excellency in Council, produce a very undesirable effect on the education imparted in this class of schools. The Bombay Code appears to recognise this; and as a remedy it provides for the concession of fixed grants for periods of years. The remedy may not be all that the case requires; in the present condition of education in India, it is impossible to establish a system in which pecuniary considerations shall not influence the teaching or the examination of the pupils; but it is undoubtedly a step in the right direction; and its adoption in other provinces has, therefore, been recommended by the Government of India.

15. Special recommendations for the education of Muhammadans were made by the Education Commission; and the Governor General in Council, in Home Department Resolution No. 7—215-25 of July 15th, 1885, reviewed the suggestions which had been made for the special treatment of this class. The Commission proposed a differential treatment of the Muhammadan community in respect to education which the Government of India found' itself unable to approve. In its Resolution just referred to, the Goverment of India pointed out that, if the Muhammadans desired to succeed in the competition of life with their Hindu fellow subjects, the way lay in taking advantage, in the same manner as other classes do, of the high education provided by the Government. The Governor General in Council is glad to think that the Muhammadans have themselves adopted this view of the subject. In 1881-82, there were 447,703 Muhammadan pupils; in 1885 86 they numbered 748 663, and in 1886-87, 752,441. The great increase in the first mentioned period must not, however, be taken as shewing that children not previously at school were brought under instruction. The increase is chiefly due to the extension of the State system of education, so as to include schools which were previously outside it. The percentage of Muhammadans to total pupils, which in 1881-82 was only 17·8, stood in 1886-87 at 22·5—practically a ratio identical with the proportion which the Muhammadan population (45 millions) bears to the total population (199 millions) of British India according to the census of 1881. But if this steady and marked advance of the Muhammadan community in regard to education be a gratifying feature of the educational statistics for the past five years, a closer examination of the figures shews much room for improvement. Although the total number of Muhammadans under instruction compares favourably with the total number of Hindus, the number of the former receiving education of an advanced type is very small relatively to the number of Hindus under similar instruction. Out of a total of 2,303,812 Hindus attending all classes of schools, private and public, in 1886-87, 316,493 were in the secondary stage, while 9,634 were attending College. On the other hand, out of

a total of 752,441 Muhammadans under instruction during the same year, only 58,222 were attending secondary schools, and only 587 attending College. Thus while one out of every seven Hindu students was receiving the higher education, only one out of thirteen Muhammadan students had passed beyond the primary stage. To this condition of things, especially regarding collegiate education, His Excellency in Council would earnestly invite the attention of the Muhammadan community, and would impress on them the necessity of their taking advantage more largely of the educational facilities within their reach. The fact that the attendance of Muhammadan students at secondary schools has since 1881-82 risen from 20,000 to over 58,000 shews, indeed, that progress is being made; but the progress might be more rapid.

16. Passing from the statistics of attendance at the various classes of Indian Schools and Colleges to the expenditure on education, we find that in 1881-82 the total expenditure on public instruction in India was, in round numbers, 186 lakhs of rupees. Four years later (in 1885-86) the total had risen to 240 lakhs; and last year it stood at a little over 252 lakhs. At the beginning of the five years, the Government bore 73 lakhs of this expenditure, while Local and Municipal funds contributed 32 lakhs; the balance of 81 lakhs, consisting of fees, subscriptions, endowments, &c., falling on the public. In the year 1885-86, the share of the Government is shewn at 80 lakhs; that of Local and Municipal bodies at 48; and that of the public at 112 lakhs. The share assigned to Local bodies, however, is not entirely the proceeds of local taxation, but includes an item of $4\frac{1}{2}$ lakhs contributed by Government; so that in effect the share of Government at this period stood at about $84\frac{1}{2}$ lakhs. Next year the shares are shown at $85\frac{1}{2}$ lakhs for Government, 49 lakhs for Local and Municipal Boards, and $117\frac{1}{2}$ lakhs for the Public. But of the 49 lakhs expended by Local bodies, $6\frac{1}{2}$ were contributed by Government; so that there has been a progressive increase in the Government expenditure. The Governor General in Council considers that the growth of the share borne by Local bodies should for the future exhibit a more marked increase than it has done since 1885; and that there should be a tendency to decrease rather than to increase in the share which now is defrayed from the public treasury.

17. The Government of India recognizes its responsibility to provide, so far as its finances permit, facilities for the education of the people. But in educational, as in all other matters, it is the policy of the Government of India to avoid entering into competition with private enterprise: it pioneers the way; but having shown the way, it recognizes no responsibility to do for the people what the people can and ought to do for themselves. When, therefore, local effort or private enterprise shows itself able and willing to supply the educational wants of the people in any locality, it is the policy of Government to retire from the field of direct instruction and to help by reasonable subventions of money the operations of independent institutions. Under this policy, it is the aim of the Government also, wherever there is vitality of private effort, to restrict official action to the maintenance of a few schools, in which the system of instruction and discipline shall afford a standard for the emulation of private or aided institutions in the neighbourhood. In pursuance of this policy, the expenditure from Provincial revenues on Government educational institutions should not ordinarily increase in proportion to the total expenditure, but should rather be a constantly diminishing quantity, provided that there is the assurance that the ground abandoned by the Government is occupied by local effort.

The gradual substitution of aided for Government schools should, in the opinion of the Government of India, be accompanied by a contraction in the number of pupils educated in the institutions still maintained by Government, more especially the High Schools and Colleges. If the Government High Schools and Colleges are to afford a standard for the emulation of other institutions, it is essential that the number of pupils attending them shall be so limited as to secure to each individual that share of personal attention which is the first requisite of a sound system of education. In giving effect to these views, it is not the wish of the Government of India that the existing accommodation in Government High Schools and Colleges should not be utlized to the fullest extent; but it is from this point of view desirable that further expenditure in expanding or increasing the number of such institutions should be incurred by Government only under exceptional circumstances.

18. Passing from the progress of education in its general aspects, the next subject which claims notice is the machinery maintained by Government for imparting instruction in colleges, and for testing the results of the teaching that is given in the schools. At present there is no distinction or line of demarcation between the European Professorial Staff and that engaged on inspection: the same officer may be engaged at one period of his service in the College lecture hall, teaching philosophy or the higher mathematics; at another period in the camp, inspecting Primary village schools. Gradually, however, it has come to be recognized that the qualities required for the one set of duties are not those required for the other, and that the usefulness of the metaphysician, or the expert in physical science, is impaired, not improved, by testing the knowledge of peasants' children in the rudiments of reading, writing and arithmetic. The Government was gradually coming to the opinion that changes in the form of the Educational Department were demanded by circumstances; and accordingly the subject formed one of the questions which were referred to the Public Service Commission.

Their opinion, briefly stated, is that the time has come when the system of a close Educational Service, the members of which would be content to enter as young men on small pay, and be ready to take up any duties the Department may assign to them, should be largely modified or entirely discontinued. They have given expression to the view that a close Educational Service in its present form is no longer called for; and while they recommend the maintenance in each Presidency and large Province of a College, with a staff of Professors capable of teaching up to the highest European literary standards under a European Principal, they consider that the recruitment of Inspectors from Europe should be considerably reduced, and their place taken by local agency. Upon these points, the Government of India has now asked for the advice of Local Governments and Administrations. Without desiring to prejudge the question, the Governor General in Council is disposed to concur in the necessity for keeping the inspecting agency separate from the teaching staff. Experience seems to show that the work of inspecting, at all events, primary and middle schools can be very thoroughly and satisfactorily performed by local agency; and as material becomes available in India for this purpose, the reduction of the more expensive graded lists of the superior branch of the Education Department as at present maintained, must of necessity be gradually carried out. Of late years native agency has been utilised to a considerable extent for purposes of inspection; and proposals to further substitute it for officers recruited in England for the graded list of the Department are now under the consideration of the Government of India.

19. In regard to the question of substituting local agency for European Professors, and Principals of Central Colleges, a different set of considerations arises; and the Governor General in Council does not feel assured that the possibility of dispensing with European Professors and Principals of such Colleges of the different Presidencies and Provinces is at present a question for practical discussion. On the question of the recruitment of such Professors for short terms of years, instead of recruiting them as at present for a long period of pensionable service, His Excellency in Council will await the further views of Local Governments; but, so far as he can at present see, he is inclined to the view that it will be advisable to recommend to the Secretary of State that this system of temporary appointment should be, at all events, tried to a moderate extent. It is very possible that obstacles may be found to exist in the way of the recruitment of specialists of high position for temporary employment in India without securing to them the benefits of leave and absentee allowances. It must also be admitted that a temporary residence in India of even 5 years effects a wrench from English connections and associations, and may affect the prospects of a specialist's ultimate employment in England. There is, on the other hand, in the opinion of the Governor General in Council, no room for doubt that a Professor permanently settled in India has never the opportunity, nor sometimes the

inclination, to keep himself abreast of the times; and that as education advances in India, the necessity for the employment of Professors who are recognised as specialists in the subjects which they are employed to teach will become more and more necessary. Whether the Government will be able to induce specialists ot a high class to accept temporary employment in India or not can only be tested by experiment.

20. Passing from the Professorial and Inspecting Staff to the class of school teachers, it is to be observed that the importance of maintaining properly conducted training schools in order to provide teachers of unquestionable character was insisted on in Home Department Circular No. $\frac{10}{382-391}$, dated 31st December 1887. The statistics of attendance at these schools deserve notice. In 1881-82 there were in British India only 97 schools for training masters attended by 3,563 pupils, and 16 institutions for training mistresses, attended by 519 pupils. In 1885-86 the numbers were 108 training schools for masters, attended by 4,333 pupils, and 27 for mistresses, attended by 616 pupils. It is true that some advance was maintained in 1886-87 when there were 112 training schools for masters, with 4,444 pupils, and 28 for mistresses attended by 672 pupils; but it is obvious that the progress made has not been great. In a later portion of this Resolution allusion will be made to the orders which have been issued by the Government of India on this important part of the educational question, and here all that need be said is that the Governor General in Council trusts that all Local Governments and Administrations will continue to give their special and sustained attention to the subject. At the present time, when there is reason to insist on the maintenance of a stricter system of discipline than has been in force in most Indian schools of recent years, it is more than ever necessary that the men entrusted with the education of the youth of the country should be of unquestionable character trained to habits of teaching and capable of maintaining by their personal influence and other means a high standard of discipline and morality in the schools over which they preside.

21. Paragraphs 104 to 125 of the Report under notice deal with the question of the transfer to Local and Municipal Boards of the administrative control over Primary and Secondary Education. It is to be understood that this administrative control is always exercised in accordance with rules prescribed by Government and subject to the general supervision of the Department of Public Instruction. In some Provinces this transfer has been of a fuller character than in others. For instance, in the Madras Presidency, the Government has, according to Sir Alfred Croft's inquiries, almost retired from the direct management of Primary and Secondary Schools; while in Bombay almost all Primary and about two-thirds of the Secondary Schools have been subordinated to these Boards. In the Punjab, also the transfer has extended, practically, to all Primary and Secondary Schools previously managed by the Department. In Bengal, on the other hand, while the transfer of rural schools is as full as in the Provinces mentioned, the case seems different in regard to schools situated in Municipalities. The information furnished in the report as to the extent to which transfers have been made in the North-Western Provinces and Oudh is not precise; but it is understood that the policy adopted there is not different from that followed elsewhere, though as full effect may not have yet been given to it. This qualified transfer of control over education from Government to Local Boards has been accompanied, as shown in paragraphs 16 and 17 above, by no decrease of the Government contributions towards education. The charges on Provincial revenues were not immediately diminished, though it is to be hoped that, gradually, local taxation for the support of Schools will, to a large extent, relieve the general tax-payer. The effect of this establishment of local control should manifest itself not only in such relief to the public finances, but also in the more efficient discharge of those duties of inspection and general supervision which Members of Local Boards will now share with the officers of the Department.

22. In paragraph 12 above reference was made to industrial schools. Upon this subject the Government of India in 1886 circulated a memorandum to all Local Governments and Administrations, in which the

position of industrial schools was set forth, and it was shown that hitherto little progress. of a substantial character had been made in promoting technical education. Since then the subject has received much attention both from the public and the various Local Governments. Technical education has been brought into prominence by the pressure of two sets of considerations, which, though cognate, are not identical. In the first place, it had been observed that the object of the Education Despatch of 1854, that " useful and practical knowledge suited to every station in life" should be " conveyed to the great mass of the people " of India, was not being attained by a State education too purely literary, and leading too exclusively to literary culture. It was accordingly re. commended by the Education Commission, and accepted by the Government of India as a reform to be desired, that a secondary school course should be introduc. ed, which should fit boys for industrial or commercial careers. This recom. mendation however, though in the right direction, was wanting in the precision necessary in a working rule; and to give it the requisite definiteness, it was suggested in the memorandum of the Home Department, referred to above, that drawing and the rudiments of the sciences should be taught in all but the most elementary schools; and that generally throughout the educational system the study of natural science and the cultivation of the faculty of observing and reasoning from observation and experiment should be encouraged. In other words, it was suggested that studies which may incline to the application of natural science and to scientific research should not be neglected in favour of literature.

23. The second class of considerations which have forced this question into prominence is concerned with the need of industrial occupation for a population rapidly outgrowing the means of support supplied by a too conservative system of agriculture. It is also concerned with the need for scientific methods to develop the material resources of India and to improve its agriculture, its products and manufactures ; so that they may better hold their place in the markets of the world, where competition is carried on with an intensity of purpose, which has been compared to the conditions of warfare. But technical education in this latter sense—that is in the sense of industrial education—is a matter not so easily dealt with as the technical education of the general preliminary character referred to in the preceding paragraph; and it therefore seems desirable that if the present impulse in its favour is to be successfully directed, the conditions of the question should be clearly understood.

24. Technical education proper is the preparation of a man to take part in producing efficiently some special article of commercial demand. It is the cultivation of the intelligence, ingenuity, taste, observation, and manipulative skill of those employed in industrial production, so that they may produce more efficiently. And thus technical education of the special, as contradistinguished from the preparatory, kind is an auxiliary of manufacture and industrial capital. In India at the present time the application of capital to industry has not been developed to the extent which in European countries has rendered the establishment of technical schools on a large scale an essential requisite of success. But the extension of railways, the introduction of mills and factories, the exploration of mineral and other products, the expansion of external trade, and the enlarged intercourse with foreign markets, ought in time to lead to the same results in India as in other countries, and create a demand for skilled labour and for educated foremen, supervisors, and managers. It may be conceded that the effect of these various influences on an Asiatic people is very gradual, and that it would be premature to establish technical schools on such a scale as in European countries, and thereby aggravate the present difficulties, by adding to the educated unemployed a new class of professional men for whom there is no commercial demand. Still a large field is open for the action of Government and public liberality in the direction of promoting special technical education suitable to the immediate requirements of the country and capable of expansion with its growing necessities.

25. The practical conclusion, then, which the Government of India draws from the foregoing premises is, that it should support technical education as an extension of general education in the sense indicated above; and, furthermore,

tive skill.

The field of operation being thus defined, it would ????? to begin with industries which are in some degree centralized, ????? ing into importance with the new growth of trade and manufactures, and which are capable of improvement by the application of scientific ???? ciples to materials and processes. At the centre of such industries a technical school will be useful. To the great railway workshops and factories may with undoubtedly great advantage be attached schools of drawing and design, and of practical instruction in the scientific principles of the handicrafts there earried on. And probably in large stations and municipal towns there will be a demand which will repay those who acquire in local industrial schools superior skill. If caution at the beginning secures success; if capital is tempted by degrees to launch itself in commercial enterprises and the development of the material resources of the country; if a larger demand for the products of skilled labour springs up—then larger developments of special technical education may be fostered in complete harmony with the sound principle that supply should follow demand.

The subject is of such extreme importance, and the insignificance of what has been attempted in India is so conspicuous, that the Governor General in Council is deeply impressed with the necessity for action in whatever way may be practicable and sound. Some Local Governments have indeed recently taken practical measures to promote technical education, and these measures have been viewed with much satisfaction by the Government of India. But as it is desirable that the steps best calculated to promote technical education should form the subject of continuous enquiry and discussion, the Governor General in Council suggests that Local Governments and Administrations should on a convenient but early opportunity take action in two ways. Impressed with the existing want of information at hand as to the extent, character, and circumstances of important local industries in every province of India, His Excellency in Council would, in the first place suggest that in each province an Industrial survey should be completed. In the second place, he would recommend that, with a view to turning the knowledge acquired by such a survey to the best account in the light of the abundant information contained in the Report of the Royal Commission on Technical Education, each Government and Administration should form a committee of educational experts and professional men, who should make suggestions from time to time for the auxiliary supply of appropriate means of technical education; for such modifications of the State system of public instruction as may aid and encourage industries and industrial employment up to the full measure of such requirement at each provincial centre as may be found to exist; and when the circumstances are opportune, for the establishment of a Technological Institute, for the enlargement of the provincial schools of Art and Design, and for the larger co-operation of the University in the promotion of the object in view.

In furtherance of these suggestions, much valuable aid can be rendered by the various Provincial Departments of Land Records and Agriculture upon which the Resolution $\frac{6}{340-50}$ of 8th December 1881 laid the duty of promoting new industries, and of leading the people to a fuller knowledge of agricultural Science.

26. The subject of discipline and moral training in schools and colleges is regarded by the Governor General in Council as one of the most important ques-

system needs improvement and change may be inferred from the suggestions which His Excellency in Council made for the consideration of Local Governments. These suggestions were—

(1) The provision of efficient training schools and colleges for teachers and the employment as teachers only of those who have given satisfaction during a course of training :

(2) the extension of a system of teaching having a direct bearing upon personal conduct :

(3) the repression of breaches of discipline in accordance with certain well-defined rules :

(4) the introduction of conduct registers :

(5) the extension of the hostel or boarding-house system to the fullest extent that the public finances or private liberality will permit :

(6) the introduction of a system of monitors to be made responsible for the conduct of the scholars while in, and as far as possible while out of, school :

(7) the exclusion from school of boys who have not reached a certain class by a certain age.

(8) the introduction of inter-school rules defining the conditions under which students should be allowed to pass from one school to another :

(9) the opening of playgrounds and gymnasia.

His Excellency in Council also suggested that while the moral supervision by Principals and Professors over students in colleges could best be rendered more effective by the example and personal qualities of the Principal and Professors, it might be possible to supplement this influence by the adoption of rules in support of authority, and the direction which the rules might take was indicated to Local Governments and Administrations. The Governor General in Council now awaits the replies to these suggestions.

27. It is true, as has been observed in the letter under notice, that, in the case of colleges even more than in the case of schools, doubts have been expressed as to the possibility of introducing distinct moral teaching where there is no religious instruction ; and in their Report the Education Commission point, as a means of meeting the difficulty, to the establishment of aided colleges in which religious teaching can be fully recognized. It is clearly stated in the circular letter from the Home Department that the Governor General in Council entirely approves of the views of the Education Commission on this point, and would gladly see an increase in the number of aided colleges and schools, in which religious instruction may be freely given. But His Excellency in Council also observed that, though there is greater difficulty in introducing moral teaching into State than into aided colleges, the difficulty does not seem to have been hitherto seriously faced by Education Departments generally ; and until failure follows an earnest effort at imparting moral instruction in colleges, he is unwilling to admit that success may not be secured.

In pursuance of this opinion attention has again been called to the proposal made by the Education Commission that an attempt should be made to prepare a moral textbook, based upon the fundamental principles of natural religion, such as may be taught in all Government and non-Government Colleges. The Government of India and the Secretary of State entertained doubts as to the wisdom of this recommendation at the time when the proposals of the Commis-

further to it here.

No. 2̶4̶7̶/̶4̶2̶

ORDER.—Ordered, that copy of the above Resolution be forwarded to the Local Governments and Administrations marginally noted and to the Revenue and Agricultural Department, for information.

Madras.	Central Provinces.
Bombay.	Burma.
Bengal.	Assam.
North-Western Provinces and Oudh.	Coorg.
Punjab.	Hyderabad.

Ordered also, that the Resolution be published in the Supplement to the *Gazette of India.*

HOME DEPARTMENT,
EDUCATION;
Simla, 13 July 1888.

(True Extract.)

A. P. MACDONNELL,
Secretary to the Government of India.

REVIEW

OF

EDUCATION IN INDIA

IN

1886.

CHAPTER I.

PRELIMINARY.

Object of the Report.—The following report is written in obedience to the orders of the Government of India communicated to me in the Home Department letter No. 124, dated the 18th May 1887, placing me on special duty for that purpose. In the letter quoted, reference was made to a Despatch from the Secretary of State, No. 43, dated the 23rd April 1885, in paragraph 7 of which "it was desired that, in order to stimulate the efforts of the various au-"thorities in the promotion of education on the lines laid down by the Supreme "Government and the Secretary of State with reference to the report of the Edu-"cation Commission, the Government of India should direct the preparation of a "general annual report embracing the important features of the several provin-"cial reports (including Madras and Bombay)." It was explained that no such general report had up to the present time been drawn up, because the provincial reports on Public Instruction prior to the year 1885-86 did not proceed on the lines referred to. The provincial reports for that year, however, contain for the first time a summary of the steps that have been taken to carry out the recommendations of the Education Commission; these have been supplemented by special reports of a later date from the Local Governments; and it has accordingly become possible to draw up the report required by the Secretary of State.

2. Scope of the Report.—The instructions conveyed in the letter cited above were that the report should be confined to "a compendium of the "information supplied by the different Local Governments as regards the con-"dition of education in each province, the methods and organisation by which "it is imparted, and the extent to which effect is being given to the recommend-"ations of the Education Commission." In accordance with these orders, the present report is confined to a statement of facts and a summary of progress, in which criticism and controversial matter are as far as possible avoided. The facts which it embodies are those contained in the report of the Education Commission and the remarks of the Local Governments thereon, in the departmental reports for the ten Provinces of India from 1881-82 to 1885-86, and in the replies sent by Local Governments to inquiries from the Home Department as to the extent to which the recommendations of the Commission have been carried out. The purpose of this report, as one which is intended, not for an exposition of views, but for a record of facts, has been steadily kept in mind; and my endeavour has been to select out of the mass such leading facts of educational interest as are most frequently sought for in a work of reference, and to arrange them in a clear and consecutive form. Where full information as to systems or courses of instruction has been given in the report of the Education Commission, I have thought it unnecessary to repeat such information at any length.

3. **Period covered by the Report.**—The figures furnished in this report are those for the 31st March 1886, the returns for the following year 1886-87 not having been accessible until the work was near completion. But it has been found possible to bring down the report to a later date than that just quoted. The Resolutions of the Local Governments upon the departmental reports for 1885-86 contain an account of all important events and declarations of educational policy up to the close of the year 1886, about which time the Resolutions were generally issued. The special reports of the Local Governments, showing the steps that had been taken to carry out the recommendations of the Commission, were also submitted at various times in the year 1886, and in one instance as late as July 1887. Hence this report may be regarded as bringing down the history of education in India to the close of the calendar year 1886.

On other grounds it has been found necessary to carry back the inquiry to an earlier date. The facts and statistics quoted by the Commission are those for the year 1881-82; and in order to present a clear view of the operations of the year 1886 in the light of the Commission's report, it is necessary to exhibit the changes that took place and the progress made in the intervening years. That necessity is rendered all the more cogent by the fact that, within this intermediate period, revised tabular statements and a new system of classification were prescribed for the Education Departments in India. Under the Resolution of the Government of India in the Home Department, No. 2—111-19, dated the 13th February 1882, a Sub-Committee of the Education Commission was appointed to revise the annual statistical returns of education. The revised forms recommended by the Sub-Committee were approved by the Government of India in the Home Department Resolution No. 9—338-358, dated the 29th October 1883, and were adopted in the annual returns of 1883-84 for all provinces of India except the Punjab, in which their introduction was postponed to the following year. The new system introduced methods of classification which differed from those employed in most provinces, especially in the treatment of primary or middle departments attached to middle and high schools; these attached departments being no longer regarded as separate institutions, but as integral parts of the schools to which they belonged. The necessary result was a large apparent reduction in the total number of schools, together with a large apparent increase in the number of pupils in secondary schools and in the cost of their maintenance; and a corresponding decrease under primary schools. By the same rules, again, definition was given to a new class —that of "schools under public management"; and while this class differed materially from the "Government schools" of the Education Commission's report, with which alone it could be compared, the connected returns showed for the first time the subordinate divisions of which the class was composed. Thirdly, the transfer of schools to the control of local or municipal boards involved in many cases the transfer of funds to meet their cost; and the amounts so transferred, though still derived from provincial revenues, were thenceforward shown in the returns of many provinces as expended by the local bodies that administered them. From all these causes it follows that no useful or even intelligible comparison can be made between the different classes of schools and scholars, the expenditure incurred in their maintenance, **and the different sources from which that expenditure was derived, for the year 1881-82 as given in the report of the Education Commission, and for the year 1886 now to be furnished, without** a full explanation of the changes introduced by the new system of classification.

Further, in accordance with the orders of Government, the report of the Education Commission took no account either of schools for Europeans and Eurasians, or of schools for technical instruction, and the figures relating to such institutions were omitted from its returns. The present report is subject to no exemptions of this kind; and it will accordingly be necessary, in order to make any comparison possible, to reproduce the figures of 1881-82 with these omissions inserted. Similar considerations apply to the statistics of education in Burma, which were excluded from the report of the Commission, but are dealt with, like those of other provinces, in the following pages. The working of Indian Universities was another excluded subject which it has equally been found necessary to consider, so far at least as any intermediate changes in their regulations have affected the course and progress of education.

In order, therefore, to bring the report of the Commission into line with the present and any future reports of the same kind, it has been found necessary to give an account of educational progress in the intervening period. The scope of this report has therefore been unavoidably enlarged, so that it includes a history of education not merely for 1886, but for the three preceding years.

4. Its Divisions.—For the reasons just stated, the report is divided into two parts; the first dealing with the three years 1881-82 to 1884-85, the second carrying the history down to the end of the year 1886. The earlier portion is merely introductory, and presents little else than a dry summary, chiefly statistical and financial, of the period to which it relates. Though it extends to some length, it has been treated as concisely as the complexity of the subject and the necessity of furnishing a full record of facts have allowed. For the sake of clearness, however, it has occasionally been judged expedient to introduce into the earlier portion explanatory matter that would have found a more fitting place in the later and more important part. Conversely, action on the lines recommended by the Commission was in many instances taken before the year 1885-86; but regard being had to the main object of the present report, it has been thought advisable to postpone to the later chapter the consideration of all such changes, so as to present them in a clear and connected form. These points being understood, the introductory portion will bring down the facts and figures as furnished by the Commission, and certain others which were excluded from their purview, to the commencement of the year with which the present report has specially to deal.

It will then be possible to take up the provincial reports for the year 1885-86, and to show, as required by the Government of India, first, the actual condition of education in each province; secondly, the methods and organisation by which it is imparted; and thirdly, the extent to which effect is being given to the recommendations of the Commission. Those parts of the subject which admit of such treatment will be illustrated by comparative tables for the separate provinces and for successive years; differences in the systems of administration will be pointed out; and a detailed account will be given of the progress made in each province on the lines which the Commission and the Government of India have laid down. Attention will be drawn to such changes as derive special importance from the recommendations of the Commission, such as the progress made in primary education, the transfer of Government institutions to local control, the acceptance of educational charges and responsibilities by local and municipal boards, and the like.

Lastly, the report will be elucidated by the seven general tables now pre-

5. Order of Subjects.—The report of the Education Commission follows one method of arrangement; the provincial reports follow another; and each includes subjects which the other omits. The present report has to pay regard to both methods of classification; but it has been found advisable to adopt the latter, with a view chiefly to convenience in the preparation of future reports of the same kind, which will necessarily be compiled from the provincial reports. The order of subjects followed in that chapter which deals with the year 1886 will therefore be as follows:

  I.—General and Statistical Summary of the year's operations.

  II.—Controlling Agencies, including the transfer of departmental institutions to local bodies, and legislation relating to local and municipal boards.

  III.—University Education.

  IV.—School Education, General—
  (*a*) Secondary Schools.
  (*b*) Primary Schools.

  V.—School Education, Special
  (*a*) Training Schools, including arrangements for the selection and training of teachers.
  (*b*) Other Schools of Special Instruction.

  VI.—Female Education.

  VII.—Education of Special Classes—
  (*a*) Europeans and Eurasians.
  (*b*) Muhammadans.

  VIII.—Private Schools.

  IX.—Discipline and Moral Training in Schools and Colleges.

  X.—Educational Conferences, including revision of the grant-in-aid rules.

This distribution, while it generally follows the order of the departmental reports, covers and includes all the subjects of chief importance discussed by the Education Commission except the Financial Summary (Chapter XII). This last may, for the present purpose, be neglected, since it is mainly historical and explanatory, and is followed by no specific recommendations. The points on which it touches may be conveniently considered under the several sections of the report and in the General Summary. The recommendations of the Commission under other heads, and the extent to which they have been carried out in the different provinces of India, will be considered in the sections specially relating to them.

CHAPTER II.

EDUCATION IN INDIA FROM THE CLOSE OF THE YEAR 1881-82 TO THE CLOSE OF THE YEAR 1884-85.

I.—SCHOOLS AND SCHOLARS.

6. General Statistics of Attendance, 1881-82 to 1884-85.—The following table exhibits in a compendious form the statistics of attendance in schools and colleges throughout India and British Burma at the close of each year from 1881-82 to 1884-85. The figures are taken from the provincial departmental reports; and it has been already explained that the departmental returns for 1881-82 differ in certain particulars from those furnished in the report of the Education Commission :—

CLASS OF INSTITUTIONS.	1881-82.		1882-83.		1883-84.		1884-85.	
	Schools.	Pupils.	Schools.	Pupils.	Schools.	Pupils.	Schools.	Pupils.
Arts Colleges, English	63	5,442	70	6,123	72	6,290	78	6,780
,, ,, Oriental	4	595	4	575	3	488	4	664
Professional Colleges	18	1,545	19	1,753	19	(a) 1,882	20	2,192
Secondary Schools, English, for boys	2,134	149,265	2,244	162,088	2,175	229,771	2,204	254,802
Secondary Schools, Vernacular, for boys	1,798	66,466	1,814	69,391	1,805	105,719	1,787	127,170
Secondary Schools, English, for girls	146	5,636	178	6,017	170	11,603	210	13,902
Secondary Schools, Vernacular, for girls	44	730	66	1,117	78	5,937	102	7,755
Primary Schools for boys	83,591	2,070,963	98,352	2,394,858	98,389	2,436,884	100,774	2,496,171
,, ,, girls	2,678	85,279	3,180	99,541	3,559	100,715	4,206	113,441
Training Schools for masters	97	3,563	108	4,046	107	4,076	113	4,265
Training Schools for mistresses	16	519	18	603	25	822	28	865
Technical and other Special Schools	125	(b) 5,068	149	(c) 5,818	139	(d) 5,866	153	(e) 6,988
TOTAL PUBLIC SCHOOLS	90,714	2,395,071	106,202	2,752,430	106,541	2,910,053	109,679	3,034,995
PRIVATE SCHOOLS	4,275	56,918	2,883	30,671	13,171	174,194	26,734	336,583
GRAND TOTAL	94,989	2,451,989	109,085	2,783,101	119,712	3,084,247	136,413	3,371,578

(a) In addition to 40 students of Law classes, included under Arts Colleges.
(b) ,, ,, 1,000 pupils of Drawing and Agricultural classes already included under Secondary Schools.
(c) ,, ,, 1,143 ,, ,, ,, ,,
(d) ,, ,, 1,372 ,, ,, ,, ,,
(e) ,, ,, 1,641 ,, ,, ,, ,,

7. Definition of Public and Private Schools.—The most general result, therefore, is that the schools of India increased, within the three years to which the table refers, from 94,989 to 136,413, and the pupils reading in them from 2,451,989 to 3,371,578. These figures, however, require further explanation to make their meaning clear. In the first place, it is necessary to explain the distinction between public and private schools which was established by the Resolution of the Government of India in the Home Department, No. 9—338-358, dated the 29th October 1883, and introduced into the returns of all provinces (except the Punjab) for the year 1883-84. Under the classification up to that time in force, the terms "public" and "private" schools had signified respectively schools under public and schools under private management. The Education Commission took exception to the term "private institutions" when applied to those schools and colleges which conform in every respect to the regulations and standards of the Education Department. "The term," it stated, "is "held to convey an invidious distinction, and to imply that these schools are not "only under private management but that they serve no public purpose. We "therefore propose to apply in future the term 'public schools' to all schools

"which form a regular and recognised part of the system of public instruction
".............Private institutions will include all indigenous schools which have
"not accepted the departmental standards of instruction, and all others in which
"the course of instruction, however advanced, does not conform to the stand-
"ards prescribed or accepted by the Department or by the University, and which
"submit to no public test. All such schools should be shown in a class by them-
"selves;" subject however to the condition that they should not be called upon
to supply any money-returns. This principle was adopted by the Sub-Committ-
tee of the Education Commission, appointed under the Resolution of the 13th
February 1882 for the revision of the annual statistical returns of education;
and in accordance with its recommendations, the Government of India, in the
Resolution of the 29th October 1883, laid down the following definitions:—

"Every school or college in which the course of study conforms to the
"standards prescribed by the Department of Public Instruction or by the Uni-
"versity, and which either is inspected by the Department, or regularly presents
"pupils at the public examinations held by the Department or by the Univer-
"sity, is called a *public* institution."

"Every school or college not coming within the above definition is called
"a *private* institution."

Then followed the division (with which we are not for the moment concerned) of public schools into those under public and those under private
management. The former class was sub-divided into (1) Government or departmental schools, (2) schools maintained by local or municipal boards, (3)
schools maintained by Native States, to which was subsequently added (4) schools
maintained by other departments of Government or in other ways. The latter
class was sub-divided into aided and unaided schools, according as they did or
did not receive aid from Government or from a local or municipal board. It
may be noticed in passing that the term "departmental institutions" in the
tables appended to the report of the Education Commission includes not only
departmental schools properly so called (that is, Government schools), but also
schools maintained by local and municipal boards. Schools maintained by Native
States are classed in those returns under unaided institutions.

8. Private Schools from 1881-82 to 1884-85.—In accordance with the
definition of public and private schools to which reference has just been made,
the provincial returns for 1883-84 included for the first time the new class of
private indigenous schools. These, indeed, had all along been shown in the returns for Bengal, in which province the whole fabric of public primary education was and is based on the indigenous system, and in which private "pathsalas" pass into public schools by almost imperceptible gradations. The 4,275
schools shown against the siding "private schools" for 1881-82, and the 2,883
schools shown against the same siding for 1882-83, are the unaided and unin-
spected pathsalas, tols, and maktabs of Bengal, which had furnished returns to
the Department, but had in no other way been affected by the departmental system. In the returns for 1883-84 every province (with one exception) rendered
an account of its private institutions, and the number accordingly rose to 13,171;
the chief contributors being Bombay with 3,081 schools, and the North-Western
Provinces and Oudh with 5,928. In the returns for the following year 1884-85,
the Punjab for the first time appears, bringing 12,716 schools to the total of 26,734.
More than half this large number of indigenous institutions in the Punjab are
small Muhammadan schools in which the Koran alone is read, the average number
of pupils in each not exceeding 10. The indigenous schools of the North-Western
Provinces and Oudh are mainly vernacular pathsalas, and these also contain only
some 10 or 11 pupils on an average,—much the same number as is found in the
indigenous pathsalas of Bengal and in the *kyoungs* of British Burma. In Assam

and Madras, for the same year 1884-85, the average number of pupils stands at 15 and 17 respectively. In the former province, where there never was an indigenous system of secular education, nearly all the private schools are of a religious kind, chiefly for Muhammadans. In the latter, in which the system of elementary instruction has been, as in Bengal, mainly erected on an indigenous basis, the private vernacular schools are those which have not yet been received into the departmental system, and in them the average number of pupils sinks to 14. In Bombay, where the primary system is almost exclusively the creation of departmental effort, the number of pupils in an indigenous elementary school is as high as 22. The general purport of these figures, so far as they relate to non-religious schools, is clear. In those provinces, such as Bengal, Burma, and Madras, in which the primary system is entirely or largely based upon indigenous material, and where therefore for many years the best of the indigenous schools have been absorbed into the departmental system, those that still remain outside it are of necessity the poorest and weakest of their class. Where, on the contrary, indigenous schools remain generally outside the departmental system and follow out on an independent course their own ideas of what is advantageous and useful, many of them will be popular and well-attended, and the average number of pupils will rise in proportion. Such is the case in Bombay; in the North-Western Provinces the indigenous schools do not seem to be very popular or successful, owing to causes described in paragraph 124 of the Education Commission's Report.

9. Public Schools and Colleges from 1881-82 to 1884-85.—We can now turn to the figures showing the progress of public institutions, that is, of those institutions that form a regular and recognised part of the system of public instruction. The total number of public schools advanced from 90,714 with 2,395,071 pupils in 1881-82, to 109,679 schools with 3,034,995 pupils in 1884-85, an increase of 21 per cent. in schools and of 27 per cent. in pupils. But this increase was attended by intermediate fluctuations that deserve notice. In the first year the schools increased to 106,202 with 2,752,430 pupils. This rapid advance was not maintained. From 1882-83 to 1883-84 the number of public schools increased from 106,202 to 106,541 only; while at the same time the increase in the number of pupils from 2,752,430 to 2,910,053, though smaller than in the previous year, is still considerable. In the following year there is again a marked increase in the number of schools, from 106,141 to 109,679; while the number of pupils rises in a slightly higher ratio, from 2,910,053 to 3,034,995. To put it briefly, the number of schools increased in the first of the three years by 17 per cent., in the second year it was nearly stationary, and in the third year it increased by 3 per cent.; while in the same three years the number of pupils increased by 15, 6, and 4 per cent. respectively. These somewhat remarkable fluctuations suggest the existence of a special cause at work. They are in fact explained to a great extent by the changes that took place in the same years in the lower primary schools of Bengal,—a point that will be more fully considered hereafter. The disturbance introduced by the special circumstances of these Bengal schools is indeed so great that it will be convenient to separate them for a moment, and look at the figures as they stand when unaffected by that cause. We thus get the following result:—

	1881-82.		1882-83.		1883-84.		1884-85.	
	Schools.	Pupils.	Schools.	Pupils.	Schools.	Pupils.	Schools.	Pupils.
Total of Public Schools in India	90,714	2,395,071	106,202	2,572,430	106,541	2,910,053	109,679	3,034,995
Lower Primary Schools of Bengal	48,844	812,339	60,337	1,016,482	61,253	1,073,934	62,863	1,121,900
TOTAL, EXCLUDING LOWER PRIMARIES IN BENGAL.	41,870	1,582,732	45,865	1,735,948	45,288	1,836,119	46,816	1,913,095

These figures present a much more natural and intelligible rate of progress both of schools and of pupils The number of pupils increases year by year in a fairly steady ratio. There is a corresponding increase in the number of schools; but it suffers an apparent check in the year 1883-84. The cause of this has now to be explained.

10. New Classification of Schools in 1883-84.—The Sub-Committee appointed for the revision of educational forms, to which reference has already been made, submitted a further recommendation, that the practice of showing the different departments of schools as separate institutions should be discontinued. This proposal was sanctioned; and accordingly a high school containing a high, a middle, and a primary department, or a middle school similarly divided, was no longer shown as three or as two schools, but as one only. The effect of this was to bring about a large apparent reduction in the number of middle and of primary schools,—a reduction amounting, in the case of middle schools, to a number equal to that of the existing high schools that had middle departments, and in the case of primary schools, to the number of high and independent middle schools together. The number of secondary schools in 1882-83 (excluding those of Bengal, in which the separation of schools into departments had never been made) exceeded 2,000; and though not all of these had primary departments attached, the greater number had; and the apparent loss of nearly 600 schools for the year 1883-84, referred to in the last paragraph, is thus seen to be merely nominal, and to be consistent with an actual and even large increase in the number of separate and independent institutions. The total number of pupils was of course unaffected by this change of classification, and, as the table shows, the number increased in 1883-84 by a little over 100,000. But the number of pupils returned under the new classification for secondary schools was increased to the full extent of the primary, or middle and primary, departments now included under middle and high schools respectively; and accordingly we find from the table in para. 6 that, while there was in that year a nominal decrease of 78 under the head of secondary schools for boys, English and vernacular, the number of their pupils increased from 231,979 to 335,490, that is, by more than 100,000. Notwithstanding these wholesale transfers, the total number of pupils in primary schools (those of Bengal being still excluded), only fell from 1,378,376 to 1,362,950, or by 15,426; that is to say, the apparent loss arising from the transfer of primary departments was made good except to the extent of about 15 per cent.

11. Summary of Progress, 1881-82 to 1884-85.—Returning to the table in para. 6, we find that Arts colleges, English, increased within these three years from 63 to 78, the number of their pupils increasing in much the same proportion. Professional colleges increased from 18 to 20, with a much larger proportionate increase, amounting to 42 per cent., in the number of their pupils. Secondary schools, English and vernacular, for boys increased from 3,932 to 3,991, notwithstanding the fact that the middle departments of high schools were no longer separately counted. The number of their pupils increased from 215,731 to 381,972, an increase, however, from which large deductions have to be made owing to the causes just explained. Secondary schools for girls increased from 190 to 312, and their pupils from 6,366 to 21,657; both sets of figures being subject to the same considerations as affect those of boys' schools. Primary schools for boys increased from 83,591 to 100,774, and their pupils from 2,070,963 to 2,496,171; or if the Bengal returns be excluded, from 34,747 schools to 37,911, and from 1,258,624 pupils to 1,374,271, to which increase should rightly be added the whole number of primary departments and their pupils, now merged in the secondary schools to which they are attached. Primary schools for girls increased from 2,678 to 4,206, and their pupils from

85,279 to 113,441—an increase which again represents less than the truth. Training schools for masters increased from 97 to 113, and the students reading in them from 3,563 to 4,265; those for mistresses increased in a still larger ratio, from 16 with 519 pupils to 28 with 865. Technical and other special schools increased from 125 to 153; but this class, as will afterwards appear, includes a number of institutions which have no concern with technical education properly so called.

12. Provincial Returns of Schools and Colleges, 1881-82 to 1884-85.—It will now be convenient to show in what proportions the general increase in public institutions above described has been distributed among the different provinces of India. In doing so, it will also be convenient to divide the schools still further according to their management; showing what increase has taken place under the respective heads of schools under public management, aided schools under private management, and unaided schools. And as the Education Commission has declared (para. 283) that "the relation of the State "to secondary is different from its relation to primary education, in that the "means of primary education may be provided without regard to local co-opera- "tion, while it is ordinarily expedient to provide the means of secondary educa- "tion only when adequate local co-operation is forthcoming," it will further be advisable to exhibit in separate tables the figures for primary schools and for all other schools. These tables are accordingly subjoined, it being understood that indigenous and other private schools are not included.

I.—Primary Schools.

	1881-82.						1884-85.					
PROVINCE.	UNDER PUBLIC MANAGEMENT.		AIDED SCHOOLS.		UNAIDED SCHOOLS.		UNDER PUBLIC MANAGEMENT.		AIDED SCHOOLS.		UNAIDED SCHOOLS.	
	Schools.	Pupils.	Schools.	Pupils.	Schools.	Pupils.	Schools.	Pupils.	Schools.	Pupils.	Schools.	Pupils.
Madras	1,265	47,218	7,480	207,961	5,811	109,575	1,211	39,447	8,657	229,331	4,431	83,972
Bombay	3,811	243,959	196	13,902	1,331	74,827	5,712	371,526	532	26,004	37	2,201
Bengal	28	916	47,375	835,444	4,376	62,038	60	1,755	61,658	1,176,173	6,164	84,833
N.-W. Provinces and Oudh	5,561	197,060	270	16,091	41	1,159	5,157	180,938	264	12,005	44	1,608
Punjab	1,550	88,264	293	15,394	...	...	1,494	76,902	297	11,917	10	282
Central Provinces	891	55,694	367	19,001	86	3,229	1,023	67,804	603	24,481	92	2,452
Burma	26	2,657	782	35,604	2,430	49,489	23	1,633	1,292	55,881	3,631	73,017
Assam	7	187	1,256	35,643	88	2,352	1,249	36,391	335	9,616	95	2,308
Berar	469	28,574	212	4,263	207	2,672	502	27,090	222	4,495	98	1,124
Coorg	57	2,978	3	91	...	...	63	3,283	4	128	...	...
TOTAL	13,665	667,507	58,234	1,183,394	14,370	305,341	16,494	806,769	73,864	1,549,981	14,602	251,827

II.—Schools other than Primary.

	Schools.	Pupils.	Schools.	Pupils.	Schools.	Pupils.	Schools.	Pupils.	Schools.	Pupils.	Schools.	Pupils.
Madras	209	8,508	348	15,332	340	5,089	247	17,943	515	45,008	88	7,762
Bombay	194	12,992	111	9,218	61	3,993	315	23,240	137	14,378	12	2,088
Bengal	299	31,163	1,428	89,835	298	30,331	308	32,279	1,588	110,452	351	37,349
N.-W. Provinces and Oudh	545	7,433	98	3,783	6	70	506	47,732	101	15,771	21	2,047
Punjab	198	5,592	43	1,177	..	...	205	35,325	45	7,985	2	582
Central Provinces	70	2,845	26	1,004	3	29	65	3,131	25	1,141	1	1
Burma	20	791	27	482	1	27	29	2,565	35	4,428	...	...
Assam	35	3,623	58	4,205	11	761	48	4,318	60	4,681	14	1,455
Berar	8	382	...	...	..	...	27	5,528	...	...	...	...
Coorg	3	164	...	...	..	...	3	415	1	16	...	...
TOTAL	1,581	73,493	2,144	125,036	720	40,300	1,753	172,476	2,507	203,860	489	51,284

	1881-82.		1884-85.	
	Schools.	Pupils.	Schools.	Pupils.
TOTAL OF PRIMARY SCHOOLS	86,269	2,156,242	104,960	2,609,612
TOTAL OF OTHER SCHOOLS	4,445	238,829	4,699	425,383
GRAND TOTAL	90,714	2,395,071	109,679	3,034,995

13. Provincial Returns of Primary Schools.—A comparison of the returns of primary schools for 1881-82 and 1884-85 is, as before, rendered difficult by changes of classification that took place in the interval. Not only were primary departments no longer counted as separate schools, but the following transfers also took effect. Primary schools in Native States in the Bombay Presidency, which in the latter year numbered 1,604 and were included among schools under public management, were in the former returned as unaided schools, and appear to have numbered about 1,300. Again, of 1,256 primary schools shown as 'aided' in the returns of Assam for 1881-82, a number amounting to nearly 1,000 were under the direct control of district officers or local boards; and schools of this class were accordingly returned in 1883-84 as being 'under public management.' If the corresponding corrections be made, it will be seen that (approximately) primary schools under public management increased from 15,965 to 16,494; aided schools from 57,234 to 73,864; and unaided schools from 13,070 to 14,602. The greatest increase in schools under public management took place in Bombay, where 600 were added to the list. Considerable additions were also made in Assam and the Central Provinces, while 400 schools of this class disappeared from the returns in the North-Western Provinces and Oudh. Aided schools (after correction of the figures for Assam) increased from 57,234 to 73,864; but towards this increase of 16,630 schools Bengal contributed no fewer than 14,283. Half of the remainder are accounted for by the increase in Madras, and the rest by Burma, Bombay, and the Central Provinces. The increase of about 1,500 in the number of unaided schools is more than accounted for by an increase of 1,800 in Bengal; an addition of 1,200 schools in Burma being counterbalanced by a reduction in Madras of nearly 1,400, mostly transferred to the aided class. The circumstances that led to these changes will be considered later on. For the moment it will be sufficient to observe that schools under public management, that is those established for the most part independently of the co-operation of the people, increased by about 530, 300 of these having been established in Native States; and that aided schools, in other words, those which depend for their existence upon the co-operation and even the initiative of the people, increased by nearly 2,350.

The returns for 1881-82 do not enable me to state how many of the schools under public management (described generally as 'Government schools' in the returns of that year) were under the direct management of the Department, and how many under that of public bodies. But it may be mentioned here that of the 16,494 primary schools under public management in 1884-85, 13,370 were under local or district boards, 390 under municipal committees, and 1,640 in Native States, leaving only 1,094 under the direct administration of the Department, of which 501 were in Berar and 323 in the Central Provinces.

14. Provincial Returns of Schools other than Primary.—The second of the two tables shown above refers to secondary schools, schools of special instruction, and colleges. Those under public management increased by 152, and aided schools under private management by 363; while the number of unaided schools fell off by 231. The greatest changes took place in Madras, which added 38 to the number of its schools under public management and 167 to that of its aided schools, while 252 disappeared from the list of unaided schools. The returns of Bombay are chiefly noticeable for a large increase of 102 in the number of schools under public management; the list of aided schools being increased by 26, and that of unaided schools reduced by 49. In Bengal there is a small increase of 9 in the number of Government institutions, while there are large additions of 160 and 53 respectively, to the list of aided and of unaided schools. In the North-Western Provinces and Oudh there is a decrease of 39 in the returns of schools under public management, which is not made up by any corresponding increase in schools under private management. Assam and Berar, which add 12 and 19 respectively to the number of Government and other publicly-managed schools, account for the remaining differences of importance. On the whole it appears, as regards secondary and other schools of this class, that there has been a considerable, and in Bombay a large, increase in the number of institutions under public management, which has not been met, except in Madras and Bengal, by any large or corresponding increase in the number of aided schools; while the number of unaided schools has been much reduced, owing to the great decrease under that head in Madras. Owing to changes already described in the mode of classification, the number of pupils has been largely augmented, even where there has been a reduction in the number of schools; and it should also be added that, but for the operation of the same cause, the increase in the number of secondary schools would have been considerably greater than the actual figures show. The different classes of institutions coming under this general head of 'schools other than primary' will be separately examined hereafter.

II.—EXPENDITURE.

15. General Statistics of Expenditure, 1881-82 to 1884-85.—The intermediate changes of classification that have affected the returns of institutions and the attendance at them, have also affected to some extent the returns of expenditure, since the cost of high and middle schools now includes that of the lower departments attached to them; the immediate result of the change having been to increase the apparent cost of expenditure on secondary schools, and to reduce by the same amount the cost of primary education. That being understood, it has not been thought necessary to show in this place the expenditure for each of the three years of the period under review. The following table compares the expenditure on different classes of institutions, and for different heads of administrative charge, for the years 1881-82 and 1884-85 only :—

CLASS OF INSTITUTION.	1881-82.			1884-85.		
	Provincial Revenues.	Other sources.	TOTAL.	Provincial Revenues.	Other sources.	TOTAL.
	R	R	R	R	R	R
Arts Colleges, English	6,89,157	5,25,630	12,14,787	7,81,022	6,62,908	14,43,930
Arts Colleges, Oriental	16,622	6,500	23,122	18,229	26,393	44,622
Professional Colleges	2,86,713	92,457	3,79,170	4,30,840	1,07,758	5,38,598
Secondary schools, English, for boys	13,82,225	25,04,698	38,86,923	13,41,592	43,24,443	56,66,035
Secondary schools, Vernacular, for boys	2,13,563	3,29,351	5,42,914	1,76,869	5,96,819	7,73,688
Secondary schools, English, for girls	97,426	2,63,540	3,60,966	1,97,445	5,85,458	7,82,903
Secondary schools, Vernacular, for girls	4,474	11,000	15,474	37,548	72,142	1,09,690
Primary schools for boys	13,41,232	53,95,534	67,36,766	12,13,237	59,53,723	71,66,960
Primary schools for girls	2,41,543	6,46,687	8,88,230	2,39,578	6,02,331	8,41,909
Training schools for Masters	2,19,201	1,04,495	3,23,696	2,53,387	2,04,238	4,57,625
Training schools for Mistresses	41,225	20,542	61,767	64,693	33,662	98,355
Technical and other special schools	3,81,203	1,85,880	5,67,083	4,13,445	3,06,902	7,20,347
TOTAL OF TUITIONAL CHARGES	49,14,584	1,00,86,314	1,50,00,898	51,67,885	1,34,76,777	1,86,44,662
University	54,886	1,22,854	1,77,740	49,000	1,63,943	2,12,943
Superintendence and control	14,81,925	2,00,973	16,82,898	14,28,447	4,43,624	18,72,071
Scholarships	3,16,079	1,92,596	5,08,675	3,51,343	2,08,412	5,59,755
Buildings	3,60,214	5,11,869	8,72,083	6,95,843	7,78,665	14,74,508
Miscellaneous	1,63,566	2,01,555	3,65,121	2,07,712	3,75,942	5,83,654
TOTAL OF NON-TUITIONAL CHARGES	23,76,670	12,29,847	36,06,517	27,32,345	16,70,586	47,02,931
GRAND TOTAL	72,91,254	1,13,16,161	1,86,07,415	79,00,230	1,54,47,363	2,33,47,593

16. General Statistics: Tuitional and Non-tuitional Expenditure.—
The most salient facts presented in the foregoing statement are the following.
The expenditure from provincial revenues on education has increased from
R72,91,254 to R79,00,230, that is, by R6,08,976, or 8⅓ per cent.; while the expenditure from other sources has increased from R1,13,16,161 to R1,54,47,363,
that is, by R41,31,202, or by 36½ per cent. It will presently appear that these
figures are not strictly accurate; and that owing to direct transfers that have been
made from provincial revenues, to district boards in the North-Western Provinces chiefly, and to municipal funds in Burma, the increase in the Government
expenditure has been greater, and that from other sources less, than the percentages here shown. But before going on to consider these details, it may be noticed that the table divides the expenditure into tuitional and non-tuitional; the
former class of charges including the direct expenditure incurred in maintaining
educational establishments; the latter including indirect charges such as those
for the Universities, for the administration of the Department in direction and
inspection, for scholarships, for buildings and furniture, and for other miscellaneous charges. The importance of this division lies in the fact that the former
class of charges are those in which, according to the Education Despatch of 1854
and the consistent policy of the Government of India, it is hoped and expected
that the people of India will bear a constantly increasing share. Nor does it
appear that this expectation is being falsified. The direct expenditure on the
maintenance of schools and colleges increased from 1½ crores in 1881-82, to one
crore and 86½ lakhs in 1884-85. Of this increase of 36½ lakhs of rupees the
table shows that only some 2½ lakhs were contributed from provincial revenues,
while about 34 lakhs were provided from "other sources," the nature of which
will be examined presently in greater detail. Liberal allowance may be made
for the transfers mentioned above from provincial revenues to local and municipal
funds, and still the general tenor of these figures will not be altered.

The second class of charges, namely, the non-tuitional, are in a greater degree matters of administration, in meeting the cost of which the co-operation of the
public, or of local bodies representing the public, can be less readily looked for.
Still, it appears that out of a total increase of 11 lakhs under this head of charge,
only 3½ lakhs came from provincial revenues, leaving 7½ lakhs to be contributed
from local sources, chiefly under the heads of 'inspection' and 'school buildings.'

17. General Statistics: Provincial Expenditure.—The total increase
of expenditure is distributed over the several provinces of India in the proportions shown below:—

	1881-82.			1884-85.				
	Provincial Revenues.	Other Sources.	TOTAL.	Provincial Revenues.	Other Sources.	TOTAL.	Provincial Revenues.	Other Sources.
	R	R	R	R	R	R	R	R
Madras	9,81,793	24,85,716	34,67,509	11,72,341	30,26,219	41,98,560	1,90,548	5,40,503
Bombay	11,28,148	22,79,360	34,07,508	12,50,084	28,92,650	41,42,734	1,21,936	6,13,290
Bengal	26,46,010	36,22,372	62,68,382	30,76,400	47,38,778	78,15,178	4,30,390	11,16,406
N.-W. Provinces and Oudh	9,28,085	11,27,347	20,55,432	6,31,187	21,61,418	27,92,605	—2,96,898	10,34,071
Punjab	6,30,198	9,54,083	15,84,281	7,14,410	12,82,449	19,96,859	84,212	3,28,366
Central Provinces	3,26,967	3,12,396	6,39,363	3,85,282	3,23,863	7,09,145	58,315	11,467
Burma	2,59,510	2,38,284	4,97,794	2,65,747	5,42,736	8,08,483	6,237	3,04,452
Assam	1,41,371	1,69,724	3,11,095	1,67,842	2,89,220	4,57,062	26,471	1,19,496
Berar	2,35,942	1,17,372	3,53,314	2,21,132	1,74,276	3,95,408	—14,810	56,904
Coorg	13,230	9,507	22,737	15,805	15,754	31,559	1,602	7,160
TOTAL	72,91,254	1,13,16,161	1,86,07,415	79,00,230	1,54,47,363	2,33,47,593	6,08,063	41,32,115

These figures seem at first sight to disclose great varieties of educational
policy. Madras, Bombay, Bengal and the Punjab have incurred increased expenditure from provincial revenues varying from 11 to 19 per cent., accompanied and explained by increased expenditure from local sources in proportions

ranging from 22 to 34 per cent. On the other hand, the North-Western Provinces and Oudh appears to have reduced its public expenditure to the extent of 32 per cent., while at the same time the expenditure from local sources has increased by 93 per cent. In the last-named province, however, there has in reality been no such striking change of policy as the figures, barely stated, seem to show. The change, such as it was, took place in 1882-83; and an account of it in the report for that year is prefaced by the remark that the year had been characterised by no "startling or sweeping reform." The nature of the change is thus described:—"The district school committees of the North-Western Provinces "have been superseded by the newly constituted district boards, which, with "wider powers and heavier responsibilities than their predecessors, have been "entrusted with the financial and administrative control of village and town "schools, and in zila schools with the management of boarding-houses, schol-"arships, and endowments, and with the general financial control of the schools "themselves. Similarly, aided schools with some exceptions have been placed "under local control as regards scrutiny of bills, passing of accounts, and "general visitation and report." (Report for 1882-83, para. 10). Again, in the report for 1884-85 (para. 3) the financial position of the district boards is explained by the statement that its income is made up from the following among other sources: (a) a share of the district rates levied under Acts III and IV of 1878 and credited to provincial revenues, (b) an additional allotment from the general provincial revenues sufficient to meet the board's further liabilities; and it is added that (a) and (b) together "constitute an allotment "from the general provincial fund, the first specifying the amount which is "literally due to the district, and the second the balance required to meet the "charges of all establishments transferred." It appears therefore that the policy thus inaugurated involved no change in the source from which the money was derived, but merely a change in its control; an assignment made from provincial revenues, and up to that time expended on Government schools, being now transferred to district boards together with the charge of the schools themselves. A comparison of the departmental returns of 1881-82 with those of 1882-83 gives the following results:—

	1881-82. R	1882-83. R
Provincial Revenues	9,28,085	3,34,763
Local Cess	5,97,541	12,51,866
Total	15,25,626	15,86,629

But in the text of the report, and in the Government Resolution upon it, the totals just given are jointly shown as "Government expenditure," and this would seem to afford a more correct representation of the facts; the large decrease in the expenditure from provincial revenues, and the corresponding increase in that from local sources, being matters of account only. The circumstances are different, however, in 1884-85. The statement of expenditure for that year stands as follows:—

	R
Provincial Revenues	6,31,187
Local Cess	13,58,579
Total	19,89,766

In this year, it is true there was a nominal increase of R1,36,000 in the Government expenditure, arising from the transfer to the educational returns of the cost of the Enginering College at Roorkee; but after deducting this sum, it appears that there has still been a considerable increase in the expenditure from provincial revenues in the strict sense of the word. In the same way the figures for Burma appear to show only a trifling increase of some 2½ per cent. in the Government expenditure, while the expenditure from local sources has more than doubled. The truth, however, is that the bulk of the additional expenditure from local sources in Burma is actually derived from, and is a charge upon, provincial funds, from which a transfer has been made for educational purposes to municipal bodies. Thus the resolution of the Chief Commissioner on the Education Report for 1881-82 states (para. 13) :—"In future the ex-"penditure from municipal funds will be largely increased. This increase will "not, however, represent any increase in municipal burdens or cause any corre-"sponding relief to provincial funds, from which latter an assignment has been "made to municipalities in consideration of their undertaking all educational "charges within their limits." Again, the Resolution on the report for 1883-84 (para. 3), after stating that the provincial expenditure increased from R2,21,282 to R2,40,788, and the municipal expenditure from R1,82,095 to R2,15,800, goes on to explain :—"The provincial expenditure on education might perhaps be "shown at R1,74,000 more and the municipal expenditure at R1,74,000 less "than the foregoing figures; inasmuch as this sum represents the amount of "provincial money recently made over to municipal and town committees for "expenditure on education." Indeed the only case in which there has been an actual decrease in the expenditure from provincial revenues appears to be that of Berar, where the increased productiveness of the educational cess in 1884-85 relieved provincial funds to a corresponding amount.

18. Expenditure from Provincial Revenues: Tuitional.—The table in paragraph 15 shows that there was a total increase of a little over 6 lakhs in the expenditure from provincial revenues, of which, in round numbers, 2½ lakhs were for tuitional and 3½ lakhs for non-tuitional charges. The increase of R2,53,000, by which the Government expenditure of 1884-85 on schools and colleges exceeds that of 1881-82, is made up of the following principal items :— (1) Arts colleges, R94,000, of which excess R49,000 has been incurred in Bengal (though some portion of this increase is merely nominal), and R11,000 in British Burma; the rest being distributed in various smaller shares over the other provinces that maintain collegiate institutions. (2) Colleges for professional education, R1,44,000; the bulk of which is explained by the transfer to the returns of the Education Department, in 1884-85, of the cost of the Roorkee Engineering College amounting to R1,36,500, previously shown as a Public Works charge. An addition of R9,000 to the cost of the Medical College at Madras accounts for the remainder of the increase. (3) Secondary schools for girls—English R1,00,000, vernacular R33,000. The chief portion of this increase arises in Madras, where there has been an addition of R59,000 to the former and of R30,000 to the latter head of charge. The increase in this and other provinces is for the most part due to the change of classification introduced in 1883-84, whereby for the first time the cost of their attached primary departments was included in that of secondary schools. Concurrently with this change, there was also a real increase in the Government expenditure, corresponding to and caused by the growth of girls' schools of this class, between 1881-82 and 1884-85, from 190 to 312. In Bengal, for example, where the change of classification did not operate, there was an actual increase of R15,000 under this head. (4) Training schools for masters and mistresses, R58,000. The increase actually amounts to R90,000, since there is a nominal decrease of R32,000 in the North-Western Provinces and Oudh, due to the transfer of the charges connected with training schools to the control of district boards. Madras shows an apparently increased expenditure of R51,000 under this head, to be reduced by R20,000 on account of stipends, which in the returns for 1881-82 were separately included under scholarships; and Burma of R17,000. (5) Schools of special instruction, R32,000. Under this head there has been an increase of R24,000 in Bombay, due to increased expenditure on medical schools and the School of Art; and a nominal increase of R18,000 in Bengal, arising from the transfer to provincial revenues of the cost of the Nawab of Moorshedabad's Madrassa, formerly charged to the Nizamut Fund. In other provinces also there has been an increase, amounting in all to R18,000, and thus the total increase of cost under this head amounts to R60,000. This is again brought back to R32,000 by a reduction of R28,000 in Madras, where the charges for medical schools have been for the most part transferred to local and municipal boards.

Against these increased charges must be set the following items of decrease:—
(1) Secondary schools for boys—English R41,000, vernacular R37,000. From what has been said above with regard to the additional charge involved in the amalgamation of attached primary departments with secondary schools—to say nothing of the general development of secondary education in a period of three years—it might have been anticipated that the cost to Government of secondary schools would have shown a considerable increase. This has in fact been the case in Bengal, Madras, Berar, and the Punjab, in which provinces there has been an increased charge to provincial revenues on account of this class of schools varying (in the order named) from R24,000 to R45,000, and amounting altogether to R1,40,000. But all this increase has been cancelled, and more than cancelled, by the transfer of secondary schools to district boards in the North-Western Provinces and Oudh, together with assignments for meeting their cost, amounting to R1,48,000 for English and R35,000 for vernacular schools. Similar transfers and assignments have been made to district boards in Assam and to municipalities in Burma, resulting in apparent reductions of R17,000 and R11,000 respectively, in the Government expenditure on secondary schools of this class. (2) Primary schools for boys, R1,28,000. The reduction is due to the combined operation of causes already named. On the one hand, the transfer of primary departments has led to a decrease of R38,000 in Madras, of R46,000 in the Punjab, and of R45,000 in Berar; while the transfer of schools to local bodies has effected a corresponding reduction of R1,64,000 in the North-Western Provinces and of R25,000 in Burma. On the other hand, there has been a real increase of R1,72,000 in the Government expenditure on primary education in Bengal, due to yearly additions to the grant made for that purpose from provincial revenues; and an increase of R18,000 in the Central Provinces.

19. Expenditure from Provincial Revenues: Non-tuitional.—The increase of R3,56,000 in the Government expenditure for non-tuitional purposes is accounted for—(1) by a large increase of R3,35,000 in the cost of buildings, which rose from R3,60,000 in 1881-82 to R6,95,000 in 1884-85. The greatest increase took place in the North-Western Provinces and Oudh, where it amounted to R1,66,000, distributed to schools under private and under public management in the proportion of 2 to 1. Increased expenditure varying from R16,000 to R33,000 was also incurred in the Central Provinces, Bombay, and Assam, of R52,000 in the Punjab, and of R74,000 in Madras; while there is a real decrease under this head of R12,000 in Bengal and a nominal decrease (by transfer to municipalities) of R24,000 in Burma. (2) There has been a decrease of R53,000 in the Government expenditure upon superintendence and control, that is, upon inspection. This is really a steadily increasing charge, and most provinces in fact exhibit an increase, which amounts to R36,000 in Madras, to R28,000 in Bombay, to R59,000 in Bengal and to R47,000 in Burma. But in the North-Western Provinces and Oudh, there has, as in other similar cases, been a large transfer of funds on this account from provincial revenues to district boards, involving an apparent reduction of R2,06,000 in the cost of inspection to Government. (3) The cost of Universities appears to have decreased by R6,000. There are only three provinces in which Government incurs any charge on this account, namely, Bombay, in which a subsidy of R27,000 a year is made to the University; the Punjab, where the local University is the constituted adviser of the Government in educational matters, and receives an annual grant of R22,000; and Burma, in which an Educational Syndicate discharges the same duties, though without the statutory powers of a University, and receives a grant for the expenses of conducting the annual examinations of schools. The reduction of R6,000 in the charges under this head is due to the disappearance of the last-named grant from the returns; but no report seems to be furnished by the Syndicate to the Burma Education Department, and it is difficult to say whether the charge is still incurred, or whether it is met by fee-receipts. (4) There has been an increase of R35,000 in the State expenditure upon scholarships, of which the largest items are in Assam and Burma, with an increase of R12,000 in each. There is an apparent decrease of R10,000 in the Government expenditure on scholarships in Madras, but this is due to the inclusion in the earlier returns of R20,000 for stipends in training schools, which are rightly shown in the returns of 1884-85 as part of the ordinary expenditure of those institutions. (5) Lastly, miscellaneous charges show an increase of R44,000, though the nature of the items is generally such as to defy analysis.

20. Expenditure from "Other Sources."—The sources of income here referred to are of many different kinds. They include, on the one hand, contributions from district and municipal funds, and, on the other, the proceeds of endowments, subscriptions, and fees. These various sources of income, though all in one sense local, and therefore rightly to be distinguished from the assignments made by Government from provincial revenues, yet differ widely in their nature and origin. Some are derived from taxation, imposed under the authority of legal enactments; others are purely private and personal, and depend on the will of individuals. Some imply self-denial and a readiness to incur sacrifices for the sake of acquiring or promoting education; from others that characteristic is absent. Elements so different need to be separately shown if clear views are to be gained as to the voluntary part the people are taking in the work of education. The following table accordingly separates for each province, for the years 1881-82 and 1884-85 respectively, the contributions made, on the one hand by local or district boards and by municipal bodies, and on the other from subscriptions, from the income of endowments, and other miscellaneous sources, and from fees:—

PROVINCE.	1881-82.				1884-85.			
	Local Funds.	Municipal Funds.	Fees.	Subscriptions, Endowments, &c.	Local Funds.	Municipal Funds.	Fees.	Subscriptions, Endowments, &c.
	R	R	R	R	R	R	R	R
Madras	5,62,534	88,018	10,10,493	8,24,671	6,36,064	1,66,211	13,76,438	8,47,511
Bombay	(a)7,64,055	80,423	5,55,300	(b)8,79,582	(a)9,10,792	97,908	7,80,983	(c)11,02,967
Bengal	9,883	24,953	23,15,634	12,71,902	5,304	71,412	31,75,104	14,90,595
N.W. Provinces and Oudh	5,97,541	(d)52,069	1,62,175	3,15,562	13,58,579	70,863	2,41,858	4,90,118
Punjab	4,49,646	(e)1,44,831	1,20,531	2,39,075	5,05,087	1,50,017	2,08,534	4,18,811
Central Provinces	1,32,256	34,815	40,546	1,04,779	1,29,725	45,464	52,193	(f)96,481
Burma	64,837	33,558	71,612	68,277	76,143	2,53,157	86,139	1,27,297
Assam	63,345	360	60,580	45,439	1,36,666	3,791	91,847	56,916
Berar	86,283	1,377	27,099	2,613	1,20,057	1,674	48,423	4,122
Coorg	7,063	...	2,224	220	7,262	1,821	4,224	2,447
TOTAL	27,37,443	4,60,404	43,66,194	37,52,120	38,85,679	8,62,318	60,65,738	46,33,628
GRAND TOTAL				1,13,16,161				1,54,47,363

(a) Exclusive of local cesses levied in Native States in Bombay.
(b) Inclusive of Native State revenues (R4,58,127) and of local cesses in Native States (R39,102).
(c) Ditto ditto (R5,73,336,, and ditto ditto (R40,666).
(d) Including grants to unaided schools (R2,276)
(e) Excluding municipal grant to the Punjab Oriental College (R6,372).
(f) Including receipts from Native State revenues (R5,146).

21. Character of Local or District Funds.—In every province of India local rates are raised under statutory provisions for expenditure upon local wants, such as roads, schools, and medical relief; and the income so raised is in nearly all cases administered by district boards having statutory powers. The various systems will be described at greater length hereafter. For the present it is sufficient to notice one special point of difference which throws doubt upon the true local (as distinguished from the provincial) origin of some portion of the expenditure said to be derived from local funds; and it is for this reason that the term "local funds" has been substituted in the foregoing statement for the "local rates or cesses" of General Table IV, from which the figures have been taken. In some parts of India—Bombay, Berar, and the Central Provinces—either there is a special educational cess, or else a definite share of the local rates is assigned by law to educational purposes. In other parts the same object is secured by an executive order specifying what share of the cess or other purely local income shall be devoted to education; this share generally varies from one-fourth to one-sixth. In others, again, education receives whatever portion can be spared after prior claims are satisfied. In Bengal no portion of the local rates has ever been assigned to education, except as regards small sums in certain non-regulation districts; and up to the close of the period with which the present report deals, the whole of the cess-income in Bengal was devoted to roads and communications, in accordance with the provisions of the Act. But whatever system be followed, Government in most provinces makes a contribution from general revenues in aid of those services, educational and other, for which the local rates are intended to provide; and the contributions may take the form either of direct assignments or of transferred sources of revenue, all of which are administered by the boards along with their other funds. Now it appears that these additional contributions are very differently treated in different provinces. In some the amount derived from the cess is kept strictly separate and distinct, and the provincial contributions are shown under their proper head as derived from provincial revenues. In others the provincial assignments to the fund are lumped up with the cess, and the heading "local rates or cesses" shows the expenditure from both sources combined. No doubt, when the accounts of a fund involve opening and closing balances, when the receipts consist of local cesses, provincial assignments, transferred sources of revenue, and other miscellaneous items, and when the expenditure is incurred not only for education but for several other services, it is a matter of difficulty to distribute the different heads of expenditure with any precision among the different sources of revenue. This is however done in Bombay, Madras, and other provinces. Where the distinction is not made, it follows that under the heading "local rates or cesses" are included certain amounts which do not spring from that source and should, strictly speaking, be transferred to the head of provincial revenues. Hence an element of uncertainty is introduced as to the true character of these payments, whether they are really derived from "local rates and cesses" as the authorised heading would lead us to suppose, or in a larger sense from "local funds" to which provincial revenues have in some measure contributed. In the next paragraph it will be shown more definitely in what provinces this uncertainty exists. A further element of uncertainty arises from the transfer, already repeatedly noticed, of the cost of primary departments to the secondary schools to which they are attached. From this last cause it will frequently appear that local bodies have been spending money on secondary at the cost of primary education, when in reality nothing of the kind has occurred.

22. Expenditure from Local Funds.—The contributions made to education from local funds increased from R27,37,443 to R38,85,679, or by R11,48,000 nearly. From what has preceded it will be understood that this increase does not imply the relief of provincial burdens to the same extent, since it is due in some measure to the transfer of funds from provincial revenues to local boards, to enable them to meet the charges of schools transferred to their control. Not that this explanation deprives the transfer of all its significance. The people learn the lesson of educational administration, even though the Government continues for the present to pay a large part of the cost. An examination of the items of increase, from whatever source derived, will at the same time be useful as showing the purposes to which local boards devote the funds entrusted to their control. The North-Western Provinces and Oudh contribute the main portion of the increase, amounting to R7,61,000. It is not probable that any considerable share of this increase was yielded by the district rates, the income from which is described as "practically stationary;" hence the increase is really debitable to provincial revenues, though as it passes to the schools through the agency of the district boards, it is formally debited to the latter. Thus, from 1881-82 to 1882-83 the expenditure from "local rates or cesses" is said to have increased from R5,97,541 to R12,51,866, while the amount debited to provincial revenues shows a nearly equivalent diminution from R9,28,085 to R3,34,763. The charge is really an administrative rather than a financial one, as has been explained in an earlier paragraph. The Director in his report for 1884-85 thus describes the difference:—"The distinction between "the amount shown as drawn from local rates or cesses and the amount shown "as drawn from provincial revenues" is that "in the first case the sum of pro- "vincial money is credited to the board and then to the school, and in the second "it is directly credited to the school. Thus the distinction is not one referring to "the source from which the fund is derived, but to the authority by which it is "administered." Of the total nominal increase of R7,61,000 between 1881-82 and 1884-85, R3,76,000 are debited to secondary schools, and R2,26,000 to inspection, these being the chief heads of administration transferred to local control. Primary schools, which accounted for more than five-sixths of the whole local fund expenditure in the North-Western Provinces in 1881-82, received in the next three years an addition of R47,000 only; due, it will be understood, to the transfer of primary departments. The remainder of the increase in the local fund expenditure, amounting to about a lakh, was spent on buildings and training schools in nearly equal measure. In Madras there has been an increase from R5,62,000 to R6,36,000, or of R74,000. It appears from the following extract from the report for 1882-83 (para. 36) that this is a real local increase independent of provincial grants. "The gross "outlay from local funds has risen by about R90,000. Out of an approximate "revenue of 15 lakhs of rupees, the local boards are spending 6¾ lakhs for educa- "tional purposes. To the liberal treatment of elementary education by local "bodies the advance of the country in this respect is largely due; but it is to be "deplored that most local boards have reached the limit, or nearly so, of the pro- "portion of income which they can reasonably be expected to devote to public "instruction." The additional expenditure has been incurred chiefly in secondary schools (R32,000), training schools (R25,000), medical schools (R17,000) and inspection (R13,000). A reduction of R14,000 in the expenditure on primary schools indicates amongst other things that these institutions have become more self-supporting, since the reduction went on even after the change of classification above referred to. In Bombay the increase of expenditure from the local cess amounts to R1,47,000, out of which R1,22,000 have been devoted to the multiplication and improvement of primary schools maintained by local boards, and R17,000 to industrial schools. This again represents a genuine increase from purely local sources, towards which the assignments from provincial revenues (separately shown in the returns) have in no way contributed. In the Punjab there is a similar increase of R55,000, by which amount the allotments for educational purposes from the proceeds of the cess have been increased. There has been an addition of R33,000 to the expenditure from this source on school buildings, and of R46,000 on secondary education, while the allotment to primary schools has nominally fallen by R23,000. In the Central Provinces little variation is shown in the expenditure from local funds; but that heading includes a small contribution from provincial revenues to the rural educational cess, the proceeds of which are never sufficient for its purposes. The increase of R73,000 in Assam is due to the growing tendency of district boards to spend on education the full share prescribed by Government, namely, 20 per cent. of the local revenue, which is not however confined to local rates, but includes certain transferred sources of income, such as rents and ferries. This last assignment was originally made to meet the cost of grants-in-aid to middle and primary schools and of scholarships, the administration of which was transferred, from the 1st April 1882, to District Committees. There is an increase of R30,000 for middle and of R21,000 for primary schools; in reference to which it should be remembered that the change of classification by which the cost of middle schools was increased in other provinces did not affect Assam. There are also additional charges of R11,000 for inspection, and of R7,000 for scholarships. In Berar there has been an increase of R34,000 (spent on primary schools and schoolhouses), the whole of which is due to the increased productiveness of the educational cess; and the same cause explains an increase of R12,000 in Burma which has been wholly devoted to primary schools.

* For the whole of India it may perhaps be estimated, by a very rough approximation, that of the total increase of R11,48,000 in the educational expenditure of local boards from 1881-82 to 1884-85, from 7½ to 8 lakhs were contributed from provincial revenues, and that from 3½ to 4 lakhs were derived from local rates.

23. Expenditure from Municipal Funds.—The uncertainty which has been shown in the last paragraph to prevail as to the true origin of the funds classed in the returns as "local," and as to the exact extent of the increase in the payments made from local rates and cesses, does not exist in the case of municipal contributions towards education. In every province except Burma, the amount shown under the latter head has been raised by municipal taxation, towards which provincial revenues seem to have in no degree contributed. But in Burma, as already explained, the large increase of R2,20,000 in the tabulated expenditure from municipal sources is almost exclusively due to the special allotments made from provincial revenues to municipal corporations. Under the scheme which came into force in that province in April 1882, nearly all Government schools and all aided schools within municipal limits were made over to the control of municipal committees, together with the grants assigned for their maintenance. Expanding sources of revenue were also made over; and the increase in municipal expenditure on education has been effected with little or no addition to municipal burdens. Throughout India, the expenditure from municipal funds increased from R4,60,404 to R8,62,318—an increase of R4,02,000, or if Burma be excluded, of R1,82,000. Towards this amount R78,000 were contributed by the municipalities of Madras, secondary education receiving R50,000 of the increase, and primary education R18,000. The remainder was spent on buildings, training schools and medical schools. In Bengal, whose municipalities had, up to the date of the Education Commission's report, been conspicuously backward in the support of education, a considerable increase is now shown, namely, from R24,953 to R71,412, or not far short of 200 per cent. There is an increase of R30,000 in the expenditure on secondary schools, chiefly in aided institutions, and of R10,000 on primary schools: each represents a real increase, since the change in the mode of classifying primary departments did not operate in Bengal. An additional sum of R5,000 has also been spent on school buildings. The increase of R19,000 in the North-Western Provinces and Oudh is made up of R25,000 for secondary schools, and of R5,000 to the Agra and Aligarh Colleges, partly met by an apparent decrease of R11,000 in the contributions to primary education. In Bombay, out of an increase of R18,000 in municipal contributions, R11,000 have been spent on primary and R5,000 on secondary schools. Of the increase of nearly R11,000 in the Central Provinces, R8,000 have been spent on primary and R2,000 on secondary schools. An apparent increase of R5,000 in the contributions of municipalities in the Punjab is explained by the omission from the returns of 1881-82 of a grant of R6,372 made by the Lahore municipality to the Oriental College. It was stated in the report of the Education Commission (paragraph 672) that the Punjab was the only province of India in which the municipal corporations acted with liberality towards education. In 1884-85 it had made no further advance in this respect, while Madras had overtaken and passed it. The still larger contributions shown under the head of municipalities in Burma spring, as already explained, from a different source.

24. Distribution of the Increase from Public Funds.—From the immediately preceding paragraphs we can now conjecturally, and by a rough approximation, amend the statement derived from the table in paragraph 15 as to the different sources from which the total increase in the educational expenditure from public funds is derived. That table gives the following distribution of the increase :—from provincial revenues 6 lakhs, from local funds $11\frac{1}{3}$ lakhs, and from municipal funds 4 lakhs. Of the increased expenditure from provincial funds about $1\frac{1}{4}$ lakhs is nominal, and arises from the transfer from one head of account to another of the cost of the Roorkee Engineering College, and of the Nizamut Madrassa in Bengal. Of expenditure that is not nominal, it appears that a retransfer of $7\frac{1}{2}$ or 8 lakhs should be made to provincial revenues from district funds, and of about 2 lakhs from municipal funds. Hence the corrected figures showing the distribution of the increase would stand approximately as follows :— from provincial revenues $14\frac{1}{4}$ lakhs, from local funds $4\frac{1}{3}$ lakhs, and from municipal funds 2 lakhs. It will be shown hereafter that such portion of these additional assignments as was devoted to primary and secondary education was met by far larger contributions from purely private sources.

25. Expenditure from Fees.—We now turn to educational receipts of a different character, those, namely, which indicate the readiness of the people to pay for education from their own private funds, and consequently afford a measure of the value they set upon it. The total amount of fee receipts advanced from R43,66,194 to R60,65,738, that is, by R16,99,544 or about 39 per cent. On reference to the table in para. 6 it will be seen that within the same period the pupils reading in all the public schools of India increased by not quite 27 per cent. The increase in fee-receipts is therefore much greater proportionately than that of pupils. This conclusion, it is necessary to observe, is not vitiated in any way by the large expansion of lower primary schools in Bengal which, as already stated, took place between 1881-82 and 1884-85. If we follow the method adopted in para. 9 above, and separate from the total fee-receipts the fees paid by pupils in these schools, amounting to R10,86,244 in the former year, and to R15,08,766 in the latter, we obtain the result that in all other public schools of India the fees increased at the same ratio of 39 per cent., while their pupils increased at the still lower ratio of 21 per cent.

26. University Fees.—But there is one class of fee-receipts which should rightly be separated from the general statement, namely, fees paid by candidates at the various University examinations. It is certainly true that these form a regular and legitimate educational charge, and are part of the ordinary cost of collegiate instruction. The reason for excluding them lies in the fact that there has been, and is, no uniformity in the mode of dealing with this charge in the different provinces of India. In Madras the fees paid by candidates increased from R67,186 in 1881-82 to R1,00,810 in 1884-85. In Bengal they decreased from R55,618 to R31,318, owing to the introduction of a new system involving the postponement of all University examinations to a later date in the year. (In the following year, it may be stated, the University fee-receipts from Bengal candidates increased to R81,000.) In the North-Western Provinces, the Punjab, and Assam, these receipts are shown in the later but not in the earlier returns. In Bombay, owing possibly to a misapprehension of the Government orders conveyed in the Resolution of the 29th October 1883, the returns of neither year include any statement of University fee-receipts; and the same omission is observed in the remaining provinces of India. On account of these differences it will be convenient to separate fees paid for examinations from the general statement of fees paid for tuition. The table in the following paragraph relates therefore to fees paid for tuition only.

27. Provincial Increase in Pupils and Tuition-Fees compared.—It will now be shown that the proportionate increase which has taken place in the number of pupils and in the amount of tuition-fees paid by them is an average struck between terms of very different values. The following table compares for each province the increase of pupils with that of fee-receipts, and shows how widely these differ in different parts of India:—

PROVINCE.	Increase of pupils per cent.	Increase of fee-receipts per cent.	Value of new fee-unit (old unit=1).
Madras	7·6	34·2	1·25
Bombay	22·2	40·6	1·15
Bengal	37·4	39·1	1·01
North-Western Provinces	15·3	45·7	1·26
Punjab	20·4	56·9	1·30
Central Provinces	21·	28·7	1·06
Burma	54·4	20·3	·78
Assam	25·6	50·5	1·20
Berar	6·5	78·7	1·68
Coorg	18·8	90·	1·60
TOTAL	26·7	38·9	1·10

With the exception of Bengal, where the increase in fee-receipts progresses at about the same rate as that of pupils, and of Burma where it is much lower, in every province of India the fees have increased at a far higher rate than the pupils have. The absolute increase in fee-receipts is greatest in the smaller and less advanced provinces—in Coorg and Berar; and again, though not so conspicuously, in the Punjab and Assam. It is this increase that measures the vitality and progressiveness of education; and obviously there is more room for expansion in the provinces just named than in Madras, Bombay, or Bengal.

But for the purposes of a financial summary such as the present, the most important point is the relative increase,—the increase, namely, of fee-receipts as compared with that of pupils; since it is this which measures the willingness of the people to pay increased fees, and the degree in which the influence of the Department has been exerted to that end. For the purpose of comparing province with province, it is worth while to consider for a moment what numerical value should rightly be assigned to such relative increase under any given set of conditions. Thus, if in any province the pupils increase at the rate of 10 per cent., and the fee-receipts at the rate of 40 per cent., it is clear that while, at the beginning of the period, 100 pupils paid 100 fee units, at the end of the period 110 pupils have come to pay 140 fee units. Hence the average fee paid by each pupil is increased in the ratio of $\frac{140}{110}$ to 1, that is, of 1·27 to 1. The last column in the preceding table shows the value of the new fee-unit compared with the old, in other words, the proportion in which the fee paid by each pupil on the average exceeds the old rate of fee. Berar and Coorg again stand easily first, with an increase of 68 and of 60 per cent.; the Punjab, the North-Western Provinces, and Madras follow some way after with rates of increase varying from 30 to 25 per cent.; and then Assam and Bombay with 20 and 15 per cent. The Central Provinces show a small increase of 6 per cent; Bengal is stationary; and Burma comes last with a loss of 22 per cent. in the average fee paid by each pupil.

In Madras, there has been a very steady increase year by year. In this province, at least as much as in any other, constant attention is paid to the levying and the increase of fees. The fee-rates for different classes of schools and for different parts of the country are regulated by a definite scale, and, under a recent order, schools which refuse to adopt this scale are not admitted to the public examinations. According to the report of the Education Commission (para. 277), the scale was fixed in 1869, and raised in 1877. It was again raised with effect from the 1st January 1884. In the following year there was an increase of R1,25,000 over the receipts for 1883-84, though there was a decrease of nearly 17,000 pupils. The increase is ascribed not only to the introduction of the new scheme of fees, but also, amongst other causes, "to the gradual levying of fees "in primary schools maintained by Boards......to the growing feeling that the "well-to-do classes should pay the approximate cost of their children's education, "and also to the new provision of the grant-in-aid code, which gives preference to "schools in which regular fees are levied." The importance of raising school-fees is dwelt upon in the Resolution of the Government of Madras on the report for 1883-84 :—" The recent enhancement of fees will result, it may be hoped, on "the one hand in an increase of educational facilities, and on the other in a rise "in the pay and so in the social position of the teachers;" and it is added, in concurrence with the view expressed by one of the Inspectors, that the general raising of the status of the teacher will do almost as much as improved normal training to improve the quality of the teaching. One of the provisions of the new fee-code was the substitution of term-fees for monthly fees in colleges; the rates varying from R25 to R31 in Government colleges, and from R24 to R25 in aided colleges, for a term of six months. This method had already been tried in Arts colleges in Bombay (see report of the Education Commission, para. 312), where it is said to have worked well. The recommendation of the Commission on this point is actually based upon the practice prevailing in Bengal, and is to the following effect :—" That to secure regularity of attendance at col-"leges, the principle be affirmed that fees, though levied monthly for the conveni-"ence of students, are to be regarded as payments for a term, and that a student "has no right to a certificate from his college for any term until the whole fee for "that term is paid" (VI. 12). With regard to the introduction of the term-fee system in Madras, the report states that "its advantages are manifold; and as "people get accustomed to it the difficulties which now seem to beset it will dis-"appear, and those parents and managers who hitherto have looked upon it with "more or less of disfavour will come to regard it with approval."

In Bengal, where, however, fees in Government colleges are higher than in any other province except Bombay, an attempt was made in 1882 to raise the rates, and Principals of colleges were consulted on the point. With one exception, they all concurred in the opinion that any increase in the rates would reduce the number of students without affording any relief to provincial revenues. The

Director in reviewing their opinions, expresses his "surprise at the practical una-"nimity of Principals of colleges on this question, even after allowing for the "well-known fact that the students who attend the colleges are generally of very "narrow means. But the conclusion to be drawn from their representations "appears to be that any increase in the fee-rates would inflict greater hard-"ship on students than would be warranted by the decrease of Government "expenditure, if any decrease could indeed be expected; which is, at least "doubtful if the probable withdrawal of students in consequence of an enhanced "fee-rate be taken into account." In Government high schools reading to the matriculation examination, proposals have recently been sanctioned for a general increase of fee-rates in all cases where they seem to be below the mark. Schools of other classes in Bengal are mostly under private managers, who may be expected in their own interests to levy fees at the highest possible rate.

The Commission had commented adversely on the low proportion of the receipts from private sources in the Punjab. In 1884 the Lieutenant-Governor gave his serious attention to this question, observing that "fees are the truest "and best source of self-support for schools, and the low rate of fees which have "hitherto been levied in the Punjab has been complained of as being one of the "leading causes of the stagnation of native educational enterprise." Strict orders were issued that fees were to be raised, especially in colleges and secondary schools, whether Government or aided, due provision being at the same time made for exemptions on the ground of poverty or special merit. Attention was similarly drawn, in the Bombay report for 1884-85, to the necessity of increasing the fee-rates throughout that province, in reference to the fact that less than 19 per cent. of the total expenditure on education was raised from this source. With regard to primary education, it was observed that "the question is "complicated by the necessity for educating the poor, and by the conditions "imposed on a Department which levies a cess for education from the rural "classes;" so that no fair comparison could be drawn, for example, between Bombay and Bengal. But in secondary schools it was thought there was much room for improvement. While departmental schools of this class raised 52 per cent. of their expenditure in fees, and aided schools 39 per cent., the proportion for board schools was only 35 per cent., and in schools maintained by Native States only 21 per cent. It should be mentioned that while a considerable proportion of the poorer pupils in primary schools in Bombay were exempted altogether from fee-payments, fees were levied, though at reduced rates, from the children of cess-payers. The same rule prevailed in Madras. On the other hand, in the North-Western Provinces, the Punjab, and to some extent in the Central Provinces, the children of cess-payers were exempted from the payment of fees, a practice which the Commission (Report, para. 194) declared to be wrong in principle.

In Berar and Coorg, where the ratio of increase is both absolutely and relatively the highest, the increase is due, not so much to the fact that in each province there has been a definite enhancement of the rate of fees in secondary schools, as to the gradual advance of pupils to higher standards, in which higher fees are payable. This consideration applies with greatest force to those provinces in which education is still backward though advancing. In the more advanced provinces the proportion from year to year of pupils in the lower to those in the higher stages of instruction exhibits less variation. The stationary rate of fees in Bengal may be illustrated by a remark of the Education Commission (Report, para. 665) that the fee-receipts are proportionately higher in that province than in any other; there is therefore less room for expansion. The relative decrease in the fee rate in Burma is due to the fact that pupils in primary schools have increased at an enormously high rate compared with those in schools of a better class; the effect of this being obviously to reduce the average rate of fees paid in all schools. Another remark is also relevant to this subject. In those provinces, such as Madras, Bengal and Burma, in which the primary system of education is mainly based upon indigenous village schools, it is believed that the fee-receipts are largely understated. Thus the Madras report for 1883-84 observes that the total average remuneration of a village schoolmaster is probably not less than R8 a month, while the returns for schools in rural tracts put it no higher than R5. In Bengal, similarly, the average income of a village teacher appears from the returns to be a little over R4 a month, while the best sources of information agree in the conclusion that his total emoluments, including contributions of all kinds in lieu of fees, are not less than R7 a month.

28. Expenditure from Subscriptions, Endowments, and Other Sources.—The income from these various sources increased from R37,52,120 to R46,33,628, or if we exclude contributions from the revenues of Native States in Bombay and the Central Provinces, and the proceeds of local cesses levied in Native States in Bombay, the income from purely private sources advanced from R32,54,891 to R40,14,480. Amongst these sources of income, the amount received from subscriptions supplies a valuable test of public spirit in the support of schools for the public benefit. The amount of fee-receipts measures the value which the people set upon the education of their own children; the amount of subscriptions that which they set upon the education of the community to which they belong. The following figures show the receipts from subscriptions in Madras, Bombay, and Bengal for 1881-82 and 1884-85:—

	1881-82.	1884-85.
	R	R
Madras	1,40,364	1,18,165
Bombay	76,400	92,722
Bengal	7,45,913	8,68,886

The reduction in Madras seems to be due chiefly to re-classification; since the income from the endowment in support of St. Joseph's College at Trichinopoly, amounting in 1884-85 to R32,000, had in the previous year been shown under the head of subscriptions. The large receipts from this source in Bengal are doubtless connected with and explained by the absence of a local cess and the poverty of the contributions from municipal funds. The Education Commission remark (Report, para. 668) that local and municipal funds "may, from one point of view, be regarded as local resources, and although "they are called forth by legal enactment, they must somewhat reduce the fund "from which voluntary educational effort could be supplied. Where, as in "Bengal, there are no local rates, it is urged that fee contributions largely take "their place;" and this consideration applies with even greater force to subscriptions. In Assam subscriptions to schools rose from R14,566 to R24,295. In other provinces there is some doubt as to the amount of subscriptions in 1881-82. In the North-Western Provinces, for example, the subscriptions appear to have fallen from R1,96,671 to R1,44,961; but the amount shown in the departmental report for 1881-82 under the head of subscriptions is transferred by the Education Commission to "other sources," not readily to be identified. Again in the Punjab the subscriptions in aid of schools are stated to have risen from R22,036 (Education Commission's report, 1881-82) to R1,54,756 (Departmental report, 1884-85), a difference which is not explained by the exclusion from the former returns of subscriptions in aid of European schools (R30,000 in 1884-85), and which seems to show that in the earlier report the amount of subscriptions was understated. In the Central Provinces there seems to have been a decline from R53,000 to R24,000. The total amount of subscriptions to schools throughout India amounted in 1884-85 to R14,48,151.

29. Proportionate Expenditure from various Sources.—We are now in a position to compare the proportions in which the total expenditure on education has been met, in each province of India, from public and from private sources of different kinds. The percentages are given in the two following tables:—

PROVINCE.	1881-82.							
	Provincial Revenues.	Local Funds.	Municipal grants.	Native States Revenues.	Total from Public Funds.	Fees.	Other Sources.	Total from Private Sources.
Madras	28·3	16·2	2·5	...	47·0	29·2	23·8	53·0
Bombay	33·1	22·4	2·4	14·6	72·5	16·3	11·2	27·5
Bengal	42·2	·2	·4	...	42·8	36·9	20·3	57·2
N.-W. Provinces	45·1	29·1	2·5	...	76·7	7·9	15·4	23·3
Punjab	39·8	28·4	9·1	...	77·3	7·6	15·1	22·7
Central Provinces	51·1	20·7	5·5	...	77·3	6·3	16·4	22·7
Burma	52·1	13·0	6·8	...	71·9	14·4	13·7	28·1
Assam	45·4	20·4	·1	...	65·9	19·5	14·6	34·1
Berar	66·8	24·4	·4	...	91·6	7·7	·7	8·4
Coorg	58·2	31·0	...	...	89·2	9·8	1·0	10·8
INDIA	39·2	14·7	2·5	2·7	59·1	23·4	17·5	40·9
	1884-85.							
Madras	27·9	15·1	4·0	...	47·0	32·8	20·2	53·0
Bombay	30·2	22·0	2·4	14·8	69·4	18·8	11·8	30·6
Bengal	39·4	·1	·9	...	40·4	40·6	19·0	59·6
N.-W. Provinces	22·5	48·6	2·6	...	73·7	8·7	17·6	26·3
Punjab	35·8	25·3	7·5	...	68·6	10·4	21·0	31·4
Central Provinces	54·3	18·3	6·4	·7	79·7	7·4	12·9	20·3
Burma	32·9	9·4	31·3	...	73·6	10·7	15·7	26·4
Assam	36·7	29·9	·8	...	67·4	20·1	12·5	32·6
Berar	55·9	30·4	·4	...	86·7	12·2	1·1	13·3
Coorg	50·1	23·0	5·8	...	78·9	13·4	7·7	21·1
INDIA	33·8	16·6	3·7	2·7	56·8	26·0	17·2	43·2

These are two instructive tables, for they show to what extent India, and the different provinces of India, have been advancing since 1881-82 in the direction of meeting the cost of education from local sources. No stress should be laid on the decrease in the cost of education to provincial revenues, from 39·2 to 33·8 per cent., since it has been pointed out that a large share of this apparent decrease implies nothing more than the transfer to the head of local or municipal funds of expenditure that is really provided for and borne by provincial revenues. The basis of a more accurate comparison is supplied by the figures showing the proportionate expenditure from public funds of every kind, including not only local and municipal grants, but the contributions made by Native States. It appears, then, that the total expenditure on education from public funds throughout India decreased from 59·1 per cent. to 56·8 per cent; and correlatively, that the expenditure from strictly private sources, including fees, subscriptions, and endowments, advanced from 40·9 to 43·2 per cent. Madras and Bengal are the two provinces in which the total expenditure from public funds is lower and that from private sources is higher than in the average for India; the amount contributed from public funds being 47 per cent. in Madras, against the same proportion in 1881-82, and 40·4 per cent. in Bengal, against

42·8 per cent. in 1881-82. In Madras there is no change in the total proportionate expenditure from public and from private sources; but there is an increased percentage under the heads of municipal grants on the one side and fees on the other, the actual receipts from each of which have increased in a high ratio. In Bombay increased fee-receipts have reduced the expenditure from provincial revenues (and from public funds generally) by 3 per cent. The high rate of expenditure from public funds, (69·4 per cent.) is partly brought about by the inclusion of Native State expenditure under that head. If the schools in Native States and the expenditure on them be neglected, the expenditure from public funds is reduced to 66·5 per cent. (provincial revenues 36·8, local funds 26·8, municipal grants 2·9), and that from private sources increased to 33·5 per cent. (fees 20·8, other sources 12·7). In Bengal the contributions from public funds are lower than anywhere else in India. They are as yet almost entirely limited to provincial grants, though municipal grants have certainly been increasing of late years in a satisfactory way. The absence of a local cess in Bengal, and the still rudimentary character of municipal enterprise in education, are largely made up for by the liberality of the contributions from purely private sources, in which respect Bengal stands at the head of all the provinces of India. In the North-Western Provinces and Oudh, provincial revenues and local funds must, for reasons already explained, be taken together, when it will be seen that public funds pay 3 per cent. less, and private sources of income 3 per cent. more, than in 1881-82. The Punjab (which of late has been keenly alive to the necessity of increasing the rates of fees in public schools, and has taken active measures to that end) shows the large decrease of 9 per cent. in the cost of education to public funds. In the Central Provinces and in Assam public funds bear an increased share of the cost; while in the latter province a transfer of funds to local boards has helped to reduce the apparent cost to provincial revenues. A similar transfer to municipalities in Burma has had a similar result. In Berar there has been a large reduction (11 per cent.) in the cost of education to the State, which has been met in nearly equal proportions by increased receipts from local funds and from fees. In Coorg large reductions in the proportionate expenditure from provincial and local funds have been met partly by municipal grants (a new source of income), and partly by increased receipts from fees and other private sources.

A further analysis of the chief heads of attendance and expenditure shown in the foregoing tables, illustrated by such extracts from the provincial reports as may serve to throw light upon them, will now afford a convenient means of showing the progress made by each class of public institutions within the period under review.

III.—COLLEGIATE EDUCATION.

30. The Indian Universities.—In paras. 304 to 306 of the report of the Education Commission a summary but sufficient account is given of the scope and character of collegiate instruction as defined and governed by the three Universities of India. In the Universities of Madras and Calcutta a course of four years leads up from matriculation to the B. A. degree, the First Examination in Arts taking place midway between these limits. In Bombay, where the matriculation standard is said to be more advanced, the course for the degree covers three years; the Previous Examination being held at the close of the first year, and the first and second B. A. Examinations at the end of the second and third years respectively, the examination for the degree being thus divided into two parts. In Bombay the degree of Bachelor of Science has also been instituted,—a degree distinct in name, but corresponding closely to the scientific side of the Arts degree in the Calcutta University. In each University the Examination for M. A.

takes place either one or two years after that for the B. A. degree. It is now desirable to state the chief changes that have taken place, between 1882 and 1885, in the constitution or the regulations of these bodies. It will be seen that in two out of the three the course for the degree in Arts has been greatly reduced in extent, more accurate and fuller knowledge being required of fewer subjects. It will also be necessary to give a brief account of the newly-constituted Punjab University.

31. The Madras University.—The most important change was the revision in 1882 of the course for the B. A. degree. Under the old regulations a knowledge of five subjects was demanded, namely, English, a second language, history, mental science, and an optional subject. Under the new regulations candidates are required to qualify in three subjects only, namely, English, a second language, and an optional subject. This revision of the courses was accompanied by correlative changes in two directions. On the one hand, the standard both of the Entrance and of the First Arts examination was raised, by the requirement either of additional subjects or of a higher passing limit; on the other the number of alternative subjects, any one of which a candidate could take up for the M. A. degree, was increased from five to eight. These eight subjects now stand as follows, the five subjects under the old regulations being also shown by way of comparison :—

Old.	New.
I. Language.	I. Mathematics and Natural Philosophy.
	II. Physics.
II. Mathematics.	III. Chemistry.
	IV. Botany and Physiology.
III. Physical Science.	V. Zoology, Geology and Physical Geography.
IV. Biology.	VI. Mental and Moral Science.
	VII. History.
V. Mental Philosophy and Sociology.	VIII. Language.

The change, it is at once evident, has been in the direction of the further division of subjects, still carrying out that idea of preferring concentration to diffusion, depth to superficial extent, which characterised the change in the B. A. course. In accordance with the same principle, the new subject of language separates, as alternative branches, English, a classical language, or the group of Dravidian languages; while under the old scheme English and a classical language had to be taken up together. The first examination under the revised curriculum for matriculation and First Arts was held in December 1884; that for B. A. and M. A. being postponed to January 1887. Other changes followed. The fees to be paid by candidates for the various examinations in Arts were increased by 20 per cent. Boards of studies, consisting of Fellows of the University possessing special qualifications in various branches, were appointed for the purpose not only of selecting text-books, but of assisting the Senate in the disposal of questions requiring the special knowledge of experts. The medical examinations were revised. A degree in teaching was instituted. The B. A. examination was divided into two parts, the examination in languages being held separately from that in the optional branches; and the study of these latter was extended and encouraged by allowing candidates to take up more than the one branch required by the regulations. A proposal was made to establish a Convocation of graduates, but this did not commend itself to the Government of India. A scheme of studies and examinations for a proposed degree of Bachelor of Science was fully discussed, without being finally adopted. During this period the number of affiliated institutions rose from 35 to 43, six colleges having been affiliated up to the F. A. standard, and two to that of the B. A. degree.

Rajaram College in the Native State of Kolhapur were also affiliated up to the First B. A. standard. The total number of institutions recognised by the University was eight.

33. The Calcutta University.—As in Madras, the courses for the B. A. and M. A. degrees have been entirely revised. The following changes were sanctioned in 1882, all of them being in the direction of limiting the range of study and requiring more exact and full knowledge of each subject taken up. Under the old regulations candidates for the B. A. degree were required to present themselves in one of two courses—A, or literary, and B, or scientific. These two courses included the following subjects:—

A.	B.
I. English.	I. English.
II. A classical language.	II. Mixed Mathematics.
III. Mixed Mathematics.	III. Inorganic Chemistry.
IV. } Two out of the following:—	IV. Physical Geography.
V.	V. One of the following:—
(a) Philosophy.	(a) Physics.
(b) History.	(b) Zoology.
(c) An advanced course of Pure Mathematics.	(c) Botany.
	(d) Geology.

Under the new regulations, the division of the course into two branches, literary and scientific, was retained, but the course was greatly reduced. It included the following subjects for the pass degree:—

A.	B.
I. English.	I. English.
II. Philosophy.	II. Mathematics.
III. One of the following:—	III. One of the following:—
(a) A classical language.	(a) Physics.
(b) History.	(b) Chemistry.
(c) Mathematics.	(c) Physiology.
	(d) Geology.

At the same time an honour course was instituted for those B. A. candidates who aimed at special distinction. The honour course in each subject included all the contents of the pass course, so that a candidate who failed to obtain honours might still secure his degree. For the M. A. degree the old division of subjects was retained, namely,—(1) Languages, (2) History, (3) Mental and

postponed from December and January to April, and the date of the M. A. Examination was shifted to November. In the following year important changes were made in the course and standards for the license and degree in engineering, and the examination was divided into two branches, civil and mechanical. The regulations for the examination of female candidates in Arts were revised. They are the same as for male candidates, with the exceptions (1) that attendance at an affiliated institution is not required, (2) that at the First Arts examination such candidates are allowed to substitute botany for physics, and either French, German, Italian, or an Indian vernacular for a classical language Female candidates were also declared admissible to the Calcutta Medical College and the examinations in medicine on the same terms as men. Between 1881-82 and 1884-85 five colleges were affiliated to the University in Arts up to the B. A. and eight to the F. A. standard; four institutions were also affiliated in law. Five of these were situated in the North-Western Provinces, four in Bengal, and the rest in the Punjab, the Central Provinces, Burma, and Ceylon.

34. The Punjab University.—The history and objects of this University, however recently established, have been involved in some doubt, and have even been the subject of acrimonious controversy; insomuch that His Honour the Lieutenant-Governor of the Punjab felt himself compelled in 1885-86 to issue a Resolution defining the relations of the University to the Oriental College and to the Society known as the Anjuman-i-Punjab, to which the College and even the University were said to have owed their existence. The Lieutenant-Governor cordially acknowleged the very great services rendered to the University by the Anjuman, and fully recognised the importance of maintaining an Oriental college, and of affording encouragement to the enlightened study of the eastern classical languages and improving the vernacular literature. But, it was added, while he had continuously and consistently advocated the establishment of an Oriental college, he had never concealed his conviction that the vernaculars of the country did not as yet afford the materials for conveying instruction of a high order, and that a knowledge of English was indispensable to any native of India who desired to prosecute high literary and scientific studies. There was no ground whatever for the assumption that the Punjab University, in its origin and constitution, was, or was intended to be, exclusively Oriental; and that character had been expressly disclaimed at the very inauguration of the Punjab University College, from which the University derived its origin. The objects which the original promoters of the Punjab University had in view may in fact be gathered from the following passage taken from the Introduction to the University Calendar. "The promoters asked [in 1865] for an *Oriental Uni-*
"*versity*. The word *Oriental* was not used to represent that the English lan-
"guage and western science were not to be encouraged and supported; but that
"the University was to bear the impress of an oriental nation; that the ori-
"ental classics and vernacular languages of the country were to be encouraged
"and developed; that the masses of the people should have the boon of the
"civilising influences of education extended to them in their own language;
"and that the institution should not be a mere body for holding examinations
"in the European curriculum only, but should teach and examine in the
"languages used by and dear to the people. The promoters therefore declared
"that the Oriental University should be a 'supreme literary body' to restore
"and revive ancient learning; a 'supreme teaching body' supporting educa-
"tional institutions marked with its own characteristics, and diffusing European
"knowledge through the medium of the vernaculars; and lastly, it was to be
"a 'supreme examining body' in all departments of knowledge, conferring
"honours and rewards upon those who distinguished themselves at its examina-
"tions." In other words the University was to be Oriental in spirit and charac-

ter, but was certainly not to be limited to the study of Oriental learning and languages.

However, to leave controversial matters, by Act XIX of 1882 the Punjab University College was raised to the status of a University, and empowered to hold examinations and grant degrees. Its leading characteristics are that it is not merely an examining but a teaching University, its functions in this respect being limited to the maintenance of the Oriental College and Law School; that the examinations in Arts are held not only in English, but also in the vernacular languages; and that an Oriental Faculty, distinct from the Faculty of Arts, has been established for the purpose of examining and conferring degrees on students of the Oriental classics. There are two examinations leading to the degree in Arts—the Intermediate, corresponding to the First Arts examination; the High Proficiency examination, corresponding to that for B. A. Those who pass the High Proficiency standard through the medium of English, receive the degree of B. A., while on those who pass it through the the medium of the vernacular is conferred the degree of B. O. L., or Bachelor of Oriental Learning. Graduates of either class are entitled to present themselves at a later date for examination by the Honours in Arts standard, and those who pass receive the degrees of M. A. and M. O. L. respectively. Similarly on the Oriental side, examinations are held in Arabic for the titles successively of Maulavi Alim and Maulavi Fázil, in Persian for the titles of Munshi Alim and Munshi Fázil; and for Vishárad and Shástri in Sanskrit. Examinations are also held in Gurmukhi, or the literature of the Sikhs. The Senate of the University further acts as the constituted adviser of the Government on educational matters. Among many important subjects referred to that body for discussion and opinion may be mentioned—vacations in schools and dates of public examinations; systems of grants-in-aid; the award of scholarships; primary standards for boys' and girls' schools; the inspection of girls' schools; proposals for a new Panjabi dictionary; the European Education Code; rules for training colleges; and tests for admission to the public service in various grades. The conduct of the middle school examination was also transferred to the University. Thus it is evident that the Punjab University occupies towards the Government of the Province a position which is not filled by any other University in India. (The Educational Syndicate of Rangoon discharges similar functions in relation to the Government of Burma; but that is a body which has not the status of a University.) At its first institution the Punjab University and the Calcutta University seemed to possess nearly equal attractions for students of the province, as judged by the number presenting themselves for the examinations of either; but in the course of a year or two the former succeeded in practically driving its competitor from the field. This result is doubtless due to the action of the Local Government in refusing to award its scholarships by the Calcutta examinations, and in confining the instruction in Government institutions to the Punjab course. The chief institutions affiliated to the University for degrees in Arts are the Lahore Government College and St. Stephen's College at Delhi; and on the Oriental side of the same Faculty, the Oriental College at Lahore, which, however, prepares the great majority of its students for the Titles examination. For the Entrance examination, whether in English or in the vernacular, and for the various examinations for Oriental titles, a much larger number of institutions are connected with the University. In 1885, 294 candidates from 40 schools (including the colleges in the Native States of Kapurthala and Patiala) passed the Entrance examination in Arts, and 29 candidates from 5 schools the Oriental examinations; while 90 candidates from 30 institutions passed one or other of the examinations for titles in Sanskrit, Arabic, and Persian. By a Resolution of 1883, Oriental titles are conferred only on those candidates who have also passed the Entrance examination.

35. Arts Colleges, English, 1881-82 to 1884-85.

—The following table compares the number of institutions of different classes and of students at these two dates:—

PROVINCE.	1881-82.								1884-85.							
	UNDER PUBLIC MANAGEMENT.		AIDED.		UNAIDED.		TOTAL.		UNDER PUBLIC MANAGEMENT.		AIDED.		UNAIDED.		TOTAL.	
	Colleges.	Students.	Colleges.	Students.	Colleges.	Students.	Colleges.	Students.	Colleges.	Students.	Colleges.	Students.	Colleges.	Students.	Colleges.	Students.
Madras	10	742	12	828	3	124	25	1,694	10	895	18	1,488	2	132	30	2,515
Bombay	3	311	2	139	1	25	6	475	3	522	2	233	1	47	6	802
Bengal	12	1,305	5	895	5	545	22	2,745	13	946	5	877	7	956	25	2,779
N.-W. Provinces	3	172	2	157	1	20	6	349	3	155	5	194	3	26	11	385
Punjab	1	103	...	...	...	...	1	103	1	186	1	39	...	...	2	225
Central Provinces	1	65	...	...	1	2	2	67	1	31	1	24	1	1	3	56
Burma	1	9	...	...	...	...	1	9	1	18	...	...	...	...	1	18
TOTAL	31	2,707	21	2,019	11	716	63	5,442	32	2,763	32	2,855	14	1,162	78	6,780

The number of colleges apparently increased from 63, with 5,442 pupils, to 78 with 6,780 pupils; but these figures do not exhaust the list of collegiate institutions. It was stated above that 43 colleges were affiliated to the University of Madras at the close of 1884-85, but the returns show only 30. Similarly in Bombay, the Baroda and Fergusson Colleges, though affiliated to the University, do not appear in the returns. In Bengal, again, mention is made of one or two institutions that occasionally send candidates to the University examinations, but furnish no returns to the Department. These excluded colleges are all under private managers, mostly unaided, and generally of small size.

Of the 15 new institutions shown in the returns, all but one were under private management, whether aided or unaided. The exception was the new college department attached to the Fyzabad High School; but as this was placed under the management of the district board, the number of purely departmental colleges remained unaltered at 31. The Agra Government College was transferred in 1883 to the management of a local body; but this was counterbalanced by the opening of a small college department in 1884 in the Government Madrassa at Calcutta—the special institution for Muhammadans.

Aided colleges increased from 21 to 32. Six of the 11 new colleges were in Madras, all but one of which owed their existence to missionary enterprise. Five institutions, which had been previously aided as schools, were raised to the rank of colleges, and a grant was given to a college before unaided. In the North-Western Provinces and Oudh, the number of aided colleges rose from two to five; the Government college at Agra having being transferred to a board of trustees with a grant-in-aid, and college classes having been opened in connexion with the Government school at Bareilly, but managed by a local body with a Government grant. The third addition is the college department of a European school at Mussoorie, since transferred to the unaided list, as the grant that it now receives under the Code is made specifically to the school department. Aid was also given to the Free Church College at Nagpore in the Central Provinces; and, on the failure of the attempt to resuscitate the old Delhi College, to St. Stephen's College then newly established at Delhi under the management of the Cambridge Mission. This last institution, it may be noticed, also receives aid from the local municipality.

Unaided colleges, including those in Native States, increased from 11 to 14, besides several that are not shown in the returns. Two of the new institutions are found in Bengal, one having been opened at Calcutta and another at Dacca, both under purely native management. A new college under missionary auspices was also opened at Agra. One of the unaided colleges at Madras was transferred to the aided list; and a nominal addition is furnished by St. John's College at Agra, which omitted in 1881-82 to supply returns to the Department. In the list of unaided colleges are included two in the Central Provinces—one with two students and another with one only—which are not of sufficient importance to rank as public institutions.

36. Attendance of Students in Arts Colleges, 1881-82 to 1884-85.

—The variation in the number of students attending different classes of colleges during this period may be thus shown. In 1881-82, 5,440 students were reading in 62 Arts Colleges, an unaided institution with two students in the Central Provinces being neglected. Of these, 2,707 were reading in 31 Government colleges, with an average of 87 students to each; 2,019 in 21 aided colleges, with an average of 96 students; and 714 in 10 unaided colleges, with an average attendance of 71. In 1884-85, 6,779 students were reading in 77 colleges; an unaided college with a single student being again excluded. Of these 2,763 were reading in 32 colleges under public management (including one under a local board), with an average attendance roll of 86; 2,855 in 32 aided colleges, with an average attendance of 89; and 1,161 in 13 unaided colleges, also with an average attendance of 89. Averages of this kind are, it must be admitted, of no great importance when a mean has to be struck between terms of widely different values—between, for example, the Presidency College of Calcutta containing 374 students in 1881-82, and the Government College at Rangoon with only nine in the same year; or between the Madras Christian College with 537 students in 1884-85, and the Free Church Aided College at Nagpore with 24; or between the unaided Metropolitan Institution of Calcutta with 506 students, and three unaided colleges in the North-Western Provinces with only 24 students between them. Again, the averages would seem to show that while Government institutions have maintained their strength unimpaired, unaided colleges have added largely to their numbers at the cost of aided colleges. But it appears on closer examination that this is not the case. The older aided colleges in Madras and those in Bombay have largely increased their average attendance, and in Bengal the numbers are practically stationary. The reduction in the average attendance of aided colleges from 96 to 89 is due to the opening of six colleges of this class in Madras with an average roll number of 26 pupils only, and of five colleges in other parts of India that together contribute only 100 pupils to the total. Even the stationary character of the attendance in Government colleges is marked by wide divergencies in different provinces. In Madras the attendance has increased by 20 per cent., in Bombay by 68 per cent., and in the Punjab by 80 per cent.; in Bengal, on the other hand, it has fallen by 27 per cent., owing to the opening of unaided colleges in the neighbourhood of the Government colleges at the Presidency, at Hoogly, and at Dacca.

Madras contributes the largest share, namely, 821 students, to the total increase of 1,338. Bombay gives a larger proportionate increase, namely, 61 per cent. against 48 in Madras; and the Punjab shows a still better result, the number of its college students being more than doubled. The Jubbulpore Government College in the Central Provinces has lost more than half its students, and the loss is not fully made up by the admissions to the newly-aided college at Nagpore; the unfavourable result of the Entrance examination for the schools of the province are accountable for the decrease.

37. Grade of Arts Colleges, 1881-82 to 1884-85.

—Colleges are classified as of the first or of the second grade, according as they carry instruction up to the standard of the B. A. degree, or to that of the First Arts or some equivalent examination intermediate between matriculation and the degree. The number of first-grade colleges increased within the period now in question from 29 to 35. To this increase of six, Bengal contributed three raised to the first grade, namely, two aided colleges and one unaided; in Madras one unaided college was similarly raised; in the Punjab one aided college; and in Burma the Government college at Rangoon. The first-grade college at Agra was transformed from a Government into an aided institution. In all, there were, at the end as at the beginning of this period, 17 Government colleges of the first grade; 11 rising to 15 aided colleges, and 1 rising to 3 unaided colleges of the same grade. The 35 first-grade colleges of 1884-85 are thus distributed:—in Bengal 15, in Madras 8, in the North-Western Provinces and Oudh 5, in Bombay 4, in the Punjab 2, and in Burma 1.

38. Expenditure on Arts Colleges, English, 1881-82 to 1884-85.—

The two subjoined statements compare the expenditure on Arts Colleges in the two years, 1881-82 and 1884-85:—

	1881-82.				
	Expenditure from				
CLASS OF INSTITUTIONS.	Provincial Revenues.	Municipal Grants.	Fees.	Subscriptions, Endowments, &c.	TOTAL.
	R	R	R	R	R
Government	6,23,516	3,000	1,68,321	73,967	8,68,804
Aided	65,641	...	73,657	1,81,002	3,20,300
Unaided	...	...	6,679	19,004*	25,683*
TOTAL	6,89,157	3,000	2,48,657	2,73,973	12,14,787

* Includes R5,964 from the revenues of Native States.

	1884-85.				
	Expenditure from				
CLASS OF INSTITUTIONS.	Provincial Revenues.	Local and Municipal Grants.	Fees.	Subscriptions, Endowments, &c.	TOTAL.
	R	R	R	R	R
Government	6,75,610	6,114	1,91,129	48,827	9,21,680
Aided	1,05,412	7,869	1,10,725	2,41,429	4,65,435
Unaided	...	...	9,970	46,845*	56,815*
TOTAL	7,81,022	13,983	3,11,824	3,37,101	14,43,930

* Includes R5,727 from the revenues of Native States.

Thus, for an increase within this period of 24 per cent. in the number of colleges and of 25 per cent. in that of college students, the Government grants increased by 13 per cent., the local income by 26 per cent., and the total expenditure by 19 per cent.

Provincial Revenues.—The expenditure from provincial revenues upon Government or departmental colleges increased by R52,094, or 8⅓ per cent. This is explained by an increase of R49,000 in Bengal, of R11,000 in Burma, and of of R4,000 in Bombay, accompanied by a decrease of R6,000 in the North-Western Provinces and of R4,000 in Madras. In Burma the Rangoon College has been raised to the first grade, and the reduction in the North-Western Provinces is due to the transfer of the Agra College to a local body. The increase in Bengal is attributed, first, to the opening of college classes for the special benefit of Muhammadan students in the Calcutta Madrassa; secondly, to the additional teaching power rendered necessary in many colleges by the introduction of the new courses and standards prescribed by the Calcutta University under its revised regulations; and thirdly, to a large decrease in fee-receipts arising from the diminished number of students in Government colleges—a circumstance which affects not the gross but the net cost. But if the expenditure by Government upon its own institutions increased to the extent of more than 8 per cent. throughout India, the Government grants to aided colleges increased during the same period by 60 per cent. The chief portion of the increase has been incurred in Madras (R13,600), where new grants have been given to six colleges; and in the North-Western Provinces (R14,400), where there has been an addition of three, including Agra, to the aided list. The Agra College now receives a grant of R5,000 a year, while its cost to Government as a departmental institution in 1881-82 was R7,800. There are new grants in the Punjab to the amount of R6,900, and of R2,300 in the Central Provinces.

Local and Municipal Grants.—Under this head there has been a considerable increase. In 1881-82 the only contribution of this kind was a municipal grant of R3,000 to the Gujarat (Government) College at Ahmedabad in Bombay. This grant was still given in 1884-85; and in addition the following municipal grants were made to aided colleges in the North-Western Provinces and the Punjab:—R4,000 to the Agra College, R1,061 to the Muhammadan Anglo-Oriental College at Aligarh, and R1,200 to St. Stephen's College at Delhi under the Cambridge Mission. From local funds the District Boards of Fyzabad and Bareilly made grants of R3,000 and R1,600 respectively, to the college departments attached to the high schools of those places.

Fees.—In ordinary circumstances the receipts from fees vary directly as the average number of students on the rolls monthly throughout the year—not, of course, as the number that may happen to be on the rolls at the end of it. Thus, in Government colleges throughout India, the fee-receipts increased almost precisely in proportion to the average attendance, namely, between 13 and 14 per cent. But in aided colleges, while the pupils in average attendance increased 39 per cent., the fee-receipts increased 50 per cent.; and in unaided colleges a still higher rate of increase is observed, namely, 59 per cent. of fees against 7 per cent. of pupils. These facts indicate a very healthy desire on the part of the managers of private colleges to increase their fees to something like the rates obtaining in departmental colleges. The average fee paid by each pupil in a Government college was, at the end as at the beginning of this period, a little over R69 for the year. In aided colleges the average fee rose from R42 to R45½, and in unaided colleges from R31 to nearly R46. The following table shows these facts in detail for the various provinces:—

PROVINCE.	1881-82.			1884-85.		
	Departmental Colleges.	Aided Colleges.	Unaided Colleges.	Departmental Colleges.	Aided Colleges.	Unaided Colleges.
	R	R	R	R	R	R
Madras	45·5	30·7	28·9	62·2	47·7	45·3
Bombay	81·7	59·0	48·2	83·6	58·0	61·2
Bengal	88·2	54·1	—*	80·9	45 2	—*
North-Western Provinces	42·9	16·5	20·9	45·3	27·4	25·3
Punjab	21·9	...	...	21·4	24·2	...
Central Provinces	20·7	...	...	24·5	22·7	...
Burma	42·7	...	...	44·9	...	...
AVERAGE FOR INDIA	69·2	42·1	30·9	69·1	45·5	45·8

* No returns received from unaided colleges in Bengal.

CHAP. II.]   COLLEGIATE EDUCATION, 1882 TO 1885.   35

The introduction, already noticed, of the term-fee system into the colleges of Madras has resulted in an increase of 73 per cent. in the fee-receipts of Government colleges, while the increase of pupils amounts to only 28 per cent. In the aided and unaided colleges of the same province the proportionate increase is still greater. There is also a large increase in the fee-rates of the unaided colleges in Bombay. In Bengal, where in 1882 the fee-receipts for each student in a Government college were higher than in any other part of India, a large reduction in the attendance at the Presidency College, with its high rate of R12 a month, has brought down the average for the whole province. A special though temporary cause has operated still further to reduce the fee-receipts, both in Government and in aided colleges; a change in the date of the University examinations having resulted in the remission of three months' fees to all students who had completed the prescribed period of attendance for two years. Many of the unaided colleges of Bengal return no statement of their expenditure, so that it is impossible to make the comparison in their case. The aided colleges in the North-Western Provinces show a large increase in the fee-rates.

Subscriptions, Endowments, and Other Sources.—It is not very easy to disentangle these various sources of income, which are not completely separated in the returns. The transfer of the Agra College endowment, yielding an income of R24,000 in 1881-82, to the new governing body of the college has caused a decrease to the same amount under the head of endowments in Government colleges. The increase of R60,000 under this head for aided colleges arises partly from the same cause, but chiefly from the enhanced contributions of missionary bodies in England and Scotland in aid of the colleges which they maintain, for the most part in Madras and in Bengal.

39. Results of University Examinations, 1881-82 and 1884-85.—
The results are compared in the following statements, showing for each province the number of successful candidates from different classes of institutions at each of the University Examinations in Arts for 1881-82 and 1884-85 :—

First Examination in Arts.

PROVINCE.	1881-82.			1884-85.			
	Government Institutions.	Other Institutions.	TOTAL.	Institutions under public management.	Aided Institutions.	Unaided Institutions and private students.	TOTAL.
Madras	144	279	423	179	164	25	368
Bombay (a)	67	40	107	177	50	8	235
Bengal	171	124	295	174 (135)	81 (90)	91 (65)	346 (290)
N.-W. Provinces	20	22	42	30 ...	41 (19)	...	72 (19)
Punjab	8	...	8	20	6	2	28
Central Provinces	10	1	11	4 (3)	3 ...	...	7 (3)
Burma	1	...	1	5	...	1	6
TOTAL FOR INDIA	421	466	887	589 (138)	345 (109)	128 (65)	1062 (312)

The numbers in brackets represent candidates at the supplementary examination of the Calcutta University held in 1884.

(a) Including the results of the 1st B. A., 1st B. Sc. and Previous Examinations.

F 2

B. A. Examination.

PROVINCE.	1881-82.			1884-85.			
	Government Institutions.	Other Institutions.	TOTAL.	Institutions under public management	Aided Institutions.	Unaided Institutions and private students.	TOTAL.
Madras	71	73	144	83	80	6	169
Bombay {	28	8	36	68	15	...	83
{	1	1	(a) 2	3	1	...	(a) 4
Bengal	59	36	95	105 (44)	86 (40)	73 (28)	264 (112)
N.-W. Provinces	5	3	8	19 ...	18 (6)	1 ...	38 (6)
Punjab	2	...	2	9	1	4	14
Burma	...	...	...	1	...	...	1
TOTAL FOR INDIA	166	121	287	288 (44)	201 (46)	84 (28)	573 (118)

The numbers in brackets represent candidates at the supplementary examination of the Calcutta University held in 1884.
(a) Candidates at the examination for the B. Sc. degree.

M. A. Examination.

Madras	...	5	5	...	...	9	9
Bombay	1	2	3	8	1	...	9
Bengal	21	5	26	(a) ...	...	...	...
N.-W. Provinces	4	...	4	(a) ...	...	...	...
Punjab	3	...	3	4	...	1	5
TOTAL FOR INDIA	29	12	41	12	1	10	23

(a) No examination was held by the Calcutta University in 1884-85 for the M. A. degree.

The immediate inference from these figures is that the number of successful candidates at the First Examination in Arts (or other examination corresponding thereto) increased from 887 to 1,062, or by nearly 20 per cent., made up of an increase of 40 per cent. among candidates from colleges under public management, and of 2 per cent. from other colleges; that the number of successful candidates for the B. A. degree increased from 287 to 573, or by 100 per cent., towards which departmental institutions contributed 73 per cent., and colleges under private management 169 per cent.; and lastly that owing to a special cause the number of M. A. graduates decreased. The following explanation is necessary in order to elucidate the tables. The last examinations of the Calcutta University under the old system were held in the cold weather of 1883-84. In introducing the new courses and standards, the University further determined, with the object of utilising the cold weather in study instead of (as before) in testing the results of study, to postpone the First Arts and B. A. examinations to April; the college session thus extending from June to March, instead of as before from January to November with a hot weather vacation. The first examinations under the new system were accordingly held in April 1885, that is to say, just after the official year 1884-85 had closed. But it has been found inconvenient to separate the examinations from the year to which they practically belong; and since the provincial reports have included the results of these examinations in the account of the year's work, it has been thought better to adopt a method which is in accordance with practice and with a reasonable view of the limits of the school year. The unbracketed figures for the year 1884-85 refer therefore to the candidates examined after the close of that year under the new system. The figures in brackets refer to a different set of candidates. After the old system had come to an end, the University held a supplementary and final examination in May 1884 for the benefit of those candidates who had failed to pass at the regular examinations held in the preceding January and February, and who therefore would have had no chance of passing by a new and different standard a year later. These examinations, though actually held within the years 1884-85, really belong to the old system; they have therefore been placed within brackets and not included in the number of successful candidates of the year. These remarks apply to Bengal, the North-Western Provinces, and the Central Provinces. Burma sent no candidates to the supplementary examination; nor did the Punjab. By 1885, indeed, the Punjab had almost entirely severed its connexion with the Calcutta University. In 1882 the candidates from schools and colleges in the Punjab were about equally divided between the Calcutta and Punjab Universities; but in 1885 (with the exception of two private students, not shown in the departmental returns or in the foregoing tables) all the Punjab candidates presented themselves at the examination of the local University.

While, under the new system, the First Arts and B. A. examinations of the Calcutta University were postponed to April, the M. A. examination was transferred from February to November. Hence from February 1884 to November 1885, there was no examination for the M. A. degree; none, therefore, fell within the official year 1884-85. The examinations of November 1885 are rightly dealt with in the reports for the year 1885-86; but for the purposes of comparison, the results of the examinations of February 1884 for Bengal and the North-Western Provinces may be included in the last of the three tables given above. From Bengal 57 candidates passed, namely, 31 from colleges under public management, 18 from aided colleges, and 8 from unaided colleges including private students. In the North-Western Provinces, 7 passed, all from Government colleges. If these results be included in the statement, it is seen that the number of M. A. graduates increased from 41 to 87, those educated in departmental colleges increasing from 29 to 50, and those educated in other colleges from 12 to 37.

40. Increasing Success of Non-departmental Colleges.—The most important result to be obtained from the foregoing figures is the evidence they afford of the prominent and rapidly increasing share which is taken by colleges under private management in the higher education of India. The figures show that while there was an increase of 40 per cent., 73 per cent., and 72 per cent. respectively in the number of successful candidates from departmental institutions at the First Arts, B. A. and M. A. examinations, the corresponding proportions of increase among candidates from institutions under private management were 2 per cent., 169 per cent., and 208 per cent., respectively. To have a complete view of the matter, the tables in the last paragraph should be compared with the statements showing the number of students in Government and other institutions at the two periods. We thus get the following:—

	1881-82.				1884-85.			
CLASS OF INSTITUTIONS.	Number of students on the rolls.	Passed at			Number of students on the rolls.	Passed at		
		F. A.	B. A.	M. A.		F. A.	B. A.	M. A.
Departmental . . .	2,707	421	166	29	2,763	589	288	50
Non-departmental .	2,735	466	121	12	4,017	473	285	37

Hence the large increase that has taken place in the number of successful candidates from Government institutions has been accompanied by an increase of only 2 per cent. in the number of their students; while the still larger proportionate increase in the number of successful candidates from colleges under private management has been attended by an increase of 47 per cent. in the roll number. The comparison is not, of course, a perfectly just one; for an increase in the roll number does not have its effect on the examinations until after the lapse of two or of four years, when the candidates go up for the F. A. and B. A. Examinations; and from this point of view the large increase in the number of successful candidates reflects still greater credit on the colleges under private management.

It may be noticed that the small percentage of increase at the First Examination in Arts, especially in non-departmental colleges, is due to a decline in the number of successful candidates from Madras. In other provinces of India there was an increase of 50 per cent. in the number of successful candidates, namely, of 48 per cent. in Government colleges, and of 52 per cent. in those under private management. In Madras there was a loss of 13 per cent., made up of an increase of 24 per cent. in Government colleges, and of a decrease of 59 per cent. in those under private managers. The fluctuations in the results of this examination at Madras are noteworthy; in the four years beginning with 1881-82 the number of passes was 423, 279, 501, and 368, respectively. This is ascribed by the Director of Public Instruction (Report for 1882-83, para. 61) partly to variations in the standard of examination, and partly to the fact that the standard for matriculation is too low, so that the standard of the First Arts examination cannot be reached in two years except by students of more than average ability. Complaints as to the variation of standard have also been made in other provinces; and the University of Calcutta has lately paid particular attention to this subject with the view of enforcing greater uniformity. The truth appears to be that differences from year to year in the percentage of successful candidates depend on several causes, among which differences in the attainments of the candidates need not be taken into account, as these would be likely to cancel each other over a large area. First of all there may be a difference in the standard at that particular examination; secondly, greater or less severity at the next preceding examination, resulting in the relegation to the following year of a greater or smaller number of candidates who will then have had three years of study instead of two; lastly, variations in the standard of the Entrance examination two years before, for if the meshes of that net are made unduly large, a greater number of fish will be stopped at the next succeeding obstacle. Sometimes all these causes operate together, and the result is a large increase or decrease in the number of successful candidates.

41. Oriental Colleges, 1881-82 to 1884-85.—The few purely Oriental colleges, so-called, that survived in India throughout this period were the relics of the old institutions, of whatever foundation, designed for the cultivation of the classical learning of the Hindus and Musulmans, especially in so far as that learning bore upon their religion, laws and customs. "This preference for "the study of the Oriental classics," to quote the report of the Education Commission, "quickly gave way to an appreciation of the larger benefits to be "derived from a knowledge of the English language and of western modes of "thought." Those specially named by the Commission were the Madrassa at Calcutta, the Sanskrit Colleges at Calcutta and Benares, the Arabic and Persian Colleges at Surat and Delhi. The Surat College had already fallen into decay before the date of the Commission's report; the Delhi College and the similarly constituted college at Agra had been absorbed into the English colleges which were engrafted upon them; the Benares Sanskrit College retained its identity indeed, but merely as a department of the English college; and English was also taught as a separate department of the Calcutta Madrassa and the Calcutta

Sanskrit College. The purely Oriental colleges then remaining were but three, namely, the Sanskrit department of the Benares College, the Oriental department of the Canning College, Lucknow, and the Oriental college at Lahore. The tables attached to the report included, in the list of Oriental colleges, four madrassas in Bengal supported from the Mohsin Endowment Fund; but these are not reckoned as colleges in the provincial reports, nor indeed, according to the Resolution of the 29th October 1883, is it right to apply the term to any institutions except those whose students are reading a course of Oriental subjects prescribed by a University.

The departmental returns of 1881-82 show four Oriental colleges with 595 students; those of 1884-85 show also four colleges with 664 students. The earlier returns included the Benares Sanskrit College, the Oriental department of the Muhammadan Anglo-Oriental College at Aligarh, and the Oriental department of the Canning College at Lucknow,—all in the North-Western Provinces; and a so-called Sanskrit College supported by local funds in Tanjore, which was afterwards transferred to the head of private institutions. In 1884-85 the same three colleges in the North-Western Provinces were returned, and to them was added the Oriental College at Lahore, which, though founded in 1870, appears to have furnished no returns to the Department in any year before 1884-85. But by this time the number of students in the Oriental department of the Aligarh College had dwindled to four.

42. The Benares College.—A far more successful institution was the Sanskrit department of the Benares College, which throughout this period gave instruction in various branches of Sanskrit learning to some 400 students. The following extract from the report of the Principal for 1882-83 may be cited as showing the character of the work which the College undertakes, and the temper of the students who are taught therein:—" Of the majority of the students, " among whom natives of all parts of India are to be found, it may be said with " greater truth than of the majority of students in the English colleges, that their " heart is in their work. The learning they acquire is in its way solid and exten- " sive, and the circumstance of their education and scholarship being of national " growth enables them—or at least the best among them—to obtain a complete "grasp and thorough mastery of the subjects they study, no room being here left for " that half culture and half scholarship which characterise so many of the young " natives who have passed through the English colleges." At the same time Dr. Thibaut expresses his regret that the pundits had no longer any opportunity of becoming acquainted with western thought and culture, except in one department, that of mathematics and astronomy, in which the superiority of European methods was so pronounced and so fully acknowledged that the best professors of that science had, for a long time back, taken pains to learn and to teach their pupils Euclid, trigonometry, and the calculus. He refers in proof to the considerable number of Sanskrit and Hindi treatises on mathematics and astronomy in their European form which had of late years been published, many of them by Benares pundits. "In other branches of Sanskrit learning, however, the " teaching continues to move entirely in the old grooves; and what we should call " a critical knowledge of Sanskrit literature and language is scarcely to be found " among pundits, however learned and acute they may be. This is all the more " to be regretted, as the English colleges have hitherto done very little for the ad- " vance of Sanskrit scholarship." The Anglo-Sanskrit department of the college was re-opened in 1884 to enable Sanskrit scholars to study European science and philosophy. In 1885 it contained 44 students.

The Benares College examines its own students, as well as those of other institutions in the Province, for the titles of Upádhyáya and Achárya. The

Oriental department of the Canning College sends its students to the examinations in Arabic and Sanskrit of the Punjab University. The Benares College further contributes to the study of Sanskrit by the issue of two publications, the *Pandit* and the *Benares Sanskrit Series*. The cost of the Benares College in 1884-85 was R15,854, of which nearly the whole was paid by Government; the Oriental department of the Canning College cost R6,476, of which R2,707 were provided by a Government grant; and the small Oriental department of the Aligarh College cost R1,360, met altogether from its own resources.

43. The Oriental College, Lahore.—This institution, which is one of the chief constituents of the Punjab University, differs from other Oriental colleges in that, while cultivating the Oriental classical languages, it also claims to impart the higher branches of European knowledge and science through the medium of the Indian vernaculars. In fact, its declared object is to embody, as a teaching institution, those principles which the Punjab University sets forth in its examinations. Translations from European works have been published under its auspices into Hindi and Urdu in such various subjects as arithmetic, algebra, Euclid, trigonometry, statics, dynamics, history, geography, psychology, logic, political economy, chemistry, physics, and astronomy. It also undertakes to prepare students through the vernaculars for the examinations of the Punjab University in law, medicine, and engineering. The great majority of the students, however, belong to the Oriental Titles department, for which, as before stated, it is necessary that they should pass the Entrance examination of the University. The special purposes of the college are explained and defended in the following extract from a report presented to the Senate:—" The chief object of the great majority of the students who enter at " the college is, not the acquisition of general knowledge, but the advanced " study of the Eastern classics. This higher training in the classics of the " country is the most distinctive feature of the Punjab University, and un- " doubtedly constitutes its special attraction for the people. It not only enables " us to attract classes who have a desire for Eastern, but none for Western, learn- " ing, but it also enables us to add improved methods and criticism to the " indigenous lines of classical teaching, and at the same time to insist upon the " acquisition of a certain amount of more general knowledge, the want of which " must always tend to place the purely Oriental student at a disadvantage in the " race of modern life. The amount of general knowledge demanded is that re- " quired for the Entrance examination of the Oriental Faculty. It is small; but " it is something gained, and to demand more at present would probably result in " our losing that little." Then, in answer to the question, why it is necessary to retain the examination for Oriental titles, when the Oriental Faculty has a complete series of Oriental degrees, it is urged that "their retention, at any rate for " the present, is essential; they enable specialists to pursue their own objects, and " they also carry out the liberal principle of the University, which has always been " to give scope and encouragement to every kind of learning, and not to repress the " desire for knowledge in its spontaneous form by enforcing a too rigid scheme " of what may appear to western scholars alone worthy of the name of Univer- " sity education. At the same time we even now hold out inducements in the " shape of more valuable scholarships, by which we hope gradually to lead our " students to follow the course for degrees rather than that for titles;" and a hope is expressed that in a few years it will be found possible to abolish all but the highest examinations for Oriental titles, which would then follow upon the attainment of the B. O. L. degree.

The college is said to labour under three disadvantages—want of funds, inefficiency of a portion of the staff, and the lack of suitable text-books (Report

CHAP. II.] COLLEGIATE EDUCATION, 1882 TO 1885. 41

for 1883-84). The second of these defects has been partly remedied by the transfer to the Oriental College of the professors of Sanskrit and Arabic attached to the Government college; a close connexion between the two institutions being maintained by a provision for the mutual interchange of students desiring to read English or the Oriental classics respectively. The want of text-books is described as a greater difficulty. "In some subjects, on the Hindi side at least, "there are absolutely no text-books, and the instruction is wholly oral. The " University is fully alive to the necessities of the case, and is gradually supplying "the want." By orders passed in 1884-85, the college was placed under the management of a committee composed of members of the Senate, who receive a fixed allotment from the University revenues and are entrusted with large powers of self-government. The college contained 119 students in its various departments in 1885. Its cost was nearly R21,000, of which only R371 appear to have been paid in fees. The Punjab Government contributes to its maintenance, not directly indeed, but indirectly by a grant of R22,000 to the Punjab University.

44. Professional Colleges, 1881-82 to 1884-85.—The number of these institutions increased from 18 to 21, and the pupils reading in them from 1,515 to 2,380. The particulars are shown in the following table :—

	1881-82.						1884-85.					
PROVINCE.	LAW.		MEDICINE.		ENGINEERING.		LAW.		MEDICINE.		ENGINEERING.	
	Institutions.	Students.	Institutions.	Students.	Institutions.	Students.	Institutions.	Students.	Institutions.	Students.	Institutions.	Students.
Madras, Government	1	112	1	76	1	9	1	127	1	116	1	19
Bombay, do.	1	136	1	283	1	151	1	180	1	370	1	(a)184
Bengal, do.	7	270	1	117	1	170	6	125	1	132	1	(b)149
Do., Unaided	1	190	...	...	...	...	2	524	...	...	...	...
N.-W. Provinces, Government	...	...	...	...			...	...	...	...	1	(c)155
N.-W. Provinces, Aided	2	31	...	...	...	...	2	94	...	...	...	...
N.-W. Provinces, Unaided	...	...	...	...	...	...	1	17	...	...	...	...
Punjab, Government	...	...	...	...			...	...	1	188	...	...
TOTAL Government	9	518	3	476	3	330	8	432	4	806	4	507
TOTAL Aided	2	31	...	...	...	...	2	94	...	...	...	...
TOTAL Unaided	1	190	...	...	...	...	3	541	...	...	...	...
GRAND TOTAL	12	739	3	476	3	330	13	1067	4	806	4	507

(a) Including 82 non-collegiate students. (c) Not reading for University degrees.
(b) ,, 107 ,, ,,

There is an addition of one to the number of law departments, of one to the number of medical colleges, and of one to that of engineering colleges. The last named is the Roorkee College, maintained by the Public Works Department of Government, and included for the first time in 1884-85 in the returns of the Education Department. The Lahore Medical School, which also existed in 1881-82, should preferably, since its affiliation to the Punjab University, be included among professional colleges. It has accordingly been entered in the foregoing statement, though in the tables appended to this report it is shown under medical schools. The only real addition is the new law department of the Benares College which, though entirely supported by fees, is under Government management, and should probably be included among departmental institutions. There has been an addition of 328 to the number of law students, of 330 (including 188 in the Lahore Medical School) to that of medical students, and a nominal increase of 177 engineering students, due to the inclusion of the Roorkee College with 155 students on its rolls. With the exception of a few law departments, all professional colleges are Government institutions;

an engineering college being maintained in four of the five Presidencies named in the table, and a medical college in all except the North-Western Provinces, where, however, there is a medical school. In Bengal, law departments are attached to six Government colleges, and are entirely supported by fees. The law department of the Presidency College was abolished at the end of 1884. It charged fees at the rate of R5 and R10 a month, and in this way returned for many years a large profit to Government over and above the salaries of the professors. But in 1881-82 the Metropolitan Institution of Calcutta, an unaided college, was affiliated to the University in law, and opened its classes with a fee-rate of R3. The result was the rapid depletion of the Presidency College classes until, on the 31st March 1884, they contained only six students, and were closed under the orders of Government in the following December. Another law department was subsequently opened in the unaided City College of Calcutta. Of the three law departments in the North-Western Provinces, two are attached to the Government Colleges at Allahabad and Benares, and are therefore under public management, though they are shown in the returns as aided and unaided respectively. The third is attached to the Canning College at Lucknow, and receives a grant-in-aid. Strictly speaking, therefore, private enterprise has not entered into the field of higher professional education except as regards three law departments, two unaided in Calcutta and the other aided at Lucknow.

The Lahore Medical School had both an English and a vernacular department, the latter being the more numerously attended. Additional classes were also formed (1) for '*hakims*' or students of the native systems of medicine, (2) for European midwives, (3) for '*dais*' or native midwives. The chief event of the year 1884-85 was the admission of women to the regular classes; of 15 candidates 11 were admitted, 4 to the English department and 7 to the vernacular.

A great impulse was given to the study of engineering in 1884-85 by the orders of the Government of India guaranteeing to each engineering college annually a certain number of appointments in the higher ranks of the Public Works Department. To the Roorkee College are allowed four and five appointments in alternate years, and to each of the other colleges one or two appointments. By earlier orders of the Government of Bengal, all appointments under road-cess committees, such as those of district engineers, were reserved to qualified students of the Seebpore College, but complaints have been made that these orders have been neglected by the appointing authorities.

45. Cost of Professional Colleges, 1881-82 to 1884-85.—The total cost of professional education connected with the University advanced from R3,75,027 to R5,95,897; or if the cost of the Roorkee Engineering College and the Lahore Medical School be excluded, to R4,02,068. In all other colleges together the Government expenditure has risen from R2,82,570 to R2,94,310, and the local expenditure from R92,457 to R1,06,858. The figures are given below:—

HEAD OF CHARGE.	1881-82.				1884-85.			
	Provincial Revenues.	Fees.	Other sources.	TOTAL.	Provincial Revenues.	Fees.	Other sources.	TOTAL.
	R	R	R	R	R	R	R	R
Law	527	39,496	7,433	47,456	—406	32,186	4,886	36,666
Medicine	1,78,157	35,607	...	2,13,764	2,13,889	53,366	2,411	2,69,666
Engineering	1,03,886	9,921	...	1,13,807	2,70,560	13,256	5,749	2,89,565
TOTAL	2,82,570	85,024	7,433	3,75,027	4,84,043	98,808	13,046	5,95,897

Law.—The law classes practically pay for themselves. Government incurs a cost of a few thousand rupees in Bombay and the North-Western Provinces, which is met by a surplus to much the same amount in Madras and Bengal. The fee-receipts have fallen from R39,000 to R32,000, and the total expenditure from R47,000 to R36,000, owing to the abolition of the law department of the Calcutta Presidency College with its costly staff of professors and high fee-payments.

Medicine.—After excluding the cost of the Lahore Medical School (R57,000, of which R53,000 was borne by Government), the total cost of the other three medical colleges of India remains nearly constant at R2,13,000. Their fee-receipts have increased from R35,000 to R50,000, chiefly owing to an increase of R12,000 in the Grant Medical College of Bombay, where the fees in 1884-85 reached such an amount as to return an actual profit of R4,000 to Government upon a total expenditure of R23,000. The total cost of the Madras Medical College amounted in the same year to nearly R39,000; but in each case the expenditure is far below that of the Calcutta Medical College, which reached the sum of R1,50,000. It is probable that this difference merely represents some variety in debiting the cost of the institution to the Medical and Education Departments respectively.

Engineering.—The cost of the Roorkee College in 1884-85 was R1,37,430, practically the whole of which was borne by Government. The total cost of the other three engineering colleges increased from R1,14,000 to R1,53,000, nearly all paid from provincial revenues, the fee-receipts amounting to R10,000 at the earlier and R13,000 at the later date. It will be seen that a much smaller proportion of the cost is met from fees in engineering than in medical colleges. The Madras Engineering College, which cost R8,000 only, is on a much smaller scale than the Poona College of Science or the Seebpore Engineering College, in each of which the expenditure amounted to eight or nine times as much.

46. Results of University Examinations, 1881-82 and 1884-85.—The results of the University Examinations in law, medicine, and engineering are subjoined. The statement includes those only who passed the final examination in each case, whether for the license or the degree:—

Province.	Law.		Medicine.		Engineering.	
	1881-82.	1884-85.	1881-82.	1884-85.	1881-82.	1884-85.
Madras	12	25(a)	4	10(b)	1	7
Bombay	5	13	14	24(b)	16	7
Bengal	67	77(c)	20	14	6	...(d)
N.-W. Provinces	2	...	...	...	...	3
Punjab	...	...	...	11	...	..
Total	86	115	38	59	23	17

(a) Including 1 Master in Law.
(b) Including 1 Doctor of Medicine.
(c) Including 42 candidates from non-departmental institutions.
(d) No examination in engineering was held in Bengal in 1884-85.

In Bengal, law classes under private management have largely taken the place of Government institutions; and of 77 candidates who took the degree of B. L. in 1884-85, 42 appeared from the former. No examination for the degree of L. C. E. or B. C. E. was held in Bengal in 1884-85, owing to a change in the date of the University Examinations. The three candidates in the North-Western Provinces passed the special examination held by the Roorkee College for its own students.

47. The Collegiate Education of Women, 1881-82 to 1884-85.—In the Report of the Education Commission (paragraph 599) it was stated that in Bengal alone had any provision been made for the higher education of women. The college department of the Bethune School in Calcutta was opened in 1879, in consequence of the success of one of its pupils at the Entrance examination of the University. From that time there have been candidates at the Entrance and

higher examinations every year. On the 31st March 1882, the college department contained six pupils reading for degrees in the Calcutta University; and in the following year two of these succeeded in obtaining the degree. The Free Church Female Normal School also contained at the same date three matriculated students who were reading for the First Arts examination. It will not be without interest to trace the University career of these young ladies and of their successors, who have taken the lead in the higher education of women in India. Miss Chandra Mukhi Bose was the first young lady in India to pass the Entrance examination. She was followed by Miss Kadambini Bose; and together they passed the B. A. examination and were admitted to the degree in 1883. The former young lady continued to read in the Bethune College classes for the M. A. degree. She obtained that degree, with honours in English, in 1884, and was subsequently appointed to be a teacher in the institution to which she owed her training. The latter, after her marriage, entered the Calcutta Medical College as Mrs. Kadambini Ganguli, where she is now pursuing her studies for the degree of Bachelor of Medicine. Two other young ladies, Miss Ellen D'Abreu and Miss Abala Das, who had passed the First Arts and the Entrance examination respectively in 1881, entered the Medical College of Madras with scholarships from the Bengal Government, which were renewed after their term had expired. By the Resolution of the 29th June 1883, female candidates were declared admissible to the Medical College of Calcutta, provided they had duly passed the First Arts examination, as required in the case of men. The Lieutenant-Governor also sanctioned special scholarships of R20 a month, tenable for five years, for all female candidates without restriction who, after passing the First Arts examination, elected to join the Medical College. Two young ladies, Miss Virginia Mitter and Miss Bidhu Mukhi Bose, took advantage of this offer and are now reading the ordinary course for the license in medicine. Four more young ladies, either then or subsequently, passed the First Arts examination, some of whom continued their studies for the B. A. degree; while others (including four Europeans) passed the Entrance examination. At the close of 1884-85, six young ladies were reading in the college classes of the Bethune School. It is not to be questioned therefore that in Bengal the higher education of women has made a fair start. In Madras and Bombay, up to 1884-85, no native female candidate had passed the Entrance examination of the University, nor was there any institution in which they could be taught to that standard. In his report for that year the Director, Mr. H. B. Grigg, observed with reference to the absence of any provision for training female students to the Entrance standard:—
"This defect is much to be regretted; and if not remedied will probably result "in Natives of India being supplanted in the advanced institutions by mistresses "imported from Europe having higher qualifications. The introduction of "French and German into the subjects of the Entrance Examination removes the "language difficulty, and there is no good reason why girls should not be "taught mathematics and physical science up to the required standard."

In the medical education of women Madras has long taken the lead. Up to 1883 female students from Bengal, who had passed the qualifying examination of the University but were nevertheless refused admission to the Calcutta Medical College, were compelled to pursue their medical studies in Madras. In 1883, as stated just above, His Honour the Lieutenant-Governor of Bengal issued a Resolution declaring the eligibility of women, provided they were otherwise qualified, to enter the Medical College as regular students for the degree or the license in medicine on equal terms with men. The following extract from the Resolution will be read with interest:—" The Lieutenant-Governor learns to "his regret that some Bengali ladies, fully qualified by educational attainments

"Rivers Thompson's opinion, clearly opposed to the public good, as well as to legi-
"timate private interests, that such a state of things should continue, and that
"the educational system of Bengal, progressive in other respects, should be
"illiberal and retrograde in this. Illiberality here has great and numerous
"evil consequences. It encourages zenana prejudices; it strengthens the
"barriers of caste; and it suppresses the natural and reasonable aspirations of
"Indian ladies to enter a profession which would find, in India of all coun-
"tries in the world, a wide sphere of action and of beneficent service. Every day
"that passes widens our knowledge of the fact that among the native community
"there are women in every position of life who would prefer death to treatment
"by a male physician; and the misery caused by neglected and unskilfully treated
"illness must be widespread and most lamentable. There is but one way
"by which this suffering can be relieved, and that is by the medical education
"of females; for, in the present conditions of Indian life, it would be useless to
"wait till opposition based upon prejudices (if such they can be called) is re-
"moved. The Lieutenant-Governor therefore considers it his duty to support
"this movement; and he looks on the objections which have been made to it, on
"the ground of the difficulty of teaching mixed classes, as unsubstantial and obso-
"lete. Experience gained in Europe, in America, and in Madras has shown that
"mixed classes can be taught without any bad results; while the aptitude of
"women for the study and profession of medicine is, in the Lieutenant-Governor's
"opinion, no longer open to discussion or doubt." A similar movement was
made the same year in Bombay. In reference to the assumed intention of the
Bombay University to admit women to medical degrees—an intention which
was carried into effect a few months later—the Government of Bombay in
May 1883 decided that a class should be opened in the Grant Medical College,
at first for non-University female students, and after the lapse of five years
for those alone who had passed the licentiate examination. The class was
opened at once with 12 students (seven Christians and five Parsis), of whom
one had passed the Entrance examination. The number increased in the following year to 17. A special examination was held for admission to the class; but
the desirability of raising the standard was even then discussed; and Mr. Lee-
Warner observed, in his report as Acting Director for 1884-85:—"Success in
"the terminal examination depends largely upon the preliminary education
"gained by the student, and in course of time it will be convenient to insist upon
"the matriculation standard as the test for entrance." At the end of 1884-85,
female students were therefore attending the medical college of each Presidency; 5 in Madras, 17 in Bombay, and 3 in Calcutta. For the attainment of a
medical degree it was necessary that a candidate should have passed the qualifying examination in Arts; but only in Calcutta was this condition required for
admission to the classes of the Medical College.

IV.—SECONDARY EDUCATION.

48. Secondary Schools for Boys, 1881-82 to 1884-85.—Secondary
schools are of two classes—upper secondary (or high) and lower secondary (or
middle), the former reading for the matriculation examination of the University, the latter for a standard short of this, which may be English, or vernacular, or a combination of the two. .Under the orders of 1883 these two classes
of schools are combined in the returns. The subjoined tables, however, which
give the results of the two examinations specified above, will show the number of
schools that send candidates to each. That number will not, it is true, correspond with the number of high and middle schools shown in the returns, for
there is always a certain number of schools included in the class, but not yet
able to undergo the test. The schools that send candidates to the examinations
are those that read the full course for high and for middle schools respectively.

Pupils.	Schools.	Pupils.	Schools.	Pupils.	Schools.	Pupils.	Schools.	Pupils.	Schools.	Pupils.	Schools.	Pupils.
6,370 35	251 21	13,467 83	221 91	4,339 393	624 116	24,196 511	156 3	13,483 133	328 21	32,365 703	65 5	6,521 177
11,170	78	7,174	56	3,812	281	22,158	210	18,405	79	10,893	12	2,088
16,186 10,467	583 791	44,225 41,623	200 76	24,244 4,351	844 1,050	84,654 56,441	62 189	16,187 11,918	676 849	58,029 47,872	220 102	28,242 6,221
2,927 3,562	67 7	2,635 241	5	50	139 462	5,612 3,803	43 432	9,313 36,396	65 11	12,946 832	13 2	1,745 191
2,238 2,736	38	946	…	…	101 126	3,184 2,736	64 127	15,015 19,089	30 1	7,812 78	2	582
2,101	16	699	…	…	55	2,800	39	2,477	21	1,071	…	…
588	18 1	363 23	1	27	32 1	978 23	16 1	2,124 76	21	3,234	…	…
…	…	…	8 1	624 65	48 44	5,193 2,984	12 16	2,343 1,498	27 27	2,673 1,845	13 1	1,364 91
2,021 1,382	29 25	2,548 1,537	…	…	7	303	26	5,454	…	…	…	…
303	…	…	…	…	2	157	2	401	1	16	…	…
157	…	…										
44,060 18,182	1,080 845	72,077 43,507	491 168	33,096 4,309	2,133 1,799	149,233 66,498	631 768	85,221 69,110	1,248 909	129,039 51,380	325 110	40,542 6,680
62,242	1,925	115,584	659	37,905	3,932	215,731	1,399	154,331	2,157	180,419	435	47,222

So far, therefore, as the table shows, English secondary schools increased between 1881-82 and 1884-85 from 2,133 with 149,233 pupils to 2,204 with 254,802 pupils; while in the same period there was a slight decrease from 1,799 to 1,787 in the number of vernacular schools, accompanied by an increase from 66,498 to 127,170 in the number of pupils. But, as has been already frequently explained, the change of classification that took place in 1883-84 render any estimate of progress very difficult, except in Bengal and Assam, where the primary classes had always been reckoned as an integral portion of the secondary school, and where therefore the change did not operate. In Bengal there was an increase in these three years of 114 English and of 90 vernacular schools, with an increase of nearly 18,000 pupils in the former and 1,000 in the latter; the increase taking place almost exclusively in the field of private enterprise. In Assam there was a smaller proportionate increase of five schools and 1,500 pupils. In other provinces, it is useless to compare the number of pupils at the two dates, as it is impossible to say what portion of the increase is due to the growth of the secondary and what to the addition of the primary classes. A comparison of the number of schools, though not free from difficulty, is more feasible. Practically every high school had a middle section, formerly reckoned a a separate school; and hence the immediate effect of the change was to reduce the number of secondary schools by a number equal to that of high schools. The number of high schools in India in 1883, Bengal and Assam being excepted, was 246; and by that amount the number of secondary English schools at once fell, in consequence of the change of classification. Adding that number, therefore, to the recorded increase of 71 schools, we arrive at 317 as an approximate estimate of the increase in the number of secondary schools teaching English. In vernacular schools this cause did not operate, as only a very few had high departments; and yet it is seen that the number actually decreased throughout India (though only to the extent of 12 schools), notwithstanding an increase of 90 schools of this class in Bengal. The reduction took place in Madras, chiefly in the last year of the period when the number fell from 101 to 29; and it is explained that the disappearing schools were mostly petty schools, that ceased to exist or at any rate to furnish returns when, owing to poor attendance and defective management, they were refused admission to the examinations under the results system. "In fact," it is added, "there can be no question that hitherto, and pos-"sibly still to some extent, schools which did not exist at all appeared in the "returns, speculative managers not unfrequently sending in detailed applications "for schools which they hoped to start, but which were never started." A similar but much smaller reduction took place in the North-Western Provinces in 1882-83, when a number of unsuccessful Government schools were reduced from the secondary to the primary class.

In addition to these local and occasional fluctuations, there is another cause of a more general and permanent character tending to reduce the number of middle vernacular schools. Just as these schools are continually being reinforced from the upper section of the primary schools, to which indeed the less successful among them again from time to time revert, so also middle vernacular are constantly being converted into middle English schools, as the desire for English education manifests itself. Especially is this the case in those provinces in which the vernacular is the medium of instruction in middle English schools, and where therefore the conversion of a vernacular into an English school means nothing more than the addition of an English class.

49. Secondary Schools classified according to Management.—For the purposes of this comparison, 55 English schools maintained by Native States, and now included with those under public management, must be transferred to the class of unaided schools, under which they were returned in 1881-82. After this correction has been made, it appears that the number of secondary schools (English) under public management increased from 562 to 576, or by 2½ per cent., and the number of aided schools from 1,080 to 1,248, or by 16 per cent.; while that of unaided schools fell from 491 to 380. The loss under the last head is confined to Madras, where the number of unaided English schools fell from 221 to 65. This loss has been partially met by an increase of 77 in the number of aided schools of the province; but the reduction mainly arises from the causes specified in the last paragraph. The largest increase in aided schools is found in Bengal, which adds 93. In other provinces there is either a slight apparent decrease or no apparent increase, implying in either case a real increase to the extent of the numerical reduction caused by change of classification.

Among vernacular schools, those under private management receiving grants-in-aid are the only section in which there is any increase, namely, from 845 to 909, or 7½ per cent.; and this is practically confined to Bengal. Schools under public management have suffered a small, and unaided schools (in Madras only) a considerable reduction. In these cases change of classification has had no effect.

The returns of 1881-82 do not enable me, nor does the report of the Education Commission, to separate the schools under public management into those managed and maintained by local or municipal boards. But the process of transfer from the former to the latter system of control was going on more or less actively throughout this period. At the end of it the figures stand thus:—
Of 631 English and 768 vernacular schools under public management, 335 of the former and 570 of the latter were managed by local and municipal boards, and 55 English schools were maintained by Native States. The schools maintained by the Department were therefore 241 English and 198 vernacular. These figures need revision, however, in one point. In the North-Western Provinces, 36 zila (or Government high English) schools, which are maintained from the funds placed at the disposal of District Boards, are returned as being "managed and maintained" by the Boards, though the management of them is in no way under their control but remains in the hands of the Department. It follows that the heading "managed and maintained" is unsuited to cases of this kind, where the institutions are managed by one authority and maintained from the funds of another.

50. Results of Public Examinations: the Entrance Examination.—
The most important public test that secondary schools have to undergo is the Entrance or matriculation examination of the different Universities,—a test which exhibits no very wide variations between one University and another as regards difficulty of standard. The Education Commission seem to have admitted the higher character of the Bombay test; but the additions that have lately been made to the Madras course will at any rate have reduced any difference that may have existed. The Commission quote the report of the Bengal Provincial Committee to the effect that the Calcutta matriculation standard "appears to "be below that attainable in present circumstances by high schools," but the changes recently made by the University have not increased the difficulty of the examination. Under the tests as they stand, the increase in the number of successful candidates throughout India, from 2,952 in the first to 4,132 in the last year of the period, is very marked. The number of competing schools and of successful candidates for each province is subjoined. For the provinces coming

SECONDARY EDUCATION, 1882 TO 1885.

under the Calcutta University, the results of the examination of April 1885 are given, as no examination was held within the year 1884-85 :—

Entrance Examination.

PROVINCE.	1881-82.								1884-85.									
	GOVERNMENT INSTITUTIONS.		OTHER INSTITUTIONS.		TOTAL.		INSTITUTIONS UNDER PUBLIC MANAGEMENT.		AIDED INSTITUTIONS.		UNAIDED INSTITUTIONS.		TOTAL.	
	Schools.	Candidates.	Schools.	Candidates.	Schools.	Candidates.	Schools.	Candidates.	Schools.	Candidates.	Schools.	Candidates.	Schools.	Candidates.
Madras	21	227	106	904	127	1,131	37	382	76	768	45	453	158	1,603a
Bombay	18	171	42	217	60	388	27	416	28	156	29	268	84	840b
Bengal	51	462	157	564	208	1,026	57	497	120	217	66	356	243	1,070c
N.-W. Provinces	25	103	32	87	57	190	24	88	39	105	2	5	65	98d
Punjab	11	81	12	34	23	115	20	158	26	111	3	34	49	303
Central Provinces	1	22	5	36	6	58	1	23	5	27	...	...	6	50
Burma	3	12	...	...	3	12	3	8	2	3	...	2	5	13
Assam	9	23	2	1	11	24	9	34	3	3	1	3	13	40
Berar	2	4	...	...	2	4	2	11	...	...	...	1	2	12
Coorg	1	4	...	...	1	4	1	3	...	...	...	...	1	3
TOTAL	142	1,109	356	1,843	498	2,952	181	1,620	299	1,390	146	1,122	626	4,132e

(a) Including 22 girls.
(b) ,, 7 ,,
(c) ,, 1 ,,
(d) Excluding 27 candidates who passed the vernacular Entrance examination of the Punjab University.
(e) Including 30 girls.

The number of schools teaching the standard has increased by 26 per cent., and that of successful candidates by 40 per cent. The inference is that the schools have become more efficient, since the increase in the number of successful candidates is too large to be accounted for by fluctuations such as have been noticed in the percentage of candidates passing from year to year. In the Madras University, indeed, the proportion of successful candidates was nearly constant, lying between 30 and 31 per cent. in both years. In Bombay, it is true, there was a considerable rise, the percentage of successful candidates varying from 28 in 1881-82 to 41 in 1884-85; but against this may be set the unfavourable results of the year 1884-85 for students examined by the Calcutta University, when only 34 per cent. passed, against 48 per cent. in 1881-82.

Of the successful candidates in 1881-82, 37½ per cent. were from departmental and 62½ per cent. from non-departmental schools; in 1884-85 the proportions were 39 and 61 per cent. respectively. Taken as a whole, therefore, the non-departmental schools have not fully kept pace with their departmental co-adjutors in the business of preparing candidates for admission to the University.

51. Results of Public Examinations: Middle School Examination.— The character and contents of this examination in each province are fully described in paragraph 254 of the report of the Education Commission. In some provinces English forms a necessary part of the standard; in others, where middle vernacular schools are regarded as filling an important place in the secondary system, there are alternative standards in English and the vernacular. Of the English standards, again, the character of some is governed by the University Entrance examination, to which they lead two years later; while others, framed in the interests of students who do not look forward to a University career, are altogether independent of University standards. In some provinces, again, the middle school test is applied not only to pupils of middle schools, but also to those pupils of high schools who are in the corresponding stage of progress; in others, no pupil of a high school is admitted to the examination. With all these differences it will be evident, first, that the passing of this test does not imply identical or even similar acquirements in different provinces; and secondly, that the number passing affords no exact measure, between province and province, of the number of pupils who have arrived at that stage. In any one province, however, the results of the examination may be held to afford some measure of progress from year to year, though even this

below :—

Middle School Examination.

PROVINCE.	1881-82.		1884-85.	
	Schools.	Candidates.	Schools.	Candidates.
Madras	234	2,484	284	4,500
Bombay	173	1,751	733	2,158
Bengal	1,361	2,858	1,415	3,769
North-Western Provinces	480	782	553	1,761
Punjab	191	1,073	230	2,148
Central Provinces	46	242	49	605
Burma	30	130	34	260
Assam	49	82	76	178
Berar	2	23	10	90
Coorg	1	9	1	20
TOTAL	2,567	9,434	3,385	15,489

Out of the total number of successful candidates, 4,180 passed the public service certificate examination (1,217 English and 2,963 vernacular), which is held in four provinces and is sometimes identical with, but generally distinct from, the middle school examination. The large increase in Madras is due to the reduction of the passing-mark in 1882, in order to utilise the examination for the purposes of school-promotion by adding a third class. Admission to the public service was restricted, as before, to those who passed in the first or second class. In Bombay, it will be noticed, the increase in successful candidates is by no means proportionate to that of competing schools. The explanation is that in 1881-82 the middle school examination was identical with that in Standard III, which was the gate of admission to the high school course and was therefore exclusively English. In 1884-85 the public service certificate examination took its place; this is divided into two branches, English for the upper grades of the service, and vernacular for the lower. The English examination is determined by Standard V, which is reached two years after admission to the high school, and is therefore passed by a much smaller number of candidates. The vernacular examination which attracts the great bulk of the candidates, is held in the sixth or highest standard of primary schools. In Bengal, the increase in the last year is partially due to the circumstance that the boys had a longer time for preparation, owing to a postponement of the date of examination. In the North-Western Provinces and Oudh there was a great rise in 1883-84, owing to the reduction of the passing-mark from 40 to 33 per cent.; and this was maintained in the following year. The middle school examinations in the Punjab were transferred in 1883-84 to the charge of the Punjab University. The change does not appear to have been attended with unmixed good. For two years bitter complaints were made against the delay in publishing the results of the examination; and in the second year (1884-85) the standard of passing is alleged to have been lowered to an almost ridiculous point. Mr. Ibbetson wrote of this examination :—"The standard was much too easy; and I have received state-
" ments from several masters of schools to the effect that boys were passed who

52. Secondary Schools for Girls, 1881-82 to 1884-85.

The following table shows the progress made in each province in secondary schools for girls, English and vernacular:—

Province.		1881-82									1884-85								
		Under Public Management.		Aided		Unaided.		Total.		Under Public Management.		Aided.		Unaided.		Total.	
		Schools.	Pupils.	Schools.	Pupils.	Schools.	Pupils.	Schools.	Pupils.	Schools.	Pupils.	Schools.	Pupils.	Schools.	Pupils.	Schools.	Pupils.
	English	4	22	44	450	10	98	58	570	4	311	76	4,646	6	240	86	5,197
	Vernacular	2	10	12	77	14	110	28	197	17	1,219	58	4,724	4	586	79	6,529
	English	...	...	28	1,581	...	...	28	1,581	2	73	47	2,740	...	...	49	2,813
	Vernacular	2	299	27	2,124	7	607	36	3,030	2	186	27	2,080	9	746	38	3,012
	English	...	...	14	509	1	19	15	527	...	...	18	957	1	20	19	977
Pro-	Vernacular	...	...	12	342	...	...	12	342	...	...	14	1,242	1	64	15	1,306
stern	English	...	...	1	6	...	...	1	6	...	...	1	48	...	...	1	48
	Vernacular	...	...	3	27	...	...	3	27	1	202	6	294	...	...	7	496
	English	...	...	...	...	...	...	...	...	...	...	1	68	...	...	1	68
ovinces	Vernacular	...	...	2	14	...	...	2	14	...	...	3	46	...	...	3	46
	English	...	...	6	73	...	...	6	73	...	...	11	1,013	...	...	11	1,013
	Vernacular	...	...	...	...	...	...	...	...	...	...	1	85	...	...	1	85
	English	...	...	1	9	...	...	1	9	1	19	...	...	...	...	1	19
	Vernacular	...	...	...	...	...	...	...	...	1	48	...	...	...	...	1	48
Total	English	6	321	121	4,597	17	705	146	5,636	10	791	184	12,061	16	1,050	210	13,902
	Vernacular	2	10	29	604	15	129	44	730	18	1,267	79	5,882	5	606	102	7,755
GRAND TOTAL		8	331	150	5,201	32	834	190	6,366	28	2,058	263	17,943	21	1,656	312	21,657

64, or 44 per cent. ; while vernacular schools have increased by 58, or 132 per cent. The main portion of the increase is found in aided schools; and in that field the chief development has taken place in Madras, which adds 28 English and 51 vernacular schools, and in Bombay, where 21 English schools have been opened. Among the smaller provinces, much enterprise has been shown in Burma, where the number of secondary schools for girls has been doubled.

53. Expenditure on Secondary Schools for Boys, 1881-82 to 1884-85.
—It is not worth while to go at any great length into the subject of expenditure on secondary schools, whether for boys or for girls, at these two dates. No exact comparison is in fact possible, since the intermediate change of classification increased the tabulated expenditure on secondary schools by the full cost of their primary departments. The following statement of expenditure on secondary schools for boys is however given, partly because the comparison may be made for some provinces which were not affected by the re-classification, and partly in order to furnish the materials for a subsequent comparison of expenditure in secondary and primary schools taken together, the differences caused by re-classification being thus got rid of.

CHAP. II.] SECONDARY EDUCATION, 1882 TO 1885. 53

Secondary Schools for Boys.

Province.	1881-82.					1884-85.				
	Provincial Revenues.	Local Funds.	Municipal Funds.	Fees.	Other Sources.	Total.	Provincial Revenues.	Local Funds.	Municipal Funds.	Fees.	Other Sources.	Total.
	R	R	R	R	R	R	R	R	R	R	R	R
Madras	1,94,768	11,172	2,900	3,23,363	1,69,368	7,00,971	2,23,559	42,305	4,868	38,432	2,42,596	12,01,060
Bombay	2,15,968	614	4,854	2,57,955	2,32,314	7,41,105	2,11,710	769	38,831	3,69,196	2,28,017	8,48,523
Bengal	5,57,813	1,412	17,813	8,06,700	5,36,833	19,20,571	5,81,732	917	47,958	12,14,528	5,90,197	24,35,332
North-Western Provinces	2,65,097	17,845	9,783	64,656	56,694	4,14,075	82,269	3,75,424	33,677	1,40,753	1,86,166	8,18,289
Punjab	1,69,636	38,820	30,096	35,172	36,710	3,10,434	2,15,487	85,289	72,056	1,14,806	92,712	5,80,350
Central Provinces	65,911	...	10,583	0,159	13,918	1,00,571	64,024	...	12,540	15,440	12,393	1,04,397
Burma	47,916	2,143	9,692	21,014	22,173	1,02,838	36,805	198	9,354	53,638	42,662	2,26,647
Assam	47,778	...	285	39,407	19,096	1,06,566	30,942	20,967	940	60,285	24,218	1,37,352
Berar	23,383	...	...	645	...	24,028	65,038	72	420	9,874	369	75,778
Orrg	7,518	...	...	1,160	...	8,678	6,895	...	340	3,811	954	12,000
Total	15,95,788	72,006	1,14,706	15,60,231	10,87,106	44,29,837	15,18,461	5,25,941	3,49,384	26,25,663	14,20,274	64,39,723

From the table it appears that the total cost of secondary schools for boys increased from R44,29,837 to R64,39,723; the cost to provincial revenues showing some reduction from R15,95,788 to R15,18,461, while the share borne by "other sources," including local and municipal funds, increased from R28,34,049 to R49,21,262. It has already been explained that the charge of secondary schools was in several provinces made over to local or municipal boards, together with grants for their maintenance; while on the other hand the cost of secondary schools increased, not only as a result of their regular and normal development, but by the inclusion of their primary departments. Hence the reduction shown above in the Government expenditure is illusory, and represents in fact merely the excess of the grants transferred to local bodies over the increased cost due to the causes just named. An illustration or two will make this clear. In Madras, the total cost of secondary schools for boys increased, owing to these causes, from 7 lakhs to 12 lakhs. But as no transfer of funds to local bodies took place, it might have been expected that provincial revenues, like other sources of income, should bear their share of the increased cost. And so indeed they have, but only to the extent of R29,000 out of the total increase of 5 lakhs. The table shows that the bulk of the increase has been borne by fees; in other words, that the schools have become much more self-supporting. The same result emerges in Bombay, where there were no primary departments to be transferred; the Government expenditure is stationary, and even shows some small reduction, and the whole of the increased cost of the schools is derived from fee-receipts. In Bengal, where the change did not operate, there is a slight increase in the Government expenditure, accompanied by a very large increase in that from private sources. But in the North-Western Provinces both causes are in full operation. The transfer of funds to local bodies effected an apparent reduction from R2,65,000 to R82,000 in the expenditure from provincial revenues; while that transfer, coupled with the addition of the cost of primary classes, brought up the expenditure from all other sources from R1,49,000 to R7,36,000. Throughout India, the expenditure from provincial and local funds taken together has increased from R16,68,000 to R20,44,000, while that from all other sources, including municipal funds, has increased from R27,62,000 to R43,95,000,—a very much higher rate of increase, the amount of which is not seriously affected by the grants made to municipalities for secondary schools in Burma. The general inference that may fairly be derived from these figures is that the increased cost of secondary education within this period has been very largely derived from local sources, and that provincial grants, whether made to the schools directly or through the medium of local bodies, have not received any material addition. For some of the larger provinces the statement might be made in more emphatic terms.

As to secondary schools for girls, it is only necessary to remark that the total expenditure on them increased, according to the returns, from R3,76,440 to R8,92,593; the provincial expenditure increasing from R1,01,900 to R2,34,993 and the local expenditure from R2,74,540 to R6,57,600. The duty of maintaining or of aiding girls' schools of this class has not been made over to local bodies to the same extent; and hence provincial revenues bear their full share of the increased cost, whether arising from additional schools or from the inclusion of the primary departments.

54. Secondary Education, Madras, 1881-82 to 1884-85.—Reference has been made in a previous paragraph to a change in the University standard for matriculation. The first examination under the new standard, which is a good deal more difficult than the old, was held in December 1884. The passing mark in vernacular languages was raised from one-fourth to one-third;

to the arithmetic test interest, discount, present worth, and stocks were added; under general knowledge, English history was included, and the standard in Indian history raised; while the whole instead of portions only of the two scientific text-books—Roscoe's *Primer of Chemistry* and Balfour Stewart's *Primer of Physics*—was required. A reduction in the percentage of successful candidates at the first examination under the new standard was ascribed, not unreasonably, to its greater difficulty. It was especially marked in the science subjects, as to which the Director notices the difficulty of securing competent men who are able to teach the subject practically, adding—"The expediency of "making elementary science a universal test for matriculation is, of course, open "to question; but there can be no question that if the test is imposed, it should "be thorough and practical, however elementary." It is suggested that under the former system the cramming of the text-books was sufficient to secure a pass in those subjects.

Changes were also made in 1882-83 in the standard of the middle school examination. The importance of this examination in Madras lies partly in the fact of its having been constituted the main gate of entry to the public service in its lower grades, but chiefly on account of its position as the "keystone" of middle and primary education, and in particular as the means by which, if at all, middle vernacular schools may hereafter be spread over the country (Report for 1881-82, paragraph 122). At present there are but few schools of that class in Madras; and, as previously noticed, the number has been decreasing year by year. The changes referred to were designed to promote greater thoroughness of instruction in language, mathematics, history and geography, to encourage candidates to study special subjects in addition to the obligatory course, and to ensure attention being paid to vernacular translation and composition—a subject alleged to have been more or less neglected in all English schools. For the purposes of school promotion, the passing standard was reduced in order to add a third class to the first and second classes of previous years; and this resulted in a large increase in the number of successful candidates. In 1883-84 the charges incurred in the secondary education of boys in municipalities were transferred from Government to the municipal boards concerned. In speaking of this transfer the Director writes:— "Judging from the experience of the past, I see no reason to fear that such "schools will not be efficiently conducted; whilst the responsibility for this "branch of education will tend to create a wider and more intelligent interest "in public education, which is no mean set-off against a slight decline of effici- "ency in that of Government schools, even if such decline should prove a fact, "which as a general rule I by no means apprehend."

In the report for 1884-85 it is stated that no institution had then begun to provide instruction for women in the matriculation course of the University. But a special examination, called the Higher Examination for Women, was instituted a few years ago, with the object of carrying their education beyond the middle standard; and schools preparing their pupils for that examination were classed as high schools, though the standard fell considerably short of that for matriculation. However, it has met with a large share of success, and is believed to have done a great deal in improving and maintaining the standard in girls' schools of the better class. In 1881-82, 55 candidates presented themselves for that examination, and 24 passed. In 1884-85, 62 candidates appeared from 26 schools, and 22 passed. For the middle school examination, 245 candidates appeared in 1881-82, and 104 passed; in 1885-86, 273 were examined and 188 passed, of whom 93 were pupils reading in high schools for girls.

55. Secondary Education, Bombay, 1881-82 to 1884-85.—A special feature distinguishes the high schools of this province, to many of which drawing and agricultural classes are attached. With a view to the more general introduction of drawing into the school course, the Government of Bombay laid down in 1880 a course of instruction called the "first grade art," which included free-hand drawing, model and object drawing, and practical geometry. For more advanced students a second grade art course was prescribed, including, in addition to the subjects given above, linear perspective and the delineation of diagrams on the black-board. In 1884-85 the number of children taught in these classes was 2,713, of whom 201 passed the examination. Again, to eight schools agricultural classes have been attached. In these classes it was intended that instruction in agricultural chemistry, in botany, and in surface geology should be given to boys willing to receive it, who would then be excused certain lessons in the ordinary course. The boys thus learn something in school about crops, manure, soils, stock, and implements, while attached to the school is a small farm in which may be practised the principles acquired in the schoolroom. The eight classes contained 89 students in 1884-85, of whom 68 passed the examination. The Bombay report for 1884-85 notices the fact, which is probably not peculiar to Bombay, that the pupils in the district high school tend to be drawn more and more from the municipal town in which the school is situated—that the high school, in fact, is ceasing to be a district school and is becoming an exclusively local school. The remedies suggested are (1) the fuller encouragement of aided enterprise, so as to provide for the requirements of rural tracts, (2) the provision of scholarships and free studentships for poor students at a distance from head-quarters, and (3) the establishment of boarding-houses.

Middle or lower secondary schools in Bombay are not looked upon as occupying any very important place in the educational chain. The school-going population is regarded as being composed for the most part of two sections, one of which is content with a good primary education, while the other and much smaller section looks forward to the Entrance examination and a University career. Hence the Bombay Department has devoted its energies to improving the primary schools of the province, which are designed and believed to be good enough for all classes of the population. But to meet the case of that further section of the people which, without desiring a high English education, looks for something beyond the ordinary course of the primary school, that course is enlarged by the addition of two vernacular classes (Standards V and VI) which may therefore be fairly regarded as coming within the sphere of secondary education, and as corresponding to middle vernacular schools in other provinces. In 1884-85, 1,783 pupils passed by Standard VI from primary schools in Bombay. This is accepted as the vernacular test for admission not only to the lower grades of the public service in that province, as the fifth (English) standard in middle and high schools is the test for admission to the higher grades. The results of both examinations are combined in the table given above in paragraph 51.

Secondary education for girls in Bombay is mostly confined to Europeans and Eurasians, the number of Hindu and Muhammadan girls at these schools being almost insignificant. Of the 22 girls who passed the Entrance examination in 1884-85, none was a Hindu or Muhammadan. The University of Bombay has opened its doors to women in every Faculty; but as Mr. Chatfield pointed out in his report for 1883-84, these changes can be of little service to native ladies until the gap between primary schools and the University is bridged by the establishment of secondary schools for girls. It is with this object that the Poona High School was opened under distinguished patronage in September 1884. At the close of that year it contained 62 girls, of whom 47 were Hindus and 15 "others."

56. Secondary Education, Bengal, 1881-82 to 1884-85.—In this province the experiment has been tried of placing the lower classes of high schools on a vernacular basis. In the two lowest classes no English is taught; in the next three English is taught as a language, all substantive instruction being imparted in the vernacular; in the four highest classes English is the medium of instruction. This system has been experimentally adopted in eight schools; but no accurate estimate can be formed of its value until the boys trained under it are ready to appear at the Entrance examination. Another matter to which attention has been given in Bengal is the necessity of restricting within moderate limits the growth of the Government high schools at head-quarters. Proposals to increase the accommodation of existing schools have not been favourably received, except in those cases in which there was no prospect of private enterprise supplying what was required. In general such proposals have been met by the order to raise the fees to such a rate as would reduce the attendance to conformity with the size of the building, and thus give encouragement to the establishment of a private school. It is maintained that overgrown classes are a serious evil; and the policy is thus defended both on the ground of efficient management and in the interests of private enterprise.

Close attention is paid in Bengal to middle schools, whether English or vernacular; indeed, the only difference between these two classes of schools is that in the former English is taught, as a language merely, in addition to the vernacular course which is common to both. The result is that it is easy for a school to pass from one class to another, according to the varying needs of village communities. A constant process of change is going on: upper primary schools begin to teach the next higher standard, and to be ranked as middle vernacular schools. Of these, some year by year take up the study of English, and finally make good their claim to be ranked as middle English schools; of these last, again, some drop the teaching of English from various causes, and fall back for a time into the ranks of middle vernacular schools. The passage from one class to the other has been rendered easier by the rules of 1882, which allow candidates from all middle schools to compete for both classes of middle scholarships, English and vernacular. In 1884-85, 26 boys passed the middle English examination from vernacular schools, and 674 boys passed the middle vernacular examination from English schools. In the case of most of these last the meaning is that they failed in the English paper only, passing in all the subjects of the vernacular course. In the examination of 1883, the first under the new rules of 1882, the qualifying pass-mark was considerably raised, and this resulted in the number of successful candidates being reduced from 2,885 to 2,111. The loss was fully made up in the two following years, when the number of passes rose to 2,512 and 3,769 respectively. In 1883-84, the cost of all Government middle vernacular schools situated within municipalities was transferred from provincial revenues to municipal funds.

In Bengal, the native community have taken the lead in the higher education of women; and we find, as a consequence, that Hindus and Native Christians are largely represented in secondary schools for girls, as is also the case in Madras.

57. Secondary Education, North-Western Provinces and Oudh, 1881-82 to 1884-85.—In the North-Western Provinces and Oudh, there are, in addition to English and vernacular schools of the ordinary character, high and middle, a few Oriental schools of an advanced type, which prepare their pupils for the Oriental Titles examination of the Punjab University in Arabic, Persian and Sanskrit. Persian was formerly the favourite language with Hindu students, but it appears that a reaction is now taking place in favour of "the ancestral, but till now almost obsolete, Sanskrit." The standard of the middle school examination was raised in 1882 by the addition of vernacular composition, the second book of Euclid, and the Sanitary Primer alternatively with a primer of biology. The immediate result was a decline in the number of successful candidates from 782 to 424. In the following year, the passing-mark was lowered from 40 to 33 per cent., and the number of passed candidates went up with a bound to 1,470 in 1883-84 and 1,761 in 1884-85. The control of Government secondary schools, and the administration of the grant-in-aid to those under private management, were in 1882-83 transferred in large measure to the newly-constituted district boards; though it should be remembered that (as explained in para. 49 above) the relation of district boards to the 36 zila schools of the province is confined to maintenance and excludes management.

58. Secondary Education, Punjab, 1881-82 to 1884-85.—It was noticed by the Education Commission that the Punjab was the only Province in which "high vernacular" schools were recognised. It was long maintained that these schools were dear to the people, who valued the old ways and their Oriental learning, and looked with dislike and suspicion on the advance of English education. In his report for 1883-84 as acting Director of Public Instruction, Mr. Ibbetson discussed this question with reference to the fact that the last vernacular high school had in that year disappeared. He came to the conclusion that these feelings were confined to a generation now passing away, and that they were shared by none in the present generation outside "the literate "section of the priestly and semi-religious classes." To the latter our whole educational system and the secular basis of our teaching were so entirely repugnant that no possible modification of our course of studies could make our schools acceptable to them; and the best hope of reaching them lay in the gradual improvement of the higher indigenous schools. Upon the merits of the question, Mr. Ibbetson was of opinion that we lost little or nothing, and gained much, by the substitution of English for the vernacular in high schools. For high vernacular schools proper text-books were wanting, as well as teachers who had received the necessary training. These wants could only be supplied by multiplying the number of those who had acquired, through the medium of English, the knowledge which they were to communicate through the vernacular. On these grounds he came to the conclusion, which has all along been insisted on in Bengal, that the spread of English education had supplied the means of establishing and multiplying vernacular schools.

There was no great increase in the number of secondary schools, though in his report for 1884-85 the officiating Director remarked that he had been much impressed when on tour "with the widespread and genuine desire on the "part of the people of the towns and large villages to secure the advantages of "secondary education for their children. They did not seem to be deterred by "the information that they would be expected to bear a portion of the extra "cost involved in raising their schools to the middle standard."

59. Secondary Education, 1881-82 to 1884-85: Other Provinces.—These may be more briefly noticed. In the Central Provinces a middle school is now apparently raised to the status of a high school, only when the people or the local municipality provide the greater part of the increased cost. This had been done in two or three cases up to 1884-85. A beginning had also been made to transfer the charge of secondary schools to district councils. In Assam the people appear to be thankful for small educational mercies. It is stated that the parents and guardians of boys bring great pressure to bear on masters to allow their children to go up for matriculation, as they consider it a recommendation to a boy to be able to say hereafter that he has appeared at the Entrance examination; "and even being able to write 'failed Entrance "candidate' after his name is a recommendation to a boy when seeking a wife." Nevertheless, the high schools are well-attended and successful, and the percentage of candidates passing the Entrance examination is just as high as in Bengal. In 1882 the control of aided middle schools was generally made over to local boards, who are said to have given the schools more liberal grants on easier terms. In Berar the number of secondary schools rose from 7 to 26, chiefly in consequence of a change of classification in 1883-84, by which the lower limit of middle schools was brought down from the seventh to the fifth standard, reckoning from the bottom. Under the new classification primary schools include standards I to IV, middle schools V to VII, and high schools VIII to XI. The high school course formerly included only the two highest standards; and hence the cost of each pupil in a high school in Berar was shown in the report of the Education Commission to be double the amount at which it would have stood had this classification been adopted. In Coorg, there was a creditable increase. A municipal school was raised from the primary to the secondary stage, and an aided school of the same class was opened. In 1881-82 there was only one school above the primary stage, namely, the Central School at Mercara, though this was then reckoned as two schools according to the existing practice. In Burma secondary education is still backward. In 1883 a new scheme was promulgated for the furtherance of education of that class. It included provision for raising 13 secondary schools to a higher grade, and for attaching boarding-houses to 20 schools. Half the cost was to be borne by the municipalities concerned, and half by Government. It was proposed to make a grant of R50,000 for this purpose from provincial revenues; but this proposal could not be carried out owing to financial exigencies. In the Resolution by the Chief Commissioner on the report for 1883-84, it is remarked:—"The progress of secondary education "in this province in other than private institutions will for the future " depend almost entirely upon the energy and liberality of the several muni- "cipal committees, to whom the management of the town schools has been " entrusted;" and a promise was added of Government assistance in all cases in which committees were unable to make, from their own funds, full provision for secondary education of which the need was shown.

V.—PRIMARY EDUCATION.

60. Primary Schools for Boys, 1881-82 to 1884-85.—Under the classification in force in 1881-82, there were two divisions of primary schools, English and vernacular. Under the orders of 1883, which relegated the chief section of English primaries (namely, the primary departments of high and middle schools) to the secondary schools to which they were attached, this division was no longer necessary, nor was it retained. Primary schools were thenceforth regarded as being in the main vernacular, and they are now accordingly shown under a single head. They consist in the different provinces either of four or of five classes, the two highest forming the upper primary section, and the classes below these the lower primary. The following table compares for each province

Pupils.	Unaided.		Total.		Under Public Management.		Aided.		Unaided.	
	Schools.	Pupils.	Schools.	Pupils.	Schools.	Pupils.	Schools.	Pupils.	Schools.	Pupils.
193,988	5,591	2,080	14,003	341,998	1,150	36,793	8,310	2,6,038	4,260	79,709
9,564	1,236	0,544	5,012	312,771	5,403	352,554	460	290	35	2,048
820,080	4,307	9,541	50,788	880,937	56	1,595	59,501	B9,188	6,028	11,855
10,876	31	917	5,582	205,166	4,988	177,078	115	6,936	36	1,382
9,525			1,526	93,919	1,358	3,205	125	630	9	255
18,106	85	3,211	1,262	74,335	959	4,612	574	23,193	87	2,254
34,612	2,428	49,411	3,223	86,680	20	1,488	1,284	5555	3,631	13,047
34,511	84	2,275	1,280	36,973	1,167	35,154	289	8,782	71	2,014
4,164	207	2,672	876	35,141	478	26,339	217	4,333	98	1,124
65			59	3,043	63	3,283	2	27		
1,135,491	13,969	291,951	83,591	2,070,963	15,842	772,401	70,877	1,180,082	14,255	243,688

The tables show a total increase of 17,183 schools and of 425,208 scholars reading in them; but the increase is really greater than this, since the figures of 1881-82 included the primary classes of secondary schools, which are excluded from those of 1884-85. It has been repeatedly stated (see paragraph 13 above) that a comparison of progress from 1881-82 to 1884-85 is rendered difficult by changes of classification that took place in the interval. To render any comparison possible, it is necessary to make the following approximate transfers and reductions in the figures of 1881-82. We have first to remove 1,220 boys' schools in Native States (Bombay and the Central Provinces) from the head of unaided schools to that of schools under public management; and also to transfer to the same head 934 schools in Assam which in 1881-82 were returned as aided schools, but which at both dates were equally under the control of public officers or bodies. We have next to deduct those primary departments of middle schools which in 1881-82 were counted as separate schools. In Bengal and Assam they were never so reckoned; in Bombay middle schools had no primary departments; in the Central Provinces they had upper primary departments, but these appear still to be reckoned as separate schools. If a rough estimate be taken of the deductions to be made on this account in the remaining provinces of India, they will amount to 820 schools under public management, 300 aided and 300 unaided schools. Hence the corrected figures for primary boys' schools in 1881-82 will be approximately and in round numbers, 14,390 schools under public management, 55,330 aided, and 12,450 unaided, or 82,170 in all. There is therefore an approximate increase of 18,604 schools, of which 1,252 were added to the number of those under public management, 15,547 to aided, and 1,805 to unaided schools. The chief provincial changes under each class may now be briefly noticed.

61. Schools under Public Management.—The various systems of public primary instruction in force in the different provinces of India are described at length in Chapter IV of the report of the Education Commission. It will be remembered that the term "under public management" includes several divisions. Of the 15,642 primary schools of this class in 1884-85, 13,098 were managed and maintained by local or municipal boards, 1,519 were in Native States, and only 1,025 were under the direct control of the Education Department. These last were mostly confined to Berar and the Central Provinces. The chief agency for the development and extension of primary instruction is therefore that of local and municipal boards. After deducting 134 primary departments in 1881-82, the number of schools so managed in Madras increased from 1,083 to 1,150. In Bombay, primary schools in Native States increased by about 300; and these being excluded, the number of schools under public management in British territory increased by 290, from 3,630 to 3,920. In Bengal, schools of this class are generally conspicuous by their absence; and if the number, small as it is, has been doubled, that result is due to the action of municipalities in certain parts. The North-Western Provinces have suffered an apparent loss of 413 schools; but, on the other hand, they must receive credit for the absorption of nearly 500 primary departments, and there is consequently a sensible increase. In the Punjab, after allowing for 178 primary departments, an advance of 132 schools has to be recorded. In Assam, after making the transfer noticed just above, there is an increase which may be estimated at nearly 230 schools. In the remaining provinces little change has been made.

Where progress has been recorded, it is attributed to the advancing prosperity of the people, their growing desire for education, and the increased ability of the local boards to meet new claims upon their funds. Where there is loss, the loss is ascribed for the most part to the prevalence of cholera or small-pox, to floods or droughts with their attendant scarcity and distress, or to other causes chiefly of a local character. Thus, in explanation of the want of progress in certain districts of the North-Western Provinces in 1882-83, it is remarked that the appreciation of primary education " is, and long must be, a plant of very slow " growth, and poor cultivators are frequently unwilling and unable to send to " school the children whose labour in the fields has an immediate and a tangible " value;" and again in 1883-84, that " the stolid apathy of the agricultural classes " in some parts of the country is an obstacle which the gods themselves would " fail to surmount." In the report for the latter year in Bombay, two counter-acting causes of a quite exceptional character deserve attention. The first was a visitation of locusts—a calamity which afflicted a large number of districts and caused great disturbance to educational work. " Masters, assistants, and in many " cases scholars, had to lend a band in the emergency, and many schools had to " be closed for months together." The second was the predicted occurrence in the following year of a conjunction of Jupiter with the sign Leo ('Sinhastha Vrihaspati'), unpropitious for marriages; the result being that every possible marriage had been arranged in the year preceding that event, with much consequent irregularity of attendance.

62. Aided Schools: Bengal.—The increase in aided schools throughout India amounts approximately to 15,550. The explanation of this large increase is found in the continued development of the policy, pursued in Bengal since 1872, of taking up indigenous schools, and inducing them by the offer of small rewards to modify their course of instruction into conformity with that recognised by the Department. In this way, through the vigilance of inspecting officers, and the readiness of the village schools to ally themselves with a system which, without doing violence to their traditional methods, ensured them the attention and sympathy of Government, and procured them some slight pecuniary gain, it resulted that year by year 6,000, 8,000 or 10,000 schools were brought under some form of departmental recognition and control. But in 1883-84 this policy was profoundly modified. It was recognised that the number of schools brought within the influence of the system was getting too great for effective supervision by the existing staff. Accordingly, in the Resolution on the departmental report for 1882-83, in which year some 12,000 new schools had been brought on the returns, a check was for the first time imposed. " It " is not," the Lieutenant-Governor observed, " his wish to discourage the estab-" lishment of new schools in districts where their number is still small in com-" parison with the extent of country and population; but there can be no doubt " that in many districts the development of the system of primary education has " already reached, if in some it has not actually exceeded, the limit compatible " with sound administration; and it is desirable that in these districts there " should be no further extension for some years. The consolidation and improve-" ment of existing schools," it was added, " should now be the main object of " local officers, and the search for old indigenous schools should be generally aban-" doued." The relations of local officers towards indigenous schools were by these orders sensibly changed. In former years no school was too humble, no group of pupils gathered together for a few months too insignificant, to be entered on the returns. The object was to find out by detailed inquiry all the existing means of instruction, with the object, or at least in the hope, of improving them hereafter. In this way as years went on, the number of schools on the returns far outgrew the limits of efficient inspection, even with all the aid that could be derived from subordinate agencies of various kinds. Under the limitations now set, the search for additional schools was for the first time laid aside, except in certain parts of the country. The result was that the returns of aided primary schools in Bengal for 1883-84 showed an increase of little more than 1,000 over those for 1882-83. The new policy was confirmed by the orders of Government on the report for 1883-84. In that report the proposal was for the first time made to give no grant to a school in which a printed book of some kind was not read. This condition had not hitherto been required. Under the system prevailing up to that time, the introduction of printed primers had been urged on the schools by the inspecting officers, and encouragement had been given to that form of learning by special grants. Under this voluntary system the number of pupils in primary boys' schools returned as reading print grew from 340,000 in 1881-82 to over 600,000 in 1883-84. But even at the later date the pupils who had not a printed primer in their hands were almost as numerous as those who had; and there were large numbers of aided schools that had as yet made no attempt to introduce books, contenting themselves with the practice of handwriting and with native and mental arithmetic. If any sacrifice was to be made, this was the class of schools that offered the fairest mark. It was certainly to be deplored that aid should be withdrawn from any, even the humblest, class of schools. "But," it was urged, "if our "resources are not yet expansive enough to include all, it is unquestionably the "last class of schools from the control and subsidy of which we should for the "moment retire; and that for two reasons. In the first place, we cannot at this "time of day consent to include in our scheme of public primary instruction any "school which permanently refuses or is unable to teach the vernacular through "the medium of printed pages. The advantage to the ryot, the artisan, or the "petty trader of being able to spell out the meaning of a printed notice is so "obvious at the present time, and will probably be so much greater at no distant "future, that we may rightly insist on the introduction of that form of learning "into every school which receives public money. In the second place, to deny "grants of money to schools which teach no printed primer is to provide them with "the best possible inducement to supply the deficiency. The sums which these "schools now receive from the primary grant are too small to make the with- "drawal of aid a matter of life or death to them; while the amounts to which "they may become entitled if they can succeed in teaching a moderate standard, "including a printed book, are considerable enough to make it worth their while "to put forth an effort to that end." The whole group of proposals made for the improvement and consolidation of primary schools may be thus summarised:—

(1) To revise the course of instruction in both upper and lower primary schools, so as to make it more practically useful to the classes for whom it was designed.
(2) To make the use of printed books obligatory in aided schools.
(3) To require, from every school seeking a reward, that it should produce at least ten boys, should have been in existence for six months, and should keep attendance and inspection registers.

All these proposals received the sanction of Government. They were duly carried out, and in the report for 1886 it will be seen how great and serious an effect was produced by the new policy.

63. Aided Schools: Bombay.—It was noticed by the Education Commission that the value of the indigenous system of elementary instruction was not sufficiently appreciated in Bombay. It is therefore of special importance to observe that the number of aided primary schools was nearly trebled during the period under report, advancing from 146 to 460, and contributing towards the net increase of the year more schools and more scholars than were furnished by the Department and by local boards taken together. As Mr. Lee-Warner remarked in his report as Acting Director for 1884-85 :—" Aided schools contribute 5,964 or "30 per cent. to the total increase of 19,542 pupils. No previous report submitted "to Government has shown such a satisfactory feature." And again—"Government can determine, by a mere glance at the figures, whether the Department has recognised the pre-eminent claims of aided institutions, and whether the response made to their applications for aid does not justify full confidence in the expansive power of private enterprise;" and in another passage he remarks—"The old theory that the work of the Department must be judged by its direct educational work, is happily superseded now by a more liberal view of its aims as an impartial director of educational effort." In the same spirit the Government of Bombay, in its Resolution on that report, characterises the outcome of the year's work in the promotion of private enterprise as "a result which must be considered satisfactory when the fact is recognised that it is impossible for Government with the means at its disposal to educate more than a very small percentage of the population, and that its efforts must be mainly directed to setting an example in each district by maintaining a high standard, and to the development of those branches of education and those localities which private enterprise is likely to neglect." From these extracts it is clear that a new departure has been taken in Bombay, though the field of its operation is as yet limited. The returns for 1884-85 show that 3,219 schools with over 70,000 scholars remain unrecognised by the Department; and the opinion that a large proportion of these are entitled to be entered as public schools and are therefore eligible for grants, is probably well founded. Especially is this true in the case of a number of schools whose headmasters, it has been ascertained, were educated in cess schools, and are reproducing in their own institutions the methods which they acquired under the departmental system. These are certainly "public schools" and eligible for aid ; and the bestowal of grants on such institutions, as well as on others that may more properly be described as indigenous, has been rendered easier by the introduction of liberal provisions having that object into the new grant-in-aid Code. The Department in Bombay, having before its eyes the excellent results obtained in past years under the system which it has fostered with such sedulous care, is naturally chary about entrusting primary education in any wholesale way to private enterprise, with its attendant risks of a lowered standard ; but there appears little reason to fear that in future years the claims of private enterprise will not receive full and generous consideration.

64. Aided Schools: Punjab.—In the Punjab the period is marked, not by any increase in the number of aided schools, but by an entire reversal of the policy governing the relations of the Department to indigenous schools. In his review of the report for 1881-82, the Lieutenant-Governor insisted on the great use that might be made of the vast mass of indigenous schools that were known to exist. To ignore them, he said, was sheer waste of so much educational material. It might not be possible to mould them into the departmental shape, but that was of itself an advantage. If education was to be diversified and free, a clear line must be drawn between departmental and popular instruction. The population was composed of various races and classes, speaking different vernaculars and accepting different creeds. Most of those who wanted their children educated wished them to have the benefit of religious teaching. Some preferred one dialect or religious character or tongue, some another. Many would choose mere technical training in mental arithmetic and bankers' accounts. These various creeds could not be satisfied by the Government schools, which must necessarily be framed on one, and that a non-religious model. The only practicable way to meet the difficulty, to secure the growth of primary education in a manner consonant with, and even springing out of, the wishes of the people, was to offer grants-in-aid to those indigenous institutions which, while maintaining their traditional character, consented to add the rudiments of a liberal education to the technical acquirements or religious knowledge gained in the *Gurmukhi* or *mahajani* schools, in the *maktabs* or *pathsalas*. The method of payment-by-results had been tried with remarkable success in Bengal and Burma, and it seemed to be the method most suited to the circumstances of the Punjab. The Government desired to add certain educational attainments to those spontaneously sought by the people, and according it offered to pay on proof of the diffusion of those attainments. The inquiry and discussion on these points were prosecuted with vigour during the next two or three years, though as yet without direct result as shown in the returns.

65. Aided Schools in Other Provinces.—It is only in Bengal, which contributed more than 13,000 schools to the total increase, and in Bombay and the Punjab which, without adding to the numbers, reversed their previous policy regarding indigenous schools, that any striking change of system took place between 1881-82 and 1884-85; and the progress of aided schools elsewhere may be more briefly noticed. In other provinces there was a total increase of about 2,200 in the number of primary boys' schools receiving aid; towards which Madras contributed approximately 1,340, the Central Provinces 225, and Burma 530. In Assam, as before explained, it is not quite easy to distinguish between aided schools and those now classed as under public management; but in both classes taken together there was an increase of about 260 schools, of which 230 have been assumed in a previous paragraph to be the increase in the number of those under public management, leaving an increase of about 30 aided schools.

In Madras there was in 1882-83 an increase of 1,750 in the number of schools earning grants. This advance was not maintained; for in 1884-85 there was a loss of 500 schools of this class, which is ascribed by the Government to the distress caused by drought in some parts of the country and by floods in others. In reference to the large increase in the earlier year, and to the fact that it was accompanied by a considerable increase in the number of unaided schools also, the following remarks by the Director are of interest, as throwing light upon the relation that subsists between aided and unaided schools in Madras—a province in which the claims of privately managed schools to grants-in-aid have always been fully recognised. After pointing out that the additions to the number of unaided schools had more than made good the loss caused by the transfer of so large a number to the aided list, Mr. Grigg continues—
"This is very satisfactory from one point of view, as it shows unmistakeably "the extension of the influence of the State educational system over indigenous "schools, and the rapid establishment of new schools. But it has its dark side, "for it shows how long the process of transfer is; one year should suffice, but "the figures seem to prove that one to three years are now required, as only one- "third of the unaided schools passed to the aided list. But this observation needs "qualification, as many schools which are aided one year, cease to be aided in the "next, or cease to exist; and in so far as they cease to be aided, they swell the "unaided list. If allowance for this retrograde movement is made, the process "of improvement will probably be found less tardy than above estimated." Much of the increase must be ascribed to better organisation of the inspecting staff; "but no efficiency of organisation could effect so rapid a change, if there were "not among the people a growing desire for instruction, and still more for in- "struction on our improved methods." Great care, it may be added, appears to be taken to prevent the indiscriminate admission of schools to the examination for result-grants—a point in which the Madras system differs from that in force in Bengal, where any school is allowed and even encouraged to offer pupils for examination, provided it satisfies certain conditions relating to course of study, organisation and stability.

In the Central Provinces aided primary schools are of two kinds. The first are private-adventure schools kept by village pundits, which are described as slowly improving, though much inferior to Government schools. They suit people who do not care to send their children to school or to pay fees regularly. The second class consists of schools started by the district officer. The masters are paid a small fixed monthly salary from a fund raised by subscriptions from the people, and the schools are aided under the result system. The master gets three-fifths of this grant, and is paid one-twelfth of his share monthly. This, in addition to his fixed pay, gives him a respectable income. The schools are inspected and supervised in the same way as Government schools, and are said to be much better than the indigenous schools kept by pundits. The drawback to these schools is the instability of the funds from which the master's fixed stipend is paid, and which are liable to suffer from a bad harvest or other causes. As to the relation of the Department to aided schools of both classes, Mr. Browning remarks—" I think Inspectors now understand that the Depart-"ment welcomes the establishment of all public schools, does not show undue "partiality to schools under public management, but is willing to aid and to "support, as far as it can, schools under private management."

An account of the system of primary education in Burma will be given hereafter. For the present it is sufficient to say that it is based entirely on the indigenous system of schools, monastic and lay, in which Burmese, Pali, and (occasionally) arithmetic have been taught for generations past; and that, with the exception of some few in which the masters receive salaries, all the primary schools of the province that receive Government money, earn it in the shape of rewards after examination in the subjects above named and in certain others. Within the period under review the standards of examination, which at first were of an elementary kind, were assimilated to those in force for Government schools. Any school that chooses is admitted to the examination for rewards; and the large increase of over 500 aided schools represents the additional number that competed with success. But notwithstanding this rapid increase in the number of aided schools, the list of those returned as unaided increased still more. These last, which constitute the great majority of the public primary schools, are in an intermediate stage; they have so far abandoned their early character as to adopt the Government standards, though they have not yet made good their claim to aid by complete success at the examinations.

Aided schools in Assam are of two kinds: either indigenous tols and maktabs, which have qualified for aid by adding a little secular instruction to their traditional course of study, or schools maintained by missionary bodies in backward tracts and among the less civilised tribes. Such increase as is shown has taken place in the former class of schools. A full account of the primary system in Assam, which is stated to have been misunderstood by the Education Commission, will be given in the following chapter.

66. Unaided Schools.—The general character of these institutions, and the relation in which they stand in different provinces to aided schools and to the Department, will have been gathered from what has preceded. After allowing for the transfer of 1,200 primary schools in Native States in Bombay to the head of institutions under public management, the provinces in which the chief changes are found are Madras, with a loss of 1,300 schools, Bengal with a gain of 1,700, and Burma with a gain of 1,200. In Madras the reduction merely means that so many schools have qualified for grants and have been transferred to the aided class. In Bengal and Burma the increase represents the additional number of schools that have begun to adopt the courses

67. Primary Schools for Girls, 1881-82 to 1884-85.

The following table presents the usual comparison for each province:—

	Total Pupils	Total Schools	Unaided Pupils	Unaided Schools	Aided Pupils	Aided Schools	Under Public Management Pupils	Under Public Management Schools
1884-85								
	20,210	579	4,263	171	13,293	347	2,654	61
	25,870	402	153	2	5,724	72	19,993	328
	40,123	2,287	978	136	36,985	2,157	160	4
	9,155	326	226	8	5,069	149	3,860	169
	8,851	309	27	1	6,227	172	3,597	136
	4,478	98	198	5	1,288	29	2,992	64
	421	11	...	...	276	8	145	3
	2,379	153	294	24	848	47	1,237	82
	13	29	...	...	162	5	751	24
	41	2	...	...	41	2	...	...
	118,441	4,206	8,139	347	69,913	2,988	35,389	871

	Total Pupils	Total Schools	Unaided Pupils	Unaided Schools	Aided Pupils	Aided Schools
	22,756	553	6,595	220	13,973	285
	19,917	326	4,283	95	4,338	50
	17,461	991	2,097	69	15,364	922
	9,144	310	242	10	5,215	140
	9,739	317	18	...	5,869	171
	3,589	82	78	1	895	17
	1,070	15	77	2	992	13
	1,209	71	...	4	1,132	67
	368	12	...	...	99	4
	26	1	...	...	26	1
	85,279	2,673	13,390	401	47,903	1,870

As in the case of boys' schools, certain corrections have to be made in the figures of 1881-82 owing to changes of classification. They are the following:—

(a) ninety-five girls' schools in Native States in Bombay are to be transferred from the head of unaided schools to that of schools under public management;

(b) to the same head are to be transferred 44 girls' schools in Assam previously reckoned as aided schools;

(c) the totals are to be reduced by the number of attached primary departments, namely, 6 in schools under public management, 78 in aided, and 24 in unaided schools.

The corrected figures for 1881-82 will, therefore, stand as follows:—740 schools under public management; 1,548 aided schools; 282 unaided schools. Consequently there is an increase within this period of 131 schools of the first kind, 1,440 of the second, and 65 of the third, or of 1,636 schools altogether. The bulk of the increase is found in Bengal, where 1,235 have been added to the number of aided girls' schools. This means for the most part that in 1,235 villages a girls' school has been opened at the instance and persuasion of the inspecting officers, either under a separate *guru* or, more often, under the *guru* of the boys' school sitting at separate hours. The only other considerable increase in this class of schools took place in Madras, where 118 have been added to the number. In schools under public management, Bombay shows the largest increase with an addition of 52, half of which, however, have been established in Native States. In Assam the relative increase is nearly as great as in Bengal, and amounts to more than 100 per cent, distributed over all classes of girls' schools. There is a similar, though much smaller, advance in Berar.

68. Primary Schools: Results of Public Examinations.—The examinations to which primary schools are subjected are the lower and upper primary examinations; the former taking place generally at the end of the second or third year of organised study, the latter two years afterwards. The results of the examinations for 1881-82 and 1884-85 are subjoined for each province:—

	1881-82.				1884-85.			
	Boys.		Girls.		Boys.		Girls.	
Province.	Upper Primary.	Lower Primary.	Upper Primary.	Lower Primary.	Upper Primary.	Lower Primary.	Upper Primary.	Lower Primary.
Madras	6,674	15,334	498	1,273	7,757	21,349	776	1,804
Bombay	7,946	21,932	230	890	12,670	30,858	426	1,247
Bengal	1,967	16,333	113	146	2,953	21,500	51	381
North-Western Provinces	6,627	14,834	29	391	4,538	13,043	150	374
Punjab	4,214	7,607	29	107	5,436	11,374	65	185
Central Provinces	3,067	6,410	63	234	5,890	9,179	106	348
Burma	337	437	41	66	639	1,916	107	279
Assam	...	683	...	1	178	1,080	...	(a)31
Berar	109	1,487	...	15	961	2,940	3	36
Coorg	...	400	...	...	Not given.			
Total	30,941	85,457	1,003	3,123	41,022	113,239	1,684	4,685

examinations appears in some instances to vary considerably from year to year. Thus in the North-Western Provinces and Oudh, the figures for the previous year 1883-84 are much higher, namely, 9,916 and 18,483 respectively; and the report explains that no comparison is possible, owing to the diversity that prevails in the method of counting and returning the passes in these standards. There is in fact no fixed upper or lower primary standard for the whole province; and it is even added that there has been no such supervision as to insure a uniform standard throughout each division. In Berar, again, the higher limit of primary schools was reduced in 1883-84 from the sixth to the fourth departmental standard. Finally—to cite the present as one instance out of many in which difficulties of comparison have arisen—the figures in the text, from which alone the details can be derived, do not always agree with those in the tables.

69. Expenditure on Primary Schools, 1881 82 to 1884 85.—As in the case of secondary schools, the causes to which frequent reference has been made render it a matter of some difficulty to compare the expenditure on primary schools at these two dates. Still the attempt in this case may be made, partly because the transfer of primary departments affected some provinces only, and partly because the allotment of funds by Government to local and municipal boards concerned primary education (which had all along been in the hands of those bodies) much less than secondary. The following tables present the necessary figures for boys' schools and girls' schools separately.

Primary Schools for Boys.

Province.	1881-82.						1884-85.					
	Provincial Revenues.	Local Funds.	Municipal Funds.	Fees.	Other sources.	Total.	Provincial Revenues.	Local Funds	Municipal Funds.	Fees.	Other sources.	
	R	R	R	R	R	R	R	R	R	R	R	
...	1,25,090	4,07,877	63,190	5,11,807	2,83,635	13,96,599	87,593	3,91,349	82,599	4,36,252	1,88,492	
...	2,46,633	5,35,391	38,357	1,90,343	2,81,889	12,92,613	2,48,474	6,60,377	44,093	2,38,735	3,50,564	
...	4,78,390	8,121	4,564	11,56,157	3,61,036	20,11,268	6,50,808	3,362	10,833	16,25,278	4,27,431	
...estern Provinces	1,68,238	4,99,424	35,650	67,184	62,505	8,33,001	4,046	5,15,031	24,901	15,674	42,475	
...	73,015	2,39,567	63,648	65,244	35,912	4,77,386	26,919	2,15,884	25,611	32,533	17,457	
...rovinces	76,168	1,11,366	19,557	22,978	34,192	2,64,461	93,863	1,22,249	25,066	29,739	26,661	
...	32,687	40,006	19,439	34,727	22,031	1,48,890	7,229	71,726	81,240	9,986	9,741	
...	11,287	49,436	75	17,992	16,052	93,842	10,670	77,794	1,101	22,684	17,153	
...	1,27,638	53,342	718	26,454	1,144	2,09,296	82,214	65,131	602	33,457	2,250	
...	2,086	6,150	...	1,064	110	9,410	1,426	7,262	1,152	398	305	
Total	13,41,232	19,50,880	2,45,198	20,93,950	11,05,506	67,36,766	12,13,237	21,30,165	2,97,193	24,43,836	10,82,529	

Primary Schools for Girls.

Province.	1881-82.						1884-85.					
	Provincial Revenues.	Local Funds.	Municipal Funds.	Fees.	Other sources.	Total.	Provincial Revenues.	Local Funds	Municipal Funds.	Fees.	Other sources.	
	R	R	R	R	R	R	R	R	R	R	R	
...	68,731	2,542	6,733	28,437	1,65,454	2,71,897	41,508	5,080	5,168	6,265	71,103	
...	27,613	43,011	1,485	4,127	50,509	1,26,645	42,419	40,393	4,717	4,113	72,018	
...	48,523	...	1,221	10,642	1,14,989	1,75,375	84,676	...	5,933	20,081	34,104	
...estern Provinces	40,627	3,182	2,811	18,553	37,636	1,02,809	6,240	23,053	2,125	7,503	41,981	
...	41,801	9,606	10,769	15,379	52,343	1,29,898	45,656	9,073	10,571	17,757	57,743	
...rovinces	5,314	11,963	1,680	4,328	8,428	32,213	14,705	4,561	3,280	4,714	11,251	
...	6,596	...	...	13,757	19,752	40,035	1,693	...	8,106	1,742	7,091	
...	643	1,698	...	24	3,239	5,604	1,019	3,849	742	41	3,584	
...	1,745	863	646	...	270	3,524	1,642	2,033	577	34	324	
...	120	...	...	...	110	230	120	...	101	15	305	
Total	2,41,543	72,865	25,345	95,747	4,52,730	8,88,230	2,39,578	98,042	41,320	62,265	3,98,904	

In Madras, it will be seen, there is a reduction of expenditure under nearly every head, due to the transfer of primary departments to secondary schools. It will be remembered (see table, para. 53) that under the head of secondary schools for boys, there was an increase in the total cost from R7,00,000 to R12,00,000 in round numbers, towards which provincial revenues and local funds each contributed about R30,000. If now these figures be combined with those given in the table above for primary schools, so as to get rid of the uncertainty arising from the transfer of primary departments, it results that the total increase for both classes of schools amounted to R2,90,000, that there was a reduction of R9,000 in the cost to provincial revenues, and an increased expenditure of R15,000 from local and of R67,000 from municipal funds, so that more than 2 lakhs of the increase was met from private sources. In Bombay, where practically no portion of the local rates is devoted to secondary education, and where also there were no primary departments to be transferred, the total increase of expenditure on primary education amounted to $2\frac{1}{3}$ lakhs, involving little or no additional charge to provincial or municipal revenues, but an increase of R1,25,000 to local funds. In Bengal, where the absence of local rates has to be made good by increased allotments from provincial funds, the provincial grants to primary schools increased from R4,78,000 to R6,51,000, or by R1,73,000. Municipal grants to primary schools increased by R6,000 and to secondary schools by R30,000; but with these exceptions the rest of the increase of 7 lakhs was met from fees and other purely private sources. In the North-Western Provinces and Oudh a different set of conditions come into play. Large primary departments were transferred, and the control of secondary schools, together with grants for their maintenance or support, was made over very generally to district boards. Combining the charges we find that, for primary and secondary schools together, the total cost in these provinces increased from R12,47,000 to R14,20,000, that the amount debited to provincial revenues decreased from R4,33,000 to R86,000, while that debited to local funds increased in a nearly corresponding measure from R5,18,000 to R8,90,000. Thus, towards the increased cost of both classes of schools taken together, public funds, local and provincial, contributed R25,000, an increase of less than 3 per cent., municipal grants R13,000, or 30 per cent., and private sources of income R1,35,000, or 45 per cent.

To consider in another light this question of the proportions in which different sources of income contributed to the increased cost of primary and secondary education, we may group the provinces according to the changes of classification that occurred in them. In Bombay and Bengal no such changes were made. In these two provinces taken together provincial revenues contributed R1,74,000 (almost exclusively in Bengal), local funds R1,21,000 (exclusively in Bombay), and municipal grants R12,000, towards the total increase of R9,54,000 in the cost of primary education. Similarly, in these two provinces the cost of secondary education increased by R6,22,000. Towards this increase provincial revenues contributed R20,000 and municipal funds (chiefly in Bengal) R35,000; the remainder of the increased cost, R5,67,000, being met from fees and other purely private sources. For the next group we make take Madras, the Punjab, Berar, and Coorg, the returns for which are affected by the transfer of primary departments; and therefore, in order to remove that source of uncertainty, the cost of primary and secondary schools will be combined. The total expenditure on these two classes of schools increased by R4,31,000. The cost to provincial revenues decreased by R14,000, local funds bore an additional share of R51,000, municipal funds of R73,000; and the balance, or R3,21,000, was met from private sources. The third group is made up of the North-Western Provinces, the Central Provinces, and Assam, in which the contribu-

able grants appear to have been made from provincial revenues to municipal funds for the support of primary and secondary schools. The increased expenditure shown under the head of municipal funds and arising from this cause amounts to R1,45,000, out of a total increase of R1,54,000 for these two classes of schools together. There is a correlative decrease of R34,000 shown under the head of provincial revenues, so that the increased cost to provincial revenues amounts to about R1,10,000.

The outcome of this laboured analysis is of some importance. After due allowance is made for the uncertainty that surrounds all calculations of this kind in the circumstances shown, it points to the reasonable inference that, except in Burma, the expansion of primary and secondary schools within the years 1882 to 1885 has taken place with very little additional cost to provincial revenues, and even to local rates, compared with the additional income derived from purely private sources. In Bombay and Bengal, out of a total increase of R15,76,000 for schools of both classes, primary schools received additional grants of R1,74,000 from provincial revenues, R1,21,000 from local rates, and R12,000 from municipalities, while secondary schools received R20,000 from provincial revenues and R35,000 from municipal grants. In the other seven provinces (excluding Burma), primary and secondary schools received R1,22,000 from provincial and local funds jointly, and R84,000 from municipal revenues out of a total increase of R7,07,000. The following statement compares the amounts received from different sources of income, as shown in the returns, for primary and secondary schools together:—

	1881-82.	1884-85.	Increase or decrease.
	R	R	R
Provincial Revenues	29,37,020	27,31,698	—2,05,322
Local Funds	20,22,886	26,56,106	+6,33,220
Municipal Funds	3,59,904	6,46,577	+2,86,673
Fees	36,54,181	50,69,499	+14,15,318
Other sources	21,92,612	25,02,803	+3,10,191
TOTAL	1,11,66,603	1,36,06,683	+24,40,080

VI.—SPECIAL INSTRUCTION.

70. Training Schools, 1881-82 to 1884-85.—The subjoined table exhibits the progress of these important institutions, for masters and mistresses separately:—

Training Schools for Masters.

PROVINCE.	1881-82.						1884-85.					
	Under public management.		Under private management.		Total.		Under public management.		Under private management.		Total.	
	Schools.	Pupils.	Schools.	Pupils.	Schools.	Pupils.	Schools.	Pupils.	Schools.	Pupils.	Schools.	Pupils.
Madras	26	642	3	157	29	799	41	937	7	218	48	1,155
Bombay	4	360	3	120	7	480	6	513	1	54	7	567
Bengal	16	672	4	335	20	1,007	16	654	6	429	22	1,083
N.-W. Provinces	18	306	...	...	18	306	10	377	1	22	11	399
Punjab	4	247	1	31	5	278	4	232	1	31	5	263
Central Provinces	3	171	...	...	3	171	3	189	...	...	3	189
Burma	3	99	1	6	4	105	3	202	...	...	3	202
Assam	6	220	3	111	9	331	9	244	3	75	12	319
Berar	1	79	...	...	1	79	1	74	...	...	1	74
Coorg	1	7	...	...	1	7	1	14	...	...	1	14
TOTAL	82	2,803	15	760	97	3,563	(a)94	3,436	(b)19	829	113	4,265

(a) Including two schools in Native States in Bombay.
(b) „ two unaided schools.

Training Schools for Mistresses.

	Schools.	Pupils.	Schools.	Pupils.	Schools.	Pupils.	Schools.	Pupils.	Schools.	Pupils.	Schools.	Pupils.
Madras	1	20	3	137	4	157	4	72	8	291	12	363
Bombay	2	73	...	...	2	73	3	98	...	...	3	98
Bengal	...	...	2	41	2	41	...	...	3	102	3	102
N.-W. Provinces	...	...	3	89	3	89	2	4	1	92	3	96
Punjab	...	...	4	142	4	142	...	...	4	148	4	148
Central Provinces	1	17	...	...	1	17	1	29	...	...	1	29
Burma	...	...	...	...	...	...	2	29	...	...	2	29
TOTAL	4	110	12	409	16	519	12	232	16	633	28	865

71. Training Schools for Masters.—There is an increase during this period of 12 schools and 633 pupils under public management; and of 4 schools and 69 pupils under private management, in all, of 16 schools and 702 pupils. The numbers should, however, be reduced by one school in the North-Western Provinces with 92 pupils, and one in the Punjab with 96 pupils; both said to have been wrongly included under the head of training schools, since they are in fact merely girls' schools in which a few pupils are sometimes trained to be teachers. In Madras alone 19 new schools were opened, chiefly through the agency of district boards, while 7 schools were closed in the North-West Provinces. Assam added three to the number of its schools, and there were smaller changes in Bengal and Burma. Half of the total increase of pupils is found in Madras. The cost of these schools increased from R3,23,696 to R4,57,625; and towards this increase Government contributed R34,186, while an additional sum of R99,743 was derived from other sources, including local funds. Of the 94 schools under public management in 1884-85, 47 were managed and maintained by the Department, 45 by district boards, and 2 in Native States. The departmental schools cost Government R2,35,620, and on their own schools district boards spent R1,38,671. Towards the support of the 19 aided schools Government contributed R17,767, and district boards R1,200, the balance of R48,228 being met from private sources.

72. Training Schools for Mistresses.—There was a much greater proportionate increase in this class of schools, which advanced from 16 to 28, the women under training increasing from 519 to 865. Private enterprise undertakes a very large share of the duty of training mistresses; and though within this period the number of schools under public management was trebled, yet they still fell short of those maintained by private agency, chiefly by missionary bodies. As before, the greatest increase is found in Madras, where three additional schools were opened under public and five under private management. The cost of all schools of this class increased from R61,767 to R98,355, R24,468 of the increase being met from provincial revenues, and R13,120 from other sources of income. Of the 12 schools under public management in 1884-85, eight were maintained by the Department, three by district boards, and one by a Native State. The eight departmental schools cost Government R38,598; and R7,276 were paid from local funds for the three schools under district boards. For the maintenance of aided schools, grants amounting to R26,105 were paid from provincial revenues, the Punjab Government being specially liberal in their support, while local boards in the North-Western Provinces contributed R2,400 towards the same object.

73. Training Schools in Madras.—The policy constantly pursued in Madras is well illustrated by the following remark of the Madras Provincial Committee, quoted in the report of the Education Commission (paragraph 180):—
"Improved masters are a pressing want. For the training of these, some addi-
"tion to the number of local normal schools seems to be required." To the same effect may be quoted an extract from the Director's report for 1882-83:—
"The conviction that the improvement of normal schools is an absolute neces-
"sity, if elementary education in rural tracts is to be developed, is gradually
"asserting itself, as may be inferred from the fact that the number of normal
"schools established by local fund boards is increasing. The increased activity
"of the boards in this direction is now being encouraged by aid from provincial
"funds." Accordingly between 1881-82 and 1884-85, 19 additional schools for masters were opened,—three under departmental management (two of this class being also closed), 14 by local boards, and four by missionary bodies. Thus it appears that the local boards undertake the chief part of the duty of training teachers. The number of schools under their direct management increased from 19 to 33, and the expenditure on them from R25,034 to R44,490. At the same time the departmental expenditure on training schools increased from R15,000 to R47,000. Notwithstanding these efforts, it appears that the impression produced upon the vast mass of primary school teachers is as yet but slight. Of 16,497 teachers employed in all elementary schools in 1884, only 1,865, or less than 12 per cent., had passed through a normal school; and the inference drawn by one of the most experienced inspectors (Mr. Garthwaite, to whose efforts the present system of training schools in Madras is mainly ascribed,) is that "the funds now employed in keeping under inspection worthless
"schools—worthless because unimproved and unimproveable, and in providing
"inspecting schoolmasters to attempt to improve them—an attempt in which they
"never are successful—would, if devoted to a temporary increase in the number
"of normal schools, soon remedy this lamentable state of things." Still, it is not all plain sailing, even if training schools be multiplied; and that point is exactly hit in the following passage from the same report:—"There is of course a
"difficulty in getting a man of that class (long-standing masters of indigenous
"schools) to leave his village and go to a strange place and rough it for a year

"on a bare subsistence allowance, leaving his school perhaps to go to pieces and "maintaining his family on credit." On the other hand,—"To admit into the "normal school not merely youths who were learners in the indigenous schools, but "youths that had no connection with any indigenous school, and no idea of where, "when their training was over, they would start a school, did not seem to me the "right way of getting the indigenous schools under trained masters. In fact, it "worked the other way; when these young men set up a school, it was never in "conjunction with the indigenous schoolmaster,. who knew nothing of him, "but rather in opposition. The parents, as usual, prefer their old friend's "school to that of this new-comer. The new-comer, finding his school not pay- "ing him, closes it; and after applying in vain for an educational appointment, "naturally claims permission to try to get a living in some other department and "is thus lost to that of education ; in which case the money and labour spent in "training him are thrown away." This is precisely the difficulty that has had to be confronted in other provinces—in Bengal, for example, where it led to a very large reduction in the number of training schools for village schoolmasters between 1874 and 1879, as pointed out by the Education Commission. It is true that the Director, Mr. Grigg, is not inclined to lay any great stress on the complaint that young men trained in these schools eventually betake them-selves to other occupations. He thinks the complaint exaggerated; but still it appears that out of 383 pupils who passed out of the training schools in 1882-83, only 281 found subsequent employment as teachers.

In 1882-83 a novel and interesting experiment, the. idea of which may have been derived from the Central Training College at Lahore, was tried in the Madras Normal School, with the object of giving definite instruction in the science and history of education. This institution (the only one of its class in Madras) is designed for the training of English teachers in secondary schools, and none are admitted but those who have passed some University examination. Three courses of lectures were instituted ; the first on psychology in its relation to education, in other words, the scientific basis of education; the second on the general history of education in Europe, more especially since the revival of learning; and the third, a development of the existing course of lectures on school method and management and on the art of teaching. The published syllabus of each set of lectures indicates a varied and thorough course of in-struction. The lectures were well attended, by several graduate teachers amongst others; and the success of the scheme was considered to be such as to justify a request being made to the University to institute a degree in the science and art of teaching. The University received the proposal favourably, and the degree was instituted and obtained the sanction of Government in 1885.

Female training schools in Madras increased from four to 12, and the pupils in them from 157 to 363. Three of the new schools were departmental and five under private management, three of the latter receiving aid. The expend-iture from provincial revenues on these schools increased from R2,886 to R21,740. Six of the 12 schools were under missionary management, and they trained altogether 261 pupils, all but six of whom were Christians. In the Government and local fund schools eight of the pupils were Eurasians, 26 native Christians, 34 Hindus (chiefly Sudras), and 4 Muhammadans. In the two unaided schools there were 18 low-caste Hindu and 12 Muhammadan women. These figures sufficiently illustrate the difficulty, already pointed out by the Education Commission, of inducing native women of good position, other than those who have adopted the Christian faith, to follow the profession of a teacher. The normal training of women has been certainly as successful in Madras as in any province of India, and it is a matter of interest and importance to observe under what conditions of difficulty it is carried on.

74. Training Schools in Bombay.—These remained unaltered throughout this period. Four schools for masters were maintained by the Department at Poona, Ahmedabad, Dharwar, and Hyderabad, two by the Native States of Rajkot and Kolhapur, and one at Ahmednagar was maintained by the Christian Vernacular Education Society. The expenditure on departmental schools remained nearly constant—about R34,000 from provincial and R16,000 from local funds; and the Ahmednagar school, previously unaided, received a grant of R1,000. The proportion of trained to untrained masters in Bombay is very different from that to which attention has just been drawn in Madras. Out of 4,242 teachers of primary schools in British territory in Bombay in 1884-85, 1,829, or 44 per cent., were trained. But in his report for that year, the officiating Director, Mr. Lee-Warner, put forward a strong appeal for more training schools, based chiefly on the removal of Government control, under the development of the local self-government policy, from the schools in rural districts and in towns. It was the right and the duty of the Department to require the appointment of fully qualified masters, but the demand must often be made in vain unless the means of training teachers were largely increased. Schools on the departmental model, he urged, though excellent in their constitution and in the results of their work, cost too much to allow of their being multiplied; and the best means of securing the required end lay partly in encouraging local boards to open less highly organised training schools as in Madras, and partly in aiding schools under private managers. The results attained in the Ahmednagar school, though undoubtedly inferior to those of a departmental training school, were good enough, if not for the best, at any rate for the generality of primary schools; and the teachers passing out from them were in any case far better than the chance employés whom the boards would pick up unless provided with better material. And again, any training school that a local board might establish could get as many pupils as it pleased of an initial standard higher than that with which the Ahmednagar authorities were content. Only in these ways, Mr. Lee-Warner argued, could the necessities of the time be met.

There were two training schools for women at Ahmedabad and Dharwar, and a third was opened in the Native State of Rajkot. The difficulty of getting women to attend these schools, and afterwards to take work as teachers, was felt in Bombay as elsewhere; but an attempt was being made to get over it by inducing the wives of schoolmasters to adopt that profession. The general complaint is that widows and unmarried girls are not trusted, while married women are rarely allowed to take part in the work. Mr. Kirkham, the Inspector, writes:—" I do not think that mistresses, as a general rule, will be able " to manage schools successfully and conciliate the respect of the people, unless " they are respectable married women living with their husbands and families in " the same place," the common practice in England and other civilised countries. Accordingly we find that in 1883-84, out of 44 students in the Poona College for mistresses, 16 were married; though the number fell to nine in the following year. One further point deserves notice. There does not seem to be anything like the same difficulty in Bombay as we have observed in Madras in inducing Hindu women of respectable position to join these schools; nor are the training schools dependent in the same way on native Christians. Out of 98 female students under training in 1884-85, only 16 were Christians, while 71 were Hindus, and the majority of the latter were Brahmans and Marathas. The remaining 11 were Parsis, Jains, and others.

75. Training Schools in Bengal.—The policy pursued in Bengal with regard to the provision of teachers for primary schools was fully explained in paragraph 180 of the report of the Education Commission. It proposed to effect a general improvement in the standard of teaching, not by imposing teachers from without on the village schools, nor even generally by compelling the teachers to come in to the district head-quarters for training, but rather by gradually infusing among the villagers a desire for a better standard, and by so improving the position and prospects of the teacher that men with higher qualifications for the work might gradually be attracted to it. The necessity of a superior training for village teachers was held to be less urgent in Bengal, where the village school course is limited by the moderate requirements of the labouring population, than in those provinces in which all classes receive their elementary education together. In pursuance of this policy, training schools for village teachers were maintained in only eight or ten of the more backward districts, where the ordinary schools of the country, upper primary or middle, were not numerous enough to furnish a constant and assured supply of young men capable of undertaking the work of an elementary teacher. Hence the policy of training every teacher, the necessity of which had been so strongly insisted on in Madras and Bombay, was deliberately abandoned in Bengal, and the supply of teachers was left to the operation of natural causes and the chances of the market. The Government of India, however, was not satisfied that this policy was a sound one; and, in its Resolution on the report of the Education Commission, declared in favour of an organised system of training schools for primary teachers. While admitting that there might be difficulties in Bengal in insisting on a normal training for all primary schoolmasters, the Government nevertheless thought it desirable that all teachers who were willing to undergo training should have opportunities of securing it, and that their doing so should be favourably recognised in the grants made to them. Up to the close of the year 1884-85 nothing more had, however, been done in that direction. In that year there were eight training schools of the lower grade, for village school teachers, and classes of the same kind were attached to three training schools of the upper grade, in which masters for middle vernacular schools are trained. The superior character of these last schools, of which there were eight in Bengal, was fully recognised by the Education Commission, which declared that the course, though exclusively vernacular, was on a level with that for the First Arts examination of the Calcutta University. At any rate, the demand for the services of trained teachers is said to be so great that all who pass at once obtain employment, and there is room for many more. Another advantage has been claimed for these training schools,—" They are the only " representatives of vernacular colleges in Bengal, and serve to maintain a high " standard of literary purity both in our vernacular schools and in vernacular " literature. It may be asserted unhesitatingly that the vast majority of the " Bengali books which issue from the press at the present day would never have " existed, but for the maintenance of a high literary standard by means of the " normal schools. The vernacular language can never disappear from society or " from education; and its cultivation to a due standard of excellence, and of " fitness for purposes of literary and scientific expression, is not unworthy the " attention of the Education Department or of Government." The 16 departmental schools were maintained in 1884-85 at a cost of R67,651, of which Government paid R66,992—an increase of R5,000 over 1881-82.

Aided training schools have increased from four to six for masters, and from two to three for mistresses. All are under missionary management. The great majority of the male pupils and all the female pupils in these schools are native Christians, and are being trained for work in the schools which the separate missions conduct, chiefly of an elementary character. But the two aided schools for mistresses in Calcutta train their pupils to a high standard, and one of them, the Free Church Female Normal School, has passed many pupils at the Entrance and First Arts examinations of the University. The cost of aided schools for masters and mistresses increased from R27,000 to R33,000, the grants-in-aid increasing from R8,000 to R10,000.

76. Training Schools in the North-Western Provinces and Oudh.—

The Education Commission wrote:—" This province has always paid syste-
" matic attention to the training of teachers, and it is estimated that 58 per cent.
" of the masters hold certificates………The department endeavours to obtain
" for these [the normal] schools young men who have passed the middle class
" vernacular examination, and who require chiefly to be trained in the art of
" teaching." The period began with six divisional training schools, for both primary and secondary teachers, in the North-Western Provinces, and twelve classes for training village teachers, which were attached to district schools in Oudh. In the following year a central school of a higher type for secondary teachers was established at Lucknow, the district classes being also retained. But a year later a change was rendered necessary by the introduction of the system of decentralisation, under which middle and primary schools were transferred to the control of district boards. All training schools were, however, to be retained under departmental management; and hence the attached classes were closed, and replaced by three training schools at divisional head-quarters. It was clearly impossible to maintain an arrangement under which, of two institutions held in the same building and under the same head-master, one should be under departmental and one under local management; but it does not appear whether any consideration was given to the alternative plan of transferring the training classes also to the district board, after the example of Madras. While they lasted, the attached training classes were said to be doing good work and to be turning out a useful class of men. The period closed with ten training schools; but notwithstanding the reduction, there was a considerable increase in the number of pupils. The course in these schools is described in the following extract, which incidentally throws a side-light on the language difficulty in Oudh:—" Every student who desires to pass the examination must qualify himself
" in reading two languages (Urdu and Hindi) and in writing three different
" characters—Persian, Nagri and Kaithi. There is no one language or character
" among the natives of these provinces, and there are very few schools in villages
" in which the two languages and the three characters are not required to be
" taught." Besides those trained in the school, uncertificated village teachers of long standing and good promise were encouraged to prepare themselves by private study for the village teachership examination. In this way the number of uncertificated teachers promised in course of time to be greatly reduced.

The returns include the training schools of these provinces among institutions "managed and maintained" by district boards; the fact being that, like the zila schools, they are entirely under departmental control, although maintained from the funds placed at the disposal of the boards, including, it will be remembered, large provincial grants. In 1881-82, R30,000 out of a total expenditure of R36,000 were paid from provincial revenues, but in 1884-85 the whole of the public expenditure, amounting to R46,000, was debited to local funds.

For the training of female teachers there were three institutions, aided (and two of them afterwards maintained) by local-fund boards at a cost of about R6,600. The third was subsequently included under girls' schools. Classes were also in some instances attached to schools under missionary management,

though these are not shown in the returns. The old difficulty recurs,—
"When girls have been trained and pronounced fit for employment, it is often
"impossible to induce them to go to the place where they are wanted."

77. Training Schools in the Punjab.—In 1881-82 the number of
teachers in departmental primary schools who held certificates of training, or
who had passed some equivalent public examination, amounted to about two-
fifths of the whole. In aided schools the number of trained teachers was
small. For admission to the Government schools a new condition was required—
that a student should have passed the middle school examination, though exceptions were still allowed in the case of teachers. Model or practising schools
were attached to each of the three departmental schools. The constitution of
these model schools underwent some criticism; and it was urged that the existing
system, under which the pupils were taught in turn by students under training
in the normal schools, should be replaced by one in which a full permanent staff
should be attached to each model school, the students under training merely
visiting the schools and taking part in the instruction. The men trained in
the normal schools were said to be in general request, though it was added that
"they cannot always hold their own when placed in sole charge in a strange
"village." The aided school at Amritsar, under the management of the Christian Vernacular Education Society, was described as an excellent institution, the
teachers passing out from which were, as a rule, in no way inferior to men of the
same class trained in the Government schools. This opinion may be compared
with that expressed by the Bombay authorities with regard to the Ahmednagar
School under the same management. For the sake of further comparison it
may be here noticed that of the third training school maintained by the Society—
that at Dindigul in Madras—the results are described as "very good." Regrets
have been expressed that the various missionary societies in the Punjab made
but little use of the Amritsar school, which might be utilised to the great advantage of the aided schools of the province; and for want of sufficient support
it was apprehended that the school might be closed. The report incidentally
discusses what is described as "the deterioration which gradually comes about in
"the mental capacity of village school teachers," as a result of their being cut off
from intercourse with educated men, and having no opportunities of exercising
thought upon any literary or political subject. In Bengal an attempt has been
made to counteract this evil by the somewhat wide distribution of a monthly
illustrated journal devoted to useful and interesting topics, and intended for
the recreation of patshala teachers and their pupils.

The Central Training College at Lahore is designed for teachers of a
higher class, both English and vernacular. There are two English classes,
one for students who have passed or read up to the First Arts or Intermediate
examination, the other, more recently instituted, being for matriculates. The
senior course is confined to the principles and practice of teaching, to translation and re-translation, and to elementary science. The junior course includes
instruction in all the subjects which the pupils will afterwards have to teach.
The vernacular class is composed of picked men who have passed through a
training school, of students who have passed the vernacular Entrance examination of the Punjab University, and of teachers sent in from schools. With
necessary modifications, the curriculum is the same as for the senior English
class. The examinations are open to all candidates, whether trained in the
school or elsewhere. The total expenditure on training institutions for masters
increased from R37,000 to R57,000 according to the returns. The difference is
probably due to the inclusion of the cost of stipends at the later date.

The four training schools for mistresses were all under private management, and all aided. They contained about 150 pupils, but only a very small

proportion of these were under training as teachers, and still fewer had passed even the lower primary examination. Indeed, Mr. Ibbetson wrote of these schools in his report as officiating Director for 1883-84:—"It is an abuse of "language to call such schools normal, and a waste of money to pay for them "as such. The system of separate normal schools for native girls has been "tried, and has failed; and all that we have are primary schools, probably of a "superior class to the rest, some of the most promising pupils of which occa- "sionally consent to serve as teachers in the immediate neighbourhood of their "homes." In the year 1883-84, to which this report relates, these four schools, though styled aided schools, drew R11,000 from provincial revenues, out of a total expenditure of R12,700. In the following year the receipts from private sources were, however, raised to R4,000, the provincial expenditure receiving only a slight addition.

78. Training Schools in Burma.—Of the training schools in Burma, Mr. Hordern, the Director, remarks:—"No more important work engages the "attention of this Department than that of the training and testing of teachers. "The examinations for teachers' certificates held by the Educational Syndicate "attract yearly increasing attention, and the value of the system is attested by "the marked increase of efficiency in the schools to which certificated masters are "attached." Certificates of two grades, English and vernacular, are awarded, and the examinations are open to all comers. The standard for the lower grade certificate is the middle school examination, and for the higher grade the University Entrance. In each case a test in practical school management is added. The number of pupils in the three Government training schools increased from 105 to 202; and 185 certificates were issued during the three years to normal school pupils and others. Certificated teachers when employed in primary schools under public management were formerly Government servants; but under the new scheme introduced in 1884-85 with the object of reducing pensionary liabilities, they were regarded as servants of the municipalities or district boards employing them. Though this plan had many advantages, it began to be feared that the reduction which it effected in the status and prospects of teachers, and the lessening of their chances of employment as the funds of local boards were more fully placed out, would tell on the attendance at training schools. Still it was not anticipated that there would be any reduction in the number of candidates for certificates. The training schools in fact were not the only agency for the supply of teachers, for the Government had invited the co-operation of grant-in-aid and indigenous schools throughout the country by the offer of grants of R100 or R200 to any school that passed a candidate at the teachership examination; and, in the year 1884-85, such certificates were awarded to 28 candidates independently trained. A further development of the new scheme was the recognition of the pupil-teacher system by the introduction of a special certificate for pupil-teachers, and by encouraging their employment in schools of all grades, especially indigenous schools. The chief drawback to the successful working of the training schools was stated to be the absence of separate boarding accommodation, which made it difficult to attract students from the interior.

The attached practising schools appear to have been taught exclusively by the students under training; and it is expressly stated that the results, though inferior to those attained when, as formerly, the model schools were under a separate staff of European masters, were yet quite good enough to justify confidence in the ability of the students to teach when sent to independent charges—a conclusion which may be compared with the opposite view expressed in the Punjab. The public expenditure on training schools increased from R18,000 to R31,000.

For the training of mistresses two classes were opened, at Rangoon and Maulmain. Though placed under teachers appointed and paid by Government, they were attached to girls' schools maintained by missionary bodies, to whom the teachers and their classes were fully subordinate. The classes were attended by 29 pupils, nearly all Burmese girls, 15 of whom obtained certificates in 1884-85; and the examiners reported that in practical school management the female students far surpassed the majority of the masters under training. For every girl who passed by the lower (or middle school) standard a grant of R30 was made to the school and of R20 to the teacher, with double these rates for any who passed by the higher standard. Under the rules for aiding girls' schools, half the salary of any certificated Burmese schoolmistress, up to a limit of R50, is paid by Government. The advantages of this liberal rule were becoming widely known and appreciated; and 11 certificated mistresses were already employed in 1885, at a cost to Government of R1,029 for the year. The Karen girls were reported as specially apt for teaching and willing to engage in it.

79. Training Schools in Other Provinces.—Of the Central Provinces, the Education Commission observed:—" In no province of India, except the small "district of Coorg, has greater success attended the efforts of the Department "to improve teachers. . . . . In the Government schools 87 per cent. of "the masters are trained." The period of instruction for village teachers was extended from one year to two. Classes in carpentry, drawing, and gymnastics were attached to some or all of the schools. In the female training school at Jubbulpore the policy of the Department was, as in Bombay, to induce the wives of teachers to qualify; and with such success that out of 29 pupils in 1884-85, 21 were the wives of teachers or of those under training for teachers. Five were widows, living some with their children, some with their mothers; and of these the Inspector observes: " Where so many women live in one compound, " some of them rude, all talkative, there have been causes for anxiety,"—a remark not without interest in reference to the proposal for the extended employment of this class of women.

In Assam the number of Government training schools was increased from 9 to 12: there were also three aided schools under missionaries. The period of tuition in Government schools was extended from one to two years. About half the teachers in training schools were certificated. Great difficulty was felt in getting pupils from distant parts to attend the schools; while if the pupils were selected from the neighbourhood of the schools, they would refuse service elsewhere. On this ground an attack was made by Mr. C. B. Clarke, who officiated as Head of the Department in 1884-85, on the whole system so far as it regarded the training of teachers for primary schools. He urged that it was of much more importance that the teachers should be taught their subjects well than that they should be taught how to teach, the latter acquirement being either superfluous or impossible according as the former condition was or was not satisfied. He was therefore in favour of closing these schools, and of utilising the ordinary middle schools of the country for the further training of village teachers,—a plan which would go far to remove the difficulty arising from the distance of the normal schools.

In the report of the Education Commission it was stated that a large proportion of the primary school teachers in Berar were foreigners, chiefly from Bombay. According to the new training college rules, all candidates for admission to the training college at Akola were required to be natives of the province; but it was alleged that they were inferior in mental capacity to men from Bombay, and also that they objected to service at a distance from their homes. In addition to the training school at head-quarters, it was proposed to

In Coorg, where, as before stated, close attention is paid to the training of teachers, the course has been extended from 6 or 12 months to three years, at the end of which time candidates are required to pass the middle school examination, and a separate examination in the art of teaching.

80. Technical and Other Special Schools.—Technical instruction, whether in schools or in colleges, was excluded from the inquiries of the Education Commission. Professional colleges, in which instruction to a University standard is given in law, medicine and engineering, were the subject of an earlier paragraph. In the following paragraphs some account will be given of the leading non-collegiate institutions for professional or technical education throughout India, together with a sketch of the progress made in various branches between 1881-82 and 1884-85. The necessary figures are contained in the statements that follow:—

PROVINCE.	1881-82.									
	ART.		MEDICINE.		ENGINEERING OR SURVEYING.		INDUSTRIAL.		OTHER.	
	Schools.	Pupils.	Schools.	Pupils.	Schools.	Pupils.	Schools.	Pupils.	Schools.	Pupils.
Madras	1	84	2	200	1	42	3	138	2	106
Bombay	1	177	3	143	1	10	7	509	27	1,029
Bengal	1	77	4	310	4	161	3	113	14	1,476
North-Western Provinces	...	...	1	39	...	...	2	152	...	...
Punjab	1	43	1	138	...	...	4	128	...	...
Central Provinces	...	...	...	...	...	...	23	440	13	369
Burma	1	58	...	...	2	37	1	17	...	...
Assam	...	...	...	...	1	60	1	12	...	...
TOTAL	5	439	11	830	9	310	44	1,509	56	2,980
	1884-85.									
Madras	1	162	5	197	1	106	5	179	2	166
Bombay	1	251	3	164	1	21	7	522	35	1,780
Bengal	1	157	6	672	4	171	5	172	16	1,556
North-Western Provinces	...	...	1	89	...	...	2	186	11	757
Punjab	1	85	...	...	...	...	4	93	2	131
Central Provinces	...	...	...	...	...	...	19	316	2	89
Burma	...	...	...	...	5	110	1	38	2	64
Assam	...	...	...	...	7	163	1	18	1	26
TOTAL	4	655	15	1,122	18	571	44	1,524	71	4,569

The general result is that there is an increase in medical and engineering (or surveying) schools, that industrial schools are stationary, and that there is a loss of one Art school. The miscellaneous institutions included under "other schools" are of very various types; and of many it may be said that they are shown under the head of special instruction because they can go under no other.

lowing passage from the report for 1882-83:—"The subject of drawing finds "a place among the optional subjects for the upper primary examination; but "no encouragement is offered to the study in middle or high schools, and under "these circumstances the class is unlikely to be popular." In the four Art schools, properly so called, the attendance increased from 381 to 655. The Madras institution was becoming more of an industrial and less of an Art school, its proper function being thus described—" to serve the development of all the "industrial arts having for their end the construction and decoration of the chief "articles, whether of metal, wood, stone, or clay, required by the exigencies of "modern life in this country." The pupils were mostly drawn from the poorer European community and from the lower or artisan classes among the Hindus. The influence of the Jamsetji Jijibhoy School of Art in Bombay was felt far beyond the limits of that institution. Drawing classes had been established in 33 high and middle schools throughout the province, under teachers trained in the school. Of 607 candidates examined in 1884-85 for certificates in drawing, only 116 were presented from the Art school itself. Of its 251 pupils more than 200 were in the elementary class; the classes for painting, sculpture, and architectural drawing numbered 51. In 1883-84 the pottery department, for which this institution had long been deservedly famous, was transferred to private control; and in the following year the metal-work and wood-engraving classes, for which little success could be claimed, were closed. The Calcutta School of Art opened the following new classes: drawing from the living model, lithography, wood-carving and metal-chasing. The lithographic class was engaged on the illustrations of a work on the Ficaceæ, by Dr. G. King, Superin. tendent of the Royal Botanical Gardens. The metal repoussé work done for the Calcutta Exhibition in 1884, was much appreciated and sold to advantage. Wood-carving was pursued under difficulties, as it is not an ancient and established industry in Bengal. To the school is attached an Art Gallery, supported by a Government grant of R10,000 a year. The Gallery has been deeply indebted ever since its foundation to the Earl of Northbrook, to whom it owes its existence, and who, since his departure from India, has devoted both labour and skill to the selection and purchase of pictures in England.. But the building in which the collection is housed is described as being "in a dilapi. "dated and almost dangerous condition, and a destructive storm might do "irreparable damage to its contents." It is believed that all the other schools of Art in India are decently or even sumptuously housed. Mr. Kipling, the Principal of the Mayo School of Art at Lahore, defines as follows the governing idea of the school,—"that the indigenous styles of art are capable of indefinite "development, and that the first thing to study is the actual work of the "country, which alone can give a rational point of departure for variety of "design and improvement of *technique*." That definition being accepted, it follows that a school of Art in the Punjab is much more favourably circumstanced than one, for example, in Bengal, where indigenous art is marked by but little variety or grace. The influence of the Mayo School was exercised in two ways,—partly by the training of pupils "in the higher and more artistic branches "of their crafts, and especially in the principles of design," and partly "by "acting as an æsthetic centre, a school of design, and the source of enlightened "criticism and advice" to the artistic industries of the province. In the latter capacity it furnished patterns and designs to be used in local industries. As a school it was steadily growing in the estimation of the public, and more than doubled its numbers in the period under review.

82. **Medical Schools.**—These schools are intended to give a medical education below that which is required for a University degree. In some the instruction is given in English, in others through the vernacular exclusively,

The number increased from 11 to 15 by the addition of three schools in Madras and of two in Bengal, in which latter province also the chief accession of pupils took place; and by the transfer of the Lahore Medical School to collegiate institutions. The three new schools in Madras were maintained by district boards; but notwithstanding this increase the total number of pupils slightly declined, owing to the abolition of the class for hospital assistants in the Madras school. The five schools cost in 1884-85 R55,000, of which R34,000 was contributed by local boards and R11,500 by municipalities. The cost to provincial revenues fell short of R2,500. In Bombay the lectures are given in English. The only incident of importance was that the medical schools, like the Grant Medical College, were thrown open to women, as they had long been in Madras. In Bengal, where the instruction in medical schools is exclusively vernacular, the pupils in the four Government schools increased from 310 to 504. These are of course conducted on the "orthodox system;" but in 1882-83 a homœopathic school was opened as a private speculation at Dacca, and its success was so pronounced as to lead to the establishment of a second at the same place two years later. The two schools had together 168 pupils, and were supported entirely by the fee-receipts, amounting to R2,184. After a three years' course the pupils are considered qualified to practise, and may expect to earn an income of R30 to R50 a month. The North-West reports contain no information about the medical school at Agra, but its popularity is attested by the increase in its numbers from 39 to 89. The Lahore Medical School, besides the students preparing for the University examination, also contained classes for hospital assistants and for European and native midwives. Provision is made in the Calcutta Medical College for the training of Burmese students, both candidates for degrees and others, all of whom receive liberal stipends from the Government of Burma during the full period of their training. Students from the Central Provinces are mostly trained in the Patna Medical School, where again scholarships are assigned by their own Government for their maintenance.

83. Engineering or Surveying Schools.—These increased from 9 to 18 and their pupils from 310 to 571, new schools having been opened in Assam and Burma. The survey schools in Burma, which increased from two to five, were designed primarily for the training of '*thugyis*,' or subordinate revenue officers, and were placed under the general superintendence of district officers. These schools were declared to be of great utility, both to the students trained in them and to the public service. Of much the same class are the seven Government survey schools opened in 1883-84 in Assam for the purpose of training '*mandals*' and '*mauzadars*' in land-surveying. The course included so much of this subject as would enable the men to keep up district maps and show new land taken up for cultivation, as well as to calculate areas. Of a different character was the Engineering School of Madras, which was intended to train candidates for subordinate appointments in the Public Works Department. The reductions made in that Department, and the consequent lack of appointments, brought down the numbers of the school at the beginning of this period, but as the prospects of employment increased the numbers rapidly rose. The course included mathematics, drawing, surveying, and engineering, up to the standard required for overseers and draughtsmen. For the latter class of candidates the demand was active and growing, and was independent of fluctuations in the Public Works staff. The Engineering School at Haidarabad in Sind is a comparatively small institution, with 21 pupils, who are being trained for sub-overseerships. The requirements of the Bombay Presidency in this respect are otherwise and more fully met by the lower department of the Poona College of Science. In 1885 the workshop and sub-overseer class of this college contained 82 students. Of the four survey schools returned for

Bengal, one is a municipal school for training '*amins*' or surveyors for the Chota Nagpore estate; the other three are Government institutions maintained at Dacca, Patna, and Cuttack, for the training of men principally for private employment. During the progress of the railways in Eastern Bengal and Behar, the passed pupils were eagerly sought for and are said to have given much satisfaction; but in 1884-85 it was reported that greater difficulty was found in obtaining employment. The course is entirely in the vernacular; and it has been suggested that the students would have better prospects if they were required to know English. Another institution of a similar class was the apprentice department attached to the Seebpore Engineering College, near Calcutta. Its object was to train up foreman mechanics; and in addition to a theoretical course, lasting for $3\frac{1}{2}$ years, each student went through a course of practical instruction in carpenter's, blacksmith's, fitter's, and moulder's work in the shops. After training, the apprentices found employment without difficulty in private firms, on tea gardens, or on steamers.

84. Industrial Schools.—This important class of schools comprises institutions of every degree of usefulness; from those in which boys are systematically taught, through several years of work, a trade by which they will afterwards earn their living, to others that only aim at making amateur carpenters or smiths, of various degrees of inefficiency, out of boys of the literate classes who attend the workshop for an hour or so daily while the fit lasts, as a relaxation from the severer studies to which alone they look for their future livelihood. To this last class of schools it is useless to offer any encouragement. Here and there a youth may perhaps be found to acquire such skill and to take such interest in the trade he has learnt as to follow it as the means of living; but there is no hope that technical education so conducted will have any large or general effect in relieving the existing pressure on the professional or clerical walks of life. All that such schools or classes do for a student is to teach him an accomplishment for his leisure hours which he never fully acquires and which he soon forgets. In the following brief sketch of the progress of industrial schools between 1881-82 and 1884-85, some account will be given of the leading institutions of the class, and also of others whose failure is instructive.

Madras.—In Madras the number of industrial schools rose from three to five, all under private management. The industrial school for Eurasians in the Black Town of Madras contained about 50 pupils, who were taught carpentry, book-binding, shoemaking, blacksmiths' work, and rattan work. They also received an elementary general education, which was described as imperfect and unsound. The receipts exceeded the cost of materials by about R50 a month, and the school further received a Government grant of R150 a month. Of 33 boys that left the school in 1883-84, 18 are known to have found employment; in the following year 10 found employment out of 26. It being understood that four or five years are generally required for learning a trade, the complaint is made that the boys will not stick to their work. Unless means, it is added, can be adopted to prevent their constant migration, such as the personal apprenticing of the lads to the Superintendent, it is useless to expect the school to become really efficient. The Nazareth Industrial School for native Christian orphans at Tinnevelly was well spoken of. The boys were taught carpentry, smith's work and tailoring; the girls lace-making.

Bombay.—In Bombay there were seven schools, one under public management, four aided, and one in a Native State. Two schools under public management were closed, and replaced by two aided institutions. One of the Government institutions (at Dharwar) was rendered unnecessary by the workshops of the new railway, in which much better practical instruction could be obtained. But the history of the other school, that at Dhulia, is an instructive instance of the class of schools that can never succeed. It was opened with ten boys, including seven Brahmans, pupils of other schools in Dhulia. An experienced workman was told off to teach them, and they worked steadily for six months. At the end of that time most of the boys, it was reported, had quitted the carpentry class " because they say their parents do not wish them " to waste any time in learning carpentry to the prejudice of their regular school " studies." Another report remarked :—" The work of a carpenter being laborious " and naturally distasteful to beginners, it is therefore necessary to offer them " scholarships to induce them to attend." The remaining Government school at Ratnagiri is of a different order. It is attended by boys of the artisan and labouring classes, who in the school are taught drawing and practical geometry, while they learn their special trades in the factory to which the school is attached.

The Fardunji Industrial School at Surat affords a good example of the difficulties into which such institutions are liable to fall, and of the measures that may be taken to restore them to a sounder condition. It was founded in 1883 by a private endowment of R50,000, and of late years it has also received a grant of R2,000 a year from Government. But notwithstanding this munificent support the school declined, until in 1883-84 the attendance had fallen to 20, and it was condemned as a " mere workshop." Mr. Little, the Executive Engineer of the division, was deputed to report on the school. He found that it had become disorganised and was working without any efficient system. He recommended the appointment of a Superintendent on R150 or R200 a month, of an assistant to teach geometry and drawing, and of four master-workmen for carving, carpentry and joiner's work, smith's work, and fitting and metal work. The course should consist of three hours' work a day in the class-room and of three hours in the shops. In the class-room should be taught (1) linear drawing, such as to enable a man to draw roughly doors, windows, roofs, boxes, &c.; (2) free-hand drawing, to include leaves, flowers, figures, and other studies useful for carving; (3) sufficient practical geometry for the construction of simple figures; (4) elementary mensuration of planes and solids for the calculation of materials. In the shops, students should master one trade before being permitted to take up a second. A course of this kind appears to combine theoretical and practical instruction in just those proportions that experience and authority alike suggest; the theoretical instruction being confined to those subjects which, by educating the student's hand and eye, help him to become a more skilful workman in the craft that he follows. But a somewhat unexpected result ensues. Mr. Little was of opinion that the re-organised school ought to secure a sale for its produce at bazar prices, but that it should not attempt to undersell the bazar. He added the explanation :—" I do not believe the school is likely " to turn out better workmen than family workshops ; but if it enables boys who " without it would have been unskilled workers, to become skilled artificers, it will " be justifying its existence as a school of industry." The question naturally arises, if such a result is all that can be secured from a permanent income of R4,000 a year, what chance is there of multiplying industrial schools, or what advantage if they could be multiplied? The recommendations were adopted, and the attendance rose in 1884-85 to 58.

The David Sassoon Reformatory at Bombay contained over 200 boys. All attended school, and all above the age of 12 were required to work for three hours a day, either in the Central Printing Press, or in the workshop attached to the institution. But the boys are all convicts ; and the inclusion of this school in the educational returns appears to be at variance with the orders conveyed in the letter to the Government of the Punjab No. 231A, dated 7th

August 1884 (copy of which was circulated to Local Governments and Administrations), that such institutions should not be included with schools for the free population.

Bengal.—Industrial schools in Bengal increased from three to five, by the opening of two schools under private management. One of these, the Mahisadal School at Midnapore, was endowed with a sum of R5,000 by a local zamindar from whom the school derives its name, and in 1884-85 it had attracted 68 pupils, 51 of whom were learning carpentry and 17 tinsmith's work. But the report for that year states that the pupils mostly come from the Midnapore College and other institutions in the neighbourhood. "One is a Master of Arts and a pleader of the "local bar, who has joined the school in order to set a good example to his fellow- "countrymen. The object of the public-spirited founders is to create a taste for "industrial arts among young people of good social standing." An institution having such objects was foredoomed to failure. The school at Dehree, maintained by the Public Works Department for the benefit of the sons of artisans employed in the canal-workshops at that place, taught a little mechanics and practical geometry, in addition to the subjects of an ordinary vernacular school. The Ranchi school, formerly under the Berlin mission, but taken over after the departure of the managing missionary by the District Committee, taught reading, writing, and arithmetic, together with carpentry and smith's work. The pupils are exclusively Kols, a race among whom these handicrafts are rare. In 1884-85 the school was pronounced a failure, owing to the incompetence of the Superintendent. In reference to the general want of success that had attended the efforts to establish industrial schools in Bengal, the following remarks of the Director may be quoted—" To be of any real utility, technical instruction requires, as a condition "of its growth and development, the existence of industrial centres, in connexion "with which corresponding schools may be opened. Such centres exist on the "continent of Europe, where technical schools abound; they do not exist, except "in a few large towns, in any part of Bengal."

North-Western Provinces.—There were two industrial schools under missionary management, one for boys at Gorakhpur and one for girls at Benares. The boys learnt weaving, shoe-making, tailoring, and baking; the girls learnt needle-work. All were native Christians. However humble in their character and aims, such schools set at any rate a salutary example for the advancement of industrial education among the general community; and they have a special value in the introduction of useful trades among a class of people who are out of caste and have no hereditary callings to follow.

Punjab.—In the Punjab there were four industrial schools, three under public management and one aided. The last was not a school, but merely an establishment in which women made and sold lace and embroidery under missionary management. The industrial school at Hoshiarpur was started with the laudable object of "providing a new career for the sons of zamindars "and other respectable persons, and thus to relieve the overcrowding from which "existing callings suffer." At first instruction was given in various arts, but after a while the school became simply a carpet-manufactory where the boys learnt reading and writing for an hour daily. The hope that boys of respectable families would be attracted to the school was not realised. The scholars belonged to the poorest families, and were attracted by so-called scholarships of 8 annas to R4 a month. As a rule they left the school as soon as they could find employment elsewhere, and it was stated that there was no instance of their entering any trade in which the instruction they had received could be turned to practical use. In 1885 it was decided to close the school, and Mr. Ibbetson reported of all the industrial schools in the Punjab that "they have a tenden-

"cy to degenerate, either into charitable institutions, or into factories supported
"by public funds. They do not introduce improved methods or special skill. The
"technical instruction they impart can be better obtained in the local work-
"shops, while the general instruction can be more effectively and more cheaply
"given in night schools." If for 'night schools' were substituted 'schools
in which drawing and other special subjects are taught,' this last sentence
would, in the opinion of many, express the true principle which should govern
technical instruction in this country.

Central Provinces.—The 23 (reduced to 19) schools in these provinces
were carpentry classes attached to training and other schools, at a cost to
Government in each case of R10 a month for a teacher. They were declared
in the report for 1883-84 to be generally unsuccessful. "If it was expected,"
Mr. Browning wrote, "that by starting these schools Brahmans and other
"high castes would be induced to take to carpentry as a means of livelihood,
"then the scheme must be pronounced a failure." Certain advantages were at
the same time claimed for these classes; they had taught that there was no
degradation in manual labour; the advantage of improved tools had been
made known. "Nevertheless, the scheme as tried by us is not the best way of
"improving carpenter's work in the country. Instead of trying to turn Brahmans
"and other high castes into carpenters, it would be better to establish Schools of
"Art at selected centres, where native workmen could be instructed in improved
"methods." Upon this report the Government ordered the classes to be closed.
They were still in existence, however, in the following year.

Burma.—Referring to industrial schools in 1884-85, Mr. Hordern wrote :—
"The value of such teaching is extending, and a good deal of unpretentious
"work in this direction is already done in some of our principal schools." In 1882
an apprentice school for Europeans and others was attached to the railway
works at Insein. They were chiefly engaged on the lathe and in the fitting of
engines, and their work was said to be remarkably good. Classes were established
for teaching mathematics to the European, and English to the native students:
The industrial school at Akyab is described as teaching carpentry, printing,
clock-making, &c. Industrial arts of various kinds were included in the course
taught by several mission schools in the province.

Assam.—The Williamson Artisan School in Assam was under the Manager
of the Jorhat Railway. It was "not successful, nor promising."

85. Other Special Schools.—This somewhat miscellaneous class need
not detain us long, though many are of considerable importance, and some
would seem to find a more appropriate place in the class considered in the
preceding paragraph. The school of ordnance artificers attached to the Gun
Factory at Madras is a purely industrial school, which gives a combined course
of theoretical and practical teaching to about 70 Europeans, of whom some are
men sent in from out-station arsenals, others young boys. The object of the
school is thus described :—"Every endeavour is put forth so to train the men
"that from the practical knowledge they acquire of the trades learnt, together
"with instruction in the principles of steam, the steam engine and machinery,
"they may be fitted to do justice to positions of trust in the service of Govern-
"ment." The Agricultural School at Saidapet gave instruction to all classes of
the population, Brahmans forming the majority. Most of the students were
sons of landholders. The course included agriculture, botany, chemistry, veterinary practice, physiology, book-keeping, mechanics, and other subjects. The
passed students were declared to be in some request; 81 had passed up to 1884-85.

The 35 "other" schools in Bombay consisted chiefly of 22 drawing and 10 agricultural classes attached to high schools throughout the Presidency. Some account of these has already been given in paragraph 55, relating to secondary education in Bombay. The drawing classes contained 2,713 pupils in 1884-85, and the agricultural classes 289. There was a steady increase and improvement year by year. The classes in agriculture were originally instituted in view of the possible institution of a degree in that subject by the University. That expectation had not been fulfilled; but meanwhile the classes, which were mainly attended by the sons of zamindars, were believed to be doing independently very useful work.

Of the 16 schools in Bengal, 11 were madrassas for the education of Muhammadans. Six of these were under departmental management and maintained either from provincial revenues or from the Mohsin Endowment Fund, and the other five had accepted more or less fully the madrassa standard and were therefore transferred from the class of unaided indigenous institutions. Two Sanskrit schools are also included among the number. Besides these, there were two music schools, and a school at Darjeeling for training Bhuteas and Lepchas to be explorers, surveyors, and interpreters. This last school has furnished most of those explorers who are known by initials in the records of the Survey Department and the Geographical Society, and who have done so much to increase our knowledge of the inner Himalayas and Tibet.

The 11 schools of the North-Western Provinces and Oudh are schools for the training of patwaris in surveying.

The 13 patwaris' schools in the Central Provinces in 1881-82 were declared two years later to be inefficient, and appear to have been closed, all but two, in 1884-85.

There was a law school with 71 students in the Punjab, and another with 6 students at Rangoon. The pupils were not matriculated members of the University.

CHAPTER III.
EDUCATION IN INDIA IN 1886.
Section I.—GENERAL SUMMARY.

86. Method of the Chapter.—The statistics of the year 1885-86 are fortunately free from those elements of uncertainty which obscured the progress of education in the three previous years. By this time the revised systems of classification were in general use, and the technical terms of education were employed uniformly in the same sense. In nearly all provinces the new Local Self-Government Acts had come into full operation. It will be necessary to give an account in some detail of the working of district and municipal boards in each province from their first institution under the new Acts; but the history of the year relates, not so much to the introduction of a new system of control, as to the development of a system already introduced and at work. Lastly, the uncertainty which has been seen to arise from the inclusion of provincial grants in the funds of local and municipal boards is confined within very narrow limits, and is generally capable of elucidation.

The following chapter deals with the progress of education to the end of 1886; and in the separate sections of it will be considered in order the topics enumerated in paragraph 5 of this report. In each section will be given, first, the figures for each province of India relating to that branch of education of which it treats; secondly, a summary of the information to be derived from the provincial reports in elucidation of those figures, together with some comparison of relative progress in the various provinces; and thirdly, a statement of the measures that have been taken in each province to carry out those recommendations of the Education Commission that relate to the subject-matter of the section. In the present section is given a summary, in the most general form, of the progress made in education of all kinds during the year 1885-86 throughout India; and it will be illustrated by tabular statements, statistical and financial, showing in a comprehensive way for each province the progress made in education of various classes, the expenditure which it has involved, and the sources from which that expenditure has been met. These various points will be developed in greater detail in the succeeding sections of this chapter.

87. General Statistics of Attendance, 1884-85 to 1885-86.—The following statement compares the attendance in different classes of institutions on the 31st March 1885 and the same date in 1886:—

CLASS OF INSTITUTIONS.	1884-85.		1885-86.		AVERAGE NUMBER OF PUPILS TO A SCHOOL IN	
	Institutions.	Pupils.	Institutions.	Pupils.	1884-85.	1885-86.
PUBLIC INSTITUTIONS.						
Colleges { Arts	82	7,444	86	8,127	91	94
{ Professional	20	2,192	24	2,411	110	100
Secondary Schools { For boys	3,991	381,972	4,083	394,508	96	97
{ „ girls	312	21,657	349	23,904	69	68
Primary Schools { For boys	100,774	2,496,171	86,363	2,415,004	25	28
{ „ girls	4,206	113,441	4,337	122,498	27	28
Special Schools	294	12,118	324	13,452	41	41
TOTAL	109,679	3,034,995	95,566	2,979,904	...	...
PRIVATE INSTITUTIONS.						
Advanced	6,276	70,560	6,384	70,744	11	11
Elementary { For boys	20,025	258,101	19,544	262,181	13	13
{ „ girls	433	7,922	873	12,251	18	14
TOTAL	26,734	336,583	26,801	345,176	...	...
GRAND TOTAL	136,413	3,371,578	122,367	3,325,080	...	...

Attention is at once struck by the remarkable decrease that has taken place in the year 1885-86 in the number both of schools and of pupils. There has been in fact a decline of 14,113 in the number of public schools (that is, schools of regular and organised instruction), and of 55,091 in the number of pupils reading in them. From the table it appears that the decrease is confined to primary schools; schools of all other classes showing an increase both in their number and in the number of their pupils. The cause of this serious loss has been already foreshadowed in paragraph 62 of the last chapter, where a sketch was given of the policy recently pursued in Bengal with the object of limiting the number of primary schools brought under inspection and receiving Government aid. A full account of the circumstances will be given below, in the section relating to Primary Education. Here it is sufficient to say that the exclusion, first from the departmental examinations for rewards, and subsequently from the returns of the inspecting officers, of small and weak indigenous schools and of those in which no printed books were read, resulted in the disappearance from the returns in Bengal of 14,875 primary schools for boys, and of 122,952 pupils reading in them. A comparison of these figures with those given just above will show that in the rest of India there is a trifling increase in the number of primary schools, and a large increase, amounting to nearly 68,000, in the number of their pupils. The increase has been general, except in the North-Western Provinces and Oudh, where there is a loss of about 7,500 pupils in primary schools. The removal of so many small schools from the returns of Bengal, and the large increase in the number of pupils elsewhere, have resulted in raising the average attendance in each school from 25 to 28.

With regard to public institutions of other classes, there is an increase of four Arts colleges and of four colleges for professional instruction, with an increase of 683 and of 219 respectively in the number of their pupils. There is a gain of 92 secondary schools, high and middle, for boys, and of 12,563 pupils reading in them. Under special instruction there is an increase of 30 schools and of 1,334 pupils reading in them. In the instruction of girls there is an increase of 37 secondary schools with 2,247 pupils, and of 131 primary schools with 9,057 pupils.

Private institutions are those in which the instruction does not conform to departmental standards. They are the indigenous schools of the country, giving instruction in subjects or after methods sanctioned by tradition and usage; and they are roughly divided into the advanced and the elementary. Of the former, which are devoted to the cultivation of the Oriental classics, the great majority are those in which Arabic or Persian is taught, the indigenous *tols* established for the study of Sanskrit forming hardly more than one-fourth of these. The latter are either village or bazar *pathsalas* of the old type, untouched by departmental influence; or *maktabs* in which the Koran is taught by rote to Muhammadan boys. The table shows that there is very little change in the numbers of these institutions; but it will be understood that the returns do not profess to give the whole number of existing institutions of this class.

88. Proportion of Scholars to Population, 1885-86.—The following table shows, for each province of India, the proportion of male and female scholars to the population of either sex of school-going age; that class being reckoned at 15 per cent. of the total male or female population. It will presently be seen (paragraph 94) that this conventional percentage has very little connexion with the facts of scholastic life in India.

Proportion of Scholars to Population, 1885-86.

PROVINCE.	POPULATION.			SCHOLARS.			Percentage of male scholars to male population of school-going age.	Percentage of female scholars to female population of school-going age.	Percentage of total scholars to total population of school-going age.
	Males.	Females.	TOTAL.	Males.	Females.	TOTAL.			
Madras . .	15,278,232	15,590,272	30,868,504	397,040	58,797	455,837	17·3	2·5	9·8
Bombay . .	11,966,936	11,225,123	23,192,059	481,922	49,205	531,127	26·8	2·9	15·2
Bengal . .	33,917,217	34,243,381	68,160,598	1,277,843	80,186	1,358,029	25·1	1·5	13·2
North-Western Provinces and Oudh . .	22,912,556	21,195,313	44,107,869	321,716	12,476	334,192	9·3	·3	5·05
Punjab . .	10,210,053	8,640,384	18,850,437	242,078	26,796	268,874	15·8	2·06	9·5
Central Provinces . .	5,827,122	5,721,389	11,548,511	98,874	5,126	104,000	11·3	·5	6·
Burma . .	1,991,005	1,745,766	3,736,771	143,715	15,217	158,932	48·1	5·8	28·3
Assam . .	2,503,703	2,377,723	4,881,426	63,997	4,626	68,623	17·04	1·3	9·3
Berar . .	1,380,492	1,292,181	2,672,623	39,816	1,202	41,018	19·2	·6	10·2
Coorg . .	100,439	77,863	178,302	3,919	529	4,448	26·01	4·5	16·6
TOTAL	106,087,755	102,109,395	208,197,150	3,070,920	254,160	3,325,080	19·2	1·6	10·6

Roughly, therefore, out of 10 children that might be at school, only 1 is actually found in school; the proportion being 1 in 4 for boys, and 1 in 62 for girls. As regards the education of boys, the highest place is taken by Burma, in which province, with its widespread system of indigenous schools, nearly half the population of school-age are actually at school. Then follow in order Bombay, Coorg, and Bengal, with a proportion of 1 in 4 boys at school. Next come Berar, Madras, Assam, and the Punjab, with proportions of 1 in 5 or 1 in 6. The lowest places are taken by the Central Provinces and the North-Western Provinces, with proportions of 1 in 9 and 1 in 11 respectively.

In the education of girls Burma again takes the lead, with the little territory of Coorg in close attendance. The spread of female education in these provinces is indicated by the proportions of 1 in 17 and 1 in 22 respectively. The next group is composed of Bombay, Madras, and the Punjab; then follow Bengal and Assam; and lastly, Berar, the Central Provinces, and the North-Western Provinces, in which group the proportion sinks from one in 166 to one in 333.

89. Schools classified according to Standard of Instruction.—The following table shows, for each province, the number of institutions of various classes and of the scholars attending them at the close of the year. The figure for male and female students are not separated.

[SEC. I.] GENERAL SUMMARY. 93

Schools classified according to Standard of Instruction, 1885-86.

PROVINCE.	COLLEGES.		SECONDARY SCHOOLS.		PRIMARY SCHOOLS.		SPECIAL SCHOOLS.		PRIVATE INSTITUTIONS.		TOTAL.	
	Institutions.	Pupils.	Schools.	Pupils.	Schools.	Pupils.	Schools.	Pupils.	Schools.	Pupils.	Schools.	Pupils.
.	34	2,992	755	66,709	13,753	360,718	75	2,559	1,397	22,859	16,014	455,837
.	12	1,674	377	37,536	7,038	419,743	65	(a)2,034	2,964	70,140	10,456	531,127
.	38	4,191	2,187	177,235	52,996	1,142,314	78	4,540	2,234	29,749	57,533	1,358,029
P. and Oth	19	1,275	609	64,813	5,405	187,247	36	1,995	7,232	78,862	13,301	3,392
.	2	307	283	44,371	1,863	91,538	16	755	12,201	131,903	14,315	268,874
Provinces .	4	79	67	3,860	1,764	99,590	19	471	...	...	1,854	104,000
.	...	20	70	8,881	5,117	146,755	16	410	208	2,866	5,412	158,932
.	...	...	105	9,965	1,799	50,291	17	572	503	7,795	2,424	68,623
.	...	...	26	4,606	894	35,839	1	102	30	471	951	41,018
.	...	...	3	436	71	3,467	1	14	32	581	107	4,448
Æ.	110	10,538	4,432	418,412	90,700	2,537,502	324	(a)13,452	26,801	345,176	122,367	3,325,080

* Ex have of 2,163 pupils in Bombay already shown in ah h schools.

No further comment on this table is now required, since these are specifically the figures which will be developed at length in the succeeding sections of this chapter.

90. Scholars classified according to Stage of Instruction.—The preceding table shows, for each province, the number of pupils in institutions of various classes. But that is a different thing from the number of pupils in each standard, a result arising from the great variety of school-systems in different provinces of India. Every student of a college is of course in the collegiate stage of instruction; but it does not follow that every pupil in a high school is in the high stage of instruction, since he may be in the middle or even the primary stage. In Bombay, for example, the pupils in secondary schools are all, with few exceptions, in the secondary stage; in Bengal the great majority of such pupils are in the primary stage. It therefore becomes necessary to discriminate pupils, in whatever schools reading, according to the stages of instruction in which they are. In the Resolution of the Government of India, dated the 29th October 1883, these stages are defined as follows:—

(1) *Lower Primary* stage, including those pupils who have not passed beyond the lower primary standard, and who are subdivided into (A) those not reading printed books, and (B) those reading printed books.

(2) *Upper Primary* stage, including those who have passed stage (1), but have not passed beyond the upper primary standard.

(3) *Middle* stage, including those who have passed stage (2), but have not passed beyond the lower secondary (or middle) standard.

(4) *High* stage, including those who have passed stage (3), but have not passed the matriculation examination.

The necessary classification is supplied in the following table. It should be understood that the table refers only to schools of organised instruction, excluding private institutions of all classes, and also excluding technical and other special schools.

Scholars classified according to Stages of Instruction, 1885-86.

PROVINCE.	PERCENTAGE OF PUPILS IN THE					
	Collegiate stage.	High stage.	Middle stage.	Upper Primary stage.	Lower Primary stage (A).	Lower Primary stage (B).
Madras		1·4	5·6	6 8	70·	15·5
Bombay	·4	2·5	4·4	28 4	32·2	32·1
Bengal		1·	2·9	5·7	54·3	35·8
North-Western Provinces and Oudh	5	·6	4·7	19·5	69·1	5·6
Punjab		·9	6 3	15·5	73 2	3 9
Central Provinces .		·4	5·3	13 2	41·8	39 3
Burma		·1	1·1	1·5	97·	·3
Assam		1·	2·6		73·9	16·7
Berar		·9	6·1		39·9	27·
Coorg		1·3	5·		67 8	...
AVERAGE FOR INDIA .					25·9	

with the fact just stated, that of all children of a school-going age, 1 child in 10, or 1 boy in 5, is actually at school. It now appears that out of 100 children at school $94\frac{1}{2}$ are in the primary stage, and $5\frac{1}{2}$ in stages higher than the primary. Of those in the primary stage, 26 read no printed books, their instruction being limited to writing and accounts. Of the rest of the primary pupils 57 are in the lower and 11 in the upper primary stage.

The provincial differences disclosed in the table are very striking, but they must be read with the important limitation that the attempt to identify the various standards throughout India has been abandoned; and that the "lower primary," for example, or the "upper primary" standard does not necessarily mark the same stage of progress in all provinces. At one end of the scale the collegiate stage, and at the other the lower (non-reading) section of the lower primary stage have fixed and definite meanings; but the intermediate stages may vary by a year or more according to the differences of provincial systems. Thus in Bombay and Berar the high schools contain four classes leading to the matriculation examination, and all the scholars in these four classes seem to have been returned in the "high stage" of instruction, while in other provinces that stage is limited to the two highest classes. On the other hand, the two classes which are added to many vernacular schools in Bombay, with the object of carrying instruction beyond the upper primary standard, are included in the upper primary stage. In the Central Provinces, which has a similar system, the pupils in these classes are returned as being in the middle stage.

The last column of the table, as to which there is no uncertainty, shows very remarkable differences. In the Central Provinces, in Bengal, and in Bombay and Berar, the attention paid in primary schools to the indigenous methods of writing and accounts is indicated by the large percentage of pupils who as yet read no printed books. In Burma and Coorg, on the other hand, every pupil learns to read from the first day that he enters a school. In a Burmese school, monastic or lay, Burmese or Pali is taught to all scholars; in the indigenous schools of Coorg every boy brings to school a book of some kind, though the choice appears to be regulated by his own fancy. The wide development of the primary system in Burma, where 97 per cent. of the pupils are in the lower primary stage, explains the small percentage of pupils in the higher standards. The same remark does not fully account for the low place occupied by Bengal in the higher stages of instruction. It will explain the position of Bengal as compared with Madras, since it appears from the table in paragraph 88 that the proportion of pupils to population is nearly 50 per cent. higher in the former than in the latter province. It will not explain it as compared with Bombay, where education is even more widely extended than in Bengal. If the standards are equal, it would follow that education is, in point of quality, much more advanced in Bombay than in either Bengal or Madras. It is impossible to settle that point with anything like certainty, but the probability of difference in the value of the standards is indicated by the small proportion of pupils (6 or 7 per cent.) in the upper primary stage in Madras and Bengal, compared with the far higher percentage, not only in Bombay, but in almost every other province of India.

91. General Estimate of Progress in 1885-86.—Whatever uncertainty may attend the value of the different provincial standards of education, will not affect an estimate of the progress made from year to year, since the separate standards, if not identical, are at any rate constant. The following table shows progress at the beginning and at the end of the year 1885-86:—

General Estimate of Progress, 1884-85 to 1885-86.

STAGE OF INSTRUCTION.	MALE SCHOLARS.				FEMALE SCHOLARS.			
	Number of Scholars.		Percentage.		Number of Scholars.		Percentage.	
	1884-85.	1885-86.	1884-85.	1885-86.	1884-85.	1885-86.	1884-85.	1885-86.
Collegiate	9,606	10,503	·34	·38	30	35	·01	·01
High	31,343	35,290	1·12	1·29	401	375	·19	·17
Middle	105,668	109,993	3·77	4·02	3,708	4,339	1·73	1·88
Upper Primary	300,934	321,052	10·72	11·73	13,254	15,641	6·17	6·81
Lower Primary (A)	1,568,016	1,567,944	55·87	57·30	120,676	132,023	56·20	57·44
Lower Primary (B)	790,938	691,604	28·18	25·28	76,664	77,444	35·70	33·69
TOTAL	2,806,505	2,736,386	100·	100·	214,733	229,857	100·	100·

The table furnishes a satisfactory record. In the case both of boys and of girls, the proportion of pupils in the lowest stage of instruction has decreased, and the corresponding increase is distributed in due proportion over all the higher stages. In the book-reading section of the lower primary stage, the proportion of boys and of girls is equal. The percentage of girls is greater in the section below that; and of course it falls off in all the higher standards.

92. Schools classified according to Management.—The following table shows the extent to which the Department in each province relies upon its own institutions, upon those maintained by district and municipal boards, and upon those which are the fruit of private effort.

SEC. I.] GENERAL SUMMARY. 97

Schools classified according to Management, 1885-86.

Province.	Departmental Institutions.		Institutions maintained by Local and Municipal Boards.		Aided Institutions.		Unaided Institutions.		Private Institutions.		Total.	
	Schools.	Pupils.	Schools.	Pupils.	Schools.	Pupils.	Schools.	Pupils.	Schools.	Pupils.	Schools.	Pupils.
Madras	143	8,908	1,414	49,534	8,897	280,530	4,163	23,956	1,397	22,859	16,014	3,837
Bombay	(a)1,893	115,988	4,698	292,291	861	48,450	40	4,258	2,964	70,140	10,456	35,127
Bengal	328	30,992	48	3,834	46,692	130,280	8,231	163,174	2,234	29,749	57,533	8,629
North-Western Provinces and Oudh	27	2,759	5,573	221,014	387	2,822	82	3,735	7,232	78,862	13,301	3,192
Punjab	111	17,565	1,625	97,400	848	20,838	30	1,168	12,201	131,903	14,315	268,874
Central Provinces	(b)326	21,151	767	51,849	631	27,726	130	3,774	...	...	1,854	104,000
Burma	21	848	42	3,712	1,325	65,308	3,816	86,198	208	2,866	5,412	158,932
Assam	65	4,549	1,293	36,424	442	16,014	121	3,841	503	7,795	2,424	68,623
Berar	586	33,040	17	1,818	226	4,476	92	1,213	30	471	951	41,018
Coorg	63	3,413	6	340	6	164	...	...	32	531	107	4,448
Total	3,563	239,213	15,483	757,766	59,815	1,621,608	16,705	361,317	26,801	345,176	122,367	3,325,080

(a) Includes 1,763 schools with 1,080 pupils in Native States.
(b) Includes 44 schools with 2,340 pupils in F udatory States.

Compared with the total number of schools, it is only in Berar, the Central Provinces and Coorg that any considerable proportion of the schools are maintained directly by the Department. It will appear hereafter that these are all primary schools. A much larger proportion of high and middle schools are so maintained; though in Bengal, which has the largest number of departmental secondary schools, the great majority are vernacular schools planted here and there to infuse a desire for a better education than the village school can supply, and transplanted as soon as the way has been prepared for the establishment of an aided school. The development of board schools has proceeded most vigorously in Bombay, the North-Western Provinces, the Punjab and Assam; largely also in the Central Provinces, and to a less extent in Madras. District boards had not, up to the close of the year 1885-86, been established in Bengal or in Burma; and though in Burma large educational powers had been given to municipal boards, those bodies preferred for the most part to aid schools rather than directly to maintain them.

Aided institutions exist in Bengal to an extent far beyond that found in any other province. Out of 59,815 aided schools in India, 46,692 are in Bengal alone, where they compose practically the whole of the primary system, as they do also in Burma. Among other provinces, Madras takes the lead in the extent to which it makes use of private agency in education, and the same policy prevails in different degrees in the Central Provinces, Berar, and Assam. Unaided institutions are either public schools of organised instruction, belonging therefore to the departmental system, though not receiving aid from the State or from local bodies; or private institutions in which the course and methods of instruction are of a purely indigenous character, owing nothing to the influence or example of the Department. Schools of the former class are, as might antecedently have been expected, most numerous in Madras, Bengal and Burma, where the primary system of education is either largely or exclusively built up on an indigenous foundation. Those of the latter class are most numerous in the Punjab and the North-Western Provinces, where the efforts of Government have not yet succeeded in bringing indigenous institutions within the circle of departmental influence. There are also many institutions of a similar kind in Madras, Bombay, Bengal and Assam.

93. Race and Creed of Scholars.—The next table distributes the pupils in public and in private institutions respectively among the main divisions of the population, namely, Europeans and Eurasians, Native Christians, Hindus, Muhammadans, and other races, in which last division are included not only the aboriginal or semi-Hinduised aboriginal races that are found throughout many parts of India, but Parsis, Sikhs and Burmese, who are confined to special provinces. The educational condition of two or three of these divisions of the population will be separately considered in later sections of this chapter.

SEC. I.] GENERAL SUMMARY. 99

or Creed of Scholars, 1885-86.

Provinces	In Public Institutions.						In Private Institutions.				
	Europeans and Eurasians.	Native Christians.	Hindus.	Muhammadans.	Others.	TOTAL.	Native Christians.	Hindus.	Muhammadans.	Others.	TOTAL.
	6,835	36,955	356,498	31,456	1,234	432,978	464	20,668	1,709	18	
	3,288	4,515	376,087	57,747	(a)19,350	460,987	241	44,027	23,009	(b)2,363	70,140
	6,118	8,164	928,814	358,459	26,725	1,328,280	60	7,654	21,383	651	29,748
	2,319	3,572	207,266	42,125	48	255,330	402	49,858	28,476	127	
	1,558	906	68,836	51,553	(c)14,118	136,971	179	21,449	108,666	(d)6,608	
	874	626	89,277	8,048	5,175	104,000	...	...	...	...	
	1,590	...	...	...	(e)154,476	156,066	...	...	...	(f)2,363	2,363
	31	1,589	42,991	9,463	6,754	60,828	...	2,222	5,515	58	7,795
	1	35	34,893	5,594	24	40,547	...	169	302	...	471
	20	122	1,120	159	2,496	3,917	3	355	...	173	531
TOTAL	22,634	56,484	2,105,782	564,604	230,400	2,979,904	1,349	146,402	184,059	13,366	345,176

(a) Including 12,316 Parsis. (b) Including 2,428 Parsis.
(c)   „   13,076 Sikhs.   (d)   „   6,403 Sikhs.
(e)   „   140,281 Burmese. (f)   „   1,830 Burmese.

To enable us to judge of the significance of these figures, and to estimate the spread of education among the different races of India, it is necessary to ascertain the number of children of school-going age in each section of the population. The following table supplies the materials for a comparison. The statistics of population are taken from the appendices to the article "India" in Vol. IV of the Imperial Gazetteer, and the number of children of school-going age is taken, as before, at 15 per cent. of the population. It will be remembered that, owing to the very limited spread of female education, the percentages for boys alone may be doubled, without risk of serious error, in all but a few small sections of the people.

RACE OR CREED.	PERCENTAGE OF SCHOLARS TO CHILDREN OF SCHOOL-GOING AGE.		
	In Public Institutions.	In Private Institutions.	TOTAL.
Hindus	10·6	·7	11·3
Muhammadans	9·3	3·1	12·4
Parsis	121·6	24·0	145·6
Sikhs	7·6	3·7	11·0
Burmese	59·4	·8	60·2
Native Christians	62·9	1·6	64·5
Europeans and Eurasians	68·	...	68·
Others	2·4	·1	2·5

The difference between the spread of education among Hindus and among Muhammadans is not so great as is often supposed. Hindus take somewhat greater advantage of schools of organised instruction; but the wide prevalence among the Muhammadan population of schools in which the Koran alone is read more than restores the balance. The "Granth schools" of the Sikhs act in the same direction. The percentage for "Burmese" relates to the Burmese proper, excluding the Karens and other races, among whom education is far less widely spread. The high proportion among Native Christians shows how carefully they are looked after by their pastors. The proportion among Europeans and Eurasians would be still higher than it is, but for the presence of the English army in India, and for the fact that the children of the wealthier classes are sent out of India before they reach the school-going age. No great value can be attached to the figures relating to "others." The population on which the percentage is based are the 17 or 18 millions of aboriginal or semi-Hinduised aboriginal races of the census report; but the pupils so classed include also those of many miscellaneous sects or races that can find no more appropriate heading.

94. Meaning of the "School-going Age."—The figures for the Parsi population are striking. The Parsis numbered 67,531 in the Bombay Presidency at the last census; and 15 per cent. of that number gives 10,130 as the number of children of school-going age. The number of Parsi children at public schools in Bombay was 12,316, which exceeds the former number by more than 20 per cent. The necessary inference is, either that Parsi children are kept at school for a longer term than is common with other sections of the people, or that the accepted proportion of 15 per cent. is too low for India. The statistics of population and of the average duration of life in India appear to lend support to the second alternative. The English ratio of 15 per cent. was arrived at in the following way. It was ascertained (1) that nearly 11 per cent. of the population were between the ages of 6 and 12, (2) that of the school-population 70 per cent. were between 6 and 12, and 30 per cent. above or below those limits; whence it followed, by a not very cogent inference, that about 15 per cent. of the whole population (as 70 : 100 :: 11 : 15) ought to be at school. This method of calculation has now been abandoned in England. The present method assumes (1) that 23·73 of the population are between the ages of 3 and 13, (2) that about one-seventh of these are children of the middle and upper classes who do not attend schools working under the Code. Hence about

20 per cent. of the population ought to be on the registers of public elementary schools, and that ratio is now taken to represent the children of school-going age. In India there is no need to make any deduction for scholars of the middle and upper classes, since about them we have full information. The census returns show that 26 per cent. of the population of India are between 5 and 15 years of age, and between these limits lie the ages of the vast majority of scholars in India. But it by no means follows that the vast majority of scholars are at school for the whole period between 5 and 15 years. Some remain for ten years and even longer; but it is probable that five years more nearly represent the normal duration of school-life for the generality of Indian scholars, some beginning earlier and some later within those limits. Thus the people as a whole would be fully educated according to their needs, even though the returns showed that only half the population, from 5 to 15 years of age, were at any given time at school. It follows that, under any ordinary acceptation of the limits of the school age, we can never expect to work up to anything like the full percentage as regards the agricultural and labouring classes, however freely schools may be multiplied. On the other hand, among a people so advanced and generally so wealthy as the Parsis, it is antecedently probable not only that all the children are educated, but that large numbers of them remain at school after the age of 15; so that the proportion of boys at school would thus exceed the assumed limit of 26 per cent. In fact, 26 per cent. of the Parsi male population amounts to 8,779; and an analysis of the returns (in which, however, the sexes are not clearly distinguished) leads to the conclusion that the number of Parsi boys at school is not less than 9,300.

In any case, it appears that the assumed proportion of 15 per cent. is too low for India. Children from 5 to 10 years of age form 15 per cent. of the population, and from 10 to 15 years of age 11 per cent; whence it follows that from 5 to 12 years of age the proportion would be about 20 per cent. That seems on the whole to be a fairer proportion to take. On the one hand we cannot expect the masses of the people to remain at school more than five years, but up to five years we should endeavour to keep them there if they are to receive a sound primary education. On the other hand, the margin left will provide for and include that large number of scholars who carry on their education to the secondary and collegiate stages. Applying this proportion of 20 per cent. to the case of Hindus, and making the necessary deduction for girls, we find that about 15 per cent. of the Hindu male population of school-going age are actually at school. The balance of 85 per cent. represents those backward castes and sections of the people who have no school-going traditions, and also those scholars who attend school for less than five years.

95. Languages learnt by Scholars.—The following table possesses interest, as showing the comparative attention paid to different languages in different provinces :—

Languages learnt by Scholars, 1885-86.

PROVINCE.	IN PUBLIC INSTITUTIONS.						IN PRIVATE INSTITUTIONS.		
	English.	Percent.	Classical language.	Percent.	Vernacular.	Percent.	English.	Classical language.	Vernacular.
Madras	77,173	17·8	9,905	2·2	422,283	97·5	1,390	1,197	22,329
Bombay	39,577	8·5	15,735	3·4	439,416	95·3	430	12,923	57,053
Bengal	105,403	8·1	71,823	5·4	1,283,455	96·6	178	25,842	4,673
North-Western Provinces	28,429	11·1	25,926	10·1	244,377	95·7	1,029	43,913	34,998
Punjab	18,293	13·3	49,973	36·4	135,083	98·6	479	91,283	39,521
Central Provinces	7,149	6·8	1,073	1·03	102,748	98·7	...	...	...
Burma	7,529	4·8	136,511	87·4	155,197	99·4	135	556	2,209
Assam	5,512	9·06	2,812	4·6	59,200	97·3	144	7,055	734
Berar	1,899	4·6	579	1·4	40,536	99·9	...	68	403
Coorg	576	14·7	19	·4	3,897	99·4	24	...	531
TOTAL	294,540	9·8	314,356	10·5	2,886,192	96·6	3,809	*182,837	162,456

* Including 85,717 pupils reading the Koran.

Madras and Coorg at one end of India, the North-Western Provinces at the other, take the lead with regard to the proportion of their pupils that learn English in public schools; while in Burma and Berar the proportion is lowest. These figures should, however, be regarded side by side with those given in an earlier table, showing the total spread of organised education in each province. In the study of classical languages Burma stands pre-eminent, her position being due to the inclusion of the Pali scriptures among the subjects of the traditional course in indigenous schools. The high place taken by the Punjab arises from the popularity of Persian in both English and vernacular schools, especially the latter. In the North-Western Provinces, also, Persian and Sanskrit are widely read in schools, though the study of Persian is said to be somewhat on the decline. Elsewhere, much less attention is paid to the Indian classics; and in the Central Provinces, Berar and Coorg, but few of the students learn any classical language.

96. General Statistics of Expenditure, 1884-85 to 1885-86.—The following table shows in a compendious form the expenditure incurred from provincial revenues, from local and municipal funds, and from private sources of all kinds, in the support of education throughout India in the years 1884-85 and 1885-86.

General Statistics of Expenditure, 1884-85 to 1885-86.

HEAD OF CHARGE.	EXPENDITURE IN 1884-85 FROM				EXPENDITURE IN 1885-86 FROM			
	Provincial Revenues.	Local and Municipal Funds.	Private Sources.	TOTAL.	Provincial Revenues.	Local and Municipal Funds.	Private Sources.	TOTAL.
	R	R	R	R	R	R	R	R
Collegiate	12,30,091	13,983	7,83,076	20,27,150	12,15,200	16,524	8,18,005	20,49,729
Secondary	17,53,454	9,09,711	46,69,151	73,32,316	18,09,078	9,60,336	49,58,056	77,27,470
Primary	14,53,529	25,67,620	39,88,522	80,09,671	14,78,082	26,53,238	38,38,377	79,69,697
Special	7,31,525	2,29,246	3,15,556	12,76,327	7,18,923	2,08,145	3,20,441	12,47,509
Universities and Direction	49,000	6,091	1,57,852	2,12,943	31,200	...	2,71,222	3,02,422
Inspection	14,28,447	3,97,743	45,881	18,72,071	15,47,635	3,85,567	47,886	19,81,088
Scholarships	3,51,343	1,09,023	99,389	5,59,755	3,62,067	1,25,216	1,07,972	5,95,255
Buildings and Furniture	6,95,843	4,35,770	3,42,895	14,74,508	5,55,531	4,14,056	5,82,759	15,52,346
Miscellaneous	2,07,712	78,810	2,97,132	5,83,654	2,49,305	74,404	2,57,389	5,81,098
TOTAL	79,00,944	47,47,997	1,06,99,454	2,33,48,395	79,67,021	48,37,486	1,12,02,107	2,40,06,614

The most general result therefore is, that of a total increase of R6,58,219 in the expenditure from all sources on education, the bulk, amounting to R5,02,653, has been derived from private sources, while provincial revenues and local funds have contributed no more than R66,077 and R89,489 respectively. These figures relate to the increase of expenditure. As to the actual expenditure in 1885-86, it should still be remembered that some share of the cost debited to district and municipal funds is derived, not from local rates, but either directly or indirectly from provincial grants. The receipts from this source are largest in the North-Western Provinces, where it was shown in the last chapter that the contributions made from provincial revenues to district funds to meet the cost of transferred services amounted in 1884-85 to something like 7½ lakhs; and there was little variation in the expenditure from this source in the following year. In Assam, similarly, the 20 per cent. share of transferred sources of income (rents, pounds, ferries, &c.) which was devoted to education in 1885-86 may be roughly estimated at from R30,000 to R35,000. In the Central Provinces an increased grant of R28,000 was made in the same year from provincial revenues to the funds of district boards to meet the cost of transferred schools. In Burma the municipal expenditure on education increased in 1885-86 by R90,000. The additional amount was allotted to schools by the various municipalities in Burma out of their general funds; but as these funds include, not only the proceeds of taxation, but contributions from provincial revenues in the form, partly of a fixed grant of R87,000 a year, and partly of a largely increasing excise revenue made over to them by the Local Government, it is difficult to say what portion of the additional expenditure on education should be debited to provincial revenues. It would perhaps not be unfair to debit these last two sources of income, (provincial grant and transferred excise revenue) with R30,000 of the increase, in addition to the R2,20,000 shown in the last chapter to have been derived from the same sources. From that point of view we probably may, without risk of serious error, amend the figures in the foregoing table by increasing the expenditure from provincial revenues by $10\frac{1}{4}$ lakhs, and by reducing that from district and municipal rates by 8 and by $2\frac{1}{4}$ lakhs respectively. If these corrections be accepted the total educational expenditure from public sources would roughly stand thus: from provincial revenues 90 lakhs, from district funds 29 lakhs, from municipal funds 9 lakhs; or 128 lakhs in all from public funds, against 112 lakhs from private sources. If, on the other hand, municipal funds be included among private contributions (as in the opinion of some they should be reckoned), the expenditure from public and from private sources will be 119 and 121 lakhs respectively.

In passing on to the different heads of expenditure, it will be noticed that under collegiate instruction, special instruction, and buildings, there is a decrease in the Government expenditure. In the provincial expenditure on colleges, there is an increase in Madras, and a decrease in Bengal and the North-Western Provinces. The decrease under special instruction is nominal, and due to the transfer of the cost of certain institutions in the Punjab to other heads. There is also a nominal decrease in the expenditure from provincial funds on Universities. The fixed grants made by Government to these corporations are R27,000 in Bombay and R22,000 in the Punjab; but the returns for the latter were not received in time, and only a small portion of the grant is shown. In secondary and primary institutions, in direction and inspection, in scholarships, and in miscellaneous charges, there is an increase in the expenditure from provincial funds. That under secondary instruction is explained by an increase of R13,000 in Madras, of R18,000 in Bombay, of R5,000 in Bengal, and of R17,000 in the North-Western Provinces, accompanied by a decrease of R5,000 in the Central Provinces, due to the transfer of secondary schools to district boards. Under the head of primary expenditure from provincial funds there have been larger changes, the chief of which are an increase of R88,000 in Bombay and of R17,000 in Madras, and a decrease of R61,000 in Bengal and of R20,000 in the Central Provinces, the last being again due to the transfer of schools to local control. The cost of inspection has increased by R1,19,000, of which the chief items are R38,000 in Madras, R51,000 in Bengal, and R17,000 in the Central Provinces.

In the expenditure from local and municipal funds, the chief heads of increase are secondary and primary schools and scholarships. As regards primary and secondary schools, there is an increase under both heads in every province except Madras and the North-West. Under secondary schools, the largest increase has taken place in Burma (R36,000) and in the Central Provinces (R32,000). Under primary education there is an increase of R33,000 in the local fund expenditure of Bombay, of R22,000 in that of the Central Provinces, and of R19,000 in Burma. It is in Burma also that an increase of R8,000 in the municipal provision for scholarships is found. There is a reduction under special instruction, due to the reorganisation of the Ratnagiri Industrial School in Bombay, and the non-recurrence of a grant of R17,000 made in 1884-85 by the local board. The local grants for inspection have been reduced by R22,000 in Madras, and increased by R13,000 in the North-Western Provinces; altogether there is a reduction of R8,000 under this head. There is also a reduction in the expenditure from these sources on buildings, and a nominal reduction of R6,000 for Universities, due to the exclusion from the returns of the grant to that amount made by the Lahore Municipality to the Punjab University.

In the expenditure from private sources there is an increase under almost every head, the chief items being R35,000 for collegiate instruction, R2,89,000 for secondary schools, and R2,40,000 for buildings. There is a reduction of R1,50,000 in the private expenditure on primary schools, arising from the reductions in Bengal. There is a large increase, amounting to R1,14,000, in the expenditure on Universities from private sources, including the fees levied from candidates at the various examinations and the proceeds of endowments. Most of the increase is however nominal. The Bombay returns show for the first time the receipts from these sources, including R42,000 from fees and R19,000 from endowments. The fee-receipts in Bengal have risen from R31,000 to R81,000, and in the North-Western Provinces from R5,000 to R11,000, owing in each case to a change in the date of the University examinations, which reduced the receipts in the previous year. On the other hand, the fee-receipts of the Punjab University, amounting to R19,000 in 1884-85, are omitted from the returns of the following year. The receipts from University fees in Madras rose from R1,07,000 to R1,29,000, an amount much larger than in any other province, and (as in the Calcutta University) more than sufficient to pay all expenses. With the exception of Assam, the other provinces show no receipts from this source.

97. Provincial Expenditure, 1884-85 to 1885-86.—The following table compares the expenditure from various sources in each province for the two years 1884-85 and 1885-86:—

Provincial Expenditure, 1884-85 to 1885-86.

PROVINCE.	1884-85.				1885-86.			
	Provincial Revenues.	Local and Municipal Funds.	Private Sources.	TOTAL.	Provincial Revenues.	Local and Municipal Funds.	Private Sources.	TOTAL.
	R	R	R	R	R	R	R	R
Madras	11,72,341	8,02,275	22,23,944	41,98,560	12,74,946	7,88,302	23,70,746	44,33,994
Bombay	12,50,798	10,08,700	18,84,038	41,43,536	14,09,138	9,27,152	21,80,861	45,17,151
Bengal	30,76,400	76,716	46,62,062	78,15,178	29,86,159	84,584	45,76,927	76,47,670
N.-W. Provinces	6,31,187	14,29,442	7,31,976	27,92,605	5,86,809	14,20,871	9,09,506	29,17,186
Punjab	7,14,410	6,55,104	6,27,345	19,96,859	6,95,667	6,45,060	5,40,159	18,80,886
Central Provinces	3,85,282	1,75,189	1,48,674	7,09,145	3,50,623	2,31,135	1,75,216	7,56,974
Burma	2,65,747	3,29,300	2,13,436	8,08,483	2,73,718	4,49,814	2,26,197	9,49,729
Assam	1,67,842	1,40,457	1,48,763	4,57,062	1,38,797	1,57,894	1,55,460	4,52,151
Berar	2,21,132	1,21,731	52,545	3,95,408	2,31,369	1,20,081	58,869	4,10,319
Coorg	15,805	9,083	6,671	31,559	19,795	12,593	8,166	40,554
TOTAL	79,00,944	47,47,997	1,06,99,454	2,33,48,395	79,67,021	48,37,486	1,12,02,107	2,40,06,614

It thus appears that every province has increased its total educational expenditure, with the exception of Bengal, the Punjab, and (to a small extent) Assam. In these three provinces the reductions amount to R2,88,000; while in the rest of India the expenditure on education has increased by R9,46,000, chiefly in Bombay, Madras, Burma, and the North-Western Provinces.

It may be convenient for purposes of reference to append here a brief financial summary of educational expenditure in each province in 1885-86. It will serve to throw light on the question how far each province has shown itself able and willing to increase its educational assignments, whether from provincial, from local, or from private sources, in accordance with the recommendations of the Commission. This important point will meet with fuller consideration later on, in connexion with the subject of an increased provision of funds for primary education. Meanwhile, one general observation may be made. If it has not been found possible to carry out the policy recommended by the Commission, so far as it involved increased expenditure, that result has uniformly arisen, not from any reluctance to accept the policy, but solely from the stringent necessity of retrenchment in all departments which was imposed by superior orders upon the Local Governments towards the close of 1884-85, and which still exerts pressure in the same direction. In the Resolution of the 23rd October 1884 the Government of India had, in the following passage, held out to the Provincial Government hopes of assistance in carrying out educational reforms :—" The " Governor General in Council will, therefore, should necessity arise, and should " a review of the financial situation of any Local Government show that it is " unable to increase expenditure on education to the extent contemplated, be " prepared to consider any claims that may reasonably be put forward for assist" ance from Imperial revenues, and to deal with them in as liberal a spirit as " the condition of Imperial finances at the time will permit." But urgent military necessities quickly put it out of the power of the Government of India to redeem any of the promises implied in those words.

Madras.—The following figures show the increase or decrease under each source of income :—

	Increase. R	Decrease. R
Provincial Revenues	1,02,605	...
Local Funds	...	23,323
Municipal Funds	9,350	
Fees	15,658	
Other sources	1,31,144	...
	2,58,757	23,323
NET INCREASE	2,35,434	

The Madras Government has undertaken to devote in future 5 per cent of its total revenues to education; and the increase of more than a lakh of rupees in the educational grants for 1885-86 affords a practical illustration of that policy. It is further to be noticed that of the total increase in the provincial grant, as much as R60,000 has been given to institutions under private management. There is an increase of R34,000 under the head of inspection; but as there is a corresponding decrease of R22,000 in the local fund expenditure under the same head, this may merely mean the transfer of charges for inspection from district boards to the Government, in return for the acceptance by the former of the charge of secondary schools, which, it will shortly be seen, have been largely made over to local control, together with grants for their maintenance. At any rate, the decrease in the expenditure by district boards on education is not otherwise accounted for. District boards and municipalities now spend from 12 to 14 per cent. of their total income on education, primary schools receiving 8 and 7 per cent. respectively. The increase in fee-receipts is explained by a large increase of R22,000 in University fees; the increase in the fees of secondary schools and colleges having been more than swallowed up by a loss of R24,000 in the fee-receipts of primary schools. Under " other sources" the chief items of increase are enhanced subscriptions of R74,000 for buildings, and of R36,000 and R15,000 towards the maintenance of secondary schools and of training schools for mistresses.

Bombay.—The following figures show the variations in expenditure:—

	Increase. R	Decrease. R
Provincial Revenues	1,58,340	...
Local Funds	...	2,25,639
Municipal Funds	1,44,091	
Fees	1,30,952	
Other sources	1,65,871	..
	5,99,254	2,25,639
NET INCREASE	3,73,615	

The wealth and liberality of the Government of Bombay, and the earnestness of its desire to follow out the recommendations of the Education Commission, are sufficiently shown by the large additions which that Government made in 1885-86 to its educational grants. The details will be explained hereafter. For the present it need only be stated that additional grants were made to the amount of R3,84,000; that the subsequent necessity of retrenchment owing to operations on the frontier reduced the actual increase in the Government expenditure to R1,72,000; and that increased fee-receipts in Government institutions reduced the net increase to R1,58,000. Of this amount (minor variations under other heads being neglected) R88,000 was spent in increased grants to primary schools under local and municipal boards, and R71,000 upon buildings. But the point of chief interest in the foregoing table is the reduction of R2,25,000 in the educational expenditure of district boards. This resulted from the adoption of a new policy, involving on the one hand the transfer from district boards to municipalities of the duty of maintaining schools within municipal areas, and on the other the acceptance by Government of increased liabilities for the support of schools under local control, whether district or municipal. The result was a great increase in municipal as well as in Government expenditure; while the transfer of management and of financial responsibility placed large sums at the disposal of district boards, which they were as yet unable to apply to the extension of education in other directions. There is a remarkable increase of R1,31,000 in fee-receipts, of which R97,000 were school-fees, chiefly in institutions under private management; the balance is accounted for by the introduction of University fees for the first time into the returns of the Department. The large increase under subscriptions and "other sources" is distributed over primary and secondary schools and buildings.

Bengal.—The following are the figures:—

	Increase. R	Decrease. R
Provincial Revenues	...	90,241
Local Funds	870	...
Municipal Funds	6,998	...
Fees	66,986	...
Other sources	...	1,52,121
	74,854	2,42,362
NET DECREASE		1,67,508

We have now come to a province less prosperously circumstanced than Madras or Bombay. Two causes were at work in Bengal in 1885-86, one operating to reduce public, and the other private expenditure. The first was the sudden call for retrenchment in all departments which was imposed upon Government by military necessities; the second was the removal of 15,000 primary schools from the cognisance of the Department. In response to the recommendations of the Education Commission the Government of Bengal had undertaken, six months before the year began, to increase its educational assignments by a yearly addition of 1½ lakhs of rupees, up to a total increase of 14 lakhs, which it hoped to reach within nine years, without aid from the Supreme Government, if the provincial income continued to advance at the existing rate of progress. This expectation was not fulfilled. Financial exigencies compelled the Government to cut down its educational estimates for 1885-86 by a lakh of rupees. The salaries of subordinate inspecting officers had lately been increased by R55,000 a year; and it accordingly became necessary to reduce building grants by R80,000, grants for primary education by R61,000, and grants to colleges by R13,000. The withdrawal of primary schools from the returns caused a falling off of R75,000 in fees and of R1,24,000 in the receipts from subscriptions. On the other hand, there was a large increase in the fee-receipts of secondary schools, and also in the fees paid by candidates at the University examinations.

North-Western Provinces.—The statement is subjoined:—

	Increase. R	Decrease. R
Provincial revenues	...	44,378
Local Funds	...	12,292
Municipal Funds	3,721	...
Fees	27,497	...
Other sources	1,50,033	...
	1,81,251	56,670
NET INCREASE	1,24,581	

The financial condition of these Provinces was much the same as that of Bengal. The educational estimates for 1885-86 included an additional assignment of R68,700, including R40,000 for primary schools. But at the beginning of the next year it became necessary to cut down the estimates by R1,00,000, in which all the new assignments were swallowed up. The figures given just above show a saving of R44,000 only; but the statement of expenditure includes special charges for the Government Book Depôt, since closed, and reductions to the amount of nearly R80,000 were actually effected under other heads. Building grants were reduced by R88,000; while a further saving under Arts colleges and medical schools allowed of increased expenditure upon secondary schools and for inspection. The reduction in local fund expenditure has taken place in primary and secondary schools, to the amount of R12,000 in each case; and there is a nearly equivalent increase under inspection. Fee-receipts have improved to the extent of R29,000 in secondary schools, thus reducing the cost to the district boards that maintain them; and University fees have also increased. On the other hand, the fees of primary schools have fallen by R6,000, owing to a reduction in their number. Contributions from subscriptions and other sources have been increased by R36,000 for secondary schools and by R1,16,000 for buildings.

Punjab.—The figures are subjoined:—

	Increase. R	Decrease. R
Provincial Revenues	...	18,743
Local Funds	...	14,211
Municipal Funds	4,167	...
Fees	...	17,124
Other sources	...	70,062
	4,167	1,20,140
NET DECREASE	...	1,15,973

P 2

In 1884 the Government of the Punjab applied to the Supreme Government for an annual grant of 2½ lakhs from Imperial revenues for the development of primary education. The request could not be granted; but in 1886 the Local Government found itself able, by the exercise of economy in other departments, to set free a lakh of rupees for that purpose, though it was not until the following year that the additional grant took effect. The foregoing figures show that in 1885-86 there was a reduction under every source of income, municipal grants alone excepted. Much of the reduction is however due to the exclusion of the returns of expenditure for the Punjab University, as before explained. This accounts for the whole of the reduction under provincial revenues, for R6,000 under municipal grants (which have therefore increased by R10,000), and for R23,000 under fees. The receipts from the last source really improved by R14,000 in colleges and secondary schools, owing to the increased attention paid to fee-rates. District boards reduced their building grants by R27,000, and gave R12,000 of the amount thus saved to primary schools. The reduction in the receipts from "other sources" is due to the exclusion of the Oriental College, Lahore, and to diminished expenditure on buildings.

Central Provinces.—The figures are as follows :—

	Increase.	Decrease.
	R	R
Provincial Revenues	...	34,659
Local Funds	44,945	
Municipal Funds	11,001	
Fees	4,083	
Other sources	22,459	...
	82,488	34,659
NET INCREASE	47,829	

In the Central Provinces, as in Madras, the Local Government has fixed the future assignment for education at 5 per cent. of the provincial revenues, and large additional sums are expected to accrue from the local cess. The transfer of primary schools from departmental to local management was largely carried out in 1885-56, with the result of transferring R28,000 from provincial revenues to the funds of district boards, under which last heading the expenditure now appears, though its actual source remains unchanged. District funds have incurred increased expenditure for buildings amounting to R20,000; and the cost to provincial revenues under that head has been reduced by a nearly equal sum. Municipal grants have been increased by R11,000, of which R5,000 has been given to secondary schools, and R4,000 to the newly founded Morris College at Nagpore. There has also been a considerable increase in the fee-receipts of secondary schools, and in the private contributions towards the cost of primary schools (R15,000) and of the Morris College R(7,000).

Burma.—The figures are subjoined :—

	Increase.	Decrease.
	R	R
Provincial Revenues	7,971	
Local Funds	30,148	
Municipal Funds	90,366	
Fees	2,185	
Other sources	10,576	...

Burma and Coorg are the only provinces in which an increase of expenditure is shown under every head. In Burma the small increase of provincial expenditure has been devoted chiefly to strengthening the Rangoon College and the improvement of primary schools. The large increase in the expenditure from local funds has been brought about by the steady enhancement of the educational share of the local cess, within the last two years, from one-tenth to one-fifth. The bulk of the increase has been devoted to primary education, including buildings for primary schools. Reference has already been made to the large increase of R90,000 in the contributions by municipalities to education. When under the arrangements of 1882 the municipalities of Burma were relieved of charges for the police, accepting in return enhanced liabilities for education, medical relief and roads, they were enabled to meet these increased charges by the transfer to them of a profitable and expanding source of income in the revenue derived from excise licenses, and by an annual grant from provincial funds fixed for five years at R87,000. Their educational expenditure was at the same time estimated at R2,63,000. By the year 1885-86 it had advanced to R3,43,000, thus exceeding by R80,000 the amount that they were required to spend on education. The increased grants have been applied to the following objects:—buildings, R48,000, secondary schools R34,000; scholarships R6,000. The expenditure from "other sources" has been incurred chiefly in the support of secondary schools and in the erection of buildings.

Assam.—The figures are these:—

	Increase. R	Decrease. R
Provincial Revenues	...	29,045
Local Funds	16,836	
Municipal Funds	601	
Fees	2,482	
Other sources	4,215	...
	24,134	29,045
NET DECREASE	...	4,911

The Chief Commissioner of Assam declined to recognise any distinction in principle between provincial funds and local rates, both alike being the proceeds of compulsory taxation, in which the voluntary element is altogether wanting and the "local" character unimportant. But he pointed out that the educational grants from both sources taken together had increased from 4·4 per cent. in 1881-82 to 5·25 per cent. in 1884-85. In 1885-86 there is a reduction in the expenditure from these sources, but the reduction in the provincial grant is more than fully accounted for by reduced expenditure on buildings. The changes under other heads are unimportant. The increase in the local cess has been devoted to primary and secondary schools, inspection and buildings.

Berar.—The statement is subjoined:—

	Increase. R	Decrease. R
Provincial Revenues	10,237	
Local Funds		6,245
Municipal Funds	4,595	
Fees	7,704	
Other Sources	...	1,380
	22,536	7,625
NET INCREASE	14,911	

The increased expenditure from provincial revenues is mainly due to building grants. There has been a slight reduction in the cost of secondary schools and some increase in that of inspection. Grants to primary schools from both municipal and district funds have been increased, but there has been a reduction of R12,000 in the cost of buildings to the local cess. Fee-receipts in Berar are rising rapidly, owing to the advance of pupils throughout the province to the higher standards in which higher fees are paid. There is also a special fund for the renewal of furniture, derived from fees paid by pupils for that purpose; it received an addition of R5,000 during the year.

Coorg.—The figures are subjoined :—

	Increase. R	Decrease. R
Provincial Revenues	3,990	...
Local Funds	3,227	
Municipal Funds	283	
Fees	918	...
Other sources	577	...
TOTAL INCREASE	8,995	...

The prosperity of this small province is sufficiently shown by the foregoing figures. The increased expenditure from provincial revenues was chiefly devoted to the improvement of the Mercara Central School and the Training School, and to bettering the position of inspecting officers. The increase from local funds was applied to the provision of furniture for primary schools. There has been a considerable increase in the fee-receipts of board schools and of those under private managers.

98. Proportionate Expenditure from Public and from Private Funds.—The following table shows the different proportions in which public and private funds respectively contribute to the support of education of different classes :—

Proportionate Expenditure on Different Classes of Education from Public and from Private Funds, 1885-86.

PROVINCE.	COLLEGIATE EDUCATION.		SECONDARY EDUCATION.		PRIMARY EDUCATION.		SPECIAL EDUCATION.		INDIRECT EXPENDITURE ON EDUCATION.*		TOTAL.	
	From Public Funds.	From Private Funds.	From Public Funds.	From Private Funds.	From Public Funds.	From Private Funds.	From Public Funds.	From Private Funds.	From Public Funds.	From Private Funds.	From Public Funds.	From Private Funds.
Madras	45·2	54·8	28·5	71·5	47·8	52·2	77·	23·	65·4	34·6	46·5	53·5
Bombay	47·7	52·3	28·4	71·6	60·8	39·2	65·3	34·7	59·	41·	51·7	48·3
Bengal	65·7	34·3	25·3	74·7	25·8	74·2	65·8	34·2	87·4	12·6	40·2	59·8
North-Western Provinces and Oudh	74·	26·	50·9	49·1	86·6	13·4	92·	8·	73·1	26·9	68·8	31·2
Punjab	77·7	22·3	62·1	37·9	73·5	26·5	80·6	19·4	76·3	23·7	71·3	28·7
Central Provinces	54·	46·	69·1	30·9	76·3	23·7	100·	...	81·3	18·7	76·9	23·1
Burma	95·7	4·3	57·1	42·9	90·7	9·3	95·3	4·7	82·2	17·8	76·2	23·8
Assam	...	...	40·6	59·4	69·2	30·8	75·1	24·9	91·1	8·9	65·6	34·4
Berar	...	...	86·1	13·9	81·1	18·9	100·	...	91·6	8·4	85·7	14·3
Coorg	...	...	64·4	35·6	91·3	8·7	100·	...	82·4	17·6	79·9	20·1
	60·	39·9	35·8	64·2	51·8	48·2	74·3	25·7	74·7	25·3	53·3	46·7

* Including Universities, superintendence, scholarships, buildings and furniture and miscellaneous charges.

The last two columns of this table may be compared with the corresponding table given in paragraph 29 of Chapter II. In the latter, the contributions made to education by Native States in Bombay were included under public funds; in

on that account, it appears that there has been a decrease in the cost of education to public funds in Bombay, the North-Western Provinces, the Central Provinces, Assam and Berar; that there has been an increase in the Punjab, in Burma and in Coorg, and that in Madras and Bengal the proportion has been practically stationary with a slight decline. As in the previous year, private funds contribute the greatest share to the cost of education in Bengal and Madras, with Bombay no great way behind. Private contributions in Assam reach a higher percentage than in any of the remaining provinces, among which the Central Provinces, Coorg and Berar occupy the lowest places.

Under collegiate education Madras and Bombay stand highest, with the Central Provinces not far below. The contributions from public funds to the cost of collegiate education in Bengal are much greater than in either of the three provinces just named. Secondary education is carried on in India at much less cost to public funds than education of any other class, the proportion being little more than one-third. In Bengal it falls to one-fourth, and in Madras and Bombay the percentage is but slightly higher. In all other provinces, Assam excepted, the proportion is above one-half. The widest differences are found under primary education, in which the cost to public funds varies from 25·8 per cent. in Bengal to 86·6 per cent. in the North-Western Provinces (where primary education is practically free) and 91 per cent. in Burma and Coorg. But the constitution of primary schools differs so widely in different parts of India, that a bare comparison of this kind has little practical value. The cost of special instruction is necessarily high; and it appears that in some provinces the entire cost is met from public funds. "Indirect" educational charges are chiefly incurred on account of administration, scholarships and buildings, in the first two of which at any rate little aid can be expected from private sources. Hence public funds pay three-fourths of the cost, though in Bombay the proportion falls to three-fifths.

99. Average Cost of the Education of each Pupil.—The following is a convenient table for reference and comparison, as showing the cost to provincial revenues, to local and municipal funds, and to private sources, of educating each pupil in institutions of different standards:—

Average Cost of educating each Pupil, 1885-86.

CLASS OF INSTITUTIONS.	COST OF EACH PUPIL TO			
	Provincial Revenues.	Local and Municipal Funds.	Private Sources.	TOTAL.
	R	R	R	R
Colleges { Arts	104·4	2·2	92·4	199·0
Colleges { Professional	178·1	...	49·4	227·5
Secondary Schools	4·5	2·4	12·4	19·3
Primary Schools	·6	1·1	1·6	3·3
Training Schools	64·3	30·6	16·9	111·8
Special Schools	50·1	7·2	29·5	86·8

The table speaks for itself, and comment is unnecessary. The statement of cost is an average derived from institutions under every form of management —departmental, local or municipal, and private, whether aided or unaided. It is obvious that for these various classes the figures will differ very widely, but all the necessary information can be obtained from General Table II appended to this report.

SECTION II.—CONTROLLING AGENCIES.

100. Different Agencies of Control.—The general question of control is discussed in Chapter VII of the Commission's report; the control of indigenous and primary schools by municipal and local boards in Chapters III and IV; the transfer of departmental institutions to such boards in Chapter VIII, and the desirability of determining the position and duties of boards by legislation in Chapter XI. The work of the Education Department—that term being understood in a large sense as including all the direct agencies, public and private, for imparting instruction in this country—is subject to control and supervision of three different kinds. The first is that of departmental officers, consisting of the Director of Public Instruction in each province and of the inspecting officers of various grades subordinate to him. Secondly, statutory bodies have been created by legislative enactment for the local administration and control of certain services of public importance, education being one. In towns these bodies are the local municipalities. In rural tracts the district is generally the administrative area; and the controlling bodies are variously known as district boards or councils, rural boards, or local fund boards, the last name expressing one of their most important functions—namely, the administration for local purposes of funds locally raised. In many cases other bodies subordinate to these have also been created by law for the administration of areas smaller than the district: these are often known as local boards. Thirdly, in two provinces of India the Government is assisted in educational matters by a permanent consultative body, to which have also been entrusted certain administrative duties. These are the Punjab University and the Educational Syndicate at Rangoon; the former of which is constituted by law, while the second has been created by executive order. I exclude from the list the various educational conferences which have met from time to time in the various provinces, at the invitation of the Government, to discuss special subjects of importance. These have, strictly speaking, no controlling powers, and an account of their proceedings and of the action that has been taken on them will be more conveniently postponed to a later section of this chapter.

101. Superior Officers of the Department.—The Director of Public Instruction in each province and the superior inspecting officers usually belong to what is known as the graded educational service, the members of which are for the most part appointed in England by the Secretary of State. Of late years, indeed, it has not unfrequently happened that members of the Covenanted Civil Service have been appointed to vacancies in the office of Director of Public Instruction. Temporary vacancies have been so filled up in the Punjab and in Bombay; permanent vacancies have been so filled up in Madras and the North-Western Provinces, where in each case the office is now held by a member of that service. The superior inspectorships have been occupied by claimants from another quarter. The Education Commission recommended (VII. 12) "that it be "distinctly laid down that Native gentlemen of approved qualifications be eligible "for the post of Inspector of schools, and that they be employed in that capacity "more frequently than has been the case hitherto." In Madras it is in contemplation to increase the number of inspectorships from seven to nine, by a redistribution of the circles which are now too large. A definite proposal has been made to create an additional inspectorship for the Godavari and Kistna districts, and it is intended to confer the appointment on a native officer. On three occasions also in the year 1885-86 temporary vacancies in these appointments were filled by native deputy inspectors. In Bombay the Local Government expressed its readiness to appoint competent native gentlemen as opportunity occurred;

and in 1885-86 two out of five inspectorships were held by natives of India. On this point Mr. Lee-Warner wrote in his report for 1884-85: "We require "longer experience before we can decide on the advantages of increasing their "number. The work of an Inspector requires the full confidence of all educa- "tional agencies, some of which are very sensitive, and a genuine sympathy with "private effort. I have been much disappointed at the attitude taken up to- "wards aided schools by many of our native head-masters. It is, perhaps, hard "to require from a Hindu gentleman, proudly conscious of the superiority of his "own caste and deeply attached to the Government system, a real interest either "in the efforts of the lower orders of Hindu society or in the Muhammadan "schools; while in the later developments of educational progress he lacks that "personal acquaintance with the technical or special schools of Europe which "helps an Inspector to encourage and to guide education in new channels. At "the same time the experiment is wisely being made; and if the difficulties of "Native Inspectors are systematically appreciated, I trust that it will in the end "be successful." The complaint of want of sympathy with aided effort has not been made in Bengal, where both primary and secondary education are mostly undertaken by private enterprise, and where, as in Bombay, two native officers have been appointed inspectors of schools and promoted to the superior graded service. In Bengal, again, joint-inspectorships have been created, one for each · of its nine divisions; and these appointments, the duties of which closely re- semble those discharged by circle inspectors, are held in every case by natives of India. In the North-Western Provinces and Oudh proposals of a more thorough-going character have been made. It is in contemplation to reduce four of the inspectorships now held by European officers in the superior grades, and to substitute for them ten native assistant inspectors on lower salaries. The native inspector of the Rohilkhand Division retired in 1885-86 "after long "and creditable service in the Department;" and a native inspector has since been appointed to the Benares Division. In the Punjab a native gentleman (in succession to a European Officer) has been permanently appointed Inspector of the Delhi Circle on the graded staff, while another has officiated for lengthened terms in a similar capacity. In the opinion of the Local Government there appears to be no reason why native gentlemen should not be generally em- ployed as inspectors (the Inspector of European schools apart), and it is believed that the prospect of such employment will do much to attract the best men to the Department and to keep them there. In the Central Provinces the same principle is accepted, as it is stated that native gentlemen have often officiated as inspectors and have also held the appointment permanently; while a native of India has long been the Director of Public Instruction in Berar.

102. Subordinate Officers of the Department.—These consist of deputy or district inspectors, one for each district, who are in all cases natives of India; and officers subordinate to these, but of the same class and general qualifications, who are known by various names, of which that of sub-deputy inspector may be taken as the type. Below these, again, there are in some pro- vinces men of a quite inferior status, whose duty it is to inspect a limited circle of village schools, and sometimes to instruct the schoolmasters in their duties. Such are the inspecting schoolmasters in Madras; the circle pundits, inspecting pundits, and chief gurus in Bengal. These are in nearly all cases men of the schoolmaster class, who have proved their practical capacity in managing and teaching elementary schools. With regard to the subordinate inspecting staff, the Commission recommended (VII. 9) "that native and other local energy be relied "upon to foster and manage all education as far as possible, but that the results "must be tested by departmental agency, and that therefore the inspecting "staff be increased so as to be adequate to the requirements of each province," and again (VII. 10), "that the remuneration of the subordinate inspecting "officers be reconsidered in each province, with due regard to their enhanced "duties and responsibilities." The Government of India remarked that "as the "Department withdraws from pushing its own institutions, its machinery for "inspection will require strengthening," since a grant-in-aid system postulates a thorough inspection of all institutions brought under it. On these points a general complaint is expressed that the inspecting agency is still far too weak for efficiency, though endeavours have been made in many provinces to remedy the defect, so far as the state of the funds has allowed. In Madras and the Central Provinces something has been done towards improving the pay of inspecting officers; in Bombay and Berar a small increase in their number has been effected. Of the Punjab it was reported in 1884 that the inspecting staff was the weakest part of the educational machinery of the province, and quite insufficient for the full and proper performance of even its existing duties. The staff has now been strengthened; but not, as Colonel Holroyd reports, "to so great an extent "as was contemplated when liberal assistance from the imperial revenues was "anticipated." The increase, however, though numerically small, is important, as it greatly improves the prospects of district inspectors. The number of assistant inspectors has been raised from four to seven; these appointments are invariably held by natives, and all who hold them may hope to become inspectors. District inspectors have also been appointed to all districts but two. In Assam the number of sub-inspectors has been increased from 14 in 1881-82 to 21; and there is now one these of officers to each sub-division, with an average of 73 schools under his inspection. In Burma the necessary proposals have been postponed to a time of greater financial prosperity. In Bengal the Director of Public Instruction wrote in 1882: "If the number of sub-inspectors in those "districts in which primary schools abound were doubled and even quadrupled, "it would still be impossible to secure such frequent inspection as would seem "to be required." In 1884 the Government of Bengal expressed the opinion that were it not for the cheaper agency of inspecting pundits and chief gurus which had been employed in Bengal with pronounced and increasing success, the existing staff of 175 sub-inspectors would have to be increased to something like 600, since each sub-inspector had an average of 387 schools to look after. As it was, the smallest increase that could be regarded as satisfactory could not be put below 80 additional officers. It was also very desirable to increase the minimum pay of this class from R30 to R50 a month. The last improvement has since been effected in all but a few cases. The proposal to augment the staff could, on financial grounds, be only partially carried out; but in 1886 ten more sub-inspectors were appointed. These changes involved an increased expenditure of over R18,000 a year.

103. Code of Rules for Inspectors.—The Commission recommended (VI. 14) that "in every province a code be drawn up for the guidance of inspect- "ing officers." Miscellaneous instructions on the subject of inspection had been from time to time issued by Local Governments and heads of departments, but it was believed that inspection would be rendered much more thorough and efficient, if these scattered orders and traditional practices were embodied in a code. Such a code, it was recommended, should prescribe in detail the routine which an officer should follow in visiting a school, the manner in which his examination should be conducted, the points to which his attention should be directed apart from the examination of scholars, and the form in which his inspection report should be drawn up. This recommendation has been generally and readily accepted. In the Central Provinces and Berar such a code already existed. In Assam the existing code was to be re-written and enlarged. In all the remaining provinces the proposal was cordially approved. The preparation of a code of this character is a work of time, but it appears that everywhere steps are being taken to carry out the project.

* At the same time, it is not only a code that is required if inspection is to be efficient and thorough and sympathetic; if it is to be a help and a guide to schoolmasters, and not a mere criticism, sometimes harsh and unintelligent, of their work. As an illustration of what inspection too often is, and of what it may become in the hands of an officer who knows his business, I quote the following extract from a report by Mr. Deighton, inspector of schools in the North-Western Provinces:—

"I have already referred to the unintelligent system of examination in "practice among the subordinate inspecting officers, by which I was so much "struck during my recent tour. Some of these officers were of course better "than others; but with the large majority of them examination was a lifeless "and wooden thing, and it was lifeless and wooden not in respect to any one "subject, but in respect to every subject, whatever its character. Literature, "history, geography; works practical like the sanitary primer, and works imagi- "native such as the *Ramayana* or the *Bostan*, were all treated with a treadmill "monotony that could not possibly awaken the slightest interest in the exami- "nee, nor, I should have thought, have satisfied the dullest examiner. If it was "literature, the most usual proceeding was to ask nothing more than the mean- "ing of a string of words, the answers being received with much the same "appreciation, whether they were right or wrong. The idea of trying to find "out whether the boy had understood what he had been reading, whether he "had any conception of the general gist of a book or a chapter of a book, whe- "ther he could accurately render a phrase or a peculiar idiom, whether on any "point he had acquired information which might be of benefit to him, whether "he could make use of the vocabulary he had acquired, whether, in short, he "was an intelligent human being or the merest of parrots, seemed to be quite "beyond the examiner's care or ability. If history is the subject, the date of a "king's accession, the number of his sons, the family he belonged to, the list of "names forming the dynasty of which he was a member, the battles he had "fought, the misfortunes he had suffered,—such details to the ordinary De- "puty Inspector constitute history. To him it is a veritable book of kings, and "humanity of any lower grade seems worth no consideration. Even with this "limitation, it might be expected that the examiner should direct some atten- "tion to the objects which these kings had in view, the causes which led to "their battles, their treatment of their subjects, their character as men, the "nature of their laws, the reforms they introduced, the sources of their wealth, "their attitude towards different religions, the public works they executed, the "ways in which they used their revenues, their system of government, and a "hundred other topics of interest It might also be expected that he should "concern himself with things lower than the divinity of a king; that he should "recognise the existence of poets, philosophers, statesmen; that he should have "something to ask and to tell of the changes of various kinds that have from "time to time taken place in the condition of the people; that some reference "should be made to the material progress of the country; that attention should "be drawn to the numerous nationalities that constitute such a geographical ex- "pression as India, to the admixture of different peoples, different customs, "different religions, as a result of conquests, immigrations, commerce; that "something should be said of the characteristics of the inhabitants of different "regions as affected by climate, by physical conformation of country, by descent; "that some effort should be made to bring down history from the clouds and "unreality, and present it to a boy's understanding as a matter with which he "has a real concern. But if history is treated in a way which looks as though

"the intention was to make it nauseous, I am not sure that geography does not
"fare worse. As a rule, an examiner, when that examiner is a Deputy In-
"spector, is satisfied if a boy can enumerate the chief cities, rivers, mountains,
"bays and lakes of a country: if he can also point them out on a map, the sum-
"mit of excellence is reached. Anything that creates an inquring interest, any
"thing that makes geography more than a list of names and a canvas picture,
"seems a matter not dreamt of in the Deputy Inspector's philosophy. What
"manner of men they are who inhabit the various divisions of an empire or of
"an hemisphere as shown in that picture matters nothing; what the race to
"which they belong, what the climate they enjoy, for what they are specially
"renowned; of what kind the products, the manufactures, the sources of wealth
"of a country; what the manner of life, the customs, the character of religion,
"the national peculiarities, the form of government, the population; whether a
"people is highly civilized or sunk in the lowest state of barbarism; how the
"shape and figure of a tract of country has been affected by the action of rivers
"or the convulsions of nature; from what causes one country has become com-
"mercial, another relies mostly on its manufactures, a third on its capacities
"for producing grain supplies—such topics, it seems, are outside the scope of
"examination. I am quite aware that most of the manuals in our schools are
"to the last degree barren, that a book like the *Áiná Táríkh Nama*, or the
"Middle Class Geography, is but an epitomidion of an epitome, the merest
"scaffolding, the skeleton of a body that needs to be clothed with flesh; and for
"this, as for other reasons, I have often thought that no history or geography
"should be taught in any but the highest class of our vernacular schools. I
"am also aware that the ability and learning to be purchased for R8 or R10 a
"month cannot be of a very high order. But the Deputy Inspectors cost us a
"good deal more than this sum, and are or ought to be far above the capacity
"of the teachers whose schools they inspect. They have read and, we will
"hope, thought about something more than is contained in the books put into
"the hands of a village schoolboy; and I am convinced that if their examina-
"tions were of a more intelligent character, the teaching they test would im-
"prove proportionately."

104. District and Municipal Boards.—A general review of the powers, duties, and resources of local boards is given in paragraphs 214, 660, and 661 of the Commission's report. It was there shown that there was a marked absence of uniformity in the treatment of local rates throughout India. In Madras, Bombay, and Bengal the local fund income was wholly at the disposal of district boards, and they had full control over their unexpended balances. In other provinces the proceeds of local rates were first credited to provincial revenues, from which a part was afterwards allotted to education; and should the boards have failed to spend their whole assignments within the year, all unexpended balances lapsed to the provincial treasury. Bombay, again, was the only province in which a fixed share of the local cess was appropriated by statutory rule to education. In other parts of India, except Bengal, education received whatever balance could be spared for its wants after other claims had been satisfied. In Bengal education received no portion of the local rate, which was by law devoted wholly to roads and communications. The proposal to introduce an educational rate into Bengal has been met by the contention that private liberality had altogether taken its place, and that the people voluntarily contributed to the advancement of education at least as much as a cess could be expected to produce.

With regard to municipalities the law was everywhere permissive, and education was a legitimate but not an imperative charge on municipal income. The result was that municipalities taken as a whole throughout India contributed to the cost of education a share altogether disproportionate to the extent of their resources. In 1882 they had been relieved of all police charges on the express understanding that they should devote a larger portion of their income to education among other local wants. There was, therefore, a special ground for the demand that municipalities should thenceforward take a much more active and liberal part in the promotion of education. A further point demanded attention. In some provinces schools within municipal limits were maintained largely at the expense of the district rates, and it was complained that the towns were thus allowed to encroach unduly on a provision that was primarily intended for the extension of education in rural tracts.

105. Recommendations of the Commission as to District and Municipal Boards.—The recommendations of the Commission under this head were chiefly determined by the considerations adduced in the last paragraph. The alleged defects being admitted, the question arose whether legislation was needed to remedy them, or whether the desired end could not be secured by executive orders without legislation. The Commission declared (paragraph 651) "that "executive orders of clear import and general application issued from 1854 to the "present time have failed more or less in all provinces to ensure uniform at- "tention to broad principles presented for general guidance," and were therefore of opinion that legislation was the only way by which the policy of Government could be made to live and last. The first recommendation proposed was of a general character, and related to primary instruction:—"That an attempt be "made to secure the fullest possible provision for, and extension of, primary "education by legislation suited to the circumstances of each province." (IV. 4.) In a later portion of the same chapter, and again in Chapter XI, the question was narrowed and defined by a series of recommendations urging the necessity of settling, by special legislation directed to that end, the educational duties and powers of district and municipal boards. The Commission refrained from expressing an opinion whether the school-boards to be constituted for educational purposes should be the town-boards and local fund committees, or whether they should be sub-committees of those boards. They proposed that the duties of local and municipal boards in controlling or assisting schools under their supervision should be regulated by local enactments suited to each province (XI. 1); that school-boards should be established for the management and control of schools in every municipal or rural area constituted for the purposes of local self-government (XI. 2), and in particular that they should exercise general control over primary school expenditure (IV. 32); that both local and municipal boards should keep a separate school fund (IV. 29); that the Local Government should declare from time to time of what funds the school fund should consist (XI. 4; IV. 30, 31); that a minimum share of the general local fund, to be fixed for each province, should be appropriated to education and paid into the school fund (IV. 31); that a fair proportion of municipal revenues, to be fixed by the Local Government for each municipality, should be in like manner paid into the municipal school fund (IV. 30); that if schools in municipalities were supported from the district fund, this should be done by means of a fixed contribution to the municipal fund (IV. 30c); that each fund should be re-credited with its own unexpended balances (IV. 30f, 31f), and that the Local Government should declare what proportion of the school fund should be assigned to any class of education (XI. 4). Other recommendations dealt with the exclusion, at the discretion of the Local Government, of any class of schools (other than primary schools) from the control of the boards, and for the independence of schools under private managers (XI. 3); with the duties of the boards in registering, aiding, or maintaining schools (XI. 5); with the appointment of teachers (XI. 6); with appeals against the orders of boards (XI. 7) and with the duties of Government and of the boards jointly in securing a due provision, within each rural or municipal area, of schools of every class (XI. 8).

106. Action taken on the Foregoing Recommendations.—In the opinion of the Commission, therefore, special Educational Acts were necessary to give permanent effect to their recommendations. It happened, however, that about this very time every Provincial Government was engaged in carrying out, by means of legislation, the principles of local self-government that had recently been declared by the Government of India. After consulting the Provincial Governments on the recommendations of the Commission, the Supreme Government observed, in the Resolution of the 23rd October 1884:—" The Local "Governments appear to be unanimous in deprecating any special educational "legislation at the present time. Under all the Acts for settling the conditions "of local self-government in municipalities and rural tracts, provision more or "less complete has been made for education; and the wish is generally expressed "that each province should be left to work on the lines laid down in the local laws, "and that any further legislative action should be deferred until it be seen "whether the results are satisfactory or the reverse. The Governor General "in Council is content for the present to accept in this matter the conclusions "of the Local Governments, in reliance upon their hearty co-operation in the "complete application of the principles now laid down by the Government of "India with the approval of the Secretary of State." The district and municipal boards were therefore ordinarily to form the school board for the area under their jurisdiction, with or without special educational sub-committees of their own, and with or without local committees for the management of individual schools or groups of schools. The important thing was that the boards should be required to give full effect to the policy of Government, and to work the grant-in-aid rules equitably and liberally, so as at once to maintain the essential character of the Government system and to encourage the development of private enterprise in education. The relations of the boards to the Department and the position and authority of inspecting officers were to be determined by each Local Government, having regard to the advancement or backwardness of each local area and to the character of the board that administered it. The local enactments did not generally constitute a separate school fund, and it would therefore be necessary for each Local Government to come to a clear understanding with the boards as to the provision to be made for education and the due appropriation of the Government subsidy.

In the paragraphs that follow some account will be given of the action that has been taken in each province of India in the direction of confirming the position and enlarging the powers of district and municipal boards in the control of education. It will be seen that the position of these bodies, especially of district boards, has been distinctly advanced in the interval. In the majority of provinces a definite share of the local fund income has been appropriated to education, not indeed by legislative enactment, but more or less effectually by executive order; and while the interests of primary education have been very generally secured, the expenditure of the fund on education of a higher class has been in some instances restricted by rule. Local bodies have been vested with complete control over the funds which they administer, including (in every province but one) their unexpended balances. Speaking generally, and exceptional cases apart, the Department has altogether retired in favour of the boards from the direct control of primary, and in a less degree of secondary, schools; and large powers, with corresponding grants in many cases from provincial revenues, have been transferred to the boards for the purpose of aiding schools under **private management. The maintenance of a continuous educational policy has been secured, not only by laying down certain general rules and principles** which the boards are to observe, but in most cases by prescribing for their guidance a detailed code for the distribution of grants-in-aid, as well as by the provision that no change of system is to be introduced without the sanction of superior authority for good cause shown. Where they had not the necessary agency already at their disposal, the boards have been furnished with a staff of inspecting officers to assist them in the discharge of their new duties. With regard to municipalities, the Local Governments have with one or two exceptions, expressed reluctance to compel these bodies, by executive order, to devote a certain minimum share of their income to education; and while they have not hesitated to express their wishes and expectations in this matter, they have for the most part been content to leave it to the municipalities concerned to fix the amount of their educational grants; in the full belief that the boards would of their own motion make adequate provision for the maintenance of schools, and that a policy of compulsion was both unnecessary and inadvisable. Still, the position and reponsibilities of the boards, whether district or municipal, and the relations in which they stand to the Department, are not so uniform that they can be covered by a general description, and in the following paragraphs a brief sketch will be given of the position which local boards now occupy in each province of India. The time has not yet come to form an estimate of the results of the policy of local self-government as applied to education.

107. District and Municipal Boards in Madras.—The educational position of district boards in Madras is determined by the Local Boards Act, V of 1884, and by the District Municipalities Act IV of the same year. The creation of a special school board was not approved, and education is administered by the district or municipal board within each area. But the Acts admit of the appointment of separate committees for separate services, so that a special educational agency can be constituted wherever it is thought necessary. Under the provisions of the Local Boards Act there is not, as formerly, any special tax levied for educational purposes, nor has any separate school-fund been created. But each district board (as also each municipality) is expected to spend upon education about one-sixth, roughly, of its revenue derived from taxation, in addition to all strictly educational receipts, such as school fees, subscriptions, endowments, &c. The amount allotted from the rates by a district board to education is expended on the maintenance of its own schools, in aiding schools under private management (a much larger number), on the training of teachers, and on inspection. District boards are held directly responsible for lower primary education only, including standards I to III. The rules framed under the Act lay down that "the provision of improved elemen-"tary education for boys is the chief duty of the district board, and to its "promotion a very large proportion of the funds allotted to education must "be devoted." The boards are not made responsible in the same way for upper primary or for secondary schools, for girls' schools, or for training and technical schools. When district boards maintain such schools, they are entitled to receive grants from provincial funds under the grant-in-aid Code, on the same terms as are offered to private managers. If, for example, a district board maintains a middle school, it draws from its own funds the entire cost of the lower primary department, but receives a grant-in-aid under the code for the upper primary and lower secondary classes. When Government middle schools have been transferred to district boards, they have generally been transferred on these terms. The authority of local boards is limited by the provision that all money expended in aiding schools under private management must be given in accordance with the rules of the grant-in-aid Code. The boards are also required to consult educational officers upon any proposals they may make for the establishment of new schools (other than primary schools) or for fresh educational expenditure, and generally to conform to the rules prescribed by the Department, *e.g.*, for the appointment of teachers. Under the District Municipalities Act, no separate school fund is created. Municipalities are required to bear the cost not only of primary, but also (except in the town of Madras) of lower secondary schools within municipal limits; and a special section of the Act makes the grant-in-aid code binding upon those bodies. Care is however taken that the interests of primary education are fully secured. The new Local Fund and Municipal Acts lay particular stress on the importance of fostering and developing this stage of instruction, and it is at any rate clear that by far the largest share of educational outlay from local funds is devoted to primary education. By the Madras Town Act the Municipal Commissioners are required to provide for the elementary education of the poorer classes only, while even in this respect their duties and obligations are not defined. It is complained that the Madras Municipality, which should take the lead among the municipalities of the Presidency, is almost debarred by the terms of the Act from making anything like the same general provision for education as similar bodies, poorer and in every way less advanced, are elsewhere required by law to make.

In accordance with the recommendations of the Education Commission, the Government of Madras has almost completely retired from the direct control of primary and secondary schools. All the departmental schools of these two classes have been transferred to district boards or municipalities, with the exception of schools in the Agency Tracts, which (it is stated) must continue to be maintained from provincial funds, and of four high schools for which the arrangements are not yet mature. Lower secondary (or middle) schools in rural circles were handed over to district boards in October 1884, on the terms specified above. The Government high schools at Chicacole, Cuddapah, Kurnool, Bellary, Palghat, Tellicherry and Cannanore have since that date been transferred to the management of the local municipalities, either on the salary-grant system, or on the understanding that Government should bear the net cost of the highest departments of the transferred institutions. With the exception of a special school for Muhammadans in Madras, there remains under the management of the Department only one high school situated within a municipality, and even this it is intended either to close or to transfer. The college at Salem was also transferred to municipal management, and received aid from the Department on the salary-grant system.

108. Expenditure by District and Municipal Boards in Madras. The sum expended from local rates on education in 1885-86 was R6,12,741 against R6,36,064 in the previous year, the reduction having taken place in grants to aided institutions. On their own schools, numbering 1,292, of which 1,150 were primary, district boards expended R2,53,003, of which R1,67,146 was for primary schools and school-buildings, and the balance for education of a higher kind (including R28,644 for 106 secondary schools and R50,981 for 33 training schools), in consideration of which they received grants-in-aid amounting to R52,128. They maintained three medical schools at a cost to local rates of R5,733, and a further cost of R21,974 was incurred in grants to medical schools under the Department. Institutions under private management are aided in accordance with the provisions of the departmental grant-in-aid code. On schools of this class the district boards expended R2,59,100, all but R12,000 of which were devoted to primary schools. The cost of inspection was R60,738.

The municipal expenditure from the rates on education was R1,75,499 against R1,66,211 in the previous year. Municipalities are now required to bear the cost of lower secondary as well as of primary education. These bodies maintained 87 primary schools at a cost to municipal rates of R22,520, and 31 secondary schools at a cost of R5,447; the fee receipts and provincial grants being nearly sufficient to cover the whole expenditure in the latter class of schools. The Salem College cost the local municipality R1,027, and the municipality of Madras maintained a training college at a cost of R580. On primary and secondary schools under private management the municipalities throughout the province spent R64,846 and R39,973 respectively. They also contributed R15,928 to the cost of medical schools, and R1,259 to training schools maintained by local boards.

109. District and Municipal Boards in Bombay.—In Bombay the Education Department is understood to concern itself but little with the direct control of elementary schools. Almost all the primary schools and more than two-thirds of the secondary schools under public management are now managed and maintained by local and municipal boards; though the controlling functions of these bodies, apart from the provision of funds, are sometimes described as being merely nominal, or at the best as limited to giving advice, while the actual administration of the schools rests as before with the officers of the Department. Committees have also been established for the local control of individual schools; and though occasionally described as apathetic, indifferent or useless, they are as often said to show signs of genuine interest in the work entrusted to them. Various estimates are formed of the results of transferring schools to municipal control. In great cities no harm is apprehended; but when the population is small and the income limited, there is room to doubt whether the transfer will be beneficial to the schools. The reports speak of "a monotonous record of decrease in the attendance," of "reckless administration," of "action characterised by haste or intemperance;" though the picture is often painted in brighter colours. Where the members of the Committee are not enlightened enough to take an intelligent interest in the management of the schools, they remain practically under the management of the Department, though the control of the inspecting officers is circuitous instead of direct. In general, the municipalities have accepted the change in a passive spirit, and will need close supervision and frequent interference.

The legal position of local and municipal boards respectively is now settled by Acts I and II of 1884. These Acts apply to all parts of the province outside the Presidency town. In Bombay itself no necessary provision is made under the existing Act of 1872 for the establishment of a local school system directed and maintained by the municipality. Schools, both primary and secondary, are maintained or supported by the municipality under that Act, but the application of its funds to such purposes is not enforced by law. A new Municipal Bill is, however, under consideration, by which it is proposed to transfer many of the departmental schools to municipal control, making the maintenance of primary schools compulsory on the town, that of secondary schools optional. Act I of 1884 (the Local Self-Government Act) reconstituted the old local fund committees as local boards. The funds which were at their disposal for educational purposes remained apparently the same as before—namely, (1) one-third of the local cess, less the amount levied within municipal limits; (2) the fees, subscriptions, and other assets of schools; (3) the provincial grant, which for many years had been fixed at R2,58,900. Government reserved the power, as in the similar case of municipal boards, of framing a Code for regulating the conduct of education by these bodies, and of imposing conditions to which the payment of grants-in-aid should be subject. After any local board had been constituted, it could no longer continue to maintain schools within municipal areas, though it was empowered to make grants-in-aid to such schools, with the sanction of Government, whenever it was satisfied that the schools provided for the needs of pupils outside the municipal area. Act II of 1884 threw upon municipalities in a definite form the duty of providing for elementary education within the municipal area. It amended the District Municipal Act of 1873, which provided that it should be the duty of every municipality to make adequate provision within the municipal district for establishing and maintaining middle class and primary schools. Under Act II of 1884 the Government took power to define what an 'adequate provision' was, and to ensure that the provision should be adequate by declaring the minimum sum that was to be devoted to education. Every municipality was therefore made responsible by law for the establishment and the adequate maintenance of the whole system of primary and middle education within the municipal area, quite apart from any aid which Government might render towards that object. The municipality was also empowered, though not compelled, to make provision for high schools. It was further enacted that the extent of the independent authority of any municipality in respect of public education, and its relations with the Education Department, should from time to time be prescribed by Government. On the other hand, Government was under no legal obligation to contribute to municipal school funds, either under the Municipal Act or under the grant-in-aid rules. The aid of Government was defined as being "entirely voluntary and "discretional, and subject to such conditions as Government may think fit to "impose in the interests of education."

But what the Government was not compelled to do by the Act, that it has nevertheless undertaken to do in the interests of education and in pursuance of the policy recommended by the Commission. It has re-adjusted the relations between local boards and municipalities in respect of the maintenance of schools within municipal limits, and it has undertaken to make large grants to municipalities and largely increased grants to local boards, so as to enable those bodies to discharge more effectually their educational duties. With regard to the first point, the Education Commission declared (paragraph 208) that an undue share of the local cess was spent in towns, the municipalities generally neglecting the duty of establishing primary schools within their limits. By Resolution No. 1204, dated the 15th July 1884, the Bombay Government restored the balance of educational expenditure. It pointed out that while the municipalities contributed to the support of schools within municipal limits only R1,14,685, in which were included the fee-receipts in those schools, the contributions from municipal funds, and the share of the local cess levied within municipal limits —in fact, every receipt for which they could claim credit, they drew from the district funds for the maintenance of those schools no less a sum than R3,38,232. It decided that the municipalities must surrender to the district funds the balance of R2,23,547, less the amount of the provincial grant to which they might fairly be held entitled, or about R31,000. The cost of municipal schools, amounting to R3,38,232, was therefore to be borne by the municipalities concerned, without imposing any burden on the district rates. To enable them to meet the additional charge thus thrown upon them without bearing too heavily on municipal resources, the Government undertook to come to their aid with a grant of one-third of the total expenditure, or, in round numbers, R1,12,000, which would cover and include the sum of R31,000 to which they could put forward a reasonable claim as their share of the original provincial grant. The remainder of the cost (namely, R2,26,232) was to be borne by municipalities, that amount including their existing contribution of R1,14,685. They would therefore be involved in a further expenditure of R1,11,547, a sum equal to about 4 per cent. of the municipal income. The contract thus made with the municipalities was to run for five years, and might, like the provincial contract, be revised at the end of that time. Meanwhile, the municipalities were bound to maintain an adequate provision of schools; and it might happen in any given case that the existing provision was not adequate and required to be supplemented. This supplementary provision might be made, within the terms of the contract, by a more economical distribution of grants, by increasing the fees, and by taking the cheaper indigenous schools into the system. But if money were spent beyond the terms of the contract in extending education, the Government of Bombay would not insist upon the letter of the agreement, but would be ready to afford additional aid in proportion to the amount so spent, until the contract came up for revision.

If however, the Resolution went on to declare, the municipalities were to be encouraged by a provincial grant equal to one-third of the cost of their primary schools, it was but equitable that equal favour should be shown to the district educational funds. The whole of the existing grant of R2,58,900 would be left at their disposal, and they would also recover from municipalities, under the arrangements described, the sum of R2,23,547 which rightly belonged to the district funds. The increased funds thus secured for district education from the cess-income amounted to R8,59,496; and the Government expressed its desire to deal out to district boards the same terms as had been offered to municipalities, by giving them, when the resources of the Government permitted, a grant of one-half that amount, or R4,29,748. This involved an increase over the existing provincial grant of R1,70,000 in round numbers, and that addition the Government declared its willingness to make. These liberal measures involved a total increase of R2,82,000 in the grants to district funds and municipalities. A beginning was at once made with the grant of R1,12,000 to municipalities. As to district boards, it was believed that the additional grants could not be utilised all at once; but the grant to these bodies was raised in 1884-85 from R2,59,000 to R2,72,000, and on the urgent representation of Mr. Lee-Warner, the officiating Director, it was still further raised, by the addition of a lakh of rupees, to R3,72,000 in the budget for 1885-86. For the same year a further grant of R28,000 was made to municipalities towards the expense of opening new schools. It may be mentioned here that an equal sum was at the same time sanctioned for result-grants payable by district boards to indigenous schools, and that the educational grant was increased in other ways, outside the control of local and municipal boards, by R1,03,000. Thus the total addition made to the educational estimates from provincial grants in 1885-86 amounted to R3,84,000. The grants were coupled with the condition that practical instruction and training in handicrafts or in the rudiments of agricultural science should, wherever possible, be introduced and encouraged.

√ **110. Expenditure by District and Municipal Boards in Bombay.**—Owing to the re-adjustment of expenditure described in the last paragraph, by which the charges incurred on schools in municipalities devolved upon municipal boards, the expenditure from the local cess decreased from R9,10,792 in 1884-85 to R6,85,153 in 1885-86, while the municipal expenditure on education increased to a similar though smaller extent. The total expenditure from local and municipal rates together fell from R10,08,700 to R9,27,152; the loss of R81,000 being nearly made up by increased provincial grants, amounting to R75,000, to schools maintained by local and municipal boards. In other words, the amount spent on these schools taken together remained nearly constant, while the increased provincial grants set free a corresponding sum for the extension of education from cess-funds, which, however, had not yet had time to take effect. This being understood, the expenditure of 1885-86 may be thus analysed. District boards expended on their own schools—numbering 4,057, of which 4,008 were primary—the sum of R6,24,608, of which R44,652 was for buildings and furniture, the provincial grants-in-aid to these schools amounting to R2,90,581. They gave grants of R21,576 to departmental institutions, chiefly training schools; of R16,304 to primary schools maintained by municipal boards; and of R22,665 to institutions under private management, half the amount being given to secondary schools.

Schools maintained by municipal boards increased, as above explained, from 24 to 641, and the expenditure on them out of municipal rates from R4,456 to R1,70,851. Among them were 64 secondary schools, involving a charge on the rates of R15,203. Further sums of R22,478 and R18,254 were spent from the same source in grants, chiefly primary, to local board schools and to schools under private management respectively. The total expenditure on education from municipal rates increased from R97,908 to R2,42,000.

111. District and Municipal Boards in Bengal.—District boards in Bengal were constituted by the Bengal Local Self-Government Act III of 1885, and they began to come into existence in selected districts towards the close of the year 1886. In the following year the Act was extended to 33 districts in Bengal. There seems, however, to be some uncertainty as to the extent of the authority with which these bodies are entrusted. Under section 62 of the Act every district board " shall be charged with, and be responsible for, the main-"tenance and management of all primary and middle schools under public man-"agement within the district,"/schools for Europeans being excepted; and under section 63 it " may with its own consent be charged with, and made respon-"sible for, the maintenance and management of any other school or class of "schools within the district."/ Section 65 empowers the Lieutenant-Governor to make grants to district boards " for expenditure on the improvement of primary "schools under private management." Section 64 authorises the formation of joint committees, composed of members delegated partly by district boards and partly by municipal commissioners, for the maintenance and management of any high English school under public management situated within a municipality. Under section 138 power is taken by the Lieutenant-Governor to make rules, consistent with the Act, regulating the maintenance and management of schools under the sections just quoted. Before adverting to these rules it is necessary to recall the definition of " public schools " and of " schools under "public management" adopted by the Government of India in the Resolution of the 29th October 1883. According to that Resolution a " public school " is one in which the course of study conforms to the standards prescribed by the Department or the University; while a " school under public management " is one which is under the direct management of Government, or of officers or committees acting on behalf of Government, or of boards exercising statutory powers. Conversely, an institution managed by private persons or associations is an institution "under private management." The rules, however, attach entirely different meanings to these well-known terms. Under Rule 104 a school under public management is defined to mean a school " in which the course of study "conforms to the standards prescribed by the Department of Public Instruction "or by the University;" in other words, a " school under public management " is identified with a " public school " as defined by the Government of India, which may be either under public or under private management. It is not quite clear what was intended by giving to the most important educational term in the rules a sense at variance with that which alone it can bear in the Act. The object appears to have been so to enlarge the definition of board schools as to be able to make over to local bodies a charge of sufficient magnitude; though the exceptional development of aided enterprise in the primary and middle school system of Bengal made it antecedently impossible that the number of board schools—that is of Government schools transferred to local management—should approach the number of such schools in other provinces. However that may be, this apparent inconsistency between the rules and the Act makes it difficult to say how far the jurisdiction of district boards in Bengal really extends. As they stand, however, the rules give district boards authority in different degrees over (1) middle schools transferred from the control of the Department, (2) grant-in-aid schools, subject to any exceptions which the Lieutenant-Governor may make, (3) primary schools; all schools in municipalities and primary schools situated in Government estates being, however, exempted from the control of the boards. (1) Over transferred middle schools the boards have complete authority; they may appoint and dismiss masters, determine the class of each school, establish new schools, and transfer or abolish any existing schools. (2) With regard to the grant-in-aid schools over which they are to exercise control, the boards are to occupy precisely the same position as the Department has held. The rules under which grants are to be given from the funds placed at the disposal of each district board are defined in detail; and the control of the board is limited by the proviso that they shall not interfere in the management of any grant-in-aid school further than is necessary to ascertain whether the conditions of the grant are being complied with. (3) District boards are also charged with the duty of maintaining and managing all primary schools under public management within the district, and of determining the rates of stipends or rewards payable to the teachers and pupils of such schools, in accordance with rules from time to time prescribed by Government. Local boards are also constituted for smaller areas than the district. As the agents of, and subject to control by, the district board, they exercise authority over such matters as may be transferred to them by that body. Again, any village or group of villages may be constituted a Union and placed under a Union Committee, which in its turn acts as the agent, and is subject to the control of, the local board, and is specially charged with the maintenance and management of primary schools within the union.

The new Municipal Bill for Calcutta is now under the consideration of the Bengal Council. It contains a provision allowing the municipality to spend money upon primary and technical education. The position of municipalities throughout the province is defined in sections 32 and 69 of the Bengal Municipal Act III of 1884. Section 32 provides that any school within a municipality, not being private property or the property of a religious institution or society, may, by order of the Local Government, be vested in the municipal commissioners. Section 69 provides that the commissioners may apply the municipal fund to the construction and repair of school-houses and the establishment and maintenance of schools either wholly or by means of grants-in-aid. The section, it will be seen, is merely permissive, as was the corresponding section in the old Act. In reference to the absence of any fixed provision for education, the Government of Bengal observed: "It may be that legislation sup-"plementary to the Municipal Act may have to be undertaken at some future "time on this point; but there are difficulties in the independence which muni-"cipalities claim in the distribution of their funds, and for the present at least it "must be left to executive action to press for a proper attention to the education-"al wants in each municipal jurisdiction." By the orders of the Local Government certain educational charges have accordingly been laid upon municipalities in Bengal in lieu of the police charges of which they were relieved in 1882. The burden of supporting departmental middle schools situated in municipal limits has been shifted from Government to the municipality concerned; and it is proposed to require the municipality to pay also a fair share of the cost of the Government high school at head-quarters, the share being roughly determined by the relative proportion in which pupils come from the town itself and from the district generally. But beyond the provision of funds, municipalities in Bengal have not yet been invested with the control or management of schools situated within limits. All such schools are retained under the management of the Department.

112. Expenditure by District and Municipal Boards in Bengal.—It has been explained that the Local Self-Government Act had not come into force up to the close of 1885-86. A small sum of R5,000 or R6,000 was spent in each year from local rates in non-regulation districts, but that was all. In the following year the educational charges defined in the last paragraph, together with others for dispensaries and medical relief, were transferred to the boards. To enable them to meet these charges, the Government placed at their disposal, first, the income from district pounds and ferries, and secondly a lump sum sufficient to balance the account. In future years the Government assignment was never to fall short of that lump sum, and might, if the state of the provincial finances permitted, exceed it; and the boards were also declared entitled to any increase in the sources of income transferred to them, as well as to the disposal of their balances. Within such limits was the further progress of education under the control of the boards confined.

The expenditure from municipal rates increased from R71,412 in 1884-85 to R81,659 in 1885-86. A share amounting to about R45,000 of this expenditure was spent in grants to secondary schools, and R17,000 on primary schools. Municipal boards themselves maintained 48 schools, 16 of which were secondary, costing R9,000; 30 primary, costing R3,000, and two industrial at a cost of R800.

113. District and Municipal Boards in the North-Western Provinces and Oudh.—District boards were constituted in these provinces by Act XIV of 1883, in supersession of the old district school committees. The changes introduced by that Act, which came into force on the 1st April 1885, had in most points been anticipated by the executive action of the Local Government in transferring to these bodies many of the duties and functions now devolving on them by law, but up to that time discharged by Government officials. It was claimed that under the new system of local self-government the authority and the financial responsibility of local boards in educational matters would be greater, and not less, than that contemplated by the Commission. The administration of primary and middle vernacular schools had always been in their hands. They had also been entrusted with important powers of supervision over the Government high schools at head-quarters, the cost of which (as also that of training schools) was charged to district funds though the administration continued to be departmental. Grants-in-aid to local schools were included in the boards' estimates; but their powers in this respect went no further than the recommendation of grants, the final sanction resting with the Department and with Government. In relation to this and other matters it was to be "under-"stood, as an essential principle, that district boards are bound to observe and "act in accordance with the general principles of administration which the "Government has from time to time laid down in regard to the several depart-"ments handed over to local control . . . . . although, so long as the "general principles are kept in view, the Lieutenant-Governor desires to leave "as much as possible to the discretion of the boards" (Resolution of the 25th February 1885). The subordinate inspecting officers were also localised, and the boards were further required to pay a proportionate share of the cost of the higher inspecting staff. Act XIV directed that district boards should provide for the establishment, management, and maintenance of schools so far as the funds at their disposal permitted. They had, however, no funds separately reserved for education. Under the previous system, special allotments had been made from provincial funds to meet the cost of specific services. Under the new regulations another method was adopted. The income of district boards consisted of (1) local rates, (2) revenue of transferred services, (3) municipal contributions, (4) assignments from provincial revenues. The necessary expenditure of the boards in the maintenance of schools as well as for all other transferred services being calculated, as afterwards in Bengal, on the average cost at the time of transfer, the provincial assignment was made as a lump sum just calculated to meet the deficiency in other sources of income. The income from district rates was described as being "practically stationary"; and the same character was given to municipal contributions. The possibility of expansion was therefore, strictly limited to the gradual development of transferred sources of revenue, which it was hoped might be improved by careful nursing; and education would be only one out of several claimants for a share in the benefits resulting from enhanced prosperity. The chances of development seem to be still further reduced by the provision that unexpended balances lapse to provincial funds. The Education Commission recommended (paragraph 216), with special reference to the case of the North-Western Provinces, that all unexpended balances of the school fund should be re-credited to the fund, but the recommendation does not appear to have been carried out.

Under the Municipal Act XV of 1883, municipalities were required to bear a share of the cost of maintaining schools within municipal areas, such share to take the form of contributions to the district boards by which the schools were to be maintained. Where it was thought advisable, the management of intra-municipal schools was to be placed under joint committees, as in Bengal. They were also empowered to aid schools under private management.

114. Expenditure by District and Municipal Boards in the North-Western Provinces.—It was explained in the preceding chapter of this report and may also be gathered from the last paragraph, that it is impossible to state what portion of local fund expenditure in the North-Western Provinces is derived from the district rates, and what from transferred sources of revenue or from direct provincial assignments. The expenditure shown in the tables under the heading "local rates or cesses" includes all these. That term must, therefore, be understood as meaning "local funds," excluding municipal contributions and the local assets of schools. The total expenditure from this source fell from R13,58,579 in 1884-85 to R13,46,287 in the following year. On institutions under their own management or financial control district boards spent R9,66,168 from local funds. The Fyzabad College is maintained by the district board at a cost to the local fund of R2,528. On secondary schools under the control of the boards R3,07,646 were spent, and on primary schools R5,05,753. Training schools cost R44,596, scholarships R26,487, and buildings R79,158. Grants to aided schools amounted to R1,15,074, of which secondary schools received R74,852 and primary schools R31,116. The inspection of all these institutions was carried out at a cost to local funds of R2,45,346.

The expenditure from municipal taxation increased from R71,260 to R74,584. The cost of municipal schools to the rates was R23,377; nearly three quarters of this amount was spent upon primary education. In the grants to aided schools a different proportion was observed; only R5,000 was devoted to primary schools, while secondary schools received R16,000. The Agra College, now under private management, also received a grant of R4,000 from the rates, and the Mahomedan Anglo-Oriental College at Aligarh a grant of a little over R1,000.

115. District and Municipal Boards in the Punjab.—Under the District Boards Act XX of 1883, the education cess, together with the cesses for roads and the district post, is merged in and becomes part of the local rate. The Act has been extended to the greater part of the province, and will, it is understood, be shortly extended to the whole. In the remaining districts the one per cent. educational cess is still separately levied; and where this is done, it is credited, together with the proceeds of the local rate and other cesses, to the district fund. Government has reserved the power of requiring district boards to expend on education a minimum sum equal to one-fourth of their cess-income; a share which amounts to considerably more than the one per cent cess, to which in fact educational expenditure has never been limited. Both local and municipal boards have full control over their own funds, except that no school can be abolished without the sanction of the Department; and they retain in their own hands all unexpended balances. The particular measures that have been taken to enlarge their powers and resources in conformity with the recommendations of the Commission are the following. In the transfer of departmental schools the Punjab Government claims to have gone further than the Commission anticipated in the immediate future; and it is stated that all schools, whether primary or secondary, that were formerly under the Department, with the single exception of practising schools attached to training institutions, have been transferred to the control of local bodies. Local and municipal boards are also to have the charge of aiding all native schools for primary and secondary education that may apply for new grants-in-aid hereafter; and their powers and duties in this respect have been clearly defined. It is in contemplation to transfer to them the administration of existing grants; and should this measure be hereafter carried into effect, the only direct charges upon provincial revenues on account of primary education will be those incurred for inspection and for the training of teachers. Most important of all, it has been determined to fix a minimum rate of expenditure on education from district and municipal funds, up to which the local bodies concerned will be required to work. In the case of district funds the proportion that must be devoted to primary education is also fixed. Up to a recent date no grant was made by Government in aid of the funds of local boards; but under orders lately issued, this policy has been virtually abandoned. Local boards have been relieved of charges for inspection and for the training of teachers, which are hereafter to be borne by provincial revenues to the amount of R66,000 a year; and this sum will therefore be set free for the extension and improvement of schools, both departmental and indigenous. Upon the latter class of schools it is proposed to expend about R25,000 a year; and that amount may be supplemented by additional grants from provincial revenues if the income of the boards is insufficient for the purpose. The primary departments and branch schools attached to institutions formerly under the management of the Department have been transferred to municipalities, together with grants for their maintenance, paid either directly or by the removal of equivalent charges. The liberality of municipal boards in the Punjab towards education called forth, it will be remembered, the specially favourable comments of the Commission.

116. Expenditure by District and Municipal Boards in the Punjab.—The expenditure from local rates and cesses fell from R5,05,087 to R4,90,876, the reduction being chiefly under the head of buildings. On their own schools district boards expended R3,15,807, thus distributed: primary, R2,23,000; secondary, R43,000; buildings, R41,200; scholarships, R7,500. Grants to departmental schools amounted to R47,000, training schools receiving R27,000 of this sum. Grants to municipal institutions were R66,800, including R36,300 to secondary schools. Altogether, district boards in the Punjab contributed from local rates R85,700 to secondary schools, R2,32,900 to primary schools, R27,000 to training schools, R55,000 for inspection, R31,000 for scholarships, and R59,000 for school buildings.

The expenditure from municipal rates increased from R1,50,017 to R1,54,184. The expenditure included a grant of R1,200 to St. Stephen's College at Delhi, the only instance in India of a contribution made by a municipality to a college under missionary management. Secondary schools received R72,416, primary schools R36,182, training, medical, and industrial schools R5,236, scholarships R7,885, buildings R21,000, and R6,091 was contributed to the expenses of the Punjab University.

117. District and Municipal Boards in the Central Provinces.— The educational cess in these provinces amounts to two per cent. of the land revenue. The standing orders provided that its proceeds should be devoted exclusively to primary education in rural tracts, with exceptions in favour of training schools, and of contributions under special sanction to town schools. These orders received legislative sanction by Act I of 1883, which created district councils for the administration of educational funds, with local boards subordinate to them; and it expressly provided for the expenditure of the local cess on primary education. To this was added a grant from provincial revenues; and the boards and councils were directed to keep a separate school account. During the year 1884-85 all departmental rural schools, except in a few districts, were transferred to the control of these bodies. As regards the course of studies, the rates of fees, and other similar matters, they are governed by rules framed by the Department, and these cannot be altered without due cause shown. Subject, however, to that condition, the control of the district boards over schools is as complete as was that formerly exercised by the Deputy Commissioners whom they have nominally superseded, though officials still have a seat on the great majority of the boards. But these rights involve, in the opinion of the Local Government, corresponding duties. A decided view is expressed as to the responsibilities of district councils in regard to the provision of funds for the promotion of education. Their tendency, it is alleged, is to increase the expenditure on education from local funds, without any attempt to provide for such increase by private liberality. On this point the Chief Commissioner has remarked:—" It was distinctly expected and intended, when the Local Self-Government Act was passed, that the district councils should not only spend public "money, but should also stimulate and systematise private liberality. It was "hoped that it might be found, on the one hand, that the people would contri-"bute more readily to funds which were managed by their own representatives, "and on the other hand, that when these representatives of the people were led "intelligently to grasp both the importance of such matters as education and "the difficulties in their way, their appeal to the liberality of the people would "be more earnest and more effective. In few places only has this expectation "been realised; but only so far as it is realised is the lesson of self-help really "learned. The Chief Commissioner has, therefore, determined to fix for a term "of years for each district the maximum expenditure on education by the dis-"trict council from public funds. No expenditure on education in excess of "this maximum will be allowed unless private liberality shall have first supplied "or secured the necessary funds."

It was acknowledged that municipalities did not spend a fair share of the rates on education, their contributions amounting in 1881-82 to only R35,000, or not more than three per cent. of their income, which was not sufficient to support the schools within municipal limits. Under the existing Act the Local Government has no power to compel a municipality to set apart certain sums or to take specific measures for the promotion of education. If the law came

under revision for other reasons, it was the opinion of the Chief Commissione.
that it might be well to give the Government power to compel the municipalities
to do their duty in this and other respects. But at present legislation was not
desirable. The committees were most anxious to do their duty and were ready
to listen to advice. It was believed that after a while they would, without compulsion, take a keen interest in the success of their schools, and that a spirit of
rivalry would in time be aroused among them which would have more effect than
the most stringent legislation.

118. Expenditure by District and Municipal Boards in the Central Provinces.—Under the new regulations a grant is made to district councils from provincial revenues, and this is included in the amount shown under the head of "local rates and cesses." The expenditure from local rates proper increased from R1,27,638 in 1884-85 to R1,46,852 in 1885-86, and the provincial subsidy from R2,087 to R27,818. In 1885-86 the total expenditure from local funds, including the provincial grant, amounted to R1,74,670, against R1,29,725 in the preceding year. The whole of it was expended in institutions maintained by the councils and boards, all of which are primary schools, with the exception of two secondary schools costing R1,300 and five industrial schools costing R700.

The expenditure on education from municipal funds increased from R45,464 in 1884-85 to R56,465. This increase, especially if compared with the expenditure of R35,000 in 1881-82, would appear to justify in some measure the opinion which the Local Government has formed as to the public spirit and liberality of these bodies in regard to education, though the Chief Commissioner draws attention to the fact that municipalities were relieved in 1882 of police charges amounting to R1,07,000, and expresses the opinion that they ought finally to contribute something like R80,000 a year to education. As a rule, municipalities were unwilling to undertake the direct management of schools; and the three primary schools shown in the returns for 1885-86 as under municipal management were, it appears, subsequently transferred to different control, the municipality continuing to aid them. The grants to other institutions included R3,711 to the Morris College at Nagpore, R17,394 to secondary schools, R29,714 to primary schools, and R5,646 for buildings and miscellaneous purposes.

119. District and Municipal Boards in Burma.—A district cess amounting to 10 per cent. of the land revenue, is levied in Burma for various local purposes. Under the orders of 1881, one-tenth of the proceeds of the cess in each district was devoted to education. In 1885-86 the share had risen to one-fifth of the cess, and the amount spent on education from that source was R1,06,291. There are, however, no district boards charged with the administration of the funds thus derived. The district committees, which are being gradually abolished and now exist in but few districts, act only as consultative bodies. The new 'rural boards' which have been formed in some districts have as yet taken no part in educational work, though it is intended to give them the status of educational councils and to entrust them with the control of funds. Unspent balances of the educational share of the cess lapse to the general district fund.

Municipal committees in Burma occupy a much more defined and important position with regard to education. With the exception of seven that had been previously constituted, these bodies acquired a legal status by the Burma Municipal Act of 1884; but two years before that time they received large educational powers, which have been steadily growing ever since. It was shown in the preceding chapter that the educational expenditure from municipal funds increased from R33,000 in 1881-82 to R2,53,000 in 1884-85; and it was explained that the increase was due to assignments from provincial funds for the discharge of specific educational duties, which were imposed in constantly increasing measure upon municipal committees in exchange for other burdens of which they had been relieved. In 1885-86 there was again an increase of nearly a lakh in the expenditure from municipal funds, which in that year exceeded by more than R80,000 the amount which, under the arrangements of 1882, the municipalities were required to spend on education. The money was derived partly from enhanced returns of the excise revenue; but chiefly from the allotment to education of a larger share of the general municipal income, including the annual grant of R87,000 at which the contributions from provincial revenues to municipalities had been fixed. The work of the committees was the subject of cordial praise. The regulations of the Department had been voluntarily accepted and applied in every municipal town; and while the transfer of the charge of educational affairs to local management had thus on the one hand been effected without break of continuity, on the other it had stimulated local interest in schools, both primary and secondary, and had in many cases led to a much more liberal provision for education than could otherwise have been anticipated—for example, in the establishment of municipal girls' schools. The interests of education in each municipality were assured by the creation of a school-fund, to which all unspent balances were re-credited.

120. Expenditure by Municipal Committees in Burma.—The expenditure from municipal funds increased from R2,53,157 in 1884-85 to R3,43,523 In 1885-86. Municipal boards maintained on their own account 37 schools: 16 secondary at a cost of R87,647, 11 primary at a cost of R19,027, 9 girls' schools costing R6,971, and a technical school costing R800. They also aided secondary schools with grants amounting to R44,729, and primary schools with grants of R68,498; buildings and furniture cost R80,000 and scholarships R24,000.

121. District and Municipal Boards in Assam.—Under Regulation III of 1879 the Chief Commissioner is empowered to allot, from the proceeds of the local rates levied under it (not exceeding one anna and four pies in the rupee of the land revenue), such amounts as he may think fit for the construction and repair of school-houses, the maintenance and inspection of schools, the training of teachers, and the establishment of scholarships. The Regulation also created district committees for the control and expenditure of this allotment, under rules to be prescribed by the Chief Commissioner. The system received an important development in 1882, when all aided primary and middle schools were made over to local boards, together with the necessary funds for their maintenance. Other heads of expenditure, such as sub-inspectors (who were afterwards again provincialised) and stipends in training schools, were at the same time localised and the requisite allotments transferred. At present the procedure is somewhat different, and no special grant is made for education. Each local board is charged with certain services, of which education is one. It is credited with (1) the full local rate levied in the district; (2) certain transferred sources of revenue, including rents, ferries, and pounds; (3) a provincial grant sufficient, with the other income, to cover the sanctioned expenditure. This provincial grant is really a grant-in-aid of public works, since the local receipts included under the other two heads are more than sufficient to meet the remainder of the charges. In 1884, Sir Charles Elliott was averse to appropriating to education, either by law or by executive order, any definite proportion of the local income. He knew of no abstract consideration which was sufficient to determine the proper ratio; and, though, as a matter of fact, the average share of the local income devoted to education was about one-fifth, yet this was a mean between terms of very different values. On the whole, the grants were largest where there was most demand for education, and smallest where the demand was lowest. That was the true ratio of variation; between the grants and the local rates no necessary relation existed, since the local rate did not vary with the population nor with the demand of the people for schools. Nor, even if it were possible, did he think such a course desirable. If a "minimum proportion" were established, it would probably come to be regarded as a sufficient allotment, and would thus have a paralysing effect upon education, by checking the growth of a disposition to support it liberally. Two years later somewhat different views prevailed. Each local board is now expected and required to spend annually on education one-fifth of its purely local receipts, including local rates, transferred heads of revenue, and opening balance; and it is stated that they mostly spend up to that limit. The income from local rates increased from R3,41,016 in 1882-83, when the boards were established, to R5,08,713 in 1885-86; and the receipts from other local sources (pounds, ferries &c.) increased from R1,50,203 to R1,81,101. Adding the opening balance of 1885-86 (R43,147), it results that the amount to be set apart for expenditure on education (one-fifth of these sums) increased from R98,244 to R1,46,592. It is evident therefore, that the resources at the disposal of local boards possess great elasticity.

Municipalities are hardly yet sufficiently developed in Assam to take any prominent part in education. At the same time, in the opinion of the Chief Commissioner, native members of municipal committees are often more eager for educational than for any other form of expenditure; and though the amount actually spent on education in Assam is small, yet the proportion it bears to the total municipal income of the province is higher than that shown in 1881-82 for any province of India except the Punjab. It is therefore, in Sir Charles Elliott's opinion, both possible and easy to induce municipalities to contribute their full share towards the education of the native population; and he holds it to be quite unnecessary to make provision, legislative or other, for "dragooning" them into doing this by levying a forced percentage on their income.

122. Expenditure by District and Municipal Boards in Assam.—
From what has preceded it will be understood that the educational expenditure from local funds in Assam is not strictly confined to local rates, but includes income from transferred services and also (so far as it is supplemented by a share in the opening balances) from provincial funds. The educational expenditure from local funds, understood in this sense, increased from R1,36,666 in 1884-85 to R1,53,502 in the following year. This last amount, it will be seen, is greater than the one-fifth share of local income which has just been mentioned as the normal educational provision for the year. On their own schools, which are exclusively primary, the local boards spent R75,650, and R13,186 on the inspection of them. They also gave grants of R25,867 to secondary schools, and of R11,722 to primary schools under other management. Inspection cost R13,186, training schools R5,590, scholarships and buildings R21,487.

Municipal expenditure on education amounted to R4,392, divided nearly equally between grants to secondary and to primary schools.

123. Local Boards in Berar and Coorg.—In Berar some of the existing municipalities have been intrusted with the management of primary schools within their limits. No district boards for the control of education have yet been formed. There is, however, an educational cess, which is levied at the rate of 3 pies in the rupee of land revenue and is administered by the Department. The proceeds are wholly allotted to education, and unspent balances can be utilised in succeeding years. The expenditure from the cess decreased from

R1,20,057 in 1884-85 to R1,13,812. There was increased expenditure on schools —all primary, costing R72,000—but a reduction in the cost of buildings. Municipalities spent R6,269 on education.

Local self-government has not yet been introduced into Coorg, and in the Chief Commissioner's opinion the country is not ripe for such a measure. A local fund for the promotion of elementary education has been created by the plough-tax, which was voluntarily imposed on themselves by the Coorgs some years ago, and is now supplemented by a provincial grant to half the amount. The expenditure from the cess increased from R7,262 to R10,489.

Municipalities in Coorg are still in their infancy; but at Mercara all vernacular education is under municipal control, and at Virajpet the control extends to education of all kinds, whether English or vernacular. In these two towns the municipal expenditure on education increased from R9,083 to R12,593.

124. Educational Expenditure of District Boards.—We are now in a position to undertake a general survey of the manner in which the boards throughout India have distributed, to the various classes of schools and the different stages of education, the funds placed at their disposal for educational purposes. The materials for this survey will be found in General Table VII for 1885-86 appended to this report. And first for district boards.

The total expenditure from district funds on education in 1885-86 was R36,93,821, against R38,83,567 in 1884-85. It has been explained in an earlier paragraph that the funds of district boards in Bombay were relieved of the charge of municipal schools to the extent of R2,25,000—an amount more than sufficient to account for the decrease just shown. The expenditure in 1885-86 was, to take the most general view, distributed in the following way:—

Head of Expenditure.	In Institutions Maintained		Total Expenditure.
	By the Boards.	Otherwise.	
	R	R	R
Colleges	2,528	...	2,528
Secondary schools for boys	3,81,485	1,60,385	5,41,870
,, ,, for girls	499	8,872	9,371
Primary schools for boys	16,23,151	4,55,335	20,78,486
,, ,, for girls	57,640	28,643	86,283
Training schools	97,710	48,690	1,46,400
Other special schools	7,567	27,259	34,826
Total Expenditure on Instruction	21,70,580	7,29,184	28,99,764
Inspection			3,74,987
Scholarships			77,310
Buildings, &c.			2,86,733
Miscellaneous			55,027
Total			36,93,821

The boards, therefore, spent on secondary schools for boys and girls little more than one-fourth of their expenditure on primary schools. If it be remembered that secondary schools include in many provinces large primary departments, and if the cost of training schools, all of which is practically incurred for the benefit of primary schools, be included under the latter head, the proportionate expenditure on secondary schools will fall to a much lower rate. It will fall to a rate lower still if the expenditure on schools maintained by the boards themselves be alone considered.

√125. **Educational Expenditure of Municipal Boards.**—If the expenditure of District Boards on education declined from 1885 to 1886, that of municipal boards increased in a more than corresponding degree, namely, from R8,61,448 to R11,40,678. The details are again given in a general form :—

HEAD OF EXPENDITURE.	IN INSTITUTIONS MAINTAINED		TOTAL EXPENDITURE.
	By the Boards.	Otherwise.	
	R	R	R
Colleges	1,027	12,969	13,996
Secondary schools for boys	1,71,395	2,15,386	3,86,781
" " for girls	4,971	16,481	21,452
Primary schools for boys	1,96,748	2,25,869	4,22,617
" " for girls	42,354	22,000	64,354
Training schools	580	3,059	3,639
Other special schools	2,309	21,713	24,022
TOTAL EXPENDITURE ON INSTRUCTION	4,19,384	5,17,477	9,36,861
Inspection			10,580
Scholarships			47,102
Buildings, &c.			1,27,941
Miscellaneous			18,194
TOTAL			11,40,678

The first point that strikes attention is that municipalities are much less fully inclined than district boards to maintain schools of their own. The expenditure by district boards on their own schools exceeded the amount of their grants to other schools in the proportion of three to one. In the municipal expenditure the balance is the other way. Again, as might be expected from the greater advancement of schools in towns, the expenditure of municipalities on secondary schools falls very little short of their expenditure on primary schools, though here again large allowance must be made for the cost of primary departments. The inspection of schools and the training of teachers is mostly provided for by other agencies; but it deserves notice that the expenditure of municipalities on technical and other special schools is as yet insignificant.

The total municipal expenditure on education in India increased, between 1881-82 and 1885-86, from R4,60,000 to R11,40,000. That of Burma, in which the circumstances were exceptional, increased from R33,000 to R2,53,000; in all other provinces taken together the expenditure was more than doubled. The Punjab remained nearly stationary, rising from R1,51,000 to R1,54,000; in Madras the expenditure rose from R88,000 to R1,75,000; in Bombay from R80,000 to R1,71,000; in the North-Western Provinces from R52,000 to R74,000; in the Central Provinces from R34,000 to 56,000; and even in Bengal it increased from R25,000 to R82,000.

126. **Enactment of an Educational Code.**—The preceding paragraphs have dealt with the recommendations of the Commission as to the powers and duties of district and municipal boards and the action that has followed on those recommendations. But the Commission's proposals did not stop there. It was certain that the functions of such bodies would be largely confined to primary education, and indeed such a limitation was suggested by more than one of their recommendations. But to the majority of the Commission it appeared that, if primary education was to be made the subject of legal enactment, it would have a bad effect if similar legislative protection was not also afforded to other branches of education. They, therefore, recommended that legal sanction should be given to a Code intended to regulate the internal organisation and

external relations of the Education Department, with power reserved to the Local Governments to cancel and modify the provisions of the Code. The recommendations to this end (XI. 10—12) fell stillborn. They were felt to be a desperate attempt to give to secondary and higher education a form of protection, financial and other, of which it hardly stood in need, and which from the nature of the case was hardly open to legislative treatment. All that it was necessary to do could very well be done by the executive action of Government. The proposals met with but scant notice or criticism, and did not survive such criticism as they received.

127. Other Controlling Agencies.—The duties, as regards general educational administration, which have been entrusted to and accepted by the Punjab University and the Educational Syndicate at Rangoon have been sufficiently described in the preceding chapter of this report. It is only necessary to add that in 1885-86 the Syndicate at Rangoon acquired a more definite status by its enrolment as a corporate body under Act XXI of 1860. Its main functions consist at present in the conduct of all provincial examinations. Hereafter it will further relieve the Education Department by undertaking the control and management of the Rangoon College.

Section III.—COLLEGIATE EDUCATION.

128. Character of Collegiate Education.—The application of the term 'college' should strictly be confined to those institutions in which the students have passed the matriculation examination, and are reading one or other of the courses prescribed by the University for its higher examinations. This is in accordance with the definition accepted by the Government of India in the Resolution of the 29th October 1883, in which colleges—that is, colleges affiliated to an Indian University—are divided into (1) Arts colleges, English, whose students have passed the matriculation examination, and are reading a course prescribed by the University for degrees in Arts; (2) Oriental colleges, whose students have passed an examination declared by the Local Government to be equal in difficulty to the matriculation examination, and are reading a course of Oriental subjects prescribed by the University; (3) Professional colleges, whose students have passed the matriculation examination, and are reading for degrees in law, medicine, or engineering. There is no uncertainty as to the first and third of these classes. With regard to Oriental colleges, there is some diversity of practice, as the term is also applied to institutions like the Benares Sanskrit College, in which the students have passed no matriculation examination, and in which the subsequent examinations and titles for which they read are conducted and conferred by their own professors. These facts will appear more clearly from the description of the several institutions to be given later on.

Professional colleges will fall to be treated more conveniently in the section relating to Special Education.

129. Changes in University Regulations.—Under this head there are not many changes of importance to record. The activity shown by the several Universities of India in the period treated of in the last chapter was followed by a year of comparative quiescence. Proposals for the creation of a new University at Allahabad, for the special purpose of regulating education in the North-Western Provinces, were indeed submitted to the Government of India, in full accordance with the hope expressed by the Commission in paragraph 324 of their report ; but the actual establishment of this institution falls into a later period. The Calcutta University has somewhat reduced the standard for the M. A. degree in physical science, which was originally framed for a two years' course of study, and was found to be too extensive for the time actually allowed. In Madras, diversity of attainments has been encouraged by allowing candidates at the M. A. Examination to pass in more than one branch before proceeding to the degree of M. A. In Madras, also, a new degree has been instituted—that of licentiate in teaching. As this is the first degree of its kind that has been instituted in India, it may be well to describe at length the subjects in which candidates will be examined. The standard is as follows :—

I.—*Principles of Education.*

(*a*) The relation of education to the science of mind.

(*b*) The various modes of mental activity and their connexion with bodily structures and functions.

(*c*) The relation of the teacher to each mode of mental activity.

(*d*) Characteristics of different ages :—

    1. Infancy and childhood.

    2. The school-age strictly so called.

3. The period succeeding the school-age when the study of science becomes possible.

(The characteristics of each period are defined in great detail.)

(e) The natural order of the acquisition of knowledge during these periods respectively, as determined by the order of development and the laws of the growth and operation of the intellectual faculties.

II.—History of Education.

(a) History of education in Europe from the rise of the Universities to the present time:—

1. Monastic schools, their management and course of instruction. The origin and development of the Universities.
2. The revival of letters, and its educational effects, *e. g.*, the Latin schools.
3. The Reformation, and the partial provision for popular education in Protestant countries.
4. The educational work of the Jesuits and of the Jansenists.
5. Changes effected under the influence of Rousseau, Pestalozzi, Froebel, and the chief British writers on education.

(b) The present state of educational practice as exhibited in Germany, Great Britain, and India.

(c) Special periods or writers to be prescribed from time to time.

III.—Methods of Teaching and School Management.

1. The site, structure, fitting and furniture of school buildings.
2. Sanitary conditions of effective teaching.
3. Physical exercises.
4. Books and appliances.
5. Registers and returns.
6. Organisation of schools.
7. Classification of scholars.
8. Means for securing discipline, order, regularity, and punctuality.
9. Distribution of school-work among the teachers.
10. The apportionment of time.
11. Order and correlation of studies.
12. The art of questioning as a means of instruction.
13. The use of lectures, of catechetical *vivâ voce* teaching from a text-book, and of catechetical *vivâ voce* teaching without a text-book.
14. Methods of teaching and of illustrating each of the subjects in an ordinary school-course, with special reference to the English and vernacular languages (including all the various branches of instruction falling under those two heads), mathematics, geography, history, and physical science.
15. Preparation of teaching notes.
16. Examination, *vivâ voce* and in writing.
17. The management of a class.
18. The use of the black-board and other material appliances.

Candidates for the degree must have already graduated, must have attended a six months' course at an affiliated institution, and must have subsequently practised their profession for six months. By special order of the Senate, exemption from attendance at the course may be granted to a teacher who for a period of 2½ years has been on the regular staff of a high school or college.

130. Arts Colleges, English, 1885-86.—The number of colleges of different classes in each province in 1885-86, and the number of students reading in them, are given in the following statement:—

Arts Colleges, English, 1885-86.

PROVINCE.	UNDER PUBLIC MANAGEMENT.		UNDER PRIVATE MANAGEMENT, AIDED.		UNDER PRIVATE MANAGEMENT, UNAIDED.		TOTAL.	
	Colleges.	Students.	Colleges.	Students.	Colleges.	Students.	Colleges.	Students.
Madras	9	938	17	1,483	4	267	30	2,688
Bombay	(a) 5	608	3	433	...	...	8	1,041
Bengal	13	949	6	875	7	1,174	26	2,998
North-Western Provinces	3	186	4	228	6	34	13	448
Punjab	1	248	1	59	...	...	2	307
Central Provinces	1	39	2	39	1	1	4	79
Burma	1	20	...	...	...	...	1	20
TOTAL	(a)33	2,988	33	3,117	18	1,476	84	7,581
TOTAL FOR 1884-85	(b)33	2,810	32	2,855	13	1,115	78	6,780

(a) Including two colleges in Native States.
(b) Including one college in a Native State.

The average number of students to a college increased from 88 to 91. The average daily attendance, calculated on the average monthly roll-number, was 92 per cent. in colleges maintained by the Department, 87 per cent. in aided colleges, and 80 per cent. in unaided colleges. The increase of six colleges is thus distributed:—two each in Bombay and the North-Western Provinces, one in the Central Provinces, and one in Bengal. In Madras there is no change in the total number; but the Government college at Salem was transferred to the management of the local municipality, and another at Bellary was reduced to the status of a high school and similarly transferred, on the retirement of Government from its management. The loss was made up by the opening of college classes in the institution maintained without Government aid by the American Mission at Guntoor. The well-known Pacheappa's College at Madras, which in previous years had received a grant, was transferred to the unaided list. In the Bombay Presidency a new college was established in the Native State of Bhaunagar; but the most important event of the year in this field was the opening of the Fergusson College at Poona by the private enterprise of a native association. The Fergusson College, now an aided institution, owes its origin to an English school founded in 1880 by a few native gentlemen, the success of which led the managers in 1884 to take a further step in advance. Under their auspices was originated the Deccan Education Society, in the government of which the original promoters of the school were assigned a leading part; and the society shortly afterwards resolved to raise the school into a college, and to call it by the name of His Excellency the Governor, in order to mark its appreciation of the interest he had evinced in the cause of private enterprise generally, and in the prosperity of the school in particular. The college, it is stated, "intends to be independent of any Euro-
"pean element in its lecture-room, and to impress upon its students the patriotic
"sentiments of its founders." At its first attempt it passed seventeen candidates

scriptions amounting to R84,000. In Bengal an addition of one has been made to the list of aided colleges by the re-opening, after a long interval, of college classes at St. Paul's School, Darjeeling, for European boys. The increase of two unaided colleges in the North-Western Provinces arises from the opening of college classes in the Ramsay High School at Almora, and also in the Allahabad High School for girls, where three young ladies were reading for the First Arts Examination. The addition of one in the Central Provinces is due to the Morris College at Nagpore, an institution which is maintained from funds subscribed by native chiefs and others in honour of Sir John Morris, the late Chief Commissioner. It receives no grant from Government, but is aided by the local municipality to the extent of R300 a month.

On the whole, the general movement has been in the direction of the Commission's recomendations. Government has retired from the direct management of two colleges, one of which has been closed and the other transferred to a local board. In six institutions under private management collegiate departments have been newly opened, and three of these have received aid either from Government or from municipal funds.

131. Classification of Arts Colleges according to Management.— Colleges are either under public or under private management; and the latter are divided into those that are aided and those that maintain themselves without aid. Of the 33 colleges under public management two are maintained by Native States in the Bombay Presidency; and two—the Salem College in Madras and the college department attached to the Fyzabad High School in Oudh—are maintained by the municipal or district board of the place. There are therefore 29 colleges under the direct management of the Department. Of these, 19 (including the Jubbulpore College, recently raised) are of the first grade, reading the full course for the B. A. degree, and 10 are of the second grade, in which the standard is limited to that of the First Arts or the Previous Examination. Five of these second-grade colleges are in Madras, and five in Calcutta. The two colleges that have been transferred to the management of local boards are both of the second grade; and that seems for the present to assign the limit both of the powers and of the inclinations of those bodies. But within that limit there seems to be an increasing tendency (which has since received further illustrations) to transfer the management of small Government colleges to local control.

The aided colleges also number 33. Of these, 18 (including the two aided colleges at Nagpore, recently raised in standard) are of the first and 15 of the second grade. The large and beneficent share which missionary energy takes in the higher education of the country is evidenced by the fact that 12 aided colleges of the first grade and eight of the second are under missionary management. Unaided colleges are 18, four of the first and 14 of the second grade; and among these also one of the former and four of the latter class are maintained by missionary bodies. If, then, all colleges, aided and unaided, under private management be taken together, and if four colleges or college departments for Europeans —two of the first and two of the second grade—be separated, it results that out of 18 colleges of the first grade and 29 of the second grade maintained by private enterprise for the benefit of natives of India, as many as 13 of the former and 12 of the latter class owe their existence to the efforts of missionary bodies. The leading institutions of this class are the Madras Christian College, the Free General Assembly's College in Bombay, the General Assembly's Institution and the Free Church Institution in Calcutta, and St. Xavier's Colleges in Bombay and Calcutta. The more prominent colleges under native management are Pacheappa's College in Madras, the Fergusson

College at Poona, and the Metropolitan, City and Ripon Colleges of Calcutta. The Metropolitan Institution had more than 550 students reading in the college department on the 31st March 1886.

Besides the two colleges maintained by local boards, five others receive grants from these bodies. Two colleges are maintained for the exclusive benefit of females; they are the Government Bethune School in Calcutta, of the first grade, and the First Arts classes attached to the unaided high school for girls at Allahabad.

132. Expenditure on Arts Colleges, English, 1885-86.—The following table exhibits the details of expenditure in 1885-86 in a convenient form:

Expenditure on Arts Colleges, 1885-86.

PROVINCE.	FROM PROVINCIAL REVENUES.			From District and Municipal Funds.	From Fees.	From other Sources.	TOTAL.
	In Colleges under public management.	In aided Colleges.	TOTAL.				
	R	R	R	R	R	R	R
Madras	1,36,564	42,216	1,78,780	M 1,027	1,20,148	1,03,131	4,03,086
Bombay	88,514	9,400	97,914	M. 3,000	58,413	(a) 72,873	2,32,200
Bengal	2,90,493	24,217	3,14,710	...	1,25,296	1,07,216	(b) 5,47,222
N.-W. Provinces	68,343	29,186	97,529	D., M. } 7,586	14,423	65,999	1,85,537
Punjab	45,797	5,400	51,197	M. 1,200	8,110	6,927	67,434
Central Provinces	9,199	2,376	11,575	M. 3,711	1,660	11,365	28,311
Burma	22,274	...	22,274	...	1,012	...	23,286
TOTAL	6,61,184	1,12,795	7,73,979	16,524	3,29,062	3,67,511	14,87,076
TOTAL FOR 1884-85	6,77,410	1,03,612	7,81,022	13,983	3,11,824	3,37,101	14,43,930

a. Including R25,092 from the revenues of Native States.
b. Excluding the expenditure in four unaided colleges in Calcutta.

133. Expenditure from Public Sources.—The general result is that there has been an increase of expenditure from every source except provincial revenues, which show a decrease of R7,000. Under provincial revenues, again, there is an increase of R9,000 in the expenditure upon grants to aided colleges, which is more than covered by the decrease of R16,000 in the Government expenditure upon colleges under departmental management. It is not necessary to lay any stress on this decrease as indicating a new departure in the Government policy. The fact is that the maintenance of the graded educational services involves a certain expenditure in salaries which has to be incurred in any case. If there is a decrease, it is probably due to causes of an accidental and temporary kind, such as the departure of officers in the higher grades on furlough or on deputation. This, in fact, is the explanation given of the decrease of R13,000 in Bengal and of R16,000 in the North-Western Provinces. It is obvious that in the comparison of one year with another, an increase may be due to corresponding causes; and this might be accepted as a sufficient explanation of the increase of R11,000 in Madras, were it not for a remark made in the Government Resolution on the report for 1885-86 to the effect that the expenditure in Government colleges has shown a tendency to increase of late years " owing " chiefly to the increased cost consequent on an improved staff."

The local bodies that now maintain or support colleges are the following:—the district board of Fyzabad, and the municipalities of Salem in Madras, Ahmedabad in Bombay, Agra and Aligarh in the North-Western Provinces, Delhi, and Nagpore.

134. Expenditure from Fees.—The importance of requiring that students of colleges shall pay fees proportionate in some degree to the cost of their education is insisted on by the Education Commission; and it is therefore desirable to examine that point in some detail. The following table shows the average yearly rate of fee paid by students in departmental, in aided, and in unaided (including Native State) institutions, for each province of India. It may be compared with the corresponding table in paragraph 38. In each case the yearly fee is calculated on the average monthly roll-number.

PROVINCE.	Departmental Colleges.	Aided Colleges.	Unaided Colleges.
	R	R	R
Madras	57·9	48·0	43 9
Bombay	86·4	(a)65·2	39·3
Bengal	71·5	49 2	(b)...
North-Western Provinces	39·7	27·9	28·6
Punjab	27·4	37·2	...
Central Provinces	29·3	14·5	27·0
Burma	48·2	...	...
AVERAGE FOR INDIA	65·4	47·6	41·3
AVERAGE IN 1884-85	69·1	45·5	45·8

(a) Excluding the Fergusson College at Poona, for which the returns of expenditure have not been given.
(b) Unaided colleges in Bengal have generally furnished no returns of expenditure.

The average yearly fee paid by students in departmental colleges throughout India fell within the year from R69 to R65, owing to diminished receipts in Madras, Bengal and the North-Western Provinces. In Madras, where with a larger monthly roll-number the total fee-receipts remain constant, the receipts in some colleges are far below what the average attendance combined with the term-fee would indicate. In Bengal, the increasing success of the privately-managed colleges in Calcutta, coupled with the high rate of fees at the Presidency College, continues to reduce the attendance at the latter institution, and thus to reduce the average fee for the province; while the remission of three months' fees to second and fourth-year students, necessitated by a change in the date of the University examinations, operated, as in the previous year, to bring down the gross receipts from that source. This last cause ceased to have effect in 1886-87, when the average yearly fee again rose to R78. There is some increase in the average fee-receipts of aided colleges throughout India, chiefly arising in Bombay and the Punjab. The opening of the Morris College at Nagpore with low rates of fees, has reduced the average for the Central Provinces. In unaided colleges there is also some reduction in the average fee, which is confined to colleges maintained by Native States in Bombay, a new institution of this class having been opened at lower rates.

Bombay and Bengal stand far above the rest of India, with average yearly fees of R86·6 and R71·8, respectively, paid by students in Government colleges. The monthly fee charged at the Elphinstone College of Bombay is R10, and at the Presidency College of Calcutta R12. In Madras, notwithstanding the close attention that has been paid to the systematisation of fee-rates, and the special recommendation of the Commission on that point (VI. 13), the yearly fee paid in the Presidency College is only R62, against R120 in Bombay, and R144 in Calcutta. Outside the Presidency towns, the fees charged are generally at the rate of R6 a month in Bombay, from R5 to R6 a month in Bengal, and from R4 to R5 a month (R50 and R60 a year) in Madras. Small Government colleges, charging lower rates of fees, such as are found in Madras and Bengal, are not encouraged in Bombay. In the North-Western Provinces, the Central Provinces and the Punjab, the yearly fee paid by students of Government colleges falls to a much lower point, though in the Central Provinces there is some improvement, and in the Punjab the rate is rapidly rising. The comparatively high fee realised in the Rangoon College is noticeable.

The fees levied in the aided colleges of Madras, Bombay and Bengal, whether in or outside the Presidency towns, are lower than the corresponding rates fixed for Government colleges at the same places. The managers of these institutions are in a position to feel the financial pulse of their students with great accuracy; and it may be inferred that, in charging lower rates, they have been guided by the desire of cheapening education, but not to such an extent that their total fee-income would suffer. The Department regards the question from a somewhat different point of view. It desires to raise fees in proportion to the greater cost of departmental institutions; but it cannot raise them beyond a certain point without depleting the classes and increasing the net cost of the institutions to provincial revenues, while at the same time education is checked. The Education Commission wished to lay down a general rule (VI. 10) that "no aided "college should be required to levy fees at the same rate as that charged in a "neighbouring Government college." This proposition was met in the following manner in para. 10 of the Secretary of State's Despatch of the 24th July 1884:—
"It is right that, so long as the expenses of such institutions [those maintained "from public funds and under official management] exceed their receipts, the "fees charged in them should be as high as possible without injuring their effi- "ciency and usefulness; nor should such institutions, by charging lower fees, "unduly compete with corresponding aided institutions. But I see no reason "why a rule should be laid down that the fees are necessarily to be *higher* than in "aided institutions." These orders do not of course forbid the levy of higher rates of fees when pupils are found sufficient to fill the classes and willing to pay them; and that this has been the practical principle adopted by the Department is clearly shown by the figures given in the table. It may be inferred that in the North-Western Provinces, the Punjab, and the Central Provinces, it has not hitherto been found possible to raise the fees in Government institutions to anything like the rate that prevails in those provinces where collegiate education is more valued; though the point may incidentally be noted that the aided college at Delhi has apparently been able to charge much higher fees than the Government college at Lahore. There is a further point worth a moment's consideration. It is observed that much lower fees are charged in those provinces which are less advanced in education. Now it is true that in an educationally backward province, both the means of education may be limited and the desire for education on its own account may be feeble. But it is also true that under such conditions there is a steady and effective demand for educated men who are natives of the province, and consequently that education has a much higher pecuniary value than it has where the competition among graduates is so great as it is in Madras, Bombay, or Bengal. Where the means of education exist, it seems a fairly reasonable inference that fees might with safety be levied at something like the rates which are paid in more advanced provinces. Active steps have been taken in this direction in the Punjab, where the Lieutenant-Governor decided in 1884 that the system of college-fees graduated according to income (a rule which in practice had been ignored) should be definitely abandoned, and that a uniform fee should be fixed at as high a rate as possible. With so liberal a system of

scholarships as prevailed in the Punjab, there was no sort of hardship in high college fees. In accordance with these views, not only have the fees been increased from a uniform rate of R2 in 1881-82 to a rate varying from R4 to R6 according to the class, but even these increased rates are to be doubled in the next five years, by annual increments of 20 per cent.; the fees in aided colleges being fixed at three-fourths of the rate prescribed for Government colleges. It may be noted that this vigorous action is not confined to colleges. In every class of schools, Government and aided, throughout the Punjab, a similar immediate enhancement has been ordered, with a similar provision for doubling these enhanced rates within a period of five years. In the Central Provinces, the fee in the Jubbulpore College has been slightly raised from R2 to R2-4 a month. In the North-Western Provinces and Oudh no attempt of this kind has been made; indeed, it is stated that the fees in Government colleges could not at present be raised except at the cost of throwing back high education.

135. Proportion of Fee-receipts to Total Expenditure.—But after all, that which has been held to justify the imposition of higher rates of fees in Government colleges is the higher rate of expenditure that their maintenance often involves. For the establishment of Government colleges a highly paid staff of European professors is employed. In colleges under native management the salaries of the professorial staff are fixed at a much lower rate; while in colleges of another class, the missionary spirit leads men whose lives are devoted to the work of education to be content with very moderate pecuniary reward. Whatever be the cause, Government colleges generally cost more than colleges under private management, and herein lies the explanation of the higher fees. The declaration of the Secretary of State above quoted deprives this comparison, it is true, of much of its significance; but still the question may possess an interest of its own. The proportion which fee-receipts in different classes of institutions bear to the total cost is shown in the following statement of percentages:—

PROVINCE.	Government Colleges.	Aided Colleges.
Madras	26·3	32·5
Bombay	26·1	37·9
Bengal	20·2	29·3
North-Western Provinces	9·5	6·9
Punjab	12·0	12·2
Central Provinces	8·8	3·7
Burma	4·8	...
AVERAGE FOR INDIA	20·6	25·5

Notwithstanding the higher fees, therefore, in Government colleges, they still bear a much lower proportion to the total cost than the fees in aided colleges. It may be well to compare these figures with the corresponding percentages obtained by the Commission. The table is given on page 280 of the report; and it appears that the proportion of fee-receipts in Government colleges throughout India has risen from 19·5 to 20·6 per cent., and in aided colleges from 23·4 to 25·5 per cent. A further comparison shows that in Madras and Bombay the percentage of fee-receipts to the total cost of Government colleges has risen from about 18 to 26 in each province; and that in aided colleges in the same two provinces the increase has been even greater, namely, from 23·7 to 32·5 per cent. in Madras, and from 21·7 to 37·9 in Bombay. In Bengal, on the other hand, while the percentage in aided colleges remains stationary, in Government colleges it has fallen from 27·5 to 20·2. It is evident that variations of this kind depend upon three causes, namely, increase or decrease (1) in the total expenditure on colleges, (2) in the prescribed fee-rate, (3) in the total fee-receipts as determined by the number of students. Of the three provinces named above, it is only in Madras that any considerable increase of cost has been incurred in the maintenance of Government colleges. This by itself would tend to lower the proportion which fee-receipts bear to the total cost; but the proportion has been more than fully recovered by the revision of the fee-rates and the increasing number of students. In Bombay the last named cause has chiefly operated. In Bengal the total fee-receipts in Government colleges have fallen by one-fourth since 1881-82. This is due to the operation of two causes : first the steady depletion of the classes in Government colleges in those places where private enterprise has successfully entered the field. Thus, in Calcutta, where the attendance at unaided colleges has increased between 1882 and 1886 from 493 to 920, the reduction of the number of students at the Presidency College from 374 to 180 means a yearly loss of more than R25,000 in fee-receipts in that institution alone. At the same time the teaching power of the college must be maintained at its full strength, since that is the only condition that justifies the levy of fees at the high rate of R12 a month. Secondly, there is a temporary cause already referred to, which arose out of a change in the date of the University examinations, and which resulted in the remission of fees for two years to the extent of one-eighth of the whole receipts from that source. This cause, while it lasted, affected aided colleges in an equal degree.

Similar considerations apply to all classes of institutions in all provinces; and on the whole it may be said that the rise or fall of the proportion that we have been considering is affected by the increase or decrease in the number of students far more than by any other cause.

136. Expenditure from Other Sources.—Under this head are included the receipts from endowments and subscriptions and those derived from missionary funds for the support of colleges. It is probable that the contributions from this last source fall little short of two lakhs of rupees a year.

137. Results of University Examinations in Arts, 1885-86.—The number of successful candidates at the different examinations of students in Arts colleges for the session 1885-86, is subjoined:—

University Examinations, 1885-86.

Province.	M. A.	B. A.	B. Sc.	First Arts or equivalent examination.
Madras	8	163	...	456
Bombay	3	69	3	(a)238
Bengal	31	410	...	636
N.-W. Provinces	2	51	...	91
Punjab	2	15	...	58
Central Provinces	...	...	...	21
Burma	...	...	...	3
TOTAL	46	708	3	a1,503
TOTAL FOR 1884-85	23	569	4	(b)1,087

(a) Including 96 who passed the 1st B. A., or 1st B. Sc. examination at Bombay.
(b) ,, 77 ,, ,, ,,

The Jubbulpore Government College and the two aided colleges at Nagpore, which were raised to the first grade in 1885-86, have as yet sent no candidates

in the number of successful candidates at all the chief examinations, which is most marked at the First Arts stage and at the M. A. degree. The M. A. candidates are the most distinguished products of the University system. The course which they follow is so framed as to give them, possibly for the first time, an insight into what education and culture really mean. For a year or two their faculties, which up to that time have been employed upon many diverse subjects of knowledge, are concentrated on one alone; and they suddenly awake to the fact, perhaps but dimly recognised at earlier stages, that the field of knowledge is vast and is not limited by their text-books. These are the men that reflect conspicuous credit on the Universities that have trained them; it is they who come to fill the highest pcsitions in professional and public life, and the enlargement of their numbers is a public gain.

138. B. A. Examination: Courses in Literature and in Science.— The candidates who took the degree of Bachelor of Arts numbered 708, while those who graduated in science were three only. At first sight this disproportion is startling, and would seem to augur ill for the prospects of scientific education in India. Bombay is the only University in which a separate degree in science has been conferred. A proposal to institute a similar degree in Madras, after having been under discussion for some years, has now apparently been shelved. But for all that, it must not be supposed that scientific education in Indian Universities is confined within the paltry limits indicated in the table. In the Universities of Madras and Calcutta, though the name is not there, the thing itself is. The point is of sufficient importance to be elucidated at greater length, by means of a comparison between the alternative courses for the B. A. degree in the Universities of Calcutta, Madras and Bombay.

Bombay.—The Bombay course in Arts comprises the following subjects:—
1. English.
2. A classical language.
3. One of the following groups:
    (a) Language and Literature.
    (b) History and Political Economy.
    (c) Logic and Moral Philosophy.
    (d) Mathematics.
    (e) Natural Science: namely, either (1) Elementary Physics and Inorganic Chemistry, or (2) Botany, Zoology and Physiology, with Vegetable and Comparative Anatomy.

The course for the degree in Science consists of three out of the following nine subjects, one at least being chosen out of subjects 3 to 8:
1. Pure Mathematics.
2. Applied Mathematics.
3. Experimental Physics, treated mathematically.
4. Chemistry, Inorganic and Organic.
5. Botany.
6. Zoology.
7. Animal Physiology.
8. Physical Geography and Geology.
9. Logic and Psychology.

Madras.—The Madras course for the B. A. degree is thus composed:—
1. English.
2. A second language (classical or vernacular).

in Chemistry.
- (*c*) General Biology, with either Botany, Animal Physiology, Zoology or Geology.
- (*d*) Mental and Moral Science.
- (*e*) History and Comparative Philology.

Calcutta.—The Calcutta University divides the Arts course into two branches, literary and scientific, in either of which the degree of B. A. may be taken. There are also separate honour and pass courses in each branch. The A or literary course is composed as follows :—
1. English.
2. Mental and Moral Science.
3. One of the following :—
   - (*a*) A classical language.
   - (*b*) History.
   - (*c*) Mathematics.

The B or scientific course is thus composed :—
1. English.
2. Mathematics.
3 One of the following :—
   - (*a*) Physics and the elements of Chemistry.
   - (*b*) Chemistry and the elements of Physics.
   - (*c*) Physiology, with either Botany or Zoology.
   - (*d*) Geology, with either Mineralogy or Physical Geography.

Punjab.—The Punjab University has established a Science Faculty separate from the Faculty of Arts. The course for the Arts degree is as follows :—
1. English.
2. A classical language.
3. One (or two) of the following :—
   - (*a*) Mathematics.
   - (*b*) History and Political Economy.
   - (*c*) Philosophy.
   - (*d*) Physical Science : namely, either (1) Physics and Chemistry, (2) Zoology and Comparative Physiology, (3) Botany, or (4) Geology.

he course for the degree of High Proficiency in Science is thus constituted :—
1. Mathematics.
2. Physics and Chemistry.
3. One (or two) of the following :—

lines, except (1) that in Madras only is a vernacular language recognised as a qualifying subject for the degree, while in other Universities it is not admitted even to the First Examination in Arts; and (2) that in Calcutta the student of literature is not allowed the option of taking up any branch of physical or natural science. The scientific course in Bombay and the Punjab and the scientific side of the Arts course in Calcutta are again constructed on similar lines, except (1) that English, which forms a necessary subject of the latter, is altogether excluded from the two former, and (2) that mathematics, optional in Bombay, is a compulsory subject at Calcutta and Lahore. Hence, then, the student who elects to take up science for his degree must at Bombay take up two and may take up three scientific subjects (mathematics being reckoned among them); at Calcutta he must take up two, but can take no more; at Madras he can only take up one.

139. Popularity of the two Courses.—In reference, therefore, to the claims of science as a part of University education, it becomes of importance to inquire what is the comparative attractiveness of scientific and of literary subjects to candidates for a University degree.

Bombay.—The answer has already been given for Bombay, where three students graduated in Science against 69 who took the degree in Arts. That does not, it is true, represent the full extent of scientific education, since those who graduate in Arts have also the option of taking up one scientific subject. From the Bombay University calendar for 1885-86, which gives the results of the examinations for the previous year, it appears that out of 83 B. A. graduates, 8 took up mathematics and 13 a scientific subject.

Madras.—It has been already stated that the Madras University has dropped the proposal to establish a separate course in Science for the B. A. degree. The scientific requirements of students are met by the provision that one subject out of the three they take up may be a scientific subject. On this point Mr. Grigg remarked in his report for 1884-85 :—" The steady and rapid increase in the "number of students taking up physical science is, a pleasing feature, and it " would be all the more so were it accompanied by an increase in the number of " those taking up mathematics . . . . . I deplore the neglect of mathe- " matics in the interests of the physical and natural sciences themselves. We are " on the eve of an important movement for the development of technical in- " struction throughout the Presidency, and I feel sure that however rapid may " be the progress for a time, the movement will speedily languish, unless accom- " panied *pari passu* by thoroughly sound instruction in mathematics." In the following year the disproportion still continued: 40 per cent. of the candidates took up physical science, but only 17 per cent. mathematics. It may be added that in his views as to the necessity of mathematics as the basis of scientific study, Mr. Grigg is at one with all the best authorities.

Calcutta.—In the Calcutta University there has been much variation from time to time in the comparative attractiveness of these two branches of study. In the examination of 712 candidates from Bengal colleges in 1885-86, 538 took the literary and only 174 the scientific course. Of those who chose the former 60 per cent. passed; of those who chose the latter only 36 per cent. The Director remarks on this point :—" The comparative success of the candidates in " the two alternative courses as indicated by these figures is not in accordance " with previous experience; and it would seem to follow that the B course as now "defined is more difficult to master than the A course. But the B course still " finds favour with the best students, as is evidenced by the fact that a majority " of the scholarship-holders take it up." The examination to which these remarks refer was the second under the new system. In that of the previous year there was a similar disparity between the number of candidates for the A and for the B course, and those who took up the latter were again less successful, though the difference was not so marked. But in the four previous years under the old system the B candidates were quite as numerous as the A, and were far more successful in the examination. These results led to the often-repeated remark that either the B course under the old system was easier than the A course, or that it was chosen by the abler students. The inference is that the native of India, or at any rate of Bengal, has no objection whatever to reading a scientific course for his degree, and that he will even choose it by preference, unless he believes that he will be placed at a disadvantage by its greater difficulty. In the North-Western Provinces, which are also examined by the Calcutta University, only 12 candidates out of 77 chose the B course in 1885-86.

Punjab.—It has already been noticed that the special course in science has as yet been taken up by no candidate. In the Arts course six candidates out of 26 from the Lahore Government College took up science as an optional subject, and it is noticeable that all these passed.

140. Comparative Success of Government and Other Colleges.—It now becomes necessary to inquire, in reference to the growing share which colleges under private management are taking in the higher education of the country, how far these colleges are successful, so far as success can be estimated by the ability of their students to pass the examinations of the University. The figures necessary for forming a judgment on this point are given below:—

M. A. Examination, 1885-86.

PROVINCE.	Government colleges.	Aided colleges.	Unaided colleges and private students.	TOTAL.
Madras	...	...	8	8
Bombay	2	1	...	3
Bengal	21	5	5	31
North-Western Provinces	1	1	...	2
Punjab	2	...	...	2
TOTAL	26	7	13	46

B. A. Examination, 1885-86.

Madras	87	71	5	163
Bombay	(*)62	10	...	72
Bengal	149	135	126	410
North-Western Provinces	23	23	5	51
Punjab	12	1	2	15
TOTAL	333	240	138	711

(*) Including 3 B. Sc. candidates.

First Arts (or equivalent) Examination, 1885-86.

Madras	211	182	63	456
Bombay	135	84	19	238
Bengal	244	139	253	636
North-Western Provinces	33	44	14	91
Punjab	41	9	8	58
Central Provinces	14	6	1	21
Burma	3	...	...	3
TOTAL	681	464	358	1,503

141. M. A. Examination.—The eight candidates from Madras were all privately educated. In his report for 1884-85 the Director stated that no provision had yet been made for teaching the M. A. course in any branch in the Presidency College, though it was hoped that the new re-organisation scheme, then awaiting the sanction of the Secretary of State, would enable the college to supply this manifest defect. A similar complaint is made by Mr. Wordsworth, Principal of the Elphinstone College, Bombay, who remarks that so long as "the provision for instruction in the higher branches of study is so inadequate, "few of the Bachelors in Arts will continue their studies, and still fewer obtain "the degree of Master of Arts." Of the three successful candidates in Bombay, one from the Elphinstone and one from the Deccan College passed in mathematics, and one from the Free General Assembly's Institution in natural science. In the North-Western Provinces and Oudh, the Muir Central College and the Canning College at Lucknow passed one candidate each in English literature. The two Punjab candidates came from the Lahore Government College; one passed in science and one in philosophy. The great majority of the candidates came from colleges in Bengal, where the number, large as it was, was much below that of previous years; the decrease being explained by the fact that this was the first examination under the new standards, which have been considerably raised in correspondence with the revised standard for the B. A. degree in honours. The noticeable fact is that colleges under private management in Bengal passed more candidates for the M. A. degree than all other colleges outside Bengal taken together. The General Assembly's Institution passed three candidates in literary subjects and one in botany; St. Xavier's College passed one in mathematics. From the unaided Metropolitan Institution two passed in English, one in physics, and one in botany. The physical student, though nominally borne on the rolls of the Metropolitan Institution, whence he took the B. A. degree, appears to have attended the science lectures of the Presidency College for the M. A. degree. Under an arrangement that has been many years in force, students of other colleges in Calcutta that do not possess the requisite appliances for scientific instruction are allowed to attend the necessary lectures in the Presidency College for the B. A. and M. A. degrees. Of Government institutions the Presidency College passed nine in physical science, one in mathematics, and six in English; the Patna College three in science; and the Sanskrit College two in Sanskrit.

I have gone into these figures in detail with the object of drawing attention to the fact that out of 38 colleges of the first grade in India in 1885-86, in only 12 have students been successfully prepared for the M. A. degree. It is true that some competed and failed, and that some others which have usually sent candidates to the examination failed to do so in this particular year. But accepting the figures as they stand, it appears that in only 7 out of 18 Government colleges, in only 4 out of 16 aided colleges, and in only one out of four unaided colleges of the first grade is the course for the M. A. degree effectively taught. It may be asserted in general that a college of the first grade numbers among its professors one or more who are qualified to impart instruction up to that standard; and if that be so, there would seem to be room for a great development of the highest form of education now obtainable in India, of the value of which to its possessors and to the State there can in these days be little doubt. If the instruction were provided, there would probably be no lack of students to take advantage of it.

Another point arises. The lamp of scientific education is chiefly fed in Government colleges, where 16 out of 26 candidates passed in scientific subjects. In colleges under private management the number was 5 out of 11, and one at least of these was taught in a Government institution. The fact is explained by the much greater cost which scientific instruction involves in the maintenance of laboratories, but it is of obvious importance as bearing on the relation of Government to scientific and technical education.

142. B. A. Examination.—In the examination for the B. A. degree, colleges under private management take a much more prominent position. From these institutions 378 candidates passed, while from Government colleges 333 passed. It is only in Bombay and the Punjab that colleges under private management fail to take a conspicuous place; in the other provinces their numerical success at the examination is either but little below or greatly above that of Government colleges. This is especially the case in Bengal, where five aided and two unaided colleges passed 243 candidates, against 149 from eight Government colleges. It is true that the colleges under private management that prepare candidates for this degree are all in Calcutta, while the Government colleges are scattered all over Bengal and are often small. But this consideration in no way detracts from the merits and usefulness of the privately managed institutions. From the unaided Metropolitan Institution 79 candidates passed; from the aided Free Church Institution 64 passed; from the Government Presidency College 75 passed. So in Madras: from the Madras Christian College 53 passed, while from the Government Presidency College 45 passed. And it is not only numerical success that these colleges can claim; the results of their teaching are often as valuable in quality as in quantity. At the B. A. examination of the Calcutta University in 1886, the first place on the class list was taken by a student of the unaided City College. This, no doubt, is an exceptional case; for while 46 per cent. of the students in Government colleges passed the B. A. examination in honours, among those from aided colleges the proportion was only 17 per cent. At the examination of the same year in Madras the first two places were taken by students of the Madras Christian College. In Bombay the first place in the examination of 1884-85 (the results of which are alone accessible to me) was taken by a student of St. Xavier's College; and it may be added that a student of the Free General Assembly's College in Bombay gained the Chancellor's medal at the M. A. examination of the following year. In the North-Western Provinces the Muir Central College at Allahabad takes the lead, and the aided colleges at Agra and Lucknow occupy a somewhat inferior but still a very creditable position.

143. Provision of Scientific Instruction.—A further question remains; whether colleges under private management are taking their due share in educating the youth of the country in physical and natural science. The following facts will supply an answer to the question. In Bombay both the Free General Assembly and St. Xavier's Colleges have established classes in science for the B. A. degree; but while 11 candidates passed the B. A. examination of 1885 in that subject from the Elphinstone College, only two candidates passed from aided colleges. In the separate examination for the degree of B. Sc. the proportion is better: out of 11 persons who have taken that degree since its institution in 1882, seven have appeared from Government and four from aided colleges, the General Assembly's Institution taking the lead among the latter. In Madras all the three Government colleges of the first grade have made provision for giving instruction in science. In the Presidency College a new chair for biology has been created; and a similar class, in addition to others, has been opened in the Madras Christian College. Among aided institutions the Madras Christian College is far in advance of the rest, though the Director anticipates that the other first-grade colleges will before long provide the means of instruction in the more important optional subjects of the new B. A. course. The number of candidates in science from the two classes of institutions is not stated. In Bengal the results are clearly given. The B or scientific course is taught in every Government college of the first grade. Out of 149 candidates for the B. A. degree from Government colleges, 41 took up that course; out of 243 candidates from other colleges, only 23 chose science. Again, of 23 candidates who took honours in that branch, 20 were students of Government colleges. In the North-Western Provinces and Oudh, the Canning College at Lucknow is the only one of its class that attempted science for the B. A. degree, and its success was limited to one student; the two Government colleges furnishing seven out of eight candidates in this subject. In the Punjab, science is taught in the Lahore Government College only. The scientific course is also to be taught in the Jubbulpore Government College, the aided college at Nagpore having selected the course in literature.

144. The Relation of Government to Collegiate Education.—The general conclusion to be drawn from these facts seems to be that while colleges under private management have taken a creditable and in some cases a brilliant part in promoting scientific education, the chief share of that duty still devolves upon Government institutions. The large or general withdrawal of Government from the direct control of high education would therefore seem to involve the substitution of literary education for scientific over a wide area, and also—though this change would operate in a somewhat narrower field—the substitution of a pass for an honour student. It is quite in this sense that Mr. Lee-Warner in his report for 1884-85, after pointing to the dearth of aided colleges in Bombay and the necessity of revising the grant-in-aid rules in a liberal spirit, remarked:—
"With the introduction of a system which would give a college reasonable
"assistance in its infancy, when its needs are greatest, we might reasonably
"anticipate that private enterprise would supply the wants of the country with
"aided Arts colleges. Government could then concentrate its attention on the
"development of technical and scientific institutions, a department in which
"the cost of apparatus and the want of teaching power render it hopeless to
"expect that native society will be able to take the first step." To a similar effect wrote Mr. Wordsworth in his report of the Elphinstone College for 1885-86:—"If no additions can be made to the professoriate staff of this
"college, it seems on all grounds desirable that the work of preparing youths
"for the Previous Examination should be carried on in the high schools or
"provincial colleges, and that this college be only open to students preparing
"for the higher examinations. With our existing staff we could teach these
"pretty effectively, and include in our course some lectures for those reading
"for the degree of M. A." It is quite clear that private agency, financial considerations apart, is everywhere competent to undertake the charge of second-grade colleges, and also generally that of first-grade colleges reading for the pass standard alone. It is no less clear that Government agency is still required, not only to maintain the highest standard of liberal education in India, but still more to develope it in its scientific branches.

145. Recommendations of the Commission as to Collegiate Education.—The Commission were precluded by their instructions from inquiring into the working of Indian Universities, and they accordingly put forward but few suggestions of a general character regarding collegiate instruction. The chief recommendations under this head are contained in Chapter VI. of the Report. They may be divided into the following groups:—

A. Extension of the Means of Education.

"1. That the attention of the Local Governments be invited to the recommendations made in the several provincial reports with regard to providing or extending the means of collegiate education in the province of Sind and at Ahmedabad in Bombay, at Bhagalpur in Bengal, and at Jabalpur in the Central Provinces; and also to the question of the establishment of an aided college at Delhi under native management.

"6. That in order to encourage diversity of culture, both on the literary and on the physical side, it is desirable in all the larger colleges, Government and aided, to make provision for more than one of the alternative courses laid down by the Universities."

B. Grants to Aided Colleges.

"2. That the rate of aid to each college be determined by the strength of the staff, the expenditure on its maintenance, the efficiency of the institution, and the wants of the locality.

"3. That provision be made for special grants to aided colleges, whenever necessary, for the supply and renewal of buildings, furniture, libraries, and other apparatus of instruction."

C. Employment of Indian Graduates.

"5. That Indian graduates, especially those who have also graduated in European Universities, be more largely employed than they have hitherto been in the colleges maintained by Government."

D. Withdrawal of Government from the Direct Management of Colleges.

The recommendations under this head are found in Chapter VIII. of the report and are as follows:—

"27. That in order to evoke and stimulate local co-operation in the transfer to private management of Government institutions for collegiate or secondary instruction, aid at specially liberal rates be offered for a term of years, wherever necessary, to any local body willing to undertake the management of any such institution under adequate guarantees of permanence and efficiency.

"32. That in dealing with the question of the withdrawal of Government from the management of existing colleges, these colleges be regarded as divided into three classes, *viz*:—

(1) Those from which it is premature for Government to consider the propriety of withdrawal, on the ground that they are, and will long continue to be, the institutions on which the higher education of the country mainly depends;

(2) Those that might be transferred with advantage, as a measure promising useful political results, to bodies of native gentlemen, provided the new managers give satisfactory guarantees that the college will be maintained (1) permanently, (2) in full efficiency, (3) in such a way as to make it adequate for all the wants of the locality;

(3) Those which have been shown to be unsuccessful, or of which the cost is out of proportion to the utility, and from which Government might advantageously withdraw, even with less stringent guarantees for permanent efficiency. Such colleges should be closed if, after due notice, no local body be formed to carry them on with such a grant-in-aid as the rules provide.

"33. That the Government of Madras be requested to consider the propriety of dealing with the second-grade Government colleges of that province on the principles applicable to the second or third class as may be deemed advisable in each case, in the light of the recommendations made by the Madras Provincial Committee.

"34. That the Government of Bombay be requested to consider the propriety of raising the Ahmedabad college to one teaching up to the B.A. standard, and of securing its full efficiency for a term of years, on the condition that after that period it be treated on the principles applicable to the second class.

"35. That the Government of Bengal be requested to consider the propriety of dealing with the Rajshahye and Krishnagar Government Colleges on the principles applicable to the second class, and with the colleges at Berhampur, Midnapur, and Chittagong on the principles applicable to the third class, as suggested by the Bengal Provincial Committee."

146. Extension of Collegiate Education.—The specific recommendations (VI. 1) made by the Commission with regard to particular colleges have been severally dealt with by the Governments concerned. The Government of Bombay explained that its aim had been to maintain a sufficient establishment of colleges without superfluity. "When time is ripe for founding colleges in "the provinces which now possess none, the Government will be prepared to "take action in this direction;" but the time had probably not yet come in Sind. "When there is even a bare sufficiency of Government colleges, it seems proper "to require some evidence of genuine local effort and enterprise before assigning "public support to new ones, and the Commission recognises this principle in the "case of the Gujarat College." The Government had already (in 1884) taken action for the further development of the Gujarat College by offering to the community of Ahmedabad terms which were believed to be liberal on the principles enunciated by the Commission. It had offered a subsidy for a full college, but had held its hand because the local co-operation appeared to be not quite adequate. In 1885, it was further stated that "Government have helped "into existence the aided Gujarat College. It is true that the scaffolding of Gov- "ernment professors must be thrown down before the College can claim to be a "monument of native aided enterprise, but the building has been commenced on "plans and estimates which aim at that final result." The Province of Sind, it was now added, had stronger claims to a provincial college, and correspondence was going on with the local authorities with the view of establishing a college under local management. The Lieutenant-Governor of Bengal could not accept the recommendation that provision for collegiate education should be made at Bhagalpore. His Honour observed :—" We should, in his view, rather retire "from, than embark further in, interference with collegiate education. At all "events, he deems the establishment of a college at Bhagalpore, with Patna "within a few hours' journey by rail, wholly unnecessary." The Jubbulpore Government College has lately been raised to the first grade, chiefly by the aid of local subscriptions amounting to R79,000, which have been invested for the benefit of the college. Further provision of the same kind has been made in non-Government institutions in the Central Provinces. The Free Church College at Nagpore has been raised to the first grade by means of large additional contributions made by the parent Society, the extra cost to Government being limited to R100 a month. The Morris College has also been established at Nagpore by the aid of private subscriptions amounting to R1,70,000, and has been placed under a committee consisting partly of official and partly of non-official members. It is aided by grants from Government and from the local municipality. No attempt appears to have been made to establish an aided college at Delhi under native management. The ground is now occupied by St. Stephen's College, established in 1883 by the Cambridge Mission.

The provision that has been or is being made in Government and aided colleges respectively for the establishment of alternative courses in literature and science has been considered in a previous paragraph.

147. Grants to Aided Colleges.—The particular recommendations under this head would apparently find a more appropriate place among those that relate to the revision of the grant-in-aid rules, where, indeed, there is a specific recommendation "that the payment-by-results system be not applied to colleges" (VIII. 5). The recommendations were accepted in all provinces; and, indeed, no change was required except in Bombay, where, under the system criticised by the Commission, aid to a college was given in the shape of a fixed grant of R100 for every student passing either of the University examinations in Arts. The objections to the system were urged in paragraphs 463 to 465 of the Commission's Report, where it was stated that the Commission could "scarcely "conceive of a college springing up under this mode of aid." The Government of Bombay was at first disinclined to accept this recommendation; but the Government of India, in calling upon the Local Government to make a change in its rules, remarked:—" Private enterprise in this branch of instruction can " never make a fair start under a system of payment by results. It is hoped, "therefore, ... that the grant-in-aid rules may in this respect be assimilated " at a very early date to those in force in Bengal." The objections to the existing method were afterwards admitted by the educational authorities in Bombay to be insuperable. The paucity of aided colleges in that province was adduced as evidence that the grant-in-aid rules for colleges were illiberal; but at the same time defects were equally alleged against the Bengal system, which gives a fixed monthly grant for a term of years, the amount being determined chiefly by the sums expended from private sources in the maintenance of the college. On the one hand the teachers employed by the Society of Jesus in St. Xavier's College were men who devoted their lives to the work of education, but who received no remuneration for their services and declined to appraise them at any money value—a compromise which had been advocated by the Commission in paragraph 459 of their Report, and which formed the subject of a special recommendation (VIII. 2). On the other, the staff of the Fergusson College at Poona was composed of men who, though they included some of the most capable students of the University, were content from purely patriotic motives to work at reduced salaries, while at the same time they believed that they would distance all rivals in the examination-room. From the motive, therefore, either of religion or of patriotism, the authorities of these colleges were unanimous in declining a grant based on expenditure. A new plan was therefore hit upon, for which its authors claimed that it removed all difficulties and combined the merits of elasticity and liberality with a due regard to economy. Under this method the grant to a college was fixed in the first instance at R2,500 for each year of the full course of three years which it taught: thus a first-grade college would receive R7,500 a year. This grant was to be given subject to two conditions: (1) that the college was maintained in efficiency; (2) that the grant did not exceed, in the case of a first-grade college, R100 a year for each student in average attendance. If, therefore, the number of students fell below 75, the grant could be reduced in proportion. Again, the grant might be raised to R10,000 a year for any college in which the increased attendance or widened courses of instruction justified a further claim upon Government assistance. The Local Government accepted the scheme provisionally, but doubted whether it did not contain a weak point in the absence of any guarantee for proportionate expenditure from private assets. Accordingly, the Government demanded an assurance that educational assets, either in money or in money's worth, to double the amount of the State grant should be actually made good by the institution claiming aid. It was anticipated that the colleges which earned R6,100 in 1884-85 would, under the new rules, receive R24,000 in the following year, and an assignment to that amount was sanctioned in the estimates. The actuals, however, only reached R9,400. Of the immediate effect of the rules a satisfactory account is given by the Director, who states that they have enabled the Free General Assembly's College to appoint an additional professor.

148. Employment of Indian Graduates.—General readiness has been expressed to accept and act upon the proposal of the Commission to employ Indian graduates, especially those who have graduated in English Universities, as professors in colleges. In Madras the graded list already contains two native graduates of distinction who are employed in the Presidency College, while the entire staff in the other two first-grade colleges, with the exception of the principals and one professor, is composed of graduates of the local University. In Bengal there are eight natives of India in the superior graded staff, or one-fifth of the whole number; six of these are employed as principals or professors of colleges, including the Principal of the Sanskrit College. Further, of the eight colleges of the first grade, only four have a full European staff; the remainder have a European principal with native professors. Four small colleges are entirely officered by natives of India. In the Punjab four Indian graduates, one of whom has graduated at Cambridge, are employed in the Government College at Lahore; though His Honour the Lieutenant-Governor believes that it will be a long time before Europeans can be dispensed with for the higher professorships. He adduces the fact that in the Muhammadan College at Aligarh, which is entirely under native management, three Englishmen, graduates of Cambridge, are employed. In the Jubbulpore College two of the four professors are Indian graduates.

149. Withdrawal of Government from the Direct Management of Colleges.—The specific recommendations of the Commission on this point are limited to the provinces of Madras, Bombay, and Bengal. The action taken in Bombay with regard to the Gujarat College has just been described. For Madras it was proposed that the Government should either withdraw from the management of, or should close, the seven colleges of the second grade that were departmentally maintained. The Government of Madras declared its policy on this point to be "to transfer to municipal and local bodies as "much as is prudent of the administration of all but the highest education, "by which means the guarantees of efficiency are likely to be more satis- "factorily attained than by transfer to a private committee;" and the Director of Public Instruction was of opinion that the only institutions which it was necessary, in the interests of education, to retain under Government management were the three first-grade colleges at the Presidency, Kumbakonam, and Rajamundry. Speedy action was taken in accordance with these views, and at the end of 1885-86 the college at Salem had been transferred to the local municipality, and the college at Bellary had been closed. There still remain in Madras five provincial colleges of the second grade.

Of the five second-grade colleges in Bengal, two are college departments attached to the Calcutta Sanskrit College and the Calcutta Madrassa. So long as Government retains control over the central institutions, it is obvious that it cannot transfer to other management the small collegiate departments attached to them. The question of closing the college classes altogether was a separate one, but the Government saw advantages in retaining at small cost in each of these institutions a department which served to leaven the orientalism of their course. With regard to the three second-grade colleges outside Calcutta a different policy was followed. By a Resolution issued in 1886, the Government of Bengal declared the Lieutenant-Governor's intention "to close the Midnapore "and Berhampore Colleges if no arrangement can be made before the 1st of May "1887 for the transfer of their charge. It is thus left to those interested to "determine for themselves whether these institutions shall continue to exist; "and the Lieutenant-Governor confidently anticipates that the public spirit and "interest in high education, for which both the important districts immediately "interested are remarkable, will be found equal to the occasion." These anticipations have been justified by the result. The Midnapore College, together with the attached collegiate school, has been taken over by the local municipality with an annual grant of R1,600, equal to the average cost of those institutions to Government for the two preceding years; and the Berhampore College and school have been transferred to the management of a local committee without a grant-in-aid for an experimental period of five years, the transfer having been rendered possible by the munificence of the Maharani Sarnamayi, C.I., who expressed her desire to provide for the cost of its maintenance without Government aid. The cost to Government of the college departments of these institutions in the last year was R869 for Midnapore, and R12,276 for Berhampore. The transfer of the Midnapore College causes no immediate reduction in the Government expenditure; but that of Berhampore will effect an ultimate saving to the full amount stated above, as soon as the officers whom the new management did not desire to retain in its service are absorbed. To both institutions large private endowments were attached, amounting to R28,000 in the case of Berhampore, and to R60,000 in that of Midnapore; and these endowments, together with the buildings and other property attached to the colleges, were made over to the control of the new managers, in accordance with a recommendation of the Commission to that effect (VIII. 28). Provision was also made for securing such of the officers as were transferred with the college in the enjoyment of their existing rights and privileges (VIII. 29). The Resolution further stated that the colleges of Rajshahye and Krishnagar, which are officered by a native staff with the exception of the European Principal, would be transferred only on condition that a body of native gentlemen could be found to give adequate guarantees for permanent and efficient management. No arrangement under such conditions had then been found possible, though tentative proposals have since been made for the transfer of the Krishnagar College.

The Government colleges in the North-Western Provinces were not the subject of any definite recommendation by the Commission. But in 1883 the management of the Agra College was transferred to a board of trustees, who received in aid of its maintenance, together with that of the attached school department, annual grants of R10,000 from the Government and of R8,000 from the municipality of Agra, in addition to the income of R22,000 a year derived from the original endowment of Babu Gangadhar Shastri, to whose munificence the college owed its origin. At the time of the transfer the trustees made an appeal to the noblemen and gentlemen of the North-Western Provinces, with the result that a lakh of rupees was added to the endowment, while the capital of the separate scholarship fund was raised from R25,000 to R45,000. The result of the transfer has been to reduce the Government expenditure on the whole institution from an average of about R30,000 to R10,000 while the attendance of students in the college department has risen from 29 to 65. The Bareilly College, which had been closed in 1876, was re-opened as a second-grade college in 1884 and placed under the management of a local committee, with a Government grant of R1,800 a year, the remainder of the income being derived from an endowment fund. Since its transfer to private management the attendance at the college has risen by 69 per cent.

150. Other Recommendations regarding Colleges.—The Commission recommended "that an attempt be made to prepare a moral text-book, based "upon the fundamental principles of natural religion, such as may be taught in "all Government and non-Government colleges;" and "that the Principal or one "of the professors in each Government and aided college deliver to each of the "college classes in every session a series of lectures on the duties of a man and a "citizen." (VI. 8, 9). The Government of India questioned the possibility of introducing such a text-book without raising a variety of burning questions; and thought it improbable that a text-book of morality, sufficiently vague and colourless to be accepted by Christians, Muhammadans, and Hindus, would do much, especially in the stage of collegiate instruction, to remedy the defects or supply the shortcomings of a purely secular education. The Secretary of State intimated his concurrence in the views of the Government of India, but added that possibly hereafter some book in the nature of a text-book of moral rules might be written of such merit as to render its use desirable. In that event the question could be reconsidered.

Recommendations 10 to 13 relate to fees and free studentships in colleges. The 10th, relating to the comparative rates of fees in Government and aided colleges, and the 13th, relating to the special case of the Presidency College in Madras, have already been considered. The others have been generally approved and acted on.

· Recommendations 14 to 19 refer to scholarships. They have been generally accepted in principle, though the consideration of some, such as the provision of scholarships to enable graduates to read for the M. A. degree or to proceed to Europe for technical instruction, has been postponed on financial grounds. The 14th recommendation invites Local Governments to consider whether the provision for scholarships tenable in colleges should exceed two per cent. of the provincial grant for education. In Bengal it amounted in 1885-86 to about 2·16 per cent. of the assignment. The only other provinces to which the recommendation seems to have applied were Assam and Berar, in which it is explained that the provision for scholarships was intended to make up to promising students for the absence of a local college in which they might continue their studies. The 18th recommendation proposed the substitution in Madras of a system of scholarships, tenable in any college, for the existing provision of free-studentships tenable in Government colleges; and the 19th invited the Government of Bombay to consider the advisability of allowing the Elphinstone and Deccan College scholarships to be made tenable in any affiliated college. It does not appear that any action has been taken on these recommendations.

151. Oriental Colleges.—The number of these institutions shown in the returns has fallen from four to two; the Oriental department of the Muhammadan College at Aligarh, which had long been declining, having finally disappeared as a separate institution, and the statistics of the Punjab Oriental College having been received too late for insertion in the provincial returns. The other two are the Government Sanskrit College at Benares and the Oriental department of the Canning College, Lucknow. An account of these institutions was given in the preceding chapter of this report. It will be noticed that the Benares Sanskrit College is not a college in the technical sense of the term, since its students do not read for any University standards. The Calcutta Sanskrit College is returned as an English college, by reason of the First Arts classes that it maintains; it is also strictly, though in a limited sense, an Oriental college, since a few of its students read for the M.A. degree in Sanskrit. For a similar reason, the Calcutta Madrassa is returned as an English second-grade college; but its standard in Arabic and in Muhammadan Law, however high, is not prescribed by any University. This institution, together with the other madrassas of Bengal which read to the same standard, will be considered in the section relating to Muhammadan Education.

The Benares Sanskrit College contained 458 students in 1885-86, all Hindus. Its wide popularity is shown by the fact that 190 of the students came from outside the North-Western Provinces, including 161 from Bengal. The students are subject to a special examination by their own professors in various branches of Sanskrit literature, proficiency in which is rewarded by the bestowal of titles. The Anglo-Sanskrit department included 48 students, mostly pundits advanced in life, whose progress in English is described as slow. The maintenance of the college involved an expenditure of R13,900 from provincial revenues, and R234 were realised from fees. The Oriental department of the Canning College contained 88 students, of whom 51 were Muhammadans. The students at this institution are examined by the Punjab University for the titles which that body confers. For the maintenance of its Oriental department, the college derived R2,533 from Government and R3,287 from the proceeds of the endowment; it also received R19 from fees.

152. The Punjab Oriental College.—This institution contained 144 students in the college department, against 119 for the previous year. The Director's report observes :—" The College affords valuable instruction of a high order "in Arabic, Persian, and Sanskrit, and provides instruction in general education "through the medium of the vernacular; but it stood in urgent need of reform. "Some improvements have been already effected, and the practice of teaching "what is opposed to modern science, such as the Ptolemic system of astronomy, "which prevailed in some branches has now, I understand, been discontinued." Colonel Holroyd was of opinion that the utility of the college would be much increased if it were brought into relation, by means of a system of stipends, with the advanced indigenous schools of the province, which would thus supply the college with picked men from all parts of the Punjab—a suggestion which the Government thought worthy of consideration. The working of the institution underwent close scrutiny during the year, the investigation of a sub-committee appointed for that purpose having, in the words of His Honour the Lieutenant-Governor, "brought to light the extraordinary condition of affairs that all the "students who were attending the College and School were stipendiaries, with the "exception of 46 who were in expectation of obtaining stipends." His Honour had previously remarked :—" It seemed nothing short of a scandal not only that "so enormous and costly a staff should be employed with so infinitesimal a re-"turn in the shape of fees, but that there should be in the Oriental College and "School so large an annual expenditure on purely charitable stipends, and that "stipends or scholarships should in some instances be drawn by the same person "for 8, 10, and even 14 years." The course of instruction was the subject of equally severe criticism at the hands of the sub-committee. The following extracts from their report will be of interest :—" With regard to the scope of the "pretensions and the operations of the Oriental College and School, the Sub-Com-"mittee found that they were out of all proportion to the available means, efficient "teaching power, and appliances. It is unfortunate that really good and valuable "work has been mixed up with various prétentious schemes which have given "rise to an erroneous impression that the institution is to a great extent a sham "of pseudo-oriental and pseudo-scientific education. In the published reports it "is represented not only as an institution for advanced instruction in Oriental Clas-"sics and for communication of knowledge on subjects of General Knowledge and "Science through the medium of the Vernaculars, but also as a school of Hindu "and Muhammadan Law, an Engineering school, a school of Medicine for two "systems, the Hindu and Muhammadan, and a resort for Central Asian students."

The sub-committee then go on to give the actual facts, as ascertained by visit and inquiry. " There are at present no classes in Hindu and Muhammadan law." The only foundation for the statement was that a salary of R10 a month was given to the Head Pundit and Head Maulavi to deliver lectures on these subjects. " They are said to have been delivered out of college hours. There is no " record in the college tables as to how many lectures had been delivered, or how " many students had attended, and they are said to have been discontinued for " several months because students did not attend." The sub-committee recommended that the allowances should be discontinued. The engineering classes were in a satisfactory state, though it was considered that drawing and surveying classes would be a more appropriate name. The sub-committee believed these classes to be very valuable, as leading to a means of livelihood in the subordinate branches of the Public Works Department, and recommended additional expenditure on them. " As regards the Medical classes, it was found that " the only instruction given to each student was half an hour a day in the study " of Arabic or Sanskrit ancient medical books........Special stipends of R1 to R3 " were paid to those attending. There were none of the appliances of a Medical " school, and they found on their visit that a person was teaching as *Hakím* who " had no special qualification beyond being the brother of one of the other teach-" ers." Such a system the sub-committee condemned as worse than useless. In its character as a resort for Central Asian students the college employed a teacher on R8 a month, at whose feet sat two scholars, zamindars from places in or on the borders of Cashmere, aged respectively 45 and 35. The first " had " joined seven years ago, but had taken two years' leave during Dr. Leitner's ab-" sence. His stipend was R5 per mensem." The other " had been here about " five months. Both had been taught their letters here. The first was able to read " a little of a Persian primer with difficulty; the other could read a few pages of " the Qurán by rote. This teacher also gave instruction in Arabic for one hour " daily to the students of medicine. The Sub-Committee proposed no reduction ' in this expenditure, as it was so slight, besides being an interesting curiosity." After these damaging strictures, the following expression of opinion will be received with relief :—" As to the real legitimate work of the Oriental College and " School, (1) the teaching of Classics to a high standard, (2) instruction in Science " and General Knowledge in the vernacular, the Sub-Committee expressed a " high opinion of its value and importance as at present conducted." It will have been noticed that the Punjab Oriental College shares with other colleges of the same class the difficulty of realising fees from students. The cost of the college in 1885-86 was R25,477, including an expenditure of R4,682 on stipends, while the fee-receipts amounted to only R578. The sub-committee remarked on the subject of stipends :—" The large expenditure in salaries to the students " showed how artificial the foundation of the institution is at present. The attend-" ance can be increased or diminished *ad libitum* by the amount of scholarships " and stipends paid. The scholarships are the rewards of merit in examinations " passed, but the stipends are awarded to those who fail to secure the former, " and are also used as an inducement to poor boys to join the institution." It was added that the few free-students in the college were hanging on in the hope of getting stipends, and would most likely disappear if they failed to secure them. One of the members of the sub-committee objected to the reduction of stipends, on the ground that from time immemorial the study of Sanskrit and Arabic had been connected with the receipt of alms, of which stipends took the place. The Education Commission referred in like manner to " the traditional " sentiment in favour of gratuitous education which still lingers in the minds " alike of Muhammadans and of Hindus," adding their belief that such a sentiment was wholly incompatible with any wide-spread scheme for education of a modern type. " The Brahman educated in a Sanskrit *tol* devoted himself to a

153. The Calcutta Sanskrit College.—Besides 19 students in the Arts classes of this college, in which also Sanskrit is taught to a much higher standard than the University requires, 25 students were reading for the Sanskrit Title examinations, and five others for the M.A. degree in Sanskrit. The college, which is under the charge of Mahámahopádhyáya Mahesh Chandra Nyáyáratna, C.I.E., was maintained at a cost (including the Arts department) of R21,458, of which R1,058 were paid in fees. The Sanskrit Title examinations held in 1885-86 were conducted by a board of examiners composed partly of professors of the college and partly of learned pundits from other places in Bengal. Seventy-two students passed in various branches of literature, law, and philosophy, and received titles corresponding to their acquirements. A Government grant of R1,500 a year is made towards the expenses of the examination, and numerous prizes and scholarships for successful students have been founded by private liberality.

SECTION IV (a).—SECONDARY EDUCATION.

154. Character and Scope of Secondary Education.—The following extract from the Report of the Education Commission (paragraph 225) may be cited as illustrating the divergent views that prevail in different parts of India as to the character of the instruction to be imparted in secondary schools, and as to the position which such schools occupy in the general scheme of education : " In some Provinces the course in secondary schools is framed with exclusive " reference to the University matriculation standard; in others, independent " standards and courses of instruction are also found. In some Provinces, but " not in all, instruction in English forms a necessary part of the course; in others, " the study of an Oriental classic is required, either as an alternative with English " or as an independent subject; in others, again, elementary science is prescribed. " In every province, history, geography, and either geometry or algebra or both, " form part of the course, though one or other of the first two subjects is some- " times taught in primary schools of the better class. But with all these differen- " ces, there is a clear line of distinction between secondary and primary educa- " tion, in that the character of the former no longer has exclusive reference to the " practical requirements of the student in after-life. In however small a degree, " it begins to be definitely associated with what is understood as liberal education, " and with the exercise of the higher faculties of thought. These are the lines " by which the character of secondary education has been determined in all " countries, and along which its development should manifestly proceed." The variety of standard above noted is, however, practically confined to lower secondary (or middle) schools. The course in upper secondary (or high) schools is governed throughout by the standard of the matriculation examination in which it ends, and that standard does not vary very widely among the different Universities of India.

155. Different Classes of Secondary Schools.—At the date of the Commission's report, secondary schools were divided into the two classes of high and middle. The Commission recommended, in order to avoid any misconception as to the meaning of the term " high school" (which had sometimes been applied to what are now known as second-grade colleges), that the use of that term should be discontinued, and that high and middle schools should be united in the returns as secondary schools (V. 3). The term " high school" has not, it is true, dropped out of use. It is still employed as a short and convenient synonym for upper secondary schools; and as the term " second-grade college " is now uniformly applied to those institutions that read up to the First Arts standard, there appears to be no objection to the continued use of the term " high school" for those in which the course is limited by the matriculation stand. ard. The returns, however, no longer show explicitly the distinction between upper and lower secondary, that is, between high and middle schools. The necessary information as to pupils may be gained from general Table V, which shows the number of scholars in the " high stage" of instruction, that is, all between the lower secondary (or middle) and the matriculation standard—a period of two years; and the necessary information as to schools may be gained ap. proximately from general Table VI, which shows the number of schools that send pupils to the Entrance examination. I say approximately, because on the one hand the table excludes those schools which have passed beyond the middle stage and are preparing pupils for the Entrance examination, without having yet reached that standard; while on the other, there are schools under private management which send candidates to the examination but furnish no returns to the Department.

According to the returns, therefore, the only recognised division of secondary schools throughout India is that into English and vernacular. The secondary system is however in reality much more complicated than this simple division would imply. The different classes of schools and the standards for which

x

they respectively read, are described at length in Chapter V of the Commission's report. Here the results may be briefly re-stated. In Bombay and the Central Provinces every pupil receives the rudiments of his education in a primary school, and must have passed either the upper or the lower primary examination before he can obtain admission into a secondary school and begin the study of English. The primary course is thus the same for all pupils, whatever their future destination. In other provinces, high and middle schools have attached primary departments, and a pupil can pass the Entrance examination from the same school in which he began his letters. In this case the study of English may either be commenced in the lowest class of the school, as in Madras, the North-Western Provinces, Burma, and usually in Bengal; or it may be postponed until the lower stage of primary instruction is passed, as in the Punjab. The requirements of pupils who do not look beyond primary, or at most beyond middle instruction are provided for in these provinces by a parallel class of schools, vernacular in the main, in which the course of study diverges more or less widely from that of the lower or middle departments of secondary schools in which English is taught. Again, after the primary standards are done with, and a pupil enters on the secondary stage, he may either, as in Madras, the North-Western Provinces, the Punjab and the Central Provinces, pursue a single and undifferentiated course through the middle to the high school standard; or a bifurcation of studies may take place, and the middle school course may terminate in a standard which differs from that at the corresponding stage in a high school. Such a bifurcation obtains in Bombay, where the ordinary middle school course, preparatory to the high school, is extended in an independent direction for two years, and ends in the public service certificate examination. It also obtains in Bengal, where the middle school course differs from that in high schools *ab initio*, and the medium of instruction is vernacular throughout. Then again, in Madras, in all the provinces of Northern India, and to some extent in Burma, there are secondary schools of purely vernacular instruction, which are a development of the ordinary primary school. The same thing exists in fact, if not in name, in Bombay and the Central Provinces, where special standards, occupying a period of two years, have been added to the primary course for the benefit of those students who desire somewhat more advanced instruction than the ordinary primary school supplies. The primary school, thus enlarged, prepares candidates for the examination qualifying for the lower grades of the public service.

156. Secondary Schools for Boys, 1885-86.—The number of secondary schools, English and vernacular, and the attendance of pupils in them, are shown for each province in the two following tables, in which the schools are classified according to management.

Secondary Schools, English, 1885-86.

PROVINCE.	MANAGED BY THE DEPARTMENT.		MANAGED BY LOCAL OR MUNICIPAL BOARDS.		AIDED SCHOOLS.		UN-AIDED SCHOOLS.		TOTAL.	
	Schools.	Pupils.	Schools.	Pupils.	Schools.	Pupils.	Schools.	Pupils.	Schools.	Pupils.
Madras	10	1,268	135	11,592	300	31,520	76	6,732	521	51,112
Bombay	(a)102	15,475	110	3,407	96	12,872	20	2,991	328	34,745
Bengal	64	16,411	7	1,537	698	60,348	227	31,330	996	109,626
N.-W. Provinces	1	514	42	8,581	78	13,730	9	909	130	23,734
Punjab	(b)34	9,537	29	6.115	32	8,307	1	373	96	24,332
Central Provinces	38	2,585	2	74	21	1,068	2	50	63	3,777
Burma	2	222	16	2,139	22	3,343	2	163	42	5,867
Assam	14	2,557	...	...	32	2,940	12	1,186	58	6,683
Berar	26	4,606	...	...	...	...	...	...	26	4,606
Coorg	1	330	1	86	1	20	...	...	3	436
TOTAL	292	53,505	342	33,531	1,280	134,148	349	43,734	2,263	264,918
TOTAL FOR 1884-85	(c)296	52,606	335	32,615	1,248	129,039	325	40,542	2,204	254,802

(a) Includes 57 schools with 4,937 pupils in Native States in Bombay.
(b) „ 4 „   „ 1,046 „ in the Punjab managed by other Departments of Government or in other ways.
(c) „ 55 „   „ 4,374 „ in Native States in Bombay; and 5 schools with 1,078 pupils in the Punjab, managed by other Departments of Government or in other ways.

Secondary Schools, Vernacular, 1885-86.

PROVINCE.	MANAGED BY THE DEPARTMENT.		MANAGED BY LOCAL OR MUNICIPAL BOARDS.		AIDED SCHOOLS.		UNAIDED SCHOOLS.		TOTAL.	
	Schools.	Pupils.	Schools.	Pupils.	Schools.	Pupils.	Schools.	Pupils.	Schools.	Pupils.
Madras	...	...	...	...	30	1,568	7	298	37	1,866
Bengal	179	9,508	9	1,417	857	47,166	96	5,853	1,141	63,944
N.-W. Provinces	1	60	433	37,219	14	1,234	9	898	457	39,411
Punjab	...	...	124	19,154	2	160	1	70	127	19,384
Burma	...	...	...	...	15	1,800	...	...	15	1,800
Assam	16	1,361	...	...	26	1,756	1	68	43	3,185
TOTAL	196	10,929	566	57,790	944	53,684	114	7,187	1,820	129,590
TOTAL FOR 1884-85	198	12,177	570	56,933	909	51,380	110	6,680	1,787	127,170

157. Secondary Schools, English : Attendance.—The total number of high and middle schools in which English is taught showed an increase of 59, with an addition of 10,116 pupils. The average number of pupils to a school increased from 115 to 117. The schools maintained by the Department, which in most provinces include the leading high schools of the country, are much the most numerously attended, with an average of 183 pupils in each. Next come unaided schools with an average of 125 pupils, and aided schools with 105. Board schools, which are for the most part confined to those of the middle class, have an attendance of 98 pupils each. The average daily attendance bore to the average monthly roll number a proportion of 84 per cent. in departmental and board schools, of 81 per cent. in aided schools, and of 82 per cent. in unaided schools. These proportions are much the same as those of the previous year : the only noticeable change being a rise of 2 per cent. in the daily attendance of unaided schools—a satisfactory indication of improved discipline.

As has already been stated, high and middle schools are combined in the returns under the common name of secondary schools. But in some cases it is possible to separate the figures for high schools ; and it is worth while to compare them for the three leading provinces. The 119 high schools of Madras have an average of 190 pupils each ; the 264 high schools of Bengal have an average of 211. In both cases the high schools have attached primary departments, though in Madras the primary departments in Government institutions are gradually being reduced. The 63 high schools of Bombay, which have no attached primary departments, have an average of 310 pupils each, a fact which bears out the remark of the Commission that the secondary schools in Bombay are very efficient, better filled than in other provinces, and well distributed.

158. Secondary Schools, English : Control.—The increase in schools is mostly confined to those under private management, aided and unaided. The changes under departmental and board schools are much smaller, the most important having taken place in Madras. In that province, the Department has retired from the direct management of secondary education as far as is at present practicable. One high school has been abolished; six more have been transferred to municipal management. Thus the number of departmental high schools has decreased from 16 to 9. Five of these are in the Agency Tracts, and must continue to be maintained from provincial funds. One is a special school for Muhammadans in the town of Madras. Of the other three, one is to be retained as the practising school for the Teachers' College, about to be transferred from Madras to Saidapet. A second is to be either made over to the local municipality or closed. In the third case there is no municipality or other local agency competent to take it over. Owing to the same policy of transfer

the number of high schools under municipal management has increased from 10 to 17. It is the same of middle schools : out of 402 schools of that class in the Madras Presidency, only one remains under the direct control of the Department, while 105 are managed by district and 12 by municipal boards. In Bengal there has been as yet no such extensive transfer. But a beginning has been made ; and in the year under report the number of secondary schools maintained by municipal bodies increased from three to seven. Municipalities took over two high schools from the control of private committees, and relieved Government of the cost of two middle vernacular schools ; the latter after transfer were converted into English schools. These are small beginnings ; but in accordance with the provisions of the Local Self-Government Act, all Government middle schools have since been transferred to district boards, which have but lately come into existence, while Government high schools are to be made over to joint committees, which have in no case yet been appointed. At the close of 1885-86 there were in Bengal 52 high and 12 middle schools maintained by the Department; four high and three middle schools maintained by municipal boards. In Bombay there is a decline of three in the number of departmental middle schools. One school has been amalgamated, one transferred to the municipality, and one closed because " the local authorities were too poor to support it accord-
" ing to the requirements of the new Act. " It is added that arrangements for the transfer of the remaining Government middle schools are in progress. No high schools are maintained by local boards or municipalities in Bombay. Of 136 middle schools under public management, 26 are maintained by the Department, 47 by local boards and 63 by municipal boards. In the North-Western Provinces no change took place within the year; but with one exception—the high school department of the Benares College—all secondary schools, whether high or middle, are maintained from funds under the control of the boards, and middle schools are also managed by them. In the Punjab there were, up to the close of 1885-86, no high schools under local boards ; of middle schools 16 were maintained by the Department, 27 by municipalities, and two by district boards. Burma is the only other province in which local bodies take a leading part in the direct control of secondary education. Two out of the four high schools and all the 14 middle schools are under municipal management—a result of the large transfer of educational powers and funds that has been made to municipalities in that province.

Among aided English schools there is a loss of 32, made up chiefly by a gain of 17 in Bombay, of 22 in Bengal, of 13 in the North-Western Provinces, and of 5 in Assam, and by a loss of 28 in Madras. The decline in the middle schools of Madras, which is spread over the whole Presidency, is not explained ; in other provinces the increase is due to the ordinary operation of the grant-in-aid rules. This is specially noticeable in Bombay, where the adoption of a liberal policy towards private effort and the addition of R10,000 to the grant-in-aid allotment have resulted in an increase of 20 per cent. to the number of aided schools, in full accordance with a recent declaration of the Government of Bombay, that the further extension of secondary education must lie in the direction of encouraging private enterprise.

159. **Secondary Schools, Vernacular.**—With the exception of two or three high schools in the Punjab and the North-Western Provinces, all the schools in this class are middle schools. Their number is affected from year to year by two different causes. On the one hand, the class is recruited from the ranks of upper primary schools, as the best of them rise in standard. On the other, middle vernacular schools, in the general educational advance, take up the teaching of English and in time become converted to middle English schools. **There was altogether an increase of 33 middle vernacular schools, and of 2,420 pupils.** The

increase was almost entirely confined to aided schools. In Burma 14 indigenous schools have worked up to the middle standard, and been included in this class. The North-Western Provinces have added 12 and Madras 8, to the number of aided schools. The average number of pupils to a school was 71, as in the previous year. Departmental schools are mostly confined to Bengal, where they have since the close of 1885-86 been transferred to the management of district boards. The average number of pupils in such schools fell from 62 to 56; a loss which is due to the transfer of some of the most flourishing schools to the middle English class, as explained just above. Board schools were much more numerously attended, with an average of 102 pupils to each—an evidence, so far as it goes, of the capacity of local boards to manage this class of schools with efficiency. In Madras, however, where schools of this class are neither numerous nor very popular, the three middle vernacular schools under local boards disappeared during the year, falling back to the rank of primary schools. Aided and unaided schools contained respectively 57 and 63 pupils. The superiority of board schools is further shown in the regularity of their attendance, the proportion being for board schools 84 per cent. of the monthly roll-number, while for other schools it sinks to about 78 per cent.

It will be seen from the table that vernacular secondary schools are confined to six provinces of India. But in Bombay, and in those neighbouring provinces which have founded their educational system on that of Bombay, something corresponding to secondary education in the vernacular is to be found in those classes (reading the 5th and 6th standards) which have been added to the ordinary course in primary schools, and which terminate in an examination qualifying for the lower grades of the public service. Their pupils are, however, ordinarily shown in the returns of primary education. Seven-eighths of the schools of this class are found in Bengal and the North-Western Provinces; and their popularity, in the former province at any rate, is shown by the fact that 84 per cent. of these schools in Bengal are under private management. One of the leading vernacular newspapers of Bengal recently wrote on this subject to the following effect:—" Those who read in " higher class English schools become utterly useless, if they fail to pass the " Entrance examination; but those, on other hand, who read in the middle " schools, often acquire a good and useful knowledge of Bengali, even though " they fail to pass the examinations. Again, it is often good for those sons of " rich people who have no great intellectual power, to read in the vernacular " schools, where they may acquire such knowledge of Bengali arithmetic and " vernacular accounts as is sure to be of great practical use to them in after-life. " Thus it is desirable to raise the status and secure the permanence of the middle " vernacular and middle English schools." The manifest liking of the people of Bengal for schools so constituted thus appears to be based on practical considerations of their relative value. Indeed, in the four provinces of Northern India, preference has always been shown for placing secondary education to a moderate standard on a vernacular basis. The Despatch of 1854 established the position of this form of education, by declaring that schools in which no English was taught might, if their standard of instruction in other subjects was sufficiently high, be placed in the same rank with English schools. The value of such education was fully recognised; the idea of imparting western education through the medium of the vernaculars was an attractive one; and its cheapness supplied a further recommendation. The consequence was that in these provinces vernacular schools above the primary standard rapidly increased. But throughout the rest of India little value appears to be set on any form of secondary education from which English is excluded.

160. Different Departments in Secondary Schools.—Except in Bombay and the Central Provinces, secondary schools in all provinces have primary departmentments attached to them, though in Madras and Berar there is a tendency towards the gradual abolition of these departments in high schools. Hence the number of pupils returned for secondary schools, while it shows how many are in what may be described as the region of secondary instruction, is by no means identical with the number in the secondary stage. The division of the pupils according to the stages of instruction which they have reached, is given in general Table V appended to this report. The returns are summarised as follows for boys in all secondary schools, so far as they have been classified.

Stage of Instruction.	Number of Pupils in 1886.	Percentage in 1886.	Number of Pupils in 1885.	Percentage in 1885.
High	35,286	9·0	31,330	8·2
Middle	106,724	27·3	102,850	27·2
Upper Primary	85,093	21·8	78,764	20·8
Lower Primary	163,940	41·9	165,858	43·8
Total	391,043	100·0	378,802	100·0

It results, therefore, that only about 36 per cent. of all the boys in secondary schools are in the secondary stage, and only 9 per cent. of the whole number are in the high stage. A further inspection of the table discloses the fact that the proportion of pupils in the lowest stage has decreased by 2 per cent., about one per cent. having been added to the topmost rank of pupils, and one per cent. to those in the upper primary stage. A comparison of this kind affords a fair measure of progress from year to year.

The statement just given shows the distribution of pupils in schools of all classes ranked as secondary, whether they be high or middle, English or vernacular, with or without primary departments, under public or under private management. If it were worth while to separate all these classes of schools, a very different distribution of the pupils would doubtless result. There is however one division of schools, that into English and vernacular, which may usefully be made, since they occupy widely different portions of the field of secondary education. The percentages showing the distribution of pupils are the following:—

Stage of Instruction.	In English Schools.	In Vernacular Schools.
High	13·3	...
Middle	32·4	17·8
Upper Primary	21·1	23·0
Lower Primary	33·2	59·2

In English secondary schools, therefore, just 46 per cent. of the pupils are in the secondary stage. Also 82 per cent. of the pupils in secondary vernacular schools are in the primary stage—a fact which shows that these institutions serve the purpose of true primary schools of a superior class, and should therefore be taken into account in any estimate of the extent and development of primary education.

161. The Teaching of English in Secondary Schools.—Of 264,918 pupils in secondary English schools in 1885-86, 224,832 actually learnt English, while 40,086 read as yet the vernacular only. In the previous year those who read English and the vernacular alone numbered respectively 211,531 and 43,271. We have therefore an increase of more than 13,000 scholars reading English, while those who read the vernacular only have suffered a decline. That the numbers of the latter class are still so large is due to the practice, differently regarded in different parts of India, of postponing the teaching of English in secondary schools until the pupil has made some advance in elementary subjects of instruction through the vernacular. In some provinces the pupils in a high school begin English and the vernacular simultaneously in the lowest or alphabet class; in others the three or four lowest classes are confined to vernacular instruction. Again, there are middle schools in which the course of instruction is drawn up on purely vernacular lines, but which have added an English class for the more advanced pupils. These, when they have reached a certain stage of proficiency, are recognised as English schools and are classed accordingly. There are others, again, which, though they have begun to teach English, have yet to make good their claim to be ranked as English schools, and are still classified as middle vernacular. The returns show that there are 7,900 pupils, nearly all in Bengal, reading English in schools of this description. All these schools will in time make their way to the middle English class.

The subjoined statement compares the total number of pupils in the secondary English schools of each province with the number of pupils reading English in them. It will not escape notice that in Bombay and the Central Provinces there are no primary departments, and that in the lower primary classes of secondary schools in the Punjab no English is taught.

PROVINCE.	Total number of pupils in English secondary schools.	Number of pupils reading English in them.
Madras	51,112	45,495
Bombay	34,745	34,745
Bengal	109,626	90,714
N.-W. Provinces	23,734	22,351
Punjab	24,332	14,828
Central Provinces	3,777	3,777
Burma	5,867	5,542
Assam	6,683	5,031
Berar	1,606	1,883
Coorg	436	436
TOTAL	264,918	224,832

In Bombay, the Central Provinces and Coorg, every pupil in a secondary school reads English. The proportion is not far short of this in the North-Western Provinces and Burma, where English is taught to the great majority of pupils in secondary schools down to the lowest primary class. In other provinces a larger number of the pupils read the vernacular only.

162. The Medium of Instruction in Secondary Schools.—A further question arises. In vernacular schools the medium of instruction is necessarily the vernacular; but in English schools should the pupils be taught through their own vernacular, or through English—to them a foreign language? The question was a familiar one in England in days not very long gone by. In the grammar schools of that country, Latin and Greek grammar were invariably taught up to quite recent times by the aid of Latin text-books, and Latin and Greek authors were elucidated for the use of schoolboys by Latin notes. At the present day juster views prevail as to the value of artificial trammels in the acquisition of knowledge, and English has altogether displaced Latin as the vehicle of instruction. In India the question still occupies debateable ground and divides the opinion of authorities. It is true that the conditions are widely different in the two countries. In England a boy learns Latin, it is presumed, as an element in a liberal education, as a recognised form of culture, as a solace for his leisure hours; but not as a language for which he will have any use in the business of life. In India, on the other hand, the Entrance examination which crowns his school course is conducted in English; throughout his subsequent University career English is exclusively employed; and familiarity with English as a spoken and living language is indispensable to success in official and professional life. These are important differences; and they furnish ground for the contention that throughout his school course an Indian boy's mind should be saturated with English; that he should be talked to and made to talk in English, that his text-books in history or geography should be in English, not indeed in order to teach him history or geography the better, but in order to familiarise him the more with English. On the other side it is urged that by following such a method, you may indeed teach him English but you will teach him nothing else, and that the main purpose of his education will be missed. Nor, again, is it conceded that you will by this method be sure of making him a more expert and fluent English scholar. To recur to the case of the schoolboy or the University man in England, it is maintained that if he had to use Latin and Latin only in his ordinary public life, if he had to conduct cases in it, to preach in it, to correspond in it, he would be enabled to discharge all these duties just as efficiently under the present as under the exploded system. It is certainly the modern theory in England that a boy's intellect should be strengthened by instruction in his own vernacular before he attempts the study of a foreign language, and that he will thus be enabled to grapple with the difficulties of the foreign language much more successfully. It is precisely in this sense that the head masters of Harrow, Winchester, and Marlborough have lately expressed their intention of postponing the study of Greek to a later stage than at present They condemn the practice of making boys begin Greek "before either their "knowledge of Latin or their mental growth has qualified them to enter on the "study of a second dead language. Our experience shows that the minds of "young boys are confused by the multiplicity of subjects taught at the same time. ". . . Boys who began [Greek] at a later age would be able with more rapidity "and less confusion to assimilate the grammar" of that language. "There "would be other considerable advantages in beginning Greek at a later age. "Time would then be set free for the study of French, geography, and the out- "lines of history; and above all for gaining such acquaintance with English "as would both stimulate interest and thought, and promote a more intelligent "study of Latin and Greek." They conclude by saying: "We are most an- "xions to do nothing that will diminish the range and influence of classical edu- "cation in England. But we believe that a change of method on the lines here "indicated would lead to a higher average of intellectual attainment in public "schools, and that, so far from injuring the cause of classical education, it would "strengthen it by removing reasonable objections, and by establishing the study "of both Latin and Greek on a more reasonable basis." If 'English education' be substituted for 'classical education,' these remarks have an obvious and apt bearing on the conditions of education in India. One further point may be noticed. In defence of the system of educating Indian boys through English in order to increase their power of familiar expression in that language, it is urged that an English parent, wishing his children to learn French colloquially, places them under a Swiss *bonne*. The difference is that the Swiss *bonne* teaches them good colloquial French, while the Hindu schoolmaster can often teach only bad colloquial English, and the lower down in the school the study of English is begun, the more pronounced is this defect. Glaring faults of idiom and of pronunciation, which sometimes disfigure the speech of even highly educated men, are in most cases due to the fact that they have begun to learn English under junior masters imperfectly acquainted with the language, and that early training has rendered these faults ineradicable.

Views so divergent have influenced, more or less consciously, the methods of secondary instruction that find favour in different parts of India. It is in high schools—in the instruction of those who are destined for the Entrance examination and a subsequent University career—that the differences emerge most clearly. Sometimes the study of English is entered on from the beginning; sometimes it is postponed for two or three years until the pupil has mastered the rudiments of education through his own vernacular. After it has been taken up, it is sometimes taught as a language merely, sometimes it is employed as the vehicle of instruction. In the former case, the school is at that stage essentially a vernacular school with instruction in the English language added; in the latter, the text-books in history, in geography, in mathematics are all in English, and the questions and explanations of the teachers are conveyed in the same tongue. When we turn to middle schools we find much greater uniformity, and a much stronger inclination—since English can be taught to only a moderate standard in the end—to impart all substantive instruction through the vernacular. It appears from the returns that besides the 40,000 pupils of secondary English schools who learn the vernacular only, there are nearly 168,000 who learn the vernacular along with English. Many of these, it is true, are pupils who are merely practised in vernacular composition for the purposes of the matriculation examination; but the great majority, it may reasonably be inferred, are those who, being in the middle stage of instruction, have not as yet acquired enough English to be able to do without vernacular teaching in the class. The question of the relative merits of the two systems is argued at length in paragraph 250 of the Commission's report, and its consideration was recommended to Local Governments. In the Resolution of the 23rd October 1884, the Government of India drew special attention to the point in the following words (paragraph 22):—" There is one method re-
" garding which no specific recommendation is made, but to which attention was
" drawn in the Resolution appointing the Commission, and which is discussed in
" paragraphs 249-50 of their report, *viz.*, the place which should be occupied by
" English and the vernacular in middle schools. The Governor-General in Council
" is disposed to agree with the Commission that for boys whose education termi-
" nates with the middle course, instruction through the vernacular is likely to be
" the most effective and satisfactory. The experience of Bengal goes, indeed, to
" show that even for lads pursuing their studies in high schools a thorough ground-
" ing conveyed through their own vernacular leads to satisfactory after-results.
" It is urged by those who take this view that many of the complaints of the
" unsatisfactory quality of the training given in the middle and high schools of
" the country are accounted for by the attempt to convey instruction through a
" foreign tongue. The boys, it is said, learn a smattering of very indifferent
" English, while their minds receive no development by the imparting to them
" of useful knowledge in a shape comprehensible to their intellects, since they
" never really assimilate the instruction imparted to them. It has been pro-
" posed to meet this difficulty by providing that English shall only be taught in
" middle schools as a language, and even then only as an extra subject when
" there is a real demand for it, and a readiness to pay for such instruction. His
" Excellency in Council commends this matter to the careful consideration of
" Local Governments and educational authorities." This important question has received attention in several provinces.

In Madras the subject of the teaching of English does not, in the opinion of the Local Government, require further action in that Presidency. As to purely vernacular schools, it is alleged, and was indeed admitted by the Commission, that the demand for English is so strong that schools from which English is excluded would be unable to exist. And as to the medium of instruction, there is no reason, it is urged, to believe that the ill effects said to have been observed in Bengal have resulted in Madras, where the knowledge of English is very much more diffused. Reference is also made to the standing orders on the subject of teaching English in Government schools, which are said to be " well " calculated to check the tendency towards a mechanical repetition of half under-" stood sentences." These orders direct special attention to translation and re-translation into English and the vernacular, as a means of ascertaining whether the pupils comprehend what they read, and of ensuring that they shall do so. It may be added that English is not taught to pupils in the lower primary stage, and that substantive instruction in the three lowest classes of an English school is invariably conveyed through the vernacular. In Bombay also no English is taught in the four lowest standards, as far as the upper primary examination; and in middle schools it is taught mainly as a language.

In the North-Western Provinces the opinion of the Government is very clearly expressed in a sense altogether opposed to that of the Commission and of the Government of India. " Instruction in special subjects," it is observed, " such as mathematics, history and geography, has for some years been conveyed " to pupils in the middle stage through the medium of the vernacular; but it " may be doubted whether the results of the experiment have been wholly " satisfactory. There appears to be a general consensus of opinion among both " teachers and inspectors that while pupils whose education stops with the " middle course derive no appreciable benefit from the practice, it is distinctly " disadvantageous to those who proceed to the University course by compelling " them to learn the same subjects first in one language and then in another. " This view appears to be supported by the diminished proportion of passes " to failures at the Entrance examination since the practice has been intro-" duced, and the subject is one which will have urgent claims on the atten-" tion of the new University." This clear expression of opinion, based as it professes to be on an experience of both systèms, is of great value. At first sight it would appear to be altogether opposed to the conclusions arrived at after similar experience in Bengal. But a closer examination leads to the belief that the contrasted views are not really irreconcileable. In the North-Western Provinces the middle school course is merely the high school course shorn of its two highest classes. There is no separate standard, as there is in Bengal, for middle schools, based on the requirements of those who proceed no higher, and altogether independent of the University. The middle school standard in the North-Western Provinces is merely a stage through which the pupil passes on his road to the Entrance examination. The experience of the North-Western Provinces is therefore to be compared with that of Bengal so far as it relates to high schools only; and in Bengal it is not insisted on that pupils in high schools should postpone the use of English as the medium of instruction until two years from matriculation. It is to the middle English school, with its separate course and standards, and not to the middle stage of high school instruction, that the views expressed in Bengal have chief reference; and the requisite experience is altogether wanting in the North-Western Provinces, where that special class of schools does not exist. With regard to the teaching of English, the opinion is very strongly held that it should begin from the lowest classes of a high school. Mr. Nesfield, Inspector of Schools, and formerly Director of Public Institution in Oudh, is convinced that a boy who reads to the upper, or even to the lower primary standard in a high school and then stops, is better educated than one who reads to the same standard in a primary school. Boys of the former class know their own vernacular quite as well as the others, and they have had their wits sharpened and their sphere of knowledge extended by learning something of English besides,—not much indeed, but enough to serve many useful purposes in after life. And they are better trained than the others, because they have had the benefit of zila school discipline under the guidance of a highly paid and experienced head-master. Furthermore, if this preparatory teaching were abolished, the upper classes would rapidly deteriorate, since it is only in the primary classes of zila schools that students can be so grounded in English as to be qualified for admission to classes where English is taught side by side with the vernacular up to the secondary stage. "It is a "necessity which has brought the primary Anglo-vernacular classes into zila "schools, and it is a necessity which will keep them there." These observations appear to have met with the approval of the Local Government.

The Punjab, with the same school system in essential points as the North-West, has come to a widely different conclusion with regard to instruction through the vernacular. The middle school standard, in both provinces alike, is that of the seventh class in a high school; and the corresponding examination has always been, and still is, conducted in the Punjab through the medium of the vernacular in all subjects. When English is taught in Government or in board schools, and generally in aided schools also, it is taught as a language, and is not employed as the medium of instruction. In the Punjab no objection has been raised to this practice; nor is it alleged that a student suffers from being compelled to learn history, or science, or Euclid, first in his own vernacular, and then by means of English text-books for the Entrance examination. Indeed, if he has been well grounded in these subjects in the middle stage through the vernacular, his subsequent study of them in English text-books would partake, partly of the character of an easy revision of matter already known, and partly of a new series of lessons in English.

Of the Central Provinces it is stated that the Education Commission misconceived the character of the system. Instruction through English was characterised in the Commission's report as the leading note of secondary education in these provinces. It is now explained that this does not represent the actual facts. In the first place, no pupil can enter a middle school or begin the study of English until he has passed the lower primary examination; in other words, his first three years of study are confined to the vernacular. In the second place, he in no case receives instruction through English until he has learnt English, as a language only, for one year more. It is only in the five highest classes of a secondary school that substantive instruction is conveyed through English. So explained, the system in the Central Provinces seems to carry out effectively the views which the Commission adopted and which the Government of India approved. Mr. Browning's remarks on this point are worth attention partly because they seem to be directed to some extent against the system which he administers:—"All the masters in our departmental middle schools are "natives of India, and are usually natives of these Provinces. There is thus "every guarantee that instruction should be conveyed through the vernacular; "and there is a danger lest English should be taught rather as a dead than as a "living language, rather by means of grammar than by conversation and by using "the language in the higher classes as a medium of instruction. Every effort "is made to counteract this tendency. I do not see why a student should not be "able to express in English all his ordinary wants and wishes after he has attend-"ed an English school for twelve months."

From what has preceded the balance of opinion may now be struck. In those provinces in which middle English schools have an independent course and standard of their own, determined by the requirements of pupils most of whom proceed no further than the middle stage, it is not denied that instruction can most usefully be imparted through the vernacular. When the middle school course is merely a section of the high school course, and is to be pursued alike by those who are preparing for the matriculation examination and by those who are not, there is still a preponderance of opinion in favour of teaching English as a language only, and of imparting substantive instruction through the vernacular. In the North-Western Provinces this method now finds no favour; but the objection to it is chiefly based on the disabilities which it is believed to impose on students preparing for matriculation. The other class of students are merely thought to derive "no appreciable advantage" from instruction through the vernacular. Greater difference of opinion prevails as to the most suitable course, from the alphabet to matriculation, for those students who are preparing for the Entrance examination. The course of nine years may conveniently be divided into three approximately equal sections. In the lowest stage of two or three years, instruction must necessarily be imparted through the vernacular almost exclusively; and the only difference of opinion arises on the point whether English should be taught at that stage. The balance of opinion appears to incline to the view that it should not then be taught, though the opposite view is very strongly held by competent authorities. In the next, or middle stage, opinion seems to lend stronger support to the employment of vernacular text-books in history and such-like subjects, more especially if a commencement of English has been postponed to this stage. In the last two, three, or four years of the course, it is by unanimous consent allowed that the vernacular should be altogether put aside (except for purposes of translation and composition), and that English text-books should be exclusively used. The whole question seems to be one which might with great profit be submitted in each province to the judgment of an Educational Conference, in which the head-masters alike of departmental and board schools and of those under private managers should be represented, and in which the practical results of different methods might, when possible, be compared.

163. Results of Examinations: Matriculation.—In a previous paragraph it was shown what proportion of pupils in secondary schools were in the high stage of instruction, or generally, within two years of matriculation. The following table, in which the results of the Entrance examination are given, will show for each province the number of secondary schools for boys that prepare candidates for that examination, in other words, the number of high schools. The matriculation standard in the various Universities of India may be ascertained from para. 256 of the Education Commission's report, and from what has been said in the preceding chapter about changes subsequently introduced. The differences are not very important. The standard everywhere includes (1) English, (2) a classical or vernacular language, (3) arithmetic, algebra to simple equations, and three or four books of Euclid, (4) the history of England and India, and geography, (5) an additional subject, such as physics or chemistry or physical geography or mensuration, always in a very elementary form.

Entrance Examination, 1886.

PROVINCE.	SCHOOLS UNDER PUBLIC MANAGEMENT.		AIDED SCHOOLS.		UNAIDED SCHOOLS, INCLUDING PRIVATE STUDENTS.		TOTAL.	
	Competing Schools.	Successful Candidates.	Competing Schools.	Successful Candidates.	Competing Schools.	Successful Candidates.	Competing Schools.	Successful Candidates.
Madras	39	434	82	850	46	611	167	(a)1,895
Bombay	19	329	30	192	23	316	72	(b)837
Bengal	57	418	132	203	76	292	265	(c)913
N.-W. Provinces	24	131	37	97	4	10	65	(d)238
Punjab	15	129	27	81	2	23	44	(e)233
Central Provinces	2	36	5	33	...	1	7	70
Burma	4	17	3	6	1	...	8	23
Assam	9	30	3	5	1	4	13	39
Berar	2	14	...	...	...	...	2	14
Coorg	1	10	...	...	...	1	1	11
TOTAL	172	1,548	317	1,464	153	1,258	642	(f)4.273
TOTAL FOR 1884-85	180	1,620	289	1,390	143	1,122	612	(g)4,132

(a) Including 7 girls. (b) Including 10 girls. (c) Including 11 girls. (d) Including 7 girls. (e) Including 3 girls.
(f) Including 40 girls and excluding 13 Oriental candidates of the Punjab University.
(g) „ 30 „ „ 29 „ „

Compared with the previous year there is a decline in the number of successful candidates in three provinces, Bombay, Bengal, and the Punjab. In Bombay the original examination failed, owing to the publication of the papers before they were given out to the candidates. The perpetrators of the fraud were not discovered, but it is stated that the University was obliged to hurry its arrangements for a second examination, and that the candidates were put to considerable inconvenience which in many instances told heavily against them. In Bengal, the remarkably low percentage of success among the candidates at this (and to a somewhat less extent at the preceding) examination, induced the authorities of the Calcutta University to institute an inquiry into its causes. It may be mentioned that in the examination of the following year the number of successful candidates at matriculation increased from 913 to 2,346. In the Punjab also, the decline in the proportion of successful candidates has attracted the notice of the Senate of the Punjab University, and a committee has been appointed with the object of ascertaining what steps should be taken to ensure fixity of standard.

The results given above may now be combined with those of previous paragraphs. Out of 2,263 secondary schools, English, 642 were high schools sufficiently advanced to send candidates for the Entrance examination. Out of 265,000 pupils in secondary schools, 35,286 were in the high stage of instruction, that is, were within two years of matriculation. Out of 12,850 candidates who presented themselves for the Entrance examination in 1885-86, 4,273, or 33 per cent., passed. If private candidates be excluded (and among them the percentage of success is very low) the proportion of successful candidates rises to 40 per cent., thus distributed :—among candidates from schools under public management, 49 per cent; from aided schools, 36½ per cent; from unaided schools 33 per cent. Schools under public management maintain, therefore, their superiority as regards efficiency of teaching over those under private management; but the latter, as a class, take a larger share of the work of preparing pupils for the Entrance examination.

164. Middle School Examination.—The result of this examination, which is generally held two years before matriculation, or at a stage corresponding thereto, may now be given. In Madras, Bombay, the North-Western Provinces, and Coorg, the test is that for admission to the public service. In the Central Provinces there is a separate test, distinct from the middle school examination. The various standards are given in paragraph 254 of the Commission's report.

Middle School Examination, 1885-86.

PROVINCE.		SCHOOLS UNDER PUBLIC MANAGEMENT.		AIDED SCHOOLS.		UNAIDED SCHOOLS, INCLUDING PRIVATE STUDENTS.		TOTAL.	
		Competing Schools.	Successful Candidates.	Competing Schools.	Successful Candidates.	Competing Schools.	Successful Candidates.	Competing Schools.	Successful Candidates.
Madras	English	88	611	156	1,252	51	673	295	2,536
Bombay	English	32	179	14	28	12	53	58	260
	Vernacular	786	1,344	17	43	81	577	884	1,964
Bengal	English	9	28	390	465	47	76	446	(a)590
	Vernacular	153	455	889	1,686	103	388	1,145	(b)3,111
N.-W. Provinces	English	37	403	51	259	16	123	103	785
	Vernacular	403	1,045	26	45	...	154	429	1,244
Punjab	English	58	597	28	266	11	145	97	1,008
	Vernacular	128	618	3	5	...	54	131	677
Central Provinces	English	35	228	13	101	1	(c)79	49	(c)408
Burma	English	13	64	16	25	2	...	31	89
	Vernacular	10	66	13	4	34	42	57	112
Assam	English	3	9	17	28	1	10	21	47
	Vernacular	15	37	38	92	1	6	54	135
Berar	English	26	137	...	...	...	...	26	137
Coorg	English	1	7	...	...	...	5	1	12
TOTAL	English	302	2,263	685	2,424	140	1,118	1,127	5,828
	Vernacular	1,495	3,565	986	1,875	219	1,267	2,700	7,289
GRAND TOTAL		1,797	5,828	1,671	4,299	359	2,385	3,827	13,115

(a) Including 21 candidates who passed the vernacular Examination from English schools.
(b)   „   582   „   „   English   „   „   vernacular schools.
(c) Including 46 vernacular candidates.

In the previous year 14,646 candidates passed the examination, so that there is a decline of more than 2,000 in the number of successful candidates. In Madras alone there was a loss of nearly 2,000, the standard for passing under the new examination scheme having been considerably raised. In the Punjab also the number of successful candidates fell off by nearly 400, owing to a similar cause. In the Central Provinces there was a considerable decrease in the number of candidates who competed for and obtained the public service certificate. In Bengal and Assam the pupils in the middle stage of high schools (about 19,000) are not, as in other provinces, subject to this examination, which is confined to candidates from middle schools proper. In the North-Western Provinces the number of successful candidates increased, though the examination is said to have been conducted more strictly than in the preceding year. It may be noted as an interesting point in the controversy as to the use of the Nagri or of the Persian character in these provinces, that two-thirds of the candidates chose the latter. It is also added that the candidates who selected Nagri were much superior as a class to those who took Persian, the proportion of passes being 44 per cent. for the former and 37 per cent. for the latter. The same difference was observed in the previous year. In Burma the total number of successful students has been affected by the disturbed state of the country, often resulting in irregular attendance.

The important place taken by purely vernacular instruction in the secondary stage is shown by the fact that more than half the candidates who passed the middle school examination were ignorant of English. To this statement it should, however, be added that the vernacular list includes nearly 2,000 candidates who passed the vernacular test for the lower grades of the public service in Bombay, and that that test, corresponding to Standard VI of vernacular schools, is not uniformly reckoned as coming within the secondary stage of instruction. The necessity of encouraging vernacular education at this stage is enforced by the recommendation of the Commission "that in every province in which "examinations for the public service are held, they be so arranged as to give "encouragement to vernacular education." (VII. 19).

165. Expenditure on Secondary Schools.—The two following tables show the amount expended from various sources on secondary schools for boys, English and vernacular, for each province of India.

Expenditure on Secondary Schools, English, 1885-86.

PROVINCE.	From Provincial Revenues.		From Local and Municipal Funds.	From Fees.	From other Sources.	TOTAL.
	In Schools under public management.	In aided Schools.				
	R	R	R	R	R	R
Madras	1,06,154	1,11,960	81,028	6,45,991	2,61,352	12,06,485
Bombay	1,25,615	97,988	52,140	4,14,273	2,85,020	9,75,036
Bengal	1,65,800	2,56,215	44,158	10,86,838	5,04,761	20,57,772
N.-W. Provinces	11,703	70,376	2,60,525	1,36,456	1,93,916	6,72,976
Punjab	1,49,232	61,743	65,222	1,07,629	78,505	4,62,331
Central Provinces	45,557	13,339	18,395	19,725	12,853	1,09,869
Burma	20,261	16,415	1,09,458	59,802	46,106	2,52,042
Assam	24,557		19,905	55,009	21,114	1,20,585
Berar	63,651	...	423	10,180	204	74,458
Coorg	7,149	1,200	172	4,621	90	13,232
TOTAL	7,19,679	6,29,236	6,51,426	25,40,524	14,03,921	59,44,786
TOTAL FOR 1884-85.	7,54,968	5,86,624	6,08,965	24,31,653	12,83,825	56,66,035

Expenditure on Secondary Schools, Vernacular, 1885-86.

PROVINCE.	From Provincial Revenues.		From Local and Municipal Funds.	From Fees.	From other Sources.	TOTAL.
	In Schools under public management.	In aided Schools.				
	R	R	R	R	R	R
Madras	...	2,329	2,404	1,561	174	6,468
Bengal	47,500	1,15,225	10,718	1,53,957	1,16,234	4,43,634
N.-W. Provinces	1,506	1,200	1,49,675	19,131	17,189	1,88,701
Punjab	701	...	94,820	12,225	1,473	1,09,219
Burma	...	203	14,089	200	496	14,988
Assam	8,767	...	6,381	8,726	4,686	28,560
TOTAL	58,474	1,18,957	2,78,087	1,95,800	1,40,252	7,91,570
TOTAL FOR 1884-85	57,906	1,18,963	2,66,360	1,94,010	1,36,449	7,73,688

From the first of these tables it appears that the total cost of English schools has increased by about R2,79,000, the increase being in a somewhat higher ratio than that of their pupils, shown above in paragraph 156. Provincial grants show a trifling increase of R8,000; but it is to be observed that this net result is made up of an increase of R43,000 in the grants to aided schools, and of a decrease of R35,000 in the provincial outlay on schools under public management. The grants made to secondary schools by local and municipal boards have advanced by R43,000, the total outlay being now about equally divided between these two classes of public bodies. The contributions of district boards are specially high in the North-Western Provinces, and the departmental expenditure low in a corresponding degree; and the same may be said of municipal contributions in Burma. These special features have been already explained as arising from the transfer of the charge of secondary schools in these provinces to local bodies, with the necessary provision for maintaining or aiding them. There is an increase of R1,09,000 in fees, which is again somewhat greater proportionately than the increase in pupils. The higher ratio is due to the enhanced fee-rates which have been introduced into most provinces in accordance with the recommendations of the Commission. In Bombay, however, where the increase under this head is much greater than elsewhere, it is ascribed to the fact that a larger percentage of pupils are now in the high stage of instruction, where they have to pay fees at increased rates. Lastly, the receipts from subscriptions and other sources have increased by R1,20,000.

Of the total cost of English secondary schools throughout India, 66 per cent. is paid from fees, subscriptions, and other private sources, 23 per cent. from provincial revenues, and 11 per cent. from local and municipal funds, in which last, however, direct grants from Government are sometimes included. The proportion contributed from private sources is greatest in Madras, Bombay, and Bengal, where it amounts to 75, 72, and 77 per cent. respectively, and in Assam, where it is 64 per cent. In the North-Western Provinces the shares paid from public and from private sources are nearly equal. In the remaining provinces private contributions are paid at lower rates. As stated just above, the largest contributions from local and municipal funds are made in the North-Western Provinces and Burma, where they amount to 39 and 43 per cent. respectively.

The cost of vernacular schools shows little variation. There has been a total increase of R18,000, two-thirds of which have been met from local and municipal funds. The proportionate share of the cost of these schools which is borne by public funds of all classes amounts to 58 per cent.

166. Recommendations of the Education Commission as to Secondary Education.—The subject of secondary education is discussed in Chapter V of the Commission's report. The chief recommendations which they made under this head may be grouped as follows :—

(*A*) *Bifurcation of Studies*—

"1. That in the upper classes of high schools there be two divisions—one leading to the Entrance examination of the Universities; the other, of a more practical character, intended to fit youths for commercial or other non-literary pursuits.

"2. That when the proposed bifurcation in secondary schools is carried out, the certificate of having passed by the final standard, or if necessary by any lower standard of either of the proposed alternative courses, be accepted as a sufficient general test of fitness for the public service."

(*B*) *Qualifications of Teachers*—

"6. That an examination in the principles and practice of teaching be instituted, success in which should hereafter be a condition of permanent employment as a teacher in any secondary school, Government or aided.

"7. That graduates wishing to attend a course of instruction in a normal school in the principles and practice of teaching be required to undergo a shorter course of training than others."

(*C*) *Fees*—

"9. That the Director of Public Instruction, in consultation with the managers of schools receiving aid from Government, determine the scale of fees to be charged and the proportion of pupils to be exempted from payment therein.

"10. That, in order to encourage the establishment of aided schools, the managers be not required to charge fees as high as those of a neighbouring Government school of the same class.

"11. That scholarship-holders as such be not exempted from payment of the ordinary fees.

(*D*) *Scholarships*—

"12. That in all provinces the system of scholarships be so arranged that, as suggested in the despatch of 1854, they may form connecting links between the different grades of institutions.

"13. That scholarships payable from public funds, including educational endowments not attached to a particular institution, be awarded after public competition without restriction, except in special cases, to students from any particular class of schools.

"14. That scholarships gained in open competition be tenable, under proper safeguards to ensure the progress of the scholarship-holder, at any approved institution for general or special instruction."

(*E*) *Moral Discipline*—

"19. That the importance of requiring inspecting officers to see that the teaching and discipline of every school are such as to exert a right influence on the manners, the conduct and the character of pupils, be re-affirmed." The consideration of this point may conveniently be postponed to a later section of this chapter, which deals with moral training and discipline.

(F) *Extension of Secondary Education—*

"23. That it be distinctly laid down that the relation of the State to secondary is different from its relation to primary education, in that the means of primary education may be provided without regard to the existence of local co-operation, while it is ordinarily expedient to provide the means of secondary education only when adequate local co-operation is forthcoming; and that therefore, in all ordinary cases, secondary schools for instruction in English be hereafter established by the State preferably on the footing of the system of grants-in-aid."

167. The Bifurcation of Studies in Secondary Schools.—In pointing out the special importance, at the present time, of giving a more practical character to school education, the Government of India observed:—" Every "variety of study should be encouraged which may serve to direct the attention "of native youth to industrial and commercial pursuits." Here there are two alternatives stated, in a somewhat more definite form than the "commercial or other non-literary pursuits" of the Commission's recommendation. The present high school course, ending with the matriculation examination, was in the opinion of the Commission, adapted chiefly for students who intended to go up to the University in order to qualify for the liberal professions or for the public service. But on the one hand there are many students who after matriculating are prevented by circumstances from going through the University course, and have therefore to betake themselves to other callings for which their education will not have specially fitted them; and on the other it is desirable, on grounds of public economical policy, to withdraw a certain proportion of the educated classes from the paths which lead to official or professional life, and to divert them into those of productive industry such as attract so large a proportion of the educated youth of Europe. Boys of the former class generally apply for clerkships in mercantile or public offices; and if they are to become clerks, it would seem to be an obvious improvement on their present course if the subjects of Sanskrit and algebra, for example, were replaced by précis-writing, by the drafting of letters, and by practice in accounts, tabular statements and percentages. So again, a boy would be better equipped for industrial pursuits if from the age of 15 to 17 he had put aside classics and begun to learn drawing and the use of simple tools. Thus far no difference of opinion was expressed by those who commented on the Commission's proposals. Doubts began to arise when the question no longer was what would be best for the students, *sua si bona norint*, but the more practical point whether, if the classes were formed, students would be found to attend them. It was at any rate certain that the establishment of the classes, if carried out on any thing like a comprehensive scale, would involve large additional cost. Incidentally the question arose whether the bifurcation ought not to be postponed until after the completion of the high school course; the ground taken being that the matriculation standard was not too advanced a test of general education and intelligence, even for students who were destined for a non-literary career. The general opinion was, however, adverse to that position; and the Government of India disposed of it with the remark that to postpone the bifurcation in the way suggested would to a great extent render its advantages futile.

The practical difficulty remained. The commercial class was unquestionably the more promising of the two, for many of the boys who flocked to our schools were the sons of office-clerks, and it would be natural for them to follow in their fathers' footsteps. But it was doubtful whether many, even of these, would make up their minds two years before matriculation to abandon the chances of a University career for the humbler, if more secure, position and emoluments which clerkship offered. The only hope of starting such classes with any chance of success lay in a declaration by the Government that appointments to junior clerkships in the public offices would preferentially be given to those who had gone through the specified course. In this way the course might be made attractive enough to induce students to take advantage in sufficient numbers of the opportunities which it offered; and the commercial class might under these conditions turn out a success. But what corresponding inducements were or could be held out to students to join the other—the industrial class? In the first place, the pupils of high schools did not belong to the classes that traditionally followed industrial callings; and if they were now to gravitate to such pursuits, it could only be in response to the attractive force of an improved worldly position. It was by no means clear, however, that that advantage would be gained. To become a civil engineer it was necessary for the student to pass through a full University course; but short of that, what position of moderate competence and respectability was open to a youth after he had passed the prescribed examination? He could not become an artisan; for, all other objections apart, he would still have to serve a long apprenticeship before he could earn a living in that way; and for all the advantage his superior education gave him, he might just as well have begun to learn his trade five or six years earlier. There were, to be sure, subordinate positions of a traditionally "respectable" kind, such as assistantships in mills and factories, for which a practical training would give increased aptitude; but outside the subject of drawing, it was doubtful whether anything of special value for such a purpose could be taught under the necessary limitations set by a "high school" course, however largely modified. The Public Works Department might, indeed, require the passing of the alternative examination as a condition of admitting a student to the special courses of instruction that led up to its subordinate appointments, but no intention of that kind had been declared. Still less was it certain that private employers of labour would give any special preference to candidates so trained, in the absence of any practical experience of what they were fit for. Let it be granted that with the increasing industrial development of the country a demand would arise for technically trained men; they would still have to acquire their technical training in institutions specially equipped for the purpose; and no, or but few, such institutions as yet existed. When technical institutions (other than those designed to supply the limited demand for civil engineers) had been provided, a need would arise for students with a somewhat more practical initial training. Meanwhile we were beginning at the wrong end, and proposing to train students in a way that offered no obvious prospects of employment.

168. Action taken on this Recommendation.—Notwithstanding these difficulties, which sprang to notice on a first consideration of the proposals that had been made, and which specially affected the more backward provinces, the local Governments generally expressed their concurrence in the aims of the Commission, and their desire to give such practical effect to them as might be possible.

Madras.—The Government of Madras fully recognised "the necessity of "giving increased prominence to the commercial, industrial, and technical side "of education, as opposed to literary studies." It was accordingly deemed desirable to begin the bifurcation of studies at a stage not only below the Entrance but below the middle school examination, which latter is accepted as the general test of fitness for the public service. The middle school standard, as now amended, contains a variety of options, including commercial, technical, scientific, and industrial subjects; and it is believed that "pupils desirous of qualify-

SECONDARY EDUCATION.

"ing for commercial and non-literary pursuits in after-life may even at this stage "acquire a knowledge of the rudiments of the special branches of study they may "choose to enter on." The revised scheme for the middle school examination comprises the following branches :—

A. First (or compulsory) language; generally English.
B. Second (or optional) language; an Indian Vernacular.
C. Geography, map-drawing, and Indian history.
D. Arithmetic.
E. Mathematics.
F. English history.
G. Introductory Science, with one of the following :—
   (1) Physical geography.
   (2) Geology.
   (3) Astronomy.
   (4) Animal physiology.
   (5) Botany.
   (6) Agriculture.
   (7) Electricity and magnetism: with possible additions to the list hereafter.
H. Music.
I. (For females only) Domestic economy.
K. Drawing.
L. Modelling.
M. Wood-engraving.

For males only.
N. Carpentry, joining, turning, and cabinet-making.
O. Ironsmith's work.
P (1) Jeweller's work.
   (2) Silversmith's work.
Q. Printing.
R. Tailoring.
S. Boot and shoe-making.

For females only.
T. Needlework: either
   (1) Industrial special branches, either—
      (i) Dress-making, or
      (ii) Boot and shoe-making (in part), or
      (iii) Native tailoring, or
   (2) (a) Plain needle-work.
       (b) Fancy needle-work.

U. Telegraphy.
V. (1) Mercantile arithmetic.
   (2) Advanced spelling and superior penmanship.
   (3) Book-keeping.
   (4) Commercial correspondence.
   (5) Commercial geography.
   (6) Short-hand writing.
   (7) Political economy.
   (8) Fire, life and marine insurance.

Male candidates have to come up in five branches, namely
(1) Compulsory language.
(2) Geography, map-drawing, and Indian history.
(3) Arithmetic.
(4) and (5) Either of the following groups :—
   (a) Mathematics and a second language.
   (b) Mathematics and science.
   (c) Mathematics and drawing or modelling.
   (d) Drawing or modelling and an industrial branch (M to U).
   (e) Two of the sub-divisions of the commercial branch, marked V.

For female candidates a slightly reduced standard is fixed. The options (b), (c), (d), and (e) are open to pupils of recognised science, art, industrial, and commercial schools respectively. The practical character which it is attempted to give to the examination in industrial subjects may be judged from the following extracts. Under carpentry: "To mark out and cut slanting double "mortice and tenon," &c. Under jeweller's work: "To file a joint groove, make "and fit joint, broach the same, and fit joint pin," &c. Under printing: "To be "able to distribute and compose at the rate of 1,000 ens per hour, and with "tolerable accuracy, from either reprint or manuscript copy, punctuating the "latter fairly well," &c. It is thus hoped that students who intend ultimately to proceed to the higher examinations in science, art, and industries, under the scheme lately promulgated in Madras for the development of technical education, may thus begin to lay the foundations at an early stage of their career. The further consideration of the scheme to which reference has just been made will be postponed to a later section of this chapter which deals with technical education. Here it is only necessary to state that it is intended, in order to render the scheme of bifurcation complete, to prolong the "modern side" into the high school, since the middle school standard is considered too low to serve as the final stage of general education, even for those who are to follow industrial and commercial pursuits. It is, however, believed that the co-operation of the University is necessary before any radical change can be effected in high schools.

As the first fruits of the new scheme, a commercial school has been opened in Madras in connexion with Pacheappa's Institution. A large proportion of the pupils of this institution are sons or wards of local and often well-to-do traders, and it was hoped that a sufficient number of these might be induced to join the new school; while the funds of the endowment removed all pecuniary difficulties. The school was opened in February 1886 with over 100 pupils, and the number increased to 153 at the close of the year. The subjects taught, in addition to the ordinary subjects of middle school education, were mercantile arithmetic, commercial correspondence, and short-hand. The following establishment was entertained:—a head-master, a graduate of eight years' standing, on R75; two assistant masters on R25 each, a writing master on R25, and a short-hand teacher on R10. The Government of Madras gave their cordial approval to the establishment of the school, considering it "likely to have most useful results "in the development of a sound commercial education."

Bombay.—It has already been stated that classes in agriculture and drawing have been attached to many secondary schools in Bombay, and that the latter especially have been attended with a gratifying measure of success. These classes however are not alternative with the matriculation course, but supplementary to it; and therefore, though they carry out the plan of giving variety and a more practical character to the instruction in high schools, they do not exactly embody the Commission's idea. Upon this last subject the Government of Bombay explained in 1884 that the purpose of the Commission was in some sense already realised in the examination qualifying for the public service, the test for which was Standard V of high schools (two years below matriculation), with the classics omitted and with other modifications. But quite apart from this, a proposal was then under the consideration of the University with the object of modifying the matriculation standard. Commenting on this proposal, the Government of Bombay observed:—"If the "University establishes a 'modern side' to the matriculation examination, the "result will in some degree carry out the views of the Commission, though this "is not exactly what the University is considering. The measure will, however, "be popular, because it is an object with parents that their boys should obtain a "certificate of the University in some shape. It is perhaps easier to entertain a "vague conception of a 'practical course' than to draw out the programme of "one suited to India, which shall at once present a really distinct course of "study, and not lower the educational standard by opening a too easy road to a "matriculation *testamur*."

In a Resolution of the following year a desire was expressed that further advance should be made in the direction of technical education; and qualified approval was given to the development of practical instruction by establishing an alternative standard in high schools, and especially by the provision of facilities for pupils desiring to learn some manual industry. Still later, in a Resolution of September 1886, it was declared that the time had come for thoroughly re-organising the high school course in science, with a view (1) to make it more thorough and practical, (2) to secure a nucleus of real scientific work in every high school, so as to discover the students who had a special aptitude in that direction, and pass them on to Science and Art Colleges with scholarships created for the purpose. Teachers of science were to be attached to every high school; and arrangements were to be made for the delivery in the school-building of a set of lectures—outside the regular course of the school, but illustrated by the school apparatus—in scientific and agricultural subjects, and especially in such as had a practical bearing upon any art or industry carried on in the neighbourhood. Drawing classes were also to be held, out of ordinary school-hours, for the instruction of persons already engaged in arts or manufactures, who were to be taught drawing without payment of a fee. By these measures it was hoped that, without a formal bifurcation of studies, the "modern side" of secondary education would be still further developed, so as to secure all the advantages of bifurcation without its attendant inconvenience and expense.

Bengal.—The proposal for the bifurcation of studies was one to which the Lieutenant-Governor would endeavour to give full effect, expressing the opinion that "it will be a great gain if we can establish schools specially adapted to the "requirements of those who are intended for commercial or other practical pur- "suits, without at the same time sacrificing a sound general education." The preliminary expense of opening new classes, requiring costly appliances and often extra teachers, was the first difficulty that stood in the way of the reform. It next became manifest, as it had also become manifest in Madras and Bombay, that without the co-operation of the University success could not be looked for with confidence. Mr. Tawney, who was officiating as Director of Public Instruction, wrote in 1886:—"I have always thought that the only way to "make technical education really popular is to induce the Calcutta University "to take it up. No subject that is not recognised by this body can in the long "run hold its place in schools.......The University can always create a demand "for the teaching of any subject by simply introducing it into its examinations. "Now there is one subject which all authorities on technical education consider "indispensable, namely, drawing.......Government might perhaps induce man- "agers of schools to appoint teachers of this subject by offering to pay their "salaries, and giving prizes and scholarships for proficiency in it. But the "University can bring about the same result by simply paying a gentleman to "examine in it." The University was accordingly addressed in this sense, with the recommendation that an alternative Entrance examination should be held of a more practical character than the present, in which the subjects of language and literature should be replaced by mechanical drawing and the elements of chemistry and physics. The alternative standard was to be compulsory on students proceeding to take up engineering, but on no others. After lengthened discussion the Senate finally decided that it was not desirable to introduce an alternative examination, that Huxley's *Introductory Primer of Science* should be substituted for mensuration, and that any candidate who desired it might also be examined in drawing. If a candidate took up and passed in this last subject, the fact was to be noted on his certificate; but success or failure in it was not otherwise to affect his passing the examination or his place in the class list.

North-Western Provinces and Oudh.—The following extract from the, report submitted by the Government of these Provinces gives a complete statement of the action that has been taken: "A circular was issued in 1884, in- "viting the opinions of educational officers and of the managers of aided schools "as to the expediency of adding a modern side to the higher sections of "secondary schools in which a practical education, distinct from the training "for the University course, might be undertaken. It was suggested by the

"Director of Public Instruction that increased attention might be given to "modern English, the newspapers of the day for instance, handwriting, both "English and Urdu, letter-writing, précis-writing, book-keeping, land survey-"ing, and the elements of political economy, physics, and chemistry. The "managers of aided schools were generally not unwilling to try the experiment, "but objected that they were unable to provide the expense of entertaining the "new masters and purchasing the necessary appliances for the additional classes "which it would be necessary to establish. Moreover, in most of these schools "the higher classes were so small, very commonly containing less than 10 pupils "each, that bifurcation was nearly impossible. Many of the best authorities "thought that the new classes would fail to attract pupils, as the only certi-"ficate valued by parents and guardians was that of having passed the Entrance "examination; and the opinion was expressed that the Entrance course, in "which good penmanship, good spelling, the power of expression, methodical "habits of thinking, good arithmetic and algebra, some knowledge of geometry, "and some power of translation, were acquired, afforded a sufficient preparation "for commercial and non-literary pursuits. With these views Sir Alfred Lyall "was disposed in the main to concur. The distinction between classical and "modern education is much more sharply defined in the curriculum of English "schools and colleges than in the course of study preparatory to admission to "the Indian Universities, and it is probable that the present course might "without material departure from the lines on which it is formed, be made "to approximate very closely to the proposed modern course. It was not "thought advisable to try an experiment which might be expensive and "had no sure prospect of immediate success, until a scheme had been drawn "up specifying in some detail the subjects and character of each of the distinct "courses, which would show whether the bifurcation was sufficiently substantial, "and so clearly different from the present line of studies as to be worth its cost. "The addition of a modern side to the educational system would probably re-act "on the course of studies prescribed as a preparation for the University; and it "was eventually decided to postpone the consideration of the subject, in which "there is no urgency, until it could be laid before the Senate of the new Uni-"versity at Allahabad."

Punjab.—In the opinion of the Government of the Punjab the question presented some difficulties, but they did not appear to be insurmountable. The main inducement to study in the Punjab, as in every other province of India and every country in the civilised world, was, with the great mass of students, the hope of personal advancement. There was a very strong desire for English education, mainly because it led to Government employment, which afforded a certain income and some valuable prizes. Hitherto the classes who sought for an English education had not turned their attention to industrial and commer-cial pursuits. They saw no opening in that direction, and an education avow-edly framed to fit them for such occupations would offer no attraction, and cer-tainly would not be accepted if it appeared to cut them off altogether from Gov-ernment employment. One solution, however, seemed to be feasible. "It is "a common complaint that youths who have passed the Entrance examination, "and often those who have advanced to a much higher standard, are not qualifi-"ed to become efficient clerks. A course of instruction in letter and précis writ-"ing, book-keeping, and accounts would in all probability prove highly popular, "whether it began at the middle school or Entrance standard, more especially if "it were followed by the award of a certificate after passing the Entrance exami-"nation. Such an arrangement would supply a much more efficient class of "men than is at present available for junior clerkships in public offices; it would "open the way to employment in banks and shops; and it would thus lead the

"students who followed it to turn their attention to commercial pursuits, and it
"would facilitate the introduction of other branches of technical instruction
"hereafter." The whole question and its proposed solution was to be laid before
the next Educational Conference.

Other Provinces.—In the Central Provinces it was believed that there was no desire for any collegiate or high school instruction that was not conducted on the model prescribed by the University. From this statement it would follow that the bifurcation of studies could not be introduced with any hope of success unless it was first adopted by the Calcutta University, for whose examinations all schools in the Central Provinces prepare their pupils. The opinion of the educational authorities in Burma was favourable to the recommendation, but its adoption depended on the action that might be taken by the Educational Syndicate. The Chief Commissioner of Assam demurred to the expense—estimated at an addition of 25 per cent. to the total cost of high schools—that the scheme would involve, and proposed to wait until the experiment had been tried in Bengal or other advanced province. He added :—" It can hardly
" be said in Assam at present that the state of society is complex, or that there
" is any considerable class whose intellectual activity is not satisfied by the exist-
" ing literature course. The want to which the Commission refer is scarcely felt
" here. We have already a special endowment of about R4,000 a year for the
" teaching of mechanical and industrial arts, but it is extremely difficult to find
" any boys in Assam who are desirous of entering on even a rudimentary course
" of such training; and only two youths have been found fit and willing in the
" last four years to accept a scholarship to complete their education at the Sibpur
" Engineering College." In Berar and Coorg it is maintained that the time has not come for the adoption of the recommendation. In the former province, where there are only two high schools, the majority of the boys trained therein are employed in Government and private offices, where they are said to acquit themselves remarkably well after a little experience. The Coorgs are described as " conservative, slow-witted, suspicious of new measures, averse to commerci-
" al pursuits, and with a preference for agriculture and the administrative service
" of Government as their means of livelihood." The province contains only one high school.

169. Qualifications of Teachers.—The Education Commission discussed a length (in paragraph 274) the diversity of views that prevailed with respect to the necessity of training teachers for secondary schools. "In France," it was stated, " the normal schools aim at giving the pupil thorough instruction much
" more in the subjects which he is intended to teach, and in those allied subjects
" which will enable him to teach them with greater fulness, insight, and power,
" than in the methods of teaching them and the professional art of the teacher.
" In the normal schools of Germany, on the other hand, the science of *Paidagogik*
" has reached a high degree of development. Mr. Matthew Arnold a few years
" ago expressed the opinion that if in some countries undue importance was attach-
" ed to that science, yet there was no justification for treating it with the ne-
" glect which it commonly received in England where middle schools were concern-
" ed." The Commission proceeded to point out that a teacher, to become efficient, had much to learn besides the things which he taught; and therefore recommended that he should be required to show, before being permanently appointed to a middle or high school, that he possessed a sufficient acquaintance with the theory and methods of teaching, as developed in the many works that have been produced on that subject. At the time of the Commission's report, there was in Madras a training school for English teachers in secondary schools; in Bengal, Assam, and the North-Western Provinces there were schools for vernacular teachers; and in the Punjab a school for teachers of both classes. Elsewhere

the certificate of having passed one or other of the University examinations was accepted as a sufficient qualification.

What has since been done in Madras has been already described in the section on collegiate education, where it was stated that the University had instituted a degree in teaching. Success in this examination is now declared to be a condition of permanent employment in Government and aided schools—presumably in the case of new appointments only. A shorter course of training is sometimes accepted in the case of graduate teachers, for whom the University regulations for the degree in teaching require an attendance of six months only in a recognised normal school. The Central Training College at Lahore was already in existence at the date of the Commission's report; it trains teachers for secondary schools, both English and vernacular. Rules regarding certificated teachers have recently been drawn up in consultation with managers of aided schools; and in future such teachers alone will be admitted to permanent employment. In Bengal, Assam, and the North-Western Provinces provision is made for training vernacular teachers in secondary schools; and in the remaining provinces vernacular secondary schools are not found. It appears, therefore, that in two provinces, and two only, have any steps been taken to carry out the recommendation of the Commission with regard to teachers in English schools. The need for such a provision has, indeed, been felt elsewhere. In his report for 1885-86 Mr. White, the Director in the North-Western Provinces, dwells at some length on the mechanical character of the teaching in zila schools, and quotes with approval the remark of an Inspector, to the effect that the teaching in these schools is little else but an attempt to cram the boys with the contents of so many books : of educating influence there is next to none. The head-master is rather the senior teacher than a head-master in the true sense of the term, making his influence felt throughout the school. Mr. White goes on to say :—" The difficulty of remedying this patent "defect in the schools is mainly, I think, due to the absence of any systematic "training of teachers for these schools, and it will not be remedied until the "establishment of a central training college for the teachers of our secondary "schools becomes possible. The time is now passed or rapidly passing in Europe "when the amateur is admissible into the profession of teaching; and the "experience of the primary schools in England has conclusively proved the "superiority of the trained master." On this last point he quotes a remark by Mr. Sedgwick in his lecture on Form Discipline :—" In ease, in resource, in "confidence, in mastery of handling, a certificated master could give points to "any average graduate, even many of the best, fresh from the Universities." That is an accepted principle as to primary schools ; but it is probable that the general absence of any similar requirement for secondary schools in India has followed from the prevalent custom in England, where—not to speak of Eton and Harrow or the Elizabethan grammar schools—the more modern foundations of Marlborough or Clifton require in their masters nothing more than the possession of a good degree, and trust to experience to give them the necessary skill in the technical part of their profession. Possibly the educational conditions of the two countries present too many points of divergence to make England a safe guide for India in this respect. At any rate, in whatever direction opinion may be tending, it appears that the question is not one an early settlement of which is, in present financial circumstances, possible. The cost of establishing a training college for the further instruction of graduates and under-graduates in the principles of teaching would certainly be great; and even where vernacular training schools for secondary teachers exist, they could not ordinarily be expanded so as to provide also for English teachers, for whose training much more elaborate provision seems to be necessary. It was not, however, the training but the examination of teachers, and the issue of certificates to them, that was the subject of the Commission's recommendation; and it would appear possible to carry out these objects at an inconsiderable cost.

170. Fees in Secondary Schools.—The recommendations in Chapter V of the Commission's report are limited to the following points: (1) that the rates of fees in aided schools should be settled by the Department in consultation with the managers; (2) that such rates should be lower than those fixed for Government schools; (3) that scholarship-holders should not be exempted from the payment of fees. A much more important recommendation under this head is to be found in Chapter VII, and runs as follows :—"That it be an instruction "to the Departments of the various provinces to aim at raising fees gradually, "cautiously, and with due regard to necessary exemptions, up to the highest "amount that will not check the spread of education, especially in colleges "secondary schools, and primary schools in towns where the value of education "is understood" (VII. 3.) The fee-rates in colleges were fully considered in the last section of this chapter. The propriety of raising the fee-rates for a certain class of pupils in primary schools will be touched upon in the next section. The rates in secondary schools have been revised, and for the most part largely increased, in nearly every province of India; a material difference being generally allowed between the rates fixed for departmental and those for aided schools, though the latter have also shared in the increase. A comparison of the rates in force in various provinces will not be without interest. In Madras the fee-code was revised in 1884, and again in 1886, and the rates for departmental secondary schools now stand at R3 a month in the high and R1-8 in the middle department. In Bengal, minimum rates have recently been sanctioned for all departmental schools on the following scale:—in the high department R2-8 a month, in the middle department, R2, and in the primary department, 12 annas to R1-8. These are minimum rates, and they are already largely exceeded in the majority of schools; indeed, in the Hindu and Hare Schools attached to the Presidency College of Calcutta, they rise to R5 in the high and middle, and R4 in the primary department. In the North-Western Provinces, the Government schools are divided into 'superior' and 'inferior' according to the circumstances of the locality and of the people, with corresponding differences in the rates of fees. In the high department the rate is either R1-8 or R2; in the middle department, 12 annas or R1; and in the primary department 6 annas to 8 annas, or 8 annas to 12 annas. These rates involve a large increase over those previously in force, though chiefly in the higher classes of the schools. The minimum rates for aided schools are fixed at 75 per cent. of the above scale. Similarly aided schools are allowed to receive free students up to a ratio of 15 per cent., while 5 per cent. only are allowed in Government schools. It is stated that the increased rates of fees have only slightly affected the attendance. In the Punjab, as previously noticed, still more vigorous measures have been taken. The fee-rate to be charged in each case varies not with the school, but with the boy, according to the circumstances of each. The lowest scale is as follows :—in the high department, R1-4 to R1-8 a month; in the middle department, 12 annas to R1; and in the primary department 2 annas to 8 annas. The other two scales, for boys in better circumstances, are formed by multiplying these rates by 2 and by 3 respectively, subject to a limit of R4 in the highest class. These rates are to be doubled in five years by annual increments of 20 per cent., so that the monthly fee thus charged in the two highest classes of a Government school will be R7 and R8 respectively,—a rate nowhere as yet approached in India. In aided schools these rates are subject to a reduction of 25 per cent. Remissions of full and of half-fees may be made up to 5 per cent. of the total number of scholars in each case. In the Central Provinces, the rates in high schools (which are composed of two classes only) varies from R1 to

R2 a month; in middle schools, including the upper primary section, the pupils are divided into three grades according to their means, paying respectively 4 annas, 8 annas, and R2. Exemptions are allowed up to a limit of 8 per cent. in cases of poverty. In Berar, there has been a general increase of about 50 per cent. on the previous rates, and it is proposed to raise them still further. As they now stand, the scale is as follows:—in the high department, R1 to R1-8; in the middle department, 6 annas to 8 annas; and in the primary department, 2 annas to 4 annas. Of Coorg it is stated that the fees have been twice raised within the last six years; and it is not thought advisable to increase them any further at present. Any action of the same kind that may have been taken in other provinces is not specially noticed. It was stated in an earlier paragraph that the fee-receipts in secondary schools had increased in 1885-86 at a greater rate than the attendance of pupils; but the full effect of the enhanced rates lately sanctioned will be more clearly seen in future years.

The recommendation that the Department should have a voice in settling the rates of fees to be levied in aided schools, was objected to in some provinces, on the ground that it involved an unnecessary interference with the independence of private managers. In others it met with approval, as a legitimate exercise of control over institutions that received aid from the State; and in those provinces in which the practice was already in force, it was declared to have given rise to no trouble or dissatisfaction. It may reasonably be urged that the principle involved in the recommendation implies not interference, but rather co-operation between two parties equally interested in the spread of a sound system of education; and from that point of view it may be compared with the recommendation in Chapter V, that in the conduct of departmental and other public examinations, the managers and teachers of non-Government schools should be associated with the officers of the Department (V. 17; VII. 20); and with the more general recommendation in Chapter VIII, that with a view to secure the co-operation of Government and non-Government institutions, the managers of the latter be consulted in matters of general educational interest (VIII. 14)—a recommendation that has resulted in the assembling of educational conferences, to the great advantage of education. If co-operation is to be fairly and effectually carried out, it can only be on the condition that each party recognises the other's interest in the educational system as a whole, and his right to some voice in its control.

In Bengal and Assam holders of middle scholarships are still allowed the privilege of free tuition in high schools.

171. Scholarships in Secondary Schools.—The recommendations on this subject are (1) that the system of scholarships should be so arranged as to enable a clever boy in a primary school to rise to the highest honours which the University can offer; (2) that they should be awarded after a perfectly open competition; (3) that they should be tenable in schools under private no less than in those under public management. These recommendations amplify the later recommendation in Chapter VIII that "with a view to secure the co-opera-"tion of Government and non-Government institutions, ... the students "[of the latter] be admitted on equal terms to competition for certificates, "scholarships, and other public distinctions." (VIII. 14). The Commission pointed out (paragraph 490) that in only four provinces—Bengal, Assam, the Central Provinces, and Berar—were the provisions of the Despatch of 1854 on this subject carried out with anything like completeness. In some provinces the chain of scholarships was not continous; in others, the competition for them was restricted to the students of Government institutions—a restriction which they declared to be inconsistent with the principle that institutions under private management should be frankly accepted as an essential part of the general system of education. It will now be shown that in every province, with one possible exception, the system of scholarships has now been or is being constructed in full conformity with this important principle.

The Government of Madras was invited by the Commission to consider the necessity of revising the system of scholarships in secondary schools in that Presidency, with a view of bringing it into greater harmony with the provisions of the Despatch of 1854 (VII. 16). On this recommendation action has been taken, but action of a somewhat peculiar kind. The Director of Public Instruction, while admitting in 1884 that the scholarship system of the province was defective, raised objections to the proposals of the Commission, on the ground chiefly that they afforded no encouragement to the private endowment of scholarships, and were not based on the grant-in-aid system, that is, the principle of self-help. Accordingly, when the question came in the following year under the consideration of the committee appointed to revise the grant in-aid Code, their proposals were based on that principle. They recognised the need of establishing a comprehensive system of scholarships, but were of opinion "that the means employed should not differ in principle from the "means employed to develope other educational objects, *viz.*, the due encourage- "ment of private agencies to provide such helps to talented students." Chapter VII of the revised Code specifies the conditions of aid; and provides that a scholarship grant may be given to the amount of one-third of the private stipend, subject to a limit of R4, R5, or R6 a month according to the class of scholarship. (This is for native schools; for European scholarships the proportion is one-half, and the money limits are somewhat higher.) It follows that the creation not merely of a chain of scholarships, with special provision for poor boys in backward tracts, but even of a single scholarship, rests on the variable and uncertain basis of private liberality. This doubtful point in the system has not escaped the notice of the Government of Madras, which is " not satisfied that this question has yet been fully dealt with," and lays stress on the general admission that a system of stipendiary scholarships is preferable to that of a large percentage of free-students. The Government has therefore called for a report, showing what advantage has been taken of the provisions of Chapter VII of the Code, with suggestions for the further extension of the system in accordance with the principles of the Despatch of 1854.

The Education Commission had pointed out, as to Bombay, that almost exclusive stress was laid in that Presidency upon free-studentships, and that stipendiary scholarships were confined to students of Government schools. In remarking on the proposals of the Commission under this head, the Acting Director considered it essential, if those proposals were to be fully and fairly carried out, to make a material addition to the allotment for scholarships, on the ground that the Government colleges and high schools had so long had a monopoly of the scholarship fund that they would raise an outcry against any attempt to make the public funds allotted to them public property. He proposed an additional grant of R10,000, to which would be added an equal amount transferred from the existing provision of R33,000 for scholarships tenable in Government schools and colleges. The fund of R20,000 thus created would then be divided according to districts, and thrown open to competition, and the successful candidates would be at liberty to prosecute their studies in any institution they might select. The following extracts from Mr. Lee-Warner's report throw a clear light on the spirit in which these proposals were made : " It may be argued that the distribution of R20,000 over the whole " Presidency would be a drop in the ocean, and that in the end the Government "colleges and high schools would probably retain what they have and gain an

"addition from the increment. But this criticism would not touch the point.
"What we want to aim at is the maintenance and the practical illustration of the
"principle that aided institutions are the care of the Department as much as
"Government institutions, and that both classes of schools have a right to share
"in the educational fund. A larger notice of the progress of aided schools in the
"annual report, and a systematic recognition of their rights as public schools
"under the fostering care of the public department, is the object to be aimed at;
"and in proportion as private enterprise is appreciated and taken into partnership
"by the State, will its credit and usefulness develope." The Local Government
expressed its full concurrence in these views, and sanctioned the additional grant
of R10,000. They added an expression of their opinion that it was undesirable
to offer the stimulus of free studentships and scholarships in high schools and
colleges to the school population generally, but that special provision should be
made for pupils living in remote or backward tracts.

The Government of the North-Western Provinces took exception to the
statement of the Commission that in those provinces a complete scholarship system had not been matured, an observation which showed, in the opinion of the
Government, that the Commission had not been accurately instructed on that
point. Under the system in force "a complete ladder was provided by which a
"boy might rise from the primary school examination to the degree of Master
"of Arts." The local boards had established a system of primary scholarships, awarded after public examination and tenable in middle schools, the
expenditure on which rose from R24,000 in 1881-82 to R39,000 in 1883-84,
though it appears to have since declined; scholarships from middle to high
schools were provided by the State; and endowments existed for the award
of scholarships tenable in colleges. It was added that all Government scholarships, which were formerly tenable at zila schools only, had been thrown open
to unrestricted public competition and might be held at any approved institution; with the single exception that scholarships for M. A. students were to
be held in the Muir Central College until equally efficient instruction up to
that standard had been provided in other colleges. On these grounds the
Local Government maintained that their rules and their policy were in complete
accord with the wishes of the Government of India.

In the Punjab revised rules for the award of scholarships to students
attending schools of all classes have been embodied in the new Code, which lays
down the general rule that "all awards of scholarships shall be by merit and in
"accordance with the results of public examinations." The governing principle
of the new scheme is that Government scholarships are to be offered for unrestricted competition within each district. The system has been so arranged as to
supply connecting links between the different grades of institutions; it has been
settled in communication with the managers of aided schools, and is described
as being in strict conformity with the recommendations of the Commission and
the instructions of the Government of India.

172. The Further Extension of Secondary Education.—The recommendation quoted above, as to the future policy to be adopted in the extension
of secondary education, may be coupled with the nearly equivalent recommendation in Chapter VIII : —" That in ordinary circumstances the future extension
"of secondary education in any district be left to the operation of the grant-in-
"aid system, as soon as the district is provided with an efficient high school,
"Government or other, along with its necessary feeders." (VIII. 11.) This
principle has been cordially accepted in all the more advanced provinces. The
recommendation, it will be observed, stops short of urging the transfer of existing
Government institutions—a matter that is dealt with later on—and insists only
on the point that their number should not increase. A glance at the first table

in this section (paragraph 156) will show that the extension of purely departmental schools of the secondary rank has been definitely arrested within the year under report. If we go back a year further and include the figures of 1884—the first year in which the recommendations of the Commission could have had any effect—we shall find that the new policy has been carried out still more decisively. The following figures are in point. They refer to English secondary schools under public management, excluding those in Native States, and also excluding a few in Bengal which have been transferred in the interval from the vernacular to the English class without change of management.

	Managed by the Department.	Managed by Local and Municipal Boards.
1883-84	282	281
1884-85	240	335
1885-86	230	342

It appears, then, that there has been not only no increase but a very noticeable decrease in the number of Government institutions in these two years. It is true that there has been a still larger increase in the number of those managed by local bodies, a result of the policy of transfer pursued in Madras and elsewhere; but there is nothing in that policy that is inconsistent with the recommendation under review. Indeed, while the recommendations in Chapter VIII of the report are chiefly aimed at the transfer of departmental institutions of this class to associations of private persons, their intermediate transfer to district and municipal boards is recognised as a useful, and often a necessary, stage in the attainment of that object (VIII. 23). The Commission pointed out that local boards bore in relation to private effort a double aspect. "They may "manage schools of their own, and in that capacity receive aid from the Depart-"ment, and thus be regarded as themselves examples of private effort. On the "other hand, they may, like the Department, dispense grants from public funds "in aid of private effort in the stricter sense" (para. 499). The Commission regarded it as a moot point how far it was desirable that local and municipal boards should manage schools of a higher class than the primary. "We have "abstained," they remarked, "from recommending that secondary schools should "be managed by local and municipal boards; but some provinces may wish to "make the experiment, and in some it is being made already" (para. 500). In Madras, for example, local boards are, for the purposes of secondary education, already regarded as private agencies. It is held that their main duties are concerned with primary education; and towards the establishment of primary schools they receive no aid from the State. With regard to secondary schools, while they are encouraged to follow the grant-in-aid system, they are allowed a free hand; and should they choose to establish schools of their own, they are treated as private managers would be treated, and receive aid from provincial funds under the Code. The secondary schools that have been made over to local boards in Madras have been generally transferred on these terms. As to the encouragement of purely private enterprise in secondary education, the policy and practice uniformly followed in Madras leave nothing to be desired.

Nowhere, indeed, has the principle directly involved in the recommendation of the Commission been contested. As was stated in an earlier paragraph, the Government of Bombay announced in 1884 that the further extension of secondary education must be carried out along the lines of private enterprise; and while increasing the allotment for grants-in-aid to secondary schools by R10,000 a year, it recognised the necessity of revising the grant-in-aid rules in a sense favourable to private managers. Among its other financial proposals, the Government of Bengal (in which province, as in Madras, private effort had always been liberally encouraged) undertook to make a regular annual addition of not less than R20,000, up to a total ultimate increase of two lakhs, to the allotment for aiding secondary schools, provided its anticipations as to the growth of the provincial revenues turned out to be well founded—an estimate of its probable resources which subsequent experience has altogether falsified. The Lieutenant-Governor of the Punjab considered that the facts of the case fully justified the criticism of the Commission, that in that province departmental agency had largely taken the place of private effort. "For the future," it was added, "it must be considered a positive instruction that this policy "shall be altered, and that for the extension of secondary education the sys-"tem of grants-in-aid is generally to be preferred to that of direct departmental "agency." In later and more detailed orders the principle has been "fully "accepted and emphatically set forth" by the Punjab Government. The orders declare that "a new school for secondary education can be established "on the grant-in-aid system only; and rules have been laid down under which "it is required that if a local body desire to raise an existing middle school to "the primary grade, or a middle school to the high grade, or to introduce "English into a vernacular school, one-third of the total expenditure of the "school must be met from private sources if provision is made for instruction "in English, and one-fourth in the case of a purely vernacular school. The "only exception allowed to this rule is in cases where it is considered necessary "to establish an additional vernacular middle school, in order to make adequate "provision for the supply of men qualified to become teachers of primary "schools, as must sometimes happen in the more backward districts of the pro-"vince." It was believed that the new Education Code of the Punjab would supply a great stimulus to the establishment of secondary schools under native management. Several schools of this class had indeed already been opened; among them the most important being the Islamia school at Amritsar. The Chief Commissioner of Assam considered that the language of the recommendation left it open to doubt whether the intention of the Commission was that no new schools of secondary instruction should be opened by the Department, a proposal in which he concurred, or that all Government high and middle schools should be gradually closed and aided schools substituted. The latter alternative did not meet with his approval, as he conceived that the time had not yet come, even in the most advanced provinces, when the Government could confine its support entirely to grants-in-aid. Government schools had a great effect in raising the tone of aided schools; and it was probable that some institutions of the former class must always be retained for that purpose. The Lieutenant-Governor of the North-Western Provinces gave expression to a similar distinction. He remarked that in all ordinary cases secondary schools for teaching English should preferably be established on the grant-in-aid footing, and this principle had in fact been followed for some years. "The same principle is ap-"plicable to schools as to railways; if the public are ready to establish them with "a certain degree of State aid, and under a certain measure of State inspection, "no one will maintain that the State should take entirely on itself the business "of establishing them. But in the present condition of education and enlighten-"ment in these Provinces, the Lieutenant-Governor and Chief Commissioner is "not prepared to rely entirely on indirect means for secondary education, or to "agree that, if local co-operation is not forthcoming, the State should decline to "provide the means of secondary education. For, in his opinion, secondary is no "less important for the welfare and advancement of the people than primary "education, and he does not see any fundamental distinction at present between "the relation of the State to primary and to secondary education." At the same time a popular demand for secondary education was growing up, and it was probable that it would, at no very distant date, require nothing more than the grant-in-aid system for its support and its further development. With that explanation, the Lieutenant-Governor accepted the principle that the future aim of the Government should be to substitute aided for departmental schools. No opportunity, it was afterwards affirmed, of encouraging private enterprise in the extension of education had been lost; and liberal grants were given wherever there was ground for believing that they would be properly spent. In pursuance of the policy thus enunciated, the Government high school (Oriental) at Gorakhpur, which had been condemned for inefficiency, was closed and replaced by an aided English school under the management of the local committee, at whose instance the transfer was effected. Aided high schools were opened at eight other places; a very large school, in which two-thirds of the cost was supplied by private liberality, was established at Lucknow in commemoration of Her Majesty's Jubilee. It was proposed to give further effect to the same principle by making it a rule that no extension of the existing buildings in Government schools should be undertaken unless at least half the necessary cost was provided by local liberality.

This last provision illustrates a collateral development of the new policy which deserves notice. It has been fully understood that the animadversions of the Commission were directed, not merely against the further development of the departmental system, but against the indefinite enlargement of existing schools. If a fair field was to be given to private enterprise, it was essential that proposals for increased establishment in Government schools, or for additional buildings to accommodate more pupils, should be carefully and jealously scrutinised. Upon the overflow of a Government school a private school might often be successfully launched; and without unduly draining the Government institution, the stream of its superfluous pupils would serve to fertilise the lower lands of private effort. The Department in Bombay urged that the Government of the province should declare itself in that sense, so that effectual resistance might be offered to the pressure that was constantly-exerted by headmasters in the direction of enlarging the Government high schools. The main object of the Government should be to maintain those schools as models, and not as the only institutions for providing high education. These views were endorsed by the Government of Bombay, which declared that the departmental high schools were not to be allowed to compete with private institutions or to monopolise an increasing educational area. The limit of accommodation being reached, further growth should be checked by imposing larger fees and higher standards. The gradual transfer of secondary education to private and local management would thus be facilitated; and meanwhile the departmental high schools were to be maintained as models for the benefit of the whole secondary system, Government and aided alike. It was stated in the last chapter that the same policy had been followed for some years in Bengal. Every application for enlarging a Government high school is met by the inquiry whether there is any chance, due encouragement being given, of private enterprise supplying the further provision required. If there is any such prospect—and the tendency is to make the most of whatever chance is alleged to exist—the fees in the Government school are raised to such a point as will supply a direct incentive to private managers to open a school for the benefit of those pupils who desire a cheaper education.

The position of the Government vernacular or model schools in Bengal, and their relation to aided schools, have been materially altered by recent orders. When primary schools were few, the theory of the Government model schools was that they were to be planted in backward parts until they had paved the way for aided schools to succeed them, and then be transplanted to parts still more backward to repeat the same process. But in recent years the backward tracts of the middle region of education have been invaded and overrun by the advanced schools of the primary system. It therefore became necessary to look to some other destination for the Government middle schools; and it was decided to re-establish them, gradually and as opportunity offered, as models of middle school education to its highest standard, including English as well as vernacular. Consequently the proper locality for such a school was no longer the most backward, but the most advanced village—short always of its being so advanced as to maintain in thorough efficiency a school of the same or a higher class. It was essential to the successful working of the principle that the Government contribution should not be increased beyond the normal rate of R25 a month; and all further expenses, whether for English or for vernacular instruction, would be paid for locally. It was thus hoped that the schools would become 'pioneer' schools in a different sense from that hitherto attached to them; and that they would show the way, as the high schools had done and were doing, not merely to the inhabitants of the village in which they were placed but to all the schools of the district. The model schools are now being made over to the management of district boards; and this may possibly be a step towards their final transfer to purely private agencies.

173. Withdrawal of Government in favour of Private Managers.— The recommendations of the Commission under this head are found in Chapter VIII. They are as follows:—

" That all Directors of Public Instruction aim at the gradual transfer to " local native management of Government schools of secondary instruction (in- " cluding schools attached to first or second grade colleges) in every case in which " the transfer can be effected without lowering the standard, or diminishing the " supply, of education, and without endangering the permanence of the institu- " tion transferred." (VIII. 30.)

" That the fact that any school raises more than 60 per cent. of its entire " expenditure from fees be taken as affording a presumption that the transfer of " such school to local management can be safely effected." (VIII. 31.)

The reference to "private parties" in the paragraph (538) that leads up to the first recommendation, shows that it is aimed at the transfer of departmental institutions, not to local statutory bodies, but to associations of private managers; and the Government of India has expressly declared, in para. 32 of the Resolution of the 23rd October 1884, that this is the policy to be finally aimed at. The language of the Resolution is very clear. " Board schools and municipal " schools are not private institutions in the sense contemplated by the Commis- " sion. What is wanted is to draw forth genuine private enterprise, and to en- " courage the transfer of Government schools and board schools to the hand " of trustees who will interest themselves in their maintenance, and thus set " free the funds of the public for the extension of education in other directions." Still, as explained in the last paragraph, the intermediate transfer of Government schools to district or municipal boards is admissible, and is recommended as a step towards the final result. From what has preceded in this section and in Section II, it will be manifest that the transfer of departmental schools, though going on actively enough, is as yet only in the first or intermediate stage. Local boards in fact supply an obvious agency of transfer, and a ready-made machinery for carrying on the transferred schools. They are also under complete official supervision, and therefore under some degree of official control; their action in educational matters can be, and most commonly is, directed by rules prescribed by higher authority, and thus continuity of administration can be secured. Further, their constitution enables them to offer guarantees of permanence which are generally wanting in the case of private associations or committees. It will **be convenient to summarise here the action that has been taken in carrying out the policy of transferring secondary schools to local boards.**

In Madras (apart from schools in the Agency Tracts, which must remain under departmental management) all high schools but four and all middle schools but one have been transferred to district boards or municipalities. In Bombay no high schools are maintained by district or municipal boards; but of middle schools, 110 are maintained by these bodies against 26 under departmental management. The new Municipal Act has made it incumbent on municipalities in Bombay (other than the Presidency Town) to make adequate provision for middle as well as for primary education; and, as a result of the late re-adjustment of educational charges, nearly 30 middle schools, which up till 1885-86 had been maintained by district boards from the local rates, were in that year transferred to the control of municipalities. In Bengal, the cost of Government middle schools within municipal limits was laid in 1883 upon municipal funds, though the schools continued to be managed departmentally; while under the recent Local Self-Government Act, district boards are charged with both the management and the maintenance of all Government middle schools within the area under their control. Government high schools in Bengal are, under the same Act, to be transferred to the management of joint committees composed of members of the district board and of the municipality. In the North-Western Provinces and Oudh, there are only two secondary schools, the cost of which is directly charged to provincial revenues; they are the Benares collegiate school and the vernacular high school at Fyzabad. All other secondary schools in the province are returned as being managed and maintained by local boards; though the funds for their maintenance are practically derived, not from local rates, but from provincial assignments, and though the high schools at head-quarter stations (zila schools), notwithstanding some powers of supervision which the boards possess, are in essentials managed by the Department. Of the Punjab, it was stated in August 1886, that all secondary schools (with the single exception of model schools attached to training schools) had been transferred to the control of local boards; but the returns for 1885-86 still show 14 high and 16 middle schools under departmental, as against 29 middle schools under local, control. In the Central Provinces local boards take little or no part in the direct maintenance of secondary schools. Only two middle schools are maintained by district boards, and none by municipalities. In Burma the reverse is the case. Two out of the four high schools and all the fourteen middle schools are under municipal management. District boards have not yet been constituted in Burma. In the remaining provinces local boards have nothing to do with the direct control of secondary education, with the exception of one municipality in Coorg.

It is evident, therefore, that throughout India the Department has retired or is retiring in a somewhat wholesale manner from the direct control of secondary schools. The withdrawal is for the present taking place in favour of district and municipal boards; but the further retirement of these bodies in favour of purely private associations is not lost sight of. The Lieutenant-Governor of the Punjab states that "every facility will be given for the transfer of board "schools to the management of associations of private persons, provided they are "able to afford adequate guarantees of permanency and efficiency;" though the opportunity has not yet arisen. Such opportunities have arisen in Bengal, where two high schools have been transferred to private management; and in the North-Western Provinces, where one has been so transferred. The Director in Bombay pointed to three reasons which might be urged against withdrawal in favour of native managers. The first was that the retirement of Government might mean the withdrawal of neutral control between opposing races and religions. The second, that the resources of Government were necessary to give secondary education that ample development along various lines, technical and other,

ests, not of one section of the community, but of native society as a whole. And finally, when the revised rules for grants-in-aid and a larger provision of funds had stimulated the growth of aided schools side by side with those which Government now maintained, we could look forward to resigning the control of secondary education into the hands of really representative bodies of native gentlemen.

One minor point may be touched before leaving this subject. The Commission included schools attached to colleges among those from which Government should finally withdraw. The difficulty attending retirement from this class of institutions is that they are mostly held in the same building with the colleges to which they are attached. It would be a doubtful boon to offer a school while withholding its local habitation; and yet the practical difficulties in the way of maintaining in the same building two institutions under different management, seem to be insuperable.

Section IV (b).—PRIMARY EDUCATION.

174. Character and Scope of Primary Education.—Since the course of instruction in primary schools must include, and cannot go very much beyond, the elements of reading, writing and arithmetic in the vernacular of the pupils, so far as these can be acquired within four or five years, it might be supposed that there was no room for any great differences in the meaning which one province or another attached to the term. The limits of primary instruction might indeed vary; and in fact we find that primary schools in some provinces include subjects and standards which in others are regarded as falling rather under secondary instruction. But this is not the only difference. A far more important point is raised in the question whether primary education shall be the same for all. In some provinces, primary instruction is carefully distinguished from the primary stage of higher instruction; and the village boy, whose education begins and ends with the primary school, goes through a course of instruction altogether different from the introductory stages of secondary and higher education. In others, no such distinction is made, and all pupils alike receive the same initial training. Lastly, there are wide differences in the system of control. In one province, primary schools are mostly departmental institutions; in another they are managed and maintained by local boards; while in a third the primary system rests more or less exclusively on a basis of indigenous village schools, and the duties of the Department, or of the local bodies that represent it, are largely confined to inspection, examination and the grant of aid.

The views of the Commission as to the character of primary instruction are expressed in the recommendation, which has also been accepted by the Government, "that primary education be regarded as the instruction of the masses, "through the vernacular, in such subjects as will best fit them for their position "in life, and be not necessarily regarded as a portion of instruction leading up to "the University" (IV. 1). The words employed in the first part of this recommendation show that it was intended to define the education that should be provided for the masses of the people, while the language of the second part indicates that a different form of primary instruction might be better suited for students destined for a University career, that is, for the bulk of pupils in high schools. The advantages and disadvantages of the "dual system," as it is called, are discussed at length in paragraph 149 of the Commission's report, though no definite opinion is expressed in favour of either system. A typical example of each may be given. In the primary schools of Bombay, a single uniform course is prescribed for all pupils as far as the upper primary (or fourth) standard. The primary school, in fact, is regarded as being, and is intended to be, not only the village school but the preparatory school for secondary education. It is true that for those pupils—a constantly increasing number—who require a more complete education in the vernacular, the course of the primary school is extended by two further standards; but as far as the upper primary stage, all pupils and all classes of society read side by side in the same school, and read the vernacular only. In Bengal a different course is followed. It is held that the primary instruction suited to each pupil varies with, and should be determined by, the highest standard that he is likely to reach; that a boy, for example, who is intended for the University, and a professional career, requires a different initial training from one whose education will end with the village school, and whose days will be spent in the humble occupations of rural life. In this system high schools necessarily have their own primary departments, in which English is for the most part taught from the beginning, and the course, from the lowest class to the highest, is governed by the final matriculation standard. In a middle school, again, the junior classes read a course different from either. Primary instruction is therefore regarded in Bengal under three separate aspects,—first, as an education designed to meet the simple requirements of the masses of the people, and therefore complete in itself so far as it goes; secondly, as that which leads to a somewhat more advanced education in the vernacular, with possibly a later infusion of English; and thirdly, as the initial stage of an English education leading to the University, and therefore justifying the study of English from the outset. The Bombay system resembles that of America, in which all classes of society read together the same course in the town or village school. The Bengal system finds a parallel in England, where children of one social class learn their elements in the board school, those of another in the commercial academy, and those of a third in the preparatory school for Eton; and where, as again in Bengal, each class pays for its elementary education at very different rates. These, then, are the two contrasted types, and to one or other of these the primary systems of other provinces more or less closely approximate. Madras occupies an intermediate position. Its system recognises the existence of attached primary departments in which English is read from the beginning; but the elementary classes, in Government high schools at any rate, are now being gradually abolished, though in high schools under private managers they are still for the most part retained. Some provision for the early teaching of English is also made in vernacular schools, where English may be optionally taught within the limits of the primary stage. In the North-Western Provinces and Oudh, there are two alternative courses throughout the primary stage—English and vernacular respectively. In the Punjab, the course is common to English and vernacular schools in the lower primary stage of three years, but diverges at the commencement of the upper primary stage. The Central Provinces follow in general the Bombay system, but English may be learnt after the lower primary stage is passed, and an upper primary section is sometimes appended to middle schools. Assam has adopted the Bengal method in its entirety, and that of Burma closely resembles it.

It follows, therefore, that in all provinces primary education—understood as the instruction provided for the masses of the people—is conducted in the vernacular exclusively; while 'the primary stage of higher education' is sometimes identical with the former throughout the whole or through a part of its course, and sometimes altogether special and different. Where they are identified, the advantage claimed for the system is that " if the higher castes can give a tone to " society, and if the example of the educated can stimulate the backward " classes, then in the Bombay system this stimulus is provided by associating " every section of the community in the class-rooms of the primary school." (Report of the Commission, para. 145). The obvious danger is lest the course be moulded to suit the requirements of those—necessarily the more influential class —who are intended for a higher education, rather than of those whose school career comes to an end at the close of the primary stage. The views of the Government of India are expressed in the following extract from the Resolution of the 23rd October 1884 (para. 16):—" It is here only necessary to remark that the " curriculum of a primary school ought, while not neglecting the preparation " necessary for any pupils who may be advancing to the secondary stage, to aim " principally at imparting instruction calculated to be of real practical benefit to " the bulk of the children whose education will terminate with the primary " course."

SEC. IV(b).]   PRIMARY EDUCATION.   197

175. Primary Schools for Boys, 1885-86.—The necessary figures are given in the following table:—

Primary Schools, 1885-86.

PROVINCE.	MANAGED BY THE DEPARTMENT.		MANAGED BY LOCAL AND MUNICIPAL BOARDS.		AIDED.		UNAIDED.		TOTAL.	
	Schools.	Pupils.	Schools.	Pupils.	Schools.	Pupils.	Schools.	Pupils.	Schools.	Pupils.
Madras	58	1,974	1,203	35,187	7,998	220,871	3,868	79,208	13,127	337,240
Bombay	29	2,037	4,349	274,206	633	25,524	17	1,163	} 6,593	391,680
Native States in ditto	...	...	...	...	...	...	1,565	88,750		
Bengal	29	833	26	647	43,015	979,077	7,640	119,129	50,710	1,099,686
North-Western Provinces	...	...	4,915	171,050	93	5,182	46	1,622	5,054	177,854
Punjab	66	6,890	1,341	68,683	131	5,703	26	689	1,564	81,965
Central Provinces	193	13,921	731	49,931	571	24,979	120	3,494	} 1,658	94,788
Native States in ditto	...	...	...	...	...	...	43	2,463		
Burma	4	262	16	997	1,269	58,754	3,813	85,987	5,102	146,000
Assam	25	347	1,185	34,808	336	10,264	78	2,074	1,624	47,493
Berar	522	27,574	13	1,623	226	4,476	92	1,213	863	34,886
Coorg	61	3,069	5	254	2	89	...	...	68	3,412
TOTAL	997	56,907	13,784	637,386	54,274	1,334,919	(a)17,308	385,792	86,363	2,415,004
TOTAL FOR 1884-85	1,025	62,979	13,098	621,138	70,877	1,480,082	(b)15,774	331,972	100,774	2,496,171

(a) Including 1,608 schools in Native States, with 91,213 pupils.
(b)   „   1,519   „   „   „   88,284   „

Here we are at once struck with the loss of 16,600 aided schools, and of 14,400 in the total number. As already stated in the General Summary, this remarkable decline is a result of the policy recently pursued in Bengal, and already described in para. 62 of Chapter II. That policy, which in the opinion of the Local Government was rendered inevitable by the continuous discovery and registration of indigenous schools to an extent far beyond the power of the Department either to inspect or to aid, involved the rigorous exclusion from the departmental examinations for rewards, and subsequently from the annual returns submitted by the inspecting officers, of all schools with less than ten pupils each, of those that had existed for less than six months, of those that failed to produce attendance and inspection registers properly kept, and of those in which no printed books were read. The result of these measures was that the number of aided schools in Bengal fell, within the year 1885-86, from 65,585 to 50,710—a loss of 14,875 schools and of 122,952 pupils. In the previous chapter it was shown that between 1881-82 and 1884-85 the number of primary schools in Bengal increased by about 14,800, and that of pupils by about 342,000. It follows therefore that the number of schools again went back in 1886 to what it was in 1882, while the number of pupils increased by about 220,000 over the attendance of the earlier year. But the general rise in the standard of education that took place in the interval is illustrated by the fact that the number of upper primary schools rose from 1,944 to 3,080; in other words, that more than 1,100 schools advanced to that very important and useful stage of elementary instruction which is marked by the upper primary standard of Bengal. Most of the schools that disappeared from the returns in 1885-86 have doubtless ceased to exist as public institutions, either by amalgamation with stronger schools in their neighbourhood, or by definitely giving up the subjects on which the Department insists, and so returning to the rank of private indigenous institutions. Some 1,600 continued to register themselves and to submit returns, and these re-appear as an addition to the unaided list. About one-third of the pupils also re-appear in that list, which exhibits an increase of 37,000. In aided lower primary schools for boys, the number of pupils not reading a printed book at once fell by 110,000, and the proportion from 44 to 40 per cent. That the proportion of non-readers is still so high is due to the fact that even in the best of the village schools there is always a considerable number of pupils who are in the 'palm-leaf' or 'plantain-leaf' stage, who learn writing and the methods of country arithmetic, but who have not yet advanced to the reading of a printed primer. The Magistrates of Bengal—in whose hands the administration of the district grant had been placed, and who, with more or less assistance from the District Committees, and through the agency of the local inspecting officers of the Department, admitted village schools to the aided list, controlled the examinations and distributed the rewards—were practically unanimous in favour of the change that had been made in getting rid of the lower fringe of aided primary schools. Those that were lost were of little educational value; while their removal made it possible to aid the useful remainder at a somewhat more liberal rate.

If, then, the disturbing element introduced by the Bengal policy be excluded, it will be found that the total number of primary schools for boys in the rest of India increased from 35,189 with 1,273,533 pupils to 35,653 with 1,315,318 pupils,—a gain of 464 schools and of 41,785 pupils. The increase is confined to board schools, district and municipal, which add 686, while aided and unaided schools show a decline of 117 and 78 schools respectively; but in each of these three classes of schools there is a gain of from 15,000 to 16,000 pupils. Departmental schools, with a slight decrease of 27 in their number, have lost about 6,000 pupils; but this last class of schools, as will presently be seen, are from their character peculiarly liable to fluctuation. The increase of pupils is greatest in Bombay and Burma; but it is common to all other parts of India with the single exception of the North-Western Provinces, in which 7,500 primary pupils have disappeared.

176. Systems of Primary Education: Departmental Schools.—The preceding table shows at a glance the general character of the systems under which primary education is carried on and controlled in each province of India. Departmental schools, it will be seen, are comparatively few. Before proceeding to give an account of those that exist, it may be well to cite the recommendation of the Commission relating to the establishment of this class of primary schools :—" That primary education be extended in backward " districts, especially in those inhabited mainly by aboriginal races, by the "instrumentality of the Department pending the creation of school-boards, or " by specially liberal grants-in-aid to those who are willing to set up and main-"tain schools" (IV. 24). It will be seen that departmental primary schools in India largely conform to the conditions here specified. It is only in Berar, the Central Provinces and Coorg that any large proportion of the primary schools are under direct departmental management. The general explanation is that in Berar and Coorg, and in large tracts of the Central Provinces, district boards have not yet been established. In other provinces, Government primary schools possess almost invariably a special character. In Madras, Bengal and Assam the great majority are schools located in hill-tracts for the benefit of aboriginal or backward races, and for the most part in places where there exists no missionary agency whose services can be utilised. In Madras they also include a few special schools for Muhammadans. In Bombay, two-thirds of the number are police schools not maintained by the Education Department; and the small remainder are either model schools attached to training colleges, or schools in such out-of-the-way places as Aden. The 66 departmental primary schools in the Punjab are apparently the separate branch schools (not primary sections) which have grown out of secondary schools in towns, and which are managed by the head-masters of those schools. In the Central Provinces, the absence of district boards in certain localities is not the only reason for the existence of departmental schools. **Primary schools in towns—whether vernacular schools or** branches of middle English schools—are still retained under departmental management, owing to the general unwillingness of municipal boards to undertake their control. A partial transfer of such schools to municipalities was, however, about to be made. The number of departmental primary schools in the Central Provinces is also decreasing year by year through the continuous transfer of such schools to district boards. In 1885-86, for example, the number was reduced from 285 to 193, that of board-schools being raised in an equal measure from 639 to 731. This reduction in the number of departmental schools in the Central Provinces is met by a nearly equivalent increase in Berar.

It may be noticed in passing, though it will already have been abundantly obvious, that the maintenance of a school in the sense of providing the funds for its support, does not always imply its management. The zila and training schools of the North-Western Provinces furnish an example. Again, the departmental primary schools situated in municipalities in the Central Provinces, are either wholly or mainly maintained from municipal funds. So also in Berar, all village schools, though managed by Government officers, are maintained from the educational cess, supplemented by a grant from provincial revenues. It is urged by the local Department that they are virtually grant-in-aid schools, except as regards management (an exception however of no slight importance), and that in some other provinces they would be called cess-schools. The reference seems to be to Bombay, since in many parts of that province the cess schools, though nominally under the control of the district boards which provide the money, are really managed and administered by departmental officers exclusively, owing to the incompetence or want of interest shown by the boards.

177. Board Schools.—Schools managed by district and municipal boards form the great majority in Bombay, the North-Western Provinces, the Punjab, the Central Provinces and Assam, and a considerable minority in Madras. The general character of the control exercised by these bodies, and of the financial resources at their disposal, has been indicated in Section II of this chapter. Schools maintained by district boards have nominally increased from 12,795 to 13,037; but a deduction of nearly 100 must be made on account of the questionable inclusion under this head of certain aided schools in Madras. The actual development of the agency of district boards is more correctly measured by an increase of 144 schools either newly opened or newly taken under their management. The general policy of increasing educational facilities by multiplying board schools is limited by the recommendation of the Commission, " that [local "and municipal] boards be required to give elementary indigenous schools free " play and development, and to establish fresh schools of their own only where the "preferable alternative of aiding suitable indigenous schools cannot be adopted" (III. 12). In the next paragraph it will be seen how far this recommendation has taken effect. The new board-schools are distributed in the following way. There is an increase of 90 schools in the Central Provinces, and of about 40 each in the Punjab and Assam. These are provinces in which the area of activity of district boards is year by year enlarging itself. In Bombay also, though there is an apparent increase of 13 only, it should be explained that in pursuance of the new financial arrangements described in Section II, between 400 and 500 schools, formerly maintained from the district cess, have been taken over by municipalities and are now supported by municipal funds. As the whole of these losses have been more than made good by the grants thus set free, district boards in Bombay must be credited with their full share of educational activity. In the North-Western Provinces there is a decrease of about 60 schools, which have been reduced by district boards in cases where the income was found insufficient to maintain in an efficient state the full number of schools originally opened. Municipal schools throughout India have increased from 303 to 747, or by 444, which is almost precisely the increase that has taken place in

Bombay alone (17 to 460) owing to the cause above specified. In other provinces the losses and gains have been trifling; but in Berar, it may be noticed, 13 primary schools were maintained by municipalities in 1885-86, while in the previous year there was only one.

As the true character of the primary system in Assam is said to have been misunderstood by the Commission, it will be necessary in this place to describe it in some detail. The Commission stated rightly that the great majority of the aided schools were new creations called forth by the offer of substantial grants, and were not adopted from any pre-existing indigenous system. They were only partially right in the further statement that the system was based, as in Bengal, on private effort. Its character is thus described by the Inspector in Assam. A private person, usually an ex-pupil of a middle or primary school, starts an adventure school, reports his having done so to the Deputy Inspector, and asks for aid. One of the inspecting officers then visits the school; and if he thinks it has a fair prospect of success he recommends a grant, which is then given by the local board if funds admit. As soon as the grant is sanctioned, the founder of the school ceases to have any voice in its management; the school is carried on according to departmental rules, and the local board has no hesitation in transferring or even dismissing the original founder; in short, the school becomes to all intents and purposes a board-school. The guru receives a monthly stipend, supplemented in many cases by rewards after examination; and he also retains all that he can collect from fees and payments in kind. Other schools have a different origin. They are purely creations of the Department, started by departmental officers in hopeful localities where the villagers undertake to provide a school-house and keep it in repair, to supplement the monthly grant by contributions in kind, and sometimes to board and lodge the guru. Once established, these schools, like the former class, fall into the rank of board-schools. A third class of board-schools is composed of those which have been started among half-civilised hill-tribes by missionary bodies, acting on behalf of the Department and employing not their own but local funds, whose aid has been invoked on the ground that the Department had not a sufficiently strong agency to carry on education in those remote tracts. Such are the schools maintained by the American Mission in Nowgong, and by the Society for the Propagation of the Gospel in Durrung. This last class of schools is to be distinguished, on the one hand, from schools independently established by missionaries in the Khasia and Jaintia hills and elsewhere, and subsidised by grants-in-aid; and on the other, from schools started and still administered by the Deputy Commissioners of the Garo and Naga hills in their official capacity. The latter are departmental, the former are aided schools.

On the merits of the whole system, Mr. C. B. Clarke, who was in charge of the Assam Education Department for two years, formed an unfavourable judgment. The teachers, in his opinion, were not properly qualified for the course they were required to teach, and the course itself was not well chosen. The gurus were sent to the training school to learn the art of teaching, when what they really needed was a better education. In the lower primary schools boys were taught multiplication and division by the English way, and an elementary reader was placed in their hands, but they were not taught arithmetic after the country methods, nor mental arithmetic, nor bazar accounts; and these last were what the people chiefly valued. "There are no schools springing up "round us," he added, "nor boys crowding into our schools. In order that this "may be the case, we have to offer the people an education they reckon worth "having. It is no use our speculating as to what we think the right course for "primary schools; we can only enforce that in a limited number of schools to be "paid for by Government. To make education spread generally, the boys and

"their parents must believe that they get money's worth for their fees, their
"slates, &c., and for the trouble of attendance"—as, Mr. Clarke urges, they do
in Bengal. "I do not believe that a single child is attracted to a *pathsala*
"in Assam by the astronomical sections in the Assamese elementary reader, or
"by the Sanitary Primer in Assamese. Government can force these things on
"the schools—and then complain of the apathy shown by the Assamese in
"lower primary education."

178. Aided Schools.—Schools of this class, those of Bengal being excluded, show a decline of 117. Aided indigenous schools form the backbone of the primary system in Madras, Bengal and Burma, and constitute no inconsiderable portion of it in the Central Provinces and Berar. The increased attention paid to aided primary schools in Bombay was noticed in paragraph 63 ; and to the observations there made it can now be added that the number of aided schools increased in 1885-86 from 460 to 633. The following extracts from the report of an Inspector of Schools in Bombay show that in that province, as in Madras and Bengal, the indigenous school is readily capable of improvement on its own lines, when departmental standards and methods are introduced without menace to the traditional subjects of instruction. "The indigenous school proper is supposed to be con-
"ducted purely on indigenous methods, but it is only in a few cases that the
"traditional method of education is now followed without modification. In
"most cases people now prefer the Government standards, the sanctioned print-
"ed books, and systematic teaching, and the school prospers according to its suc-
"cess in introducing these. Many of the head-masters are young men, who
"having received their education in Government schools, are well acquainted
"with these features, and do their best to reproduce them in their private
"adventure schools...... The use of printed books, copy-slips and maps used in
"Government schools is constantly on the increase, though particular attention
"perhaps is paid to Modi manuscript reading, Modi writing, the elaborate native
"multiplication tables and mental arithmetic, these subjects being such as all can
"appreciate the usefulness of. Most of the schools examined are reported to be
"in a satisfactory state of progress." Another Inspector reports that half the aided indigenous schools "compare well with our rural schools, except that
"they are generally ill equipped. The rest of the schools are conducted mostly
"by Lingayat priests, teachers of the old type, who instruct in reading, writing
"and mental arithmetic. All of them, however, are said to use printed
"books."

The Inspector adds his belief that, where attendance and inspection registers are introduced, and other changes insisted on, "the schools will improve
"and become more permanent than at present, and will then form no insignificant
"factor in the system of national education." An exception to this satisfactory record is supplied by the Urdu (or Koran) schools for Muhammadans, the masters of which, and the parents of boys attending them, are said to be extremely averse to the introduction of any secular subject into the course. The missionary schools in Bombay, as elsewhere, are said to be well equipped and well managed. The total number of private indigenous schools of all kinds in the Presidency (including some 800 Koran schools) is about 3,000 ; so that the Department, in aiding between one-fourth and one-fifth of that number, has already made a considerable impression on what has sometimes been described as intractable material.

It was stated in the last chapter (para. 65) that there was a loss of 500 aided schools, that is, of schools that failed to earn grants at the annual examination, in the Madras Presidency in 1884-85. There was a further loss of more than 300 schools in 1885-86. The cause is not specially explained ; but the loss was partly made good by an increase of nearly 5,000 pupils, in those schools that succeeded in earning grants, over the total numbers of the previous year. But the number of schools earning or competing for grants is so large, that fluctuations of this kind are not only inevitable but unimportant. The departmental system dominates not only the 8,000 schools that earn, but the 4,000 that as yet fail to earn grants, and schools of these two classes are nearly ten times as numerous as those under public management. Aided schools in the Central Provinces either belong to missionary associations, or are indigenous. Schools under the management of recognised societies often receive fixed grants-in-aid; indigenous schools are aided by results. The latter conform to the departmental standards for primary schools, use the same books, and endeavour to introduce the same methods of instruction. The newly-opened indigenous schools are taught generally by pupils trained in the departmental schools, and occasionally by certificated teachers. Some of the masters in aided schools are said to earn so good a livelihood as to render them liable to assessment. There are in all 571 aided schools, against 731 under the management of local boards, and 193 managed by the Department. Perhaps it may be said without invidiousness that the system followed in the Central Provinces appears to combine in the most useful and practical way all methods of agency, turning each to good account. In Assam, the aided schools are either schools established by missionaries in the Khasia and Jaintia Hills, in Goalpara, and among the Garos and Nagas, or indigenous Sanskrit and Arabic schools in which an attempt is being made to introduce a little secular instruction under the stimulus of a grant-in-aid. The additional schools (47) in 1885-86 are for the most part of the last class, which now includes about 150 schools, or something less than half the whole number. With regard to the educational aspect of missionary work the Inspector observes :—" The improved economy of the Christians, who spend "nothing on witchcraft by eggs or fowls, or on changing of wives, or on alco- "holic drinks, greatly aids them in educating their children." Aided schools in the North-Western Provinces have fallen from 115 to 93. They are mostly branches of missionary schools, and are said to vary greatly in number from time to time. Instead of the usual fixed grant, a system of payment by results was applied to some schools of the class; the managing bodies speak favourably of the change and recommend its extension. The Director expresses the hope that it may hereafter be extended to indigenous schools, which still remain altogether outside the area of systematic instruction. In the Punjab vigorous attempts had been made to grapple with the vast mass of indigenous material that was known to exist. Exhaustive inquiries were set on foot in order to ascertain the character and constitution of the different classes of indigenous schools, the course of studies, the attendance of pupils, the qualifications of the teachers, their capacity for improvement, and their willingness to be improved. In his report for 1882-83, Colonel Holroyd supplied a mass of varied and interesting information on these points, and expressed a guarded opinion as to the possibility of aiding and improving the schools. But up to 1885-86 little or nothing was actually done to that end. While the returns for that year showed more than 12,000 indigenous schools in the province, aided schools for boys numbered only 131, and these were mostly either lower primary branches of Anglo-vernacular (middle) schools, or schools specially established for low-caste boys. Liberal rules for the encouragement of indigenous institutions have, however, since been framed. In Berar, out of about 350 indigenous schools, less than 30 remain outside departmental supervision. Of those classed as public schools by reason of having adopted departmental standards, 226 are aided and 92 are as yet unaided. Revised rules, offering more liberal grants for attendance and proficiency, came into operation in 1884-85, with the result that most of the indigenous schools enrolled themselves as candidates for aid. It is no matter for surprise that the aided indigenous schools are declared to be as yet far inferior to the State schools. In the words of one Deputy Commissioner, "nothing really fit as yet comes into competition with our Government institu- "tions, and the so-called indigenous and private schools present very poor stuff "in the shape of education." The departmental report states that incompetent masters are gradually being replaced by men trained in the Government schools, and that the indigenous schools are steadily improving in efficiency.

179. Unaided Schools.—It is only in Madras, Bengal and Burma that this class of schools occupies any large or important place. In the systems of those provinces, built up as they are almost exclusively on an indigenous foundation, unaided schools play a distinct and recognised part. They constitute, in fact, that section of indigenous schools which, having abandoned the traditional methods in their narrow and exclusive form, are aiming at, but have not yet reached, the departmental standards based on and including them. An increase of 400 schools in Madras is partly explained by the reduction of 300, previously noted, in the number of aided schools. Similarly in Bengal, the wholesale withdrawal of aid from schools that did not comply with the new conditions, resulted in the final disappearance of most from the returns of the Department, the amalgamation of a certain number with neighbouring institutions of a more stable kind, and the transfer to the unaided class of 1,600 schools which had more independence and vitality, and which still conformed to the departmental standards in however rudimentary a form. In Burma, the place filled by unaided schools is still more conspicuous and important. Unaided schools which have adopted the departmental standards outnumber aided schools in the proportion of three to one, and all are advancing towards the goal of successful competition at the annual examinations.

One or two further points relating to the use and value of unaided schools in the educational systems of these provinces may be of interest. First, the proportion which unaided schools, more or less conforming to the departmental type, bear to private, indigenous, unreformed institutions, so far as these are known to exist. The returns supply the following figures:—

	Unaided Schools.	Private Institutions.
Madras	3,868	1,397
Bengal	7,640	2,234
Burma	3,813	5,412

Except in Burma, therefore, what is known as the "outer circle" of indigenous institutions has been reduced to comparatively small dimensions. Secondly, we may examine the actual educational value of the schools classed as unaided, judged by the number of their pupils who are in the book-reading and in the upper primary stage. The figures are subjoined:—

	Upper primary stage.	Reading printed books	Total pupils.
Madras	1,639	61,495	79,208
Bengal	637	56,472	119,129
Burma	...	81,956	85,987

The first two columns of figures measure in an appreciable way the advance already made by this class of schools during their present intermediate stage. In all, or in nearly all these cases, the introduction of printed books has been the direct result of departmental influence and example.

Though it is only in the three provinces above named that unaided schools figure largely in the returns, yet it is admitted that elsewhere also public primary schools exist which find no place in the departmental statements. In Bombay, for example, where the value of the "outer circle" of educational activity did not appear to the Commission to be sufficiently appreciated, it is believed that a large number of schools, which are unrecognised by the Department, nevertheless conform to its standards. The returns show only 19 unaided schools for Bombay, leading to the impression, which is authoritatively believed to be erroneous, that the Department has incorporated almost every primary school which has any claim to be called public. Even in Madras, the number of unaided indigenous schools outside the circle of State supervision appears to have been largely understated; in a later return for the same date it is shown as 3,427. In Bengal, again, the rule excluding from the category of recognised schools all those with less than ten pupils, appears unnecessarily to have been applied to private institutions. This was corrected in the following year, when the number rose to 4,221, the average attendance falling from 14 to 11.

180. Primary Education in Burma.—As the Report of the Commission furnished no account of the educational system of Burma, it is now necessary to describe it in some detail. As is well known, the system of primary education in that province, as in Bengal and Madras, is almost exclusively founded on the indigenous schools of the province, which have grown up from remote times as an offshoot of the Buddhist religion, and in which the instruction given is so efficient, that, in the words of the Local Government, "it is "hardly too much to say that no child passes out of one of the indigenous schools "of Burma without being able to read and write Burmese fairly well." The following extract from a special report submitted by the Director, Mr. Hordern, in 1881, supplies a vivid and interesting sketch of the national system of primary education:—

"The province is exceptionally fortunate in possessing a widespread machi-"nery of primary vernacular education indigenous to the country, intimately "associated with the religious beliefs of the people, and thus endeared to them "both by venerable antiquity and by their most sacred associations.

"The religion of Buddhism has overspread the country from end to end "with religious houses, founded, endowed, and maintained by the piety of the lay "population, which also provides lavishly for the religious all the necessaries of "life, and such luxuries as it is lawful for them to enjoy. The remotest village is "not without its *Kyoung*, a substantial timber edifice of quaint construction, "conspicuous from afar with triple-turreted roof, and often richly ornamented "with carving. This building is at once the Buddhist monastery and the village "school where every boy first learns to read and write, his teachers being the "shaven and yellow-clad monks, who thus make return for the liberal mainten-"ance and profound veneration accorded to them by the laity; and if every village "has its monastic school, the outskirts of every town is rendered picturesque by "its extensive groups of religious houses, every one of which has also its knot of "teachers and pupils.

"In addition to the monastic schools thus scattered over the face of the "country, there exist in the larger villages a parallel institution called the house-"school, which forms a no less important part of the indigenous machinery. "Perhaps in no country of the world is the occupation of a teacher of youth held "in such universal respect as in Burma; and when the pious Buddhist layman lays "aside active labour, and desires to spend his later years in meritorious work which "will prepare him for a future state and earn for him the rewards of virtue, he "very frequently adopts the profession of a schoolmaster: he throws open his "whole house, excepting one small room or corner set apart for himself and his "family, and receives as many pupils as he can accommodate.

"The distinguishing feature of these schools, and that which gives to them "**their greatest value, is that they afford instruction to girls as well as boys, the** "**strictness of the Buddhist monastic vows forbidding** the admission of girls to

"the monastic school. These lay schools are not scattered like the monasteries
"throughout the rural villages, but no town of considerable size is without several.
"It is to them, mainly, that the women of Burma owe the education they receive,
"and in the competition with monastic schools for the rewards of the Education
"Department, the lay schools have hitherto shown themselves superior to their
"more numerous rivals."

In schools of both kinds the instruction was the same, and was given exclusively through the Burmese language. It included (1) reading and writing the vernacular; (2) the learning by rote of Pali verses, the text-books used being the Pali scriptures of Buddhism with Burmese paraphrases, and the Burmese versions of the Pali *Jataka*, or stories of the several existences of Gautama; (3) in exceptional cases, elementary arithmetic. The writing materials were the *parabike*, or book of thick blackened paper, with soap-stone pencil. Working, therefore, upon the materials which such a system supplied, the Department endeavoured to extend and systematise the teaching of arithmetic, and gradually to introduce instruction in other subjects, such as the geography and history of Burma, grammar, surveying and mensuration, and simple sanitary laws, while retaining in its integrity the indigenous curriculum. These ends were gained by visiting and inspecting the indigenous schools; by the distribution of approved text-books either free or at low rates; by holding periodical examinations, on the results of which money-grants were made to the schools according to fixed standards; by posting trained assistant-teachers, paid from public funds, to successful schools when the head-teachers sought such aid; and by establishing scholarships for promising pupils, tenable in upper primary and middle schools. After some years of indifferent success, the efforts of the Department were at length rewarded by finding the teachers of lay and monastic schools alike disposed to accept with cheerfulness the visits, the inspection, and the guidance of educational officers. In the Resolution of Government on the departmental report for 1879-80, from which these statements are derived, it is remarked that "the "teachers of indigenous schools are now for the most part ready to adopt, and the "parents of the pupils are eager to buy, the improved Burmese text-books which "are now issued at cheap rates by the Educational Department." One apparent difficulty remains to be explained; namely, how it was possible to offer the inducement of money-grants to the members of an ascetic order bound by vows of the strictest poverty. The explanation is that each monastery has its recognised patrons among the influential lay residents, and that any grant earned by a monastic school is paid to the lay patrons on behalf of the monks. It is also optional for the teachers of an indigenous school to receive a supply of books, maps, or school apparatus in lieu of a money grant.

At the outset, the standards of examination, though following the same general lines, were easier than those prescribed for the few Government schools that had been established in large towns and villages as models and examples for the indigenous schools to imitate and follow. In 1881-82 pupils of indigenous schools passed for the first time the full departmental tests; and a year or two later the standards of examination for Government and for indigenous schools were fully assimilated. The lay schools have uniformly surpassed the monastic schools in popularity and efficiency, and the improved standards were accepted much more readily by the former than by the latter; but schools of both classes professed their willingness to endeavour to work up to them. It thus became possible to gauge the work of indigenous schools by a standard test recognised throughout India; to compare schools of indigenous growth with others under foreign management; and at the same time to constitute them efficient feeders to schools of a higher grade. The lower primary standard comprised Burmese, Pali, arithmetic (including tables and the four simple rules), and the geography of

Burma and the four quarters; the upper primary standard included the same two languages, more advanced arithmetic and geography, together with an optional subject which might be either the history of Burma, or drawing, or elementary physiology, or an advanced course in Pali. Below these is an examination for rewards by a standard a year short of the lower primary; and any school earning a grant by success at this examination is classed as an aided school. In 1881-82 the number of indigenous schools under inspection was 3,172; in 1885-86 it had advanced to 5,081. In 1881-82 the number of pupils earning result-grants was 3,349; in 1885-86 the number passing by a higher standard was 9,182. In 1881-82 a few pupils passed for the first time the full departmental tests; four years later, 2,096 pupils of indigenous schools passed the lower primary, and 452 the upper primary examination; while 15 schools of the same origin had gone even beyond that standard and were included in the middle class. In 1881-82, assistant masters, trained and paid by Government, were attached to 78 indigenous schools; in 1885-86, the number of trained teachers thus employed was 216. The importance of replacing the indigenous teachers by trained masters has been recognised from the first. "It "cannot be too plainly insisted," wrote the Director in 1883, "that in the hands of "untrained masters the standard of teaching in indigenous schools can never be "materially raised by any system of examination and reward; and that one means "alone can be really effectual to this end, namely, the gradual supersession of "untrained masters by masters trained to the teaching profession." The establishment of independent schools under trained teachers was also encouraged by specially liberal rules. The trained masters are declared to be much more successful than monastic teachers of the old type, and their schools to be more numerously attended, notwithstanding the general levy of fees in them. The admission of girls to read side by side with the boys also increases the popularity of the new schools in a country where the position of women is one of great independence.

All these measures obviously involved increased expenditure. The cost of the system is not given for 1881-82, but the expenditure in grants to indigenous schools, which in 1879-80 was less than R28,000, rose in 1884-85 to nearly R1,22,000; and it became necessary to reduce the rates of result-grants. The effect of the measure was to set free additional funds for the employment of trained teachers. A year earlier the status of trained teachers sent out to village schools was modified. They were no longer regarded as Government servants, but as officers employed by the municipalities or district committees who found their salaries.

It will now be understood why the number of unaided schools is still so large. To pass by a standard and to earn a grant, a pupil must pass in all the subjects of that standard; and the number of indigenous schools in which all the necessary subjects are taught is still small. It is nevertheless maintained that the results already achieved, even in the schools classed as unaided, amount to a revolution in the national system of education. In fairness it should be added that the moral influence of the new system of education has not escaped criticism. It has been alleged that the young Burmans leave school earlier than before, and with scantier acquirements; that they marry earlier, and show a greater tendency to be "fast;" that they are less under the restraint of the law of Buddhism, and are more easily led astray by the temptations of the world; finally, that they neglect their own language for the sake of a smattering of English. These gloomy views, however, are not shared by the higher authorities.

Such, then, were the arrangements made for promoting elementary education on an indigenous basis among the Burmese. But the system thus established offered no corresponding advantages to the Karen population, and for them it became necessary to make special provision. The Karens are described as a section of the people entirely distinct from the Burmese, in relation to whom they have long held the position of a subject race, and by whom they are regarded almost as savages. Although scattered throughout the same districts, they live to this day altogether apart from the Burmese; a despised and timid people, dwelling in villages of their own and speaking their own language. Their religious ideas, so far as they possess any, have yielded to the exhortations of Christian missionaries, especially the American Baptists, and throughout whole districts they have embraced Christianity. Among this people the missionaries have founded small village schools; and to these schools, though essentially of foreign origin, have been extended the benefits of the system designed for the encouragement of indigenous institutions. But fears were expressed that the sight of a Burmese inspecting officer in their remote and secluded villages, far from encouraging them, would put to flight both teachers and pupils; and accordingly a staff of Deputy Inspectors of their own race was appointed. The steps thus taken have been attended with no small measure of success. The number of Karen primary schools under inspection increased from 139 in 1881-82 to 426, and the pupils in them from 2,562 to 10,796. In 1881-82 112 Karen pupils passed the examination for rewards; in 1885-86, 457 passed the lower, and 82 the upper primary examination. In the last year, also, certificated Karen teachers began to open independent schools of their own in the hope of obtaining Government aid. Progress so marked can hardly fail to raise the status of this depressed people, and to increase their sense of independence and self-respect.

181. Provincial Standards of Examination for Primary Schools.— Such being the general character of the systems in force in the various provinces of India, the next step is to ascertain the educational results of each system as tested by the public examinations held at certain fixed stages of progress. The stages selected are those known as the upper and lower primary standards. It is necessary, however, in the first instance, to explain the action taken by the Education Commission with regard to these standards. The Commission recommended "that the upper and lower primary examinations be "not made compulsory in any province" (IV.2). Their meaning was this. The Government of India had, on the report of the Committee of 1878, endeavoured to set up these two standards as fixed landmarks in the primary system of each province, so that every pupil, on his arrival at either stage, was required to pass a test which the definitions professed to render uniform for the whole of India. But it was soon found that the provincial systems, which had grown up on separate and independent lines, could not easily be forced into a common shape, or tested by uniform measures of progress. It was difficult to identify the proposed standards with those already in use; or if they could be identified, the particular standards selected had no special significance or value in a system which included others of equal importance. The Commission accordingly recommended that the project of imposing fixed and uniform tests should be abandoned; and that if any attempt at comparison were made, one or more of the standards already in use in each province should be accepted as a sufficient, if not an entirely accurate, basis of comparison. In Bombay, where primary instruction is carried up to a fifth and a sixth standard, the second and the fourth were declared to correspond most nearly to the lower and upper primary standards. In the Central Provinces, though generally following the Bombay model, the third and fourth were selected; the two standards below these occupying, it should be observed, only half-a-year each. In Madras, where the standards of primary instruction are limited to four, the third was taken to represent the lower, and the fourth the upper primary standard. In Bengal, where there was no definite classification of pupils by annual stages of progress, the standards of the two existing examinations for primary scholarships were accepted, though the higher of the two was declared to go much beyond that of the upper primary standard as defined by the Committee. In the North-Western Provinces and the Punjab, the standards selected were those of the third and the fifth year of study. It will be obvious from this description that the so-called equivalent standards have been selected in a somewhat arbitrary fashion, and that from the nature of the case no exact comparison can be made between province and province. The following statement of the provincial standards for the upper primary examination, which marks the higher limit of the primary course, is taken from para. 172 of the report of the Education Commission, and may serve as a guide for such comparison as is feasible. Against each province are shown the subjects required for that examination, in addition to vernacular reading, writing and arithmetic.

Madras.—Geography of Asia. Not more than two subjects from the following list may also be taken up at the option of the candidate:—(1) English, (2) vernacular poetry, (3) history, (4) the sanitary primer, (5) agriculture.

Bombay.—History and geography of India. One of the following subjects may be optionally added:—(1) drawing, (2) agriculture, (3) handicraft.

Bengal.—(1) History and geography of Bengal, (2) Euclid, part of Book I, (3) mensuration (added in 1885), (4) elements of physics, (5) the sanitary primer, together with another work on hygiene. (All these are compulsory; there are no optional subjects; and a candidate, to pass the examination, must pass under every head.)

North-Western Provinces.—One of the following:—(1) history, (2) geography, (3) sanitation, (4) mensuration. (The report of the Commission includes all these as part of the standard; but it appears from the departmental report for 1882-83, paragraph 317, that the subjects are alternative, only one out of the list being required.)

Punjab.—(1) English or Persian, (2) geography, (3) mensuration. (All are compulsory.)

In the first three provinces, arithmetic includes native methods of account; in the last two it is generally confined to European arithmetic, the standard in which is much the same in all provinces.

182. Comparative Progress as tested by Public Examinations.—With the foregoing explanation, the results of the examinations which in each province are declared to correspond most nearly to the upper and lower primary standards may now be given. The subjoined table shows the number of pupils passing by each standard. The figures for Coorg are not returned.

PROVINCE.	Upper Primary Standard.	Lower Primary Standard.	TOTAL PUPILS IN PRIMARY SCHOOLS.
Madras	8,478	22,115	337,240
Bombay	13,161	30,948	391,680
Bengal	4,092	20,018	1,099,686
North-Western Provinces	4,418	12,911	177,854
Punjab	6,051	12,316	81,965
Central Provinces	5,954	9,124	94,788
Burma	691	2,268	146,000
Assam	230	1,181	47,493
Berar	1,180	3,175	34,886

There is an increase in the number passing by each standard, especially by the upper primary. There is a slight diminution in the number of lower primary passes in Bombay and the North-Western Provinces, and a large decrease amounting to nearly 1,500 in Bengal. From this serious loss, the Director drew the conclusion that the small schools excluded from aid under the new system must have contained many pupils who were qualified to pass the lower primary examination, and who had therefore lost the advantage of that incentive to progress which the examination supplied; adding, "there is no use in disguising "from ourselves the fact, that in a large part of Bengal we have been com- "pelled to part with control over good and promising educational material." This conclusion may, however, be modified, if the results of both examinations are considered. There was certainly a decrease of 542 in the number of schools that succeeded at the lower primary examination; but it also appears that there was an increase of 581 in the number of successful schools at the upper primary stage; and since, under the Bengal rules, a school has to make its choice, and cannot send candidates for both the upper and the lower scholarship, the meaning may well be that some 500 schools passed from the lower to the upper primary stage, and were replaced by only inconsiderable additions from below.

It must be repeated that the comparison between province and province should not be unduly pressed. So far as can be judged from the mere enumeration of subjects—certainly a very imperfect test—the standard in the Punjab appears to be higher than that in the North-Western Provinces, and the standard in Bengal higher than in either Madras or Bombay. The standards may be compared from another point of view. From the diagrams given in paragraph 228 of the Commission's report, it will be seen that the upper primary standard (or its equivalent in English schools) falls short of the matriculation standard by seven years in Bombay, by five years in Madras, and by four years in Bengal. The Bombay matriculation standard is said to be a year in advance of that of other Indian Universities; and if this claim be allowed, the upper primary standard in Bombay would still appear to be lower than that in Madras and Bengal. If, then, the third and fifth standards in Bombay be taken, instead of the second and fourth, as equivalents of the lower and upper primary standards as these are understood elsewhere, the number of pass pupils would amount to 6,210 and 21,723 (Report for 1885-86, paragraph 79.) The assumption may possibly do something less than justice to the advancement of education in that Presidency; but if it be for the moment admitted, it would appear that Bombay and Madras, with something like the same total spread of education, are not very far apart in the quality of their primary schools. (This comparison is, however, subject to the further consideration that the population of Bombay is only about three-fourths of that of Madras—23 millions and 31 millions respectively by the census of 1881.) Bengal, with a population of 68 millions, or nearly three times as great as Bombay and more than twice as great as Madras, has a school population, it appears from the table, about three times as large as in either province. It should therefore have, if equal progress had been made in the quality of instruction, about 60,000 pupils passing annually by the lower standard and about 20,000 by the upper. The actual numbers, as given in the table, are far short of these limits; and the inference would seem to be inevitable that not more than one pupil in Bengal passes by either test, when, from the analogy of other provinces, we should expect to find three or more. But in drawing such a conclusion, one fact of cardinal importance is lost sight of. In Madras and Bombay all pupils, in whatever schools reading, are required to pass the specified tests—pupils who are going on to middle and to high schools no less than pupils whose education ceases at an earlier stage. In Bengal, on the other hand (and the same is true of Burma and Assam), pupils in middle and high schools are not called upon to pass any public examination at the lower and upper primary stages; and consequently the numbers shown in the table are short of the truth by the whole body of primary pupils in such schools. These must therefore be taken into account. In the secondary schools of Bengal, the number of pupils in the lower primary stage, which occupies three years, is 76,000; in the upper primary stage, occupying two years, 46,000; in the middle stage, also of two years, 37,000. A moment's consideration of these figures will show, that not less than 20,000 pupils in secondary schools are passing each year from the lower to the upper primary stage, and not less than 18,000 from the upper primary to the middle stage. These numbers should therefore be added to those given in the table; and it follows that the total number of pupils passing from the lower primary to the upper, and from the upper to the middle stage in Bengal, amounts to 40,000 and 22,000 respectively. As far, then, as upper primary education is concerned, Bengal appears to be in no way behind other provinces; and indeed the upper primary schools that form so valuable an element in the Bengal system need fear no comparison with those of any other part of India. At the lower primary stage, notwithstanding the additions just made, there is still a marked deficiency; we find that some 40,000 pupils pass by that standard when there should be 60,000. This, there can be no doubt, is a necessary result of the Bengal primary system. The materials with which that system works are not, as in most other provinces, institutions founded and maintained by departmental officers, and therefore established from the beginning in a condition of at least fair efficiency; they are indigenous schools, with all the faults to which such institutions are prone, and which can be only gradually removed. There is no definite system, as there is in Madras, by which trained teachers are substituted with the least possible delay for the indigenous schoolmasters; these schoolmasters are retained, they are encouraged to do their best and to introduce new subjects of instruction, and in course of time, when the value of the new teaching begins to be appreciated, they are replaced without violence by younger and more competent men who have received a better education than their predecessors. In all these matters the Bengal system conforms to the recommendations of the Commission "that a steady and gradual improvement "in indigenous schools be aimed at, with as little immediate interference with "their *personnel* or curriculum as possible" (III. 5); and "that the standards "of examination be arranged to suit each province, with the view of preserving "all that is valued by the people in the indigenous systems, and of encouraging "by special grants the gradual introduction of useful subjects of instruction" (III. 6). Hence the progress of improvement is slow; but that progress is being made is sufficiently shown by the fact that, within the last eight years the number of pupils passing the lower primary examination in Bengal has increased from 5,000 to 20,000 a year. Relatively, therefore, the rate of increase is rapid, and it has been brought about by adherence to the policy just described.

The North-Western Provinces and Oudh, with a population of 44 millions

progress is shown in the Central Provinces, with a population of 10 millions—only half the size of the Punjab; while the primary pupils in the former province are more numerous and in almost the same stage of advancement. Assam, with a population of 5 millions, half that of the Central Provinces, has the same proportion of primary pupils; and Burma, with a population of 3¾ millions, a far higher proportion. In these two provinces the comparison is rendered difficult, as in Bengal, by the inclusion of primary pupils in secondary schools; but it is probable that the Central Provinces are much more advanced than either as regards the quality of instruction. Berar, with a population of 2⅔ millions, more than holds its own in the comparison. It stands, in fact, in point of numbers and progress, almost precisely on a par with Bombay, whose system and example it has largely followed.

In the next paragraph will be considered the cost at which these various results have been attained.

183. Expenditure on Primary Schools for Boys, 1885-86.—In the following table is shown the expenditure incurred from various sources in the maintenance of primary schools for boys:—

Expenditure on Primary Schools, 1885-86.

PROVINCE.	FROM PROVINCIAL REVENUES		From Local Funds.	From Municipal Funds.	From Fees.	From other Sources.	TOTAL.
	In Schools under public management.	In aided Schools.					
	R	R	R	R	R	R	R
Madras .	30,417	64,899	3,89,175	82,440	4,11,389	1,87,807	11,66,127
Bombay .	3,29,900	16,366	5,72,670	1,57,458	2,81,528	3,84,733	17,42,655
Bengal .	2,794	5,83,905	3,693	11,832	15,51,580	2,99,226	24,53,030
N.-W. Provs.	...	4,888	5,01,670	24,470	8,909	30,057	5,69,994
Punjab .	12,071	13,648	2,24,163	24,768	33,412	17,170	3,25,232
Central Provs.	41,091	31,554	1,42,431	26,440	30,255	35,239	3,07,010
Burma .	4,220	5,725	89,881	85,676	6,260	8,589	2,00,351
Assam .	1,246	7,481	82,635	1,256	22,465	18,570	1,33,653
Berar .	77,457	5,795	67,892	4,666	35,372	1,668	1,92,850
Coorg .	1,508	260	7,969	1,416	497	178	11,828
TOTAL .	5,00,704	7,34,521	20,82,179	4,20,422	23,81,667	9,83,237	71,02,730
Total for 1884-85 .	4,34,360	7,78,877	21,30,165	2,97,193	24,43,836	10,82,529	71,66,960

There has therefore been a decrease of R64,000 in the total expenditure on primary schools. This is made up of the following items:—(1) an increase of R22,000 in the expenditure from provincial revenues and of R1,23,000 from municipal funds, met by a decrease of R48,000 in the expenditure from local funds, or a net increase of R97,000 in the expenditure from public funds; and (2) a decrease of R62,000 in fees and of R99,000 in the receipts from other sources, or a total decrease of R1,61,000 in the expenditure from private funds. The widest differences are found in Bombay, in which the total primary expenditure has risen by R2,00,000, and in Bengal, where it has fallen by R2,65,000. It has been noticed, in Section II of this chapter, with what liberality the Government of Bombay responded to the invitation of the Government of India to increase its educational assignments in accordance with the recommendations of the Commission. The total educational grant in Bombay for 1884-85 amounted to R15,58,000. In the following year it was increased by R3,84,000, up to a total of R19,42,000. The actual expenditure for the year fell short of this amount by R1,85,000, "owing to reductions ordered by Government in consequence of the expense of military operations on the North-West Frontier;" but still the expenditure from Government Treasuries exceeded that of the previous year by R1,72,000. The chief constituents of the increase are the following:—contributions by Government to municipal boards to enable them to undertake the charge of schools within municipal limits, R82,000 (out of R1,12,000 sanctioned, as explained in Section II); grants-in-aid R17,000, and building grants R62,000, these last two items being departmentally ascribed to "the "prosperity of the old schools and the admission of new schools to our registers." There was a further increase of R10,000 under the head of training schools. It follows that the whole, or very nearly the whole, of the increase above noted in the Government expenditure was devoted directly or indirectly to the advancement of primary education, though the increase actually debited to this head amounted to only R98,000. The contributions made by municipalities from their own funds in consequence of the new charges laid upon them, were augmented to the extent of R1,13,000; while the same cause, affording as it did immediate relief to local funds, diminished the expenditure from that source by R88,000. Finally, the increased receipts from fees in primary schools amounted to R43,000. The increase is distributed over all classes of schools, and is far in advance of the increased attendance.

Very different was the financial condition of Bengal during the same period. The allotment from provincial revenues for education in that province in 1884-85 was R34,07,000. In September 1884 the Government of Bengal, in reporting to the Government of India upon the proposals of the Commission, admitted its responsibility for increased expenditure on education to the amount, finally, of R14,00,000 a year, if the recommendations of the Commission were to be carried out in any thing like completeness. Of the total increase, 10 lakhs were to be devoted to the direct improvement of primary schools. After a review of the ways and means at his disposal, the Lieutenant-Governor estimated that, at the then existing rate of development of the revenue, he would be able to work up to the total additional grant required in nine years, by a continuous enhancement of the educational allotment to the amount approximately of R1,50,000 a year. The progress of events quickly falsified the anticipations of this letter. Urgent orders came from the Government of India to reduce expenditure, and education suffered along with other services. The allotment for education in the sanctioned estimates for 1885-86 was reduced to R33,07,000, or by exactly one lakh of rupees; and the actual expenditure of the year fell short of this by R22,000, as the result of repeated exhortations to further economy. The reductions fell with much severity upon primary schools for boys, the provincial expenditure under that head dropping by R64,000—from R6,51,000 to R5,87,000. Collegiate education suffered to the extent of R12,000, and building-grants were reduced by R80,000. On the other hand, the Government, following out on that point a specific recommendation of the Commission, had just raised the pay and increased the staff of Sub-Inspectors, involving an addition of R52,000 to their cost. The primary grant in Bengal (including grants to girls' schools and other expenditure shown under different heads) had been steadily growing year by year, from R5,00,000 in 1881-82 to nearly R8,00,000 in 1884-85. It was irksome to the authorities to be forced to reduce the expenditure under that head of all others; but such a step was really inevitable in face of the pressure then brought to bear. Officers of the Department could not be summarily dismissed, nor their salaries reduced; and grants-in-aid are fixed for a term of years. Primary education has no similar protection; and whenever a period of financial difficulty comes, primary education is among the first to suffer. Fortunately, the evils of a diminished grant were to some extent alleviated. The reduction of the primary allotment for each district, taken along with the orders that had independently been issued for the withdrawal of aid from the weaker schools, combined to bring about that large decrease in the number of aided schools to which attention has already been drawn. The schools that remained did not get the full benefit of the decrease, but still they benefited to some extent. The number of schools was reduced by 23 per cent., while the primary allotment suffered to the amount of 10 per cent. only, so that it was still possible to give larger grants than in the previous year. The total reduction in the expenditure on primary schools for boys in Bengal amounts, as above noted, to R2,65,000, of which R64,000 was saved to provincial revenues. The remainder is explained by the withdrawal of 15,000 schools from the returns, involving a reduction of R74,000 in fees, and of R1,28,000 in the receipts from other sources.

The variations of expenditure in other provinces are less striking. In Madras, notwithstanding an increase of 5,000 pupils, there is a diminution of R20,000 in the fee-receipts of aided schools. The result is attributed to laxity in the collection of fees in old-established schools, arising from the opening of private-adventure schools in their neighbourhood, and from the disturbing effect produced by their competition. In the Central Provinces there is a decrease of R20,000 in the grants from provincial revenues to primary schools, and an increase to the same amount in the payments from local funds; the change being attributable to the transfer of a number of schools, as already noticed, to the control of district boards. There is an increase of R18,000 in the expenditure from local funds in Burma, caused by the additional sums earned by indigenous schools in result-grants. Assam and Berar have also increased their contributions from the same source.

184. Comparative Cost of Primary Schools.—The different systems of primary education have now been described, and an attempt has been made to form some estimate of their success in spreading elementary instruction. It remains to ascertain at what cost a primary school is maintained in the different provinces of India. A comparison of the tables given in the preceding paragraph, and in paragraph 175 of this section leads to the following results, which show the yearly cost of each school to public funds (including provincial, local, and municipal), and to private funds respectively. For the purposes of this statement it is necessary to exclude unaided schools under private managers. The table therefore includes all departmental and board schools, aided schools, and schools maintained by Native States. The nearest rupee is taken.

Province.	Cost of a Primary School.		Total annual cost.
	To Public Funds.	To Private Funds.	
	R	R	R
Madras	61	65	126
Bombay	164	101	265
Bengal	14	43	57
N.-W. Provinces	106	8	114
Punjab	178	38	216
Central Provinces	157	43	200
Burma	144	11	155
Assam	60	26	86
Berar	202	48	250
Coorg	164	10	174

This table is an interesting one; but for the purpose of an accurate comparison two considerations have to be supplied. The first is that the average attendance of a school differs widely from province to province. Where the indigenous system is largely utilised, as in Madras or Bengal, the number of pupils to a school varies from 20 to 30; while, in Bombay, the Punjab, the

Central Provinces and Coorg, where the departmental system prevails, the number ranges from 50 to 60. The second point to be remembered is the different duties which primary schools discharge in different provinces. In Bombay a primary school not only supplies the artisan or the cultivator with all the education he will ever acquire; it is also the preparatory school in which the future graduate receives his elementary training. Such schools are necessarily more costly than, for example, those of Bengal, where the primary school is designed for the simple needs of the rural population only. Madras occupies an intermediate position between these two opposed types of primary instruction, and the character of the three systems is fairly reflected in the last column of the foregoing table.

The former of these two sources of uncertainty may at once be removed by comparing the cost, not of each school, but of educating each pupil in different provinces. The following table accordingly shows the average number of pupils to a school, the cost of their education to public and private funds, and the total cost :—

Province.	Average number of Pupils to a School.	Cost of each Pupil's education.		
		To Public Funds.	To Private Funds.	Total.
		R	R	R
Madras	28	2·2	2·3	4·5
Bombay	59	2·8	1·7	4·5
Bengal	23	·6	1·9	·5
N.-W. Provinces	35	3 0	·2	·2
Punjab	53	3·4	·6	·0
Central Provinces	59	2·6	·8	4
Burma	47	3·1	·2	·3
Assam	29	2·0	·9	·9
Berar	44	4 6	1·1	·7
Coorg	50	3·3	·2	·5

In the previous table it was shown that a primary school in Madras is maintained at less than half the total cost of a similar school in Bombay; but it now appears that, owing to the great difference in their size, the cost of educating each pupil is precisely the same in both provinces. From causes already explained, the local receipts of primary schools in Madras are much higher than in Bombay, where remissions or reductions of fees to the children of cess-payers are largely made. In Berar, the local receipts rise to a respectable height, but the total cost of education is greater than in any other province. In the North-Western Provinces (where, again, the fact that the educational cess is ultimately paid by the agricultural classes is regarded as a sufficient reason for admitting them free of charge), in Burma, and in Coorg, local receipts are exceptionally low. They are highest in Madras and Bengal; and it will be remembered that in both provinces the receipts under this head have been declared to be uniformly understated. In Bengal, for example, it is not credited that the total receipts of a village teacher fall short of R5 a month, as the first of the two tables in this paragraph would indicate.

The most striking fact presented in the second table is the low cost to public funds of a primary pupil in Bengal,—no more than 10 annas a head—while

of the instruction to be obtained in primary schools would certainly improve. What the actual quality of that instruction is, has been discussed in a previous paragraph. There is little room for question that, taken all round, the village schools in Bengal fall far short, in point of efficiency, of those more elaborate and more highly organised institutions which in other provinces serve also the earlier purposes of secondary instruction. It has been shown that, owing to their very gradual development, the large majority of village schools in Bengal have not yet reached that moderate stage of instruction which is represented by the lower primary standard. Judged by the example of the most advanced provinces, the schools of Bengal should pass 60,000 pupils a year through that standard; while the actual figures (see paragraph 182) show 20,000 pupils passing from secondary schools, and 20,000, instead of the balance of 40,000, passing from primary schools. At the same time, these last schools are maintained at a cost of only 10 annas a pupil (the cost to public funds being alone reckoned), while in other provinces the cost rises to R2-8 or R3 on an average. Efficiency certainly varies with cost; but it results from these figures, that while the efficiency of primary schools in Bengal, as compared with other advanced provinces, may be approximately represented by the fraction $\frac{1}{2}$, their cost is represented by $\frac{1}{4}$ or $\frac{1}{5}$. The reasonable inference is that in the village system of Bengal, money's worth is secured for the money spent.

185. Comparative Cost of Primary Schools and Primary Departments.—The "dual system," to which reference was made in an earlier paragraph of this section, may now be considered in another light—that of comparative cost. The Commission, while giving full expression to the merits of the system as claimed by its advocates, expressed a doubt (page 95 of the report) whether there must not be "a waste of money and of power, no matter how care-"fully the system is organised, in employing the superior masters of a secondary "school to teach children elementary knowledge." The suggested inference is that any gain which might accrue from separating primary pupils into two or more classes, and giving the poorer class a cheaper education suited to their special requirements, would be more or less fully counterbalanced by the increased cost of educating the richer classes of pupils in primary standards through the more costly agency of a secondary school. The figures do not seem to bear out this inference. In order to exhibit the comparison for the two provinces, Bombay and Bengal, whose systems of instruction offer the most complete contrast in this respect, it is necessary to exclude the cost of European schools, in which different standards and methods of instruction prevail, and in which the cost is exceptionally high. In the subjoined statement the cost is calculated for all secondary English schools for native boys, including those under public management and aided schools; and the average is based on the monthly roll-number.

	Annual cost of each pupil in a secondary school to public funds.	Total annual cost.
	R	R
Bombay	8·8	27·7
Bengal	5·3	17·9

In the preceding paragraph it was shown that the cost of a primary pupil in Bengal, both to public and to private funds, is much lower than in Bombay. It now appears that the same is true also for pupils in secondary schools. The comparison may be pushed even further. If the cost of pupils in high and middle schools in Bombay be compared with that of pupils in high schools alone in Bengal, the comparison will still be in favour of the latter province. The cost of each pupil in a high school in Bengal (unaided schools being as before excluded) is R7·2 to public funds and R24·2 altogether. Naturally, the smaller salaries paid to the lower masters in a secondary school on the combined system, have the effect of reducing the average total cost of a pupil throughout the school; while, on the other hand, the high fees which are levied in even the lowest classes of such a school greatly reduce the cost of the whole institution to public funds. Of this last advantage the Bombay system is necessarily deprived, since it is understood that all pupils in a primary school in Bombay, whatever their social status, read on terms of equality, and therefore at fee-rates which are not beyond the means of the poorer pupils. Fees are levied from the 6,000 pupils in the primary stage of Government high schools in Bengal at a minimum rate of from 12 annas to R1·8 a month, according to the class in which they read; and in high schools under private managers, as well as in middle schools of both classes, the corresponding rates, though smaller, are still considerable. Similarly, in the primary departments of high schools (as distinguished from primary schools) in the North-Western Provinces and the Punjab, the monthly fee rises to 12 annas and R1·8 respectively. On comparing the average attendance with the annual fee-receipts in board schools in Bombay, it appears that the average fee paid by pupils in these schools,—rich as well as poor, the son of the cultivator as well as the incipient B. A.—amounts to less than 12 annas a year. In municipal schools the average yearly fee rises to 14 annas, and in the municipalities of the most advanced Division to 17 annas; and it is probable that in some of the larger towns a very much higher rate is fixed. But the rate in any case must not exceed the means of the poorer class of pupils. The dual system recognises the principle that a boy belonging to the better class, and destined for a higher education, has no natural right, during the first few years of his school career, to a share in that free, or nearly free, education which is provided from the rates for the masses. During these years it requires him to pay fees at a rate which more than covers the cost of his education at that stage, and which helps to reduce the cost of educating him as he advances further. The dual system, therefore, tends to economical working in secondary, as well as in primary, schools. The comparison made above is of course financial only. As regards literary proficiency, the Bengal authorities would probably admit that the primary schools of Bombay are far in advance of the average of village schools in Bengal, including (as these last do) schools in every stage of progress, and paying exaggerated attention (as in the opinion of some they also do) to subjects of merely practical utility. But the superior economy and efficiency of the dual system find also a warm defender in Mr. Nesfield, the Inspector in Oudh, who might hesitate to make a similar admission of inferiority with regard to the *halkabandi* schools of the North-Western Provinces.

186. Recommendations of the Commission as to Primary Education.—These recommendations, and the action that has followed upon them in the different provinces, may now be considered in detail. Some of them have already been discussed. In an earlier part of this section, consideration was given to the proposed definition of primary instruction (IV. 1), and to the discontinuance, as compulsory tests, of the upper and lower primary examinations (IV. 2). In Section II of this chapter were discussed the recommendations dealing with legislation, whether generally for the extension and improvement of primary schools (IV. 4), or specially for the constitution of district and municipal boards as school boards, with defined sources of income and with general control over primary school expenditure (IV. 29—32). Before examining the remaining proposals, including those that relate to the aiding of indigenous schools in Chapter III of the report, attention may be drawn to one which dominates all the rest, and which enunciates an important and far-reaching principle of educational policy. It runs thus :—" That while every "branch of education may justly claim the fostering care of the State, it is "desirable in the present circumstances of the country to declare the elementary "education of the masses, its provision, extension and improvement, to be that "part of the educational system to which the strenuous efforts of the State "should now be directed in a still larger measure than heretofore " (IV. 3). With this may be connected a later recommendation which presents the same policy under its financial aspect :—" That primary education be declared to be "that part of the whole system of public instruction which possesses an almost "exclusive claim upon local funds set apart for education, and a large claim on "provincial revenues" (IV. 28). These points of general policy will be considered in the next paragraph. The other leading recommendations may be grouped under the following heads :—(1) agencies for the extension of primary education (III. 1, 12; IV. 5, 24); methods of aiding primary schools (IV. 7); revision and improvement of primary standards, both in schools of the departmental type (IV. 9), and in aided indigenous schools (III. 5, 6); independence of private managers (IV. 10, 11; V. 22) physical, moral, and religious instruction (IV. 12—14); provision of training schools (IV. 15, 16); fees and exemptions (IV. 17—19); elementary educational tests for public servants (IV. 20, 21); night schools (IV. 22); schools for special classes of the community (IV. 25, 26); control of education by district and municipal boards (IV. 33—36). These proposals will be considered in order.

187. Superior claims of Primary Education upon Public Effort and Public Funds.—The recommendations dealing with this important principle were quoted in the last paragraph. They received the cordial support of the Government of India, which declared them to be in full accordance with the views repeatedly expressed by Her Majesty's Government and renewed in the Resolution appointing the Commission. In that Resolution it was stated that while it would be contrary to the policy of the Government of India to check or hinder in any degree the further progress of high or middle education, yet that the different branches of public instruction should, for the future move forward together and with more equal steps than before; that the development of elementary education called for more systematic attention than it had always received; and that secondary education should, if possible, be made more self-supporting. The opinions expressed by the Local Governments upon the policy propounded by the Commission were almost unanimously to the same effect. So far back as 1882 the Government of the Punjab had anticipated that policy. Sir Charles Aitchison was convinced that a very considerable extension of primary instruction had then become the first educational requirement of the province. Under a settled Government peasants unable to read, write or reckon easily fell the prey of designing men who had these advantages. But it was not only as the shield of the poor that primary education was one of the first requirements of the day; it was also the chief instrument for the attainment of certain public objects then rising into prominence. " The system of local self-govern-"ment, the principle of popular election, and the encouragement of private en-"terprise and diversity of pursuit—all presuppose that the mass of the population "will be gradually enfranchised from gross ignorance, and will by degrees attain "at least that elementary knowledge which, as society settles, becomes one of the "first conditions of self-defence, self-reliance, self-help, and self-advancement." The policy recommended by the Commission was altogether in this vein. Some authorities, indeed, as the Chief Commissioner of Assam, held that the recommendation did not go far enough; that it was a vague and qualified declaration of policy, bearing on its face the marks of compromise. Sir Charles Elliott would have preferred to declare in the most simple and positive manner, that the first duty of the State in the disposal of funds devoted to education was to foster and encourage primary schools, without limiting the force of the declaration by reference to "present circumstances," to the claims of other forms of education, and to the strenuous efforts that had already been directed to the spread of primary schools. Sir Alfred Lyall held a somewhat different view, to which reference was made in the preceding section of this chapter. He maintained that "secondary is no less important for the welfare and advancement of "the people than primary education; and he does not see any fundamental dis- "tinction at present between the relation of the State to primary and to secondary "education." The Commission's recommendation could only be fully accepted on the assumption that secondary education would live and thrive even though it received but little encouragement from the State. That might or might not be true; and it was probably true in various degrees in different parts of India.

With regard to the connected financial recommendation, the Governments of the Punjab and Assam demurred to the distinction which the Commission proposed to make between the claims of primary education upon provincial and upon local funds respectively. Both Governments criticised adversely the declaration of the Commission, in paragraph 215 of the report, that "local "funds, even when raised by legislative sanction from any district," are "equi- "valent to funds raised by the people themselves," and that "local expenditure "on primary education should be supplemented by a provincial contribution." Such funds, in Sir Charles Aitchison's opinion, differed in no way from ordinary taxation, except that they were devoted by law to a specific purpose. "They "neither indicate nor stimulate voluntary effort. To a large extent these local "funds are merely public money, formerly administered by the Provincial "Government, which has more or less recently been transferred to be ad- "ministered by local bodies. From that point of view, the difference between "local and provincial finances is mainly one of account and agency of admi- "nistration; and to treat local funds in the same way as if they were funds "voluntarily raised by persons anxious to extend education, seems to His "Honour to be a cardinal error in principle." The discussion was not one of merely academic interest. It involved the maintenance or the discontinuance of the policy that had long prevailed in the Punjab, under which primary schools maintained by local boards were entitled to no assistance from provincial revenues; though it was true that in 1883 a permanent grant of R8,000 a year (in the form of a remission of contributions for other purposes) had been made to district boards for the extension of primary schools. The strictures of Sir Charles Elliott were to the same effect. He could find no ground whatever for the assertion that local expenditure on primary education should be supplemented by a provincial contribution. A local rate, he urged, was a form of taxation instituted for a special purpose; it was assessed and collected like the land revenue; and it was more unpopular than the land revenue because it was of newer origin, and contained, at least in the people's eyes, wider possibilities of expansion. "No one would pay it if he were not compell- "ed by the coercive processes of the law to do so; and it seems to me a mere "playing with words to call it 'a form of self-help,' or to liken it to funds raised "by the people themselves." The conditions differed, however, from those of the Punjab in this important respect, that in Assam (as stated above in Section II) provincial grants had all along been made in aid of local funds; in fact, the impossibility of separating them furnished the Chief Commissioner with a further argument in support of his criticism. In passing orders on these objections, the Government of India admitted that local cesses were from **one point of view simply a form of taxation; but quoted, as decisive of the question, the Secretary of State's definite acceptance of the principle that provincial funds should, for educational purposes, be distributed as far as possible in proportion to the amounts raised by local rates.** It was not, however, necessary to make a special point of this in the case of the Punjab, where, the Governor General in Council was satisfied, the best use would be made of all available resources, provincial or local, and where private liberality had already shown itself so capable of expansion. From what has already been stated in Section II with reference to the grants made from provincial revenues to local funds in the Punjab, it would appear that the confidence expressed by the Government of India has been amply justified.

It will not be without interest to cite the views prevailing in other provinces on this important point of principle. The North-West report for 1884-85, after explaining that the district fund is not to be distinguished in character from the general provincial fund, goes on to remark:—" From the point of view " of this Department, the essential distinction is between the local contributions " to the school fund and the allotments from the general provincial fund; we " require to know the extent to which the people are taxing themselves for the " education of their children, and the extent to which the general provincial " fund is burdened for the purpose. In distinguishing therefore between the " sources whence the expenditure on schools is met, it will generally be suffi- " cient to class provincial expenditure and local rate and cess expenditure under " one head, as distinguished from the local contributions, shown under the heads " of fees, municipal allotments, endowments and subscriptions. Between " these two groups the distinction is radical and very important." But in Bombay a different view has always prevailed as to the relation of the local cess to provincial funds. In that province (as indeed was also the case in the North-West) the local cess was originally a voluntary rate; and though it has in later days received legislative sanction, its origin still causes it to be regarded as different in kind from the proceeds of ordinary taxation, as having an essentially local character, and as possessing a claim to a supplementary grant from provincial revenues. It has already been stated how fully this claim is recognised by the Government of Bombay.

188. Action taken by the Local Governments.—But whether the Local Governments applauded the policy recommended by the Commission, or whether on any point of principle they demurred to it, they have at any rate in practice shown no reluctance to carry it out, or to accept the new responsibilities which it imposed upon them. In some provinces, indeed, no change was required, since the policy recommended for adoption was already in force. This was the case in Bombay, Berar and Coorg, with regard to both district and municipal grants for education; practically all of the former, and nearly all of the latter being devoted, either directly or indirectly, to the extension and improvement of primary schools. It was also the case in Madras, the Central Provinces and Burma (and less conspicuously in the Punjab, the North-Western Provinces and Assam) with respect to district funds, the bulk of which in these provinces was applied to the same purpose. It has already been observed in Section II, that municipalities throughout India have shown themselves much more inclined than district boards to aid secondary schools; and the Local Governments have not expressed any desire to confine the educational expenditure of these bodies to the support of primary schools, though this seems to be the meaning of the Commission's recommendation. Nor, again, in those provinces in which the funds of district boards have been applied in any degree to secondary education, does there appear to be any intention of withdrawing that support. In fact, the recommendation of the Commission in this chapter does not seem altogether consistent with those of Chapter VIII to which reference has already been made. The Commission, while aiming at the final transfer of secondary schools from the control of the Department to that of private associations (VIII. 30), nevertheless recognised the necessity of making them over in some instances to local bodies as an intermediate stage in the transfer (VIII. 23). In another recommendation, which relates to the aiding of schools by local and municipal boards, it is declared to be, not their sole duty, but an "important part of their "duty," to make provision for the primary education of the children of the poor (VIII. 24). This uncertainty of opinion is reflected in the variety of provincial systems, which some to a greater and some to a less extent, have asserted the duty or recognised the right of district and municipal boards to aid or to maintain secondary schools. Nor does any change of policy, or anything like rigid uniformity, seem to be called for. If in any province local boards are believed to make undue provision for education other than primary, the responsibility thrown upon the Local Government of making increased grants from provincial revenues for the benefit of primary education only becomes the clearer and more pronounced. We can now inquire in what provinces that duty has been recognised and acted upon.

In Madras, the rules framed under the Local Boards Act of 1884 laid down that "the provision of improved elementary education for boys is the chief "duty of the district board, and to its promotion a very large proportion of the "funds allotted to education must be devoted." The share of the local fund income devoted to education had increased in four years, up to 1884-85, from 9 to nearly 13 per cent.; and the corresponding share of the total municipal income from 6 to 14 per cent. As 72 per cent. of the former class of funds, and 51 per cent. of the latter were devoted directly to primary education (without reckoning indirect expenditure, such as that for inspection and for buildings), the Government of Madras considered that a sufficient and a growing provision was secured for primary education from those funds, and that the necessity for additional grants from provincial revenues was less urgent. It impressed on the Director the necessity of making the general policy of Government on this subject fully understood and acted on by all departmental officers, in order that the claim of primary education to the most careful attention of the Department and to the largest share of funds should be steadily kept in sight. At the same time the Government announced its intention of assigning to education in future an amount equal to 5 per cent. of its total revenues, the rate to which expenditure had been for some years approximating; and in the benefits of any resulting increase to the educational grant, primary education would have its due share. That share would, it was anticipated, be further enhanced by the gradual increase in the fee-rates of secondary schools, tending to reduce the proportionate expenditure on secondary education. The liberal grants made from provincial revenues to district and municipal boards in Bombay have already been described in detail. The Bombay Government has thoroughly accepted the principle of making grants to local funds from provincial revenues in full proportion to the amounts assigned to education from those funds; the proportion adopted being one rupee for every two rupees of local income. In calling upon municipalities to undertake the charge of schools within municipal limits, and in requiring district boards to spend upon primary education the funds thus set free, the Bombay Government was not displaying generosity at the expense of others; it was deliberately adding to its own burdens. The measures taken involved an immediate increase of R2,82,000 in the direct annual expenditure from provincial revenues on primary schools, chiefly by means of additional grants to local boards of both classes; and a further grant of R56,000 to district boards as soon as the latter were able to place out all the funds appropriated to education from the local cess. Outside all this was the expenditure on building grants, chiefly to primary schools, for which an increase of R45,000 was sanctioned in 1885-86. In Bengal, local funds did not exist, and municipal funds for educational purposes were as yet quite inadequate. The special responsibility thrown upon Government by such a condition of things was fully admitted; and the Government of Bengal declared its intention of increasing the annual grant for primary education, then amounting to nearly eight lakhs, by an addition of ten lakhs a year, up to a total annual expenditure of 18 lakhs. This result it hoped to reach in nine years by successive annual increments, spread over that period, in the grant for primary education. But these anticipations, built upon the expectation of an expanding revenue, were rudely dissipated by the urgent necessity for retrenchment; and the primary grant for 1885-86 fell to R7,45,000. Much the same thing took place in the North-Western Provinces. An increased provision of nearly R70,000, including R40,000 for primary education, was sanctioned from provincial revenues for 1885-86; but subsequent financial pressure brought about a reduction in the educational estimates to the extent of R1,00,000, in which the new allotments were included. The financial position in the Punjab was much more favourable. In 1883, local bodies had been relieved of charges to the amount of R8,000 a year, which was thus set free for the establishment of primary schools. In 1886 it was found possible, by the exercise of economy in other departments, and by the substitution of a Native for a European Inspector of Schools, to provide an additional lakh and something over for expenditure on primary education in the following year. Local bodies were to be relieved of further charges for inspection and the training of teachers to the amount of R58,000; an addition of R14,000 was sanctioned for girls' schools; and the balance was reserved for re-organising the normal schools and for strengthening and improving the subordinate inspecting staff—charges which now fell upon provincial revenues. In the Central Provinces, Burma and Assam, a general intention was expressed of keeping the grants for primary education abreast of the provincial income; though the Local Governments were generally unable to make any special additional assignments for that purpose. In the Central Provinces a steady increase of the grant was ensured by the undertaking of the Government to fix the educational allotment at 5 per cent. of the provincial income. The educational cess, which was almost exclusively devoted to primary education, was of an elastic character, and was expected to increase by 25 per cent. within the next 15 years. In Burma little hope was entertained, in view of other and more pressing claims, of increasing the grant to education from provincial revenues, though Sir Charles Bernard expressed his willingness, as a step in that direction, to re-grant each year to education all unexpended balances of the previous year. The share of the local cess devoted to education, which from 1881 to 1884, had remained at one-tenth of the proceeds of the cess, had within the next two years been raised to one-fifth. Municipalities in Burma were also taking an active interest in education, and had in many instances begun to spend much larger sums on that object than they were required to do, or were enabled to do by the provincial grants placed at their disposal. In Assam, Sir Charles Elliott objected to the distinction between provincial and local funds; but he pointed out that the educational expenditure from both sources together had increased from 4·4 per cent. of the combined provincial and local income in 1881-82, to 5·25 per cent. in 1884-85. In all these cases it was to be understood that primary education was to get its full share of any increase in the general educational allotment. In Coorg, the Chief Commissioner has increased the provincial grants to education, mostly primary, by more than 50 per cent.; and in Berar, it is proposed when the existing assignments for primary schools have been fully employed, either to increase the rate of the educational cess, or to give an additional grant from provincial revenues.

The foregoing account may now be tested and illustrated by the statistical returns of expenditure. The necessary figures are supplied in columns 8a, 8b, and 8c of General Table IV for 1885-86. To determine rightly the amounts devoted to primary education from provincial, local and municipal funds respectively, it is first of all necessary to separate "direct" from "indirect" expenditure on education. The latter head of expenditure includes charges for inspection, scholarships, buildings, and the like, which are incurred in furtherance of all classes of education, though the distribution of indirect, will naturally follow in its main lines that of direct, expenditure. In other words, the greater the share spent on primary schools directly, the greater also will be that spent on the inspection of primary schools and on buildings to house them. Hence we may regard the proportion of direct expenditure that is devoted to primary education as roughly representing the corresponding proportion of the total expenditure; at any rate it will probably be not less than this. Again, since the expenditure of local and municipal boards upon training schools is almost wholly devoted to the training of primary school teachers, that charge should rightly be included in the expenditure from local and municipal funds on primary education. Training schools maintained from provincial revenues are largely engaged in the training of teachers for secondary schools, and their cost cannot therefore be included under primary education. In appears, then, that out of a total direct (or tuitional) expenditure from provincial revenues, amounting in 1885-86 to R52,21,283, the amount spent from that source on primary education was R14,78,082, or 28·3 per cent. of the direct, and presumably also of the total expenditure. Out of direct educational expenditure from district funds amounting in the same year to R29,03,515, the primary expenditure (including cost of training schools) was R23,14,862, or 79·7 per cent. Lastly, out of municipal expenditure on the maintenance of schools amounting to R9,34,728, the primary share was R4,88,415, or 52·3 per cent. (It may be noted that the total educational expenditure, direct and indirect, from these sources in 1885-86 was—provincial, R79,67,021; local, R36,99,995; municipal, R11,37,491.) The subjoined statement shows for each province of India (1) the percentage of direct to total educational expenditure; (2) the percentage of primary to direct expenditure, which may also be approximately regarded as the percentage of primary to total expenditure.

Province.	Nature of expenditure.	Source of Expenditure.		
		Provincial.	Local.	Municipal.
Madras	Direct	66·0	83·5	86·7
	Primary	17·4	86·8	58·8
Bombay	Direct	67·4	91·8	96·5
	Primary	39·9	97·7	79·7
Bengal	Direct	68·4	*73·8	95·1
	Primary	33·4	*81·1	24·9
North-Western Provinces	Direct	63·5	73·6	93·5
	Primary	2·5	59·9	40·7
Punjab	Direct	64·2	70·4	75·6
	Primary	15·4	75·1	22·1
Central Provinces	Direct	54·0	85·5	90·9
	Primary	46·9	·7	58·
Burma	Direct	47·1	87·0	66·3
	Primary	9·3	7·2	39·8
Assam	Direct	44·4	77·4	92·2
	Primary	15·5	78·3	57·4
Berar	Direct	67·9	63·5	93·4
	Primary	53·6	99·8	94·0
Coorg	Direct	59·3	76·0	80·7
	Primary	17·4	100·0	90·0

It will be understood that the value of this comparison is affected by the two causes to which frequent reference has been made:—*first*, the direct contributions made from provincial funds to district funds in the North-Western Provinces, the Central Provinces and Assam, which contributions are shown under local fund expenditure; *secondly*, the fact that in seven provinces (Bombay, the Central Provinces, and Berar being excluded) the cost of the primary departments attached to secondary schools is not included in the statement. Thus the exceptionally low rate of primary expenditure from local funds in the North-Western Provinces is partially explained by the large sums spent from that source on middle vernacular schools, in which five-sixths of the pupils are in the primary stage. In Bengal there are practically no local rates, and the share of the provincial expenditure devoted to primary education should be by so much the higher. The proportion is, in fact, far greater than in any other province except the three named just above, in which the cost of every pupil in the primary stage is debited to primary education. It is even twice as high as in Madras, where the primary departments of high schools (at least of Government high schools) are gradually being withdrawn in favour of the Bombay system. Still, in view of the fact that primary education in Bengal has hardly any other public source of maintenance except provincial revenues, the expenditure from that source—less than one-third of the direct, and much less than one-fourth of the total expenditure on education—can hardly be deemed sufficient. It is to be hoped that the financial circumstances of the Bengal Government may so far improve as to enable it to carry out the intention, which it formed in 1884, of increasing the grant for primary education within a few years by ten lakhs of rupees.

189. Agencies and Means for extending Primary Education.—The reluctance which the Commission felt towards extending primary education by the exclusive agency of departmental or board schools, is exhibited in the following recommendations:—

"That all indigenous schools, whether high or low, be recognised and encouraged, if they serve any purpose of secular education whatsoever" (III. 1).

"That where indigenous schools exist, the principle of aiding and improving them be recognised as an important means of extending elementary education" (IV. 5).

"That [local and municipal] boards be required to give elementary indigenous schools free play and development, and to establish fresh schools of their own only when the proposed alternative of aiding suitable indigenous schools cannot be adopted" (III. 12).

"That primary education be extended in backward districts, especially in those inhabited mainly by aboriginal races, by the instrumentality of the Department pending the creation of school boards, or by specially liberal grants-in-aid to those who are willing to set up and maintain schools" (IV. 24).

The general purpose of these recommendations is clear. Wherever they exist in any form such as to promise useful development, indigenous schools are to be aided. Where they do not exist, boards may establish schools of their own. In those exceptionally backward tracts which have not yet been placed under the control of local boards, departmental schools may be established; or preferably, liberal aid may be given to schools set on foot and maintained by missionary bodies—practically the only agency in operation for such a purpose.

In Madras, Bengal, the Central Provinces, Burma and Berar, these recommendations inculcated no new policy. In Bengal and Burma there are practically no primary schools except those of indigenous origin. Of the Central Provinces, the Commission reported that "the incorporation of the whole "indigenous system into the departmental scheme is merely a question of time." In 1882 there were 316 indigenous schools receiving aid in these provinces. The number registered for aid now amounts to about 700, and nearly the whole body of existing schools has been brought within the system of public instruction, so cordial has been the recognition of their claims by local and municipal boards, and so liberal the aid granted from provincial revenues. From an earlier paragraph it will be clear that similar success has been attained in Berar, chiefly as the result of an increase of 50 per cent. lately sanctioned in the rates of aid to indigenous schools. The Director in Madras reports that the local boards of that province do not open schools of their own, except in places where adequate provision has not already been made by indigenous or other private agency. It is added that at the rate of progress which has prevailed for the last five years in Madras, all the indigenous schools will in a short time be brought under State supervision, provided that the funds at the disposal of the Department and of the local boards admit of any substantial addition to the outlay on primary education. The further development of the indigenous system in Bengal depends on, and is limited by, the same condition.

But it is not alone in those provinces in which such a policy has been pursued in time past, that the claims of indigenous schools are now receiving attention. It has been noticed in a previous paragraph that Bombay has begun to recognise in a liberal spirit the claims and the value of these institutions. Special rules for the encouragement of such schools have indeed been in existence for many years past, but up to the date of the Commission's report very few had taken advantage of them. In 1884 the rules were revised in the spirit of the Commission's recommendations, with the result that there was a large increase in the next two years in the number of schools claiming and receiving aid; and a special grant of R56,000 for the further development of this class of schools was sanctioned for the following year. The rules provide that indigenous schools are eligible for grants-in-aid, provided (1) they serve any purpose of useful secular education; (2) they maintain an average monthly attendance of 15 pupils; (3) they keep attendance registers and submit simple returns; (4) they are open to inspection. Schools so registered may receive grants varying from R15 to R60 a year, according to attendance. Schools for girls will receive grants at double rates. As soon as an indigenous school adopts the departmental standards, it may be transferred to the list of results-schools and thus become eligible for higher grants. In the Punjab, also, where a similar awakening has taken place, special rules for aiding elementary indigenous schools have been framed, and a grant of R25,000 has been set aside for this purpose. The rules will supply the means of improving indigenous schools without destroying their distinctive character. The grants are paid, partly for attendance, if the Inspector is satisfied with the general condition and appearance of the school; partly for passes in reading, writing, arithmetic and geography, under special standards framed for the purpose; and partly for the qualifications of teachers. This last provision will, it is hoped, induce existing teachers to employ assistants able to give instruction in arithmetic and geography, and will encourage them to make their "sons and probable successors" qualify themselves for these posts, in accordance with a recommendation of the Commission to that effect (III. 4). Grants to indigenous schools in the Punjab are payable under these rules by local and municipal boards, supplemented, if necessary, by contributions from provincial revenues. The weakness of the indigenous system in Assam has already

been described; but no effort seems to be spared to turn to good educational account such schools as exist. The following remarks by the Chief Commissioner throw light on the wishes and intentions of the Government with regard to these institutions :—" The desirability of attracting indigenous schools
" into the circle of departmental influence, and of building on an approved and
" popular foundation such as they present, is fully recognised ; the departmental
" officers are instructed to do all in their power to induce the gurus to come
" under Government inspection and to receive aid; and it is our standing prac-
" tice not to start a departmental school in a place where an indigenous school
" exists which is willing and fit to be utilised for our purposes. Everything
" that we can devise has been done to make it known to the masters of these
" indigenous schools that the Education Department is ready to give them help
" either in the form of monthly salaries, if their schools are brought into the
" list of aided schools, or in the form of payment-by-results if they present their
" pupils at the periodical examinations which are held for the purpose of testing
" the progress of primary and indigenous schools alike, or by a combination of
" these two systems. All that is required of them is that they should adopt the
" standards and the course of teaching laid down by the Department for primary
" schools; and they are at liberty to carry on their own method of religious instruc-
" tion without interference. The sums set apart for such rewards are given from
" the local funds, and it is a part of the local boards' duties to supervise these
" payments and make the system popular." The main difficulty is that the only indigenous schools in Assam are *tols* and *maktabs*, that is to say, not secular but religious schools, teaching respectively Sanskrit and the Koran. Mr. C. B. Clarke says of them that even when they are in receipt of rewards for teaching practical subjects, they " give way as little as they can to the pressure of " the Government officers to teach vernacular reading, writing, and arithmetic."

In the North-Western Provinces and Oudh an inquiry has been prosecuted into the number and character of the indigenous schools. The latest information shows that there are altogether about 7,200 institutions of the kind in the province, of which about 5,000 are elementary schools, teaching the current ' Kaithi' hand and bazar arithmetic, and the rest are institutions, more or less advanced, for giving instruction in Sanskrit, Arabic or Persian. Altogether they contain about 80,000 pupils, of whom 28,000 are Muhammadans. The character of these schools was all along said to preclude any great hope of their being generally incorporated into the departmental system, and the experience of many years seemed to confirm that belief; but in order to give any that desired it an opportunity of improvement and of bettering their position, a code of rules was drawn up for the award to indigenous schools of grants-in-aid according to results. The rules were widely published, but the result was singularly disappointing. Up to July 1887, out of the thousands that are known to exist, only one institution of the class, a Muhammadan school near Lucknow, had applied to be enrolled. These indigenous schools, it is explained, owe their existence to the special educational requirements which they alone supply, and which cannot be readily incorporated with the general scheme of instruction in public schools. It is apprehended by the managers of these institutions that inspection by Government officers may affect their distinctive and essential character, and, *pro tanto*, diminish their value in the eyes of their supporters. On the other hand, in the opinion of the Government, it is not easy to see where improvement is to lay hold of a school if the teachers and the course of teaching are to be very slightly touched. The dilemma is a formidable one, though it has been grappled with in much the same form elsewhere. It is admitted, indeed, in all provinces that the so-called religious schools, Sanskrit or Arabic, afford but stubborn educational material to work upon;

but it seems to follow from the facts just stated that the 'Kaithi' schools of the North-West are much more limited in range, and much more slenderly adapted to the purposes of general instruction, than similar institutions elsewhere. The most reasonable explanation seems to be that the existence of a widespread Government system of primary education has intensified the points of difference between the departmental and the indigenous school; and by limiting the pupils of the latter strictly to those classes that demand nothing beyond the 'technical' instruction which it has always supplied, has finally extruded from its course everything that could connect it with education in a larger and more liberal sense. In Coorg, a difficulty of another kind presents itself. The difficulty lies not in the distinctive character, but in the paucity of indigenous schools, owing to the absence of any professional or hereditary class of teachers. In such schools as exist, the most satisfactory results are obtained in arithmetic. "To writing," it is stated, "little attention is given; in reading, no method is "followed. Each boy brings what book he likes; and such books are generally "relics of antiquity which, even if their meaning were understood, it would be "of little use for the pupil to study. As a rule, the meaning is not understood, "and no attempt is made by the teacher to explain it." No aid has hitherto been given to indigenous schools; but they are now to be sought out and to receive attention.

190. Special Measures for Aboriginal and Backward Races.—It has always been admitted that the education of the aboriginal races is surrounded by circumstances of unusual difficulty. Their poverty, the absence of any indigenous educational system among them, the generally inaccessible character of the tracts they inhabit, their exclusive ways, and their distrust of foreign civilisation, delayed the success of the first attempts to introduce even elementary education among them. In the course of centuries the influence of Hinduism has, no doubt, greatly modified the habits and ideas of these races; while of late years a considerable number of them have been benefited by the labours of Christian missionaries, who have shown themselves, in many parts of the country, the true pioneers of civilisation among these backward people. Still, they remain a people apart; and if education is to take root and spread among them, exceptional measures are necessary. The Commission recommended that, for the special benefit of aboriginal tribes, either departmental schools should be established, or liberal aid should be given to missionary bodies. The recommendation to this effect (IV. 24), which was quoted at the beginning of the last paragraph, may be considered along with the special recommendations as to aboriginal tribes and low castes which are dealt with in Chapter IX of the Commission's report. In that chapter it is stated that the problem of educating the aboriginal races of India practically concerned three provinces only; namely, Bengal and Assam with 2½ millions of aborigines, the Central Provinces with 1¾ millions, and Bombay with nearly a million. The rest of India (exclusive of the Native States) contained in all only about 160,000 people of these races. The greatest advances in educating them had been made in Bengal and Assam, where such success as had been attained was due partly to the direct instrumentality of the State, but chiefly to the zeal of missionary societies, who carried on their work with effectual help and encouragement from Government. In Bombay some slight success had been achieved, and a still smaller measure in the Central Provinces. Elsewhere the field of work was much narrower; but hardly an attempt, it was alleged, had been made to cultivate it. The recommendations put forward by the Commission included the exemption of aboriginal pupils from fee-payments; the grant of special allowances to any schools that taught them; **and the training of some among them to become schoolmasters to their own people.** With the object of enabling them to hold their own in their dealings with more civilised neighbours, it was also proposed that the vernacular of the neighbouring community should be either the medium of instruction, or an additional subject of instruction if the education of the tribe was carried on in their own vernacular.

The number of pupils of aboriginal races at school cannot be determined with any thing like accuracy, since the prescribed forms of return have no separate heading for them. The head "Others" in General Table III, includes not only aboriginal races, but various minor sects which have discarded the principal religions of the country. Again, many pupils of aboriginal races are classed either as Hindus or as Christians when they have embraced either Hinduism or Christianity without forfeiting their tribal character. In Bengal and Assam, for example, Native Christians (who are shown under a separate heading in the table) are, in the great majority of cases, converts of aboriginal race. The Commission estimated the number of aboriginal (including Christianised) pupils in 1881-82 at about 24,000 in Bengal and Assam, 2,738 in Bombay, and 1,055 in the Central Provinces. According to the best estimate that I can frame for 1885-86, there appear to be 29,900 aboriginal pupils in Bengal, 6,500 in Assam, 3,358 in Bombay, and 2,422 in the Central Provinces. In other parts of India the numbers are insignificant. Still, a considerable advance seems to have been made since the date of the Commission's report.

In Bengal, there are various agencies at work, chiefly missionary. The division of Chota (or Chutia) Nagpore offers the largest field for their labours. It contains the great tribe of the Kols (divided into the Hos and Mundas), the Uraons and many Santhals. The education of these races has been taken in hand by the Berlin Evangelical Mission, the Society for the Propagation of the Gospel, the Free Church Mission, and latterly by St. Xavier's. In the Santhal Parganas and the adjoining district of Bhagulpore, the Church Mission Society receives a grant of R7,800 a year in aid of its work amongst the Santhals and Paharias. The Swedish Home Mission also undertakes a share in the work of Santhal education. A third agency for educating the Santhal population is the Government. A special scheme, which had not come into operation when the Commission wrote, has been organised for supplementing the labours of the Missionary Societies by the direct instrumentality of the Department. The Church Mission Society were the first pioneers of education among this race, but their work is limited by the means at their disposal, and they can cover only a comparatively small field. The Government of Bengal has been well aware of the importance of extending education among this race, with whom troubles, chiefly born of ignorance, have from time to time arisen; and it was therefore decided to establish additional schools under the direct instrumentality of the Department. These schools have been organised in close correspondence with the existing village system of the Santhals, and great care has been taken to work in co-operation and alliance with the missionary body, so as to avoid any conflict between the two sets of schools. The teachers, who are either Bengali-knowing Santhals, or Santhali-knowing Bengalis, receive stipends of R4 or R6 a month; more than 100 schools have been established and are now working with success; and a proposal has been received for the establishment of a training school for teachers of this race. Their ignorance, and the need of educating them, are illustrated by an incident quoted by the Commissioner of Orissa, where also Santhals are found. A decline in the number of pupils at the Santhal schools was attributed to a panic caused by the death of an inspecting pundit and of a promising young scholar, both belonging to that race. "The Santhal inspecting pundit was a young "man who had shown great zeal in the cause of Santhal education, and his "death was looked upon as a mark of displeasure of the offended gods." In the western districts, again, the education of this widely distributed race is carried on by the American Baptist Mission and the Wesleyan Mission; while in the district of Darjeeling, on the northern frontier, the Scotch Mission carries on the same civilising work among the Bhutias of Sikkim and the Paharias of Nepal. The Scotch Mission in Darjeeling, and the Church Mission in a part of Bhagulpore, practically occupy the position of agents of the Government, a portion of the primary allotment being made over to them for promoting education among the aboriginal races. Elsewhere the work is undertaken directly by the Department. This is the case in the Hill Tracts of Chittagong, among the half-Burmese tribes on the frontier; with the backward races on the slopes of the Garo Hills bordering on Assam; and with the forest tribes dwelling in the wilder parts of Orissa and its Tributary States. An institution of a special kind is the Bhutia Boarding School at Darjeeling, in which Bhuteas and Lepchas are trained to be explorers, surveyors and interpreters, and to the pupils of which (known to the public in the records of the Survey Department under the safe obscurity of initial letters) we owe much of our recent knowledge of the Trans-Himalayan tracts.

The Chief Commissioner of Assam demurred to the account given by the Commission of aboriginal education in that province. They could hardly, he thought, have been aware of the large proportion which the aboriginal races bore to the population of Assam, or of the efforts that had been made to extend education among them. The sketch, given in an earlier paragraph, of the primary system in Assam will have made it clear that the education of aboriginal tribes has been carried far beyond the schools maintained by Welsh Missionaries in the Khasia hills, to which alone reference is made in the report. Sir Charles Elliott pointed out that, besides these, schools have been planted by the American Mission among the Garos and Nagas, and among the Mikirs of Nowgong; and that the Society for the Propagation of the Gospel was doing similar work among the Kacharis in Durrung. A few schools of the same kind had also been established here and there by local boards, and a few more by district officers; but nearly all that had been done for the education of aboriginal races in Assam had been done by the missionaries, acting sometimes as agents for the Government, and sometimes as independent managers receiving liberal State aid. Altogether there were returned for 1885-86 between 6,000 and 7,000 pupils belonging to some twenty aboriginal tribes, the chief among them being the Khasis, Manipuris and Kacharis; besides, an unknown proportion of the 1,600 pupils returned as Native Christians. These figures mark a great advance upon the 1843 scholars of the Commission's report, and even upon the much larger estimate framed by the Chief Commissioner for 1882-83.

For Bombay the Commission estimated 2,738 aboriginal pupils at school. The departmental returns for 1883-84 and 1884-85 show 2,389 and 2,622 pupils respectively. The number rose in 1885-86 to 3,358; but the following remarks of the Acting Director in his report for 1884-85 throw light on the true state of the problem:—The conditions of the aborigines cannot be regard-"ed without an admission of the absolute failure of the Department to grapple "with the question. Not three in a thousand of this interesting population are at "school. In fact 930,000 persons are still lying outside the pale of our efforts. "I think that the education of aboriginal tribes should form a section of the chap-"ter on Special Classes. The conspicuous failure of the Department might then "stimulate effort, and attract private philanthropic enterprise. Experience else-"where has shown that the Brahman schoolmaster fails as a teacher of backward "tribes; our first need therefore is for teachers, and teachers belonging to

"the hill or forest-tribes would be the best instruments. To attract them
"would require special interest and devotion to the work, while our com-
"mon-place school would have to be replaced by a sort of combined indi-
"genous school and technical school. No other agency but private could
"supply these needs; and therefore I trust that Government will take into
"consideration our admission of failure, the neglected position of the forest and
"hill-tribes, and the need for encouraging by special grants any private agency
"which will attempt to teach the Bhils, Kolis and other aboriginal tribes." These
remarks point directly to the subsidising of any missionary bodies that will undertake the task; but it appears from a statement of the Bombay Government in 1884
that there is in that province nothing like the same extent of missionary agency
that is found in some other parts of India. Meanwhile, the Department has to
do what it can with an agency which, for this work, is admitted to be inferior.
It is stated in the report for 1885-86 with regard to the Surat district:—" The
" great difficulty experienced in these hilly tracts is to find a master who can stay
"all the year round in a malarious climate. We are now seeking for Bhil
"masters for these schools in the hills; but if these cannot be secured, it is
"probable that the schools cannot be maintained in the rains, which is just the
"time when the children can most easily avail themselves of them."

In the Central Provinces there were 2,422 aboriginal children at school in
1885-86,—much more than double the number in 1881-82. To these should be
added some proportion of the 626 Native Christian pupils. Some indigenous
schools in Mandla, chiefly for Gond children, have been registered for aid; and
elsewhere special schools for Gonds have been opened. But the Inspector-
General admits that "special efforts have still to be made for the more syste-
"matic education of aboriginal tribes." The Chief Commissioner in 1884 observed:—" It is not easy to see how, without a very large expenditure, a system
"of primary education for these tribes can be organised, in which their own
"languages are to be the medium of instruction. The first and essential step in
"dealing with them is to win their confidence, and it is impossible for the itin-
"erant officers of the Department to do this. The Chief Commissioner doubts
"if any one but an English officer, who specially devoted himself to the task
"and had peculiar qualifications for it, could succeed. The Gonds, as the jungle
"becomes cleared, and as they become more settled in their habits, are gradually
"assimilating themselves to the Hindus beside whom they live. But it is difficult
"to get them to come to school, and very difficult to teach them. The Chief
"Commissioner believes that missionaries who will live among them, and give
"themselves up to learning their language and acquiring influence over them,
"have more chance of success than Government has, unless it organises a regular
"departmental mission to the Gonds and other aboriginals." The missionary
bodies working in the province were accordingly consulted on this point, but
they had no suggestions to offer. The aboriginal population are so scattered
and live generally in such small villages, that it is difficult to introduce any
sort of school system except at a disproportionate expense. Mr. Browning
recommends the appointment of a few peripatetic schoolmasters for the education of these children of the jungle. In Madras, special exemptions from fees
and special rates of grant have been sanctioned in favour of aboriginal pupils
and other backward sections of the population; and the Government has established several schools in the Agency Tracts of the Northern Circars for the benefit
of the hill tribes that inhabit them. In Berar, attempts have been made to open
schools for aborigines; but they have mostly been closed for want of pupils.

As to low-caste children, the Commission desired, in Chapter IX, not
only to establish special schools or classes for their education, but still more to
reinforce, with due caution, the principle that no boy should be refused admis-

sion to any Government school merely on the ground of caste. To the same effect are the recommendations in Chapters III and IV, that board schools and aided schools, not registered as special schools, should be open to all classes and castes of the community, and that such a proportion of non-exclusive schools should be maintained as to make due provision for the education of the depressed or neglected castes (III, 8, 9; IV, 25, 26). The proposal to establish special schools, or to give special rates of aid to those schools in which low-caste children were taught, met with general favour. Special schools for degraded castes have been established, some by missionary, some by departmental agency, in Bengal and the Central Provinces, the North-Western Provinces, Berar and Coorg; and schools for thieving or plundering tribes in Bengal and the Punjab. In Burma, the caste difficulty does not arise; but the measures taken in that province for promoting education among the Karens have been already described; and a beginning has been made, through the agency of the Karen missionaries, of educating the Chins, another depressed race who make their homes in remote and malarious jungles. In many provinces special rates of aid are sanctioned for schools that educate pupils of degraded castes. In Madras, Bombay and Berar, Government and board schools are open to all classes without restriction; and in Bombay, at any rate, the strict enforcement of the rule is not alleged to have created difficulty. Elsewhere, too, the principle is admitted, provided it is held as a pious opinion, and not pushed too far or acted on too hastily. In the opinion of the Punjab Government, "as a matter of practical politics, the appli-"cation of it may wait on circumstances." In that province low-caste pupils are freely admissible to all schools under public management, and are sometimes found in abundance. "As a general rule, however, public opinion keeps them "out. Wanting as they are in all desire for education, it is not to be expected that "they should intrude into schools where they would be shunned and looked down "upon by the other boys." The North-West Government considered the recommendation unobjectionable in principle, but the special declaration of it unnecessary. "So long as prejudice is against them, low-caste children are not likely "to attempt to force themselves into schools where they are not welcome." Of the existence and vitality of such prejudices there is abundant evidence. The Chief Commissioner of the Central Provinces declares it impossible to run counter to the feelings of the people in a matter of this kind. We must wait until caste prejudices are weaker, and until these low castes become less barbarous in their habits by some improvement in their material condition. "They "must cease to eat carrion, and be able to afford themselves proper food. Until "there is a radical change in their condition and habits, it is impossible to expect "the better castes, who it must be remembered are also the better classes, to "associate with them willingly in our schools." Sir Charles Elliott regards the principle as an excellent one; but it is necessary to wink at its infraction. The difficulties imposed by the national instinct for ceremonial purity are very great; and up to a short time ago, Hindu and Muhummadan boys would not sit on the same bench. That prejudice has died away; but the time has not yet come in Assam when a boy of certain degraded castes could be admitted into a primary school. In Coorg, similar prejudices are alleged to exist in full strength. Perhaps the best criterion of the existence of the feeling is to be found in the practice of indigenous schools. In some of the aided indigenous schools of Madras, Pariahs are admitted, but from many (especially near the centres of religious thought) they are excluded; and the Government of Madras believes that the enforcement of the proposed rule "would deal a severe blow at "the popularity of supervised education, and would lead many masters to with-"draw their schools from inspection." Apparently, the doctrine of equal rights has still a good deal of way to make.

On a cognate point some shrewd observations are made by Mr. Nesfield, Inspector of Schools in Oudh, whose zeal for the advancement of education is tempered by his exceptional knowledge of the social conditions prevailing among the tribes and castes that people Upper India. He is speaking, not of the right of the lower castes to go to school, but of the very slight value which the right possesses for members of those castes in the present conditions of Indian society:—"It is disappointing, after all the trouble that is taken to "make them what they are, to find how little use many of the students are "able to make of the knowledge that they have gained, after leaving school. "This remark applies especially to those whose position in life, as determined "by the caste and occupation in which they were born, is below that of priest, "landlord, writer, and trader. In one school there was a boy of the Kurmi "caste, which is one of the most industrious agricultural castes in Upper "India. He had passed a very good examination in the third or highest stand-"ard of village schools; and after telling him that he had now completed all "that the village school could give him, I inquired what occupation he in-"tended to follow. His answer at once was—*service; what else?* I advised "him to revert to agriculture, as there was scarcely any chance of his getting "literary employment; but at this piece of advice he seemed to be surprised and "even angry. At another school I met a Pási, a semi-hunting caste, much "lower in every respect than that of Kurmi, the agriculturist. He was a boy "of quick understanding, and had completed the village school course in "Nagri as well as Urdu, and could read and write both characters with equal "facility. He asked me what he has to do next. I could hardly tell him to "go back to pig-rearing, trapping birds, and digging vermin out of the earth "for food; and yet I scarcely saw what other opening was in store for him. "At another school there was the son of a Chuhra, or village sweeper, a caste "even lower than that of Pási, in fact the lowest of all the castes properly so "called. He was asked with others to write an original composition on the "comparative advantages of trade and service as a career. Very naturally, "considering the caste to which he belonged, he expressed a decided preference "for trade. Yet who would enter into mercantile transactions with a sweeper "even if a man of that caste could be started in such a calling? Everything "that he touches would be considered as polluted; and no one would buy "grain or cloth from his shop, if he could buy them from any other. There "seems to be no opening in store for this very intelligent youth, but that of "scavengering, mat-making, trapping, &c., all of which are far below the more "cultivated tastes that he has acquired by attending school. And in such "pursuits he is not likely to evince the same degree of skill or enjoy the same "contentment, as one who has grown up wholly illiterate. In these and such "like ways the attempts made by the State to raise the condition of the "masses, and place new facilities of self-advancement within their reach, are "thwarted by the absence of opportunities and by the caste prejudices of the "country."

191. Methods of Aiding Primary Schools.—There is a general concurrence in the recommendation (IV. 7) that where primary schools under private management are aided, the amount of aid should be determined by the results of examination. The "combined" system of Madras is also approved, under which teachers are paid partly by a fixed monthly salary, partly by results. Under this system the fixed stipend is regarded as an advance payable out of the total amount earned after examination; and the method of combined payment has been found well suited for backward parts of the country. In Bengal, where the amount at the disposal of the Department is not large enough to provide a monthly salary, however small, for the teachers of primary schools, and where, consequently, the almost universal introduction of the results-system has been found inevitable, an exception has been made in the case of the most backward tracts, where, if schools are to be kept going at all, the scanty payments of a poor and indifferent community must be supplemented by monthly stipends. In the North-Western Provinces there are no aided indigenous schools; but the missionary schools that receive aid no longer receive fixed monthly grants, but are, under the new Code, to be aided according to results. In Assam a similar change has been made. Under the revised rules the old system of monthly stipends has been discontinued, and schools are now aided either by rewards alone, or by fixed monthly payments combined with rewards. In the Punjab and the Central Provinces a further step has been taken, by extending the method of payment-by-results to schools maintained from district funds, the salaries of the teachers undergoing revision according to the results the schools may show. In the Punjab, with the object of removing the possibility of suspicion or complaint, the District Inspector is not allowed to examine the schools in his own district except under the supervision of the Assistant Inspector; a precaution which does not appear to have been adopted elsewhere. The weak point in the system of payment-by-results, already fully recognised in Bengal and other provinces where this method is in wide operation, is the possibility it allows of clever children being passed on from school to school, and presented for examination at each, so as to secure a larger grant. The system of 'chief gurus' or 'inspecting schoolmasters'—officers employed in Madras and Bengal to supervise, below the regular inspecting staff, a small number of schools with whose teachers and pupils they become closely acquainted—has tended to put a stop to this evil.

192. Revision of Standards in Primary Schools.—The recommendation may be quoted in full:—"That the standards of primary examination in each "province be revised with a view to simplification and to the larger introduc- "tion of practical subjects, such as native methods of arithmetic, accounts, and "mensuration, the elements of natural and physical science, and their application "to agriculture, health, and the industrial arts; but that no attempt be made to "secure general uniformity throughout India" (IV. 9). A similar recommendation as to indigenous schools (III. 6) enjoined the retention of all that is valued by the people in the indigenous systems, and the encouragement by special grants of the gradual introduction of useful subjects of instruction. The principle was stated in the following form by the Government of India, in commenting on the Commission's recommendations:—" The curriculum of a pri- "mary school ought, while not neglecting the preparation necessary for any "pupils who may be advancing to the secondary stage, to aim principally at "imparting instruction calculated to be of real practical benefit to the bulk of "the children whose education will terminate with the primary course." No objection was raised by the Local Governments to the policy thus enforced; but the recommendation as to the larger introduction of useful subjects met with active criticism, on the ground that the particular subjects recommended did not seem to tend towards the 'simplification' of the course. The Governor of Madras observed:—"In a country where so little education of any sort has been till "recently available for the masses, to ask a child under primary instruc- "tion to master the elements of science, and their application to agriculture "and the arts, is to ask too much." This was in confirmation of the opinion expressed by the Director, that a child, during the four years of his primary course, ought to confine his attention to reading, writing and arithmetic, with possibly the elements of history and geography. If at that stage he attempted any higher flight, the attempt could only be made at the expense of the more necessary parts of instruction. In the Central Provinces, 'simplification' was understood to mean reduction; and, in practical agreement with the Madras opinion, regret was expressed at the proposed abandonment of history and geography, and the limitation of the primary course to reading, writing and arithmetic. In Bengal, native methods of account and mensuration had always taken a leading place in the indigenous schools, as well as in the more fully organised schools of later growth. For some years, too, the Sanitary Primer, together with another book intended to explain its meaning, had been introduced into all schools reading up to the lower primary standard; but it was doubtful whether anything to which the name of 'science' or 'agriculture' was applicable could be usefully taught in primary schools. In Assam, again, the Government had no hope, for the present at any rate, of being able to introduce "the elements of natural and physical science and their application to "agriculture and the industrial arts" into the primary school course. These subjects were beyond the capacities both of teachers and of boys, even if the ordinary course were not already long enough. The Sanitary Primer was indeed read, under the express orders of the Government of India, but its usefulness was open to doubt. To much the same effect was the opinion of the Chief Commissioner of Burma, who 'despaired' of being able to introduce any additional subjects into the primary school course, where the Sanitary Primer was already found to be a severe tax on the understanding of children. Nor was it any use to teach native methods of arithmetic. This subject had seldom found a place in monastic schools of the old type; and in those of the new, such arithmetic as was taught was wisely taught after European methods.

The recommendation of the Commission should be read in the light of their explanatory warning that the course in primary schools should be recognised as really useful, and should give no ground for the belief that elementary education unfitted the children of the poor for their ordinary duties and made them discontented with their lot in life. The arithmetic that they needed was no academic science, but the common methods of reckoning used in every bazar; the mensuration that they needed was such a knowledge of the well-understood rules for measuring fields as would enable them to hold their own with the zamindar or his agent. If these could be secured in the earlier stages, but only on that condition, further efforts of the same kind might follow as education progressed. Any advance beyond the necessary rudiments that might then be possible should follow the lines, not of a literary, but of a practically useful education. "The elements of natural and physical science, "and their application to agriculture, health, and the industrial arts" was, as we have seen, the concrete form which the recommendation took; and it is to this portion of the recommendation that objections have mostly been raised —partly perhaps from inattention to the fact that the proposed additions, if made at all, were to be made at the highest stages of the primary course. However that may be, nothing like uniform action has followed on the recommendation of the Commission. In Bombay, no change seems to have been made in the standards; nor indeed is the necessity of giving the course a more practical turn in any way so obvious when the children of the literate as well as of the labouring classes read side by side in the same school. In Madras the standards of primary education have been revised so as to include under the optional subjects not only mensuration, agriculture, drawing and modelling, and hygiene, but also vernacular poetry, English grammar, English history, Indian history, geography and mathematics. The compulsory subjects are limited to reading, writing and arithmetic, in which last are included mental arithmetic and bazar accounts. In Bengal, the Sanitary Primer was condemned as too difficult for the lower primary course, and its place was taken at that stage by an easier work more specially adapted to the province. In the upper primary course, in which the elements of physics had all along been included, mensuration was added to geometry. In the North-Western Provinces, many changes have been made. Native methods of arithmetic and mental calculation, such as may be used in ordinary bazar business, have been introduced; mensuration is taught, and the Sanitary Primer is in use in all schools. A text-book of village accounts is to be prescribed for the upper primary classes; and a series of Readers, containing such general information as may serve to expand the minds of the pupils, is being compiled under the supervision of a committee of native gentlemen. An Agricultural Primer written by Mr. Fuller, and published with the approval of the Department of Agriculture, is in use as a Reader; but a doubt is expressed whether any useful knowledge of agricultural science can be conveyed to boys at this stage of their education. The book was widely and authoritatively recommended; but it does not appear that in any other province it has been adopted for use in schools. In the Punjab, the Central Provinces, Berar and Coorg, the standards have been revised in the sense contemplated by the Commission, by the introduction of mensuration and other subjects of practical utility. In Coorg, short and simple treatises on vaccination, cattle breeding, hygiene and agriculture have been prescribed for use in primary schools. In Assam alone has no change of this kind been found possible. It will be a long time, it is alleged, before the teachers of primary schools in Assam can teach the necessary subjects.

193· **Physical, Moral and Religious Instruction.**—The question of moral training will be considered later on in a separate section. That of physical training is not altogether unconnected with it, for laziness is the parent of many vices; but it will be convenient to supply in this place such brief notice of the subject as may be demanded by the recommendation "that physical develop-"ment be promoted by the encouragement of native games, gymnastics, school "drill and other exercises" (IV. 12). The necessity of physical training seems perhaps to emerge more clearly in secondary and other schools in towns than in primary schools, most of which are situated in villages where a life of activity in the open air needs no artificial supplement. Still, some attention is now paid to this matter in provinces other than the three named by the Commission— Bombay, the Central Provinces and Bengal. Under the Madras grant-in-aid Code (Chapter III, Art. 44), "schools may claim aid for gymnastics by results, "under rules approved by the Director. The subject shall be taught accord-"ing to Maclaren's or Forrest's or some similar system, and shall include exer-"cises on the horse, parallel bars and horizontal bar......No school shall be "admitted to examination which doesnot present one-half of its pupils on the rolls "at the date of examination, or receive a grant which does not pass three-fifths "of those presented.......Grants at half rates will be allowed in rural primary "schools for such native gymnastic exercises and according to such rules as may "be approved by the Director." In the Punjab, which is said to have been long pre-eminent for the success with which cricket has been cultivated in the larger schools, and in Berar, physical training and native games have been introduced, more or less generally, into primary and training schools. Nor is the subject neglected in Burma.

The recommendation regarding religious instruction (IV. 14) was merely intended to secure to parents and children, after the transfer of schools to the control of local and municipal boards, the same religious freedom which they enjoyed whilst the schools were under Government management. The sanc-

194. Fees and Exemptions.—The Commission recommended "that pupils "in municipal and board schools be not entirely exempted from the payment of "fees merely on the ground that they are the children of rate-payers." (IV. 17). The object of the recommendation was to assimilate the practice in the North-Western Provinces, the Punjab, and the Central Provinces to that prevailing in Madras and Bombay. Upon this point the Government of India observed:— "The weight of authority is in favour of the soundness of the principle of "charging some fees to all scholars not specially exempted on the ground of "poverty; and the Government of India is itself in favour of this course, though "there may be cases where local circumstances may render advisable the more "favourable treatment of the children of cess-payers in respect of the amount "of fee." In Madras the collection of fees in primary schools has now been made compulsory. The Chief Commissioner of the Central Provinces pointed out that the question of fees in primary schools would henceforth rest with the local boards, who would be at liberty to charge all classes alike if they thought fit to do so. For his own part he demurred to the recommendation, on the ground that if one class of the community was specially taxed for a certain object, it could fairly claim some advantage in return. As a matter of fact, the trading and official classes made more use of the schools than the agricultural class, at whose expense they were maintained, but who were not even now very eager to send their children to school. The Commission had not ignored these considerations; but their recommendation was based chiefly on the principle of fairness to those agriculturists who paid the cess but who had no school at their doors. The levy of fees, they urged, would mark the necessary difference, and would go some way towards the establishment of schools in tracts that were now without them. Cases of hardship would be alleviated by the next ensuing recommendation (IV. 18), providing for the exemption of poor students from the payment of fees. It may be added that the force of the Commission's argument has been increased by the general abandonment, under subsequent legislation, of special cesses devoted to education. The Central Provinces—one of the few administrations in which a special educational cess exists, has met the difficulty propounded by the Chief Commissioner in the following way. Exemptions are allowed in each school, in cases of poverty, up to one-sixth of the roll-number of pupils. The rest of the pupils have to pay one, two, or four annas a month according to income; the terms being made easier for those who derive their income from land than for others. In the Punjab also the principle has been partially accepted; the children of agriculturists being still allowed to read free in the lower departments of primary schools, while in the upper departments half-rates are charged. In the North-Western Provinces proper, the agricultural classes have been admitted to primary schools without payment of fees; indeed, though exceptions are sometimes made in the case of other classes, it may be said that primary education has practically been free for all. In Oudh, the practice of taking small fees has been much more common, though this has been done without much system or rule. The Lieutenant-Governor has now approved the principle of charging a nominal fee, not to exceed two annas in the highest class, for all pupils alike; and this will be recommended for adoption to the district boards, in whom the management of primary schools is vested. It is not anticipated that any opposition will be raised to the measure, or that, with so low a scale of fees, any exemptions on the score of poverty will be necessary.

The foregoing statements refer exclusively to the fees paid in primary schools proper. In the primary departments of high schools in all these provinces, much higher fees are levied, and in most they have lately been considerably raised. In the Punjab, for example, the revised rates of fees in the primary classes of high schools range from 2 to 8 annas, or from 4 to 12 annas, or from 6 annas to R1-8 according to the means of the scholar. In the North-Western Provinces they vary from 6 to 12 annas. In Berar the rates in the lowest classes have been raised 50 per cent., and it is proposed to make a further increase.

It was also recommended by the Commission that fees should be levied in all aided schools, though the proceeds were to be left entirely at the disposal of the managers (IV. 19). The Government of India held that this principle was correct, and in accordance with the rule embodied in paragraph 54 of the Despatch of 1854; and that if any exceptions were allowed, they should be confined to the lowest classes of indigenous aided schools. The recommendation was, however, objected to by some, on the ground that it involved an unnecessary interference with the rights of private managers—a contention the principle of which can hardly now be accepted; and by others on the special ground that missionary bodies would prefer to sever their connexion with the State system rather than submit to such a condition. To this last objection it may be replied that missionary bodies have always shown themselves disposed, on grounds both of private interest and of public policy, to levy fees in schools so far as this could be done with safety; and that exceptional cases, such as those of the poor, of backward and aboriginal races, and of girls, are sufficiently covered by the recognised rules for exemption.

195. Night Schools.—From the nature of the case there can be no very large or steady demand for institutions of this class, except in towns. Artisans attached to factories, and others who as boys have been deprived of the advantage of education, cannot fail to recognise the benefits, pecuniary and other, which a knowledge of reading, writing and accounts would place within their reach. In rural tracts the advantages are not so forcibly pressed upon their notice, and the difficulties of establishing such schools among a scattered population are much greater. The Commission in recommending that "night schools be encouraged wherever practicable" (IV. 22), pointed to the successful efforts of Bombay in this field. In the departmental reports of that province the pupils are described as being "of the right class," namely, cultivators, cow-herds, artisans and day labourers; though admission is not refused to boys who are unemployed during the day, and who seem to be attracted by the free tuition offered. Since 1881-82 the number of night schools in Bombay has increased from 134 with 3,919 pupils to 239 with 6,758 pupils. Mr. Lee-Warner, while believing that there is a fair and genuine demand for night schools in large cities, expresses some doubt about those attached to board schools in rural tracts, since a natural desire on the part of schoolmasters to augment their salaries may have something to do with their establishment. This is the burden of the latest reports on the subject in Bombay with regard to night schools of this class; and it is worth while noticing with what limitations and drawbacks the work is carried on in the province in which most attention seems to have been paid to it. One Inspector writes :—"The agricultural classes "cannot generally have a very strong desire for night schools. They will "not, after a day's physical hard labour, sustain any mental strain at night. They "want such schools out of mere novelty, or for the sake of masters who put them "up to apply for them in their own interest,..........desiring to add a few rupees "to their scanty salaries." Another writes :—" In small villages they are of

"selves in having night schools opened. With proper inspection and examina-
"tion there is little danger of these schools becoming a mere sham."

In Bengal the number of night schools is said to be probably above 1,000. There is considerable difference of opinion as to their value, except in large centres of population, but the opinion is often unfavourable. The Assistant Inspector of the Patna Division has no doubt that the greater number of them are mere shams: in one district "not one of them does the work it should;" in another, they "gain rewards under false pretences;" in a third, 48 schools were visited unexpectedly and found not at work. The Assistant Inspector adds: "The people of this province have not yet got a sufficient taste for "learning to make them attend a night school after a hard day's work in the "fields. As an experiment I opened a night school in my own compound, and "gave it a fair trial of nearly a year. At first a large number of pupils joined, "but the novelty soon wore off, and it degenerated into an ordinary pathsala "held in the evening." Another inspecting officer takes a different view of the value of these schools; though he is alive to the danger that day-scholars of other schools may be fraudulently registered as pupils of night schools in order to gain enhanced rewards for the teacher. Of the backward division of Chota Nagpore, the Assistant Inspector writes: "It must not be understood "that the usefulness of these institutions admits of any question. On the "contrary, the larger the number of such schools opened in these districts, the "better it is for the people, who are for the most part agricultural labourers." But there is no question about the value of such schools as those maintained by the East Indian Railway Company at Jamalpore and other manufacturing centres, for the benefit of apprentices and others employed by day in the workshops.

In Madras, where night schools have also been established in considerable numbers, and where they are recognised and protected by the grant-in-aid Code, a somewhat different opinion is expressed. The Officiating Director thinks these schools eminently adapted to certain localities, "especially to rural "tracts," though no reasons are adduced for this opinion. The number of schools rose within the year from 291, with 5,420 pupils, to 312, with 6,972 pupils. All are aided on the results system. The managers are required to certify that the scholars are unable or unfit to attend day schools of a suitable standard; and no scholar under 12 years of age is admissible. In Madras, as also in Bombay and the Punjab, special provision has been made in the new grant-in-aid Code for the encouragement of night schools. Other provinces content themselves with the general statement that night schools are eligible for aid and are encouraged wherever practicable. In Berar and Coorg they are said to have failed.

196.—District and Municipal Boards.—The general position of these bodies with regard to primary education has already been sufficiently considered. The latest recommendations of the Commission in this chapter relate to certain questions of control, of which the most important are these:—"That "municipal and local boards administering funds in aid of primary schools adopt "the rules prescribed by the Department for aiding such schools, and introduce "no change therein without the sanction of the Department" (IV. 36); and "that the first appointment of schoolmasters in municipal or local board "schools be left to the town or district boards, with the proviso that the "masters be certificated or approved by the Department; and their subsequent "promotion or removal be regulated by the boards, subject to the approval of the "Department" (IV 33). The importance of the first of these recommendations, which is designed to secure continuity of policy, has been fully recognised and acted upon; and in all provinces the Local Government has taken power, under the Acts regulating local self-government, to prescribe and define the rules under which schools shall be administered and aided. It will not of course be denied that, if local bodies come up to the expectations that have been formed of them, the inevitable and advantageous result, as time goes on, will be to introduce much greater variety and flexibility into educational systems than is possible under the direct administration of a central Department. But even in educational matters the advantages of variety have their limits. In most provinces changes in the rules prescribed for the guidance of local bodies have been provided for, but only with the sanction of the Local Government; and thus the accumulated experience of the Department will apply the necessary regulative force.

The second recommendation has been jealously scrutinised from different points of view; partly in the interests of the teachers, who were to be protected from capricious or interested action; partly in the interests of the boards, whose power and independence it was desired to maintain; and partly in the general interests of education. Thus in Madras, the North-Western Provinces, Burma and Assam, the "approval of the Department" to the appointment and dismissal of teachers is deprecated as needlessly restricting the power of the boards, as striking at the root of all authority and responsibility, and as being certain to create unsatisfactory relations between the boards and the Department. In Bombay, on the other hand, the continued efficiency of the teaching is regarded as the matter of chief importance; and the Local Government prefers to surround the right of appointment with every form of departmental safeguard.

197. Other Recommendations as to Primary Education.—These require only a brief notice. The provision of the means of training teachers for primary schools (IV. 15) will be considered in the next section. The establishment of schools for special classes of the community, and the right of all castes alike to share in the benefits of education (IV. 25, 26) have been already dealt with. The independence of private managers of schools was the object of the 10th and 11th recommendations, which enforced the right of such managers to choose their own text-books, and to determine their own school promotions, independently of departmental regulations. The recommendation that in filling up the lowest offices under Government, preference should be given to candidates who can read and write (IV. 20), was intended to supply a practical incentive to the lowest classes of the people to educate themselves. All these recommendations have met with entire approval; the last, however, with certain obvious limitations as to menial offices. The position of *lambardars* in the North-Western Provinces, who were made the subject of a special recommendation (IV. 21), is said to have been misunderstood; and it is urged that in the case of these officers, character, good sense, and personal influence are of more importance than ability to read and write. The same objections do not apply to *patwaris*, who are now required to have passed the upper primary standard before being admitted to the special schools that have been established for their instruction. The Government of India, in pointing out the importance of the Commission's proposal on this head, recommended to the consideration of other Governments the admirable arrangements in force in the Madras and Bombay Presidencies for securing proper educational qualifications in candidates for public employment. Special rules of the same tenor have since been introduced into the Punjab, the Central Provinces, and Assam.

Section V.—SPECIAL INSTRUCTION.

(a) Training Schools.

198. Character and Scope of Special Instruction.—The earlier sections of this chapter have dealt with the different branches of general education, in other words, the education that is designed to cultivate the intelligence of the pupils and to fit them for the ordinary duties arising in different walks of life. We now turn to education of another class, namely, that which qualifies pupils for the special occupations in which a technical training is required. This falls into two divisions: (a) the training required for teachers, which in an educational report should occupy the foremost place; (b) the special instruction offered to those who wish to qualify for the various branches of professional artistic, or industrial life, so far as these can be made the subject of instruction in schools or colleges. The first division of this section relates, therefore, to training schools for masters and mistresses. The general arrangements in force in each province for the selection and training of teachers were described in some detail in Chapter II, paragraphs 73 to 79.

199. Training Schools for Masters, 1885-86.—The following statement shows the number of these institutions on the 31st March 1886:—

Training Schools for Masters.

PROVINCE.	MAINTAINED BY THE DEPARTMENT.		MAINTAINED BY LOCAL AND MUNICIPAL BOARDS.		AIDED.		UNAIDED.		TOTAL.	
	Schools.	Pupils.	Schools.	Pupils.	Schools.	Pupils.	Schools.	Pupils.	Schools.	Pupils.
Madras	(a) 5	145	33	792	5	195	1	8	44	1,140
Bombay	4	446	...	...	1	59	(b) 2	87	7	592
Bengal	16	683	...	...	6	459	...	...	22	1,142
N.-W. Provinces	...	...	10	353	1	23	...	...	11	376
Punjab	4	223	...	...	1	33	...	...	5	256
Central Provinces	3	188	...	...	...	...	...	...	3	188
Burma	3	167	...	...	...	...	...	...	3	167
Assam	7	226	3	56	2	83	...	...	12	365
Berar	1	102	...	...	...	...	...	...	1	102
Coorg	1	14	...	...	...	...	...	...	1	14
TOTAL	44	2,194	46	1,201	16	852	(b) 3	95	109	4,342
TOTAL IN 1884-85	47	2,212	45	1,136	17	790	(b) 4	127	113	4,265

(a) Including the Teachers' College in Madras.
(b) Including two schools in Native States in Bombay.

The loss of four schools is confined to Madras, where five Government or local fund schools, and one unaided school maintained by the American Mission, were closed. A new board school was opened, and the Teachers' College at Madras was recognised as a separate institution. This, and a similar training college in the Punjab, are the only institutions in which teachers are trained for employment in English secondary schools. In Assam an aided mission school was closed, and a new board school opened. There is some increase of pupils in Bombay, Bengal, Assam, and Berar. Elsewhere the number has fallen off.

Divided according to race, they include 754 Native Christians, 2,794 Hindus, 424 Muhammadans, and 370 belonging to other races. English was learnt by 443 students, nearly all of whom were in aided schools. With the exception of the two training colleges above mentioned in Madras and the Punjab, in which teachers are trained for employment in English schools, no English is taught in any Government training school. All the aided schools are under missionary management. One or other of the classical languages is taught to 1,458 students. The period of instruction varies. It extends to two years in the North-Western Provinces, the Central Provinces and Berar, and to three years in Bombay and Coorg, and also in the first-grade schools of Bengal for the training of teachers for middle schools. On the other hand, the course in the lower-grade schools of Bengal for the training of gurus is generally for six months only, though it occasionally extends to one year, the term usually prescribed in other provinces. To successful students certificates of various grades are issued, according to the time during which they have been under training. In 1885-86, 1,528 students obtained certificates, 522 of the upper and 1,006 of the lower grade.

200. Training Schools for Mistresses, 1885-86.—The figures for these institutions are subjoined:—

Training Schools for Mistresses.

PROVINCE.	MAINTAINED BY THE DEPARTMENT.		MAINTAINED BY LOCAL AND MUNICIPAL BOARDS.		AIDED.		UNAIDED.		TOTAL.	
	Schools.	Pupils.	Schools.	Pupils.	Schools.	Pupils.	Schools.	Pupils.	Schools.	Pupils.
Madras	2	51	1	21	9	219	...	...	12	291
Bombay	2	84	...	...	...	...	(a) 2	13	4	97
Bengal	...	...	...	...	3	116	...	...	3	116
N.-W. Provinces	...	...	2	4	...	...	...	...	2	4
Punjab	...	...	...	...	3	55	...	...	3	55
Central Provinces	1	8	...	...	...	...	...	...	1	28
Burma	2	25	...	...	...	...	...	...	2	25
TOTAL	7	188	3	25	15	390	(a) 2	13	27	616
TOTAL IN 1884-85	8	196	3	28	14	603	(b) 3	38	28	865

(a) Including two schools in Native States in Bombay.
(b) Including one school in Native States in Bombay.

The changes in this class of schools were unimportant. In Madras one Government and one unaided school were closed, and two new schools under missionary management received grants-in-aid; but the number of pupils suffered some reduction. In Bombay a school for mistresses was opened in the Native State of Rajkot. The aided schools are nearly all maintained by missionary bodies. Of the total number under instruction, 22 were Europeans or Eurasians, 368 Native Christians, 143 Hindus, 36 Muhammadans, and 47 of other races. Also, 204 of the pupils learnt English—a proportion much higher than in training schools for masters, and due to the large number of native

201. Expenditure on Training Schools.—The necessary figures are contained in the following statements:—

Training Schools for Masters.

PROVINCE.	From Provincial Revenues.		From Local and Municipal Funds.	From other Sources.	TOTAL.
	In Schools under public management.	In aided Schools.			
	R	R	R	R	R
Madras	33,305	8,407	50,281	18,219	1,10,212
Bombay	35,492	1,000	14,472	17 320	68,284
Bengal	65,960	5,758	.	11,410	83,128
N.-W. Provinces	...	...	45,076	1,540	46,616
Punjab	20,668	3,000	26,813	4,360	54,841
Central Provinces	21,120	...	...	...	21,120
Burma	12,716	2,157	5,590	1,470	21,933
Assam	9,343	...	...	...	9,343
Berar	1,357	...	...	...	1,357
Coorg	32,339	...	..	...	32,339
TOTAL	2,32,300	20,322	1,42,232	54,319	4,49,173
TOTAL FOR 1884-85	2,35,620	17,767	1,42,776	61,462	4,57,625

The total cost of these schools declined from R4,57,625 to R4,49,173, reductions in Madras accounting for half the difference. The grants to aided schools are very small, since the Department has always acknowledged its responsibility in the maintenance of training schools, either from its own funds or from those of local boards. Municipalities contribute but a small share to the cost of these institutions, the grants amounting to R1,839 only. Only one school of this class (in Madras) was maintained by a municipality, and even that has since been closed. Fees are seldom levied in training schools, and the receipts from this source amounted to only R1,525.

Training Schools for Mistresses.

PROVINCE.	From Provincial Revenues.		From Local and Municipal Funds.	From other Sources.	TOTAL.
	In Schools under public management.	In aided Schools.			
	R	R	R	R	R
Madras	11,904	11,983	2.709	15,049	41,645
Bombay	20,436	...	3,778	1,648	25,862
Bengal	...	4,720	...	9,715	14,435
North-Western Provinces	...	...	120	18	138
Punjab	...	5,356	1,200	2,070	8,626
Central Provinces	4,947	...	...	...	4,947
Burma	3,558	...	...	...	3,558
TOTAL	40,845	22,059	7,807	28,500	99,211
TOTAL FOR 1884-85	38,588	26,105	11,976	21,686	98,355

Two schools in the North-Western Provinces and the Punjab, returned in 1884-85 as training schools, have now been transferred to their proper class of girls' schools, and there is a reduction on that account of R14,000 in the total expenditure. On the other hand, there has been an increase of R11,000 in Madras, arising from the opening of two aided schools, and of R3,000 in departmental institutions in Bombay. Aided enterprise occupies a much larger space in this field than in that of training schools for masters—a result arising from the important part taken by missionary enterprise in the training of mistresses for girls' schools. . Fee-receipts amounted to R2,166.

202. Training Schools in Madras.—The number of training schools for men, which had largely increased in the two previous years, fell from 48 with 1,155 pupils, to 44 with 1,140 pupils. These were maintained at a cost of R1,10,212, of which R41,712 were paid from provincial revenues, and R50,281 from local funds. The Madras Normal School was reorganised under the name of the Teachers' College, and affiliated to the University for the new degree in teaching. The course prescribed by the University for that degree has been detailed in an earlier section. At the close of the year nine B. A. graduates were being prepared for the degree; and there were 35 other students under training who had passed either the matriculation or the First Arts examination. The institution was maintained at a cost of R12,282 to provincial revenues. Nothing was received from fees.

The two sections of the Teachers' College are shown as separate institutions in the returns. Of the other three Government training schools, one is a special school for Muhammadans in the town of Madras, containing, however, only eight pupils. The Moplah board school at Calicut, with 25 students, is also attended by Muhammadans only. It was explained in the last chapter (para. 73) that the maintenance and management of all, or nearly all, the training schools in Madras had been entrusted to local boards. The same policy was pursued in the year under report, when three Government schools were closed, and one was transferred to a district board. No pupil in a Government or board school (other than the Teachers' College) is taught English; in aided schools 119 pupils out of 195 learn English, and these are mostly native Christians. The number of trained teachers, who either obtained employment or joined their old appointments during the year, was 511. The drawbacks that attend the training of village teachers—whether teachers brought in from their schools, or new men intending to adopt that profession—were also discussed in the paragraph just quoted. With regard to the former class, the difficulty lies in inducing them to come in; and it disappears when they have been actually trained and are ready to return to their former duties. With the latter class it is just then that the difficulty begins; and it is this class that furnishes the failures of the system—the men who, disappointed in the hope of getting teacherships, or of keeping them in the teeth of village opposition, betake themselves finally to other callings. The difficulty is naturally intensified if new students are trained in excess of the number of probable vacancies caused by the retirement of village teachers of the old stamp; and a regard to the teachings of experience on that point might possibly make things easier. Many a village that sides with its own teacher while he is still able and willing to work, and resents the intrusion of an interloper, will be the first to recognise the latter's superior value when no question of sentiment stands in the way. These remarks apply to aided schools only; in Government or board schools (a much smaller number) newly-trained teachers are alone employed.

In the 12 training schools for mistresses the number of students fell from 363 to 291. The cost of these institutions was R41,645, of which R23,887 was paid from provincial revenues, and R2,709 from local funds. The reduction in the number of students is ascribed to certain new restrictions introduced by the grant-in-aid Code. Under these rules no student can be admitted to a recognised training school of any grade without having passed the general educational test of the grade. This regulation had the effect of relegating many pupils from the training to the practising department. Other rules were introduced with the object of providing that Government money should not be thrown away on those who had no fixed intention of becoming teachers. But though reduced in numbers, the students were conspicuously successful at the examinations for certificates. Fifty-two passed the examination in school management, 18 the higher examination for women, 22 the middle, and 100 the upper primary examination. Of the passed students, 75 gained employment during the year. The largest schools are the Government Normal School and the Christian Normal School, both in Madras, and the "Sarah Tucker" School at Palamcottah. They are also among the most successful. The Government School at Madras provides for 38 stipendiary pupils, of whom 18 are Hindus or Muhammadans, 12 native Christians, and 8 Europeans or Eurasians. All these receive scholarships varying from R6 to R12 a month; and a further allowance of R5 a month is made for any parent or guardian of a native student who comes to reside in Madras for the purpose of taking charge of her ward. Before any student is admitted, her guardian must undertake to repay the amount received in stipends if the pupil does not remain to complete the full course of one or two years, and also if she fails subsequently to serve for two years as a teacher. Pupils must have passed the upper primary or middle school examination before admission. The course of study is sound and thorough. Besides the subjects of general instruction and school management, it includes drilling, marching, and singing, and also needle and fancy-work. The latter is said to be "in very good taste," a remark not without significance in a country where the attempt to introduce the wool-work and other female accomplishments of Europe has resulted, for the most part, in violent combinations of the primary colours, calculated to offend the eye and to permanently degrade the national taste. The Hobart Normal School in Madras is an institution for Muhammadans only. Here, too, the ornamental needle-work is highly spoken of; and some of it was thought good enough to be sent to the London Exhibition.

203. Training Schools in Bombay.—No steps appear to have been taken to carry out the suggestion referred to in the last chapter, to open more training schools for men on a cheaper footing. There were, as in the previous year, four Government and one aided school, and two schools maintained by Native States. All these schools were kept up at a cost of R68,284, of which R36,492 were paid from provincial revenues, and R14,472 from the district cess. Though few in number, the four Government schools have an exceptionally large attendance, averaging 111 pupils. Much attention has all along been paid in Bombay to the maintenance of these schools at the highest pitch of efficiency; and proposals for strengthening the establishment were made in 1885 by the Acting Director and accepted by the Government. Mr. Lee-Warner speaks of "the paramount importance to this Department of a well-equipped primary system." A sound standard of initial qualifications is demanded, and the course extends over three years. Of the Ahmednagar aided school a very favourable account is given; "the instruction was substantial, the management good, and the discipline admirable." The two schools in Native States are also highly spoken of. The number of trained teachers in British districts rose from 44 to 46 per cent; and it is stated that some of the untrained teachers are equal to the best of the trained men. Attention is being paid to the requirements of Muhammadans in the Ahmedabad training school, where it is proposed to give them instruction in the vernacular, as well as in Urdu, so as to fit them for general employment. To all the Government training colleges a practising school is attached. These schools are almost the only exception to the rule under which the administration of primary education has been transferred to district and municipal boards. The schools are intended to be models of primary schools; and the excellence of the Poona practising school is attested by its popularity, while the high rate of fees makes it almost self-supporting.

The female training schools increased from three to four. The cost amounted to R25,862, including R20,436 from provincial revenues and R3,778 from local funds. Of all these institutions a good account is given. Of the Government school at Poona it is stated, in reference to the complaint that the elder generation of mistresses could not teach:—"This reproach certainly cannot lie "now. The students of the highest class can teach with animation and skill, "and are manifestly not without the feminine tact that makes female teachers so "valuable in all civilised countries." In the Ahmedabed school, similarly, the Inspector was "specially struck with the improvement shown in the teaching "power of the higher classes, the women of which gave lessons before me in oral "method." A new school was established at Rajkot by the Chiefs of Kathiawar, to commemorate the name of Colonel Barton, late Political Agent. Further development was given in all schools to the plan of inducing the wives of schoolmasters to come under training, with the view of being appointed teachers in girls' schools. There were 25 married students out of a total number of 97.

204. Training Schools in Bengal.—The number of training schools for masters was the same as in the previous year (22); the pupils increased from 1,083 to 1,142. They were maintained at a cost of R83,128, including R71,718 from provincial revenues. Of the 16 Government schools, eight are first-grade institutions for the training of vernacular masters in secondary schools. The pupils in these institutions are required to pass the middle standard before admission to the school; and they then undergo an elaborate course of instruction for three years. It is to the excellence of these institutions that the high position and the popularity of middle schools in Bengal (all of which are on a vernacular basis) must be attributed. No middle school is entitled to a grant-in-aid unless it employs a fully-trained teacher; and the training schools of the province are actually unable to meet the demand for such. Nor is provision wanting for the supply of competent teachers to upper primary schools. The head-masters of these schools are either the best of the old village teachers, men of superior capacity who have brought themselves abreast of the new requirements; or they are men who have been trained for a year in a first-grade normal school; or they have received their education in a middle school. This last is a rapidly increasing class; and it is to the extended employment of such men that the authorities in Bengal look for the further development of upper primary education. The number of upper primary schools increased, between 1881 and 1886, from 1,700 to 3,000, and the number of scholars passing the corresponding examination advanced in a still higher ratio. Their continued increase is only checked by financial limitations, which tend more and more to diminish the earnings of a teacher of this class as the number of schools increases.

The direct provision for the supply of trained teachers to primary schools is far more limited. Up to the close of 1885-86 it was confined (1) to ten Government schools or training classes of the lower grade, in which either actual teachers or candidates for teacherships were trained during a course extending usually over six months; (2) to the trained students of the six aided schools. These last were maintained by missionary bodies, for the exclusive benefit of the primary schools under their management; and four of them were attended only by Santhals, Kols, Bhuteas, and other aboriginal races. It follows that the direct provision for training teachers of primary schools for the Hindu and Muhammadan population of Bengal was limited to 12 Government or aided schools with 187 pupils. From the Government schools 181 pupils passed

TRAINING SCHOOLS.

on the village schools, nor even generally by compelling teachers to come in for training; but rather by gradually infusing among the villagers a desire for a better standard of education, and by so improving the position and prospects of the teacher that men with higher qualifications might be gradually attracted to the work. It was added that the Government of India was not satisfied that this policy was sound; and desired that all teachers who were willing to undergo training should have opportunities of securing it, and that trained teachers should be eligible for higher grants. Action has now been taken in Bengal in accordance with these orders. After much discussion as to ways and means, and as to the difficulty (strongly felt in Madras also) of either compelling gurus to come in and be trained, or of replacing them by newly-trained men, it was at length decided to utilise for this purpose the middle vernacular schools, Government and aided, existing in large numbers over the whole of Bengal, with an average of 25 schools to a district, all under trained pundits. Free tuition was accordingly offered to all gurus or intending gurus, certified to be so by the District Deputy Inspector, in any one out of a large number of selected schools of this class; and the head-masters were to receive from Government a reward of one rupee a month for every guru under training; the course was to last for one year, and to conform either to the upper primary standard or to the special standard for lower-grade training schools. According to the last report, the number of such classes was 104, with an average of 3 pupils to each. For the first year a provision of R6,000 was made in the estimates, sufficient for the training of 500 village teachers; but it was believed that as the advantages of the scheme became known, a much larger grant would be necessary. The scheme is a simple one; but it must always be remembered that in Bengal the elementary education of what may be called the literate classes is separately provided for in middle and high schools; and that the primary schools, especially the lower primary, have only to make provision for the simple requirements of the labouring population in their daily lives. This circumstance separates Bengal by a wide interval from those provinces in which all classes of the people attend the same elementary school, even though only a few, comparatively, may reach the higher standards taught in it. But, however simple and inexpensive, it is claimed for the new Bengal scheme that it possesses many advantages, and promises to become widely popular. In the first place, a guru need never go far from his own home, and that fact disposes of an enormous difficulty; when the gurus in the neighbourhood of one middle school have been trained, a class can be formed in another, 10 or 12 miles off; the head-masters of middle schools have all undergone a careful normal school training, and are familiar with the art of teaching and with the best methods of school management; their own middle school in its lower classes furnishes a practising school at hand; and lastly, an addition of a few rupees a month to the salary of a teacher is no inconsiderable attraction, and constitutes him a zealous apostle of the scheme to all the gurus in his neighbourhood. The inducement to the guru to come in and be trained is not as yet so clear. If the financial position of the Government of Bengal allowed it so to increase the allotments to district boards as to enable them to replace the present system of rewards by one of stipends—a tendency, it may be observed, that many district boards are even now manifesting—it would be easy to grant higher stipends to trained teachers, in accordance with the suggestions of the Government of India. But if payment goes by the results of examination, the only course open is to try to persuade the guru that training will increase his reward-earning power; and that is an argument which is likely to appeal to him much less forcibly than the promise of an increased stipend.

There were, as in the previous year, three aided boarding schools for mistresses; the nominal attendance rose from 102 to 116, though not all of these are expected to become teachers. They cost R14,435, towards which Government paid R4,720. All are under missionary management, and are intended to train teachers for the girls' schools maintained by those bodies. The pupils, with the exception of eight Eurasians, are all Native Christians. The Free Church Normal School was mentioned in the last chapter as one of the two institutions that train pupils for the Entrance and First Arts examinations.

205. Training Schools in the North-Western Provinces.—The training schools for masters were ten under district boards and one aided; the number of pupils fell from 399 to 376. Of the total cost of R47,641, R45,981 was paid from local funds, and nothing from Government. The course extends over two years. Certificates of qualification were given to 264 pupil-teachers, half in the upper, and half in the lower grade. There was much variation in the standards of passing, which differ widely from circle to circle, the proportion of successful candidates ranging from 33 to 100 per cent. The irregularity in these results points, it is stated, to the need of a common provincial test. The students in Oudh were among the least successful; and the complaint is repeated that in that province those who intend to become village teachers have to acquire both forms of the vernacular. The Director's report points to the difficulty that is thrown in the way of popular education by the fact that two vernaculars, possessing characters so utterly different as the Persian and the Nagri, are so widely current in Upper India. "There is scarcely a village in "which the residents all write the same character; and hence there is much to be "said in defence of those who, in order to put an end to this discrepancy, and to "silence the conflicting but irreconcileable claims of Urdu and Nagri, would "supersede both of the vernacular characters by the substitution of the Roman "character in their place."

206. Training Schools in the Punjab.—The Central Training College at Lahore comprises three classes: two English and one vernacular. The two English classes train teachers for secondary and primary English schools (or departments) respectively, the vernacular class for secondary vernacular schools. The teachers for primary vernacular schools are trained in the other normal schools of the province. The number of pupils in the college increased from 52 to 72; 39 in the English classes and 33 in the vernacular class. The two English classes have hitherto been trained to a great extent in common; and to that circumstance is ascribed the comparative failure of the junior class at the certificate examination. It is pointed out that the duties to be discharged by these two classes of students are very different in character. The junior class will be employed almost exclusively in imparting the elements of English to the pupils of primary schools or departments; and all that is required in their course is that they shall themselves be well grounded in English, and in the art of teaching English. On the other hand, the senior class will be employed, if in high schools, in teaching not only English but other subjects through the medium of English; if in middle schools, in teaching English and in superintending the teaching of other subjects through the vernacular. Hence the requirements of this class are much more comprehensive; and a corresponding distinction is henceforward to be made in the method of training them. With one exception, all the students who passed out with certificates from the English classes had obtained employment on salaries averaging R60 a month. The vernacular students had not been so successful; but it was anticipated that the new rules for grants-in-aid, and the rules about to be promulgated for board schools, would open an assured career for certificated teachers.

There were three training schools for mistresses, all aided, containing 55 pupils. The largest was the Amritsar School, recently made over by the Christian Vernacular Education Society to the Church Missionary Society. The latter body had, however, decided to abolish the institution—a result possibly due to the Director's adverse comments in the previous year. It was, however, hoped that the decision would be re-considered; since the work which the school had done in supplying teachers to the vernacular schools of the city was of a useful kind, though the initial qualifications demanded of the students were too low to admit of their being turned into really capable teachers.

207. Training Schools in Other Provinces.—In the Central Provinces there has been no change. The three Government training schools were maintained in full efficiency, and included, as before, classes for gymnastics, drawing, and carpentry. They numbered 178 students at the close of the year, exclusive of 164 who had passed out with certificates at the close of their two years' course. The language employed in these schools is Hindi. There are also three classes for the training of Uriya teachers in the Sambalpur district. Each pupil in a normal school signs an agreement that he will serve in the Department for two years, under penalty not only of returning the amount he has received in stipends, but of paying a fee for his tuition. The policy of engaging the wives of teachers to be trained as mistresses was pursued with success. It is stated that the number of secondary schools is too small to require a constant and steady flow of new teachers, and that it is at present premature to establish training schools for teachers in such schools.

In the last chapter reference was made to the system of capitation-grants for teachers' certificates in Burma, under which a grant-in-aid or indigenous school could claim R100 or R200 for passing a pupil at the certificate examination. This system worked with increased success during 1885-86, when the number of students so passing increased from 25 to 55 (16 of whom were from indigenous schools), notwithstanding the fact that higher qualifications were demanded in that year. Some difficulty was beginning to be felt as to the employment of students who had passed through a regular training in normal schools; since both local and municipal funds were feeling the strain of their existing educational expenditure, and were unable to establish new schools. The only course apparently open to trained teachers was to establish schools of their own; a result not only desirable in itself but actively encouraged by the liberal aid offered to schools so conducted. Among the methods of testing the results of work was the introduction of a plan whereby head-masters of training schools were encouraged to spend a part of the vacation in tours among those indigenous schools to which trained teachers had been attached.

The need of improved teachers for Assam was again strongly insisted on. Mr. C. B. Clarke, Officiating Inspector of Schools, repeated his attack on the lower-grade normal schools of the province, and recommended their abolition in favour of the new Bengal system of training-classes attached to middle schools. This proposal was not accepted by the Government. A somewhat similar method has, however, been adopted in Berar, where pupil-teachers are attached to selected middle schools with stipends of R4 a month for two years. They present themselves at the annual examinations for certificates along with the regular students of the training school. There were in 1885-86 25 such pupil-teachers, in addition to 77 regular students. The Mercara Training School in Coorg contained 14 students, who are required to have passed the upper primary examination before admission, and to present themselves, after a course of three years, for examination by the middle school test.

208. Recommendations of the Commission as to Training Schools.— The provision of a well-judged system of primary schools was a point to which the Government of India attached great importance, drawing special attention to the necessity of increasing the provision in Bengal. The specific proposals made by the Commission under this head relate to both primary and secondary schools. Those relating to primary schools are the following:—

"That the supply of normal schools, whether Government or aided, be so "localised as to provide for the local requirements of all primary schools, whether "Government or aided, within the division under each Inspector" (IV.15).

"That the first charges on provincial funds assigned for primary education "be the cost of its direction and inspection, and the provision of adequate normal "schools" (IV. 16).

The object of the second recommendation appears to have been misunderstood in some instances. It has been taken to mean that the provision of training schools is properly a charge on provincial revenues and on no other source of income; and in provinces where these institutions have hitherto been maintained by local bodies, the question has been discussed whether the necessary transfer to provincial revenues and departmental management should now be made. The intention of the Commission appears merely to have been that in any province in which a due supply of training schools, whether under departmental, under local, or under private management, did not exist, the necessary provision should be made from provincial funds.

The localisation of training schools practically comes to the same thing as an increase in their number, the object being to provide for the local wants of districts or divisions. In 1885-86 this policy was either initiated or carried out in Bengal and Berar. It was shown in the last chapter that the same policy had been pursued in the three previous years in Madras, where local boards had been very active; in the North-Western Provinces, where a training school had been established at the head-quarters of each division, but where also an opposite movement had resulted in the abolition of district training classes; and in Assam where three Government schools had been opened. In other provinces it is stated either that the existing provision is adequate, or that proposals for increase have been dropped for want of funds.

209. Special Requirements for Teachers in Secondary Schools.— The recommendation as to the training of teachers in secondary schools runs thus:—

"That an examination in the principles and practice of teaching be institu-"ted, success in which should hereafter be a condition of permanent employment "as a teacher in any secondary school, Government or aided " (V. 6).

This recommendation was put forward by the Commission as an alternative to requiring every teacher in a secondary school to go through a course of normal training. The Commission set a high value, for all who intended to become teachers, on a preliminary training in practical work with a class. "It is in "this way chiefly that the future schoolmaster will learn how to engage and "keep the attention of a whole class, how to correct and check the wandering "or listless scholar, how to put together in their due order the materials of a les-"son, and how to select those illustrations which give life to instruction and "arouse the interest of the pupils." But if in the absence of training schools for secondary teachers, and still more of practising schools attached to such institutions, opportunities of this kind were wanting, the only practicable alternative

seem to have been taken to carry out the recommendation of the Commission, so far as it relates to teachers in English schools. In those provinces where importance is attached to secondary vernacular schools, provision is very generally made for the training of teachers to serve in them. For teacherships in English schools, the certificate of having passed a University examination has been and is commonly regarded as affording sufficient evidence of capacity; though the general reluctance to establish a training school for English teachers—necessarily a costly institution—is probably due quite as much to financial exigencies as to any doubt of its utility. The two exceptions are supplied by the Teachers' College of Madras and the Central Training College at Lahore, an account of which has been given in the preceding paragraphs. But the provision made under this head in Madras is not confined to the establishment of a Teachers' College, which after all can turn out only a few trained teachers every year. The provincial report states that an examination in the principles and practice of teaching is held, and that success in the examination is a condition of permanent employment in secondary schools, whether Government or aided. In its comments on the report of the Commission, the Madras Government in 1884 objected to a similar recommendation in Chapter VIII, that "teachers in non-Government institutions be allowed to present them-"selves for examination for any grade of certificate required by the grant-in-"aid rules, without being compelled to attend a normal school" (VIII. 1). It held that this would be a retrograde step, as involving the practical abolition of normal training for superior teachers. The Government of India suggested the reference of this question to a Conference, with the result that the objections at first entertained to the proposal appear to have been removed. The revised grant-in-aid rules of 1885 throw further light on the practice in force in Madras. Salary-grants at different rates are given in aided schools for all teachers, whether trained in a normal school or not, who have satisfied certain tests. These include among others (1) the general education test of the grade for which the teacher is a candidate; (2) the test in the principles of method and of school management prescribed for the grade. The general education test is of three grades: (*a*, or collegiate), the B. A. degree examination; (*b*, or secondary), the First Arts or Entrance examination; (*c*, or primary), the middle school or upper primary examination. The first two are required in the case of teachers in secondary schools of different classes. The 'school management test' for teachers in high schools includes the following subjects:—

(*a*) To answer questions on the best methods of teaching English and vernacular reading, spelling, grammar, composition, translation, writing, arithmetic, geography, and history in a high school.

(*b*) To answer questions on the art of oral teaching generally.

(*c*) To answer questions on the form of school registers, the mode of keeping them and of making returns from them, and regarding the correct forms of official correspondance.

(*d*) To write notes of a lesson on a given subject.

(*e*) To answer questions on the organisation of a high school.

(*f*) To answer questions connected with moral discipline, as affecting the character and conduct of the pupils of a high school.

Similar, but slightly lower qualifications are required of teachers in middle schools. It may be added that the certificate is not actually given until a favourable report has been made by the Inspector of the candidate's ability to teach a class in school, and as to the general character of his work. Subject (*f*) has an obvious bearing on the relation of training schools for English teachers to school discipline.

In the Punjab also it is stated that an examination in the principles and practice of teaching for persons employed in secondary schools has long been in force in connexion with the Central Training College. Certificated teachers alone are henceforward to be employed in Government and board schools; and special staff-grants are given for such teachers in aided schools. The examination for the certificate includes 'school management' and 'the practice of teaching.' For the former of these subjects certain text-books on the art of teaching are prescribed, and a knowledge of the registers and returns of the Department is also demanded. For the latter, each candidate is required to give a lesson for half an hour in the presence of the Inspector.

(b) OTHER SCHOOLS OF SPECIAL INSTRUCTION.

210. Professional and Technical Education.—In the following section some account will be given of the progress of professional and technical instruction, whether carried on in colleges or in schools. It will include a statement, first, of the chief institutions affiliated to the University in which are taught the courses required for degrees in law, medicine and engineering; and secondly, of the various non-collegiate institutions for artistic, technical, or industrial education, in which the course of instruction is either below or outside the standards recognised by the University. It will also contain an account of the schemes and proposals that have been promulgated in different provinces for the further development of technical education, in response to the increased attention that has recently been given to that subject.

211. Professional Colleges, 1885-86.—The subjoined table shows the number of colleges, or departments of colleges in law, medicine and engineering, and the number of students reading in them on the 31st March 1886:—

Professional Colleges.

	LAW.		MEDICINE.		ENGINEERING.	
	Institutions	Students	Institutions	Students	Institutions	Students
Madras, Government	1	141	1	(a) 136	1	18
Bombay, ditto	2	221	1	(b) 296	1	116
Bengal, ditto	6	110	1	(c) 152	1	(d) 156
Ditto, Unaided	4	772	...	...	...	...
N.-W. Provinces, Government	1	61	...	...	1	(e) 154
Ditto, Aided	1	48	...	...	...	...
Ditto, Unaided	1	18	...	...	...	...
Punjab, Government	...	...	1	183	...	...
Total { Government	10	533	4	767	4	444
Aided	1	48	...	...	...	...
Unaided	5	790	...	...	...	...
GRAND TOTAL	16	1,371	4	767	4	(f) 444
TOTAL IN 1884-85	13	1,067	4	806	4	(g) 507

212. Law Departments.—These are in all cases attached to Arts colleges, since the University requires that candidates for the degree of B. L. shall have taken the B. A. degree, and the two courses are sometimes read, in part at any rate, simultaneously. In Madras a course of two years, and in Bombay a course of three years, is required subsequently to graduation. In Bengal and the North-Western Provinces, which come under the regulations of the Calcutta University, the course is for three years, of which two must be subsequent to the degree. The number of Government law departments increased from 8 to 10, by the opening of a law class at Poona, and by the transfer to this head of the class attached to the Muir College, Allahabad, returned in the previous year as aided. This explains also the reduction of one in the number of aided law departments. Unaided classes increased from 3 to 5, by the opening of two classes in connexion with the Ripou College of Calcutta and the Jagannath College of Dacca, both unaided institutions. The number of students in Government institutions has increased by 66. In those under private management the number has risen from 541 to 790; and, as explained in the previous chapter, the legal education of students in Calcutta is now entirely in the hands of unaided institutions. The six Government classes in Bengal are attached to Government colleges in the mofussil.

213. Medical Colleges.—The institutions which exist in India for the training of students for the License in Medicine and Surgery, or for the degree of Bachelor of Medicine, as well as for the higher degree of Doctor of Medicine, are the medical colleges of Madras and Calcutta, the Grant Medical College of Bombay, and the Lahore Medical School. The total number of students fell from 806 to 767,—a loss which is due to the withdrawal of a large number of students from the Grant Medical College just before the examinations. In Madras and Calcutta there was some increase in the number.

The qualification for the License in Medicine and Surgery differs from that required for the Bachelor of Medicine degree, both in the preliminary educational test and in the final standard of examination. In Madras the initial qualification for the license is the University Entrance examination; and the course extends over four years, divided into two parts by the first and second Licentiate examination. For the degree, candidates must have passed the First Arts examination, and have subsequently studied medicine for five years; during the course of which they have to pass one preliminary scientific and two professional examinations. To those students who have graduated in Arts, taking physical science, before entering on their medical course, the preliminary scientific examination and one year of study are remitted. In Bombay the only examination below that for the Doctor's degree is that for the license. A candidate must have passed the matriculation examination and have studied medicine for four years, during which he has to undergo three examinations. In Calcutta, candidates, whether for the degree or for the license, must have passed the First Arts examination; and in either case the course extends over five years. The only difference is the requirement of comparative anatomy and physiology for the degree; a similar distinction being made in Madras. The Lahore Medical School exists for the benefit of students from the North-Western Provinces as well of those from the Punjab, and both alike are eligible for the Government scholarships tenable in the institution. Of its 183 students, 65 learn English and 118 the vernacular, corresponding to the English and the Oriental side respectively of the Medical Faculty. But even of those who are reading for the diploma or license which the University confers, all are not necessarily matriculated; and there are many men both in the English and in the vernacular classes, who, though belonging to the school, have no connexion with the University. For admission to the English licentiate class a student must have passed the Entrance examination and must study for five years, undergoing two examinations in that time. Only the license is awarded. On the Oriental side four classes of certificates are given; of which the two chief are attainable after passing the Entrance examination (not necessarily in English), and of having thereafter been engaged for four years in the study of either the European or the indigenous system of medicine. Unconnected with the University are the civil hospital assistants, the military students, and the female students.

214. **Engineering Colleges.**—These institutions were four, as in the previous year; and the number of collegiate students rose from 163 to 186. It was explained in the last chapter that not all of the students belong to the University. The Roorkee College, though affiliated to the Calcutta University, sends up no candidates for degrees in Engineering, but awards certificates of various classes to its students after a college examination. Of 156 students of the Seebpore Civil Engineering College in Bengal, 52 have passed the Entrance examination and are reading for the degree, while 104 belong to the class of mechanical apprentices, who read a lower standard. The corresponding class in the Poona College of Science has now been excluded from the returns of that institution, and is separately shown as a technical school. The connexion of the higher and lower departments of engineering colleges is however so close, and the parts they respectively play in the development of industry are so nearly allied, that it will be convenient to consider them together.

The requirements of the Madras University for the degree of Bachelor of Civil Engineering are that a candidate shall have passed the First Examination in Arts, and shall have subsequently read for two years in an engineering college. All candidates for the degree are examined in mathematics, natural philosophy, mensuration, and the framing of estimates; those for the civil branch are also examined in surveying and levelling, constructive engineering, and architectural and topographical drawing; those for the mechanical branch in mechanical engineering and machine drawing. The Madras College of Engineering was completely re-organised during the year at considerable cost. The college department contained 18 students reading for the University degree in civil or mechanical engineering. The theoretical course extends over three years. It is followed by a practical course of two years; the first of which is spent in the workshops of the Public Works Department, in a course of carpentry, smith's work, founding and fitting; and the second in attendance on works in progress, during which the student learns brick-making, masonry, quarrying, accounts and other similar subjects. For the second year he receives subsistence allowance at the rate of R25 or R50 a month. The subordinate department contained 167 students, against 106 in the preceding year. This department includes four separate classes for (1) engineer subordinates, who go through a theoretical course of two and a half years, followed by a practical course of two years similar to that required for engineers; (2) surveyors and (3) draughtsmen, in each of which a two years' course is prescribed; (4) sub-overseers and artisans, who are entitled to certificates after one year of study. Fees are charged at the rate of R16 a month to engineers, and at the rate of from R4 to R6 a month in the first three subordinate classes. For the sub-overseer class a registration fee of R5 is alone required. Certificates were issued to 13 students of the subordinate engineer class, to 18 draughts-

qualifications to two years or to one and a half. The examination comprises (1) mathematics and natural philosophy, (2) experimental and natural science, (3) civil engineering, (4) one out of the following list :—(*a*) analytical geometry and the differential and integral calculus, (*b*) optics and astronomy, (*c*) mining and metallurgy, (*d*) architecture, (*e*) mechanical engineering, (*f*) chemical analysis, (*g*) botany and meteorology. Candidates must also pass a practical test in experimental science and mechanical engineering.

Instruction in the University course, both theoretical and practical, is given in the Poona College of Science with its attached workshops; and the advancement of Bombay in this matter is attested by the 116 students on the rolls of the college, while Calcutta has only 52, and Madras 18. The other departments of the college are (1) the agricultural and (2) the forest class, which are confined to matriculated students though they read for no University degree; (3) the mechanic and sub-overseer classes, containing 72 and 18 students respectively. In consequence of the steady increase in the former class of students, and in order to make the instruction in the workshop attached to the college as complete as possible, sanction was given during the year of report to the appointment of a draughtsman, a pattern-maker, a foreman turner, a moulder and a blacksmith. It is stated that the shops worked at a profit of R775 during the year, though the principle on which the accounts are drawn up is not explained. Nineteen of the workshop apprentices completed their course; of whom four left and obtained employment, while 12 joined the sub-overseer class. Of 18 students in the latter class six passed the qualifying examination for the Public Works Department.

For the License in Engineering of the Calcutta University a candidate must have passed the Entrance examination, and have subsequently studied for four years in an affiliated institution. If he has passed the First Arts examination, he will be entitled to the degree of B.E. The course comprises the following subjects : mathematics, engineering construction, geodesy, drawing, and either natural science or machinery, according as the candidate selects the civil or the mechanical branch of the course. The course in mathematics is exceptionally high and includes, besides other subjects, analytical geometry, the differential and integral calculus, and hydrostatics. Proposals are under consideration for reducing the extent of this compulsory course. The Government Civil Engineering College at Seebpore, near Calcutta, is the institution in which candidates are prepared for the University degree during a course of five years. In the first four each student, in addition to his theoretical course, works for three hours a day in the shops; and in the cold season those of the second and third years go into camp for three months, and execute a practical survey of the country in which they may happen to be. The last year, after the University examination is passed, is spent entirely on public works in progress, including a course of brick-making. During the first four years students have to pay a monthly fee of R8. It has been proposed to separate the theoretical from the practical portion of the course, to reduce the former from four years to three, and to spend the latter partly in the workshops and partly on works in progress—a change which would bring the course into conformity with that of Madras. It should be added that the course in mechanical engineering is not yet taught in the Seebpore College. This defect is, however, partly provided for in the subordinate department of the college, that for mechanical overseers or foreman mechanics. Since the establishment of the class in 1880, about 50 students a year have joined this class, and about 35 a year have passed out with certificates. A special examination of an elementary kind, chiefly in English and mathematics, is held for admission to the class. The students are passed through a five-year course of technical training, in which a sufficient knowledge of engineering theory, surveying and drawing, is combined with a full practical knowledge of workshop methods, and practice in the use of hand and machine tools. Students of this class are apprenticed for the full term of five years to the superintendent of the adjoining workshops under the Public Works Department, so that they may be qualified under the Act for the charge of the engines of inland river-steamers. During their first three and a half years they attend the shops for three hours daily; one year in the carpenter's, one year in the blacksmith's, one year in the fitter's, and six months in the moulder's shop. Then, after passing a practical examination, as well as an examination in the theoretical course which now comes to an end, they are required to go for five and a half hours daily into any one shop which they may select for the remaining eighteen months of their apprenticeship. It is stated that ex-students of this class almost invariably obtain good and remunerative employment, and that the supply is not equal to the demand. Six students with Government scholarships from Burma have joined this class.

The Thomason Civil Engineering College at Roorkee is maintained by the Public Works Department of Government for the requirements of the public service; and it has no connexion with any University. It is, however, noticed in this place since it discharges the same functions as those that are so connected. The college contains three departments. Candidates for the engineer class have to pass an examination in English and Hindustani (and also in a third language if their vernacular is English); in elementary science, in drawing, and in mathematics to a somewhat high standard. The course of study extends over two years, at the end of which time an examination is held in mathematics, applied mechanics, experimental science, civil engineering, drawing, and surveying. Students of this class are educated for the engineer branch of the Public Works Department, in which four and five appointments in alternate years are guaranteed to the best of those who pass. (For comparison it may here be repeated that the number of guaranteed appointments for the students of the Poona College is two a year; of the Seebpore College, two and one in alternate years; of the Madras College, one a year.) The upper subordinate class at Roorkee is intended to provide men for overseerships, and the lower subordinate for sub-overseerships, in the Public Works Department. The course for the former extends over three years, of which the last is devoted to practical training on works in progress. The course for lower subordinates is limited to a year and a half. The final examination for upper and for lower subordinates includes mathematics, engineering, drawing, and surveying, to different standards for the two classes. In 1885-86, 22 passed by the upper and 33 by the lower standard.

215. Results of University Examinations, 1885-86.—The following statement shows the number of those who passed the final examinations of the University (or in the case of Roorkee, of the college) in law, medicine, and engineering:—

Province.	Law.	Medicine.	Engineering.
Madras	(a) 38	(b) 26	3
Bombay	17	39	13
Bengal	(c) 120	(d) 32	3
North-Western Provinces	...	...	4
Punjab	...	7	...
Total	175	104	23

The number, and the increase in the number, of engineering students show very poorly beside the corresponding figures for law and medicine. There is a decline from 7 to 9 in Madras, of which no explanation is given. In Bengal it was the complaint for many years that the University examiners, who are officers of the Public Works Department, were for some reason or other out of touch with the course taught in the college and with the capabilities of students; and a committee has been appointed with the object of bringing about such adjustment as may be possible between the conditions of a collegiate course and the requirements of actual employment.

216. Cost of Professional Colleges, 1885-86.—The total cost of professional education of this class amounted to R5,94,818, showing a very slight increase on the expenditure of the previous year. There is a large increase in fee-receipts, producing a corresponding reduction in the cost to provincial funds. The necessary figures are subjoined:—

Profession.	Provincial Revenues.	Fees.	Other Sources.	Total.
	R	R	R	R
Law	1,082	42,415	5,339	48,836
Medicine*	2,11,672	54,678	3,863	2,70,213
Engineering	2,60,032	15,548	189	2,75,769
Total	4,72,786	1,12,641	9,391	5,94,818
Total for 1884-85	4,84,043	98,808	13,046	5,95,897

* The cost of the Lahore Medical School is included, though in General Tables III and IV it is shown under Medical Schools.

The increase in the number of law classes has brought about a corresponding increase of cost, nearly all of which is however borne by private sources. The law-classes are more than self-supporting in Bengal and Madras; they cost Government R3,848 in Bombay, and R7,798 in the North-Western Provinces.

The total cost of medical colleges remained nearly stationary, with some increase in fee-receipts. The Grant Medical College, with an average roll-number of 284, was maintained at a total cost of R25,000, which was more than fully met by fee-receipts alone. The Madras College cost R43,000, deriving R16,183 in fees from 125 students. The Calcutta College, with 169 students, cost R1,48,000, of which only R9,000 were paid in fees. The Lahore Medical School, with 183 students, all of whom either receive scholarships or read free, was maintained at a cost of R54,000, towards which the local municipality contributed a little over R2,000. It thus appears that the Bombay Medical College, with something less than twice as many students as that at Calcutta, receives three times as much in fees as the latter institution, and is maintained at one-sixth of the cost. The cost may be a mere matter of the adjustment of accounts between two departments; but the difference in fee-rates is considerable. Still more conspicuous is the difference between Calcutta and Madras; the average yearly fee paid by medical students in Calcutta being R57, in Madras R130.

The cost of engineering colleges was reduced by R14,000, of which R10,000 fell as a saving to provincial revenues. Fee-receipts increased from R13,000 to R15,000. The following figures show the average roll-number of engineering students at each college, the total cost of its maintenance, and the fee-receipts:—

	Students.	Fees.	Total cost.
		R	R
Madras	18	4,115	8,146
Poona	112	5,872	63,728
Calcutta	154	5,561	68,968
Roorkee	154	...	134,909

The differences in the total cost of these institutions are striking. It may be that the cost is estimated on different principles in Madras and in other provinces; at any rate it is difficult to reconcile the small cost at Madras with the staff employed. The attached school cost over R30,000. The average fee paid by students at Madras appears from the above figures to be R228 a year; the fee regularly chargeable is R16 a month. At Poona it works out to R52 a year, and at Calcutta to R36 a year; but this last rate is reduced by the inclusion of mechanical apprentices, who form the majority of the students. The 52 engineer students pay a fee of R8 a month.

217. Results of University Examinations.—The subjoined statement shows the number of those who graduated in 1885-86 in law, medicine, and engineering:—

Province.	Law.	Medicine.	Engineering.
Madras	38	18	3
Bombay	17	39	13
Bengal	120	32	3
North-Western Provinces	...	...	4
Punjab	...	7	...
Total	175	96	23
Total in 1884-85	115	59	17

There is a considerable increase in the number of graduates in all subjects. Of the 120 law students passing in Bengal, 98 received their instruction in non-Government colleges. The four successful candidates from the Roorkee College received their certificates as engineers from the college authorities, and not from the University.

218. Technical and Other Special Schools.—The following table includes all schools of special instruction which are not affiliated to the University:—

Province.	1885-86.									
	Art.		Medicine.		Engineering or Surveying.		Industrial.		Other.	
	Schools.	Pupils.	Schools.	Pupils.	Schools.	Pupils.	Schools.	Pupils.	Schools.	Pupils.
Madras	1	(a) 176	5	(c) 184	1	167	10	(d) 295	3	315
Bombay	1	(b) 227	3	155	1	19	8	(e) 665	41	2,442
Bengal	1	163	6	600	4	208	8	(f) 446	34	(i)1,865
N.-W. Provinces	...	...	1	105	...	...	2	(g) 186	20	1,324
Punjab	1	71	...	...	...	...	5	(h) 107	1	83
Central Provinces	...	...	...	...	...	...	15	255	...	...
Burma	...	...	...	...	9	164	1	48	...	6
Assam	...	...	...	...	...	....	1	22	4	185
Total	4	637	15	1,044	15	558	50	2,024	104	6,220
Total for 1884-85	4	655	15	1,122	18	571	44	1,524	71	4,569

as "other schools." In the last chapter a brief account was given of all the foregoing classes of schools. Full information with regard to institutions for technical instruction as they existed throughout India in 1884-85, may also be obtained from the "Note on Technical Education in India" which was drawn up by command of His Excellency the Viceroy in 1886. It will therefore be only necessary in this place to notice any changes of importance that took place in the year 1886.

219. Schools of Art.—The number of students slightly declined, the greatest decrease being found in the Bombay school. Of Madras it is stated that there is no genuine demand for the serious study of Fine Art, and the industrial character of the school is becoming more and more pronounced. The pupils showed very well in the industrial branches of the middle school examination; and it is believed that the introduction of the new scheme of technical instruction has increased the usefulness and popularity of the school. The pottery department was in active and successful operation; and further improvements were expected from the recent discovery of kaolin in the province, and from the results obtained from experiments with new colours in the decoration of pottery. To the school is attached a museum, which was visited by 75,000 persons in the course of the year. In the Bombay school there was again a decline in the classes for painting, sculpture, and architecture, which numbered only 41 students out of 227; and an increase in the elementary or drawing class, in which there were 220 students. The strength of the drawing classes attached to 33 high schools throughout the Presidency continued to increase; and of 117 candidates who obtained the first-grade art certificate, only 12 belonged to the School of Art in Bombay. Certificates of two higher grades were also awarded; and for these the school supplied the great majority of the candidates, including all who competed for the highest grade certificate. For certificates of all grades 772 candidates appeared and 169 passed, while the number of those who learnt drawing during the year increased from 2,713 to 4,033. The subject is evidently making way. The Principal of the School of Art refers to the fact that drawing is now regarded as the necessary basis of technical instruction, and quotes the recommendation of the Royal Commissioners that it should be made a compulsory subject in elementary schools, and treated in all respects as concurrent with writing throughout the standards. This cannot yet be done even in Bombay; but liberal rules have lately been sanctioned for the encouragement of drawing in grant-in-aid schools, and a sum of R10,000 was provided in the budget for this purpose. The only innovation introduced into the course of the Calcutta School was a class of fresco painting, conducted on the lines of ancient Indian art. This form of decoration has, it is alleged, been so much neglected, and at the present day has become so deeply tinged by the admixture of European elements, that it is difficult to find in the productions of native artists any genuine impress of the local character. But the students take little interest in the subject, and there were only eight who attended the fresco class. The Principal adds:—"If our 163 students were asked which "branch of the profession they would rather cultivate, the majority of them "would answer, portrait-painting. A decorative painter is not held in great "esteem among Indians, and is considered little better than a common "mechanic. The Musalmans on this point show better judgment." The lithographic, wood-carving and metal-chasing classes were, however, carried on with such success as is possible in a province where there is little indigenous art of a high character, and where therefore the feeling for art has to be created rather than evoked. The Mayo School at Lahore was largely occupied with preparing and despatching to the Indo-Colonial Exhibition in London a collection of objects representing the art and industry of the province. As a specimen of its own work it contributed the carved wooden screen which attracted so much admiration as the façade of the Punjab Court. It also took a large part in designing articles for the Exhibition, and in directing the work of artisans unconnected with the school. The modelling class had to contend with a special difficulty in the fact, noticed by Mr. Kipling, Principal of the school, that "the ancient Mahomedan prescription against plastic representa-"tion has still more force than is generally supposed." The absence of relief decoration in public buildings also diminished the popularity of this class. Practical geometry was taught with much success to a class containing many pupils of the carpenter caste; and there was also a special class for teaching carpentry of a superior kind, including architectural and constructive design. Of the students who left the school during the year, five obtained good appointments as wood-carvers, draughtsmen, and decorative painters, in places where their special acquirements could be turned to account.

The cost of the four Schools of Art amounted to R99,590; of which R6,773 was paid in fees and R19,943 was derived from other sources, including endowments and the sale-proceeds of manufactured articles. The balance (R72,874) was met from provincial revenues.

220. Medical Schools.—There is little change to record. The number of students declined in all schools with the exception of that at Agra, of which, however, no account is given in the report. The Lahore Medical School has been described above as containing other classes besides those reading for the University license. The event of chief importance in that institution was the appointment of a lady, Dr. Bielby, to teach midwifery to the female students, the number of whom is, however, not stated. In the school at Madras eight students were females. Sanction has recently been given to the opening of a class for female students in the Campbell Medical School in Calcutta. Burma has no medical school of its own; but it sends seven students to the Calcutta Medical College to qualify for the grade of assistant surgeon, and eleven to Madras for that of hospital assistant. All these students enjoy Government scholarships. The attendance at the two homœopathic schools at Dacca in Bengal slightly fell off—from 168 to 157. In these institutions the instruction is not exclusively vernacular, as 155 students are taught in English. The cost, that of the Lahore School being excluded, amounted to R1,91,574; of which R1,22,604 was contributed by the State, R27,403 by district boards, R16,168 by municipalities, R16,388 from fees, and R9,011 from other sources. With the exception of a sum of R500 in Bombay, all the contributions by district and municipal boards are made in Madras.

221. Engineering and Surveying Schools.—No exact principle seems to be followed in distinguishing these schools from industrial or from 'other' schools; and institutions of much the same character may be found in any one of these three classes. Differences of classification apart, the only important changes are that two new Government survey schools for the training of subordinate revenue officers have been opened in Burma, and that seven schools of a similar kind in Assam have ceased to be under the control of the Education Department and are no longer included in the returns. The school department of the Madras College of Engineering has more than doubled its numbers (73 to 167) in the last two years; it trains overseers, draughtsmen and surveyors for the Public Works Department. The subordinate departments of the engineering colleges at Poona and Seebpore (near Calcutta) pay almost exclusive attention to the mechanical branches of engineering, and are therefore not included in this class. Some account has already been given of these three

improvement has taken place in the school of surveying at Haidarabad in Sind, owing to the provision of facilities for practical work in the field. The survey schools of Bengal are said to answer every practical purpose, and their passed pupils to be in large demand with the employers of labour in railways and other works. The examination of these schools for certificates at the close of the three years' course is conducted by the Executive Engineer of the division.

222. **Industrial Schools.**—An increase of five schools in Madras, of three in Bengal, and of one each in Bombay and the Punjab, has been met by the closing of four carpentry classes attached to schools in the Central Provinces. The increase in Madras is ascribed to the recognition and the liberal encouragement of industrial schools in the grant-in-aid Code. Of the new schools, one taught carpentry and smith's work, and another carpentry; the remaining three (for girls) gave their attention to lace-making. Nearly all these schools are under missionary management. This is the case also with several of the schools in Bombay, including a new school opened in the year by the Free Church Mission. It is also stated that the founder of the American Mission School at Sirur has returned from America laden with appliances for teaching two or three trades suitable to the locality. The wooden roof of a mission church was made entirely by the pupils in one of these schools, and the work was described as excellent. That the benefits of industrial schools of this unpretending class are necessarily confined to pupils of a special communion does not detract from their usefulness; and it is entirely consistent with the purpose which missionary bodies have steadily followed in India that they should devote their educational funds and energies to work of such unquestioned utility. The Government grants made to aided industrial schools in Bombay amount to ·R7,652 annually, and in Madras to R3,690. In other provinces the amounts are smaller. The Ratnagiri factory belongs to the district board, which also maintains in connexion with it a school with 152 carpenter-pupils. The school has been re-organised, and the Government grant increased from R1,500 to R3,000. The cost of the school, as distinguished from the factory, is not stated; but it appears to have been maintained from the Government grant and the profits of the workshop, without any charge upon the district funds. The industrial training was reported to be " most efficient, the workshops being the most completely equipped "of the kind in the Presidency. ' At present the work is mainly in wood, and "the furniture manufactured here has gained a certain reputation. Many " hundred boys have passed through this school and are to be found in the " workshops of all parts of the Presidency." General instruction is also given in the school up to vernacular standard V, which is a year above the upper primary standard of Bombay. The Fardunji School of Surat was maintained at a cost of R6,718, including the Government grant of R2,000 and the proceeds of the endowment. Twenty-six pupils passed out during the year, of whom 10 joined mills or workshops as fitters, and 16 became carpenters. The theoretical course includes mensuration, practical geometry, mechanics, and mechanical drawing. The points in which improvement might be effected were, first, additional attention to drawing, " for to the artisan drawing is a " branch of the greatest importance," and secondly, an extension of the period of training. Parents, it was stated, declined to bind their children to remain in the school for even two or three years. (It will be remembered that in the subordinate department of the Seebpore College, all pupils are apprenticed for a term of five years.)

In Bengal four new schools were opened, and the Dehree School, maintained by the Public Works Department, was omitted from the educational returns. The new schools were all under private management, and were aided either by Government or by the local municipalities. They were of a very humble character, the average cost not exceeding R500 a year for each school. One of them taught "carpentry, clock-repairing, and electro-plating," and afterwards "drawing "and soap-making." "Ivory-work, bidri-work and embroidery" were also to be introduced, these being arts indigenous to the locality. A second took up "draw- "ing, carpentry and clock-repairing." Another, "carpentry, tinsmith's work, "and wicker-work." Another, "the simple industrial arts, such as rope-making, "carpentry, and needle-work." It is a serious question whether schools of this kind deserve active encouragement—whether in fact they possess any element of permanence, or serve any useful purpose which could not be better attained by other means. Pupils cannot be taught the trades of clock-repairing or electro-plating unless articles are sent to be electro-plated and clocks or watches to be repaired—unless, that is, the school is a going business concern. In that case it is a shop, and it differs from other shops of the same kind in three points only. On the one hand the pupils are taught not only their trades, but the rudiments of general education; and again, the name of a school may attract to an industrial calling pupils to whom the bare idea of trade would not be alluring. On the other, a school set up *ad hoc* would not be able to secure the same skill in the teachers as could be found in the most thriving shops; there would be less demand for its productions, and consequently less excellence and variety in its work. The same may be said of local indigenous arts, such as ivory or bidri-work. As to rope-making or soap-boiling it is impossible to suppose in the present day that handicraft can compete with manufactures, either in quality or in price. The true idea of a trade-school seems to be, not to teach the trade, but to take those apprentices and others who are independently learning the trade, and to give them additional instruction in special schools which, by educating the hand and eye and by cultivating the intelligence, may help them to become more skilful workmen in their own crafts. These remarks apply to those cases only in which the artisan-instructor for the technical school is locally procured. They do not apply to those cases in which a new industry is to be taught, or where a higher standard of skill, as, for instance, in carpentry or cabinet-making, is to be introduced. In such cases the teacher must be obtained elsewhere, and generally at much greater cost than these small schools can afford. Experience, it should be added, does not confirm the belief that the literate classes will be attracted in any numbers to industrial occupations by the device of technical schools, except those of a superior kind.

223. Other Schools.—In this class are included schools of Sanskrit, schools of Arabic, music schools, and many miscellaneous institutions that find no appropriate place under other heads. It is only necessary to notice the more important. The new school in Madras is the commercial class, already noticed under Secondary Education, attached to Pacheappa's School. The other two are the industrial schools attached to the Gun Factory, and the agricultural school at Saidapet, of which an account was given in Chapter II. In Bombay there have been slight variations in the number of drawing and agricultural classes attached to high schools; otherwise there is no change. The other important schools shown under this head are the mechanical department and the forest class attached to the Poona College of Science, both of which were described in the last chapter. No account is given in the educational reports of the Imperial Forest School at Dehra Dun in the North-Western Provinces. In Bengal there is no real increase; some advanced *maktabs* having been erroneously included under this head. In the North-Western Provinces, the number of schools for *patwaris* has increased from 11 to 19. They are strictly survey schools. In the Punjab, the only school under this head is the veterinary school at Lahore. The school in Assam is a Muhammadan *maktab*; and there is a small law school in Burma.

224. General Schemes of Technical Instruction.—It is obvious from, what has preceded that, apart from the higher instruction in law, medicine and engineering, required for the attainment of University degrees, there is not as yet in India anything like a general or systematic provision of technical instruction, such as the needs of an advanced community would seem to demand. The provision that exists is partial and fragmentary, directed by no guiding principle, often valuable and successful, but just as often missing success for reasons which are not very clear. The cry has gone up for more technical instruction, and that on two grounds: first, to increase the productive power of India as a manufacturing country; and secondly, to relieve the pressure on the learned and literate professions, for many years largely overcrowded, by providing for the educated classes fresh and lucrative occupation in the lines of commercial and manufacturing industry. The Department has been anxious to respond to the call, but has not known how. In default of setting up a system of industrial education of its own, it has been prompt to aid schools established by private effort even when their utility was questionable, so that no chance might be lost, and in the hope that somehow light might come. But the problem was an obscure one; all the conditions were strange; the social and industrial circumstances of India were so different from those of European countries that the experience of the latter seemed likely to throw but little light on the question. In the Resolution of the 23rd October 1884, the Government of India called the attention of all Local Governments to the need that existed for more sustained and systematic efforts in this direction. The question has thus for the first time come under definite and detailed discussion : and in the following paragraphs an account will be given of the action taken in some of the larger provinces to carry out the views of the Supreme Government.

225. The Madras Scheme.—In the section on Secondary Education it was explained how, under the new system, the bifurcation of studies in Madras was introduced into the middle school course, in the belief that pupils destined for a scientific or industrial training might, even at that early stage, find their advantage in the specialisation of study. It is from this point that the scheme of technical instruction, properly so called, begins. The course is defined by two standards; the preliminary, corresponding generally to the stage of progress marked by the ' Entrance examination, and the advanced, corresponding to that of the First Arts, though in some cases the test stops for the present at the preliminary stage.

The scheme is explicitly based upon the system of scientific and technical instruction at first elaborated by the Science and Art Department at South Kensington, and more recently developed by the City and Guilds of London Institute. The measures taken by these bodies for extending and improving technical education in science and art were, first, to institute a system of examinations in special subjects, thus creating a demand for trained teaching, and then to train teachers to meet that demand. The Madras proposals included these two essential points; and they supplemented them (1) by a system of liberal grants-in-aid both for qualified teachers and for pupils passing by fixed standards, whether in ordinary or in special schools; (2) by special grants for museums, plant, apparatus, and chemicals; (3) by the award of certificates, prizes, and scholarships in different branches of science, art and industry ; (4) by such a development of the teaching staff of existing institutions as would enable them not merely to provide the instruction in science and art that was now chiefly needed, but also to train up teachers for those subjects. These institutions would serve as models; but a much more extensive provision was required if technical instruction was to be established on a wide and solid basis. It was hoped that the direct inducements offered by the grant-in-aid rules would lead to the establishment under private managers, in large and increasing numbers, of schools or classes for instruction in various branches of science and art.

The object of the Government in instituting these examinations was thus defined :—" To encourage advanced instruction in science and art, especially " in those kinds of knowledge which bear upon the different branches of indus- " try now existing in this Presidency or suitable for it; and to furnish a means " of testing, wholly or in part, the qualifications of persons desirous of becom- " ing—

"I. (*a*) Science, (*b*) Art, or (*c*) Technical Teachers; or

"II. Mechanical engineers; mechanical draughtsmen; electrical engineers; telegraphists; builders; designers; engravers; decorative or art workmen in any branch of artistic industry included in this notification; or

"III. Scientific agriculturists; foresters; veterinarians; or

"IV. Managers or foremen of manufacturing, printing, and other industrial establishments suitable for this Presidency; or

"V. Employés in posts in the Revenue, Revenue Survey, Public Works, Education, Agriculture, Forest, Sanitation, Cattle Disease, Vaccination, or other departments which require a practical knowledge of any of the branches of science, art, or industry in which it is proposed to examine, and for employment in which Government may, from time to time, see fit to recognise these examinations as a test; or

"VI. Employés in similar posts under district boards and municipal councils, or under private employers."

The subjects of examination were numerous and varied. The syllabus enumerated 66 branches of science, art, and industry, for each of which the standard of examination, whether preliminary or advanced, was defined in detail. The scientific portion comprised 36 subjects, including pure and applied mathematics, applied mechanics, the various branches of civil and mechanical engineering, the physical sciences, the natural sciences, together with agriculture and its allied subjects, and hygiene. The Fine Art section included drawing, painting, and design; modelling, engraving on wood and copper; etching and photography. The industrial section included 25 trades, covering nearly the whole range of the industrial arts. It comprised painting, several branches of the carpenter's art, including carriage-building, the tanning of leather and making it into boots and shoes, goldsmith's and jeweller's work, the repair of clocks and watches, the processes involved in the manufacture and design of textile fabrics, pottery, glass and paper-making, tailoring and the making of lace, the manufacture of tobacco, bread-baking, cookery, and the tuning of musical instruments.

These subjects could, it was believed, be taken up and taught in various degrees by the institutions already in existence for special and professional instruction. The chief of them were the Civil Engineering College, the School of Arts, and the Agricultural College. Different branches of science could also be added to the course in existing colleges for general instruction; and it was

was "not knowledge acting on material progress merely indirectly, but "knowledge which directly bears upon industrial development." The graduate in science of the Madras University did not, it was pointed out, learn his subject in such a way as would enable him to gain his living in any industrial pursuit in which the practical application of science was required. It was hoped that this would not be the case with those who gained the diplomas of the proposed examinations; but that they would " either as prao-"tical agriculturists, or veterinarians, or builders, or machinists, or telegraphists, "or electro-metallurgists, or designers, or cabinet-makers, or painters, or in "some other industrial pursuit, be competent to earn a livelihood." In the same way the artisan who was independently learning or practising his trade might find the advantage of attending classes for instruction in those scientific principles which bore on his particular craft, and thus make himself a more intelligent and capable workman. In the words of the Government Notification instituting these examinations,—" No candidate shall receive marks in "any science, art, or industry subject who, in the opinion of the examiners, "fails to show such an understanding of its principles as is necessary for a "useful practical application thereof;" and still more definitely, the "certifi-"cates shall certify that the holder is qualified to earn his livelihood by the "profession or trade in which he has been examined."

The work of the Department naturally ended with the provision of the means of technical instruction. It was a different question whether the demand for such instruction existed or would arise—an effective demand growing out of the needs of industrial life, and not merely a factitious demand created by the desire of obtaining certificates and prizes. In that condition obviously lies the justification of any large scheme of technical instruction. The state of manufacturing industry, of agriculture, of various arts, was held to justify confidence on this important point. "Good veterinarians will find "their services in demand, and so will good builders . . . . Trained machinists "have hitherto had to be brought out from England : a local supply would meet "a demand slowly but surely tending to increase. In all manufacturing indus-"tries . . . . there is a want of foremen and managers possessing higher tech-"nical knowledge; this is because the cost of imported skilled labour is often too "high to allow of its employment except by large capitalists, and it is often for "want of such that establishments do indifferently both industrially and financial-"ly. The workmen are generally so ignorant as to be unfit to rise to the higher "positions, while outsiders possessing the superior intelligence that is requisite in "a foreman or manager lack the practical skill. Men possessed of both qualifica-"tions are wanted, and would, as the value of the certified employé's labour be-"comes known, find many establishments willing to engage them. It is partly "on this account that certain industries, such as pottery, glass-making, carpet-"weaving and paper-making have been introduced into the test; because it is "hoped that in the Madras School of Arts arrangements may be made for their "study by a superior class of men, and that, as the fact becomes apparent that "improved productions will sell at higher prices, private capital may be invested "in large establishments, for which a superior class of workmen, foremen, and "managers will be necessary. At present pottery, for instance, is almost entirely "in the hands of individual workmen, whose want of means prevents their in-"vesting in the plant that is essential to improved working." The professed object of the system of examinations was therefore to test and certify to the possession of qualifications for which, it was alleged, an effective demand existed, and the wide acquisition of which would lead to increased and improved production in the arts and manufactures of the country.

226. The Bombay Scheme.—The Government of Bombay looked at the matter from a different point. "Examinations," it said, "will occupy a second-"ary position, because examinations are considered a corollary of good education, "but no sure test of it. The success of the scheme will depend on good teaching "rather than on multiplicity of examinations." And again :—"The scheme is not "academic . . . . because it is not intended for the academic but for the pro-"ducing classes. Its success cannot be tested by examinations, but rather by exhi-"bitions, and by statistics of imports and exports, prices and wages." In fact the Government of Bombay narrowed the question down to these two points—the classes to be technically educated, and the means of educating them. A preliminary expression of its views on the purpose and limits of technical instruction in India may here be summarised. Technical instruction aimed at the application to each art or industry of the scientific principles which governed and explained its processes. It did not supersede general education; it carried it to a higher stage, but in a special direction and for definite practical purposes. It could not create manufactures; it presupposed their existence and the possibility of their improvement. Technical education would supply skilled labour for the improvement of industries; but there was another indispensable factor, namely, capital. These three conditions—existing industries, capital, and skilled labour —determined the limits within which technical education could be usefully promoted; and they brought into prominence the great difference in the circumstances of England and of India. India was an agricultural country : and except in the Presidency town there were few manufactures. There was also but little capital seeking investment; and very little of that enterprising spirit which accepts the risks attendant on the investment of capital in new undertakings. There were, however, in India a number of highly artistic crafts, distinguished by great excellence in the disposition of form and colour, and with a well-marked individuality peculiar to the country. Their processes might be improved by modern science; but the first condition for reviving them was capital.

The provision of technical instruction had therefore to be considered under three main heads : (1) agriculture, (2) art industries, (3) mechanical industries. The best way of proceeding seemed to be to ascertain by careful inquiry local and special wants, and in correspondence therewith to establish or develope institutions for scientific instruction which would conform to, and not go much beyond, the actual desires and requirements of native managers, foremen, and artisans; improving them gradually, increasing their number, and developing their ingenuity and taste. The institutions to be established might be either disciplinary or professional. The object of the former was to give the pupil such general preliminary training as would enable him, when he afterwards selected his special occupation, to make faster and more intelligent progress than he would otherwise have done. In the latter, the object was to teach some particular art or industry with such completeness that at the end of his course the pupil could at once begin to practise it for his livelihood. In general, and more especially with regard to the mechanical industries, the establishment of the latter class of schools was not for the Government to undertake. It was a matter for the consideration of special trades and special localities, though Government aid might properly be given to such institutions. Their object would be the improvement of the manipulative skill already existing, by encouraging and holding up for imitation a higher style of finish. Such schools would be of the greatest use to the sons of handicraftsmen who practised special arts as a hereditary calling. The active co-operation of municipal and local boards and of private benefactors should be invited for the establishment of special trade-schools of this class. What Government might rightly concern itself with was the provision of such general scientific or artistic instruction in the different branches named as would give intending workmen a better start and better equipment for entering on their special career, whatever it might be.

The first of the industries was agriculture and its allied occupations. For teaching the higher agriculture, the Poona College of Science might be at once selected as the central institution. It possessed an experimental farm, workshops, machinery, the apparatus for physical and chemical instruction, geological and botanical museums, and a drawing school. Whatever else was shown to be necessary would be provided. Similarly, the agricultural teaching in high schools should be so improved as to form a fitting preparation for the advanced course in the College of Science. The agricultural classes now existing should be made both useful and attractive to the sons of actual cultivators; and local committees should be encouraged by the offer of aid to open similar classes where there seemed to be a demand for them.

For art teaching, the Bombay School of Art should be the centre of the efforts of Government. There were indigenous arts of a high degree of excellence, such as wood-carving, pottery, art metal-work, embroidery, enamelling, which could be taken in hand by the school with the object of resuscitating and fostering the artistic processes now on the wane. This could be done by procuring the best native workman in his own special branch, by giving him in the school a room or workshop fitted up with all the appliances of his art, by paying him a salary as a teacher in addition to profits on sales, and by stipulating that no work should be produced except what was artistically beautiful in design and finish. With all these aids it might be anticipated that the existing level of excellence would be maintained and raised. In connexion with the School of Art, rules had also been recently promulgated for the encouragement of drawing in ordinary schools by means of grants-in-aid, for which purpose an allotment of R10,000 a year had been sanctioned. In this way, through an unpretentious beginning, the School of Art might help to promote the diffusion of art throughout the Presidency in much the same way as South Kensington had done for the United Kingdom.

With regard to mechanical industries, the first question was the establishment of a technological institute on an adequate scale, with professors who must be appointed from Europe. This was held to be too ambitious for present requirements; and the best means of affording scientific and technical instruction of the advanced character that such an institute was intended to supply would be to send selected students, who had received a general though unapplied education in science, first to a cotton mill in Bombay, and afterwards to England or Germany where each might receive a full course of instruction, theoretical and practical, in his special branch. Apart, however, from the idea of a technological institute, it seemed possible to establish in Bombay, near the mills and railway workshops, an institution in which instruction might be given in those sciences which were necessary for the practical requirements, on the one hand of managers and foremen, and on the other of skilled artisan and operatives. The subjects to be taught in such an institution—introduced not all at once, but gradually and as the need developed itself—would be physics, practical mechanics, chemistry applied to the arts, the knowledge and sources of raw materials, the nature of tools, dyeing and bleaching, the drawing of plans and designs, the theory of colour and beauty, the manipulation of cotton, jute, wool and silk, their processes of manufacture and their conversion into woven fabrics, the construction of steam and other engines. The course of instruction in such a school must always be governed by its practical purpose, namely, to give the students a grasp of scientific facts which they could readily apply to any trade, and thus to constitute a training school for managers and foremen. Its location near the mills and shops was necessary, first, for the convenience of those employed therein; and, secondly, to afford opportunities for practical illustration of the lectures. For skilled artisans and operatives instruction of a lower kind would be provided. This could be given in evening classes, and should be confined to reading and writing, arithmetic, geometry, drawing, and modelling in clay. Such an institution could most usefully be started and managed by a representative committee, with aid from Government. Liberal aid would be given on condition that Government was represented on the committee, and that the institution was placed at first under a skilled technologist from England. Its establishment might usefully be preceded by an industrial exhibition, to which, it was anticipated, local manufacturers would send machines and other articles used in the various industries, with the object of presenting them afterwards to the Institute.

227. The Bengal Scheme.—In Bengal it is not so much that any definite scheme has been authoritatively adopted, as that several proposals of widely different character and scope have been submitted for the consideration of the Local Government, which meanwhile is prevented from taking action by the uncertainty of the financial outlook. It is difficult to make even a beginning without knowing the form and dimensions which the complete system will finally take. In the words of one of the experts consulted, it is essential that a scheme of technical instruction, no matter how small the beginning may be, should be a work of progress, not one of vacillation, nor at any stage one of retrogression. Meanwhile there is no lack of suggestions, and even of detailed projects, which have been advanced by persons entitled to speak with authority. The earliest of these proposals were made by Mr. A. Pedler, Professor of Chemistry in the Presidency College, and a former student of the Royal School of Mines, and by Mr. E. F. Mondy, Professor of Physics in the Civil Engineering College at Seebpore, and a Whitworth Scholar.

I.—Mr. Pedler, at the outset of his Note, puts a necessary limitation on the meaning of the term 'technical instruction.' This, he says, "cannot be con-"sidered to include the acquirement of sufficient technical skill in any trade, "industry, or profession, which can only be gained in the arts and manufactures "by the prolonged manual or other training which is obtained in the workshop. ". . . No system of technical instruction, however elaborate, could be devised, "which would turn out experienced workmen or manufacturers, or persons prac-"tically acquainted with the trades or professions they will subsequently have to "carry on." Technical instruction may therefore be defined to be, general and practical instruction in those sciences and arts, the principles of which are applicable to various employments in life. It should, therefore, follow general instruction; and it may, in different circumstances, either precede, accompany, or follow the actual manual practice of the trade or art concerned.

A preliminary condition is essential. It is, that general instruction, as supplied in the ordinary schools, should be so modified as to include elementary science and drawing—acquirements which for purposes of general education are as good as others, and which are indispensable as the foundation of technical education. Technical education, properly so called, would begin at a later stage. It would consist, first, of the further development of science, including the general principles common to all trades and industries; and, secondly, of the application of those principles to the special trade or industry to be followed. The persons to be instructed are of three classes, namely, artisans, foremen or managers, and teachers. The standard of instruction for these three classes would vary in character and would be in an ascending scale of difficulty. The higher instruction, whether for foremen or for teachers, would be carried on in

English, and preferably at a central institution. The lower instruction, to be imparted in the vernacular, would be much more widely diffused at local centres of industry. The higher instruction must necessarily precede the lower, so as to secure a supply of teachers for artisan classes in the vernacular. Mr. Pedler's Note is, therefore, chiefly confined to the higher education; and this, he thinks, should preferably be carried on in an institution to be closely connected with the Presidency College, the scientific lectures of which could be utilised for the benefit of technical as well as of general education.

The trades and professions which might be made the subject of technical instruction are divided into four groups, namely, (A) Applications of science; (B) Applications of art; (C) Agriculture; (D) Commerce. The courses of instruction for these classes would in many points overlap; and with the establishment of a central institution the teaching power would be economised. The sub-divisions of group A, which may be taken as a sample, include medicine and engineering: but as these are provided for in special colleges, they are not further considered in the Note. Group A will also include (1) industries dependent on the application of chemistry, such as dyeing, paper-making, sugar-refining, glass-manufacture, and many others; (2) those dependent on applications of geology and metallurgy, such as the industries connected with mining; (3) those dependent on electricity, such as telegraph-engineering; (4) those dependent partly on physical, partly on mechanical science, such as the textile industries; (5) those which are chiefly mechanical, such as the manufacture of cutlery, locks, electro-plate, clocks and watches, &c.

The scheme, therefore, in this and in its other developments, contemplates the establishment of a central technological institute, capable of being finally made adequate to the requirements of all existing trades and industries. Mr. Pedler guards himself, however, from the inference that all the corresponding courses of instruction should be started at once. Its fundamental principles once settled, it might begin on a moderate scale, applicable to those industries in which improved teaching seemed to be most required and most easily provided; and be enlarged hereafter in response to the demands of the community and the teachings of experience. But it would be a manifest mistake to commence any limited scheme which would be subsequently found unfit for expansion.

A brief sketch is given of the lines on which the lower or vernacular classes for artisans, to be established subsequently, should proceed. No workman can perform his work intelligently without an understanding of the general principles on which his work depends; and thus the course should include drawing in all its branches, elementary mathematics, chemistry and physics, practical mechanics, and general workshop instruction in the use of tools for working in wood and metals. The classes should be held in the evening; theoretical should be rigidly subordinated to practical instruction; and much attention would have to be given to the practical training of the workshop. In the foundation of such local vernacular schools, influential native gentlemen and committees might be invited and expected to co-operate.

II.—Mr. Mondy speaks with the authority of one who has intimate personal knowledge of the School of Naval Architecture and Marine Engineering at Portsmouth, of which he states his belief that "no technical school has ever "yet turned out such a body of competent professional men," and which indeed he takes as his model. That school is based on a system of apprenticeship; not indeed the old and now exploded system, under which the apprentices learnt only what the master-workmen could teach them, but the modern system under which the apprentices secure, not only a good workshop training, but such further instruction in the science and principles underlying their craft as will make them more intelligent and skilful workmen. The Naval School at Portsmouth is recruited from apprentices in the dockyard, each of whom is bound for a term of seven years, and is placed under a workman who instructs him in the practice of his craft. During a portion of this period the apprentice attends school on certain afternoons and evenings, where he learns mathematics and mechanics chiefly; but his attention is mainly given at this stage to the practical training. At the end of about four years, the more competent of the apprentices are drafted into the Naval School, when their ordinary work in the shops is discontinued, and their time, during the remainder of their period of apprenticeship, is divided between the school and the drawing-office; subject, however, to the condition that they have to spend the summer months of the three years' course in a dockyard or marine-engineering works. Of the men turned out by this system, Sir E. J. Reed, who was himself trained under it, said in the House of Commons in 1879 that he "did not believe there was a more "practical body of men in the country than the technical officers of the Ad- "miralty and Royal Dockyards. Nearly every man among them had begun "his profession with apprenticeship and had acquainted himself with the use of "tools." Mr. Mondy adds that there is scarcely a large shipbuilding establishment in the kingdom that has not at some time owned one or more of the pupils of the school among its responsible officers; that the whole Board of Construction of the Admiralty, together with a vast number of subordinate officers and skilled workmen, are taken from its past students; and that to this school belongs in the main the credit of the great revolution in the construction of the navies of the world that has taken place in the past twenty-five years; while nearer home it has for some time supplied the Bombay Dockyard with its Chief Constructors.

Institutions of this form, or that may be readily moulded to take this form, already exist in India. There is, for example, the system of apprenticeship in force in the Locomotive and Carriage Departments of the East Indian Railway. Apprentices are taken at 15 years of age, are bound for five years, and receive liberal and increasing rates of pay. During their term of apprenticeship they are required to attend the night school for three or four evenings a week. The apprentices are selected without any examination, probably with very little general instruction of any kind; and hence the standard attainable in the night school is very low. But the system follows the correct principle and contains the germ of improvement. It would be well for employers of labour, or failing them even for Government, to establish schools on a similar plan in the neighbourhood of all great industrial centres. They should be subject to examination and inspection, and should be supported and encouraged by grants-in-aid, and especially by scholarships for the more promising pupils, tenable in technical schools of a higher stamp.

But the most advanced and successful institution of the kind is the Civil Engineering College at Seebpore. The students are divided into two classes, engineers and apprentices. The preliminary test for admission to either class is purely literary; for the engineer class it is the Entrance examination, for the apprentice class a special college examination of a lower standard is held. For apprentices, it is true, no technical knowledge previous to admission is necessary, except that they would be far better equipped for their work if they had learnt drawing and elementary science at school. But for engineers Mr. Mondy thinks the present system altogether faulty. Following the example of the Naval School, he would have the engineer classes recruited exclusively from the apprentices in the lower department, and from other similar institutions elsewhere, so that

neering profession by their work both in class and in the shop. Furthermore, he believes the existing combination of school and shop-work, which is in force for both classes at Seebpore, to be unsound. The apprentices spend about four hours a day in the school and three hours in the workshop; and in addition, they pass their last eighteen months of apprenticeship in the workshop exclusively. Notwithstanding that proviso, it is clear that shop-work of three hours a day is altogether insufficient to turn out a competent workman; while at the same time it is a fatal hindrance to the studies of the schoolroom, especially in a hot climate. During the whole time of apprenticeship, be it five years or less, the theoretical instruction should be strictly subordinated to practical work, and should be given in evening or other occasional classes. In the engineer classes it has already been found necessary to reduce the time spent in the shops, originally fixed at two and a half hours a day, on account of its interference with the severe study which the University course demands. On the understanding that these classes are to be recruited from apprentices who have gone through a systematic training in the shops, Mr. Mondy is of opinion that manual work should be entirely suspended at this stage of an engineer's education, except so far as concerns the making of models or the carrying on of mechanical experiments in illustration of the course, for which purpose a workshop should be provided, fitted with the usual benches and machine-tools and with motive power. The present combination of theoretical and practical work necessitates a long period of rest. Under the proposed system no long holidays would be necessary, and the time now devoted to them could be usefully spent in visiting and taking part in works in progress. In this way also the term spent in college could be shortened. The practical professions to which the proposed system may be held to apply are civil and mechanical engineering, mining, metallurgy, architecture, telegraphy and naval construction.

To clear the ground, it may here be stated that Mr. Mondy's proposals are incompatible with the existing system under which the higher education in engineering is controlled by the University, since all candidates for its degrees must have passed the Entrance examination. In order to carry them out, the connexion of the Seebpore College with the University must be severed—a proposal which has been independently mooted. A further difficulty lies in the fact that the apprentice classes elsewhere, unlike that at Seebpore, will generally be composed of men who have no knowledge of English, and are therefore unable to profit by the advanced instruction which the college supplies.

All that has preceded relates to those industries in which skilled labour is of the chief importance. Mr. Mondy next turns to the manufacturing industries, in which manual skill is of subordinate value, and scientific principles and processes are more prominently involved. The second stage in the foregoing scheme, that is, the initial practical course immediately following on general education at school, should here be replaced by a sound scientific education of a general character; to be followed finally by special technical courses adapted to the particular requirements of different branches of industry. A scheme of this kind would apply, not only to manufactures, involving close attention to industrial chemistry, but also to such practical professions as agriculture, forestry, and geology, in each of which it would be advisable for the student to spend some months of each year in field work or out-door practice.

A word is added as to the value of technological museums, which are described as the necessary accompaniment of every system of technical instruction. The collections should include specimens of all materials of economic value belonging to the animal, vegetable, or mineral kingdom, with products of the various stages of manufacturing the raw material into the finished article of commerce; together with a series of models or actual examples of the machines and appliances used or produced in the manufacturing arts and practical industries. A central museum of this character in India should contain collections of all industries now at work in the country, and of those which are likely at any future time to be introduced; while local museums would be confined to illustrative specimens of the local industries and manufactures.

III.—Mr. F. J. Spring, Under-Secretary to the Government of Bengal in the Public Works Department, has devoted much study to the question of technical instruction, and has written much on the subject. It has been alleged that the chief obstacle to the success of any scheme of technical instruction in India, however theoretically perfect, is the absence of capital. Without capital their can be no manufactures, and therefore no means of employing those who have received a technical education aimed at the improvement of manufactures. On that point Mr. Spring remarks:—"European capital is lying in millions, "only waiting for investment in Indian industrial enterprise when it shall have "been proved that such investment is likely to be profitable." If it be asked—Where are the arts, where are the manufactures, where are the industries to be fostered and encouraged?—the answer is, They will surely come; industrial education will show the way to capital.

Mr. Spring's suggestions cover, however, much wider ground than the introduction of new industries. They are divided under the following heads: agricultural instruction, trade schools, technical schools for indigenous handicraftsmen, factory schools for artisans, factory schools for foremen, survey schools, training schools, and technical colleges.

(1) Agricultural instruction can best be imparted, not in special schools or classes, but as a part of the course in ordinary schools for general instruction. The proper text-book suited to each class of schools should be drawn up by the Agricultural Department, and should contain such things as the ordinary ryot ought to know; such things, for example, as the use of ground-bone manure, the advantages of light or deep ploughing, the amount of juice to be extracted from a given quantity of sugarcane, the rearing of cattle, the improvement of breeds, and the treatment of common diseases.

(2) Trade schools are intended to supply a deficiency of ordinary craftsmen in certain localities, where the caste system of hereditary apprenticeship does not exist. Thus in backward places like Chota Nagpore, there are very few carpenters or smiths such as are found elsewhere, and those few of very inferior quality. The same may be said of certain communities, such as Eurasians and Native Christians, which have no hereditary system of apprenticeship. In these cases it is necessary to establish trade-schools, as the missionaries have so frequently done, not primarily with the object of improving, but with that of introducing, the industries whose want is felt. If a workman of superior skill can be engaged, and if the pupils can be taught to read and write while they are learning their trade, it will be so much the better; but the immediate object is to create artisans such as are found in more thriving communities.

(3) Of an entirely different kind are the technical schools which have been or may be established with the object of improving the quality of indigenous industries, such as the leather trade of Cawnpore, the glass trade of Patna and Bombay, the silk industry of many parts of Bengal and the Central Provinces, the pottery, cutlery, and metal-work trades which have existed in different localities for many generations, and which are threatened with extinction in the competition with European manufactures. With the distinctive characteristics of these arts, with local specialities of form and colour, it is essential not to interfere. These are the qualities which alone enable them to hold their own, and any attempt at "improvement" in these points might end in the ruin of the industry. The instruction should be confined strictly to *technique*, as to

which the indigenous trades have much to learn from western science; and it is probable that instruction so limited might be made of immense advantage to the hereditary artificers, who are sufficiently alive to their own interests to adopt with eagerness any method which they see to be an improvement upon their traditional processes. At the centre of some indigenous industry a model factory should be opened on a scale not far beyond that of those around it, and placed under a scientifically trained workman who would generally have to be imported from Europe. To this factory should be invited at stated times the leading men of the trade, who might thus be taught such improvements of method as they might afterwards, without much trouble or expense, carry out in their own work. As soon as the model factory had done its work in one place, it should be closed and transferred to another. In this way it might be possible so to improve those arts which are not purely decorative, as to make them capable of supplying the requirements of the great services of the country, which now look to English manufacturers for their current needs.

As an alternative to the establishment of local factories to serve as models to Indian artificers, another plan for the improvement of indigenous industries has also been suggested, to which a passing reference may now be given. If a central technological institute is at any time established, its Principal will be (or should be) a man who has made a study of the history and processes of manufactures. He need not be a master of any one trade; but he will be familiar with machines in general, he will be acquainted with labour-saving appliances, and he will know what are the successive improvements, chemical or mechanical, by which the principal manufactures have been brought to their present state of perfection. Such men are to be found in Europe—men of wide information, of shrewd business capacity, and of practical experience and manual skill. A weaver from Dacca, a glass-worker from Patna, or a silk-spinner from Nasik, is brought down with the rude appliances of his craft, and is located for a year in the central institute, where he will carry on his manufacture under the trained eye of the Principal. It is reasonable to suppose that the latter, with his practical experience and skill, and with an ample technological library at his command, would be able to discover, in the traditional processes of manufacture, faults capable of easy remedy, and practicable improvements such as to increase the value or the outturn of the work. An essential condition is that the workman, having practised and acquired skill in the new processes, and having recognised their money-value to himself, should carry them back to his home and continue to practise them. Nothing more is then required; for the improved machines or processes, provided they are simple enough for general adoption, will certainly and in no long time drive out the old. A good deal is said about the conservative character of the Indian workman, but in practice it has not been found to prevent the adoption of new means of making money, where the means are easy and the profit sure.

(4) In the establishment of schools for factory operatives we touch firmer ground. They will generally be night schools, in which apprentices and artisans can be taught those things which will train their intelligence and make them better and more skilful workmen. The "universal language of drawing" is an essential element in all schools of this class. There is scarcely a trade in which ability to understand a sketch is not of the greatest assistance to a workman. Instruction should also be given in the materials, the processes, and all that relates to the manufacture and distribution of the products of the special industry concerned. Schools of such a kind should be established, as part of a regular and organised system, in connexion with the locomotive and carriage manufactories of railways, with the cotton-mills of Bombay, the jute-mills and paper-mills of Bengal, the sugar factories of Bengal and the North-Western Provinces, and in all well-established centres of European enterprise.

(5) For the training of foremen and managers there are two opposing systems. One is that of a central institute, in which men without previous experience are trained through some years of class-work and shop-work to such a standard of intelligence and manual skill as will enable them to become efficient foremen in any kind of industry. The alleged drawback to this system is that, rightly or wrongly, employers of labour are unwilling to trust the control of workshops and machinery to men with whose merits they are unacquainted, and who have had no previous training in the particular industry which they will be called on to supervise. This defect does not attach to the alternative scheme, under which advanced instruction is given to selected men, in the factory schools just referred to, in such subjects as mathematics, mechanics, drawing, modelling, and the special technology of their trade. With such a training, picked workmen from the factories could gradually be brought to take the place of the foremen and managers now imported at great expense from Europe. An example is given from the weaving school at Glasgow, a student from which would, after a two years' course of instruction, be competent to take a picture, cut cards for it, put it in the loom, weave it, and calculate its cost. It is hoped that the proprietors of some of the great Indian mills may establish schools of this class for the benefit, primarily of their operatives, but ultimately of their business.

(6) Survey schools of a cheap and unpretentious kind are much needed and easy to establish. In Bengal there is no hereditary class of *amins* (who in other provinces where they exist are generally incompetent); and for the purposes of the newly-constituted Agricultural Department it is of great importance to train up a class of vernacular surveyors on low pay, who should be able, not indeed to lay out a line of railway, but to survey an area and measure fields. The best way would be to teach simple area-surveying to a large number of village schoolmasters and others, who would be able, when called upon, to take up jobs of this kind in addition to their regular duties. (Mr. Spring refers to the course of surveying taught in the engineering colleges, and considers it too ambitious for the purpose that he has in view. He is apparently not aware that in Bengal extensive provision of the kind that he desires is already made; not only in the vernacular survey schools at Dacca, Patna, and Cuttack, but still more largely by the inclusion of mensuration and surveying in the course of instruction in all training schools for masters, as well as in the standard examinations of middle and primary schools.)

(7) For the training of teachers, Mr. Spring looks forward to a time when there will be established in each Presidency " a central school of industrial art, " or normal technical institute," which will be able to supply teachers for every subordinate technical school, however advanced may be the instruction required. Meanwhile the instructors must be obtained from different sources. For trade and apprenticeship schools the best workman procurable must be obtained; and the elementary general instruction which the pupils are to receive must be provided in the ordinary way. Such schools should have an eye to the sale of their manufactured articles, and the proceeds of sales will go some way towards paying the cost of establishment. Factory schools may be placed under selected men who have passed out from the engineering colleges. Competent men can easily be found to teach elementary surveying to large vernacular classes. For the technical schools designed for the improvement of indigenous industries, artistic and other, it will generally be necessary to procure specially skilled men from Europe.

(8) Of the engineering colleges Mr. Spring expresses the opinion that their theoretical instruction is overdone. The work which falls to a passed student on obtaining employment is for many years of so commonplace a character

that he has no opportunity for utilising the high mathematics and somewhat advanced science which he has been learning with so much pains. The inference is that a modification of the existing course in the direction of simplicity and greater thoroughness would turn out a more useful man all round. At the same time the dissociation of these colleges from the University is deprecated as a retrograde step.

Meanwhile the course and constitution of the Seebpore Engineering College, the most important school of technical instruction in Bengal, are undergoing careful investigation at the hands of a committee. It is understood that the form which its recommendations are likely to take includes the separation of the manual from the theoretical course, the simplification of the latter, and its reduction from four years to three; a compulsory course of instruction for six months in the nature and use of tools; an optional course of eighteen months' practical training, spent partly in the workshop and partly in the brickfields or on works in progress; the recognition of a college certificate for those students who either fail at, or do not attempt, the University examination; and the reservation of the highest appointments in the gift of the Government for those candidates who have attained the B. E. degree and have also passed through the final practical course of eighteen months. The course for apprentices will be liable to similar modification. Of the five years which they are now required to serve, the first three and a half are devoted to manual and class work jointly; one year being passed in the carpenter's shop, one year in the blacksmith's, one year in the fitter's, and six months in the moulding shop. Then for the remaining eighteen months of their apprenticeship, which is confined to manual work, they spend five and a half hours a day in any shop they may select. The value of this course is attested by the active demand that exists for the passed apprentices, who obtain good employment without difficulty and are a thoroughly well-trained and useful class of men. The changes which have been proposed are the following:—the simplification of the theoretical course, which is thought to be somewhat too advanced for this class of artisans; its reduction to three years; the separation of students, after their combined manual and theoretical course of three years, into two classes, one for civil and one for mechanical apprentices, who should devote the remaining two years to practical work in the field or the shops; and the drafting of mechanical apprentices for their final two years to the great railway and other workshops. Connected with this is a useful proposal to connect the hill schools, which are attended largely by the sons of railway employés, with the Seebpore College and the railway workshops, leading ultimately to railway employment.

In addition to the classes for engineers, civil overseers or clerks of works, and foremen mechanics, it has also been proposed to establish classes for land and estate management, for veterinary practice, for telegraphic employ, for account-keeping, and for the scientific and practical instruction of superior artisans. If these proposals were carried out, the Seebpore College would acquire much of the character of a central technological institute, except that it would not concern itself with the training of workmen or managers for special manufacturing industries.

IV. Mr. C. H. Tawney, Officiating Director of Public Instruction in Bengal, while commending large schemes like those of Mr. Pedler as indicating an ultimate object of effort, is content for the present with proposals of a more moderate scope. The University of Calcutta has rejected the plan of an alternative Entrance examination of a practical character, and Mr. Tawney is of opinion that a departmental examination of the same kind should now be instituted, with classes leading up to it in selected high schools, and a system of rewards for teachers who qualify in drawing. He is also desirous of attaching to selected high schools practical classes varying with the locality; in one place a commercial, in another an agricultural class; while upon other schools technical branches might be grafted, looking up and leading to the Engineering College or the School of Art. Detached and isolated industrial schools, having no definite connexion with the general system of education, he regards with little favour. But what he chiefly advocates, as being at once easy to carry out and of assured practical utility, is the establishment of schools or classes in connexion with railway workshops for the instruction, in different subjects and standards, of the apprentices, operatives, and foremen employed therein. For such schools the co-operation of the railway authorities would be essential. A central technological institute belongs, probably, to a more or less distant future; but meanwhile our preliminary and tentative efforts should be directed by, and take their shape from, a governing idea of this character, so that all parts may fall into their right places in a general scheme of technical instruction as the system is gradually developed.

228. General Remarks on Technical Instruction.—From all that has preceded, and from the Note on Technical Education drawn up by command of the Viceroy, it will now be possible to elicit some general principles for practical guidance, and to ascertain what technical education can and what it cannot do. In the first place it is abundantly clear that technical education will not create trades; except in a few well-defined instances, it must follow in the wake of trades already established. Nor, when the trades exist, will technical education by itself create skilled artisans. The artisans must learn their trade independently; and the office of technical instruction is to make them more capable and skilful workmen, either by teaching them improved processes in the art which they already practise, or by educating the hand and eye in drawing, modelling, and the use of tools of precision, or by instructing the students in those branches of mathematics or science or technology with which their art is directly concerned. The exceptions to the rule are found in those cases in which the appliances of the art are so compact and handy that the school is itself the factory; such are the trades of wood-engraving, wood-carving, metal-chasing, and similar applications of Fine Art to industry. The School of Art may thus be made, as it has been made, the means not only of improving existing trades, but of introducing them into places where they are as yet unknown. Other instances of the same kind have been already referred to, such as the opening of a carpentry school and shop in places or among communities where the trade does not exist; or again, that most useful class of trade-schools in which a standard of skill beyond that of the bazar is secured by the employment, for example, of Chinese carpenters or of those who have been trained in workshops on the European scale. But with these well-marked exceptions, technical instruction must follow and cannot create trades or industries. This condition being understood, it is possible to grapple with the question how far existing arts and industries can be improved by a well-devised scheme of technical instruction. The method which seems to carry the greatest promise of permanent utility is, not to borrow a scheme from other countries in which the industrial conditions may be altogether different, but to start from the sure basis of facts, and to consider for each province, each district, each large town or commercial centre, what are the industries which exist and in which increased skill is attainable, and by what means in each case the necessary improvement can be effected.

The chief drawback to technical education hitherto has been its fragmentary and isolated character, its want of a governing principle. To be effective, **technical education should be combined into a comprehensive system, in which** the lower course not only serves its own special purposes, but leads to a more complete course elsewhere. The factory school, for example, should not merely train the intelligence, the dexterity, and the observing powers of the artisans and apprentices who attend it, but should be so framed as to help forward promising pupils to more advanced instruction in an engineering college or a technological institute. The lower course should be ancillary to, and governed by, the higher. Again, if technical branches are opened in connexion with high schools, it is not sufficient that they should be of a "practical" character, that they should teach drawing or chemistry instead of history or languages, in the hope that in some undefined way industries will thereby be extended or improved. They should be established with a definite aim and to serve a definite purpose; and by this their course will be determined. To take an example, already cited, from the hill schools for Europeans: the practical course should be such as to qualify the pupils for admission to the engineering college which they are afterwards to join. It may even go beyond the actual requirements of the initial examination, provided the advance is always along the lines of the future course. In this way the question—difficult enough on *a priori* grounds—whether the "bifurcation" of studies should begin at or below the middle stage of secondary schools, will be decided in each case by the special needs it is intended to serve. This condition will not prevent the special course from having an independent value of its own, such as is claimed, for example, for the drawing and agricultural classes of Bombay. The drawing course is not less valuable because it also forms the best preparation for the Bombay School of Art; while, as a matter of history, the agricultural classes were originally established for the benefit of students intended for the Poona College of Science, and finally, it was hoped for a degree in Agriculture. Only by attending to this condition of mutual dependence and subordination will technical instruction in India lose that isolated and fragmentary character which has hitherto been a hindrance and a reproach to it, as the Note of the Home Department clearly shows. And it will not be forgotten that when once technical schools have been started on an interdependent and mutually related basis, it will be possible to require of candidates for admission to the higher institutions something more than the merely literary knowledge which they now bring.

But it is necessary to guard against another danger, clearly seen by many. It is that of narrowing the intelligence by giving a technical bent to instruction at too early a stage. General intelligence—that cultivation and enlightenment which proceed from an all-round development of the mental powers, from the play of the faculties upon diverse objects of thought—is as necessary to the engineer as to the lawyer or doctor. The lines of the engineer's business are indeed so specialised, so exclusively technical—much more so, it is probable, than the lawyer's or the doctors—that there would seem to be peculiar need to give breadth to his earlier education, in order to counteract that narrowing influence in after life, and enable him to hold his own in the competition he will have to meet. An engineer of great practical experience has publicly stated that to enter upon the engineering profession, a boy needs nothing more than a good general education, the best that can be given him up to the age of 16 or 18. This of course would not preclude the choice of some subjects as being more suitable than others for the future engineer, provided they had the same value as instruments of mental training; nor would it preclude the acquirement of an accomplishment like drawing, useful in nearly every walk of life, and particularly useful to the engineer. But the warning against too great specialisation of study in early years is worth consideration by those who have to deal practically with this question.

Another point of cardinal importance is that any scheme of technical instruction, to be successful, must be governed by the extent of the actual or probable demand; the demand existing at any time not merely for technical instruction, but for the technically instructed. All has not been done when we have opened classes for technical instruction in this or that branch, or even when we have filled them. We must satisfy ourselves, first, that the instruction is sought for on its own account, and not merely in response to the artificial stimulus of scholarships or rewards, or to the attractions of novelty; and secondly, that in the existing conditions of industrial life, the men so educated will find useful and lucrative employment. If a commercial class is to be opened, teaching, for example, book-keeping, short-hand, and political economy, a necessary preliminary would be to ascertain whether these are the precise acquirements which employers of that kind of labour look for in their clerks, or which those engaged in commerce on their own account have found most useful. It would seem that the Education Department cannot answer this question until the Chambers of Commerce and the great railway companies have been consulted. So again, if it is a question of an agricultural class; it is necessary to find out by exact inquiry from the Agricultural Department or from district officers, what things a ryot or a landholder (according to the class of school) ought to know and does not; or what acquirements in agriculture and the connected sciences will give a man a marketable value as the manager of a large estate.

It has been urged with much force that in estimating the extent of the demand, we should take into account the probable enlargement of the demand which will result from a supply of the means of technical instruction. Besides the industries that exist, other industries, it is urged, for which there seems to be ample room, stand ready to be called into existence as soon as the conditions are favourable. At present the difficulty is two-fold : capital waits for skilled labour; skilled labour waits for capital. There is no demand for technical. instruction, because the industries in which it could be utilised do not exist. The industries do not exist because, in the absence of indigenous skilled labour, capital cannot be employed on them to advantage. Provide technical instruction, and each obstacle disappears in turn. India has already an enormous advantage in the low rate of wages for factory hands; that advantage would be greatly increased if the skilled labour of the native manager could be substituted for the more costly agency of the foreman imported from Europe. Meanwhile, capital is shy of entering into competition with the old and highly-developed industries of Europe, while the cost of management, added to the other causes that hamper a new industry, renders uncertain the prospect of a return for its outlay. Such is the contention; but the argument must not be pushed too far. Jute and cotton mills, sugar mills, paper mills, are all examples of European industries successfully transplanted to India; but in every case, it is believed, managers have been imported from Europe to establish them. There is a great demand in India for the more simple manufactures, such as glass, soap, and matches; but it will probably be found that capital will not risk itself upon them without the aid of European supervision. Practical experience is an absolutely essential condition ; not to be superseded by any degree of theoretical skill, which can only acquire the necessary experience through a series of costly and perhaps disastrous experiments. To take an illustrative case. It is stated in a recent report on the trade of India that $3\frac{1}{2}$ millions of umbrellas were imported into India in 1886-87. If any one were to establish an umbrella manufactory to meet this enormous demand, he would probably prefer as his manager a man who had already spent some years in the business, to a student who had learnt the principles of umbrella-making in a technological institute.

It seems unlikely therefore that the establishment of a central technological college will, of itself, go far to create or introduce new industries in competition with those of Europe. But when once the industries have been established, technological education may come to their aid by supplying them with trained men able to fill at first subordinate positions, and afterwards places of greater responsibility and power as practical experience is gained. It has also been shown of what service such a central institute might be in giving further scientific and technological instruction to those who gave signs of ability in local factories and factory schools. For such purposes the civil engineering colleges, in their mechanical branches, form technological institutes of a special kind. The trained students of these colleges go out to take either independent or subordinate charge of the machinery of mills and factories; while in the same colleges advanced instruction may hereafter be supplied to that useful class of pupils who have received some training and shown some promise in local workshops. For the present it seems that the development of the Indian engineering colleges to the highest attainable point of efficiency is the best and most practicable means of forwarding technical instruction. Machinery has still to be imported in large quantities from abroad, and that constitutes a further drawback to be establishment of new industries. The training of large numbers of students as mechanical engineers may help to pave the way hereafter to the local manufacture of machinery in increasing quantities; and meanwhile the men thus trained will not have lost their labour, for they will find congenial and suitable employment in factories and mills. Not necessarily as managers; for the European employer of labour knows the average Dundee mechanic, his merits and his defects; knows, for example, that if anything goes wrong with the machinery, he can be trusted to turn to and work for thirty-six hours at a stretch to avert a catastrophe; while he has not the same assurance about the student of an engineering college in India, because as yet he knows him not. That consideration affords a further ground for urging that the instruction given in engineering colleges should be as thorough and practical as possible. A technological college in a more comprehensive sense is not so immediately pressing a necessity; and it is an essential condition that, when started, it should be started on a moderate scale, and in close subordination to the actual state of manufacturing industry, whether indigenous or transplanted. Factory schools for workmen, in which advanced classes might be opened as the need developes itself, should be established wherever practicable, but always with the co-operation of the managers, who would be indeed the best persons to undertake them. The standard of general education is not so high among Indian as among English operatives, and it would be a mistake to look for equal results at the outset; but so far as they go, there can be little doubt about the utility of factory schools. By a wise development of art teaching in the Schools of Art new industries can be gradually taught and established; though here again it would be a mistake to expect great results among communities that have not in any high degree the hereditary artistic faculty, as in Bengal. The final, if not very satisfactory, conclusion seems to be that technical education can only advance rapidly in a country where the industries and manufactures are highly developed; that India is not such a country; and that it is a fallacy to suppose that any scheme of technical instruction will open out a royal road to industrial prosperity, the attainment of which depends upon far different conditions.

Section VI.—FEMALE EDUCATION.

229. Difficulties in the way of Female Education.—The obstacles that beset the progress of female education in India, as explained by the Education Commission, may be summarised as follows:—(1) There is no demand, in the case of girls and women, for education as a means of livelihood; and thus the most effective stimulus to the spread of education is removed. Some desire exists for the education of girls on independent grounds; but however genuine, it is of recent origin, of slow growth, and of very limited extent. (2) The system of child-marriage necessitates the seclusion of girls at an age when their education has scarcely begun. (3) The supply of teachers for girls' schools is both insufficient in quantity and inferior in quality; and under the present social conditions of India there is no class likely to yield a large and steady supply of female teachers. (4) The State system of instruction, as regards control, inspection, and text-books, has been framed with a view to the requirements of boys; and it needs modification in many important points if the education of girls is to receive due encouragement. To these difficulties may be added the belief, perhaps more widely felt than expressed, that the general education of women means a social revolution the extent of which cannot be foreseen. Native gentlemen, advanced and enlightened enough in ordinary matters, are hampered by the dread that when the women of the country begin to be educated and to learn independence, harassing times are in store for them. They may thoroughly allow that when the process has been completed, the nation will rise in intelligence, in character, and in all the graces of life. But they are none the less apprehensive that while the process of education is going on; while the lessons of emancipation are being learnt and stability has not yet been reached; while, in short, society is slowly struggling to adjust itself to the new conditions: the period of transition will be marked by the loosening of social ties, the upheaval of customary ways, and by prolonged and severe domestic embarrassment. There is, it is true, an advanced section of the community that is entirely out of sympathy with these views. In abandoning child-marriage they have got rid of the chief obstacle to female education; and it is among them, consequently, that female education has made the greatest progress in quantity and still more in quality. Girls of this section of the community remain at school long enough to complete the high school course and to pass the Entrance examination; while in Bengal a considerable number have advanced to a still higher standard, and have been admitted in Convocation to the degrees of B. A. and M. A., amid the loud plaudits of the male students. The Native Christian community are in like manner subject to no necessary restrictions as to early marriage; and missionary effort has been steadily directed for many years to the education of Christian girls. No doubt, the standard of education is generally low; for, on the one hand, it is not among the prosperous or leisured classes that conversions to Christianity are mostly made, and, on the other, custom still goes for a great deal, even among converts, in determining the age at which a girl should marry. But it is important to remember that the first female candidate to matriculate at any Indian University was a Native Christian, educated at the Mission School at Dehra Dun in the North-Western Provinces.

The foregoing remarks do not of course apply to European and Eurasian girls, who are educated to the same extent as boys are, and who in fact supply three-fifths of the pupils in English secondary girls' schools. Nor do they apply to Parsis and Jews. But outside these small and well-marked classes, the demand for female education is much less active and spontaneous. It may indeed be said hardly to exist. Girls' schools, it is true, are being established all over the country in steadily, if not rapidly, increasing numbers; and the increase in attendance goes on at a still greater rate. But the figures given in the first section of this chapter enable us to supply an accurate test of the nature and extent of the demand. They show that out of 40,000 females in India, that is, out of about 6,000 girls of a school-going age, no more than 100 girls are at school. They show, further, that out of this 100, only 2 girls have advanced beyond the primary standard, while nearly 34 are in that rudimentary stage in which the simplest printed primer is not yet read. If the classes above-named, among whom there is a real and effective desire for education, be separated, the percentage of those in the secondary stage will be reduced still further. In fact, the people of India at large encourage or tolerate the education of their girls only up to an age and in standards at which it can do little good or, according to the point of view, little harm. That it has made such progress as it has made is probably due to several causes. Girls' schools are to some extent the fashion; they are regarded as a mark of civilisation and enlightenment; they are the theme of constant exhortations addressed to the people by educational and other officers; and those who are urged to establish them have an uneasy feeling that they can put forward no valid grounds for the refusal they would often prefer to give. There appear, however, to be great varieties of provincial feeling. In Madras and Bombay, the desire for female education, however limited, is said to be steady and genuine. In Bengal, a different view is expressed, though within the limited region of high education a remarkable beginning has been made. In the North-Western Provinces, Sir Alfred Lyall was of opinion that the mere establishment of schools would do little towards the spread of education among women; "before any considerable progress is obtained, the natives must them-
" selves lend their co-operation and full assent to the administrative measures
" of Government, and a public opinion less indifferent to the education of
" women must be formed." In the Punjab, similarly, Sir Charles Aitchison was convinced that the difficulties which beset female education were not to be solved either by the recommendations of the Commission or by the most zealous action of Government, though the healthy growth of public opinion among the native community might be hastened by sympathetic action and by liberal and judicious aid on the part of Government officers. In the Punjab, and also in the Central Provinces, there was no difficulty about low-caste girls; the difficulty was to induce girls of respectable position to come to school. As to Sind, the feeling is thus expressed. It is only in large municipalities, where the Chairmen of the school boards are enlightened men, that any advance in female education is to be looked for. In such places, also, the agitation against early marriage, which is now being carried on by the reforming Hindu party, will tend to keep girls longer at school. "But in the " districts and the small municipal towns," writes the Inspector, "I fear we " can expect no progress for some time to come, as the feeling of the mass of " the people is undoubtedly adverse to female education."

230. Primary Schools for Girls, 1885-86.—The subjoined table shows the number of primary schools for girls in each province of India; and in the last column the number of girls reading in boys' schools:

Primary Schools for Girls.

PROVINCE.	MANAGED BY THE DEPARTMENT.		MANAGED BY LOCAL AND MUNICIPAL BOARDS.		AIDED.		UNAIDED.		TOTAL.		REMARKS.
	Schools.	Pupils.	Schools.	Pupils.	Schools.	Pupils.	Schools.	Pupils.	Schools.	Pupils.	
											Girls in Boys' Schools.
Madras	30	1,807	34	1,541	370	13,795	192	6,335	626	23,478	21.075
Bombay	135a	7,135	236	14,497	71	6,327	3	104	445	28,063	14,284
Bengal	...	...	4	159	2,038	38,521	244	3,948	2,286	42,628	33,208
N.-W. Provinces	...	...	170	3,796	173	5,411	8	186	351	9,393	
Punjab	2	122	129	3,385	167	6,044	1	22	299	9,573	
Central Provinces	37b	1,775	29	1,241	34	1,572	6	214	106	4,802	259
Burma	...	...	8	470	7	285	...	...	15	755	12,720
Assam	1	26	105	1,560	43	884	26	328	175	2,798	1,850
Berar	37	758	4	195	...	...	...	...	31	953	151
Coorg	...	...	...	...	3	55	...	...	3	55	425
TOTAL	232	11,623	719	26,844	2,906	72,894	480	11,137	4,337	122,498	88,922
TOTAL FOR 1884-85	209c	10,423	662	24,966	2,988	69,913	347	8,139	4,206	113,441	80,149

a Including 133 schools with 6,921 pupils in Native States.
b Including one school with 77 pupils in a Native State.
c Including 121 schools with 6,370 pupils in Native States.

Madras and Bombay contribute additions of 47 and 43 schools respectively to the total. There is an increase in the number of schools in every province except two. In Bengal the general policy followed with regard to small and weak schools has had some effect upon schools for girls also; there is a loss of nine schools in that province, but on the other hand a gain of 2,500 pupils. In the Punjab ten schools have been closed, and there is a loss of 278 pupils. Altogether there is a gain of 131 girls' schools and of 9,057 pupils reading in them. There is also an increase of 3,773 in the number of girls reading in boys' schools.

In considering the classification of schools under different heads of control, it will appear that the number of aided schools has fallen, and that of unaided schools increased. This result arises in Bengal, where more than 100 schools previously aided have been transferred to the unaided class. The primary girls' schools maintained by district and municipal boards are three times as numer-

231. Secondary Schools for Girls, 1885-86.

The details are given in the following table:—

Secondary Schools for Girls.

Province.	Managed by the Department.		Managed by Local and Municipal Boards.		Aided.		Unaided.		Total.		Remarks.
	Schools.	Pupils.	Schools.	Pupils.	Schools.	Pupils.	Schools.	Pupils.	Schools.	Pupils.	
Madras—											Girls in Boys' Schools.
English	1	165	1	72	104	5,977	6	398	112	6,612	772
Vernacular	20	1,676	3	279	58	4,685	4	479	85	7,119	154
Bombay—											
English	1	69	1	17	47	2,705	...	...	49	2,791	401
Bengal—											
English	2	201	...	...	28	2,158	5	498	35	2,857	462
Vernacular	...	...	...	...	15	808	...	...	15	808	688
N.-W. Provinces—											
English	...	...	...	...	17	1,443	3	68	20	1,511	...
Vernacular	...	...	...	...	2	157	...	...	2	157	...
Punjab—											
English	1	208	...	...	8	399	...	...	9	607	...
Vernacular	...	...	...	...	1	48	...	...	1	48	...
Central Provinces—											
English	...	...	...	...	3	68	1	15	4	83	7
Burma—											
English	...	...	1	88	10	963	...	...	11	1,051	389
Vernacular	...	...	...	...	2	163	...	...	2	163	319
Assam—											
English	1	10	...	...	...	...	...	...	1	10	...
Vernacular	...	...	...	...	3	87	...	...	3	87	37
Total—											
English	6	653	3	177	217	13,713	15	979	241	15,522	3,246 girls' in boys' schools.
Vernacular	20	1,676	3	279	81	5,948	4	479	108	8,382	
	26	2,329	6	456	298	19,661	19	1,458	349	23,904	
Total for 1884-85—											
English	7	688	3	103	184	12,061	16	1,050	210	13,902	2,716 girls in boys' schools.
Vernacular	12	902	5	317	80	5,930	5	606	102	7,755	
	19	1,590	8	420	264	17,991	21	1,656	312	21,657	

Madras again comes to the front with an increase of 26 English and 6 vernacular schools for girls. In Bengal there is some slight falling-off in schools of both classes. The advancement of Madras in female education is shown by the fact that the secondary schools for girls in that province outnumber those in the rest of India together in the ratio of nearly 4 to 3. This superiority may be explained, in close accordance with what has preceded, by the large place taken by the Native Christian community in the population of Madras. In other provinces the changes are unimportant. It will be noticed that local boards maintain only six secondary schools for girls, of which four are in Madras, one of these being the Lawrence Asylum for European children at Ootacamund. The other two are municipal schools in Bombay and in Burma.

Of 23,900 girls in secondary schools, 322 are in the high and 3,965 in the middle stage, making a total of 4,287 pupils, or 18 per cent., in the secondary stage of instruction. In secondary schools for boys, the proportion of pupils in the secondary stage is 36 per cent. In other words, half the girls who might be expected to pass on to the middle stage of instruction bring their school course to a close at the primary stage; a result which is in full agreement with the other facts relating to female education. The proportionate distribution, among the different stages of instruction, of all girls reading in schools whether for girls or for boys, was shown in the table given in paragraph 91 of Section I of this chapter, where it appeared that 91 per cent. were in the lower primary stage of instruction (including 34 per cent. not reading print), 7 per cent. in the upper primary stage, and 2 per cent. in the secondary stage.

232. Higher Education of Women: the Countess of Dufferin's Fund.—The collegiate education of women makes, as might have been anticipated, but slow progress. The number of female students in Arts colleges rose from 6 to 10, including five Hindus in Bengal, two Parsis in Bombay, and three Europeans at Allahabad in the North-Western Provinces, besides some few others in Bengal who are not shown in the returns. It is in the direction of special education that the greatest interest has been aroused and the strongest impulse given, through the beneficent movement for providing medical aid to the women of India with which the name of Her Excellency the Countess of Dufferin is associated. The time for reporting the results of this movement has not yet arrived; but its effects are already seen in the increased attention that is being paid in all provinces to the medical education of women. If medical aid is to be brought near to Indian women, that result, it is evident, cannot be attained by means of lady-doctors brought from England; a much cheaper agency must be provided by educating, to different degrees of skill, women whose home is in this country, whether they are of Indian or of European extraction. And thus it has come about that in nearly all provinces the establishment or the extension of medical classes, English or vernacular, for women, has now become a matter of practical interest and importance. The prospect of a career for women thus for the first time held out will, it is not unreasonable to suppose, react with salutary effect upon general education, the objection to which has hitherto been that it led to nothing.

233. Race and Creed of Girls at School.—The differences that were shown, in paragraph 93 of Section I, to exist with regard to the spread of education among the various races of India, are intensified when female scholars alone are considered. Unfortunately the returns do not separate the pupils of each race into boys and girls, so that only an approximate estimate can be formed. Such an estimate we can obtain by taking the returns of primary and secondary schools for girls, in which the pupils are classified according to race or creed. It will not be accurate, because amongst other differences it will not include the girls reading in boys' schools, a proportion which is often considerable. In Burma, indeed, hardly any girls are found except in mixed schools; but as the great bulk of these scholars are Burmese, they can be included in the computation for that race without much risk of error. The subjoined figures give, for each of the chief races of India, a rough estimate of the proportion which the girls at school bear to the girls of school-going age, taken as before at 15 per cent. of the female population.

Percentage of Girls at School.

Race or Creed.	In Public Schools.	In Private Schools.	TOTAL.
Hindus	·96	·1	·97
Muhammadans	·54	·32	·86
Parsis	55·4	15·1	70·5
Sikhs	1·88	·16	2·04
Burmese	10·6	...	10·6
Native Christians	35·3		35·3
Europeans and Eurasians	65·0		65·0

A comparison of these figures with those given in the table, paragraph 93, will not be without interest. In that table, which included children of both sexes, the Parsis were shown to be far ahead of the rest of India in the zeal which they displayed in the education of their children. Next came Europeans and Eurasians, Native Christians, and Burmese, with between 60 and 70 per cent. of their children at school. Muhammadans, Hindus, and Sikhs followed with 11 and 12 per cent. The Parsis are still ahead, educating 70 per cent. of their girls, and the Europeans follow closely with 65 per cent. Native Christian girls fall to 35 per cent., and Burmese still lower to 10 or 11 per cent., though from what is known of this last race it is probable that there is a good deal of female education in Burma which never enters into the returns. Sikhs show 2 per cent., while the general body of the Hindu and Muhammadan population have less than 1 per cent. of their girls at school. The percentage among Muhammadans would be still less if schools of recognised instruction were alone considered; but the proportion is brought up, as in the case of boys, by the large number of Muhammadan girls that read the Koran in indigenous *maktabs*.

The distaste of Hindus and Muhammadans for the advanced education of their girls is even more distinctly marked. Of 15,500 girls in English secondary schools, 9,000 are Europeans and Eurasians, 3,445 are Native Christians, 1,379 are "others" (including Brahmos, Parsis, Sikhs, and Burmese); while the vast Hindu population is represented by 1,755, and the Muhammadans by 7 only.

234. Expenditure on Girls' Schools in 1885-86.—The following table shows the expenditure from different sources in each province :—

Expenditure on Secondary and Primary Schools for Girls in 1885-86.

PROVINCE.	FROM PROVINCIAL REVENUES.		From Local and Municipal Funds.	From Fees.	From other Sources.	TOTAL.
	In Schools under public management.	In aided Schools.				
	R	R	R	R	R	R
Madras	47,015	1,21,202	11,401	44,816	1,93,411	4,17,845
Bombay	31,652	40,573	54,941	55,239	1,29,385	3,11,790
Bengal	17,205	1,27,488	7,264	1,44,457	2,05,965	5,02,409
N.-W. Provinces	...	38,101	46,218	67,856	1,29,882	2,82,057
Punjab	9,351	52,103	20,632	29,947	79,786	1,91,819
Central Provinces	7,176	10,601	8,443	4,636	15,305	46,161
Assam	2,955	775	7,111	3,146	3,920	17,907
Berar	996	...	5,155	693	47	6,891
Coorg	...	264	110	24	406	804
Burma	...	18,132	20,185	14,045	28,036	80,398
TOTAL	1,16,350	4,09,239	1,81,460	3,64,889	7,86,143	18,58,081
TOTAL FOR 1884-85	1,05,779	3,68,792	1,74,648	3,38,747	7,46,536	17,34,502

There has been a large increase, amounting to R1,24,000, in the total expenditure on girls' schools. Towards this increase, R51,000 have been contributed from provincial revenues, R7,000 from local and municipal funds, R26,000 from schooling-fees, and R40,000 from subscriptions and other sources. Altogether, 38 per cent. of the cost of maintaining girls' schools is paid from public funds, and 62 per cent. from fees and other private sources. The general proportion for primary and secondary schools of all classes, as may be gathered from the table in para. 96 of Section I, is 44 per cent. from public and 56 per cent. from private funds. At first sight a different result might have been expected; the explanation lies in the fact that girls' schools are for the most part supported by private agencies, while of boys' schools a much larger proportion is maintained either by Government or by local boards, involving consequently a much greater charge on public funds.

235. Female Education in different Provinces.—In this paragraph will be noticed the leading facts in the progress of female education in the various provinces of India, including the collegiate education of women and their training in professional or technical subjects.

Madras.—It was explained in Chapter II that a "high school for girls" in Madras is one that educates pupils not, as elsewhere, for matriculation at the University, but to a standard considerably below that. Seven girls are shown in the returns as having passed the Entrance examination; but from the University Calendar it appears probable that these are European pupils educated in such institutions as the Doveton Girls' School at Madras, or Bishop Cotton's School at Bangalore. No Hindu or Muhammadan girl has yet matriculated at the Madras University. Not that generous encouragement is wanting. It is stated that His Highness the Maharaja of Vizianagram has, with his usual liberality, offered for competition a three years' scholarship of the value of R10 rising to R20 a month, to enable a girl to read for the Entrance examination, together with a prize of R300 and a gold medal on her passing it. The scholarship is open to Hindu girls who have passed the middle school examination. A Muhammadan gentleman in Madras has also offered a scholarship to any Muhammadan girl who passes the upper primary examination in English, to enable her to continue her studies for the Entrance examination; but as yet no Muhammadan girl has fulfilled the first condition, though several have passed the upper primary examination in the vernacular. Even in "high schools," in the restricted sense explained above, the pupils are exclusively Europeans and Eurasians or Native Christians; and the Inspectress remarks that "high schools for caste Hindu girls have not yet been found possible." The number of high schools of this class has fallen from 25 to 22, and that of their pupils in the high departments from 152 to 95. The last reduction is explained by the "comparatively disastrous" results of the middle school examination under the revised scheme, in which the raising of the standard affected girls even more prejudicially than boys. Only 35 candidates from high schools passed that examination, against 93 in the previous year. There were also 32 successful candidates from middle schools. In the higher examination for women 41 candidates passed. Middle schools for girls increased from 139 to 175, and their pupils (of whom the great majority are in the primary departments) from 11,574 to 13,636. Of these 6,468 were Hindus, and only 40 Muhammadans. Over 5,000 pupils in secondary schools learnt English. Primary schools increased from 579 with 20,210 pupils to 626 with 23,478 pupils, the increase having taken place in schools aided by results. About 15,500 girls were presented for examination under the first four standards, and 12,100 passed; the percentage of girls passing being greater in each standard than that of boys. Besides the pupils in girls' schools, there were also 772 girls reading in secondary schools for boys, and 21,025 girls in primary schools. Six young ladies were reading in the Madras Medical College, two of these being scholarship-holders from Bengal, and eight in the attached school department. The number of girls under instruction in the School of Art fell from 31 to 20. In industrial schools 31 girls received instruction in lace-making.

Bombay.—Ten young ladies passed the matriculation examination in 1886, of whom seven were Europeans and three were Parsis. In the previous year 19 Europeans, two Native Christians and one Parsi passed the same examination. Two Parsi ladies were reading in the Free General Assembly's College for the B. A. examination, with the object of ultimately proceeding to the degree in medicine. One of these has since taken the B. A. degree; being thus distinguished as the first lady-graduate in Western India. But, as stated in the last chapter, no Hindu or Muhammadan girl in the Bombay Presidency has yet passed the Entrance examination. It was with the object of remedying this defect that the Poona High School for girls was established in 1884. There was in 1886 an attendance of 69 pupils; the expenditure amounted to R17,000, of which one-third was contributed from private sources and the remainder by Government. The school is said to have been very fortunate in its teaching staff, and a good beginning has been made. A large proportion of the pupils are grown-up girls. This is the only high school of its class in the province; and as yet none of the pupils are in the high department.

The number of middle schools remains the same at 49, with 2,791 pupils, all of whom learn English. The great majority of the pupils are Europeans and Eurasians, Portuguese and Native Christians; there are 390 Parsis to 121 Hindus, and only 3 Muhammadans. The number of primary schools increased from 402 with 25,870 pupils to 445 with 28,063 pupils. Of these 22,419 were Hindus, 2,426 Parsis, and 2,180 Muhammadans. Grave doubts had been expressed as to the wisdom of transferring girls' schools to municipal control; but the results are said to have justified the measure. In some cases, when reductions in educational expenditure have been proposed, girls' school have been spared; in other cases efforts have been made to secure the services of trained mistresses. One of the best girls' school in Gujarat is managed by a municipality. But there are not wanting indications, even in Bombay, of the slight, almost the unreal, character of the demand for female education. It seems not to be taken quite seriously; apparently in the belief that anything will do where girls are concerned. For instance, "there is still the tendency to relegate the girls to a "hovel, while the boys enjoy a finely built and airy school." Again, "parents "often refuse to provide their girls with slates and books, not on the ground of "their poverty, but, because they hold such expenditure to be useless." Again, it is stated that less than one-third of the girl-pupils are presented for examination. This is accounted for by "the large number of little children who come "to school, but do not remain long enough or attend with sufficient regularity "to appear under the standards." The proportion is, however, much the same as in Madras, where 15,000 girls were presented for examination, out of about 45,000 reading in boys' as well as in girls' schools.

The Grant Medical College contained 18 female students, of whom four had passed the Entrance examination; and the Principal reported that he had received several applications, which could not yet be complied with, for the services of qualified female doctors at outlying stations. In the School of Art at Bombay twelve girls were undergoing instruction.

Bengal.—Eleven candidates passed the Entrance examination of 1886, of whom nine were Europeans, and two were Hindu girls from the Bethune School at Calcutta and the Eden School at Dacca, both of which are Government institutions for the education of Native girls. There were no candidates from the Bethune School at the First Arts examination; but a European girl passed from the Doveton Institution, and a Native Christian from the Free Church Normal School. Of three candidates from the Bethune School for the B. A. degree, two passed, one taking honours in Sanskrit. Two other pupils of the same institution passed for the degree in the following year. In 1886 a noteworthy appointment was made by the Government of Bengal. It was stated in the last chapter (para. 47) that Miss Chandra Mukhi Bose, the first native lady in India to pass the Entrance examination, took the degree of M. A., with honours in English, in 1884, and was thereafter appointed to be a teacher in the Bethune School, in which she had been trained for her degree. In 1886 the Lady Superintendent of that institution retired, and Miss Bose was appointed to succeed her, being thus placed in educational and administrative charge of an important college and school, with a full staff of professors and teachers, male and female, and with 142 pupils on its rolls. Besides male graduates for the college classes, she is assisted by Miss Kamini Sen, B. A., also a former pupil of the institution.

There were in Bengal five high schools for girls, with 482 pupils, of whom 44 were in the high departments. Two were the Government schools at Calcutta and Dacca beforenamed; one was an aided school in Calcutta, chiefly for Native Christians, though attended also by a few Hindu and Muhammadan girls; and two were the Doveton and La Martiniere schools for Europeans. Middle schools were 45; 30 English with 2,375 pupils, and 15 vernacular with 808 pupils. Two-thirds of the pupils in secondary schools for girls were Europeans and Eurasians; there were 481 Native Christians, 684 Hindus, but only 3 Muhammadans. Besides these, there were 1,150 girls reading in secondary schools for boys. Primary schools for girls were nearly stationary, but their pupils increased by 2,500 up to 42,628. Among these the European pupils numbered only 500; there were 33,000 Hindus and 5,800 Muhammadans. There were also 33,200 girls reading in primary schools for boys. In Calcutta the work of female education is chiefly entrusted to the great missionary societies. These maintain altogether two training schools, one high and four middle and 14 primary schools, besides a number of zenana agencies employing 116 teachers, who go from house to house and are reckoned for convenience as 116 schools. The number of pupils under instruction was 3,542, and the grants made to the societies by Government amounted to R2,380 a month, or R28,560 a year. Further provision was made for establishing and aiding girls' schools in Calcutta outside the sphere of missionary work by the rules of 1884, under which capitation grants, limited to a maximum of R10 a month, are made for girls' schools or classes conforming to certain conditions. Under this system 1,359 girls were receiving instruction, at a monthly cost to Government of R89. In Calcutta and the neighbourhood an Inspectress of schools has been for some years employed. From the examination-returns of 4,086 pupils reading in zenanas and in girls' schools, it appears that 1,803 were infants, that 1,573 passed by her standards and that 710 were rejected. Outside Calcutta, missionary effort makes itself felt in many parts; and there are also several purely native associations at work for the promotion of female education both in schools and in zenanas. The chief of these is the Uttarpara Society, which holds examinations of girls' schools in six districts, and awards prizes and scholarships on the results. Each year also native girls compete with success at the examinations for Government scholarships, upper and lower primary, open to boys and girls alike. But it is not to be denied that the general standard of education in the hundreds of girls' schools scattered over Bengal is painfully low; nor can it well be otherwise when girls are withdrawn from school at the age of 9 or 10. The evil would not be remedied by the substitution of women for men as teachers; and even if female teachers could be generally provided, it is doubtful whether the increased cost would be justified by the slender results attainable. The *guru* of a boys' school can and does take charge of an infant girls' class in addition to his other duties for a trifling remuneration; and although the instruction he can give them is of the most rudimentary kind, the people readily send their children to his care. In many cases, it is true, the little pupils gain a sound knowledge of the elements of learning before they quit the school; in some few, again, a scholarship is won and the pupil is marked out for a higher stage of learning. But perhaps the most valuable result of the education of these future wives and mothers lies in the next generation and not in this. It is no slight gain to children to be brought up by mothers who have inhaled in any degree the intellectual atmosphere, who remember with pride their own small attainments, and who, it may be hoped, will try to secure for their daughters a fuller draught of learning.

Besides five young ladies reading for the Arts degree in the college classes of the Bethune School, three more are studying in the Medical College for degrees in medicine. A further departure was taken in 1886, by the opening of a class for female students who were not qualified, by passing the First Arts examination, for admission to the college as regular students for the degree. For the benefit of such students it was ordered that girls who had passed either the Entrance or a special preliminary examination might be admitted to the college; and that after a three years' course of classes and practical instruction, and on passing the final college examinations, they should receive a certificate qualifying them to practise medicine, surgery, and midwifery. Under these regulations, 21 European and Eurasian students were admitted to the class. A hostel for the exclusive accommodation of female students of medicine has been erected through the characteristic liberality of the Maharani Sarnamayi, C.I., who contributed a lakh and a half of rupees for that purpose. A grant for the creation of scholarships tenable by students of these classes was at the same time made by Sir Walter deSouza. Proposals have also been made, and in one instance carried into effect, for attaching female classes to the four Government vernacular schools of medicine in Bengal.

North-Western Provinces.—The Allahabad high school for girls has opened college classes in which three European young ladies, after matriculation, are studying the University course in Arts. There are also 22 high and middle schools, including 13 for Europeans and Eurasians, and the remainder chiefly for Native Christians. From these schools 7 pupils, all Europeans or Native Christians, passed the Entrance examination of 1886. With regard to the condition of girls' schools generally, the following extract from the report by Mr. White, the Director, puts the facts in a clear, if not a hopeful, light:—
"The vernacular primary schools for girls maintained by the district boards "out of public funds are doing little or no work, and are condemned as ineffec- "tive and unreal by all the Inspectors except Mr. Nesfield, who has found a few "doing well. Among the aided schools of this class we find education almost "stationary, large numbers of girls nominally learning, but only five in every 100 "getting beyond the lowest classes. It is only in the schools of the Anglo- "vernacular class, and a few missionary middle schools for Christian girls, that "any amount of real work is being done. Among these we have some excellent " institutions, from which we may hope to obtain educated native women who " will become the chief instruments of extending instruction among their coun- " trywomen. It is clear that efforts to extend education among the people, until " we have trained female teachers available to put in charge of the schools, will " be attended with little or no success. At present the best course will be to aid " the schools managed by ladies connected with missionary societies." Mr. White also notices the fact that in the Lucknow District, where the schools have the advantage of superintendence by a special Inspectress, greater progress is recorded.

Punjab.—Female education is said to be in a very backward condition in this province. His Honour the Lieutenant-Governor drew attention in 1884 to the fact that while in India generally there had been an enormous increase in the number of girls at school, in the Punjab the number had steadily and rapidly declined; so that from 1,029 schools and 19,561 scholars in 1865-66, the number fell to 465 schools and 11,819 scholars in 1871-72, and to 311 schools and 9,353 scholars in 1882. The quality of the education had doubtless improved, and in recent years there were still more hopeful signs,—among others that three Native Christian girls passed the Entrance examination in 1886. Two schools are singled out for special mention, as owing their origin entirely to native effort. They are the Arya Samaj School at Ferozepore, and the Anglo-vernacular School at Lahore; the former maintained chiefly for orphans, the latter attended by the children of Government officials and other persons of good social standing. Col. Holroyd remarks :—"There is "no doubt that the good example set by the missionaries and the native com- "munity will bear fruit, and the establishment of the Anglo-vernacular Girls' "School at Lahore is a proof that the desire to provide a good education for "their daughters is making itself felt amongst the educated natives." But as regards the ordinary girls' school in the districts, while there is no difficulty in obtaining scholars, chiefly from the poorer classes, the girls who attend school carry little away with them. "The schools are overfull and under- "taught" is the remark of one lady. There is no regular Inspectress; but in many of the large towns the services of ladies have for the last few years been utilised in the inspection of girls' schools.

Other Provinces.—In the Central Provinces a somewhat less desponding view is taken. Mr. Browning, while stating that there has been no marked advance, nor any serious decline, observes :—"The schools will improve when "they are really wanted by the people." That presents the situation concisely enough, and it may be applied with equal truth to the rest of India. In Assam, the circumstances of female education are much the same as in Bengal. The plan, introduced in 1885-86, of giving the *guru* four annas a month for each girl in his school who could read a little, had the effect of doubling the number of girls in boys' schools. In Burma, we enter an entirely new region, where female education has always been looked on with favour. Hitherto girls have been educated in lay schools only; but in the year under report a remark- able advance was made by the opening of girls' classes in two monastic schools. Mr. Hordern, the Director, remarks that if so good an example should be generally followed, the greatest barrier to the extension of female education in the province will be removed. As might be expected in a province where the education of girls is in accord with popular feeling, the control of girls' schools by municipalities is said to have been entirely successful.

236. Recommendations of the Commission as to Female Educa- tion.—It cannot be said that the recommendations made by the Commission mark out any new line of policy. Their character is mainly tentative and pro- visional. They enumerate obstacles to be removed and aid to be applied, in anti- cipation of the time when the greatest obstacle of all, the apathy of the people, will have disappeared. The road may be cleared and smoothed, though the machine does not yet march. The recommendations are 27 in number, and may be grouped in the following way :—After reciting that female education should be treated as a legitimate charge on provincial, on local, and on municipal funds, and should receive special encouragement (X. 1), and further that all female schools, whether on a religious basis or not, should be eligible for aid so far as they produce any secular results, such as a knowledge of reading and writing (X. 2), the Commission proceed to recommend that the grant-in-aid Codes in the various provinces should be revised so as to afford aid to girls' schools on easier terms as regards rates of aid, the attendance of scholars, the standards of instruction, fees, scholarships, the teaching of English, and the provision of boarding accommodation (X. 3—11). Mixed schools, other than infant schools, are not suited to the conditions of the country, and should not therefore be encouraged except in places where girls' schools could not be maintained (X.12—13). Girls' schools were not to be placed under the management of local boards or municipalities, except at the desire of those bodies, and even then the control was to be surrounded by certain safeguards (X. 14, 15). As to the teachers, masters were to be gradually replaced by mistresses; and with that object additional training schools for women should be provided, and liberal aid afforded to those under private management; inducements should be offered to the wives of schoolmasters, to widows, and to Eurasian young women, to qualify themselves as teachers; the examination for teachers' certificates should be open to all candidates wherever trained; and a system of pupil-teacherships should be established (X. 16—22). Additional recommendations provided for grants to zenana agencies and to local associations for the promotion of female education; for an increase to the female inspecting agency; for the revision of text-books, and for the establishment of an alternative standard for high schools, corresponding to the matriculation examination, but having no relation to any University course (X. 6, 23—27). In its brief comment on these recommendations the Government of India "had nothing to add to what the Commission say "on the subject of female education. All their proposals appear to be suitable, "and are generally approved by Local Governments."

237. Action taken on these Recommendations.—It has just been stated that the Local Governments expressed general approval of the recommendations of the Commission. An opportunity for carrying them into effect was soon afterwards afforded by the Conferences that met together in many provinces of India for the discussion of educational questions. The results of these meetings and of the action independently taken by Government, so far as concerns female education, will now be shortly stated.

238. Grant-in-aid Rules.—Under the revised Code in Madras the rates of aid for girls have been raised from 75 per cent. above those for boys to 100 per cent., and a yearly grant, varying from 12 annas to R3-8 according to standard, is made for plain needlework. In Bombay, also, the rates for girls are double those for boys, except for attendance, and an additional grant of R 2 is made for needlework. In Bengal aid is given either by fixed monthly grants or by capitation grants. In the former case the maximum rate is fixed at one-half the total expenditure, or higher than that generally allowed for boys' schools; in the latter the capitation grant of 4 annas a month (R 3 a year) for every girl under regular and efficient instruction, which was sanctioned in 1884 for schools in Calcutta, has been extended to the rest of Bengal. In the North-Western Provinces the mission schools, on which the higher education of women chiefly depends, have been treated in an exceptional way, altogether outside the grant-in-aid rules; each school receiving such aid as, added to the private resources of the school, will suffice to maintain it in efficiency. In the Punjab, where an additional grant of R14,000 a year has been sanctioned for the support of girls' schools, and in Berar, double grants are given; in Burma the grants for girls are raised 50 per cent. The standards of instruction have been generally simplified by the introduction of subjects specially suited to the requirements of girls. Much attention is given to needlework, and the standards in that subject are generally graduated after the model of the English Code. In Madras and Bengal domestic management and lessons on health are included in the course; in the Central Provinces cookery. The question of fees is a delicate and difficult one. There is no reluctance on the part of school managers to levy fees, and the principle that fees should be paid is admitted to be sound; but in practice many compromises have to be made. If, as is often and even commonly the case, parents reckon the education of their girls as having no money value, and therefore refuse to pay fees, it is felt to be on the whole better that the girls should be educated free than that the enforcement of a strict rule should drive them from the school. The number of girls at school may indeed convey a false impression of the existing demand; but the fact that there is no general demand being once admitted, there is no further objection on that ground to getting as many girls as possible to come to school. The following figures are of interest, as showing the extent of the demand for female education when measured by fee-payments. In primary schools for boys, fees amount to more than 33 per cent. of the whole expenditure; in primary schools for girls they fall to 6 per cent. In middle vernacular schools, which are for the most part primary schools with a small middle department at the top, the proportions are much the same. With secondary English schools we seem to enter on a new region, where the demand for the education of girls, so far as it exists, is steady and genuine; for in schools for girls the fee-receipts rise at once to 25 per cent. against 43 per cent. in boys' schools. Unfortunately the inference has little value, for the bulk of the receipts is derived from European schools, in which girls pay fees at much the same rate as boys. The Commission recommended (X. 9) that liberal aid should be offered for the establishment, in suitable localities, of girls' schools in which English as well as the vernacular is taught. In practice the obstacle is found to lie, not in the insufficiency of the rates of aid, but in the absence of any demand for such instruction except over a very limited area. Some steps have been taken towards carrying out the recommendation (X. 8) for the provision of special scholarships for girls. In the Madras Code such a provision has been made, but only on the principle of supplementing by a Government grant the amounts contributed for this purpose from private sources. In Bengal, the primary and middle scholarships are open to girls as well as to boys, and girls are sometimes successful in the competition. The Conference that lately sat in Calcutta recommended a separate provision of scholarships for girls at the lower primary, upper primary, and middle stages of progress; a principle of which the Government expressed its approval, though the expenditure could not be at once sanctioned. In the North-Western Provinces one scholarship has already been awarded to a Rajput girl, and others will be provided as soon as candidates are forthcoming. In the Punjab a larger scheme has been sanctioned. Special scholarships will be awarded to all girls of purely vernacular schools who pass the lower primary examination in reading, writing, and arithmetic, up to a limit of 20 per cent. of the number on the rolls; and a reward of R10 will be given to every girl who passes the upper primary examination in the same subjects. In Burma also, and to some extent in the Central Provinces, provision is made for girls' scholarships; in Berar the time for such an advance is said to be far distant.

239. Mixed Schools.—The Commission recommended that mixed schools for boys and girls, other than infant schools, should not be encouraged, as being unsuited to the conditions of the country. By "infant schools" appears to be meant (Report, paragraph 612) schools for children under seven years of age. In the educational returns of India no statistics of age are given, so that it is impossible to say how many of the 100,000 girls returned as reading in boys' schools in 1885-86 are infants in that sense. But as girls do not generally come to school before six years of age, it is probable that a large number of the pupils are between 7 and 10. For adult girls, or those above the age of 10 or 11, it is not questioned that separate schools are necessary; but for girls below that age there is some difference of opinion. The Government of Bengal was strongly opposed to the Commission's recommendation as being unsuited to the circumstances of that province. It remarked:—" General opinion testifies to the " great success which attends these [mixed] schools, and to their entire agree-" ment with social conditions in this province. The experience of every in-" specting officer in Bengal confirms the high value which the Bengal Provin-" cial Committee attached to mixed schools. The competition between the girls " and the boys in these schools is of the utmost value in stimulating the pro-" gress of both. It must of course be understood that these girls are practically " all under 10 years of age, and that condition assigns the only necessary limit " to the extension of the mixed school system. Never has any hint of danger or " difficulty been suggested by any resident of the mofussil or by any native " witness. For these reasons, as well as for others of a more general character, " the Lieutenant-Governor altogether opposes the Commission's recommendation " on this point." The recommendation was also declared by the Chief Commissioner to be inapplicable to Burma. The increase of the total number of girls in boys' schools, from 42,000 in 1881-82 to 86,000 (excluding Burma) in 1885-86, seems to show that the presence in boys' schools of girls above the age of seven does no great violence to native feeling. Since the date of the Education Commission's report the number in Bengal has increased from 23,000 to 35,000, in Madras from 14,000 to 22,000, and in Bombay from 4,000 to 17,000. Burma is the only other province in which a large number of girls (13,500) read in boys' schools; indeed in Burma there is very little separate provision for the instruction of girls, who regularly attend boys' schools and are beginning to be received into monastic schools also. Throughout India the great bulk of the girl-pupils read in primary schools for boys; the number in secondary schools for boys is only 3,246. As a matter of purely native feeling, unaffected by departmental influence, it is worth notice that 11,500 girls read in indigenous pathsalas, tols, and maktabs, though the majority of them appear to be found in the Koran schools of the Punjab. A few years ago a grown-up lady, Ram Bai, applied for admission to one of the Sanskrit tols of Nuddea, in Bengal, and was received on equal terms with the rest of the students.

240. District and Municipal Boards.—The Education Commission was of opinion that it was premature for local boards to undertake the control of girls' schools, on the ground that native public opinion had not yet decided either as to the expediency of school-life for girls, or as to the claims of female education on municipal funds. This apprehension has not generally been acted upon or indeed justified. A reference to the table in paragraph 230 will show that the number of primary girls' schools maintained by local and municipal boards is three-fold that of departmental schools. Bombay, with 236 schools so maintained, stands in advance of the rest; and is followed by the North-Western Provinces with 170 schools, the Punjab with 129, and Assam with 105. The contributions made by these bodies towards female education has also advanced from R1,08,000 in 1881-82 to R1,81,000 in 1885-86. Bombay no longer contributes half of this amount, as in 1881-82; it is in other provinces that the advance has been made. But in Bombay, as stated a few pages back, the management of girls' schools by municipalities is said to have been entirely successful; and in Burma the same bodies are declared to have shown exceptional and unexpected liberality towards female education. The Chief Commissioner indeed deprecates any form of departmental control over these bodies, such as the Commission recommends in regard to the appointment and removal of teachers; "boards must be trusted in these as in other matters." In the North-Western Provinces primary schools for girls are placed under the management of district boards equally with those for boys; and the control of female education appears to be regarded as part of the process of educating these bodies to a sense of their duties in that respect. In Bengal, where there are only two Government girls' schools, aided girls' schools have been expressly retained for the present under departmental control. In Madras, where again primary schools under public management are few compared with those maintained by private agency, girls' schools managed by local and municipal boards are being gradually taken over by Government.

241. Teachers in Girls' Schools.—The Commission admitted equally the objections that existed to the general employment of male teachers in girls' schools, and the difficulty of replacing them by female teachers. These points have found further illustration in preceding paragraphs. The substance of the Commission's recommendations on this head may be repeated. With the object of gradually superseding male by female teachers, additional training schools for women should be provided, and liberal aid afforded to those under private management; inducements should be offered to the wives of schoolmasters, to widows, and to Eurasian young women to qualify as teachers; the examination for teachers' certificates should be open to all candidates, whether from training schools or not; and a system of pupil teacherships should be established. It was shown in the last section of this chapter that the number and attendance of training schools for women showed no advance; and indeed it would seem that the establishment of these institutions must follow, and can do little to create, a demand for female education. Moreover it has been shown that aided training schools for women are mostly maintained by missionary bodies, with the object of supplying their own schools with teachers, and therefore do nothing for promoting female education among the people in general. The employment as teachers of the wives of schoolmasters does not seem to make much way. It is too early to expect that a practice, common enough and perhaps the regular rule in England, should strike root in the very different soil of India, where the wife, even of a schoolmaster, has very seldom received anything beyond the merest rudiments of education as a girl. Thus, in the Central Provinces, it is reported that the Sisters of St. Francis de Sales offered to train schoolmistresses, but no pundits could be found willing to send their wives for instruction. In Bombay the plan, as already stated, has met with greater success. In Madras a provision to the same effect appears in the new grant-in-aid Code. In the Punjab, which is declared to be better off in regard to female teachers than any other province except Madras, inducements of a valuable kind have now been held out, not only to the wives, but to widowed sisters and other female relatives of pundits, to qualify themselves for employment as teachers. To such women a reward of R30 is offered for passing the lower, and of R50 for passing the upper primary examination. When qualified, these teachers will be eligible for salaries of R10 to R20 a month—a material addition to the joint income; and increased house-accommodation will also be provided for teachers whose wives are so employed. Towards the education of widows as teachers little definite action appears to have been taken, though in the Madras Code inducements are now offered to widows to qualify. Apart from the social effacement of widows in the Hindu system, the employment of a woman, if young and therefore teachable, in independent charge, is opposed to Hindu sentiment and to the conditions of Hindu society, whether she be unmarried or a widow. It seems that as a rule she could only undertake such work when under the protection of a Christian mission. Young Eurasian women can be, and are, trained as teachers in considerable numbers; but they can only be employed in or near large towns, and generally in the service of the mission which has trained them. Doubts are expressed as to the efficacy of the pupil-teacher system, based on the elementary character of girls' schools, and the tender age at which pupils generally finish their education. Even if the system had the effect of keeping girls longer at school, it might do so without really increasing the provision of teachers. On that subject the remarks of one of the Provincial Committees are in point. After allowing that it would be possible to fill a boarding school with grown-up pupils, whether young Brahmo ladies, married women whose husbands were anxious to have them instructed, or Hindu widows whose relatives felt the burden of supporting them, the Committee observed :—" But it can hardly be assumed that " the pupils would in their turn become teachers. The married woman, when "her education was complete, would go back to her husband's house. The "educated Brahmo girl, even if she became a teacher, would soon be sought "after as an eligible wife. The widow, if elderly, could derive little profit "from her training after a life spent in ignorance; it still young, the condi"tions of Hindu society are not such that she could go off to a strange place " to undertake the charge of a school."

242. Zenana Agencies, &c.—Little information can be gathered from the reports as to any increased help offered to religious and secular associations for carrying on the education of women in the zenana. In Bengal, as stated in an earlier paragraph, very large grants are given to zenana agencies at work in Calcutta and the metropolitan districts. Several native associations, instituted for the purpose of holding periodical examinations of women taught by their fathers or brothers at home, have also been aided; and there is no doubt that a good deal of this home education goes on of which the Department hears nothing. In Madras also zenana teaching is recognised in the grant-in-aid Code. In the Punjab, grants have been allowed in some instances for zenana classes, but the rules have not yet been embodied in the Code. Among secular agencies, the National Indian Association occupies a prominent place. It has its headquarters in London, and branches have been established in Madras, Calcutta, Bombay, and Poona. The Society was founded by Miss Carpenter in 1871, " in " aid of social progress and education in India. " Its chief object is to promote education among the women of India on non-missionary principles, partly by sending out teachers to the zenanas, and partly by grants in-aid and scholarships to schools and pupils. The Association, one of whose objects is to promote social intercourse among different classes in India, is well regarded, even though it has not in all cases succeeded in gaining a commanding position. In Bombay, and especially in Madras, it appears to have been much more successful than in Calcutta; a result which may very well be due to the fact that in Calcutta the missionary agencies "hold the field," receiving large Government grants, commanding almost unlimited supplies from the Home Societies, and practically covering the entire ground to be occupied. For it is a noticeable fact that in Calcutta the missionary character of zenana instruction seems to arouse little or no opposition. Hindu householders appear to be satisfied that the slight element of Christian teaching which the zenana ladies can impart in the course of their lessons can have little effect against the force of daily custom and tradition.

The need of more inspectresses of girls' schools is fully admitted. That they have not yet been appointed in greater numbers is due solely to financial exigencies.

SECTION VII.—EDUCATION OF SPECIAL CLASSES.

(a) EUROPEANS AND EURASIANS.

243. Need of Special Measures: Lord Canning's Minute.—The exceptional position occupied in India by children of European extraction, and the necessity of employing special means for the education of this class, are questions that have long occupied the attention of the Government. Shortly after the Mutiny, Lord Canning wrote:—

"If measures for educating these children are not promptly and vigorously encouraged and aided by the Government, we shall soon find ourselves embarrassed in all large towns and stations with a floating population of Indianised English, loosely brought up, and exhibiting most of the worst qualities of both races; whilst the Eurasian population, already so numerous that the means of education offered to it are quite inadequate, will increase more rapidly than ever. I can hardly imagine a more profitless, unmanageable community than one so composed. It might be long before it would grow to what would be called a class dangerous to the State; but very few years will make it, if neglected, a glaring reproach to the Government, and to the faith which it will, however ignorant and vicious, nominally profess. On the other hand, if cared for betimes, it will become a source of strength to British rule and usefulness to India.

"The Eurasian class have an especial claim upon us. The presence of a British Government has called them into being; they serve the Government in many respects more efficiently than the natives can as yet serve it, and more cheaply and conveniently than Europeans can do so; and they are a class which, while it draws little or no support from its connection with England, is without that deep root in, and hold of the soil of India from which our native public servants, through their families and relatives, derive advantage."

The condition of this class has not in the meantime improved by comparison with their neighbours. When Lord Canning wrote, the Universities of India had just been established; and however true it may at that time have been that Eurasians could "serve the Government more efficiently than natives can as "yet serve it," the spread of University education has had the effect of at any rate reducing that difference. For those occupations in which intelligence and education are the chief requisites, Eurasians can no longer put forward any exceptional claim. It is perhaps hardly true to say that they cannot live as cheaply as the natives of the country; but it is undoubtedly true that, class for class, the Eurasian, with a more costly standard of living, requires higher wages to maintain himself in respectability and comfort, as he understands them, than the Hindu or the Muhammadan does. Consequently the Eurasian is even more heavily handicapped now than he was when Lord Canning wrote. The joint-family system secures a Hindu against absolute want. The Eurasian has no resource of that kind; and failure to obtain employment would mean the imminent risk of starvation, were it not for the extreme liberality of this class towards one another, and for the fact that the pressure of circumstances imposes upon each man the necessity of labour, and thus reduces the number of idle members who, under the joint-family system, lay so heavy a burden upon the Hindu bread-winner.

244. Lord Lytton's Minute.—Upon Lord Canning's Minute, little or no action was taken. In 1874 the Local Governments were asked for detailed information as to the number of European and Eurasian children who attended and who did not attend school; and were invited to report what measures were needed, and could be undertaken from provincial resources, for promoting the education and welfare of poor Europeans and Eurasians. The replies to that call disclosed the following facts :—

(1) that out of an estimated total of 26,649 European and Eurasian children of school-going age in India, 15,067 were actually under in-

struction, of whom about 56 per cent. were boys and 44 per cent. girls;

(2) that Government spent on these schools about R1,75,000 a year;
(3) that there were two large classes of children who received no education, namely, the children of the very poor in the Presidency and other large cities, and the children of Europeans and Eurasians living at out-stations which could not support a school;
(4) that the Local Governments, while admitting that further measures were in some instances needed, were yet unable to set aside from their provincial grants additional sums for children of these classes, without injustice to the vast native population.

It thus appeared that there were between eleven and twelve thousand European and Eurasian children in India, growing up without any education at all, "a scandal to the English name and English Government." It was on the basis of these facts that Lord Lytton took up the question as Viceroy in 1879. Lord Canning's warning, His Excellency considered, had been amply justified by the event. Though there might be exaggeration in the numbers furnished, the importance which the whole question had assumed could hardly be exaggerated. The presence of a large number of uneducated persons of this class undoubtedly constituted "a great social and political danger." In the face of increasing native competition it was not easy to provide a remedy; but there were still some forms of employment for which persons of European blood were best fitted. "There is a great and growing demand for skilled labour "of a kind for which Europeans are specially valued. The extension of railways, "and the development of English enterprise in manufactures, in trade, in planta- "tions, and in other branches of industry, lead at the present time to a constant "importation of labour from England; but if young Englishmen could be well "brought up and educated in India itself, their knowledge of the country and "the people would give them great advantages, and their qualifications for em- "ployment in India would often be better than those of their competitors from · "home." Other openings would be found in many of the public departments and offices; and it might be proper to reserve for them a certain proportion of posts of this kind. Lastly, there was the army, which offered an honourable career to boys of pure European parentage; and for this purpose the Lawrence Military Asylums might be utilised much more fully than they had hitherto been. These Asylums had been founded for the benefit of soldiers' sons; but the tendency of the existing system was to make the pupils look down on soldiering as something derogatory, instead of regarding it as the most legitimate and honourable calling for the great bulk of their number. Such being the opportunities for employment, Lord Lytton went on to consider the measures that Government might rightly take towards increasing the means of education available for boys of the poorer classes, to which he was careful to limit his proposals. Having sketched in outline a scheme for elementary schools for children in the plains, for boarding schools in the hills, for industrial schools, girls' schools, fee-remissions, the training of teachers, and inspection, His Excellency touched upon the question of compulsory education, which, he thought, might possibly be necessary in view of the indifference shown by many parents to the education of their children. The whole question was then referred to a Committee.

245. Archdeacon Baly's Report.—Of this Committee the Ven'ble Archdeacon Baly was a leading member. Indeed it was principally through his inquiries conducted for many years all over Upper India, and through the zeal and enthusiasm which he had devoted to the task of ameliorating the condition of the European races and of interesting persons in authority in their welfare, that the question had once more been brought to the front. Within a few months the Archdeacon submitted a preliminary report, in which the subject was discussed with great ability and with intimate knowledge. The leading recommendations in this report were the introduction (1) of a more searching system of Government inspection and control, grants-in-aid being determined strictly by the results attained; (2) of compulsory education, applied as a last resource; and (3) of a local educational rate, confined to Europeans, to be locally expended and auxiliary to voluntary effort. These were all declared to be necessary to a sound educational system: the first, to ensure both for the State and for parents that a full return was had for the money expended on education; the second, to protect children in extreme cases against the carelessness and selfishness of parents; the third, to secure for schools which were only aided by Government that settled and sufficient measure of public support which was absolutely necessary for their maintenance, but which voluntary contributions, necessarily fluctuating and inadequate, had hitherto failed to supply. Thus the general principle to be adopted was that of aiding private effort. It was useless, if not impossible, for Government to undertake the entire charge and maintenance of these schools. A far better course was for the Government to supplement, by a system of adequate grants-in-aid, the sums received from school fees and local resources; and to entrust the administration of the school to local committees, subject to a carefully considered system of Government inspection, financial as well as educational. In order to apply that principle completely, two things were necessary; the first, that rules affecting the standard of education, the mode of inspection, the assessment of the grants-in-aid, and the conditions required from school-committees, should be laid down by the Government of India and made uniform for the whole of Upper India,—in other words, that an Educational Code should be sanctioned; the second, that a fixed and separate grant should be made in the provincial estimates for the support of European schools. Lord Lytton had suggested that whatever measures were taken should be confined to the poorer classes. Archdeacon Baly was not of that opinion; he urged that middle and high schools should equally be provided for in the Code, on the ground that these too needed all the support the State could give them if they were to be maintained in even tolerable efficiency. He also strongly advocated the encouragement of hill schools to the utmost possible extent, by reason of the permanent improvement in health and *physique* to be secured by residence in a hill climate during the period of adolescence. But while the general system of State education was to be on the basis of grants-in-aid, there were certain institutions of a special kind which should be directly managed and maintained by the Government. These were (1) orphanages and free schools at the Presidency towns or other central situations; (2) Military schools, such as the Lawrence Asylums; (3) technical and industrial schools; (4) a training college for the whole Presidency. All schools, whether Government or aided, should be placed under the supervision of a European Inspector, in whose hands should be placed the detailed administration of the Code.

246. Resolution of the Government of India thereon.—After consulting the Local Governments on the Archdeacon's preliminary report, the Government of India, in a Resolution dated the 8th October 1881, published the results of its inquiries, and declared the policy which it proposed to follow in supporting European education. It appeared that in the Bengal Presidency, including all the provinces of Upper and Central India, to which Archdeacon Baly's report had now narrowed the inquiry, out of about 13,500 European and Eurasian children of school-going age, some 5,000 were growing up in absolute ignorance. In the opinion of the Governor General in Council, the statistics furnished by Local Governments revealed a state of things from every point of view lamentable, and certain to become in the end, to use Lord Canning's words, a glaring reproach to the Government. The necessity of adopting special measures for the education of a class which laboured under many disadvantages was clearly set forth in the following passage:—

"It has been rightly said that one very special reason why Government cannot afford to ignore the growing up in India of an uninstructed European population is that, in the case of the European, his capacity for self-maintenance depends entirely upon the education he receives. He cannot support himself in this country by working as a day-labourer, or by adopting the avocation of the Native peasant. An uneducated European almost necessarily becomes an idle and profitless, and often a dangerous, member of the community. On the other hand, it must be remembered that he, or his English ancestor, was brought out to India originally to do work that could only be done by a European, a fact which in itself gives him some claim to consideration. The climate is uncongenial to him, the cost of living is necessarily disproportionate to his means, and he is deprived at the same time of the educational opportunities which are now available at home even to the poorest of the working class. In all these respects the European parent is placed at a disadvantage, and it thus becomes necessary for the Government to come to his assistance. For the same reasons the Government cannot, in rendering its aid, confine itself to subsidising and directing merely the primary education of Europeans, but must, contrary to the practice at home, assist also the schools designed for the middle, and even to some extent those for the higher, education of this class of its subjects. It is, however, to be remembered that the standard of education in Government aided primary schools in England is at least as high as the standard for middle schools in this country."

The argument that European children should be required to attend the ordinary schools of the country, much as there was to recommend it, could not be maintained in face of the strong objections that European parents had to placing their children in schools where they would receive no religious instruction, and where the whole atmosphere of the place would be non-Christian. Nor would such an alternative provide for the education of girls. The necessity of making special provision for Europeans being thus established, the question of ways and means assumed importance. To a local educational rate to be levied on Europeans only, as proposed by the Archdeacon, there were grave and fatal objections; and with that the connected proposal for a compulsory system of education fell to the ground. The necessary provision must be made by imperial or provincial funds coming to the aid of local effort. For free schools and orphanages special measures were required. In Bengal the munificent bequest of £80,000, made by the late Misses Bruce for the education and maintenance of poor Eurasian girls, could probably be so employed as to render unnecessary any further grant from Government on account of the poorer classes. In the North-Western Provinces and Oudh, the local school at Allahabad could be developed into a central free boarding school to accommodate at least 300 children; and towards that object the Government was prepared to contribute 1½ lakhs of rupees from imperial funds. For the needs of the Punjab it would probably be sufficient to assist and extend the existing railway schools; but the Government of India would consider in a liberal spirit any application which the Local Government might make for further building accommodation at Lahore. The foregoing arrangements would, it was hoped, provide all that was necessary in the way of building accommodation for free schools and orphanages. For their efficient maintenance, as well as for the maintenance of schools for Europeans above the indigent class, recourse must be had to private contributions assisted by Government grants-in-aid, to be given in accordance with the educational work done by each, and without reference to denominational distinctions. Schools in the hills and schools in the plains were to be aided on equal terms. The gravest difficulties arose in those stations where the permanent European population was not large enough to build or to maintain a school, but where there was still a sufficient number, 12 or more, of European children to make a school desirable. In such cases the Local Government would be justified in building schools from its own funds, preference being given to those places where the European population was largest, where voluntary contributions towards the cost of building and maintenance were offered, and where a local committee would afterwards undertake to manage the school. It was the wish of the Government of India that a school should finally be provided at every place where an average daily attendance of 12 scholars could be secured. The rest, who would still form a large residue, should be provided for in central boarding schools; and to that aid a system of free passes over State and guaranteed railways should be introduced. Scholarships, to be awarded entirely by competition without the introduction of any eleemosynary element, should also be established, so as to enable boys of ability to rise from lower schools to higher, and finally to the University.

But the most powerful help that could be given to European education in India lay undoubtedly in the introduction of a system of grants-in-aid, at once liberal and strict. At present there was no security that the money given by Government was spent in the most economical and profitable manner. Grants were calculated solely with reference to the supposed needs of the schools, and hardly at all with reference to their efficiency; no inducement was held out to the managers to improve their arangements, or to the scholars to show increased diligence. All this should be replaced by a carefully devised system of grants-in-aid according to results. There would be difficulty at first owing to the want of trained teachers; especially as it was held that the establishment of a training college by Government was now at any rate premature, and that denominational colleges, to which however grants might be rightly given, did not as yet exist. In any case, it was an essential point to introduce the system gradually, and with such temporary adaptations as would enable all really sound institutions to bear the change without injury. But it was necessary that the Local Governments should be guided by some uniform rules, and that managers of schools should know the terms upon which they might hope for Government aid and the amount of assistance they might claim. A small Committee was therefore appointed to draft a Code for regulating the conduct of European education in the Bengal Presidency. Of this Committee Archdeacon Baly was a prominent member. Two other members represented the Roman Catholic and Nonconformist communities, and the Director of Public Instruction in Bengal was President. It was hoped that, after taking into account the proceeds of the Bruce legacy, a final addition of one lakh a year to the existing Government expenditure of about two lakhs would meet the requirements of European education in the whole of the Bengal Presidency,—an addition which could easily be met from provincial revenues. In Bombay and Madras it was understood that sufficient provision was already made for European education, though that belief was not based on detailed inquiries such as had been made in Bengal. A review of the question in the light of the foregoing remarks was therefore recommended to the Governments of those Presidencies, and also to the Chief Commissioner of British Burma. The Resolution concluded with a reference to technical education, and to the desirability of reserving a certain amount of employment in the public service for youths of European extraction.

247. Draft Code for European Schools in the Bengal Presidency.—In July 1882 the Committee submitted a draft Code to the Government of India, and in February 1883 the orders of that Government were issued. The Code mainly followed, as to its form, the English and Scotch Codes; and in obedience to the instructions of the Government of India, it was based on the principle of payment according to results. Grants were given for attendance and for instruction. The attendance grant was payable for every scholar in average daily attendance, the rate diminishing as the number of scholars decreased, from R12 a year for the first 25 scholars, down to R3 a scholar after the number of 75 had been reached. The instruction grant was payable for each scholar who, after completing a prescribed number of attendances (240 in the year), passed the examination in the subjects of his standard; these subjects being divided into 'elementary,' 'class,' and 'special,' with grants of R5, R3, and R5, respectively, for each scholar passing in any subject of those branches. The elementary subjects were reading, writing, and arithmetic, which all scholars were required to take up, and to pass in two of them in order to earn a grant. The class subjects—namely, those optional subjects which, if taken up at all, were to be taken up by every scholar in a class—included object-lessons (in primary schools only), English, geography, history, mathematics, elementary science, and (for girls) needlework and domestic economy. Provided 50 per cent. of the scholars examined satisfied the Inspector, a grant was payable for each that passed; but the grant was to be reduced or cancelled if the school as a whole did badly in the elementary subjects. The special subjects, which might optionally be taken up by individual scholars, comprised an Indian vernacular (also recognised as a class subject), a European language, botany, and drawing. Grants were also given for discipline and organisation, for singing, for drill and gymnastics, and for boarders; a maximum grant being fixed in each case, and the amount claimable being determined by the Inspector's opinion of the efficiency of the school in these respects.

But while based generally on English models, the draft Code diverged from them at many important points. In some it merely anticipated changes that were simultaneously being made in the English Code, such as the introduction of a seventh standard of elementary instruction. In others a change was necessitated by the different conditions of Indian life, which required, for example, the knowledge of an Indian vernacular, of Indian history in addition to English, and of a double set of weights and measures. The treatment of class subjects differed in one important point from that of the English Code, which allows only two to be taken up. The draft Code on the contrary fixed a minimum of four, on the ground that four class subjects (for example, English grammar, geography, history, and algebra) in addition to the elementary subjects, was not too heavy a burden for boys of eleven or twelve years of age, as indeed the practice of the best European schools showed. Again, while the seven standards for elementary schools in England might fairly be taken to cover not only primary schools, but those classed under Indian standards as middle, it was also necessary to determine a course and rates of aid for high schools. Difficulties, too, were presented by the variety of races and by the mixed character of European schools in India. The term 'European' was used in the Code to signify "any person of European descent, pure or mixed, who "retains European habits and modes of life;" but it was admitted that the definition would, on the one hand, include some that had no claim to special privileges, such as the Portuguese of Bombay, the Feringhis of other parts of India, and the Indo-Chinese of Calcutta; while on the other it would exclude Armenians, whose claim to be admitted to the benefits of the Code might reasonably be based alike on the social affinities of the race and on the practice prevailing in European schools. The decision in all doubtful cases was finally left to the Local Government. Some uncertainty attended even the definition of a European school, since scholars of other races were not in all cases refused admission. Under the draft Code no grant was to be made to any school in which European scholars did not form the majority; though the proportion of non-Europeans was afterwards reduced. No grant was in any case to be claimed under the Code for non-European scholars. The question of admitting "private adventure" schools was keenly discussed. The Committee finally recommended by a bare majority that they should be declared ineligible for grants. This recommendation was overruled by the Government of India, on the ground that it was not advisable to dispense with any form of agency, provided that the education it gave was satisfactory; and thus a further divergence from the English Code resulted.

Similarly, while the method of payment according to results was generally followed, the inapplicability of that method in certain cases was clearly foreseen, and the necessity of occasional exceptions recognised. These were confined to the allowance of special grants to schools in places where there was a small or poor European population; to free schools and orphanages in aid of their boarding charges; and for the boarding-out of children residing in places where there was no school. Exceptions of an opposite character were made when the circumstances of the school were such that the full grant payable under the Code could not fairly be claimed. Thus, the grant to a school was not to exceed its income from all other sources; no grant was to be made to any school whose income from other sources was sufficient to maintain it in efficiency; and finally, in the case of high schools, if the full grant was in the opinion of the Department unnecessary, a reduction was to be made in its amount.

Of the seven standards introduced by the Code, Standards I to IV constituted the primary course of instruction, and V to VII the middle course. Schools were divided into departments corresponding to these standards; and thus a middle school contained a primary as well as a middle department, just as a high school might comprise a high, a middle, and a primary department. In high schools two alternative standards were proposed, each estimated to occupy two years from Standard VII. The first was that of the matriculation examination of the University. The standard alternative to this included a higher course of English reading than the University prescribes; the substitution of a modern European language for Latin or an Indian vernacular; an extension of the arithmetical course, with the addition of book-keeping; and the introduction of political economy and commercial geography. Geometrical drawing, elementary physics, and elementary chemistry were also included as optional subjects. Suitable changes were made in the corresponding course for girls' schools. The greater value which the Committee assigned to this alternative standard was marked by the award of higher grants to schools taking it up. But the Government of India dissented from the recommendation of the Committee that the Entrance examination should be recognised in the Code. The University standard had been proposed as an alternative, partly by reason of the value which it carried in the labour market, and partly because it was actually taught in high schools for Europeans. But the Committee admitted its inferiority to the other, and even anticipated a time when the University examination might be ignored, as the standard of European education advanced under the operation of the Code. Consequently, in the opinion of the Government of India, there was no need to recognise the Entrance examination at all. The alternative course proposed by the Committee was admittedly superior, not only in its higher standard, but in its more practical character; and it alone should be recognised as qualifying for grants.

Careful attention was paid to the qualifications of teachers; a point of much difficulty owing to the absence in many schools of a properly trained staff, and the impossibility of at once replacing the existing teachers by others. Provision was made for a thorough classification of teachers then in employ; for securing that those hereafter to be employed should be properly qualified; and for the development of an efficient pupil-teacher system. None but certificated teachers and pupil-teachers were recognised in the draft Code; but the award of certificates, both provisional and permanent, to teachers already employed but not otherwise certificated, was provided for by articles of temporary operation, since struck out. On the assumption that the establishment of an unsectarian training college by Government was an impracticable measure, the articles of the Code bearing on the training of teachers were designed to facilitate the establishment of denominational training colleges. Very liberal grants were also offered towards the cost of school-buildings. The maximum rate was fixed at one-half of the total cost in places where the people might reasonably be expected to help themselves, and at two-thirds of the cost where liberal contributions could not be looked for. The Code was completed by the provision of a moderate system of scholarships, primary and middle, to enable deserving scholars to go on with their education in a middle, a high, or a technical school.

The rates of aid were fixed with reference to the instruction of the Government of India that the additional expenditure was to be estimated at about one lakh of rupees a year. But it was admitted that it was impossible to forecast with any approach to accuracy the financial effect of the Code grants, since the information at the disposal of the Committee gave a very imperfect account of the educational status, judged by the Code standards, of the scholars already at school, and none at all of the 5,000 new scholars whom it was hoped to attract. The Committee therefore proposed that for the first two years the schools should be examined under the Code standards, and the results recorded for future guidance; but that during that period no change should be made in the grants then enjoyed by the schools. The information obtained during this experimental period would enable the Department to judge of the sufficiency and suitability of the rates proposed, and to modify them in any way that experience might show to be necessary. This proposal was accepted by the Government, with the modification that the provisions of the Code regarding pupil-teachers, building grants, and scholarships should be introduced at once, and also that the Code as a whole should be applied to all new schools.

248. Provisional Introduction of the Draft Code.—The actual introduction of the Code was therefore postponed for two years, after which the probable effect of its operation could be fairly estimated. The judgment formed by the local authorities during the experimental period was on the whole favourable. In Bengal the first year of trial was declared to be satisfactory. "The Code has done and will do good in schools of all classes;" though even at that early period the Inspector, Mr. Nash, apprehended "some "danger of its eventually putting too much pressure upon both teachers and "scholars." The scale of grants was, however, found in the following year to be too high; and if a large increase in the total amount was to be avoided, reduced grants would have to be given both for attendance and for instruction. In the North-Western Provinces and Oudh the schools were smaller and the instruction less advanced than in Bengal. Very few schools, it was alleged at the outset, would gain by the new Code, even liberally interpreted; many would be ruined if its regulations were rigidly observed. The results of the second experimental year confirmed these anticipations. Of 49 schools examined under the Code, though 16 earned more than their previous grants, 23 earned less. Thus, the grant to the Allahabad boys' school, the largest in the province, fell from R6,600 to R2,873; and yet the existing grant was declared to be, in the circumstances, not too large. In the Punjab, the European community had all along been well provided with schools; and in the year preceding the provisional introduction of the Code, their position had been greatly improved by the allotment of additional grants amounting to R1,580 a month, and of R12,000 in building grants. The difficulty lay rather in the carelessness and apathy of the parents, and in the sickliness that prevailed among European children in the plains during the hot weather. With necessary modifications, the Code could be advantageously introduced into the Punjab. From the Central Provinces a favourable report was also given. The standards and rates of aid were on the whole suitable; but the provisions regarding pupil-teachers were found impracticable, and it would be necessary to raise by a year the limits of age for scholarships.

249. Confirmation of the Code.—It had been found expedient to appoint in every province a separate Inspector of European schools; and when the experimental period had come to an end, these officers met together in a Conference to compare the results of their experience. The recommendations of the Conference tended generally in the direction of restricting the extent of direct interference by the Department, and of recognising local differences in regard to the amount of grants. The rates for attendance were generally reduced, while those for instruction were considerably raised according to a somewhat complicated scale; the increase being slight in Bengal, greater in the North-Western and the Central Provinces, and greatest of all in the Punjab. Throughout these differences the object was the same; namely, in the transition from fixed grants to grants under the Code, to disturb the existing grant to each school as little as possible, and especially to avoid any sudden and large reduction in the monthly grant to a deserving school. These proposals were accepted by the Government of India; which furthermore, in order to confirm the principle of recognising local differences, authorised the Local Governments to modify from time to time the rates of grants and scholarships, subject only to the general control of the Supreme Government. With regard to the final standard of high schools, the Conference recommended that as no school had introduced the additional subjects proposed for the Entrance examination, nor had any attempted the new Code standard, it was useless to prescribe either one or the other, and that it should be left to each Local Government to fix its own standard. This recommendation, however, the Governor General in Council was unable to accept. The Entrance examination of the University had been declared by the Government of India to be an unsuitable standard for schools of this class, in which it was essential to endeavour to introduce education of a more practical character. If the proposal were adopted, the certain effect would be to make the University Entrance examination the sole and general standard, without even the very moderate improvements proposed in the existing schedule. Nevertheless, the Government of India consented to withdraw its embargo upon the University course; and it was now made optional with the Local Governments to aid by fixed grants those high schools which taught the Entrance standard alone. At the same time the Code system of grants was confined to the alternative standard; and the superior position thus assigned to it was confirmed by the declaration that, in making appointments to the Government service, preference was to be given to candidates who had passed by that standard. Important changes were made in the rules relating to teachers' certificates. By the draft Code it was provided that every teacher in an aided school was to be certificated. For a provisional certificate of the lowest class, a teacher must have passed either the final examination of pupil-teachers or the University Entrance examination. The Conference believed that under these rules it would be impossible, for some years to come and until training colleges were established, to keep up the supply of teachers, especially in girls' schools. It was not desirable to lower the qualification for certificates, and the only alternative was to allow uncertificated persons to be appointed as teachers, provided they possessed certain inferior qualifications. The recommendations under this head were accepted by the Government. Many changes were also proposed and sanctioned in the subjects prescribed for the different examinations, while the principle was upheld that no diversities should be permitted in the provincial standards. This last regulation was necessitated by the constant transfers from province to province to which the children of railway servants were liable. Among other changes were the following. The definition of Europeans was narrowed. The permissible proportion of non-Europeans in a school was reduced from 50 to 25 per cent. The conscience clause was restricted to day schools. It was removed in the case of boarding schools, on the ground that it was to some extent open to parents to select their own boarding schools; and if they chose one that insisted on a certain form of religious instruction, they did so with their eyes open. In day schools, on the other hand, there was generally no choice; and the conscience clause was necessary for the protection of parents.

After a year's working under the Code, in May 1886 the Conference of Inspectors again met. They had been invited by the Government of India to consider two points chiefly. The first was the desirability of substituting collective examination, that is, examination by classes, for the examination of individual scholars. It was thought that the proposed system would lead to an economy of time and finally of expenditure, without in any way lowering the standard of efficiency. These views, however, did not commend themselves to the Conference. In their opinion, the method of collective examination failed to attain the most important object of instruction, namely, improvement in the methods of teaching and the gradual raising of the standard. They held that a careful individual examination of the scholars afforded a valuable lesson to the teachers, bringing to light defects in the method of instruction and showing how they could be remedied. They added that the abolition of individual examination, involving the abolition of scholars' registers, would be very unpopular with parents. The results of each year's examination were entered in the scholars' registers, and parents looked upon these as a test of the merits of a school. After the children left school they retained their scholars' registers, and often used them as certificates of proficiency when seeking employment. The Government of India, while allowing that these objections had weight, decided that a trial should be given to the system of collective examination in one or two of the less important subjects in selected schools.

The second matter referred to the Conference was the amendment of the final standard for high schools. In sanctioning the recommendations of the Conference on this point, the Government of India suggested the introduction of drawing and physics, no longer as optional, but as compulsory subjects in the final examination. It was also suggested that drawing should be made an elementary subject in all standards, and elementary science a class subject in the primary, as it already was in the middle standards. These suggestions were in full conformity with the policy, steadily pursued by the Government of India, of giving European scholars a better and more useful and practical education than they could ever secure under standards that were finally dominated by the University course. Other changes were at the same time made. In the Lower Provinces the attendance grant to any school was limited to R600 a year. The instruction grants were simplified and somewhat reduced, the same rate being fixed for elementary, class, and special subjects; namely, R4 for each subject in Bengal, R5 in the North-Western and Central Provinces, and R6 in the Punjab. The grants were actually earned for the year with which the examination ended, but for the sake of simplicity and for the convenience of schools, one-twelfth of the amount so earned was taken to be the monthly grant payable to the school for the following year.

250. Extension to other Provinces.—Meanwhile the Government of India had recommended the Code to the consideration of Local Governments outside the Bengal Presidency, namely, Madras, Bombay, and Burma. In Madras the adoption of the Code was the subject of long deliberation. It was finally decided that the existing grant-in-aid rules, with certain additions and alterations derived from the Bengal Code, should be retained. Provision was accordingly made for the award of scholarships, for the grant of aid to boarding schools and orphanages, and for grants to industrial schools. Special standards of examination, with special rates for result-grants, were also applied to European schools. In 1885-86 a sum of R14,000 was paid in boarding and clothing grants for the poorest class of European pupils. At the same time, it was urged in Madras that the Eurasian question was practically identical with that of technical education. In solving the latter, the former also was solved. Men were willing to work, but could get no employment. Half the community had "no "careers open to them except to become vagrants, beggars, or dependents on "charity." The only remedy was to teach them trades. In Bombay the recommendation of the Government of India received attention; and in the recent revision of the grant-in-aid Code for that Presidency, the Bengal standards appear to have made their influence felt. The grants obtainable by European schools were also framed on a liberal scale; they varied from R10 to R50 in standards I to VI, as against a scale of R6 to R30 in Anglo-vernacular schools,—a difference considerably greater than that provided by the Madras Code. In Burma there had been in existence since 1882 a system of exceptional liberality for the encouragment of European education; and its authors claimed for it that it exactly suited the needs of the province and required no alteration. The grant-in-aid rules offered, for European pupils reading in any school, result-grants at double the rates payable for native children; while for the help of fatherless children and for those of exceptionally poor parents, free boarding-stipends were offered—60 for poor children and 120 for orphans annually. Finally, 30 free apprenticeships were created, for the purpose of enabling European boys, after leaving school, to learn handicrafts and to obtain employment in railways, dockyards, and the like. This last portion of the scheme is said to have been attended with conspicuous success. The general conclusion expressed by the local authorities is that "ample provision exists for the education of "children of European descent, that full advantage is generally taken of the "facilities offered, and that the liberality of Government in the matter is repaid "by the results."

251. Results of its Introduction.—It will now have become evident that one of the chief difficulties that attended the introduction of the Code was that of so adjusting the scale of grants to the needs of different schools and different provinces that, on the one hand, no serious and sudden reduction should be made in the amounts earned by efficient schools, and on the other that the provincial assignments for European education should be kept within moderate limits of increase. There was danger that, under any uniform scale of grants, the protection which it afforded to one class of schools would necessitate undue liberality towards another. It was found, however, after a year's experience, that the checks and safeguards provided by the Code worked satisfactorily. In Bengal the Inspector writes:—"On the whole "it may be stated that good schools have generally obtained an increase "of grant, and that in every case where a school has lost a considerable "portion of its grant, this is the result of bad teaching or bad management." In the North-Western Provinces:—"The primary schools alone have gained "anything; all others have received diminished grants. But from what "I have seen of the working of the Code, I think the grants which can be "earned under it are ample for the support of the schools; and its application has appeared harsh only in the case of those schools which had been receiving aid quite out of proportion to the amount of work they were doing." In the Central Provinces the provisions of the Code were said to be generally acceptable to the managers of European schools. In the Punjab the introduction of the Code was postponed for a further year; but the Inspector anticipated satisfactory results from the examinations.

252. Attendance in European Schools.—A more important question was that of the increase in the attendance of European scholars which had taken place under the stimulus of the Code. In earlier paragraphs it has been stated that in 1875-76 the number of children of school-age in India (Burma being apparently excluded from this calculation) was 26,649, of whom 15,067 were at school. About 1879 the number of children of school-age in the Bengal Presidency (including all India except Bombay, Madras and Burma) was about 13,500, of whom about 8,500 were at school. In the following statement a comparison is made between 1881-82, before the Code was in existence, and 1885-86, when it was in full operation. For the sake of getting a connected view, the figures for Madras, Bombay and Burma are also included.

Province.	1881-82.	1885-86.
Madras	6,034	6,835
Bombay	2,906	3,288
Bengal	5,232	6,118
N.-W. Provinces	1,641	2,319
Punjab	827	1,558
Central Provinces	785	874
Burma	1,233	1,590
Assam	40	31
Berar	51	1
Coorg	1	20
TOTAL	18,750	22,634

Therefore in the ten years between 1875-76, when the question again came to the front, and 1885-86, the number of European children at schools in India increased from 15,067 to 22,634, or by a little over 50 per cent; a greater proportionate increase having taken place in the last four years of the decade than in the first six. Next, if we consider the Bengal Presidency alone, in 1879 there were "some 8,500" children at school. In 1882, as may be collected from the foregoing table, the returns show definitely 8,577 children within the same limits, while in 1886 the number had advanced to 10,921. That is to say, of the 5,000 children whom Archdeacon Baly's report showed to be growing up in ignorance, very nearly one-half have now been brought to school. The bulk of the increase may fairly be placed to the credit of the Code, with the additional facilities and inducements that it affords for the education of children. That all have not yet been brought in need occasion no surprise. The indifference of parents of the lower classes, European and Eurasian, combined with the extreme poverty of many, will always account for a large margin of children going uneducated. In towns, some of the children have no clothes to wear, and their parents are ashamed to send them to school; others again, in quarters where few of their class reside, are too far from existing day-schools to be able to attend them. In distant places there are, all taken together, hundreds of children who have no school at hand, and whose parents cannot afford to send them to a boarding school. Cases of the last kind are, it is true, provided for in the Code; but objection to charitable relief prevents many decent parents from taking advantage of the privilege. Without going into details for the different provinces, the figures given above for Berar will supply an apt illustration of the unsettled state of the floating European population in India, and of the difficulties attending their instruction. In 1881-82 there were 57 children under instruction at three schools for Europeans. The attendance at one of the schools dwindled from 20 to 6 in the following year, and the school was accordingly closed, the number of children at school in Berar thus falling to 39. "The Eurasian population," says the report, "of each of the districts and "railway stations in Berar is so much unfixed, that it is not possible to calculate "upon it at any one time for the establishment of a school of the smallest kind." In the following year one of the two remaining schools was closed " for want of "teachers," though it received a grant of R65 a month. The number of scholars in the single remaining school at Akola had now fallen to 15. Next year the office of the Judicial Commissioner was removed from Akola; many of the Eurasian inhabitants were transferred with it, and the Akola school, after coming down to an attendance of three pupils, was closed. Another small school was, however, opened elsewhere under the Church Mission Society. It was taught by a matriculated Native Christian and his wife, and was attended at the close of 1884-85 by 11 pupils, "children of office subordinates, who but for it would be "running wild about the station." Next year this school shared the fate of the rest. It was stated:—"There has been some race prejudice at work, which "has somewhat affected the utility of the school;" in fact it had come to be attended by Native Christians only. The single European pupil at school in Berar at the close of 1885-86 was reading in the Akola high school. Well may the Director of Public Instruction say.—" Under the peculiar circumstances of the "province, the provisions of the Code of regulations for European schools cannot "be strictly applied to Berar."

253. Expenditure in European Schools.—In 1875-76 the Government expenditure on European education in the whole of India was about R1,75,000. In 1879-80 it was estimated at a little over 2 lakhs for the Bengal Presidency and Burma. The returns of expenditure upon European schools are not given with any thing like completeness in the provincial reports; but the following figures for the year 1885-86 supply, so far as they are known, an interesting comparison with those of the earlier date:—

	1879-80.	1885-86.	
	Government, Expenditure.	Government, Expenditure.	Total Expenditure.
Madras	...	...	...
Bombay	...	1,15,300	3,24,796
Bengal	72,000	1,61,346	5,94,716
N.-W. Provinces	53,600	64,723	3,35,185
Punjab	46,200	83,435	2,83,954
Central Provinces	12,600	22,527	55,175
Burma	11,000		
Assam	4,000	6,432	14,438
Berar	1,200	...	...
Coorg		1,200	2,793

Thus for the Bengal Presidency alone, excluding Burma, the Government expenditure on European schools increased from R1,90,000 to nearly R3,40,000. The increase of a lakh of rupees, which the Government of India anticipated, has thus been largely exceeded. The amount payable for attendance and instruction could be foreseen and provided for. But there was one element of expendi-

sarily resulted in increased demands for accommodation. Large sums have been raised by private subscription; and with these in their hands the managers of European schools have been enabled to claim as large or even larger grants from the Government, both for boarding and for day-school accommodation. In Bengal the expenditure on building grants in 1883-84 was R12,500. In 1884-85 it rose to R95,000. In 1885-86 the amount originally sanctioned was R85,000; but at the beginning of the year the amount was reduced and many grants were ordered to stand over until the following year, so that the expenditure was brought down to R35,000. In the following year it rose to R1,11,000. To the Calcutta Free School building additions were made for the accommodation of 100 more children; the cost was estimated at, and actually exceeded, R1,00,000, and two-thirds of the expenditure was met by a Government grant of R66,666, spread over three years. It will be remembered that the Government of India offered in 1886 to make a grant of 1½ lakhs of rupees from Imperial revenues to the Government of the North-Western Provinces, in order to enable it to expand the Allahabad City School into a boarding school for poor pupils in the whole of the province. A Committee sat in 1884 to consider this question; but it does not appear from the reports that any action has yet been taken. In the Punjab R40,000 were spent in building grants in the two years 1884-85 and 1885-86.

One further point deserves notice. If the number of European children at school be compared with the cost of educating them, it will be evident that the grant paid for the instruction of a European is far in excess of that paid for a native scholar. This difference results from, and is justified by, the much greater cost of European schools, both in establishment and in buildings. From the figures given at the beginning of this paragraph it will be seen that the proportion which the Government grants bear to the total expenditure in European schools is 26½ per cent. in the provinces under the Code and 35½ per cent. in Bombay, or 28 per cent. altogether. From the table in para 98, Section I of this chapter, it appears that the grants paid to secondary schools of all classes in India from public sources amount to 36 per cent. of the total cost, and to primary schools 52 per cent. "Public sources," it will be remembered, include not only provincial revenues but local and municipal funds, from the latter of which European schools derive no aid. Hence from the point of view of expenditure, the grants to European schools are not open to the charge of extravagance.

254. Improvement in Standard of Instruction.—Though the Code was in general well received by managers, and though the ordering of definite standards and tests has given a healthy stimulus to European education, it is early yet to attempt to measure the improvement that its introduction has effected. Still, we are not without some indications to guide us in forming such an estimate. Thus, the report for the North-Western Provinces shows the classification of pupils in European schools according to the seven standards of the code. A comparison for two years is given :—

	I	II	III	IV	V	VI	VII
1885	254	300	319	293	176	107	66
1886	244	290	334	325	194	127	76

That is to say, the pupils reading the lower standards have diminished, and those reading the higher standards have largely increased. The number of pupils passing by the different standards shows a similar advance. The best test of efficiency is the proportion of scholars that pass and earn instruction grants in the elementary subjects of reading, writing and arithmetic. The following are the approximate percentages for two years; those for boys and girls not being separated in the returns for 1884-85:—

	1884-85.	1885-86.	
		Boys.	Girls.
High Schools	80	92	97
Middle „	79	84	91
Primary „	79	85	77*
TOTAL	79	88	92

There is no doubt about the improvement of standard. The girls have done much better than the boys.

In Bengal there is a similar improvement. The following figures show the proportion of scholars that earned instruction grants in the three elementary subjects, by passing in at least two of them:

	1884-85.	1885-86.
High Schools	78·6	85·4
Middle „	87·6	89·0
Primary „	86·2	87·7
TOTAL	85·4	88·3

Besides the improvement in standard, which is most conspicuous in the case of high schools, there is also a large increase in the number of pupils presented in the middle standards, especially in Standard V, and a corresponding decrease under the primary standards, I to IV. The increase of attendance in the higher classes is ascribed to two causes, both referable to the introduction of the Code. First, the improvement in the teaching brought about by systematic investigation into its results has enabled the scholars to pass more rapidly from the primary into the middle standards; and secondly, many of the children remain at school longer than they did before.

255. Alleged Defects of the Code.—Even at this early stage the Code has not escaped sharp criticism, whether expressed in words or with equal significance in actions. A few lines above, reference was made to " the improvement " in the teaching brought about by systematic investigation into its results;" and that such improvement is taking place there is no reason for doubt. But it was stated in paragraph 248 that on the first introduction of the Code into Bengal, some danger was apprehended of its eventually putting too much pressure upon both teachers and scholars. That is one of the points to which criticism has since directed itself,—over pressure. Another is the rigid and mechanical character of the Code, as hindering free development along various lines, and confining all instruction within one narrow channel. The objections are directed not against this particular Code, but against Code education in general, and the system of payment-by-results involved in it. After two years' trial, the managers of one of the great high schools of Calcutta resigned their grant of R200 a month rather than remain under the Code, because they felt that a Code, as such, limited their freedom in the matter of teaching, and prevented them from imparting so sound, thorough, and varied an education as they could give when released from its influence. Then as to pressure, and the bad education resulting from it, the Rector of another high school of established position

India, writes to the same effect: " Under the present system clever children are "kept back; average ones experience no great difficulty in passing, but do not " necessarily do the best they might; and dull ones have a bad time of it in "school." He also speaks of the evil consequences "when managers are "nervously expectant as to the results of the examination, and teachers' reputa- "tions are at stake and their minds and bodies in a state of tumult." All this is in complete accordance with the general tenor of the evidence given before the Royal Commission now sitting in England to inquire into the working of the Elementary Education Acts; evidence which may be summed up in the words of one witness,—" The Code drives the teacher, and the teacher has in turn to drive "the boy," and often at a pace beyond the boy's powers of healthy progress. That education should not be subordinated to pecuniary considerations; that teachers should work with an eye, less to the line of the Inspector's questions, and more to the requirements of sound instruction; that clever boys should not lose their chances of advancement, nor dull ones be forced beyond their capacity; that there are higher aims in the work of the teacher than filling boys with knowledge of the kind that leads to passes and result-grants,—these objections have long since been raised in England, and echoes of them are now beginning to be heard in India. No doubt the progress of schools must be tested if they enjoy Government grants, and with that object pupils must be examined; but it is urged that examinations should not so completely dominate the educational system; that Inspectors should inspect more and examine less; that the most important work of the Inspector is to see how the teacher teaches, not how the scholar answers; and that the status of a school should not be settled so absolutely by the performances of its pupils at a single examination.

At the same time, these criticisms should not blind us to the very different conditions that prevail in England and in India. Mr. Matthew Arnold, who is no friend to the method of payment-by-results, appears to admit in his evidence before the Royal Commissioners, that individual examination must for the present be retained in England, because the teachers do not as a body come up to that standard which alone would justify the adoption of a more elastic system. If that is true in England, it is still more true in India, where the paucity of thoroughly qualified teachers is the greatest obstacle to progress. Notwithstanding that defect, there is no room for doubt that very great improvement has been effected in European schools by the operation of the Code. This result has been attained through the system of individual examination, by which the position of each scholar is assigned and the amount of the grant determined. Remove that incentive to exertion, and in the opinion of many experienced judges the schools will fall back to a point not far short of that from which they have been raised with so much pains and care. It may be possible to relax the rigour of examination; but if this is done, the experiment should be tried in the first instance within a narrow range, and with adequate provision for examination at certain definite stages of progress.

256. The Bruce Legacy.—Reference has already been made to this munificent bequest. Miss Sarah and Miss Mary Ann Bruce were the daughters of Mr. Alexander Bruce, who had amassed a large fortune as an indigo planter in Bengal. Miss Sarah Bruce died in 1878 and her younger sister in 1880, after making wills expressed in identical terms. The trusts created under these wills were that the bequests should be applied " for or towards the founda- "tion and endowment of an institution at Calcutta or at any place within 50 " miles thereof for the education and maintenance of half-caste or Eurasian " female children, whether legitimate or otherwise, and in particular orphans " or those deserted by their parents, such children to be admitted only between

"the ages of 5 and 10 years, and to be maintained until they can be provided
"for in some respectable and useful station in life." The amount of the
legacies was about £45,000, to be increased hereafter by a further sum of
£22,000 on the cessation of certain life interests; altogether about £67,000.
Transferred to India, with additions on account of interest, the first portion of
the legacy produced a sum of R6,45,900, now invested in Government securities and yielding an annual income of R25,836.

The question, what was an "institution" within the meaning of the wills,
was keenly debated. Was it necessary to build and maintain a separate home
and school; or would it be sufficient if the girls to be benefited by the trust were
placed in one or more existing institutions having similar objects? The latter
course, if only it was consistent with the trust, would allow of the funds being
more economically applied and spread over a wider area; while it would also solve
the religious difficulty which now began to loom large. The wills made no
reference to religious distinctions, made poverty and necessity the sole grounds
for admission to the benefits of the trust; but it was quite clear that if religious
distinctions were ignored, the necessary result would be to deprive the majority
of the class for whom the trust was devised from any share in its benefits. The
majority of Eurasians in Bengal were Roman Catholics; and in matters of education the Roman Church claimed absolute control over both the secular and
the religious instruction of pupils professing that creed. Hence, if the school
was established on an undenominational basis, with permission to the ministers
of different denominations to impart religious instruction at stated times, no
Roman Catholic child would be permitted to join it. It was finally decided
that the question should be settled by the High Court, and a friendly suit (the
Advocate General of Bengal *versus* the Secretary of State for India) was instituted for the construction of the wills and for the framing of a scheme for
administering the trust. By a decree of the High Court, dated the 28th
August 1886, a scheme was sanctioned giving an extended meaning to the term
"institution." It was declared that "an institution shall be established for the
"purpose of carrying out the trusts for the benefit of half-caste or Eurasian
"female children, contained in the wills of Miss Sarah Bruce and Miss Mary
"Ann Bruce, and of administering the funds provided for that purpose. The
"institution shall be called the Bruce Institution," and "shall be under the
"management of twelve governors .... The governors shall provide an office in
"Calcutta at which .... the business of the institution shall be carried on ....
"The girls to receive the benefits of the institution shall be elected by the Gov-
"ernors ... Each girl who has been elected shall be educated and maintained by
"the governors at such suitable boarding school as they may from time to time
"select. In selecting from time to time the school at which the girls shall be
"educated and maintained, the governors shall take into account ...... the reli-
"gious denomination of the school and all other circumstances which they may
"deem material." By this felicitous interpretation all difficulties were removed.
The religious difficulty disappeared; and no portion of the funds being spent
upon buildings, the benefits of the trust could be more widely extended, while
the schools selected by the governors would themselves benefit by the increase
in their income, and thus be made capable of greater usefulness.

The governing body consisted of five *ex-officio* governors, and seven others
nominated in the first instance by the High Court for a term of three years,

interested. The first election of girls to the benefits of the foundation took place in March 1887. It was estimated that after the cost of a small clerical establishment had been provided for, the income of the institution would suffice to maintain 150 children. But it was considered undesirable to appoint any thing like that number to begin with; for if the full number were elected at once, no, or but few, further elections could take place for several years. At the first election therefore 69 girls were elected to the foundation, a number subsequently increased to 78. Elections are to be held annually.

(b) MUHAMMADANS.

257. Muhammadan Education: its Early Difficulties.—The special obstacles which beset the education and the social progress of Muhammadans have been the theme of frequent deliberation by the Government in India. In 1871 the Government issued a Resolution upon the state of Muhammadan education, in which the inability or unwillingness of the Muhammadan community to take advantage of the State system of education was pointed out as the chief drawback to their advancement in times past. After expressing regret that so large and important a class should anywhere stand aloof from active co-operation with the educational system, and thus lose the advantages, both material and social, which the other subjects of the empire enjoyed, His Excellency the Earl of Mayo in Council directed, with a view to removing such disabilities as were capable of removal by the action of Government, that further and more systematic encouragement and recognition should be given to the classical and vernacular languages of the Muhammadans in the Government schools and colleges; that in avowedly English schools established in Muhammadan districts, the appointment of qualified Muhammadan teachers of English should be encouraged; that assistance should be given to Muhammadans by grants-in-aid to enable them to open schools of their own; and that greater encouragement should be given to the creation of a vernacular literature for the Muhammadans. The whole subject was commended to the attention of Local Governments and of the three Universities of India. This was the beginning of the more recent agitation on the subject.

The reports received from Local Governments in reply to this Resolution showed how closely the question of language was connected with the educational difficulty. These reports were reviewed by His Excellency the Earl of Northbrook in 1873. Wherever, it appeared, the ordinary vernacular of the country was Hindustani or Urdu, written in the Persian character, or, again, where the Muhammadans used a form of the country dialect, there the Muhammadans occupied their proper position in the primary and secondary schools founded or aided by the State. But where, on the other hand, they spoke a language different from that of the majority of the population, or expressed in a different character, there the special arrangements necessary to meet these circumstances had not always been organised, with the inevitable result that the claims of the Musulman community were disregarded. The obstacles which kept the Muhammadan students apart from the ordinary school system naturally grew stronger as the higher standards of education were reached. With a strictly limited grant for educational purposes, it was not possible to maintain a double educational agency; and consequently it was in the high schools, the colleges, and the Universities that the absence or backwardness of Muhammadans was most conspicuous. The reports all agreed that the existing system had not attracted them to the higher ranges of the educational course, or induced them to persevere up to the point at which studies impress real culture and fit young men for success in the services and the open professions. The Resolution went on to observe :—

"How far this state of things can be attributed to the want of a connected "scheme of courses of instruction suitable for Muhammadans, leading up "through the lower to the higher standards, and how far to the general "disinclination of Muhammadans to exchange their earlier modes of study "for others more consonant with modern habits of thought, is a question "which need not here be closely examined. It may be conjectured that, at "the present epoch, Muhammadans are discovering that the ancient paths "are unprofitable to stand upon, while their traditions and natural predilections "still hold them back from setting out energetically upon newly opened roads. "For while it is confessed that Muhammadans nowhere appear in satisfactory "strength upon the lists of our higher schools, colleges, or universities; on the "other hand those institutions which have purposely preserved the ancient "exclusively Muhammadan type, and which have been restricted to instruction "in the languages and sciences which belong peculiarly to Muhammadanism, "have also been found to be falling gradually, but steadily, into neglect. We "may perhaps assume, therefore, that the Muhammadans are not so much "averse to the subjects which the English Government has decided to teach, "as to the modes or machinery through which teaching is offered. And if "it thus appear that, to the traditions and reasonable hesitation which keep "aloof our Muhammadan fellow-subjects, are added certain obstacles which "our system itself interposes—either by using a language that is unfamiliar "or machinery that is uncongenial—it is plain that many of the drawbacks "to the universality of our educational system are susceptible of removal.

"His Excellency in Council, therefore, perceives with gratification from "the reports now before him that judicious endeavours are being made to diminish, so far as they can be remedied, these inequalities in the distribution "of State aid, and to place the Muhammadans, wherever this may be possible, "upon a more even footing with the general community throughout the whole "course of our public instruction."

258. Report of the Education Commission.—Upon these lines, then, the Local Governments proceeded with regard to Muhammadan education; and the results of their efforts were reviewed at length by the Education Commission in 1883. In the discussions to which reference has just been made, much greater stress was laid on the educational than on what may be called the social or historical difficulties that contributed to the backwardness of Muhammadans. The Commission, however, touched on all these points, though, as was natural, the educational difficulties attracted the greatest share of their notice. The Commission recounted the many causes to which, from one point of view or another, had been ascribed the facts which all admitted, even though those facts appeared sometimes to have been exaggerated. What the causes were, the Commission remarked, which deterred the Muhammadans from the higher English education was debated even among themselves. While some held that the absence of instruction in the tenets of their faith, and still more the injurious effects of English education in creating a disbelief in religion, were the main obstacles, others, though a small minority, were of opinion that religion had little to do with the question. Some contended that the system of education prevailing in Government schools and colleges corrupted the morals and manners of the pupils, and that for this reason the better classes would not subject their sons to dangerous contact. The small proportion of Muhammadan teachers in Government institutions; the unwillingness of Government educational officers to accept the coun-

Government schools; the practice among the well-to-do Muhammadans of educating their children at home; the indolence and improvidence too common among them; their hereditary love of the profession of arms; the absence of friendly intercourse between Muhammadans and Englishmen; the unwillingness felt by the better born to associate with those lower in the social scale; the poverty nearly general among Muhammadans; the coldness of Government towards the race; the use in Government schools of books whose tone was hostile or scornful towards the Muhammadan religion : these and a variety of other causes had been put forward at different times by members of the Muhammadan community to account for the scant appreciation which English education had received at their hands. But, concluded the Commission, while all such causes may have combined towards a general result, "a candid Muhammadan would probably admit that the most "powerful factors are to be found in pride of race, a memory of by-gone supe-"riority, religious fears, and a not unnatural attachment to the learning of "Islam."

But having thus lightly touched on those general conditions adverse to Muhammadan progress, which it was impossible altogether to ignore, the Commission went on to consider more closely the special obstacles imposed by the system of public instruction and to formulate specific proposals for the further encouragement of Muhammadan education. These recommendations and the action taken upon them will hereafter be considered in detail ; but for the present it is sufficient to quote the general account which the Commission gives of the existing difficulties, and of its proposals for their removal :—

"Apart from the social and historical conditions of the Muhammadan "community in India, there are causes of a strictly educational character which "heavily weight it in the race of life. The teaching of the mosque must pre-"cede the lessons of the school. The one object of a young Hindu is to "obtain an education which will fit him for an official or a professional career. "But before the young Muhammadan is allowed to turn his thoughts to secu-"lar instruction, he must commonly pass some years in going through a course "of sacred learning. The Muhammadan boy, therefore, enters school later "than the Hindu. In the second place, he very often leaves school at an ear-"lier age. The Muhammadan parent belonging to the better classes is usually "poorer than the Hindu parent in a corresponding social position. He cannot "afford to give his son so complete an education. In the third place, irrespec-"tively of his worldly means, the Muhammadan parent often chooses for his "son while at school an education which will secure for him an honoured place "among the learned of his own community, rather than one which will com-"mand a success in the modern professions or in official life. The years which "the young Hindu gives to English and Mathematics in a public school, the "young Muhammadan devotes in a Madrissa to Arabic and the law and theo-"logy of Islam. When such an education is completed, it is to the vocation of "a man of learning, rather than to the more profitable professions, that the "thoughts of a promising Muhammadan youth naturally turn. The above are "the three principal causes of an educational character which retard the pros-"perity of the Musulmans. It would be beyond the province of a strictly "Educational Report to attempt generalisations based upon the social or histo-"rical conditions which affect the Muhammadan community in India.

"The recommendations we proceed to make have been framed, we believe, "not merely with a regard to justice, but with a leaning towards generosity. "They are based not more upon the suggestions contained in the Provincial Re-"ports than upon the evidence of witnesses and the representations of public "bodies. They deal, we think, with every form of complaint that is grounded "in fact, and they contemplate the various circumstances of various localities.

"Few of them, indeed, are of general application; many of them, we trust, will before long be rendered obsolete. Special encouragement to any class is in itself an evil; and it will be a sore reproach to the Musulmans if the pride they have shown in other matters does not stir them up to a course of honourable activity; to a determination that whatever their backwardness in the past, they will not suffer themselves to be outstripped in the future; to a conviction that self-help and self-sacrifice are at once nobler principles of conduct and surer paths to worldly success than sectarian reserve or the hope of exceptional indulgence."

259. General Effect of the Commission's Proposals.—The Government of His Excellency the present Viceroy reviewed, in a Resolution of July 1885, the general character and results of the proposals made by the Commission. It remarked, in reference to an important memorial that had been submitted by the National Muhammadan Association on the position and claims of the Muhammadan community in British India:—" It is only by frankly placing themselves in line with the Hindus, and taking full advantage of the Government system of high, and especially of English education, that the Muhammadans can hope fairly to hold their own in respect of the better description of State appointments. - This is clearly seen by the memorialists themselves, and the reports of Local Governments show that in most provinces a real advance has been made in this respect. –The object of the Commission is to attract Muhammadan scholars by giving adequate prominence to those subjects to which their parents attach importance, and to hold out special inducements to a backward class; but in applying the recommendations, due regard is everywere to be paid to local circumstances, and care must be taken to avoid unnecessary widening of the line between Muhammadans and other classes of the community." On the whole, the Governor General in Council was satisfied that the attention which had been once more drawn to the subject of Muhammadan education would have the best results. The memorialists recognised the fact that the Muhammadans, if they were to succeed at all, must rise to the educational level of the day, and their prayer for assistance to enable them to rise had been fully met by the measures taken in all provinces.

We can now therefore turn to the tabulated statements showing the educational progress of Muhammadans.

260. Progress of Education among Muhammadans.—The following statement shows how great has been the numerical progress in the four years following that on which the Commission's report was based:—

PROVINCE.	Percentage of Muhammadans to total population.	1881-82.		1885-86.	
		Muhammadan pupils.	Percentage to total pupils.	Muhammadan pupils.	Percentage to total pupils.
Madras	6·1	25,565	6·5	33,165	7·2
Bombay	10·9	63,972*	14·7	80,756	15·2
Bengal	28·6	262,108†	23·8	379,842	27·9
North-Western Provinces	12·	36,855	16·8	70,600	21·1
Punjab	48·2	41,900	38·2	155,219	57·7
Central Provinces	2·	5,929	7·2	8,048	7·7
Burma					...
Assam					21·8
Berar					14·3
Coorg					3·5
TOTAL					23·6

SEC. VII (b).] MUHAMMADAN EDUCATION. 315

It appears from this table that, whereas in 1881-82 the proportion of Muhammadans returned as attending school was below their place in the population, by 1885-86 it had gone considerably beyond that limit. The great increase in the Punjab was due to the large number of indigenous Koran schools that had in the interval been discovered and brought on the returns. As these schools had all along existed, no real addition to the sum of Muhammadan education, and of course none to that of English education, is indicated by the figures. Consequently it becomes necessary to divide Muhammadan pupils according to the class of institutions in which they read.

261. Classification of Muhammadan Pupils.—Accordingly, in the following table the pupils are classed according as they read in English colleges, whether for liberal or for professional education, in secondary schools, or in primary schools. These are the facts chiefly worth notice as showing the general educational status of the community. The number of Muhammadans in Oriental colleges, or under training as teachers, or reading in miscellaneous schools of technical instruction, can be seen from General Table III; and the extent and distribution of indigenous schools for Muhammadans will be treated in a later section.

PROVINCE.	IN ARTS COLLEGES (ENGLISH).		IN PROFESSIONAL COLLEGES.		IN SECONDARY SCHOOLS.		IN PRIMARY SCHOOLS.	
	Muhammadans.	Percentage of Muhammadans.	Muhammadans.	Percentage of Muhammadans.	Muhammadans.	Percentage of Muhammadans.	Muhammadans.	Percentage of Muhammadans.
Madras	42	1·5	3	·1	3,269	4·9	28,043	7·7
Bombay	24	2·3	7	1·1	1,638	4·3	55,872	13·3
Bengal	140	4·7	35	·3	20,609	11·6	335,807	29·3
N.-W. Provinces	63	14·1	30	10·7	13,898	21·4	27,889	14·8
Punjab	56	18·2	57	31·1	13,844	31·2	37,284	40·7
Central Provinces	5	6·3	...	...	417	10·8	7,592	7·6
Burma	...	...	...	...	...	...	...	...
Assam	...	...	...	...	1,488	14·9	7,810	15·5
Berar	...	...	...	...	276	·6	5,301	14·7
Coorg	...	...	...	...	8	1·9	151	4·3
TOTAL	330	4·4	132	5·1	55,447	13·5	505,749	21·1

Thus it is only in primary schools that the percentage of Muhammadan pupils (21·1) exceeds the proportion of that community to the whole population (19·1). As we proceed to the higher stages of instruction the proportion of Muhammadan pupils rapidly declines. Still, by comparison with 1881-82, a striking advance is recorded. From 1881-82 to 1885-86, great as was the progress made in the education of all classes, that of the Muhammadan community was exceptionally rapid. The number of Muhammadans reading in Arts colleges increased from 197, or 3·6 per cent. of the whole number of students in those institutions, to 330 or 4·4 per cent. In colleges for instruction in law, medicine and engineering, the number increased from 73 to 132, and the percentage from 4·3 to 5·1. In secondary schools the number increased from 20,000 to 55,000; but these figures afford no real guide, since in the interval the number of pupils in secondary schools had been increased by their primary departments. Percentages furnish a surer test; and the proportion of Muhammadan pupils in secondary schools increased during this period from 9·3 to 13·5 per cent. There is no reason to be dissatisfied with a record of progress such as these figures supply.

262. Progress of Muhammadans in Different Provinces.—The provincial statements of progress are not without interest. In the Punjab, Muhammadan students of English Arts colleges have increased from 13 to 56, and the percentage from 12·6 to 18·2; but as the population-percentage is 48·2, there is still abundant room for increase. Muhammadans in the Punjab take more kindly to professional, especially to medical, colleges; and the number of pupils of that race reading in the Lahore Medical School has advanced from 38 to 57, with a percentage increasing from 27·6 to 31·1. In Madras the proportion of Muhammadan pupils in colleges, whether for Arts or for the professions, shows a slight decline, though there is some increase in the number of students, 30 to 42, in Arts colleges. In Bombay the number of college students has risen from 7 to 24; but the proportion is only one-fifth of what it should be. In this Presidency, as in Madras, Muhammadans are hardly found in the professional colleges. In Bengal there has been a steady advance. In the North-Western Provinces and Oudh the increase has been very large; and the proportion of Muhammadan students in Arts colleges (14·1) and in professional colleges (10·7) either exceeds or nearly approaches the population ratio of 12 per cent. In none other of the greater provinces is this balance attained.

263. Success at University Examinations.—On this point no comparison can be made with the results of earlier years. The new forms of return show the number of students of each race or creed passing at the various examinations; but these forms were not introduced until 1883-84, and not even then in all provinces. Still it may be useful to show the number of Muhammadan students who passed the examinations of the University in 1886, and the proportion which they bore to the total number of successful candidates. In that year there was no Muhammadan Master of Arts, though in previous and in subsequent years Muhammadans have taken that degree. There were 33 Bachelors, or 4·6 per cent. of the whole number. At the First Arts or other intermediate examination 70 Muhammadans passed, and 138 at matriculation; giving proportions of 2 and 3·2 per cent. respectively. Among 175 successful candidates at the various examinations in law, not one was a Muhammadan. Of 269 who passed one or other of the medical examinations, 6 were Muhammadans, or 2·2 per cent. In engineering one candidate passed out of 188, or about ½ per cent. It has been stated that the proportion of Muhammadan students reading in general and professional colleges is about 4 per cent. The foregoing results appear, therefore, to fall short of what might have been expected; but it must be remembered that the students at any given time in college do not come up for examination until 2, 3 and 4 years later.

264. Recommendations of the Commission as to Muhammadans.—Such being the position of Muhammadan education so far as it can be shown in a tabular and numerical form, it remains to consider what special measures of encouragement were thought advisable by the Education Commission, and what steps have been taken in the various provinces to carry out their recommendations. A passage from the Commission's report, explaining the spirit and bearing of those recommendations, was quoted a few paragraphs back; and it appeared that it was the intention of the Commission to treat the Muhammadan claims not merely with justice, but "with a leaning towards generosity." This view of their claims the Governor General in Council supported, expressing the opinion that "in view of the backward condition into which in some "provinces the members of that community have fallen," it was desirable "to "give them in some respects exceptional assistance." The proposals of the Commission covered the whole field of education, and indeed went beyond it into the domain of public life and employment. Indigenous schools for

Muhammadans were to be liberally encouraged to add purely secular subjects to their curriculum (IX. 2). In public primary schools for Muhammadans special standards should be prescribed (IX. 3). In primary and middle schools Hindustani, as the Muhammadan vernacular, should be freely recognised (IX. 4, 5), and Persian in high schools (IX. 6). Higher English education for Muhammadans both in schools and in colleges, being that form of education of which they stood most in need, should be liberally encouraged (IX. 7). A graduated chain of scholarships, leading from the primary school through all intermediate stages up to the B.A. degree, and also a system of free scholarships in schools under public management, should be established for the exclusive benefit of Muhammadans (IX. 8, 9). The benefits of Muhammadan educational endowments should be reserved for Muhammadans, and should be applied, as far as possible, to the promotion of English education among them (IX. 10, 11). Special provision should be made to increase the number of Muhammadan teachers and Muhammadan inspecting officers (IX. 12, 13, 14). In the annual reports on public instruction a special section was to be devoted to Muhammadan education (IX. 16), and the extended employment of Muhammadans in public offices was commended to the special attention of Local Governments (IX. 17).

Such were the recommendations which the Commission, not without doubt and reservation, finally adopted as its policy. "Few of them," it declared, " are of general application; many of them, we trust, will before long be rendered "obsolete. Special encouragement to any class is in itself an evil." It was not therefore to be expected that the recommendations would escape, nor have they escaped, criticism. The chief objections were the following :—First, it was not to the interest of the Muhammadans themselves that they should be offered special facilities for learning Hindustani and Persian, instead of the vernacular of the country in which they were to be employed. (This objection, so far as it relates to Persian, seems to spring from a misapprehension. Persian was not to supersede the vernacular, but to take the place of Sanskrit, which was taught as a second language to Hindu boys in high schools). Secondly, it was still less to the interest of Muhammadans to establish special schools for their benefit. The spirit of exclusiveness or "separatism" had been the worst foe of the Muhammadans; and it was a duty incumbent on the Government to repress and discourage rather than to foster it. Muhammadan boys could not begin too early to learn the lessons of tolerance and emulation in association with those amid whom their lives were to be spent. Lastly, it was unfair to other sections of the community to establish scholarships for the special benefit of Muhammadans, while these last were also allowed to compete on equal terms for the State scholarships that were open to all. There was danger lest sympathy with the Muhammadans might result in unfairness to other classes. The Education Commission, in their "leaning towards generosity," seemed to have overstepped the limits of justice.

The Commission's proposals, and the objections taken to them, were discussed in the Resolution of the Government of India of July 1885 before mentioned. The Government attached special importance to the requirement that a special section of the annual reports on public instruction should be devoted to Muhammadan education; and it was ordered that the reports should be precise and detailed, so that the Government might be kept fully informed of the state and progress of the Muhammadan community. A liberal provision of scholarships was declared to be an essential part of the accepted policy of giving Muhammadans facilities for securing a better education and fitting themselves to take a larger part in public and professional life. In Bengal and other places where Muhammadan education was backward, the appointment of special inspecting officers to inquire into the causes that hindered, and the means of developing it, would probably have a good effect.

265. Action taken in Madras.—Upon the recommendations of the Commission the Madras Government remarked:—" Special encouragement is "already held out to Muhammadan education, and a further advance is con-"templated in this direction, though not exactly on the lines suggested by the "Commission. It is not thought desirable to dissociate this class so distinctly "from the ordinary scheme of teaching; as, except in a few localities, Muham-"madans avail themselves freely of the advantages of the existing system. "Thus, neither special schools nor special normal classes seem necessary; while "the recommendations as to the Persian and Hindustani languages are hardly "applicable to the peculiar linguistic conditions of the South, and ignore the "extent to which the Muhammadans use its vernacular languages. At the same "time the object of the recommendations meets with cordial approval." In fact, the condition of the Muhammadans in Southern India was, from an educational point of view, by no means unsatisfactory, and more recent orders have tended to improve it. All funds, provincial, local, and municipal are bound by the grant-in-aid Code to give special encouragement to Muhammadan education, the sanctioned rates being 25˙per cent. above those allowed for other schools. Muhammadan boys in all schools are allowed to read at half rates. Nine scholarships of R15 or R10 a month are awarded to Muhammadan pupils on the results of the First Arts and Entrance examinations; though the system has not been extended for the benefit of pupils in primary and secondary schools. Muhammadan schools have a special curriculum in Hindustani; though the experiment of separate schools has not been successful, and is not in fact necessary, except to some extent in Madras and one or two large Muhammadan centres, and for the Moplahs on the western coast. In the opinion of the Madras Government it is undesirable to accentuate the difference between Muhammadans and Hindus by making Hindustani instead of the current vernacular the medium of instruction, whenever the Muhammadans show themselves ready to attend the ordinary schools of the country. As the Director, Mr. Grigg, put it, "boys have more to gain than to lose by mixing at school with the "children of other sections of the population." But in Madras town there is a Government high school, the Madrassa-i-Azam, for the exclusive benefit of Muhammadans. It was raised to the full high school standard in January 1887, when the matriculation class was opened. For the training of Muhammadan teachers there are two special normal schools, one at Madras and the other for Moplah teachers at Calicut. There is a Deputy Inspector of Muhammadan schools, and four inspecting schoolmasters for primary schools. The necessity of appointing at least two more Muhammadan Deputy Inspectors is insisted on.

The condition of the Moplahs, dwelling for the most part in the Malabar district on the western coast, has received particular attention. The large decrease in the number of Moplah pupils in 1884-85 was the subject of special notice in the Government Resolution of March 1886, where it was stated that " the progress of education among this race is a matter to which the Govern-"ment attach great importance, and no effort should be spared to promote it." The loss of pupils was ascribed to the fluctuating policy of the district board, in giving or withholding the full grants to Moplah schools. During the past ten years little progress has in fact been made in the education of this backward race. There is hardly any demand for secondary education among them; and the efforts of the Department have been practically confined to bringing under inspection the mosque schools in which the Koran alone was formerly read, and inducing the *mullah* to employ a teacher to give that instruction in the rudiments which he himself was too ignorant to impart. The success of the

SEC. VII (b).] MUHAMMADAN EDUCATION. 319

scheme depended on the stability of the grants; and uncertainty on that point has greatly shaken the faith of Moplah schoolmasters in the value of State support. In the Resolution on the report for the following year, the Government noticed with satisfaction some improvement in the condition of Moplah education.

266. Action taken in Bombay.—It was noticed in the report of the Education Commission that a monthly grant of R500 was made by Government towards the support of a high school established in Bombay by the Society known as the Anjuman-i-Islam. In 1885-86 the income of this school was composed of the Government grant and of R571 from fees, without any other contribution from private sources. With this income it educated 139 pupils, 39 of whom were in the high and 100 in the middle school, all learning Hindustani and English. But the condition of the school had not given satisfaction to the Department, which complained that the results did not come up, either in quantity or in quality, to the standard which might reasonably be expected from so liberal a grant. The objects of the Society were not limited to the establishment of a high school in Bombay. It was a further part of its programme to promote secular education among Muhammadans throughout the Presidency; both by improving the mosque schools, and by establishing primary and other schools of the ordinary kind for the exclusive benefit of Muhammadans. The results as to the mosque schools were declared to be slight and disappointing. The subject of special schools for Muhammadans gave rise to keen controversy, first started in a memorial of the Anjuman-i-Islam to His Excellency the Governor. In this memorial it was alleged or suggested that the recommendations of the Commission had not been acted upon in Bombay, and that the Muhammadan community had been neglected by the Department. The second of these charges was traversed in detail by Mr. Lee-Warner, the Acting Director, who had no difficulty in showing that, throughout the Presidency, Muhammadans occupied a larger place in the attendance at public schools than they did in the population—a point which is illustrated by the tables given a few pages back. The recommendations of the Commission, Mr. Lee-Warner also urged, did not apply with any force to the Muhammadans of Bombay; although where special remedies were needed they had been applied. A Muhammadan Deputy Inspector had been sanctioned for Hindustani schools in each Division; and in every Division except one, for which a qualified officer could not be found, a Muhammadan graduate had been appointed. In the training colleges improvements had been effected which, though short of what the circumstances required, had succeeded in attracting an increased number of Muhammadan candidates for the post of schoolmaster. Lastly, a material addition had been made to the number of schools, already considerable, opened for the special benefit of Muhammadans. But though this had been done in deference to Muhammadan sentiment, the wisdom of the policy of separation was directly challenged. In Sind, where the Muhammadans preponderated, special schools were no doubt necessary; but in the rest of the Presidency, where the community formed small colonies in the midst of the Hindu population, the sooner Muhammadan boys took up the vernacular and qualified in the subjects taught to the people amongst whom their livelihood must be earned, the better for their own interests. That the feeling in favour of separate schools existed was not open to doubt. In the North-Eastern Division the Inspector was forced to the conclusion that Muhammadans often refused to learn English even when offered free scholarships, and that their exclusion from secondary education was due, not, as had been sometimes alleged, to combinations of other castes against them, but to their own determination to have no part in it. It was certainly the fact that in many places they preferred the study of their own classical languages to such an acquaintance with English and the vernacular as would alone enable them to compete with the races among whom they lived. But yet in other parts Muhammadans seemed to recognise the value of an early application to the vernacular, and of joining the ordinary public schools. The final conclusion was that it was no true kindness to the Muhammadan community to dangle before them impracticable schemes of separation; that the desire for special schools should at least not be fostered by the Department; that the Department should urge and encourage Muhammadans to resort freely to the public schools, and should open special Hindustani schools only if the demand for them was genuine and strong. The further measures that were recommended as suitable for Bombay were the following :—

(i) the establishment of an aided Muhammadan college in the town of Bombay;
(ii) the reservation of a fixed proportion of scholarships tenable in colleges and secondary schools;
(iii) recognition of the claims of poor Muhammadan boys to free studentships;
(iv) the establishment of special primary and even of special Anglo-vernacular schools in large centres of Muhammadan population where a genuine demand for them existed;
(v) an increase of scholarships for Muhammadans in training colleges; and
(vi) perhaps some concession in regard to the rules reserving high revenue appointments for graduates of the University, and certainly some changes in the public service examination.

267. Action taken in Bengal.—It has been stated in an earlier part of this report that in 1884 college classes reading to the First Arts standard were opened in the Calcutta Madrassa. But notwithstanding this alteration in the status of the institution, the concession granted to Muhammadan students by previous orders was continued—namely, that of reading in any Calcutta college, under public or under private management, at one-third of the regular fees, the other two-thirds being paid from the Mohsin Fund. The result has been that students have for the most part preferred to join the other colleges, in which they could read continuously to the B. A. degree; and the number of students in the Madrassa classes has never exceeded 20. The latest proposal, which has been favourably received by the Government, is to close these classes, and to allow the Madrassa students, while nominally belonging to the Madrassa college department, to attend the lectures of the Presidency College for their degree. With regard to the provision of special scholarships, the Government of Bengal in 1885 expressed the opinion that if in any locality the number of Muhammadans who gained scholarships was not in due proportion to their numbers and position, a fair case would have been made for exceptional, though perhaps also for temporary, treatment. Under later orders the following special scholarships were sanctioned:—Twenty of R7 a month, tenable for two years at any affiliated college by Muhammadans passing the Entrance examination; ten of R10 and ten of R7 a month, to be similarly awarded for two years on the results of the First Arts examination; two of R25 a month, tenable for one year, to enable Muhammadans, after passing the B. A. examination, to read for the M. A. degree. No special scholarships tenable in middle and high schools were created, as the Government considered that it was in University education that assistance was chiefly needed. For the purpose of more fully ascertaining the needs of Muhammadan education and the means of providing for them, the appointment of two Muhammadan Assistant Inspectors, on salaries of R200 to 300 a month, has been sanctioned by the Government of India and the Secretary of State. These officers will superintend Muhammadan education throughout the districts of one or of two divisions. The establishment of special schools for Muhammadans is not viewed with favour in Bengal; in the opinion of the Lieutenant-Governor "little is gained by such separatism." A grant of R100 a month has recently been sanctioned for the Anglo-Arabic school at Patna, which, though founded and managed by Muhammadans, is open to and attended by Hindus, and in which, in addition to English, Sanskrit is taught as well as Arabic and Persian. On another side, the Muhammadan maktabs throughout Bengal have been encouraged to introduce, in however elementary a form, secular subjects of instruction; and secularised maktabs form a not inconsiderable, sometimes even a valuable, addition to the primary system. This is rendered possible by the fact that in most parts of Bengal proper the Muhammadan element is the product not of immigration but of conversion. Consequently, the vernacular of the Muhammadan peasant is Bengali, or that special dialect of it known as Musulman-Bengali—the language of a popular literature already extensive. In Behar, Hindustani is recognised as the language which, however widely it differs from the Maithili, Magadhi, or Bhojpuri dialect which the Hindu peasant alone employs at home, is at any rate the common talk of towns, and the language of official use and of current vernacular literature. Thus understood, the Hindustani language may be regarded as the common property of Hindus and Muhammadans, and the medium of communication between them. Written in the Nagri character, it is accepted as Hindi; written in the Persian character, it is accepted as Urdu; though it is true that this common description is hardly applicable to the higher branches of literature, involving complex conceptions for which expression must be found, not in the popular vocabulary, but in terms derived from Sanskrit or from Arabic and Persian sources. This common language it is the policy of the Government to foster and develope. In it the Notifications of the Government in the *Hindi Gazette* are published, and in it school books are written. Nagri, or its cursive equivalent Kaithi, is also recognised as the official character, and that fact determines a further point in the educational policy of Government. The Hindustani school books are printed, according to their higher or lower standard, in the Nagri or Kaithi character, employed as it is by nine-tenths of the population of Behar. For the benefit of Musulmans they are also printed in the Persian character; but on condition that the other must also be learnt and practised. Thus the effect of the educational system in Behar is to make the Hindu peasant acquire, outside his own local dialect, the language of the Muhammadan invader, now the *lingua franca* of India; and on the other hand, to remove the isolation of the Muhammadan and to bring him into closer connexion with the public life of the province, by making him learn the character which all his Hindu neighbours use, and which is formally recognised and officially employed by the State. It is asserted that the objections to this policy, loud as they were at first, are fast dying away, and that the Muhammadan community is beginning to appreciate the solid advantages which it brings them.

The Calcutta Madrassa is maintained from provincial revenues; the local madrassas at Dacca, Chittagong, Hooghly, and Rajshahye are maintained from the Mohsin Endowment. The Calcutta Madrassa contained 1,100 students, nearly all of the Sunni sect, of whom 339 were in the Arabic department, or Madrassa proper, and the remainder learnt English and Persian, from the rudiments up to the standard of the First Examination in Arts. Important changes have recently been introduced into the Arabic department, where 75 students now learn English as an optional subject. In the other four madrassas there are nearly 700 students, and in three of these the standard of instruction in Arabic is as high as that of the Calcutta Madrassa, the students of all four madrassas being subject to a common examination once a year. In the Dacca and Chittagong madrassas there is a separate English department, attended by 125 and 114 students respectively. In Dacca the English standard is that of the University Entrance examination, at which candidates from this madrassa pass every year.

268. Action taken in the North-Western Provinces.—In 1884 the Local Government declared that the recommendations of the Commission were not applicable to these provinces, and that no special measures were necessary. The same opinion was repeated in 1887, when it was shown that the Muhammadans either held their own, or more than held their own, in the attendance rolls of institutions of every class; indeed throughout the province the proportion of Muhammadans under instruction is 40 per thousand, and that of Hindus only 26 per thousand. In secondary schools the preponderance is as 9 to 5. But no account of Muhammadan education in the North-West would be complete without some reference to the Anglo-Oriental college at Aligarh; that "noble college," in the words of the Education Commission, in which the learning of Europe is combined with instruction in the Muhammadan faith; where upright conduct and the manners of gentlemen are cultivated with sedulous care; and where "a healthy discipline varied by healthy amusement preserves much of the "influence of home life, while fostering a manliness of character which home life "would fail to give." With this college, the work of enlightened effort and enthusiasm, the name of Sir Syed Ahmed will always be connected. Young as it is, it has already given indubitable signs of the high place it aspires to take among the colleges of the North-West; and at the last examination of the University for the B. A. degree it passed eight out of its eleven candidates, five of them taking honours in literary subjects.

269. Muhammadan Education in Other Provinces.—In the Punjab no special measures are, in the opinion of the Lieutenant-Governor, required. Muhammadan students reading in colleges increased in 1886 by 50 per cent., a much more rapid rate of increase than that of Hindus, though the Hindus are still four times as numerous as the Muhammadans, while occupying about the same place in the population. Many officers of the superior inspecting staff are Muhammadans. The new grant-in-aid rules offer specially favourable rates to indigenous schools, and it is hoped that many teachers of maktabs will take advantage of them. In the Central Provinces, similarly, no special measures are said to be required. In proportion to their number, just three times as many Muhammadans are at school as boys of other religions, the aboriginal races excepted. There were a number of separate schools for Muhammadans; and educated Muhammadans had no difficulty in finding employment. In Burma, Muhammadans form so small a portion, and that by no means the most helpless portion, of the community that no exceptional treatment is called for. The Chief Commissioner of Assam (Sir Charles Elliott) was opposed to the recommendations of the Commission as inapplicable to that province. The Muhammadans, he said, belong by birth to the lowest castes; and their inferiority in learning is chiefly due to their having been unable to shake off that defect in their pedigree. They are by no means an impoverished class; they speak the same vernacular as the Hindus of the district, and there is no reason why they should not frequent the primary schools in equal numbers. Furthermore, the feeling in the province is such that, of two candidates, a Hindu and a Muhammadan, other things being equal, most officers would prefer to appoint the Musulman. In Coorg the Muhammadans form a very small minority of the population; and in Berar, where Muhammadans attend school even more freely than Hindus, the policy recommended by the Commission is already largely in force.

SECTION VIII.—PRIVATE INSTITUTIONS.

270. Meaning of the Term.—Under the previously accepted meaning of this term, " private schools " meant simply those under private management. The Education Commission pointed out that the term so used conveyed the invidious suggestion that a school under private management could serve no public purpose—a suggestion opposed to notorious facts. They accordingly confined the application of the term to " all indigenous schools which have not accepted " the departmental standards of instruction, and all others in which the course " of instruction, however advanced, does not conform to the standards prescribed " or accepted by the Department or the University, and which submit to no public " test." Practically, therefore, an account of the private institutions of India will be confined to those indigenous schools, whether for advanced or for elementary instruction, which have survived the creation of the departmental system and still retain their hold upon the affections or the interest of the people. It was with exclusive regard to this class of institutions that, in the Resolution appointing the Commission, the Government of India directed attention to " the extent to which indigenous schools exist in different parts of " the country, and are or can be utilised as a part of the educational sys- " tem," adding its opinion that the utmost possible use should be made of such schools.

271. Recommendations of the Commission as to Indigenous Schools.—With this opinion of the Government the Education Commission expressed their full agreement. They found that in many provinces indigenous schools entered largely into the system of public elementary instruction; that in some that system had been almost entirely created out of indigenous material; and that in all, under wise and sympathetic direction, the indigenous schools could be made to render valuable aid as an adjunct of the departmental system. They accordingly recommended that all indigenous schools, whether high or low, should be recognised and encouraged, if they served any purpose of secular education (III. 1); that the best method of encouraging indigenous schools of a high order and desiring recognition should be ascertained in communication with pundits, maulavis and others interested in the subject (III. 2); that to elementary schools aid should be given on the results of examination, the standards being so arranged as to retain those elements that were specially valued by the people, and to interfere as little as possible with the general character of the schools, while gradually introducing useful subjects of instruction (III. 3, 5, 6); and that municipal and local boards should be specially required to foster and develope indigenous institutions (III. 8—14). The effect of this declaration of policy, which received the cordial support of the Government of India and the Secretary of State, has been set forth in previous paragraphs, where it has been shown to what extent the system of public instruction in India has gained by the larger inclusion of the popular element. Indigenous schools have from the beginning formed the backbone of the primary system in Madras, Bengal, and Burma, and have been widely utilised in the Central Provinces and Berar. Under the influence of the policy now authoritatively recommended, they are receiving careful and generous attention in Bombay, the Punjab, and Assam. It is only in the North-Western Provinces and Coorg that the attempt to bring indigenous schools within the circle of departmental influence has failed. These facts have been set forth in the section relating to Primary Education, to which, indeed, the consideration of this subject, so far as it relates to the aiding of indigenous schools, more naturally falls. Indigenous pathsalas, it has already been stated, pass by imperceptible gradations into the class of public primary schools, at first unaided, and then at length qualifying for aid. That class of indigenous schools requires no further notice in this place; and attention will now be confined to those indigenous institutions, high and low, which prefer to stand upon the ancient ways, and whose adherence to their traditional methods has been in no way shaken by departmental exhortations.

272. Extent of Indigenous Instruction, 1885-86.—The following statement shows the number of indigenous and other private schools of various classes returned as existing on the 31st March 1886:—

Advanced Institutions, teaching—

		Schools.	Pupils.
(a) Arabic or Persian		4,933	53,997
(b) Sanskrit		1,404	16,331
(c) Other Oriental classics		47	416
	TOTAL	6,384	70,744

Elementary Institutions, teaching—

			Schools.	Pupils.
(a) A vernacular only or mainly	for boys		10,573	152,791
	for girls		197	2,880
(b) The Koran	for boys		8,230	89,260
	for girls		659	8,289
(c) Other subjects	for boys		741	20,130
	for girls		17	1,082
	TOTAL		20,417	274,432
	GRAND TOTAL		26,801	345,176

This list does not pretend to be complete, and there is reason to believe that it is not in all respects accurate. Thus, the classification originally proposed by the Committee and accepted by the Government of India, did not include Koran schools. In 1884 the Government of the Punjab represented that these schools could not be shown under any of the existing heads, because they did not teach the vernacular and were not advanced institutions teaching Arabic. The Government of India accordingly authorised their being shown under a separate heading; and this order was communicated to Local Governments. It appears, however, that the separation has not in all cases been made; and that of the 5,000 schools, more or less, returned as "advanced institutions teaching "Arabic," a large number, and probably the great majority, are nothing more than maktabs in which the reading of the Koran is taught by rote without any un-

ing their distribution over the different provinces of India. The table shows the number of schools only, not that of pupils:—

PROVINCE.	INSTITUTIONS TEACHING				
	Arabic or Persian.	Sanskrit.	Vernacular.	Koran.	Miscellaneous.
Madras	17	16	1,322	...	42
Bombay	84	6	1,667	888	313
Bengal	1,302	577	234		121
North-Western Provinces	1,573	567	2,052	...	...
Punjab	1,930	166	2,226	7,607	271
Central Provinces	...	...	...	...	
Burma			154	50	4
Assam	24	97(a)	31	344	7
Berar	3		27	...	...
Coorg	...	...	32	...	...
TOTAL	4,933	1,404	10,745	8,889	758

(a) Including 25 elementary tols included under vernacular schools in the provincial returns.

The 47 schools teaching some "other Oriental classic" have been omitted from this table. With the exception of six schools for Parsis in Bombay, in which the religious books of that sect are probably taught, the rest are merely schools in which the language is not specified, almost all in the North-Western Provinces. Koran schools, it will be seen, are separated in only four provinces. The 1,300 "advanced Arabic" institutions in Bengal are practically all of this character; and doubtless also many of those in the North-Western Provinces. Others are probably Persian schools of different degrees of advancement; and in the Punjab report it is explicitly stated that many of these are quite elementary, though returned as advanced institutions in the forms prescribed by the Government. This is equally true of the Sanskrit tols returned in large numbers for Bengal and the North-Western Provinces; in the great majority of cases elementary instruction in Sanskrit can alone be given. In vernacular schools—indigenous pathsalas for the most part—a striking contrast is afforded between Bengal and Burma on the one hand, and the Punjab and North-Western Provinces on the other. In the latter two provinces the mass of indigenous schools remain outside of, and unaffected by, the Department; in the former there is but a small remnant, among the thousands known to the Department, to which that description applies. The Central Provinces return shows no "private" institutions of any class. It is believed that all have been absorbed more or less completely into the departmental system.

274. Private Schools in Madras.—Indigenous schools for advanced instruction are very few in number, and but little information can be gathered about them. None of them, it is stated, have ever applied for recognition or aid. They have no settled curriculum, and most of them no fixed teaching staff. The course of study is said to vary with the knowledge and wishes of the students seeking admission. More precise information is now being collected from the managers of these schools. The relation of the Madras Government to the indigenous village schools of the province has been fully described in earlier sections of this report. Its policy has been to improve the existing schools, and to aid them under the results-system as soon as the managers, who are also in most cases the masters, conform sufficiently to the grant-in-aid rules. The number of indigenous schools not under departmental supervision has thus been diminishing year by year; and from the rate of progress in past years it is anticipated that all the schools which now exist, as well as those which may meanwhile come into existence, will in no long time be brought under supervision, provided the funds at the disposal of the Department and of the local boards keep pace with local requirements.

275. Private Schools in Bombay.—Schools for teaching the Koran are separately shown; and there remain 84 "advanced institutions teaching Arabic "or Persian," of which no information is given. In the few Sanskrit schools the pupils either read the Veda or confine themselves to the learning of a single Shastra. The course of instruction in indigenous vernacular schools in Bombay, and the new departure taken with regard to them, have already been described. About one-fourth of the known schools are now in receipt of aid, and the number is steadily increasing. But many seem to prefer a position of independence, and refuse to hear the voice of the Department or of the local boards even when they bring gifts in their hands. Mr. Giles, one of the Bombay Inspectors, writes:—

"I tried three schools in one morning in Ahmedabad city a few months ago, and the answers I received were characteristic. After reminding the masters what a fine *tamasha* had been held when the Education Commission came, and how they and their schools had attended and had enjoyed sweetmeats and seen fireworks, and no harm had in consequence happened to them, I proposed that they should come to my house to consider with me the offers of the Department in the grant-in-aid rules. One man told me he would come, but did not put in an appearance; another said he would think about it, which was a polite refusal; and the third said that he wished to have nothing to do with any Department or aid of any kind."

It has been stated before that the indigenous schools in Bombay are exceptionally well attended; and that fact may explain the independent attitude of the teachers. While, in other parts of India, indigenous institutions, whether for elementary or for advanced instruction, contain generally some 10 or 12 pupils, the indigenous vernacular schools of Bombay have an average of more than 25. The rural schools of this class are largely itinerant and therefore difficult to influence. Still, it is believed that the old-fashioned school is doomed. In another generation men fairly educated will take them up, and work them either as aided schools or, if independent, with some ad.. mixture of modern elements. The new grant-in-aid rules further provide that advanced indigenous schools, if they satisfy certain conditions, may be aided under special conditions applicable to each case. The Koran schools almost entirely stand aloof from the offers of the Department. Few of these, it is stated, could be utilised for educational purposes, owing to the dense ignorance of their teachers in subjects of secular concern.

276. Private Schools in Bengal.—The necessary correction being made as to the Koran schools, there remain a certain number of indigenous institu. tions in which Arabic, Persian and Urdu literature are studied. The more elementary are known in Bengal as maktabs; the more advanced as madrassas, and in these theology, philosophy and law are often taught to a high standard. The tols are the indigenous institutions of the country for the prosecution of Sanskrit studies. Sanskrit is the only language taught in them; and the pupils, after learning Sanskrit grammar, study one or more of the following special subjects:—*Smriti* or Hindu law and theology, *Nyaya* or logic, *Kavya* or *literæ humaniores*, *Alankara* or rhetoric, and Sanskrit works on medicine. The *kyoung* is the modern representative of the ancient Buddhist Vihara, or monas. tery. In Bengal it is confined to the district bordering on Burma, whence both the name and the thing have in fact been introduced for the benefit of the Mug or Buddhist population of those parts. As in Burma, instruction is given to students of that faith in Pali, the language of their sacred books, by a *raoli*, the local name equivalent to the Burmese *phoongyee* or monk.

The Education Commission stated what had been done to revive the Sanskrit schools of Bengal. The tols of Nuddea had for half a century received a monthly subsidy from the Government in order to help the pundits 'in their self-imposed duty of feeding as well as instructing their pupils free of charge. The grant has recently been increased from R100 to R150 a month. The teachers of these tols are scholars renowned far beyond the limits of Bengal; and, in the words of the provincial report, they "have attracted students "from all parts of India, from Tirhoot and Travancore, Sind and Assam, who "resort thither to finish their education." Four or five years are usually occupied in acquiring a thorough knowledge of grammar and the lexicon. Afterwards they betake themselves to special branches of Sanskrit learning ; so that most of the students are grown-up men, and some, who take up one subject after another, are far advanced in years. In Calcutta a central examination is held annually for the award of Sanskrit titles to those students of tols who show proficiency in Sanskrit learning. In the last two years from 60 to 80 candidates have presented themselves, and on about half of these titles have been conferred. The Nuddea tols take no part in these examinations, and stand in no need of encouragement of that kind. The "Saraswat Samaj" of Eastern Bengal is an association of local pundits having for its object the systematic improvement of tols. It has laid down four standards of examination, and no pupil may appear at any higher standard who has not passed by one of the lower tests ; consequently all tols that place themselves under the Samaj have to observe fixed courses of study. An association having similar objects has recently been established in Behar, chiefly through the influence of Mr. Pope, the local Inspector of Schools. Unlike the Dacca Samaj, which institutes tests and standards of its own, the Behar Association seeks to qualify the tols to pass the Sanskrit Title Examination ; and with that object it has framed subordinate courses and tests for the encouragement of those tols that require to be brought up to the Calcutta standard by easy stages. Both these associations enjoy a grant of R500 a year from the Government. The Sanskrit Title Examination is now held, not only in Calcutta, but also at Patna and Cuttack, for the convenience of students living in Behar and Orissa.

Nothing need be said in this section as to the character and status of the indigenous pathsalas of Bengal—the material out of which the whole primary system is constructed. It may be mentioned that the efforts of the Department to bring Muhammadan maktabs and Koran schools under inspection, and to add some useful elements to their courses of study, have met with some share of success.

277. Private Schools in the North-Western Provinces.—The character of the indigenous vernacular schools, in which are taught nothing beyond the current Kaithi hand and bazar arithmetic, has been described in an earlier section, where also it was shown how entire had been the failure to connect these schools, however slightly, with the departmental system, or to raise their standard of instruction. Very little information can be gleaned from the reports as to the constitution of schools of a higher class. On this subject the Local Government remarks :—" Any information that could be furnished as to the " character of the education given at the schools which are supported entirely " by private effort, and the classes of the population from which their scholars " are drawn, would be of great value."

278. Private Schools in the Punjab.—In the Punjab, on the contrary, the information is at once ample and precise. The inquiries set on foot in 1882-83, disclosed the existence of 13,109 schools with 135,384 pupils. The schools were classified as follows:—(1) Persian, (2) Persian and Koran, (3) purely Koran, (4) Arabic, (5) Gurmukhi, (6) Nagri, (7) Sanskrit, (8) Mahajani; besides others of a miscellaneous kind. The schools in which the Koran alone was read were by far the most numerous, and formed more than half of the total number. Those in which Persian was read in addition to the Koran came next, and after them the Gurmukhi schools for Sikh children. The general average showed only about 10 pupils to a school, and in 5,400 schools the attendance did not exceed six. The standard of attainments recognised as fitting a man for the office of teacher may be estimated from the fact that 5,200 teachers in these schools could not read a printed book, 5,800 could not write, and 9,600 knew no arithmetic. The Koran schools were generally held in mosques; the pupils learned portions of the Koran (of course in Arabic) by rote, but were not taught the meaning. The teachers were for the most part wholly illiterate. Some were blind or otherwise disabled. Of some it was reported that they were blacksmiths or carpenters, who knew the Koran by heart but were unable to follow their own calling. Some were artisans plying their ordinary trade. The idea that education should be gratuitous often prevailed, but in most cases the teachers were paid either by the students or by the community that maintained the mosque in which the school was held. The hours of instruction were so fixed as to allow the students time for their regular pursuits, agricultural or other. In some cases the students were itinerant vagabonds who gained their living by begging. Occasionally these were well known to the authorities as bad characters, in league with thieves. The Persian-Koran schools for the most part resembled the Koran schools in general character, with a little Persian added to the course. In a few, however, the students were taught not only to read but to translate the Koran, and were also taught Persian, Urdu, and elementary arithmetic. The purely Persian schools were maintained in general for the better class of pupils,—often for those destined afterwards for an English education. Translation was taught, but rarely grammar. Some of the teachers were able men. So also in the Arabic schools, many were distinguished as men of learning and ability and were highly respected. They devoted themselves to one or more of the special subjects of theology, law, logic, philosophy, grammar and medicine; but arithmetic was generally held in contempt. The Sanskrit schools resemble the tols of other provinces. The teachers sometimes earn a living by visiting neighbouring towns and villages where they recite the Purans, the Ramayan and the Mahabharata, devoting themselves on their return to the work of tuition. Some act as medical advisers, others as astrologers. The students are provided with food by their teachers or by other charitable persons. In some cases a high degree of proficiency is attained in Sanskrit grammar and literature; but the instruction appears to be chiefly religious. This is the case too in the Gurmukhi schools, where the boys are taught portions of the religious books of the Sikhs, which they learn by heart. The schools are held in Sikh temples and taught by the attached priests, who are mostly religious mendicants. Most of the teachers can read and write; they often teach their pupils writing, and occasionally arithmetic and accounts. In the mahajani schools, which are intended for the sons of tradesmen and are much the same all over India, the boys are taught to write letters and names and figures on the ground, or on boards sprinkled with sand; and they learn elaborate multiplication-tables, in which fractional factors are included. Some are taught compound addition, or book-keeping, or the writing of bills of exchange. About half the teachers are able to read a printed book and to write, and about half know elementary arithmetic outside the multiplication-table.

From all this it appears that the indigenous schools differ very widely in character, and do not always afford promising material for educational efforts. The pupils in Koran schools—and these form the majority—are sent there not to learn what is useful, but to fulfil a religious obligation. But the great difficulty lies in the ignorance of the teachers in schools of nearly every class. The present policy of the Punjab Government rests on the hope that, if it is made worth their while by rewards paid according to results, capable teachers will add paying subjects to their course, and thus the fashion will gradually spread. The boys, it is supposed, will learn whatever their teachers bid them learn. From the beginning many of the schools have expressed their desire to qualify for grants.

279. Girls in Private Schools.—The returns in General Table III, for private institutions, throw a side-light on the question of female education. It appears that there are about 12,000 girls reading in schools of their own, and the same number reading in boys' schools. The great majority of these are doubtless Muhammadan girls reading in Koran schools. The necessary allowance on this account may be made, and still it will appear that the customs of the country are not averse to the general education of girls, nor even to their instruction in the same schools with boys. The force of this last inference is, however, weakened by a fact noticed in the Punjab report that it is not the custom to teach the Koran to mixed schools of boys and girls. The boys are taught in the mosque, and the girls by the *mullah* at his own house.

SECTION IX.—DISCIPLINE AND MORAL TRAINING IN SCHOOLS AND COLLEGES.

280. Recommendations of the Commission.—Upon the question of discipline and moral training in schools, the report of the Commission dwelt at some length. After pointing out the connexion of physical education with this subject, the bearing which it had on the formation of a manly type of character in rescuing boys from the habits and vices of idlers, the Commission went on to consider the possibility and the limits of direct moral training as an element in school life. Much had been advanced in evidence and in memorials regarding the importance of moral teaching, and the lowered standard of conduct which had resulted from its neglect. There was a widespread feeling, they stated, that something should be done to develope the sense of right and wrong in the minds of scholars of all grades. "Some have advocated the preparation " of a moral text-book; others of a manual for the guidance of masters; whilst " others, again, think that the object will be more surely gained by introducing " lessons having a moral bearing into the ordinary reading-books.............. Un- " doubtedly they [text-books] offer one means of conveying moral teaching to " pupils. But even where their importance is recognized, we doubt whether the " teachers take sufficient advantage of any opportunities open to them of instil- " ling moral principles and habits into the minds of their pupils.. .... It is, of " course, impossible to secure that every teacher shall be a man of such moral " character as to lend weight to his precepts. But the inspection of a school " should, at any rate, include a careful enquiry whether the boys have had their " attention directed to the moral significance of the lessons they have read. A " simple manual for the guidance of teachers may assist them in this part of their " duty; while the knowledge that some enquiry will be made by the Inspector " will keep the subject before their minds. Nor should the moral value of strict " and careful discipline be left out of sight. When a boy knows and keeps his " proper place in the school, he will be in some degree trained to keep it in the " world also. Manners afford some indication of moral training, and should on " no account be regarded as beyond the teacher's care. It appears that a good " deal of what is sometimes described as moral deterioration in Indian school- " boys is in reality a departure from the gentle and respectful manners of old " times. .... On the whole, though no general measure can secure moral " training in primary schools, careful and constant attention may have some " effect in promoting it. We therefore recommend that all inspecting officers " and teachers be directed to see that the teaching and discipline of every school " are such as to exert a right influence on the manners, the conduct and the " character of the children, and that for the guidance of the masters a special " manual be prepared." The supreme value of religious instruction as the basis of moral teaching was admitted and indeed insisted upon; but the principle of religious neutrality required that the Government, while freely permitting aided schools under private management to teach their own religious doctrines, should abstain in its own schools from any instruction of the kind. All the more necessary, therefore, was it to seek to develope, in institutions under public management, a sound system of moral instruction based on principles of conduct that were common to all creeds.

281. Boarding Houses: Inter-school Rules.—Outside the range of direct instruction, the Commission pointed to two means by which discipline could be enforced and maintained; these were the establishment of hostels or boarding-houses in connexion with colleges, and the issue of rules governing the transfer of pupils from school to school. In their scheme of discipline, but few

Indian colleges made any systematic provision for control over the pursuits of their students out of college hours. Yet that was the one thing which would enable the professor to exercise the moral influence of a close and watchful discipline, and give him a hold upon the lives of those whose intellects he trained with such sedulous elaboration. The other means suggested had to do rather with the technical requirements of discipline than with the obligations of conduct in a wider sense. In towns where there were several schools, there was a danger of discipline being injured and the tone of education lowered by too keen a competition for pupils. Many schools lived entirely upon their fees, and were often obliged to wink at infractions of discipline for fear their pupils would leave them. Pressure of the same kind was brought to bear in order to secure the promotion of pupils who were not fit for promotion. The pupils grew to believe that they were conferring a favour by their attendance, and thus became masters of the situation. It was easy to see how discipline melted away under these relaxing influences. The hold of masters upon their pupils could, however, be restored if all schools would agree to accept rules, framed in the interests of all, setting bounds to the right of transfer and of re-admission. The Commission therefore recommended " that managers " of schools in competition be invited by the Department to agree to rules " providing, as far as the circumstances of the locality allow, (1) that, except " at specified times, a pupil of one school be not admitted to another without a " certificate from his previous school; (2) that any fees due to that school have " been paid; (3) that he do not obtain promotion to a higher class by changing " his school" (VII. 4).

282. A Moral Text-Book for Colleges.—So far all were agreed. There was no doubt that moral training was as necessary to the student as intellectual or physical training, and no dissent from the principle that a system in which moral training was wholly neglected would be unworthy of the name of education. Nor, again was there any difference of opinion as to the moral value of the regard for law and order, of the respect for superiors, of the obedience, regularity, and attention to duty which every well-conducted college was calculated to promote. Difficulties began when the question was raised whether good could be done by distinct moral teaching in institutions of the status of colleges, over and above the moral supervision which all admitted to be good and useful, and which all desired to see made more thorough. The question was keenly debated, and the two following recommendations were carried by a narrow majority:—(1) "That an attempt be made to prepare a moral text-book based "upon the fundamental principles of natural religion, such as may be taught in "all Government and non-Government colleges" (VI. 8); (2) "that the " Principal or one of the Professors in each Government and aided college deliver " to each of the college classes in every session a series of lectures on the duties " of a man and a citizen" (VI. 9). These proposals met with very scanty support from the Local Governments. In Madras, "no belief is reposed in the " virtues of a suitable moral text-book, based upon the fundamental principles " of natural religion, even were its preparation possible. Nor is any credit given " to the efficacy of lectures on the duties of a man and a citizen. The proposal " would necessitate a scrutiny of the professor's social and political views, to " which this Government is in the strongest manner opposed." His Excellency the Governor of Bombay was not prepared to say that the proposal was impracticable, but thought it no easy matter to arrange a text-book which would be generally acceptable, or which could be pressed on both Government and non-Government colleges. The Lieutenant-Governor of the North-Western Provinces was unable to support the project. He thought it no part of the functions of a Government in India to draw up a code of morality and issue it officially for the instruction of students, since these could hardly be charged with ignorance of the commonly accepted code of civilised communities, or with an acceptance of principles contrary to that code. Nor could Sir Alfred Lyall approve of a course of lectures on the duty of a man and a citizen. Possibly no two professors would agree as to what this duty consisted in; and it was clearly undesirable to introduce into schools and colleges discussions on subjects that opened out such a very wide field of debate. The Chief Commissioner of the Central Provinces did not like the proposals. Without a religious basis, a moral text-book could be little better than a collection of copy-book maxims. The course of a student's reading and the influence of his professors were far more potent factors in his moral education, and had produced results in the matters of honesty, truthfulness, and general good-conduct, such as no text-book of morality could achieve. Fortified by this almost unanimous expression of opinion, the Government of India, as stated in an earlier section, disallowed the recommendations of the Commission on the ground that the introduction of the proposed text-book would raise a variety of burning questions without doing any tangible good; and the Secretary of State confirmed this view of the matter, subject to the possibility of re-opening the question at some future time, should a text-book of eminent merit be in the meanwhile produced.

283. Action taken on these Recommendations.—The Commission had recommended or suggested the use of a moral text-book not only in colleges but in schools. As to colleges the question was for the present dropped; and indeed it seemed to be felt that there was some incongruity in prescribing a compendium of moral precepts for students who, in their college lectures on moral science and the ethical systems, were critically analysing the foundations on which the very nature of moral obligation rested. For schools the case was different; but even in the case of schools it was not by a single primer, supposing a satisfactory work to be produced, that the difficulty could be solved. For primary, for middle and for high schools—even for the different classes of these schools if the instruction was to be continuous and thorough—it would be necessary to fix separate primers, advancing from standard to standard according to the complexity of the moral notions which they enforced. But the ordinary reading-books used in each class in most cases conveyed, and in all could be made to convey, lessons in conduct suited to the understanding of students at different stages of moral growth. It is not therefore matter for surprise that the subsequent reports of the Local Governments contain no reference to direct moral instruction as a part of the school course. But with regard to what may be called the external agencies for promoting discipline, definite action has been taken in many provinces. The attachment of boarding-houses to colleges had been strongly recommended by the Commission. Sir Charles Elliott pointed out that the need was at least as great in relation to students in high schools. That principle had been thoroughly acted upon in Assam, where boarding-houses had been attached to every high school and to the training school at Gauhati. They had been met by an obstinate clamour that caste prejudices would be against them; but these prophecies had been signally falsified, and with one exception every boarding-house was full and more than full. This extension of the system was therefore recommended by the Government of India to Local Governments. I have been unable to find in the Madras and Bombay reports any account of what has been done in this direction; though it may incidentally be noticed that particular attention is paid in both Presidencies to physical education, to the establishment of gymnasia, and to the encouragement of sports among students in high schools. In Bengal, hostels have been maintained for some years with much success in connexion with all the larger colleges of the mofussil.

Another very important step has been taken for the benefit of students in Calcutta colleges. Some years ago a strong representation was made to Sir Ashley Eden, then Lieutenant-Governor, as to the difficulties and temptations to which students whose homes were at a distance were exposed when they came to reside in Calcutta. Sir Ashley Eden took up the scheme warmly, promised his hearty support, and indicated his desire to give up for the purposes of the hostel a piece of land in the neighbourhood of the colleges, valued at over a lakh of rupees. He backed this offer by a liberal donation from his private purse. Subscription lists were opened, and in a short time R50,000 were collected. The grant of the land was confirmed by Sir Rivers Thompson; and his successor, Sir Steuart Bayley has recently laid the foundation-stone of what promises to be a highly useful institution. Hostels have also been attached to several high schools; and under general rules recently issued, a capitation allowance of one rupee or eight annas a month is offered for each inmate of any hostel that may hereafter be opened. In the North-Western Provinces boarding-houses have been attached to all high schools, and are being extended to many schools of the middle class. In 1886, the number of boarders was 2,825; and the accomodation in many districts is said to be insufficient for the demand. In the Punjab boarding-houses have been established to an extent unparalleled, it is believed, in any other part of India. They are attached not only to high schools, but to the great majority of secondary schools of all classes under the management of public bodies. Rules for their management and support have been embodied in the grant-in-aid Code. In Assam and Coorg ample provision is made for boarders.

Rules governing the transfer of pupils from school to school are in force in Madras, Bombay, Bengal, the North-Western Provinces, Assam, and possibly elsewhere. The following summary of the rules in the North-Western Provinces may be taken as a general description of those now in force. They provide that a boy on admission to a secondary English school, Government or aided, shall, except for some sufficient reason to the contrary, remain at the same school till the end of the school-year, and that if obliged to leave within that time he shall receive a certificate showing what stage of education he has attained, and what character he bore; that if he leaves at the end of the school-year, the master shall give him a written certificate showing whether he has passed or failed at the final examination; that the grant of any certificate shall be made conditional on his having paid all sums due by him to the school he is leaving; and that he shall not be admitted to another school except on the production of one of the above certificates. He will not be placed in a higher class in his new, unless he has passed the final examination at his previous school; and he will not receive promotion within three months of his admission. In Bengal it is further provided that an offending school shall be reported to the University. These rules have in all cases been drawn up in conference with the private managers of schools; and it is hoped that they will prove an efficient safeguard against lax discipline, though this will depend upon the spirit in which the headmasters carry them out. It is on them, on their loyalty and co-operation, that the successful working of these rules depends.

284. Discipline in Schools in Bengal.—Apart from these extraneous aids, no special action seems to have been taken for the further enforcement of discipline in Indian schools. Indeed the question seems to have aroused no special interest; and it would appear that in most provinces of India the character and conduct of students are not such as to call for inquiry, still less for any strong remedial measures. In one province only has special attention been drawn to the subject. The public misconduct of certain school-boys in the town of Dacca led the Government of Bengal in 1884 to call on the Director of Public

Instruction for a report as to the want of discipline and the spirit of insubordination that were alleged to prevail among school-boys as a class, and as to the uecessity of maintaining stricter discipline in schools and colleges. Magistrates, District Committees, Inspectors of schools, Principals of colleges and Head Masters of schools were consulted, and a valuable mass of evidence and opinion acquired. The general character of the evidence may be thus summarised. There is some slight tendency to insubordination occasionally shown by school-boys towards their teachers within the walls of the school-room and when subject to its restraints, though nothing that the rules in force are not perfectly competent to deal with. Sometimes, but much more rarely, there is a sudden and violent outbreak of lawlessness, in which all the pupils of a class or of a college are involved, and in which for the moment discipline is entirely at an end. These outbreaks, in nearly every case, spring from some fancied slight put upon one of their number. Outside the school-room and when released from its discipline, school-boys as a class are growing impatient of control, and are losing even the form of respect for authority. There is no clear difference in this respect between the pupils of Government schools and of those under private management. The causes, it is alleged, are to be found partly in the character of the teachers, partly in the authorised course and system of instruction; but chiefly in the peculiar conditions of Hindu society at the present day, and the circumstances which permit and even encourage a spirit of lawlessness in the young. There is great difference of opinion as to the remedial measures to be employed; some holding that all such measures must be unavailing until Hindu society has worked out its own reformation; others that we may usefully have recourse to systematic moral training, the introduction of a boarding school system, and the adoption of stricter rules for enforcing discipline.

285. Recent Inquiries by the Government of India.—Still more recently the Government of India has had under its consideration the question of school discipline, and has addressed Local Governments on the subject. In the opinion of the Government "the general extension in India of education "on these principles has in some measure resulted in the growth of tendencies "unfavourable to discipline and favourable to irreverence in the rising genera- "tion. Such tendencies are probably inseparable from that emancipation of "thought which is one of the most noticeable results of our educational system. "But though inevitable under the circumstances of this country, they are "nevertheless, it will be admitted, tendencies which need control and direction, "so far as control and direction can be supplied by a judicious system of scho- "lastic discipline, and of such moral training as our policy of strict neutrality "on religious matters enables us to apply." The Government proceeds to define the standard of education to be aimed at, and declares that the only standard to which it is possible to appeal in educational matters is that recognised in the highest class of schools and colleges in England, since indigenous education furnishes no traditions which can be referred to for guidance in such matters. The remedies for the evils which are believed to exist are then considered in some detail; both those which emerge from the remarks of the Education Commission, and certain others which the Government of India think likely to be productive of "a healthy tone of feeling, self-restraint, reverence "for and submission to authority." The whole subject is commended to the early and careful attention of Local Governments, on the ground that the true interests of education are bound up with the solution of the problems in question. Nor is it believed that the problem is a hopeless one. "It is some- "times observed by the opponents of our educational system that the want of "reverence and the insubordination which is sometimes imputed to Indian "students is merely part of a wider movement over which it would be vain to

"attempt to exercise any control; and that while Western civilization is sapping
"the framework of Indian society, it is unequal to laying the foundation stone
"of reconstruction. A general statement of this character cannot be accepted
"as any argument against the adoption of measures to remedy an acknowledged
"evil. The magnitude of the change in native society may well have been ex-
"aggerated; but even if it be allowed that change is taking place to the fullest
"extent supposed, the old order must be replaced by a new one; and there is
"hope that the new may be better than the old. Let it be granted that Euro-
"pean intellectual training has cut loose the rising generation from many of
"the moral and social bonds of their forefathers: other forms of restraint must
"sooner or later take their place. Western education, if persevered in, must
"in time bring with it Western principles of discipline and self-control.
"The intellectual part of the process has made good progress; it remains to
"introduce the moral element which forms the most prominent factor of the
"European theory of education. The reforms of system indicated in the
"foregoing paragraphs have this object in view, although they may not be all
"that is required. They seek to fill the vacuum which a purely intellectual
"training has created, and to mitigate the evils of a one-sided development."

As the question is still under consideration, no further observations seem to be now required.

Section X.—EDUCATIONAL CONFERENCES.

286. Co-operation between the Department and Private Managers.—The VIIIth chapter of the report of the Commission dealt with the "External Relations of the Department to Individuals and Public Bodies." It was therein laid down, as the first condition of the success of private effort, that institutions under private managers could not be successful unless they were frankly accepted as part of the general scheme of education. They formed in some provinces by far the largest, in all an important part of the educational apparatus of the country, no less than those maintained directly by the Department; whence it followed that those who assisted the State by maintaining them should be allowed their due share of influence in determining questions of general educational policy. The Head of the Department must still be the controlling authority in the last resort; but in all matters that concerned the education of the community at large, he should be guided as much by the views of persons interested in aided education as by those of departmental officers. The time had not come when a representative board should be set up to control or influence the educational executive; but meanwhile a useful substitute for such a board might be provided by free and frequent consultation between the Director and those whose co-operation the State had invited and profited by. They therefore recommended "that conferences of officers of the Education "Department with managers of aided and unaided schools be held from time to "time for the discussion of questions affecting education" (VII. 2). In the same recommendation it was proposed that conferences of departmental officers—of the Director with the Inspectors, and of the Inspector with the officers subordinate to him—should also be held from time to time.

Several modes in which the assistance of the Department could be extended to private enterprise have been considered in earlier paragraphs of this report. The leading recommendation of the Commission on this point proceeded on the assumption that, efficiency being equal, an aided was to be preferred to a departmental institution: "that, whilst existing State institutions of the higher "order should be maintained in complete efficiency wherever they are necessary, "the improvement and extension of private institutions be the principal care of "the Department" (VIII. 10). This improvement was to be effected by leaving private managers free to develope their institutions in any way consistent with efficiency and with the protection of neighbouring institutions from unfair competition; by liberal rates of aid so long as aid was needed; by co-operation as to the fees to be charged in Government and in aided institutions; by impartiality in the award of scholarships; and by many other methods, all based on the principle that private managers were jointly and equally interested with Government in the spread of a sound system of education, and all intended to pave the way for the final withdrawal of Government from its own institutions and for their transfer to private control. These points have already been treated at sufficient length.

287. Revision of the Grant-in-aid Rules.—The grant-in-aid rules are the formal expression of the policy of Government in its dealings with private enterprise. They declare for each province the conditions on which Government offers its assistance to private agency. It therefore became necessary, if effect was to be given to the new and more generous policy advocated by the Commission, to embody in the official Code rules conforming to it. One of the earliest recommendations of the Commission in this chapter ran as follows:—
"that with the object of rendering assistance to schools in the form best suited

"to the circumstances of each province, and thus to call forth the largest amount "of local co-operation, the grant-in-aid rules be revised by the local Governments "in concert with the managers of schools" (VIII. 8). The Commission went on to consider in detail the principles to be embodied in the Code. It recommended that greater latitude as to the course of instruction be allowed to managers of aided schools, and variety in the course be encouraged by grants for special subjects; that the proximity of a Government school be not regarded as of itself a sufficient reason for refusing aid; that larger proportionate grants should be given (a) to schools in backward districts, and (b) to those in which large private funds could not be looked for, such as schools for girls and for low-caste and aboriginal races; that no grant be given to an institution in which the fees were sufficient for all requirements; that the maximum grant-in-aid be limited to one-half of the total expenditure; and that this maximum be allowed only to girls' schools, primary schools, and training schools. The Commission also required that every application for a grant-in-aid should receive an official reply; and that a periodically increasing provision for grants-in-aid should be made in the educational budget of each province.

The Government of India considered that all these points should be referred to a Conference in each province, in which managers of schools should be associated with departmental officers. Other matters with which a Conference might deal were the inter-school rules; the question of substituting for training in a normal school an examination in the principles and practice of teaching; and the position of the vernacular as the medium of instruction in secondary schools. These last points have been separately dealt with in earlier paragraphs.

288. Permanent Consultative Boards.—Before describing the steps that have been taken to carry out the proposal for Provincial Conferences, a brief notice may be given of the alternative plan for the appointment in each province of a permanent consultative board. After full deliberation this proposal was rejected by the Commission, on the ground that any advantages that such a board might secure would be purchased at the price of efficient administration. It was essential that the responsibility of the Head of the Department to the Government should be absolute. "To interpose a consultative board "between the Government and its responsible officers would be to destroy re-"sponsibility and to replace expedition by delay. A board such as that proposed "must contain representatives of many conflicting interests; its members must "include men of various creeds; advocates of the higher and advocates of the "lower education; representatives of departmental agency and representatives "of private effort; delegates from the districts as well as residents in the Pre-"sidency towns. A board so composed would be perpetually engaged in the "discussion of first principles; and if action were to wait on their settlement by "the board, prompt action would be impossible." All the good to be obtained from such boards could be equally well secured by the occasional and even frequent association of departmental officers with others interested in education. Under existing arrangements, the relations of departmental officers to persons outside the Department were too exclusively confined to official correspondence; and no opportunity was given for that free interchange of ideas, and that healthy contact with outside opinion, which personal intercourse could alone or could best secure. But most educational principles had by this time been settled; the machine was in steady working, and it was only occasionally that it needed to be brought under the light of outside criticism. Unless there was something to discuss, a permanent consultative board would either have nothing to do, or its interference would be meddlesome; and all the advantages that it promised could be secured by the appointment of a Conference as occasion required.

The Government of India highly commended the proposal to hold periodical Conferences, departmental as well as general, and hoped that no time would be lost in inaugurating them. It was added that if any Government desired to try the plan of a permanent consultative board, the Government of India would not object to this. The principle of such boards has long been adopted in the Punjab and in Burma, where questions of general educational interest have regularly been referred to the Punjab University and the Educational Syndicate respectively. In the North-Western Provinces it is stated that " the " Senate of the new University will naturally take the place of a permanent and " responsible consultative board, to whom all questions materially affecting the " education of the provinces will be referred." In the Central Provinces the Local Government has cordially accepted the plan of a permanent board. But in the older and larger provinces the proposal is viewed with no favour. It appears to be felt that a highly-organised Department stands in no need of, and would only be hampered by, a permanent adjunct of this kind. In Bengal, for example, the General Committee of Public Instruction, established in 1823, gave place in 1842 to a stronger body, the Council of Education, which was itself replaced in 1855 by the Education Department with the Director of Public Instruction at its head. To return to a General Committee would be to ignore the very different conditions that now prevail. A permanent board, however necessary in those earlier times when every educational question was an open one and no system of administration had been fixed, is thought to be incompatible with the complex organisation and settled principles of the present day. The same argument is used in Madras.

289. Educational Conferences: Madras.—The Madras Government in 1884 expressed the opinion that the free interchange of ideas could really be effected without a Conference. In that Presidency the interest in education was so acute that the Department could not, even if it would, ignore outside opinion. But in deference to the strong approval of the Government of India, steps were taken to carry out the proposal. Conferences were to be called together, but only as important subjects for discussion arose. The objections to an annual or other fixed periodical Conference were, the interruption of work without in all cases sufficient cause, the loss of freshness and spontaneity which an annual Conference would be liable to involve, and the risk of hampering the educational administration by the creation of a board of irresponsible advisers. Conferences for the discussion of specific questions might render valuable aid to the Director, but it was undesirable on many grounds to allow them to become fixed and formal meetings, or to develope into the position of a consultative board. The Conferences should be so constituted as to be representative of the leading educational interests of the Presidency. Government should be represented by officers of the Education Department, selected on account of their special knowledge of the questions coming up for discussion. Municipalities and district boards should also have a few chosen representatives, more especially when the matter for consideration had to do with primary education. Institutions under the direct management of native gentlemen should be fully represented; and each of the great missionary societies engaged in educational work should be invited to send a delegate. The principle of Conferences has been carried out on these lines more fully in Madras than in any other province of India. The subjects submitted for discussion to different bodies of persons at different times have been the following:—(1) the rates of fees to be levied in the various classes of schools, Government and aided, resulting in the " school-fee notification " by which all are bound; (2) the conditions of aid for

Of these the last was the most important, as having the most general application, and as affecting the whole system of aided education in a Presidency where aided effort has been chiefly relied on. The Committee appointed to deal with this question included three departmental officers, five representatives of missionary societies, one of the Muhammadan, and one of the Hindu community interested in education, and one Inspectress of girls' schools. The report of the Committee, which was sanctioned without alteration by the Government in June 1885, is a record of thorough and careful work, in which a generous recognition of the rights of private managers is tempered by the conviction that they should make every effort to increase their private resources, and that no undue strain should be put upon the Government funds. The Committee took under consideration not only the specific recommendations of the Commission, but all the complaints that had from time to time been brought to the notice of the Department as to the provisions or the working of the Code. A brief summary of the leading provisions of the revised Code may now be given. The Committee held that the rule limiting the grant to one-half the total expenditure, while it was needlessly liberal to prosperous schools, would press with undue severity upon those that were struggling. They maintained that a school receiving aid from the State was bound to furnish a complete account of its financial position, and that the rate of aid should be the amount actually needed to maintain it in efficiency. Further, in order to provide against the growth of large surplus balances as the local income of a school increased, it was laid down that if the income from all sources, including the grant, exceeded the genuine expenditure of the school by more than 10 per cent., the excess was to be recovered from the grant of the following year. This provision is in full accordance with the principle declared in paragraph 475 of the report of the Commission, that State aid should not be a source of profit to a school, that the grant should be reduced as the need for it diminished, and that self-support was the goal at which every aided institution should finally aim. A provision strictly correlative to this was that schools in which the majority of the pupils were poor should be entitled to exceptional privileges; and in this category the Committee included schools for Muhammadans, for hill-tribes, and for "Parayas" and other backward classes. The articles defining the qualifications of teachers were made more stringent, by requiring that every new teacher should possess not only general education but technical skill. At the same time the grants to training schools were given on easier terms, on the ground that money spent on their improvement "is, in the long run, a great national economy." The stability of results-schools was recognised and encouraged by placing on a permanent list of those eligible for aid, all schools that had taught the fourth standard in towns or the third standard in rural tracts with fair success for three years. In the case of new schools, the sanctioning authority was required to consider not only the financial needs of each school in reference to the funds available, but the number and character of existing schools and the educational wants of the neighbourhood. The standards of instruction were thoroughly revised with the object of making them more simple and practical. In infant schools "action songs" and the occupations of the Kindergarten were introduced. In the lower standards object-lessons were included; and these were to be followed by elementary lessons on animals and plants, with special reference to agriculture and to the substances employed in the arts and manufactures of the district. The standards in geography followed the now generally accepted principle of proceeding from the known to the unknown, from the concrete and particular to the abstract and general. Beginning with a plan of the school-room, they took the learner by successive stages to the district, India, and the

World. Drawing, hygiene, and mensuration were introduced as optional subjects. Specially favourable grants were given to girls' schools, the rates of aid in excess of those for boys' schools being raised from 75 to 100 per cent. The results-system was declared inapplicable to high schools, in accordance with the clearly implied opinion of the Commission that the line at which that system was applicable "should be drawn at any rate below colleges." Finally, as an important and useful matter of administration, the independent power of sanction allowed to Inspectors of schools was extended to grants of R15 a month.

290. **Bombay.**—The Government of Bombay appears to have accepted the objections expressed by Mr. Lee-Warner in the following passage to the appointment of consultative boards:—" Consultative boards have been compared to " screens, and it is not desirable that the responsibility of the Director or of the " Inspectors should be sheltered under a pretence of conferences. No one can " have been in charge of this office for even a month without learning the irre- " concilable character of many differences of opinion on educational matters. " Religious differences, caste inequalities, and social prejudices are accentuated " when educational topics are under discussion. The Mussalman community is "not yet unanimous in thinking that an English education is desirable; the " local boards are doubtful of the advantages of adequate fees; and school com- " mittees are unwilling to accept the theory of the equal rights of all classes of " the community." Still, Mr. Lee-Warner held it to be desirable to bring public opinion to a focus, and to enable difficulties to adjust themselves by a compromise. Conferences were accordingly held, at first by the Inspectors with the representatives of aided schools in each circle, and finally by the Director in consultation with the representatives of all educational interests. As a result of their discussion a draft Code was prepared, with enhanced rates of grants-in-aid. This was sanctioned by the Government of Bombay in 1887, though the proposed increase in the rates of aid had to be dropped on account of financial pressure. The rules are very much simpler and less detailed than those of the Madras Code. They contain one provision which has apparently been ignored in all other provincial Codes, though the principle which it involves was clearly recognised by the Education Commission. The Commission (page 417 of the report) declared it to be " an important element of the grant- "in-aid system that part of the expense of the aided institution should be pro- " vided by its managers from resources of their own," that is, exclusive of fee-receipts. This condition finds no place in the Madras Code; and in Bengal, after long discussion, it has been held that it is impossible to introduce into the rules any effective distinction between subscriptions and fees, though the amount of guaranteed subscriptions has to be shown in every application for a grant, and though the receipts from that source are known to be large. In the Bombay rules, the sanction of a grant is determined by the amount of subscriptions amongst other things. In another point the Bombay rules are exceptionally stringent, in providing that the grant shall in no case exceed one-half of the local assets, that is, one-third of the total expenditure. The maximum limit fixed by the Commission, and generally accepted elsewhere, is one-half of the total expenditure. But the most important change now introduced into the rules is the abandonment in certain cases of the principle of payment by results —hitherto the invariable practice in Bombay for all classes of institutions, and one on which the Commission commented adversely. The rules for colleges have been described in Section III of this chapter. The revised grant-in-aid Code extends the same exemption to certain classes of schools. Those whose permanent character is established may be put by the Department on a special list, entitling them to receive a fixed grant annually for a term of

years. Such schools shall continue to teach the recognised standards; subject, however, to the important condition that modifications may be introduced with the sanction of the Department. Another provision tending to relax the rigour of payment by results is found in the rule that "schools will ordinarily be exa. "mined and inspected in alternate years," receiving for the year of inspection a grant equal to that earned in the previous year.

291. Bengal.—A conference of Inspectors of Schools in the Lower Provinces was held in 1884; and inter-provincial conferences have also been held of Inspectors of European schools in the Bengal Presidency. Two educational conferences, attended by the teachers and managers of European schools, were held in Calcutta in 1886 and 1887 for the discussion of the European Code. The holding of a more general conference was proposed and sanctioned, but was put off owing to the illness of the Director, which compelled him to take furlough in 1885. In the cold weather succeeding his return a conference was held for the purpose of discussing (1) the revision of the grant-in-aid rules; (2) the course and standards of female education and the means of encouraging and extending it; (3) the inter-school rules. The members included two representatives of the Calcutta Missionary Conference; one from each of the leading Muhammadan Associations; three Principals of unaided colleges under native management; four ladies representing missionary agencies for female education; two representatives of the unsectarian education of Hindu girls; an Inspector and an Inspectress of schools; the Director of Public Instruction being President. In reporting the results of the Conference to the Government, the Director stated that the duty which they had undertaken "involved not only close attention, but much sacrifice of comfort as the "hot weather advanced; and I have to thank the members for the readiness "with which, in many cases, they gave up private engagements in order to "attend the meetings of the Conference. I have also to thank them for "the courteous and considerate spirit in which the various questions were "discussed. Differences of opinion there were; but when the members were "actuated by the single desire to promote the best interests of education, "with due regard on the one hand to the position and claims of the Depart- "ment, and on the other to the requirements of private managers, it was easy "to arrive at a fair conclusion. In nearly every case, after the subject had been "fully discussed, the decision of the Conference was unanimous." The revision of the grant-in-aid rules occupied the chief portion of the time. The leading provisions of the new rules were these:—Municipal contributions were treated as grants from public, and no longer as grants from private, sources. The effect of this was to diminish the amount claimable from the Department by a school already in receipt of a grant from any municipality. Of an opposite tendency were the rules, (1) increasing the maximum rate of aid allowable to colleges; (2) extending to high schools in backward districts, where large local contributions could not be expected, the more favourable rates allowed in such cases to middle schools; (3) relaxation of the fee-rule in training schools, girls' schools, night schools for adults, and schools for aborigines and low castes; (4) provision for free scholars in aided schools; (5) loans to school managers for the erection of buildings. The maximum grant (half of the total expenditure) was allowed to primary schools, girls' schools, and training and technical schools, and could not be exceeded "except in special cases, under special orders of Government." The Conference raised strong objections to the former rule that, "a grant "should ordinarily be reduced on renewal," and proposed the following amended form :—" A grant may be reduced on renewal, if this can be done without loss "of efficiency." But the Government of Bengal considered that the proposed rule would have the effect of abolishing an important principle of the grant-in•

aid system—the gradual transfer of Government aid from old-established to new and struggling institutions. It was only by enforcing this principle that funds could be secured for the development of education in the more backward parts of the country without increasing the total allotment for grants-in-aid, which might not always be within the power of Government. The rule was accordingly modified into the following form :—" A grant should ordinarily be reduced " on renewal when this can be done without serious loss of efficiency." It was at the same time provided that notice of any proposed reduction should in every case be given to the managers, so as to allow them an opportunity of stating their objections. Subject to the modifications just mentioned, all the proposals of the Conference were confirmed.

The discussions that followed on the subject of female education led to the adoption of improved standards for girls' schools and zenana agencies in Calcutta and the suburbs, and these standards were so prepared as to be capable of extension to rural tracts. Special scholarships for girls were also provided, and a scale of rewards instituted for female teachers passing by certain prescribed standards. Finally, in order to bring the schools in Calcutta and its neighbourhood under more systematic supervision, it was proposed to appoint at least one additional Inspectress. With the exception of this last proposal, which was held in abeyance on financial grounds, the new rules were approved. The rules governing the transfer of pupils from school to school were extended by the Conference to colleges, and a new rule rendered an offending school or college liable to be reported to the University. The revised rules applied only to Calcutta, and were provisionally sanctioned for one year; on the understanding that their extension to the whole of Bengal, in substitution of the existing transfer rules, was to be considered at a later date.

292. North-Western Provinces and Oudh.—It has already been stated that the Government intends to look to the Senate of the Allahabad University as a permanent consultative board for educational questions. Conversely, the University will look to the Department for advice and information as to the modifications necessary to bring the course in secondary schools into conformity with the new college courses; and in order to discharge that duty it will be necessary to hold a general conference of the managers and masters of aided and unaided schools. General instructions have been issued to the Director that he or the Inspectors should at their discretion invite to a conference any officers who can conveniently be spared from current duties. In accordance with these instructions, the new rules for the regulation of grants-in-aid to primary schools, the draft rules for the distribution of the grant-in-aid to secondary schools, the new scale of fees for Government and aided schools, and the rules for regulating the relations of competing schools to one another in the matter of the admission of pupils, have all been drawn up after full discussion with the managers of the schools affected. The regulations as to fees and transfer rules, which have been so framed as fully to protect the interests of private managers, have already been described. With regard to the support of aided education, the action of the Local Government has, it is stated, conformed in all respects to the wishes of the Government of India. No opportunity has been lost of encouraging private effort in the extension of education, with the result that liberal contributions have been made for this purpose from private sources. In order to give effect to the principles approved by the Government of India for the distribution of grants-in-aid, rules have been drafted by the Director, and introduced provisionally into all Anglo-vernacular schools. They have been in operation for a year; the Inspectors have been directed to ascertain and report the effects of their working; and a final Code of rules based on the experience thus obtained will shortly be prepared. The draft rules are framed in a liberal spirit. It is provided that a grant shall not exceed (1) half the tuitional expenditure, or (2) the amount needed to enable the school with its other sources of income to maintain an efficient teaching staff. Within these limits the grant will be regulated by regard to the average attendance, the quality of the tuition, discipline and appliances, the proposed expenditure, and the sources from which it will be met. Sudden changes are to be avoided as being likely to impair the stability of aided institutions; and the redistribution of the grants, in accordance with the principles now for the first time clearly asserted, will be effected gradually and with caution. The knowledge gained in dealing with Anglo-vernacular schools will be utilised in drawing up rules for aiding vernacular schools.

293. **Punjab.**—In matters relating to the general educational policy of Government, the Punjab University has long been recognised as its responsible adviser. But in questions that require for their solution the technical skill of experts, other measures are necessary; and it has been arranged that departmental conferences, and conferences of educational officers with others interested in education, shall be held annually in Lahore. Conferences of both kinds were held in 1886. In the departmental conference the following among other matters were discussed:—reorganisation of the inspecting staff; improvement of training schools; distribution of the lakh of rupees allotted to primary education; payment by results; primary schools for girls; measures for facilitating the rise of schools to a higher class. The recommendations of the Conference were generally carried out. The General Conference was occupied with the discussion of the grant-in-aid Code. The new Code provides that no school, the income of which from fees and endowments is sufficient to maintain it in efficiency, shall be entitled to a grant. Subject to that condition, no grant is to be refused to a primary vernacular school on the ground of want of funds; a grant may be refused to a secondary school or department on that ground; grants both to primary and to secondary schools are paid partly according to attendance and the results of examination, and partly on the scale of salaries; grants to colleges and to schools of special instruction are to be determined on their merits in each case. But the total grant to any school is not to exceed half the tuitional expenditure. The general results of the Conference are thus described in the Resolution of the Punjab Government:—" The new grant-in-aid rules for colleges and public "schools, which provide for the introduction of a system of payment by results, "will, it is believed, do much for the improvement of secondary schools and the "extension of primary education; and the rules for grants to indigenous schools "will afford the means of making throughout the Punjab a systematic effort to "improve these institutions without destroying their distinctive character. The "grant-in-aid rules, together with those regarding certificated teachers, will "ensure the employment of trained men in the aided schools of the province. "The standards of examination of primary schools have been revised; a series of "standards has been laid down for the determination of grants by results to indi- "genous schools; and the rules regarding certificate examinations have been recast "and embodied in the Code. A substantial increase in the rates of tuition fees for "secondary schools has been effected, and provision has been made for a further "annual increase in the case of Anglo-vernacular schools and Arts colleges. Vari- "ous points with regard to scholarships that still demanded consideration have "been embodied in the Code. The regulations regarding boarding-houses are cal- "culated to insure the efficient management of these institutions, which now hold "a very important place in the educational system of the province." It is added that the first General Conference has proved eminently successful, not only as regards the work already accomplished, which is by no means inconsiderable, but also as regards the hope that it holds out for the future. The proceedings

were thoroughly harmonious, though opinions were freely expressed; and the result has shown the great advantage of submitting educational questions of general interest to the discussion of such a body as that of which the Conference consisted.

294. Other Provinces.—Nowhere in fact has the recommendation to refer educational questions to the judgment of persons outside the Department been overlooked. In the Central Provinces a permanent board has been appointed consisting of 13 members, five of whom are managers of aided high schools and colleges, one is a pleader, and the others are officers interested in education. Only two officers of the Education Department belong to the board. The board have selected the middle school examiners, have settled the fee rates, and, after the touring season, will assemble again to consider such business as may be brought before them. In Burma, the holding of periodical conferences for the discussion of educational matters has had full consideration; detailed proposals have been submitted to the Local Government for carrying out the measure, but their adeption has been deferred for want of funds. In Berar, all the higher educational officers meet at Akola or Amraoti once a year and discuss educational subjects. The proceedings are reported to the Resident, and an abstract is published in the annual report. The meetings are open to the public, and such educated private gentlemen as are supposed to take an interest in public instruction are invited to attend.

295. General Results.—The educational conferences that have been held throughout India appear to have had the best effect. It may be doubted whether any part of the work of the Education Commission has been more productive of good. In the holding of conferences between departmental officers and private persons interested in education, the spirit which animated the Commission finds, in fact, its most complete expression. If any fault was to be found with the Departments in India, it was the besetting sin of 'departmentalism;' the tendency to regard aided schools not as allies to be welcomed, but as rivals to be feared; the belief that a Government school was in itself a better thing, and needed more vigilant protection and defence, than an aided school. That heresy it was the business of the Commission to destroy. The earlier paragraphs of this report have shown that, if not altogether destroyed, it is fast dying away. Beliefs of this kind cannot thrive in the atmosphere of a conference in which outside opinion is allowed free expression on equal terms. The declared object of conferences is that private effort may be encouraged and may profit; but it is no less certain that departmental officers, and the system which they represent, will derive equal benefit from the free interchange of ideas and of experience which a conference allows. Misunderstanding is often removed by a clearer insight into motives; and when once the distrust that is born of ignorance gives place to co-operation and cordiality on the one side as on the other, the education which both alike have at heart cannot fail to make steadier progress. The education of the people, by whatever agency accomplished, is, after all, the object for which the Department exists. Conferences, if frankly accepted (as they have been accepted) as part of the educational machinery, will probably do more than anything else to create the feeling which the Commission recognised as the necessary condition of a sound educational system; that in the success of aided institutions the Department is closely interested, that for their success it may fairly take credit, and that by their success it should be judged.

STATISTICAL TABLES.

INDEX.

GENERAL TABLES.

Table.		Page
I.	Abstract Return of Colleges, Schools, and Scholars in the seVeral ProVinces in India for 1885-86	349
II.	Abstract Return of Expenditure on Public Instruction in the seVeral ProVinces in India for 1885-86	350—351
III.	Return of Colleges, Schools, and Scholars in the seVeral ProVinces in India for 1885-86	352—353
IV.	Return of Expenditure on Public Instruction in the seVeral ProVinces in India for 1885-86	354—355
V.	Return of the Stages of Instruction of Pupils in Public Schools for General Education in the seVeral ProVinces in India for 1885-86	356—357
VI.	Return showing the Results of Prescribed Examinations in the seVeral ProVinces in India for 1885-86	358—359
VII.	Return showing the Distribution of Local Fund and Municipal Expenditure on Public Instruction in the seVeral ProVinces in India for 1885-86	360—361

STATISTICAL TABLES.

the several Provinces comprised in British India for the Official Year 1885-86.
(For Details see General Table III.)

AND POPULATION.			INSTITUTIONS.	UNIVERSITY EDUCATION.		PUBLIC INSTITUTIONS. SCHOOL EDUCATION, GENERAL.		SCHOOL EDUCATION, SPECIAL.	PRIVATE INSTITUTIONS.		GRAND TOTAL.	PERCENTAGE OF	REMARKS.
NUMBER OF TOWNS AND VILLAGES.*	POPULATION.			Arts Colleges.	Professional Colleges.	Secondary Schools.	Primary Schools.	Training Schools.	Advanced.	Elementary.			
2	3	4		5	6	7	8	9	12	13	14	15	16
		For Males				4,083	86,363	108	6,384	19,544	} 116,781	} Institutions to number of towns and villages. 20·15	
		For Females				349	4,337	27	...	873	5,586	·96	
		Total			84	4,432	90,700	135	6,384	20,417	122,367	21·11	
Towns . 1,360 Males . 106,087,755		Males				392,698	2,333,385	4,289	70,209	251,567	} 3,079,920	} Male scholars to male population of school-going age.† 19·29	
Villages . 578,144 Females . 102,109,395													
Total . 579,504 Total . 208,197,150		Females			7	25,714	204,117	660	535	22,865	254,160	} Female scholars to female population of school-going age.† 1·65	

Abstract Return of Expenditure on Public Instruction in t

		TOTAL DIRECT EXPENDITURE ON PUBLIC INSTRUCTION					
		University Education.		School Education, General.		School Education, Special.	
		Arts Colleges.	Professional Colleges.	Secondary Schools.	Primary Schools.	Training Schools	All othe
		1	2	3	4	5	
1. Institutions	For Males	R 15,07,050	R 5,42,679	R 67,36,356	R 71,02,730	4,49 173	
	„ Females	...	...	9,91,114	8,66,967	99,211	
	Total	15,07,050	5,42,679	77,27,470	79,69,697	5,48,384	
2. (a)—Percentages of Provincial Expenditure included in columns 2—17 to Total Provincial Expenditure on Public Instruction		9 92	5 33	22·71	18 55		
(b)—Percentages of Local Fund Expenditure included in columns 2—17 to Total Local Fund Expenditure on Public Instruction			...	14·92	58·61		
(c)—Percentages of Municipal Expenditure included in columns 2—17 to Total Municipal Expenditure on Public Instruction		1·23	...	35·89	42·62		
(d)—Percentages of Total Expenditure in columns 2—17 to Total Expenditure on Public Instruction		6·27	2·26	32·18	33·19		2 ç
Average* annual cost of educating each pupil in—		R a. p.	R a. p.	R a. p.	R a. p.	R a. p.	
Departmental Institutions	Cost to Provincial Revenues	209 13 7	212 14 11	12 13 4	2 15 9	111 7 10	
	„ to Local and Municipal Funds	0 14 11	...	1 1 6	1 15 9	21 1 2	
	Total Cost	281 12 4	290 9 6	26 9 8	5 12 0	132 15 10	
Local and Municipal Fund Schools†	Cost to Provincial Revenues	...	...	1 0 8	0 9 3	13 6 1	
	„ to Local and Municipal Funds	104 8 11	...	6 13 4	3 0 10	84 3 6	
	Total Cost	122 8 0	...	11 11 5	4 1 2	97 12 1	
Institutions in Native States	Cost to Native State Revenues	448 1 1	...	21 11 2	3 6 6	123 12 9	
	„ to Local and Municipal Funds	...	...	1 2 9	0 6 11		
	Total Cost	504 5 8	...	29 7 6	4 9 8	123 13 9	
Other Departmental Institutions	Cost to Provincial Revenues	..	679 11 1	1 5 7	4 11 .		
	„ to Local and Municipal Funds	...	...	0 8 0			
	Total Cost	...	702 0 10	23 15 1	14 4		
Aided Institutions	Cost to Provincial Revenues	40 7 5	19 3 4	4 14 6	0 11 5	32 8 0	
	„ to Local and Municipal Funds	3 7 11	...	1 7 7	0 6 11	1 6 8	
	Total Cost	176 1 0	44 4 11	21 11 11	3 2 10		
	Total Cost						

ovinces comprised in British India for the Official Year 1885-86.
(eral Table IV.)

	TOTAL INDIRECT EXPENDITURE ON PUBLIC INSTRUCTION.							TOTAL EXPENDITURE ON PUBLIC INSTRUCTION.	REMARKS
	Direction.	Inspection.	Scholarships.	Buildings.	Special grants for Furniture and Apparatus.	Miscellaneous.	TOTAL.		
	10	11	12	13	14	15	16	17	
	R 3,11,519	R 16,69,569	R 5,95,255	R 14,54,687	R 97,659	R 5,81,098	R 50,12,209	R 2,20,49,322	
	...	...	...	...	...	...	...	19,57,292	
	31,519	16,69,569	5,95,255	14,54,687	97,659	5,81,098	50,12,209	2,40,06,614	
·39	3·89	15·54	4·54	6·45	·53	3·13	34·47	100·	
...	...	10·14	2·12	7·58	·15	1·53	21·52	100·	
...	...	·90	4·11	10·83	·41	1·57	17·82	100·	
1·26	1·29	6·95	2·47	6·06	·46	2·42	20·91	100·	

The annual cost is calculated on the direct expenditure only. The average cost of educating each pupil is obtained by dividing the direct expenditure by number on the rolls monthly during the year.
The average cost of each pupil in Local and Municipal Schools is obtained from the figures given in General Table VII.
Fractions of a rupee are omitted, except in the columns showing the average annual cost of educating each pupil.

CLASS OF INSTITUTION.	Number of Institutions.	Number of scholars on the rolls on 31st March.	Average number on the rolls monthly during the year.	Average daily attendance.	Number of Institutions.	Number of scholars on the rolls on 31st March.	Average number on the rolls monthly during the year.	Average daily attendance.	Number of Institutions.	Number of scholars on the rolls on 31st March.	Average number on the rolls monthly during the year.	Average daily attendance.	Number of Institutions.
1	2	3	4	5	6	7	8	9	10	11	12	13	
UNIVERSITY EDUCATION.													
Arts Colleges.													
English	29	2,870	2,778	2,545	2	50	34	30	2	68	56	47	
Oriental	1	458	439	404	...	...	...	...	...	...	...	...	
Colleges or Departments of Colleges for Professional Training.													
Law	9	472	487	422	...	...	...	...	...	...	...	...	
Medicine	3	584	578	557	...	...	...	...	...	...	...	...	
Engineering	3	293	284	253	...	...	...	...	...	...	...	...	
Teaching	1	9	6	5	...	...	...	...	...	...	...	...	
TOTAL UNIVERSITY EDUCATION	46	4,686	4,572	4,186									
SCHOOL EDUCATION, GENERAL.													
Secondary Schools.													
For Boys { English	231	47,522	46,311	39,018	342	33,531	33,383	27,929	57	4,937	4,595	3,858	
Vernacular	196	10,929	9,987	7,798	566	57,790	55,646	46,628	...	...	...	...	
For Girls { English	5	445	417	317	3	177	149	123	...	...	...	...	
Vernacular	20	1,676	1,504	1,076	3	279	227	139	...	...	...	...	
TOTAL SECONDARY SCHOOLS	452	60,572	58,219	48,209					57	4,937	4,595	3,858	
Primary Schools.													
For Boys	996	56,843	55,613	41,703	13,784	637,386	619,777	474,848					
For Girls	97	4,569	4,353	3,057	719	26,844	25,861	17,355					
TOTAL PRIMARY SCHOOLS	1,093	61,412	59,966	44,760	14,503	664,230	645,638	492,203	1,742	98,211	96,249	72,632	
SCHOOL EDUCATION, SPECIAL.													
Schools for Special Instruction.													
Training Schools for Masters	43	2,185	2,124	1,838	46	1,201	1,157	1,042	2	87	88	75	
Training Schools for Mistresses	7	188	184	159	3	25	25	19	2	13	12	10	
Schools of Art	4	637	597	457	...	...	...	...	...	...	...	...	
Law Schools	1	6	6	2	...	...	...	...	...	...	...	...	
Medical Schools	9	721	778	672	3	61	62	61	...	...	...	...	
Engineering and Surveying Schools	12	481	498	402	2	25	22	15	...	...	...	...	
Industrial Schools	12	198	218	170	8	321	328	255	1	104	109	66	
Madrasahs	7	1,124	1,156	911	...	...	...	...	...	...	...	...	
Other Schools	38	339 (1,825)	319 (1,678)	273 (1,337)	2	76	56	43	1	... (324)	... (315)	... (291)	
TOTAL SCHOOLS FOR SPECIAL INSTRUCTIONS.	133	5,879 (1,825)	5,880 (1,678)		64	1,709	1,650	1,435	6	204 (324)	209 (315)	151 (291)	
TOTAL OF COLLEGES AND SCHOOLS—PUBLIC INSTRUCTION													

TABLE III.

Provinces comprised in British India for the Official Year 1885-86.

Number of Institutions	Number of scholars on the rolls on 31st March	Average number on the rolls monthly during the year	Average daily attendance	Grand total of Public Institutions	Grand total of scholars on the 31st of March	English	A Classical language	A Vernacular language	Europeans and Eurasians	Native Christians	Hindus	Muhammadans	Aboriginal races and others	REMARK
22	23	24	25	26	27	28	29	30	31a	31b	31c	31d	31e	
18	1,476	1,415	1,127	84	7,581	7,540	5,135	2,015	108	251	6,574	330	318	10 Girls.
...	...	...	...	2	546	42	505	41	...	...	495	51	...	
5	790	779	560	16	1,371	1,182	...	...	12	18	1,258	46	37	
...	...	...	...	3	584	448	...	...	141	29	233	9	172	27 Girls.
...	...	...	...	4	447	275	...	...	117	8	275	20	27	
...	...	...	...	1	9	9	...	...	...	2	7	...	...	
23	2,266	2,194	1,687	110	10,538	9,496	5,640	2,056	378	308	8,842	456	554	37 Girls.
349	43,734	41,028	33,848	2,263	264,918	224,832	71,413	207,732	9,868	8,675	200,728	30,850	14,797	2,078 Girls.
114	7,187	6,682	5,096	1,820	129,590	7,910	16,771	128,158	1	332	100,770	24,494	3,993	1,168 Girls.
15	979	835	706	241	15,522	13,417	861	6,812	3,936	3,445	1,755	7	1,379	1,388 Boys.
4	479	448	394	108	8,382	213	83	8,457	18	2,442	5,626	96	200	48 Boys.
482	52,379	48,993	40,044	4,432	418,412	246,372	89,128	351,159	18,823	14,894	308,879	55,447	20,369	{3,246 Girls. / 1,436 Boys.}
15,700	294,579	287,941	241,960	86,268	2,415,004	33,382	214,687	2,403,522	1,236	30,616	1,691,804	489,306	202,042	83,922 Girls.
480	11,137	10,086	7,756	4,337	122,498	3,639	1,594	120,859	1,847	8,978	88,635	16,443	6,595	2,303 Boys.
16,180	305,716	298,027	249,716	90,700	2,537,502	37,021	216,281	2,524,381	3,083	39,594	1,780,439	505,749	208,637	{83,922 Girls. / 2,303 Boys.}
742	1	8	8	8	108	4,333	434	1,458	4,246	...	752	2,787	424	370	44 Girls.
410	...	...	...	...	27	616	204	25	593	22	368	143	36	47	
...	...	...	...	...	4	637	...	...	71	75	30	413	47	72	32 Girls.
...	3	30	42	32	4	45	...	...	...	3	...	37	2	3	
...	2	157	158	131	16	1,127	220	...	718	42	82	859	210	34	8 Girls.
...	...	...	...	...	15	558	101	...	158	58	23	304	30	143	
1,107	896	8	215	211	171	50	2,024	128	6	948	64	424	1,119	300	117	186 Girls.
...	...	3	192	184	122	10	1,316	423	1,207	171	...	...	1	1,315	...	
558 (18)	468 (14)	3	345	319	262	90	2,696 (2,163)	141	611	1,691	86	9	1,959	588	54	8 Girls.
20	956	922	726	324	13,452 (2,163)	1,651	3,307	8,596	350	1,688	7,622	2,952	840	278 Girls.
16,705	361,327	350,136	292,173	95,566	2,970,904 (2,163)	294,540	314,356	2,886,192	22,634	56,484	2,105,782	564,604	230,409	{87,683 Girls in Boys / 3,739 Boys in Girls}

...	...	...	...	4,933	53,097	308	50,248	4,257	1	8	14,195	47,143	328	535 Girls.
...	...	...	...	1,404	16,331	...	16,242	239	...	...	8,919	...	31	
...	...	...	...	47	416	...	416	...	...	...	13	...	107	
MAINLY	For Boys			10,573	152,791	1,648	27,634	125,818	1	978	106,179	38,168	7,565	11,402 Girls in Boys
	,, Girls			197	2,680	18	427	2,472	...	120	1,235	1,398	126	878 Boys in Girls
	For Boys			8,230	80,260	...	79,479	9,176	...	64	4,001	82,861	2,334	
	,, Girls			659	8,289	...	...	6,238	...	...	69	8,208	12	
TO DEPARTMENTAL STANDARDS	For Boys			...	13	13	...	...	13	...	...	...	...	
	,, Girls			1	...	...	...	...	...	...	...	...	...	
STANDARDS	For Boys			711	20,130	1,822	1,978	17,702	1	177	11,759	5,916	2,277	12,027 Girls in Boys
	,, Girls			16	1,069	...	175	894	...	2	33	265	769	878 Boys in Girls
						3,809	182,837	162,456	17	1,349	146,402	184,059	13,349	
GRAND TOTAL						298,349	497,193	3,048,648	22,651	57,833	2,252,184	748,663	243,749	{99,510 Total Girls Schools. / 4,617 Total Boys Schools.}

	Maintained by the Department.						Maintained by Local Fund and Municipal Boards.						Under Public M
EXPENDITURE.	Provincial Revenues.	Local Rates or Cesses.	Municipal Funds.	Fees.	Subscriptions.	Endowments and other Sources.	TOTAL.	Provincial Revenues.	Local Rates or Cesses.	Municipal Funds.	Fees.	Subscriptions.	Endowments and other Sources.	TOTAL.	Native State Revenues.
	2a	2b	2c	2d	2e	2f	2	3a	3b	3c	3d	3e	3f	3	
	R	R	R	R	R	R	R	R	R	R	R	R	R	R	
Arts Colleges.															
. . . .	6,61,184	...	3,000	1,83,448	44	44,659	8,92,335	...	2,528	1,027	610	...	...	4,165	25,09
. . . .	13,901	...	...	...	...	234	14,135	...	...	...	...	...	...	...	...
or Departments of *...es for Professional* *ining.*															
. . . .	−257	...	...	32,121	...	2,967	34,831	...	...	...	...	...	...	...	...
c . .	1,61,876	...	...	52,597	...	1,804	2,16,277	...	...	...	...	...	...	...	...
:ring . .	1,25,123	...	...	15,548	...	189	1,40,860	...	...	...	...	...	...	...	...
.g . .	1,797	...	...	.	...	...	1,797	...	...	...	...	...	...	...	...
TOTAL UNIVERSITY EDUCATION .	9,63,614	...	3,000	2,83,714	44	49,853	13,00,225	...	2,528	1,027	610	...	...	4,165	
ndary Schools.															
{ English .	6,41,913	7,714	53,188	6,60,229	6,081	31,253	14,00,378	76,158	2,12,479	1,49,611	2,27,068	3,035	70,768	7,39,119	
s { Vernacular .	57,773	609	625	24,774	4,918	25	88,724	701	2,07,341	36,443	35,157	2,259	2,968	2,84,869	
{ English .	34,482	...	1,500	8,112	630	1,832	46,556	16,320	...	4,487	713	..	691	22,211	
s { Vernacular .	12,988	126	...	357	...	...	13,471	169	499	484	...	...	...	1,152	
ECONDARY SCHOOLS	7,47,156	8,449	55,313	6,93,472	11,629	33,110	15,49,129	93,348	4,20,319	1,91,025	2,62,938	5,294	74,427	10,47,351	
imary Schools.															
s . .	1,48,886	73,117	39,326	42,691	2,336	1,087	3,07,643	3,51,420	16,46,966	2,19,388	2,70,274	5,825	8,248	25,02,121	
ls . .	30,238	3,887	2,697	450	165	14	37,451	22,033	61,431	43,192	1,601	757	1,723	1,30,737	
MARY SCHOOLS	1,79,124	77,004	42,423	43,141	2,501	1,101	3,45,094	3,73,453	17,08,397	2,62,580	2,71,875	6,582	9,971	26,32,858	
for Special Instruc- *tions.*															
{ Schools for rs . . .	2,17,169	44,862	...	726	...	213	2,62,970	15,131	94,881	1,839	15	...	154	1,12,020	0,770
{ Schools for ..scs . .	40,160	3,178	600	...	...	34	43,972	685	2,829	...	...	...	18	3,532	1,610
of Art . .	72,874	...	...	6,773	...	19,943	99,590	...	...	...	...	...	...	...	...
.oo s . .	400	...	...	...	...	. .	400	...	...	...	...	...	...	...	...
Schools .	1,07,616	22,474	15,928	14,078	...	2,983	1,63,079	...	4,939	240	...	...	6,028	11,197	...
ring and Surveying s . .	39,593	...	...	7,106	...	599	47,298	19	...	1,146	...	...	...	1,165	...
al Schools .	3,614	...	24	...	...	3,380	7,018	1,500	1,091	720	...	...	22,204	25,515	4,853
:hs . .	25,515	...	...	4,859	...	24,732	55,106	...	.	...	...	...	...	...	...
hools .	68,533	...	1,290	2,658	...	9,812	82,293	...	1,137	443	...	1,027	...	2,507	660
:CIAL SCHOOLS .	5,75,474	70,514	17,842	36,200	...	61,696	7,61,726	17,335	1,04,857	4,388	15	1,027	28,404	1,56,026	
	...	...	...	...	...	...	...	...	...	...	...	...	...		
	...	...	...	...	...	...	...	...	...	...	...	...	...		
	...	...	...	...	...	...	...	...	...	...	...	...	...		
oual Colleges	...	...	...	...	...	...	...	...	...	...	...	...	...		
ry Schools .	...	...	...	...	...		...	...	...		...				
" . .	...	...	...	...	...			...							
than	.	...													
	...	...	...	...	...										
Apparatus (special	...	...	...	...											

ritish India for the Official Year 1885-86.

		UNDER PRIVATE MANAGEMENT.										EXPENDITURE FROM			
		Aided by the Department or by Local Fund or Municipal Boards.						Unaided.							
TOTAL.	Provincial Revenues.	Local Rates or Cesses.	Municipal Funds.	Fees.	Subscriptions.	Endowments and other Sources.	TOTAL.	Fees.	Subscriptions.	Endowments and other Sources.	TOTAL.	Provincial Revenues.	Local Rates or Cesses.	Municipal Funds.	Fees.
	6a	6b	6c	6d	6e	6f	6	7a	7b	7c	7	8a	8b	8c	8d
R	R	R	R	R	R	R	R	R	R	R	R	R	R	R	R
...	1,12,795	...	9,969	1,26,492	22,47	2,24,645	4,95,948	16,310	9,506	40,568	66,384	7,73,979	2,528	13,965	3,29,062
...	2,533	...	...	19	...	3,287	5,839	...	...	...	...	16,434	...	...	19
4,800	999	...	...	505	...	800	2,304	6,829	...	...	6,911	1,082	...	...	42,415
...	...	...	...	...	...	...	...	...	...	...	...	1,61,876	...	...	52,597
1,34,909	...	...	...	...	...	...	...	...	...	...	...	2,60,032	...	...	15,548
...	...	...	...	...	...	...	...	...	...	...	...	1,797	...	...	...
	1,16,327	...	9,969	1,27,016	22,047	2,28,732	5,04,091	23,149	9,506	40,640	73,295				
23,200	6,29,236	1,01,065	1,26,539	12,27,569	3,26,307	6,04,292	30,15,008	3,96,017	79,565(a)	1,56,073	6,31,655	13,48,915	3,21,258	3,30,168(b)	25,40,524
...	1,18,957	13,524	19,545	1,25,186	90,604	9,234	3,77,050	10,683	14,742	15,502	40,927	1,77,431	2,21,474	56,613	1,95,800
5,320	1,87,373	6,746	12,365	2,98,156	48,584	2,39,321	7,92,545	402	1,040	3,357	4,709	2,38,175	6,746	18,342	3,07,383
...	31,400	2,000	2,616	5,162	17,740	40,994	99,912	...	4,387	761	5,148	44,557	2,625	3,100	5,519
	9,66,966	1,23,335	1,61,065	16,56,073	4,83,235	8,93,841	42,84,515	4,07,102	99,734	1,75,693	6,82,529				
	7,34,521	3,62,096	1,61,508	17,19,109	1,69,880	3,38,179	34,85,293	2,97,196	24,807	80,725	4,02,728				
	1,90,466	20,965	18,345	47,898	1,27,462	2,08,286	6,13,422	2,033	13,013	30,176	45,222				
	9,24,987	3,83,061	1,79,853	17,67,007	2,97,342	5,46,465	40,98,715	2,99,229	37,820	1,10,901	4,47,950				
...	20,322	650	...	782	12,022	28,817	62,593	...	...	818	818	2,52,622	1,40,393	1,839	1,525
...	22,059	...	1,200	2,166	8,869	15,799	50,093	...	...	...	...	62,904	6,007	1,800	2,166
...	...	...	...	...	...	...	...	...	...	...	...	72,874	...	...	6,773
...	...	...	...	...	...	...	...	1,955	...	...	1,955	400	...	...	1,055
...,059	68,924	...	...	...	...	...	...	2,310	...	...	2,310	1,72,400	27,403	18,249	16,388
...	...	...	...	...	...	...	...	...	...	...	...	39,612	...	1,146	7,106
...	10,077	1,080	2,004	1,029	3,043	29,220	46,453	2	1,322	5,385	6,709	15,191	2,171	3,748	1,031
...	...	...	...	...	...	...	...	16,963	12,000	1,607	30,570	25,515	...	...	21,822
...,600	34,316	...	208	831	2,806	293	5,086	255	...	1,773	2,028	77,405	4,448	1,941	6,215
1,03,240	53,406	1,730	3,412	4,808	26,740	74,129	1,64,225	21,485	13,322	9,583	44,390				
...	...	...	...	...	...	...	...	...	...	...	...	31,200	...	...	2,65,539
...	...	...	...	...	...	...	...	...	...	...	...	3,09,820	...	...	1,699
...	...	...	...	...	...	...	...	...	...	...	...	12,37,815	3,75,344	10,123	7,211
...	...	...	...	...	...	...	...	...	...	...	...	1,38,429	447	2,817	980
...	...	...	...	...	...	...	...	...	...	...	...	37,402	52	192	...
...	...	...	...	...	...	...	...	...	...	...	...	1,26,154	66,679	24,590	2,224
...	...	...	...	...	...	...	...	...	...	...	...	11,403	8,582	11,336	1,250
...	...	...	...	...	...	...	...	...	...	...	...	48,679	2,697	7,824	...
...	...	...	...	...	...	...	...	...	...	...	...	5,12,507	2,80,392	1,23,269	4,574
...	...	...	...	...	...	...	...	...	...	...	...	42,024	5,723	4,671	12,264
...	...	...	...	...	...	...	...	...	...	...	...	1,49,305	56,564	17,840	...
	...	...	...	...	...	...	...	...	...	...	...				
	20,61,686	5,08,126	3,54,299	35,54,904	8,29,364	17,43,167	90,52,546	7,50,965	1,60,382	3,36,817	12,48,164				

CLASS OF SCHOOLS.

SECONDARY SCHOOLS—

For Boys.
- Departmental { English / Vernacular
- Local Fund { English / Vernacular
- Municipal { English / Vernacular
- Native States { English / Vernacular
- Other Departments { English / Vernacular
- Aided { English / Vernacular
- Unaided { English / Vernacular

TOTAL

For Girls.
- Departmental { English / Vernacular
- Local Fund { English / Vernacular
- Municipal { English / Vernacular
- Native States { English / Vernacular
- Other Departments { English / Vernacular
- Aided { English / Vernacular
- Unaided { English / Vernacular

TOTAL

TOTAL SECONDARY SCHOOLS

PRIMARY SCHOOLS—

For Boys.
- Departmental
- Local Fund
- Municipal
- Native States
- Other Departments
- Aided
- Unaided

TOTAL

- Departmental
- Local Fund
- Municipal

in the several Provinces comprised in British India at the end of -86.

		LOWER PRIMARY STAGE.						TOTAL.			REMARKS
		COMPRISING ALL PUPILS WHO HAVE NOT PASSED BEYOND THE LOWER PRIMARY STAGE.									
		Reading Printed Books.			Not Reading Printed Books.						
		4			5						
Girls.	TOTAL.	Boys.	Girls.	TOTAL.	Boys.	Girls.	TOTAL.	Boys.	Girls.	TOTAL.	
,256	9	9,265	8,188	20	8,208	821	9	830	49,004	48	49,052	
,081	4	3,085	4,993	19	5,012	1,973	2	1,975	12,320	26	12,346	
,683	5	3,688	6,300	116	6,416	190	70	260	16,720	196	16,916	
,757	...	9,757	25,064	...	25,064	2,126	...	2,126	45,275	...	45,275	
,725	7	2,732	5,412	27	5,439	358	12	370	15,030	48	15,078	
,737	...	1,737	6,494	...	6,494	909	...	909	11,098	...	11,098	
...	...	...	...	...	...	...	...	...	4,937	...	4,937	
...	...	...	...	...	...	...	...	...	...	...	...	
273	...	273	629	...	629	...	...	...	1,046	...	1,046	
...	...	...	...	...	...	...	...	...	...	...	...	
,901	323	30,224	47,693	847	48,540	4,698	167	4,865	132,544	1,604	134,148	
,382	57	13,439	24,730	768	25,498	6,223	241	6,464	52,601	1,083	53,684	
,545	26	9,571	11,688	118	11,806	1,201	22	1,223	43,354	186	43,540	No details of pils. Do. 18
,753	4	1,757	3,186	30	3,216	1,064	21	1,085	7,114	55	7,169	
435	85,528	144,377	1,945	146,322	19,563	544	20,107	391,043	3,246	394,289	
	64	64	18	194	212	...	8	8	18	417	435	
	74	74	...	1,137	1,137	...	395	395	...	1,676	1,676	
	...	...	...	49	49	...	50	50	...	112	112	
1	29	30	34	69	103	...	4	4	35	142	177	
	2	2	...	138	138	...	25	25	...	167	167	
	...	...	...	...	...	...	...	...	...	...	...	
	46	46	...	117	117	...	...	...	...	208	208	
...	...	...	...	...	...	...	...	...	...	...	...	
143	2,685	2,828	731	5,748	6,479	318	1,028	1,346	1,245	12,468	13,713	
	691	691	25	3,643	3,663	15	934	949	40	5,908	5,948	
16	163	179	24	320	344	39	210	249	97	882	979	
	69	69	...	333	333	...	10	10	...	479	479	
3,827	3,987	832	11,748	12,580	372	2,664	3,036	1,435	22,459	23,894		
4,262	89,515	145,209	13,693	158,902	19,935	3,208	23,143	392,478	25,705	418,183	
,237	65	12,302	28,730	518	29,248	14,518	59	14,577	56,868	642	57,510	
,280	499	110,779	292,966	5,409	298,375	94,378	10,229	104,607	497,624	16,137	513,761	
,778	84	31,862	52,782	538	53,320	35,373	1,150	36,523	121,205	1,773	122,978	
,793	41	29,834	36,127	190	36,317	24,326	736	25,062	90,246	967	91,213	
25	...	25	...	39	39	...	...	...	64	...	64	
,388	673	49,061	808,948	33,197	842,145	422,867	20,314	443,181	1,280,732	54,187	1,334,919	
	34	3,133	201,736	7,588	209,324	79,511	2,594	82,105	284,363	10,216	294,579	
1,396	236,996	1,421,328	47,440	1,468,768	670,973	35,082	706,055	2,331,102	83,922	2,415,024		
	360	360	...	2,660	2,660	...	1,690	1,690	...	4,728	4,728	
	1,108	1,111	102	7,464	7,566	38	4,550	4,588	143	13,123	13,266	
	1,759	1,762	65	6,376	6,441	38	5,178	5,216	106	13,313	13,419	
	928	928	...	2,589	2,589	...	3,481	3,481	...	6,998	6,998	
	12	12	...	44	44	...	...	...	...	56	56	
	5,472	5,625	1,139	45,446	46,585	529	20,010	20,539	1,822	71,072	72,894	
	344	384	101	6,311	6,412	91	4,245	4,336	232	10,905	11,137	
9,983	10,182	1,407	70,890	72,297	696	39,154	39,850	2,303	120,195	122,498		
11,379	247,178	1,422,735	118,330	1,541,065	671,669	74,236	745,905	2,333,405	204,117	2,537,522		
15,641	336,693	1,567,944	132,023	1,699,967	691,604	77,444	769,048	2,725,883	229,822	2,955,705		

EDUCATION—GENERAL TABLE VI.

esults of Prescribed Examinations in the several Provinces comprised in British India during the Official 1885-86.

*Aided Institutions.	Other Institutions.	Number of Ex			Number Pa				Race or Creed of Pas			LARS.	F
		Institutions under public management.	Aided Institutions.	Other Institutions.	Total.	Institutions under public management.	Aided Institutions.	Other Institutions.	Europeans and Eurasians.	Native Christians.	Hindus.	Others.	
3	4	6	7	8		11	12	13	16a	16b	16c		
		46	13	8	84	26			...	...	16c		
		1	...		1	...			...	...			
					(a)1,459	330			⎱ 35	...	604		
					2	2				...	2		
					3	3				...	66		
					247	70				1	1		
					2	2			⎰	...	42		
					147	41				...	8		
					16	10							
					(c)2,811	505			⎱ 65	...	59		
					487	64			⎰	...	02		
					3	...							

Honours in Medicine		5	...								(not known.) 3 3		
" Medicine		1	...								3		
		1	...								...		
		1	...								3		
Engineering.											(not known.)		
1 E.		1	...										
2 E.		2	...										
3 C.		3	...										
4		1	...										
5 College		1	...							3			
For Boys		173	304	630	3,333	4,000	2,991	2,715	1,447	861	399	4,261	109	175	3,380	138
Public Service " Girls		2	15	17	5	40	...	9	20	...	3	25	15	5	...	...
English		66	65	161	1,108	820	51	794	287	7	190	1,066	1	16	855	187
Vernacular		1,189	43	1,313	5,554	229	497	2,922	88	140	637	3,254	...	2	2,764	487
For Boys		513	1,563	2,327	4,996	8,425	1,934	2,747	3,934	648	763	(e)8,795	161	297	5,448	342
" Girls		1	42	61	1	280	79	46	100	8	132	22		2	
For Boys		2,099	2,908	5,175	15,910	10,847	567	629	5,488	315	199	17,018	107	31	12,624	2,739
" Girls		34	53	89	202	476	8		195	7		337	80	20	154	8
Lower Primary For Boys		3,170	12,420	15,743	28,568	54,424	586	394	23,943	327	253	44,907	135	75	32,117	8,626
Examination. " Girls		123	234	360	641	3,379	23	2	957	12	2	1,339	139	79	682	60
" Examin		...	...	...	...	290	...	...	215	...	...	215	...	...	215	...
SCHOOLS FOR SPEC INSTRUCTION.														
Upper		28	21	52	868	92	2	13	575	1	5	614	...	1	398	90
Lower		73	9	108	1,381	103	116	45	846	77	20	1,020	4	1	432	84
fcr Masters. Upper		5	9	15	35	66	...	...	25	1	...	59	...	...	11	...
Training School Examination Lower		6	11	18	65	144	4	...	45	4	...	146	8	...	26	7
for Mistresses.		8	...	8	111	...	...	6	103	...	...	108	...	...	...	7
Medical Examination		38	...	50	71	...	...	164	62	...	5	62	...	...	29	...
		37	2	43	367	17	27	3	162	6	3	110	6	7	13	5
		5	1	8	70	49	58	...	55	7	1	171	...	...	24	6
		6	...	10	95	...	6	...	70	4	...	111	...	7	76	1
													74		74	

(a) Of these three were females from Bengal.
(b) Of these two were females from Bengal.
(c) Of these two were females from Bengal.
(d) No details of 196 candidates from Burma.
(e) No details of 137 candidates from Berar, and of 603 candidates from Bengal.

Return showing the Distribution of Local Fund and M

OBJECTS OF EXPENDITURE.	Number of Institutions.	Number of scholars on the rolls on 31st March.	Average number of pupils monthly during the year.	Average daily attendance.	Provincial Grants.	Local Rates or Cesses.	Municipal Grants.	Fees.	Subscriptions.
1	2	3	4	5	6	7	8		
					R	R	R	R	R
UNIVERSITY EDUCATION.									
Arts Colleges.									
English		11	12	10	...	2,528	...	135	...
SCHOOL EDUCATION, GENERAL.									
Secondary Schools.									
For Boys { English	15	16,990	16,913	14,177	31,693	2,00,332	9,311	1,08,119	1,
For Boys { Vernacular	487	45,275	43,574	36,679	...	1,81,153	5,348	20,790	1,
For Girls { English	...	...	...	...	...	...	...	...	...
For Girls { Vernacular		112	79	60	...	499	...	...	...
TOTAL	68	62,377	60,566	50,916	31,693	3,81,984	14,659		
Primary Schools.									
For Boys	13,037	563,566	546,341	418,576	2,77,187	(c)16,23,151	24,835	2,09,109	5,2
For Girls	483	14,481	14,087	9,694	11,950	57,640	838	1,128	4
TOTAL	13,520	578,047	560,428	428,270	2,89,137	16,80,791	25,673		
SCHOOL EDUCATION, SPECIAL. *Schools of Special Instruction.*									
Training Schools for Masters	45	1,181	1,137	1,026	14,429	94,881	1,259	15	.
Ditto for Mistresses	2	25	25	19	685	2,829	...	...	...
Medical Schools	3	61	62	61	...	5,733	240	...	...
Engineering and Surveying Schools	...	...	...	...	...	...	...	...	...
Industrial Schools	6	258	259	199	1,500	707	...	...	...
Other Schools	1	9	8	7	...	1,127	...	...	...
TOTAL	58	1,534	1,491	1,312	16,614	1,05,277	1,499		
Inspection	...	...	...			...	...	...	...
SCHOLARSHIP HOLDERS. Arts Colleges	...	...	...			...	228	...	...
Professional Colleges	...	...	...			...	...	...	...
Secondary Schools	...	...	...					.	.
Primary Schools	...	...	...					.	.
Special Schools other than Training Schools	...	...	...					.	.
Buildings	...	.	.						

TABLE VII.

in the several Provinces comprised in British India for the Official Year 1885-86.

				In Institutions maintained by Municipal Boards.									
Number of Institutions.	Number of scholars on the rolls on the 31st March.	Average number on the rolls monthly during the year.	Average daily attendance.	Provincial Grants.	Municipal Grants.	Local Fund Grants.	Fees.	Subscriptions.	Endowments and other sources.	Total.	The Department.	Local Fund Boards.	Private persons or Associations.
18	19	20	21	22	23	24	25	26	27	28	29	30	31
				R	R	R	R	R	R	R	R	R	R
1	39	22	20	...	1,027	...	475	...	...	1,502	3,000	...	9,969
149	16,249	16,168	13,468	22,785	140,300	12,147	117,062	1,735	827	294,856	58,042	9,311	1,21,915
79	12,515	12,072	9,919	701	31,095	26,188	14,367	496	244	73,091	772	5,348	19,398
2	105	82	62	...	4,487	...	437	...	48	4,972	1,500	...	12,365
2	167	148	79	169	484	...	...	...	...	653	48	...	2,568
232	29,036	28,470	23,558	23,655	1,76,366	38,335	1,31,866	2,231	2,119	3,73,572	60,362	14,659	1,56,246
747	73,820	73,435	56,274	74,233	1,96,748	21,620	61,165	613	683	3,55,062	39,696	25,414	1,61,338
236	12,363	11,775	7,660	10,083	42,354	3,791	473	300	66	57,067	2,989	976	18,053
983	86,183	85,210	63,934	84,316	2,39,102	25,411	61,638	913	749	4,12,129	42,685	26,390	1,79,391
1	20	20	16	702	580	...	...	...	...	1,282	...	1,259	...
...	...	...	...	...	...	...	...	...	...	...	600	...	1,200
...	...	...	...	...	...	...	...	...	...	...	15,928	240	...
2	25	22	15	19	1,146	...	...	...	...	1,165	...	...	...
2	63	69	56	...	720	384	...	...	364	1,468	24	...	1,912
1	67	48	36	...	443	...	...	1,027	...	1,470	1,290	...	208
6	175	159	123	721	2,889	384	...	1,027	364	5,385	17,842	1,499	3,350
...	...	...	...	...	...	...	...	...	...	...	...	...	...
...	...	...	...	...	...	...	...	...	...	...	2,267	228	322
...	...	...	...	...	...	...	...	...	...	...	192	...	...
...	...	...	...	...	9,554	11,439	60	211	129	21,393	3,577	3,521	7,696
...	...	...	...	...	4,295	72	...	...	...	4,367	82	...	6,693
...	...	...	...	...	...	...	...	...	458	458	1,659	...	599
...	...	...	...	3,550	82,857	9,236	...	...	...	95,643	17,200	1,304	20,473
...	...	...	...	120	2,375	...	...	10	...	2,505	1,140	32	1,049
...	...	...	...	1	9,382	2,697	110	...	724	12,914	42	...	276
...	...	...	...	3,671	1,08,463	23,444	180	221	1,311	1,37,280	26,249	5,085	37,108
1,222	1,25,433	1,13,861	87,625	1,12,363	5,27,847	87,574	1,94,159	4,386	3,543	9,29,868	1,50,138	47,633	3,86,064

Lightning Source UK Ltd.
Milton Keynes UK
UKOW06f1931271017
311772UK00013B/795/P